EDUCATION OFFICE.

FREDERICTON, N. B., February 15th, 1902.

SIR,—

I have the honor to transmit to you, to be laid before His Honor the Lieutenant Governor, the Annual Report on the Common Schools of the Province for the School year, 1900-1.

I have the honor to be, Sir,

Your obedient servant,

J. R. INCH,
Chief Supt. of Education.

TO THE HON. L. J. TWEEDIE,
Provincial Secretary.

CONTENTS.

Part I.—General Report.

Part II.—Statistical Tables.

CONTENTS.

Part III.—Appendices.

APPENDIX A.

APPENDIX B.

APPENDIX C.

APPENDIX D.

APPENDIX E.

PART I.

GENERAL REPORT

NORTHUMBERLAND COUNTY GRAMMAR SCHOOL, CHATHAM, N. B.

ANNUAL REPORT

OF THE

SCHOOLS OF NEW BRUNSWICK,

SCHOOL YEAR, 1901-2.

PART I---GENERAL REPORT.

To His Honor, the Honorable Jabez Bunting Snowball, Lieutenant Governor of the Province of New Brunswick.

MAY IT PLEASE YOUR HONOR :—

I beg tq snbmit, as required by law, my Report on the Public Schools of the Province for the School Year 1900-1.

By the provisions of "The Schools' Act, 1900," the School Year now begins on the first day of July and ends on the thirtieth day of June in each year.

The Tabular Statements given in Parts II. and III., are for the School Year ending June 30th, 1901. The Inspectors' Reports cover the whole of the :elendar year, 1901.

The following summary of the Statistical Tables (See Part II) presents a neral comparison of the work of the two terms under review, with that of the .rresponding terms of the previous twelve months :—

Statisical Abstract.

TABLE I.—NUMBER OF SCHOOLS, TEACHERS, PUPILS, ETC.

	First Term. 1900		Second Term. 1901.
Number of Schools, ...	1812	....	1741
Decrease, ...	3	Decrease,	30
Number of Teachers, ...	1893	....	1841
The same,		Decrease,	15
Number of Pupils, ...	57,629	....	60,420
Decrease, ...	1,296	Decrease,	1,024

TABLE II.—PROPORTION OF POPULATION AT SCHOOL, AGE AND SEX OF PUPILS, PERCENTAGE OF ATTENDANCE.

	First Term. 1900		Second Term. 1901.
Proportion of population at school,..	1 in 5.57	....	1 in 5.31
Decrease on corresponding term last year, ...	1 in 247.08	....	1 in 313.7
Number of Pupils under five years of age, ...	225	....	187
Decrease, ...	34	Decrease,	125
Number between 5 and 15, ...	55,111	....	56,485
Decrease, ...	1,005	Decrease,	522
Number over 15 years,....	2,293	....	3,748
Decrease, ...	257	Decrease,	377
Number of Boys, ...	28,435	....	30,870
Decrease, ...	1,024	Decrease,	680
Number of Girls, ...	29,194	....	29,550
Decrease, ...	272	Decrease,	344
Grand total number of days made by pupils enrolled, ...	3,233,208	....	4,288,235
Decrease, ...	206,794	Decrease,	618½
Average number of pupils daily present during time schools were in session, ...	37,160	....	37,717
Decrease, ...	1,892	Increase,	188
Average number daily present for the full term, ...	35,656	....	35,251

Decrease, ...	930	Decrease,	92
Percentage daily present during time schools were in session, ...	64.48	....	62.42
Decrease, ...	1.79	Increase,	1.35
Percentage daily present during full term,....	61.87	....	58.34
Increase, ...	.21	Increase,	.82

The following table shows the enrolment and percentage of average attendance for the Province for full term, from 1890 to 1901, inclusive:

Year.	Enrolment.		Percentage of Attendance for Full Term.	
	June.	December.	June.	December
1890	58,570	55,622	50.96	57.36
1891	59,568	56,217	52.40	59.82
1892	60,786	56,547	53.45	62.38
1893	60,154	57 195	54.58	61.89
1894	61,280	57,282	56.04	63.36
1895	62,518	57,889	57.62	62.93
1896	61,918	57,200	55.64	62.63
1897	61,908	58,174	55.94	64.16
1898	63,333	59,457	57.03	61.12
1899	63,536	58,925	55.69	62.08
1900	61,444	57,629	57.52	61.87
1901	60,420	......	58.34	......

THE FOLLOWING TABLE SHOWS THE ENROLMENT IN THE CITIES AND INCORPORATED TOWNS FOR THE LAST NINE YEARS:

	1893		1894		1895		1896		1897		1898		1899		1900		1901
	June.	Dec.	June.	Dec.	June.	Dec.	June.	Dec.	June.	Dec.	June.	Dec.	June.	Dec.	June.	Dec.	June
St. John	6601	6619	6412	6721	6543	6606	6326	6566	6413	6709	6711	6986	6792	6952	6753	7160	6991
Fredericton	1146	1185	1160	1227	1213	1225	1212	1243	1225	1209	1181	1203	1169	1231	1184	1214	1152
Moncton..........	1535	1614	1571	1632	1663	1708	1660	1716	1680	1749	1678	1741	1682	1825	1736	1718	1693
St. Stephen..	547	598	585	595	592	592	581	580	565	581	560	583	545	555	541	545	542
Milltown	443	362	354	370	362	369	379	381	385	389	377	370	371	371	*382	368	363
Woodstock.......	651	638	643	680	656	638	643	678	688	713	712	719	674	662	644	652	652
Marysville	224	261	246	281	276	301	300	324	314	338	300	316	304	322	319	305	302
Campbellton......	305	337	324	348	353	378	343	388	382	370	355	373	367	407	416	401	376
Chatham.........	.....	.....	.....	.....	.....	....	941	942	973	980	1019	1024	1004	1018	989	933	934
Newcastle	.....	.....	.....	.....	.....	.....	.....	.....	.....	.....	.....	.....	.....	.....	478	497	475

* This includes Night School.

THE FOLLOWING TABLE SHOWS THE PERCENTAGE OF ENROLLED PUPILS DAILY PRESENT ON AN AVERAGE IN CITIES AND TOWNS FROM 1893 TO 1901:

	1893		1894		1895		1896		1897		1898		1899		1900		1901
	June.	Dec.	June.	Dec.	June.	Dec.	June.	Dec.	June.	Dec.	June.	Dec.	June.	Dec.	June.	Dec.	June.
St. John..........	74.58	82.08	79.00	82.69	80.41	80.72	76.72	83.27	76.39	83.05	77.80	81.40	77.27	82.60	77.64	81.70	79.96
Frederictun	82.24	85.18	80.77	86.22	82.86	85.26	82.48	87.70	80.07	89.23	82.17	85.82	82.58	86.25	81.33	82.88	81.13
Moncton	78.70	78.26	79.64	82.51	78.65	83.21	79.37	83.92	76.66	82,27	76.11	83.31	82.31	84.64	81.36	81.90	80.03
St. Stephen.......	80.10	84.80	84.79	87.72	82.68	81.85	80.79	84.65	83.74	83.43	83.69	73.85	83.01	84.96	85.60	84.63	86.18
Milltown	72.98	86.71	82.66	94.61	85.99	90.37	85.06	89.15	86.24	86.32	86.12	79.77	81.06	88.11	82.31	86.40	85.90
Woodstock	77.34	82.23	79.81	83.12	79.10	79.97	81.95	82.42	81.39	86.67	81.16	80.71	80.77	84.23	74.04	82.39	79.05
Marysville	70.00	72.94	68.26	67.53	69.21	74.10	65.63	75.16	63,37	75.50	70.25	77.18	70.73	75.88	65.48	69.71	63.37
Campbellton.. ...	78.07	70.00	74.44	75.85	78.53	78.29	77.67	77.31	72.78	82.77	76.68	84.93	81.52	78.00	81.05	80.33	71.17
Chatham.........	......	......	......	......	......	......	75.90	81.39	77.45	81.43	76.96	83.98	80.13	80.80	77.05	83.05	79.00
Newcastle,.....	......	......	......	......	......	......	......	......	......	......	......	......	......	......	72.19	72.97	76.20

As anticipated in my last Annual Report, the statistics for the two terms under review, show a further decrease in the number of schools in operation and the number of pupils enrolled, as compared with the corresponding terms of recent years. The principal cause of this falling off was, without doubt, the closing of the schools in many districts on account of the prevalence of small-pox and other epidemic diseases.

Another cause more particularly affecting the rural districts, was the difficulty of obtaining teachers. This is a condition of things so detrimental to educational progress, that public attention cannot be too strongly directed to the causes which have brought it about.

THE SCARCITY OF TEACHERS.

By reference to the Normal School Report, it will be seen that the average enrolment of candidates for the teaching profession during the last ten years was 273; but as a porti n of those enrolled were already licensed teachers who were seeking advance of class, it may be estimated that from 240 to 250 new candidates present themselves each year. This number would provide for vacancies caused by the annual withdrawal of about one-eighth of the total number of teachers employed, and this proportion, under ordinary circumstances, ought to be sufficient to meet the requirements of the schools.

But under existing conditions a much larger proportion than 12½ per cent. of trained teachers of the higher classes seek and obtain other employments. There are now many more avenues of activity than formerly, opening up before educated and energetic young people of both sexes, and these new fields of usefulness give promise of much better financial rewards and their cultivation is attended with less nervous strain and self-denial than are usually associated with the charge of a country school. The inevitable results are the withdrawal annually from the teaching profession of hundreds of our best qualified teachers and the consequent closing of the schools or, what is scarcely a less evil, placing them in charge of teachers of imperfect education and utterly incompetent for the proper discharge of the functions of a teacher.

The time has come when some remedy must be found for this growing evil; otherwise, every effort which has been made to raise the standards of efficiency in the schools by supplying them with a better educated and better trained class of teachers will be rendered abortive. A young man or woman who has spent years in acquiring the necessary education, who has undergone professional training and successfully passed the prescribed examinations, has a right to claim a reasonably remunerative salary from some source. If the public revenues are too limited to admit of increased provincial grants, and if no further assistance can be expected by the augmentation of the County Fund then, I respectfully submit, that by legal enactment, the school districts, in proportion to their taxable valuation, should be required to contribute an amount which, when added to the provincial grant, will make up salaries sufficient to command the services of properly educated and well qualified teachers.

In my last Annual Report, I gave a list of twenty school districts, having a taxable valuation ranging from $109,350 to $55,000, in which the highest sum contributed by the district towards the teacher's salary was $185 and the lowest $85. These were all comparatively wealthy districts. In the poor districts, so called, the regular Provincial Grants to the teachers and the County Fund Grants to the Trustees are increased from 25 to 33½ per cent. Even with this help it is not reasonable to expect that large salaries can be given in such districts; but they should be required to contribute according to their ability, for it is demoralizing to permit even the poorest of districts to become possessed of the idea that they need incur no financial responsibility for the support of a school in their midst. The minimum sum they should be required to contribute towards the teacher's salary should equal the Provincial Grant. Cases have come under my notice during the present year in which the teachers accepted as salary the Provincial Grant only, and the amount of the County Fund was more than sufficient to pay all other expenses, as fuel, &c.; so that in these cases, the schools, instead of being a financial charge upon the districts, were actually a source of income.

It might be supposed that authority had been invested in the Board of Education, or in the Chief Superintendent to warrant the withholding of the Provincial Grant and the County Fund in such cases; but this is not the fact. Under Section 23 of the Schools' Act, the districts are not required to provide more than may be found necessary "in further payment of teachers' salarie, over and above the sums provided by the Province and County, and any sum required for other school purposes during the year." The amount, if any voted at the Annual School Meetings is absolutely within the control of the majority of ratepayers present. The employment of the teacher and the amount of salary contributed by the district is determined by the Local School Board, and it often happens that a majority of the School Board have no other interest in the school than to protect themselves and fellow-ratepayers from taxation. The results are, in many cases, what might be expected when the educational interests of the community are left, without limitation, in the hands of ignorant and narrow-minded men, who have no proper conception os the importance of the trust committed to their charge. When obliged to open the school, they employ the person who will accept the position at the lowes figure, without regard to any other consideration.

In order to protect the higher class teachers from competition, as to salary with teachers holding a Third Class or a Local License, the Board of Education some years ago passed the following regulation:

"Third Class Teachers shall not be employed (except as class room assistants) in districts having an assessable valuation of fifteen thousand dollars or upwards, unless by the written consent of the Chief Superintendent.'

In the exercise of the discretion thus given him, the Chief Superintendent has granted permission for the employment of Third Class or Local Licensed Teachers in such districts, only on the recommendation of the Inspectors, and when assured that the closing of the schools indefinitely was the alternative. And yet in the majority of cases in which Trustees have applied for such permission, there is strong ground for the belief that teachers of the Second Class could have been obtained, if a reasonable salary had been offered, and proper efforts had been made at or before the beginning of the term.

In regard to the granting of Local Licenses, it may be said that for several years such licenses have been almost exclusively limited to the Counties of Madawaska and Gloucester, principally the former, where the supply of French speaking trained teachers was very much below the requirements. But during the last year, in order to prevent the closing of the schools, I have been induced to grant Local Licenses in every County of the Province. I need scarcely say thatthe majority ofthose for whom Local Licenses are asked, are young girls living at their own homes in the community where they are to teach, that they have had little or no experience of life outside of their own narrow circle, that their education is but little in advance of that of the pupils whom they are expected to teach, and that neither in manner nor speech are they fitted for the discharge of a teacher's duties.

The only effectual remedy for the evils I have pointed out is to provide in some way for an adequate system of salaries, graded according to the class, experience, ability and length of service of the teacher. In order to aid in providing adequate salaries, County School Districts should be consolidated [illegible]ever possible, provision should be made for taking the children to a [illegible]ral school, and all school districts, large or small, should be required to [illegible]ibute for educational purposes, not less than fifty cents on every hundred dollars of the taxable valuation. Some of the poorer districts contribute double that amount at present.

By reference to Tables IV. and VIII., it will be seen that the average salary of the 24 First Class Male Teachers employed during the term ending June 30th. 1901, was $520.10 an increase of $56.77 on the previous year; and that the average salary of the 305 First Class Female Teachers employed during the same term was $312.69, an increase of $5.88 on the previous year. The increase in these averages results from the smaller number of these classes employed, and the fact that a larger proportion than formerly are employed in the graded schools of cities and towns.

The average salaries of teachers of the Second and Third Classes show a small decrease with one exception.

TABLE III.—Subjects of Instruction.

The following summary of Table III, shows the number of pupils receiving instruction in each subject, both in the Common Schools and in the Superior and Grammar Schools :

COMMON SCHOOL GRADES, I. TO VIII. INCLUSIVE.— YEAR ENDED JUNE 30TH, 1901.

	Dec. Term. 1900.	June Term. 1901.
Reading and Spelling, etc	55,932	58,731
Writing and Print Script	55,616	58,552
Number and Arithmetic	55,759	58,432
Drawing	54,761	57,385
Health Lessons	51,840	54,545
Nature Lessons	50,457	53,847
Lessons in Morals, etc	53,079	55,661
Physical Exercises	48,457	50,166
Singing	32,808	34,130
Geography	31,342	34,288
English Grammar, etc	30,365	33,355
History	19,768	22,178
Algebra	3,167	4,129
French (Optional)	3,897	3,224
Latin (Optional)	1,734	1,552
Sewing, etc. (Optional)	161	193

HIGH SCHOOL GRADES, IX. TO XII. INCLUSIVE.— YEAR ENDED JUNE 30TH, 1901.

	DEC. TERM. 1900.	JUNE TERM. 1901.
English Language and Literature	1,652	1,611
Latin	1,270	1,147
Greek	217	206
French	874	882
Arithmetic	1,351	1,412
Geometry	1,621	1,585
Algebra	1,595	1,609
Trigonometry	73	107
Book-keeping	903	957
History and Geography	1,616	1,566
Industrial Drawing	792	778
Botany	1,249	1,381
Chemistry	385	618
Physiology and Hygiene	569	566
Physics	552	766

In regard to most of the other Tables given in Part II, it is scarcely necessary to summarize.

Disbursement of Provincial Grants.

By reference to Tabless IX and XIX, it will be seen that the Provincial Grants to the Common, Superior and Grammar Schools, amounted to $163,951.73, a decrease of $4,272.99 on the disbursement of the previous year. This decrease was principally on account of the smaller number of common schools in operation.

The following statement shows the annual expenditure since 1891, in relation to the number of schools open during the term ending June 30th, and the number of teachers of each class employed :

YEAR.	No. of Schools.	TEACHERS OF EACH CLASS.					PROVINCIAL GRANT.
		Grammar School.	Sup. and Class I.	Class II.	Class III.	Totals.	
1891	1536	14	274	765	579	1632	$137,679 03
1892	1585	14	304	783	568	1669	142,681 21
1893	1614	14	345	787	547	1693	147,669 71
1894	1653	14	360	786	589	1749	150.882 20
1895	1695	13	382	827	568	1790	156,341 65
1896	1720	13	423	839	554	1829	158,135 23
1897	1737	17	440	840	534	1831	161,445 94
1898	1778	20	427	904	513	1864	163,021 86
1899	1806	25	464	894	529	1912	167,988 40
1900	1771	25	452	881	498	1856	168,224 72
1901	1741	23	429	911	478	1841	163,951 73

The total expenditure during the year 1900-1901 for the maintenance of the Grammar, Superior and Common Schools is approximately as follows:

District Assessments (approximate)	$346,623.49
County Fund	90,492.16
Provincial Grants	163,224.72
Total	$600,340.37

Amount per pupil enrolled nearly $9.00.

The total amount of Provincial moneys disbursed by the Chief Superintendent for the year ended June 30th. 1901, was $190,100.26.

The County Fund.

The total amount of the County Funds distributed during the year (See Tables X and XI) was $94,428.30, of which $5,302.40 was given as an additional grant to Poor Districts, $2,325 to the School for the Blind, and $1,611.14 to the School for the Deaf and Dumb.

The County Fund for the next decade is to be based on the Census Returns of 1901. At the rate of 30 cents per head of the population (as provided by the law) the fund should yield for the several counties as follows:

County.	Population.	Amount.		
Albert	10,925	$3,277 50	Decrease,	$13 80
Carleton	21,621	6,486 30	"	272 40
Charlotte	22,415	6,724 50	"	401 10
Gloucester	27,936	8,380 80	Increase,	911 70
Kent	23,958	7,187 40	"	33 90
Kings	21,655	6,496 50	Decrease,	429 60
Madawaska	12,311	3,693 30	Increase,	539 70
Northumberland	28,543	8,562 90	"	849 00
Queens	11,177	3,353 10	Decrease,	292 50
Restigouche	10,586	3,175 80	Increase,	683 40
St. John	51,759	15,527 70	"	655 50
Sunbury	5,729	1,718 70	Decrease,	9 90
Victoria	8,825	2,647 50	Increase,	336 00
Westmorland	42,060	12,618 00	"	174 90
York (not including Fredericton)	24,503	7,350 90	"	7 80
Total (not including Fredericton)	324,003	$97,200 90		$2,772 60

The decrease of this Fund in Albert, Carleton, Charlotte, Kings, Queens and Sunbury demands the careful consideration of the rate-payers at the next Annual School Meetings in these counties. The amounts voted for assessment upon the several districts should be increased in order to provide for the deficiency in the County Fund.

Grants to the School for the Blind, Halifax and to the School for the Deaf and Dumb, Fredericton.

Under the provisions of 55 Vic., Cap 8 and 9, and amending Acts, the ..itions above named received for the year ended June 30, 1901, the follow- ..ums:

SCHOOL FOR THE BLIND.

From Provincial Treasury		$2,325 00
From County Fund :		
Albert County, 3 pupils, ...	$ 225 00	
Carleton County, 2 pupils,....	150 00	
Charlotte County, 2 pupils,....	150 00	
Kent County, 5 pupils, ...	375 00	
Kings County, 2 pupils, ...	150 00	
Northumberland County, 1 pupil, ...	75 00	
Saint John County, 6 pupils, ...	450 00	
Westmorland County, 8 pupils, ...	600 00	
York County, 2 pupils, ...	150 00	
		2,325 00
Total grant from New Brunswick for 31 pupils, ..		$4,650 00

SCHOOL FOR THE DEAF AND DUMB.

From County Fund :		
Albert County, 1 pupil, ...	$ 60 00	
Carleton County, 5 pupils,....	258 68	
Charlotte County, 1 pupil,....	60 00	
Kings County, 5 pupils, ...	270 00	
Madawaska, County, 1 pupil, ...	60 00	
Northumberland County, 1 pupil, ...	30 00	
Queens County, 1 pupil, ...	60 00	
Restigouche County, 2 pupils, ...	120 00	
Saint John County, 2 pupils, ...	120 00	
Westmorland County, 8 pupils, ...	480 00	
York County, 2 pupils, ...	92 46	
		$ 1,611 14
By Special Legislative Grant from Provincial Revenues,		500 00
Total, ...		$ 2,111 14

I direct attention to Appendix D of this report, in which will be found many interesting facts in regard to the work of these beneficient institutions.

Superior and Grammar Schools.

The number of Superior Schools in operation during the year was 49, and the number of Grammar Schools 13. Twenty-three teachers received the Grammar School Provincial Grant. The total number of pupils enrolled in the High School Grades (IX.-XII.) was 949 in the Grammar Schools, and 579 in the Superior Schools. For details see Tables XII. and XIII.

The following table shows the Superior Schools which had 10 pupils or more above Grade VIII.:

	First Term.	Second Term.
St. Stephen High School,	56	53
Harkins' Academy, Newcastle	38	33
Superior School, Dorchester	36	30
" " Milltown	28	29
" " Sackville	27	23
" " Petitcodiac	24	22
" " Havelock Corner	18	23
" " St. Martins	20	21
" " Rexton	9	30
" " Shediac	19	19
" " St. George	17	20
" " Middle Sackville	16	19
" " Hillsboro	15	18
" " Hartland	13	15
" " Centreville	13	16
" " Salisbury	11	15
" " Hampton Sation	11	14
" " Miltord	12	9
" " Hopewell Hill	12	8
" " Bass River	11	8
" " Port Elgin	9	10
" " Fairville	10	7
" " Florenceville	..	14
" North Head, Grand Manan	..	13

To show the gradual and healthy expansion of our High School work since 1900, I append the following figures:

No. of Pupils in Grades IX. to XII. in Gtammar and Superior Schools.

	Term Ended December.	Term Ended June.
1890-1	574	610
1891-2	701	694
1892-3	782	724
1893-4	738	806
1894-5	1155	1060
1895-6	1093	1099
1996-7	1220	1228
1897-8	1469	1523
1898-9	1495	1510
1899-1900	1565	1545
1900-1	1543	1528

DEPARTMENTAL EXAMINATIONS.

These examinations consist of:

(1) The High School Entrance Examinations (See Regulation 46, School Manual) held during the month of June at the several Grammar Schools, and such of the Superior Schools as apply for the same. They cover the work of Grades I. to VIII. inclusive, or the Common School Grades. Those who successfully pass these examinations receive a certificate which is intended to serve a two-fold purpose; for pupils who do not intend to continue longer at school it serves as a diploma given under the authority of the Education Department, testifying that the holder has completed satisfactorily the course of studies of the Common Schools; for pupils who intend to continue their studies it serves as a certificate of admittance to the High School classes.

(2) The High School Leaving Examinations (See Regulation 45, School Manual) held the first week in July at different examination stations throughout the province. They cover the work of Grades IX., X. and XI. of the Grammar Schools. Diplomas are granted to those who successfully pass these examinations.

(3) The University Matriculation Examatinions held at the same time and stations as the Leaving Examinations.

(4) The Normal School Entrance Examinations held at the same time and places as the two former. Candidates for admittance to the Normal School and Licensed Teachers seeking for advance of Class are required to pass these examinations.

(5) The Normal School Closing Examinations, held at the Normal School, Fredericton, and at St. John and Chatham, beginning on the second Tuesday of June, and for Third Class Candidates in December and May of each year.

The following were the results of these several examinations during the past year:

High School Entrance Examinations.

I.—Grammar Schools.

Name of School.	No. of Candidates.	Passed Division I.	Passed Division II.	Passed Division III.	Failed.
Albert County Grammar School	9	7	2	....	....
Carleton " " "	49	5	12	31	1
Charlotte " " "	35	8	12	13	2
Gloucester County Grammar School	12	1	1	2	8
Kent " " "	8	5	2	....	1
Kings " " "	20	5	12	3	...
Northumberland County Grammar School	37	4	23	9	1
Queens " " "	6	....	....	5	1
Restigouche " " "	17	4	9	3	1
St. John " " "	258	123	107	8	20
Victoria " " "	8	3	3	2	....
Westmorland "	85	22	43	18	2
York " " "	95	24	43	24	4
	639	211	269	118	41

II.—Superior Schools.

Name of School.	Number Entered for Examination.	Passed Division I.	Passed Division II.	Passed Division III.	Failed.
Centreville	22	8	10	4	..
Florenceville	6	3	3	..	..
St. George	5	2	1	..	2
Moore's Mills	8	3	4	1	..
St. Stephen	38	18	19	1	..
Milltown	21	10	10	1	..
Rexton	14	8	6	..	..
Havelock	7	..	6	1	.
Apohaqui	5	..	1	4	..
Douglastown	6	6	..	..	..
Newcastle	14	1	8	5	..
Chipman	14	6	7	1	..
Dalhousie	10	1	6	3	..
Fairville	16	1	6	7	2
Milford	5	2	2	1	..
St. Martins	19	2	4	7	6
Fredericton Junction	10	2	2	6	..
Dorchester	23	6	13	4	..
Sackville	36	11	14	11	..
Salisbury	6	..	..	4	2
Shediac	7	2	3	2	..
Superior Schools	292	92	125	63	12
Grammar Schools	639	211	269	118	41
Total, 1900-1	931	303	394	181	53
Total, 1899-1900	776	220	269	230	57
Increase	155	83	125	..	..
Decrease	..	..	..	49	4

High School Leaving Examinations.

Only ten candidates presented themselves for these examinations, of whom two passed in the Second Division, six in the Third Division and two failed ot pass. The following are the names of those who passed in Second Division :

Mary K. Kelly, Fredericton Grammar School.
William T. McKnight, Harkins' Academy, Newcastle.

University Matriculation Examinations.

Seventy-four candidates presented themselves for these examinations, of whom three passed in Division I; twenty-eight in Division II; thirty-two in Division III; eleven failed to pass.

The following are the names of those who passed in Division I. and II, arranged in the order of highest marks :

DIVISION I.

	Anna J. Purdy,	Fredericton Grammar School.
	Mary E. Lawson,	" " "
	Roy C. Alward,	" " "

DIVISION II.

1.	Clara G. Turner,	Fredericton Grammar School.
2.	J. D. McCarthy	" " "
3.	Gertrude H. Lawson,	St. John Grammar School.
4.	Mae E. Perkins,	" " "
5.	Willard B. Smith,	" " "
6.	Mary Lenihan,	Fredericton Grammar School.
7.	Martha A. Osborne,	Milltown Grammar School.
8.	Pearl E. Babbitt,	Fredericton Grammar School.
9.	John S. Smiley,	Milltown Superior School.
10.	L. Elta Brown,	St. John Grammar School.
11.	Mary M. Winslow,	Woodstock Grammar School.
12.	George S. Whittaker,	St. John Grammar School.
13.	Bessie M. Wilson,	" " "
14.	Henry G. Hoben,	Fredericton Grammar School.
	Ethel E. Day,	" " "
	Henrietta Ruel,	" " "
	John McNaughton,	Chatham Grammar School.

18. May B. Pinder, ... Fredericton Grammar School.
19. Margaret Maloney .... St. Andrews Grammar School.
20. Edith G. Cummings, ... St. John Grammar School.
21. Burton M. Hill, ... St. Stephen Superior School.
22. Blanche M. Fraser, ... Chatham Grammar School.
23. Minnie P. Spragg, ... St. John Grammar School.
24. Kate Little, ... Campbellton Grammar School.
25. G. Estelle Carruthers, ... Chatham Grammar School.
26. Lulu M. Murray, ... Milltown Superior School.
27. Maurice E Peters, ... St. John Grammar School.
28. Madge Parkinson .... " " "

The examiners in the Matriculation and Leaving Examinations were .

Professor W. T. Raymond, B. A., University of New Brunswick.
" S. W. Hunton, M. A., " Mount Allison.
" A. M. Scott, M. A., Ph. D., " New Brunswick.
" John Brittain, Normal School.

Normal School Entrance Examinations and Preliminary Examinations for Advance of Class.

Number examined for Class I..................	172
" " " " II..................	335
" " " " III..................	8
Total..............................	515
Number obtained Class I.	57
" " " II....................	206
" " " III....................	135
" failed to classify	117
	515

CLASS I.

The following candidates made 65 per cent. and upward (arranged in order of highest marks):

*Josephine R. Cormier .... St. John.
Percy R. Hayward .... Ashland, Carleton Co.
Raymond Peters .... Florenceville, Carleton Co.

*Jessie E. McLean..............St. John.
Sarah L. Brown,................Snider Mountain, Kings Co.
Margaret Wilson................Moncton.
Arthur W. Barbour,.............Cape Enrage.
*Annie McGuiggan,.. ....St. John.
Lena M. Kearney, ...Upper Woodstock.
John M. Keefe,.................Lakeville, Carleton Co.
Perthenia J. O Leary,............Sussex.
Annie J. Shanklin,..............Shanklin, St. John.
Addie M. Hartt,................Fredericton Junction.
*May Agnes Gillen,.............St. John.
Allan R. Reid,..................Centreville, Carleton Co.
Abram Cronkite,................Campbell Settlement, York Co.
Goldwin Lord,..................Lord's Cove, Charlotte Co.
W. Millen Crawford, ...Debec, Carleton Co.
*Marguerite G. Legere, ...St. John.
Bessie M. Wright, ...Shannonvale, Restigouche Co.
*Evangeline LeBlanc, ...St. John.

Class II.

The following candidates for Class II. obtained 60 per cent. and upwar (arranged in order of highest marks):

Ethel J. McMurray,.............Prince William, York Co.
*Maggie J. Phelan,..............Chatham.
Minnie E. O'Brien,..............Ellenstown, Northumberland Co.
Florence G. DeMille, ...Goshen, Albert Co.
Beatrice Newman, ...Millerton, Northumberland Co.
Robert A. Simpson,.............Chapman, Westmorland Co.
Hester G. Sleep,................Jerusalem, Queens Co.
Inez L. Day,...................Benton, Carleton Co.
*Bessie M. Dysart,..............Cocagne, Kent Co.
Gaynelle E. Long...............Good's Corner, Carleton Co.
Annie Williston,................Newcastle, Northumberland Co.
*Sadie B. Hogan,................Newcastle, Northumberland Co.
*Mary G. Mitchell,..............Welsh Pool, Charlotte Co.
Effie M. Hayward,...............Lincoln, Sunbury Co.
Annie G. Mitton, ...Middle Coverdale, Albert Co.

Mabel McFarlane................Apohaqui, Kings Co.
Madge J. Ricketson,.............Hatfield's Point, Kings Co.
Verna B. Murch,................Bear Island, York Co.
Lola J. Thorne,.................Havelock, Kings Co.
Pearl V. Dennison,..............Stanley, York Co.
Elizabeth Anderson,.............Fredericton.
Lorenzo W. Wadlin,.............Beaver Harbour, Charlotte Co.
Medley F. Miller,..............Middle Southampton, York Co.
Oscar J. Allen,.................Bayfield, Westmorland Co.
Percy A. Fitzpatrick............Port Elgin, Westmorland Co.
Louisa Trail,...................Lower Southampton, York Co.
Mary M. Lindsay,...............Williamstown, Carleton Co.
Willie P. Day,.................McDonald's Point, Queens Co.
Minnie L. Seely,................Ashland, Carleton Co.
Nellie Harmon,.................Peel, Carleton Co.
Jennie N. Bell,.................Tay Creek, York Co.
Sadie A. Cameron,..............Fairley, Northumberland Co.
Georgia W. Barnes,.............Cambridge, Queens Co.
Damie Kennedy,................Hartland, Carleton Co.
Bessie W. Pickett,..............Kingston, Kings Co.
Sadie E. Inch,..................Fredericton.
Georgia A. Sherwood,...........Shannon, Queens Co.
Rhoda J. Corbett,...............Williamstown, Carleton Co.
Bertie H. Plummer,............Upper Gagetown.
Ida McGarrigle,................Nerepis Station, Kings Co.
Robert A. Taylor,...............Chapman, Westmorland Co.
Belle Eddy,....................Clifton, Gloucester Co.
Lena M. Firlotte,...............Jacquet River, Restigouche Co.

The following tabular statement gives the details for each examining station:

*Candidates whose names are marked with an asterisk, wrote an optional paper in French; one-seventh of the marks given for the French paper were added to the general average of the marks given for the other papers.

NORMAL SCHOOL ENTRANCE EXAMINATIONS, 1901.

STATIONS.	No. Presented at Each Station for Examination.	Number of Candidates Presented for the Various Classes with Results. Class I. No. Examined for this Class.	No. Obtained 1st Class.	No. Obtained 2nd Class.	No. Obtained 3rd Class.	No. that Failed to Obtain any Class.	Class II. No. Examined for this Class.	No. Obtained 2nd Class.	No. Obtained 3rd Class.	No. that Failed to Obtain any Class.	Class III. No. Examined for this Class.	No. Obtained 3rd Class.	No. that Failed to Obtain any Class.	SUMMARY. Total Results for Each Class. No. Obtained 1st Class.	No. Obtained 2nd Class.	No. Obtained 3rd Class.	No that Failed to Obtain any Class.
No. 1, Fredericton	77	19	8	4	3	4	56	26	17	13	2	..	2	8	30	20	19
" 2, St. John	74	34	9	16	7	2	38	18	9	11	2	1	1	9	34	17	14
" 3, Moncton	72	26	4	12	8	2	46	18	16	12	..	..	..	4	30	24	14
" 4, St. Stephen	46	21	9	9	2	1	23	5	6	12	2	..	2	9	14	8	15
" 5, Woodstock	68	19	10	6	3	..	49	22	15	12	..	..	..	10	28	18	12
" 6, Chatham	45	12	3	7	1	1	31	10	12	9	2	..	2	3	17	13	12
" 7, Sussex	48	15	4	8	2	1	33	13	9	11	..	..	..	4	21	11	12
" 8, Campbellton	12	5	2	2	..	1	7	5	1	1	..	..	..	2	7	1	2
" 9, Bathurst	16	3	1	1	1	..	13	4	3	6	..	..	..	1	5	4	6
" 10, Hillsboro	35	11	4	7	..	..	24	10	8	6	..	..	..	4	17	8	6
" 11, Andover	22	7	3	2	2	..	15	1	9	5	..	..	..	3	3	11	5
Total	515	172	57	74	29	12	335	132	105	98	8	1	7	57	206	135	117
1900	458	118	23	43	38	14	334	101	91	142	6	..	6	23	144	129	162
Increase	57	54	34	31	..	..	..	31	14	..	2	1	1	34	52	6	..
Decrease	..	..	..	..	10	2	8	..	..	44	..	..	..	..	..	..	45

Normal School Closing Examinations.

The full details of the final Examinations for License held in December 1900, and May, 1901, for the French Department and for the Third Class Candidates of the English Department, and the closing examinations for the higher classes held at Fredericton and St. John, on June 11th, 1901, and the three following days, are given in Table XV, page A 35, to which reference is directed.

The total number admitted to these examinations (including those who were examined for advance of class) was 246. The following is a summary of results:

	No. Examined.	No. Passed.
Grammar School Class..........	11	8
Class I.......................	57	40
Class II......	114	114
Class III.....................	64	75
Failed to be classed.............		9
	246	246

Ten other candidates stood a partial examination for Grammar School Class, and nine of those who gained Class I, or had previously held a First Class License, qualified for Superior School License. At the July examinations 22 other First Class Teachers received the Superior School Certificate.

The names of the successful candidates for Grammar School and Superior School Licenses are given on pages A 36, A 37 and A 38, Part II.

CLASS I.

The following named candidates made 70 per cent. and upwards at the Closing Examinations for Provincial License (arranged in order of the highest marks):

Isabella Reed, ...St. John.
Ruel E. McClintock,.............Centreville, Carleton Co.
Lavina A. McTaggart,............River Charlo, Restigouche Co.
Edna L. Golding,................Fredericton.
*Angus M. Dewar,..............Milltown.
*Annie L Pinder,.. ....Fredericton.
Helen E. Mullin, ...Fredericton.

*Mabel E. McLeod,..............Penobsquis, Kings Co.
Mary Augusta Knight,............Boiestown.
Emily A. Crisp, ...Jacksonville, Carleton Co.
Lena M. Miller,..................Dalhousie.
Lena B. McLeod, ...Farmerston, Carleton Co.
Edward S. McQuaid,..............Alma, Albert Co.
Jennie M. Munro,................St. John.
*Mary M. McInerney,.............Rexton, Kent Co.

CLASS II.

The following candidates made 70 per cent. and upward on Second Class Examination papers. (Arranged in order of the highest marks.)

Katherine Eva McLean,............Charlo Station, Rest. Co.
*Jessie Edwards McLean........... St. John.
Perthenia J. O'Leary,...............Foster's Croft, Kings Co.
Ernest W. Sheils,..................Gagetewn.
Arthur E. Floyd,...................Clover Hill, Kings Co.
*Annie J. Finnegan. ....Peter's Mills, Kent Co.
*Lulu P. Smith,....................Fredericton.
John Law,.......................Gagetown.
Sarah A. Cameron,.......... .....Fairley, North. Co.
Ada A. P. Miller,..................Tay Settlement, York Co.
*Bessie May Wright,...............Shannonvale, Rest. Co.
Abram Cronkhite,..................Campbell Settlement, York Co.
Ida Justine Kierstead,.............Dawson Settlement, Albert Co.
George Nelson Somers,.............Port Elgin West. Co.
Linda M. Ultican,..................Jacquet River, Rest. Co.
Percy S. Bailey,...................Oak Bay, Char. CO.

EXAMINERS.

Mathematics.—Chancellor Harrison and Prof. S M. Dixon, B. A.
English Language and Literature.—H. S. Bridges, M. A., Ph. D.
Latin and Greek.—H. S. Bridges, M. A., Ph. D.
Physioloy and Botany.—Prof. L. W. Bailey, M. A , Ph.D., F.R.S.C.
Physics and Chemistry.—Prof. A. M. Scott, Ph.D.
School System.—G. W. Mersereau, M. A.
Teaching and School Management, etc—G. U. Hay, M. A., Ph.B.
Industrial Drawing, Book-keeping, etc.—Mr. J. Vroom.
French and General History.—Prof. W. T. Raymond, M. A.

[illegible]be candidates whose names are marked with an asterisk took an optional paper in French. One-seventh of [illegible] made in the French papers were added to the average made on the other papers.

The dates at which the next Departmental Examinations will begin are as follows:

High School Entrance, Monday, June 23rd, 1902.
High School Leaving, Wednesday, July 2nd, 1902.
University Matriculation, Wednesday, July 2nd, 1902.
Normal School Entrance, etc., Wednesday, July 2nd, 1902.
Normal School Closing, Tuesday, June 10th. 1902.
Normal School for French Department, Tuesday, May 27th, 1902.
Normal School for Third Class, Tuesday, Dec. 16th, 1902.

The stations at which the University Matriculation, the High School Leaving and the Normal School Entrance examinations will be held are:

Fredericton, St. John, Moncton, St. Stephen, Woodstock, Chatham, Sussex, Campbellton, Bathurst, Hillsboro and Andover.

Candidates for Superior Class Certificates may be examined either during the Closing examinations in June or the Entrance examinations in July.

POOR DISTRICTS.

These districts, which have an assessable valuation of $1200 or less, receive from 25 to 33⅓ per cent. additional grants from the provincial revenues and the County Fund. It has been hoped from year to year that the number of these districts would decrease, but the tendency has been in the opposite direction. The organization of districts in new settlements, the division of some old districts and, in some cases, the successful efforts made by interested parties to keep the assessable valuation as given upon the district lists at a figure much lower than the actual value of the assessable property, have all contributed to increase rather than diminish the number of districts demanding this special aid. The operation of the change in the Schools Act, making the property within the boundaries of any school district taxable for the benefit of such district, without regard to the place of residence of the owner, has been for the advantage of the poorer districts, and will tend in that direction more and more. The total special aid granted to the Poor Districts during the year has been $8,339.56 from the Provincial revenues and $5,272.70 from the County Fund, or $13,612.26 from both sources.

The total number of Poor Districts for the calendar year 1902 are as follows:

Albert County.

Parish of Alma,	Nos. 3, 6, 7, 8, 9, ...	5
" Coverdale,	" 6, 7 (and Hillsboro), *8, 9, 11, 12, 15 (and Salisbury), ...	7
" Elgin,	" 4, 5, *6, 7, *9, *13, 15, 17, 18, 19, 20	11
" Harvey,	" 6, 7 (and Alma), *8, *10, ...	4
" Hillsboro,	" 8, *9, *11, (and Elgin) 12, 13 (and Elgin), 15, ...	6
" Hopewell,	" *4, 5 (and Hillsboro), 9,	3
		36

Carleton County.

Parish of Aberdeen,	Nos. 2, 7, 8, 9, 10, 11, 13 (and Kent), ...	7
" Brighton,	" 11, 17, 18, 19, 19½, ...	5
" Kent,	" *1½, (and Peel), *9, 19, ...	3
" Northampton,	" *8, 11 (and Southampton),	2
" Peel,	" 5, ...	1
" Wicklow,	" *8.	1
" Wilmot,	" *14, 17, ...	2
" Woodstock,	" 11, 13, ...	2
		23

Charlotte County.

Parish of Clarendon,	Nos. 1, 3, 9 (and Blissville)	3
" Dumbarton,	" 1, 4, 5, *7, *7½.	5
" Grand Manan,	" 7, *9, ...	2
" Lepreaux,	" 1, *2, (and Musquash), 5,	3
" Penfield,	" *6, ...	1
" St. David,	" *2, *7, ...	2
" St. George,	" 7, 8, 8½, (and Dumbarton), 9, 10, 11, *15,.	[illegible]
" St. James,	" *4, *4½, (St. David), *5, 8, *10 11, *13, *19, ...	8
" St. Patrick,	" *4, *6, 9, (and St. George), *10, ...	4
" St. Stephen,	" *2, 7½, (and St. James), ...	2
" West Isles,	" 1, *5½, 6½, 8, ...	4
		41

GLOUCESTER COUNTY.

Parish of Bathurst,	Nos. 3, 4, 6, 7, *8, 10, 11, ...	[illegible]
" Beresford,	" *7, (and Bathurst), 7½, (and Bath), 8, *8½, 9, *10A, (and Bathurst), 11, 12, 13, 13½, 14, 15, 16, ...	13
" Caraquet,	" 1, 3, 4, 4½, ...	4
" Inkerman,	" 1, 4, 5, 7, *8, ...	5
" New Bandon,	" 1, 3½, 4½, 5½, 7, 10, ...	6
" Paquetville,	" 1, 2, *4, 5, ...	4
" Saumarez,	" 2, *2½, *4, ...	3
" Shippegan,	" 1½, *3, *3½, 5, *6½, 8, 8½, 9, 9½, 10, 10½	11
		53

KENT COUNTY.

Parish of Acadieville,	Nos. 1, 2, 3, 4, *5, 6, 7, 8, 9, ...	9
" Carleton,	" 2. 4, 6, 8, 9, 10, ...	6
" Dundas,	" *5, 5½, 6A (and Moncton), *10A (and Moncton) 11, ...	5
" Harcourt,	" 1, 6, 7, 7½, 10, 11, ...	6
" Richibucto,	" 3, 5, 7, 9, 9A, 11, 13, ...	7
" St. Louis,	" 1, *5, *8, *9, (and Richibucto), 10, 11,	6
" St. Mary's,	" 5, 7, 7½, *14, ...	4
" St. Paul,	" 1, 2, 3, *4, 5, 6, 7 (and St. Mary's), 9,	8
" Weldford,	" 2½, 4, 5½ (and St. Mary's), 7, 11, 12, 13, 17, 18, *20, 21, 22, 23, 24, ...	14
" Wellington.	" *12½, 13, 15, 16, 17, 18, ...	6
		71

KINGS COUNTY.

Parish of Cardwell,	Nos. 4, *8, 10 (and Sussex), ...	3
" Hammond,	" 1 (and Waterford), 2, *3, *5, 8 (and Sussex, ...	5
" Havelock,	" *5, 6, 11, 15, ...	4
Kars,	" 4, 6, ...	2
" Kingston,	" 8, 9, 14, *15, ...	4
Norton,	" 9, *11 (and Sussex), ...	2
" Rothesay,	" *6, ...	1
" Springfield,	" *4, *5, *6 (and Johnston), *13, 14, 18, 21, ...	[illegible]

KINGS COUNTY.—Continued.

Parish of Studholm,	" 1, 2, *5, *6, *19, *26, ...	6
" Sussex,	" 4 (and Waterford), *8, 11, 12, 14. 15,	6
" Upham,	" 25 (and St. Martins), ...	1
" Waterford,	" 1, 3, 4 (and Cardwell), *6, 7, 9, ...	6
" Westfield,	" 5 (and Greenwich), *8, 9,*10,*12,*13,	6
		53

MADAWASKA COUNTY.

Partsh of Madawaska,	Nos. 3, 4, 4½ 5, 6, ...	5
" St. Anne,	" *2, 5, 6, 7, ...	4
" St. Basil,	" 2, 5, 8, 9, 10, ...	5
" St. Francis,	" *5, 6, 7, 8, 9, 10, 11, 13, 14, ...	9
" St. Hilaire,	" 5, 6, 7, 8, 9, ...	5
" St. Jacques,	" 2, 3, 4, 5, ...	4
" St. Leonard,	" 7, 8, ...	2
		34

NORTHUMBERLAND COUNTY.

Parish of Alnwick,	Nos. *1, *2, 8½, *12, 14, ...	5
" Blackville,	" 1½, 3, 3½, 9, 12, 13, ...	6
" Blissfield,	" 1, *1½ (and Blackville), *2, *2½, 3, ...	5
" Glenelg,	" *3, 5, 6, 8, 8½, 9, ...	6
" Hardwicke.	" 3, 6, ...	2
" Ludlow,	" 1, *1½, 2, 4, 5, ...	5
" Nelson,	" 6, *6½, 7, ...	3
" Newcastle,	" *2½, ...	1
Northesk,	" *1, 3, 11½, ...	3
" Rogerville,	" 1, 2, 3A (and Acadieville), 10½, *11, *13, *14, *15, 16 (and Acadieville), ..	9
Southesk,	" 7, *7½, ...	2
		47

QUEENS COUNTY.

ish of Brunswick,	Nos. *3, 4, 5, 7, 23 (and Salisbury), ...	5
Cambridge,	" *6, (and Waterboro), *7, *9, ...	3
Canning,	" 3, 4, *6, ...	3

QUEENS COUNTY.—Continued.

Parish of Chipman,	" 2, 3, 7, *9, 12, 13, (and Waterboro), 14, (and Waterboro), 16, (and Harcourt),	8
" Gagetown,	" *1, ...	1
" Hampstead,	" 3, (and Gagetown), 10, ...	2
" Johnston,	" 2, 6, *6 (and Springfield), 8, *9, *11, (and Wickham), *12, 13, *15, (and Springfield), 17, ...	10
" Petersville,	" 2, *13, 16, ...	3
" Waterboro,	" *2, 3, *5, *8, (and Johnston), 9, ...	5
" Wickham,	" *10, *12, (and Johnston), ...	2
		42

RESTIGOUCHE COUNTY.

Parish of Addington,	Nos. *2½, 3, ...	2
" Balmoral,	" 1, 4, 5, 6, (and Addington), ...	4
" Colborne,	" 1½ (and Balmoral), 4, ...	2
" Dalhousie,	" 4, ...	1
" Durham,	" 1½, *5, 9, 10, 11, ...	5
Eldon,	" *1.	1
		15

ST. JOHN COUNTY.

Parish of Musquash,	Nos. *7, *8, 9, ...	3
" St. Martins,	" 1, *3, *3½, *4, 9, *11, *12, *23, (and Simonds), 30, ...	9
" Simonds,	" *14, *15, *16, *20, *21, (Bdr), 22 (Bdr),	6
		18

SUNBURY COUNTY.

Parish of Blissville,	Nos. *5, *6, 7, 8, 9 (and Clarendon), ...	5
" Burton,	" 6, *8, 9, 10, 11, 12, 13, ...	7
" Gladstone,	" *2, *3, 5, 6, 8, 9 (and New Maryland),	6
Lincoln,	" 6, ...	1
" Maugerville,	" 4 (and St. Mary's), ...	1
" Northfield,	" 1, 2, *3, 5, ...	4
" Sheffield,	" 1A (and Canning), 3, 6, *7, ...	4
		28

VICTORIA COUNTY.

Parish of Andover,	Nos. 6, 8, ...	2
" Drummond,	" 1½, 2, 3, 5, 6, 8½, 9, 11, 12, 13, 14,	11
" Gordon,	" *2, 3, 7, *8, 9 (and Lorne), ...	5
" Grand Falls,	" *2, 3, *4, 5, 8, 10, *11, ...	7
" Lorne,	" 1, 2, 5, 8, ...	4
" Perth,	" 3, 5, 6, 7, *8 (and Drummond), 10, *11 *12, *13, ...	9
		38

WESTMORLAND COUNTY.

Parish of Botsford,	Nos. *4, 20, 22, 23, ...	4
" Dorchester,	" *4 (and Sackville, 15, 26, ...	3
" Moncton,	" *6A (and Dundas), *20, * 21, 22, *24, 25, 26, *30, 32, 33, ...	10
" Sackville,	" 1, 3, 4, 15' 17, 18, ...	6
" Salisbury,	" 9, 14, 23 (and Hav. and Bruns.), 25,	4
" Shediac,	" 22, 23, 24, 26, ...	4
" Westmorland,	" 11 (and Sackville), ...	1
		32

YORK COUNTY.

Parish of Bright,	Nos. *6½, *7½ 9, *11 (and Southampton),...	4
" Canterbury,	" *5, 10, 10½, 12, 20, 22, 24, ...	7
" Douglas.	" 12, 14, *16, 20, ...	4
" Kingsclear,	" *7, *8, 9, 12, ...	4
" Manners Sutton	" 7, 9, 10, 11	4
" McAdam,	" *7, ...	1
" New Maryland,	" . 1A, *3, ...	2
" North Lake,	" *13½, 17, 18, 19½, ...	4
" Prince William,	" 6, ...	1
" St. Mary's,	" 9, 10, 11, 14, 15, ...	5
" Southampton,	" *8, *10, 13, 14, 15, *16, 17, 18, 19. .	9
" Stanley,	" *1½, *2, 4, 6½, *9, 14*, 16, 17, ...	8
		53
	Total for 1902, ...	585
	Increose, ...	1

* Districts marked * to receive one-quarter rate.

School House Grants to Poor Districts.

By vote of the Legislature the sum of $1,000 was appropriated at the last session to assist Poor Districts in building and furnishing school houses.

The following grants from this appropriation were made during the year ending October 31st, 1901:

ALBERT COUNTY.

Parish of Elgin, No. 6, ...		$ 30 00

CARLETON COUNTY.

Parish of Kent, No. 8, ...	$15 00	
" Kent, No. 9, ...	20 00	
" Kent, No. 16, ...	15 00	
		50.00

CHARLOTTE COUNTY.

Parish of St. James, No. 1, ...	$45 00	
" St. Stephen, No. 6, ...	25 00	
		70 00

GLOUCESTER COUNTY.

Parish of Bathurst, No. 15, ...	$25 00	
" Beresford, No. 13½,	10 00	
" Caraquet, No. 1, ...	15 00	
" Shippegan, No. 3½	20 00	
" Shippegan, No. 8, ...	20 00	
		90 00

KENT COUNTY.

Parish of Acadieville, No. 8,	$25 00	
" of Acadieville, No. 9, ...	25 00	
" Carleton, No. 10, ...	25 00	
		75 00

KINGS COUNTY.

Parish of Kingston, No. 2, ...	$25 00	
" Sussex, No. 8, ...	25 00	
		50 00

MADAWASKA COUNTY.

Parish of St. Basil, No. 8.	$25 00	
" St. Francis, No. 13......	25 00	
	———	50 00

NORTHUMBERLAND COUNTY.

Parish of Alnwick, No. 7, ...	$20 00	
" Alnwick, No. 8½, ...	20 00	
" Blackville, No. 13, ...	25 00	
" Blissfield and Blackville, No. 1½	25 00	
" Blissfield, No. 3, ...	15 00	
" Glenelg, No. 3, ...	25 00	
	———	130 00

QUEENS COUNTY.

Parish of Canning, No. 2, ...	$10 00	
" Canning, No. 3, ...	10 00	
" Hampstead and Greenwich, No. 6......	15 00	
" Johnston, No. 13, ...	20 00	
" Petersville, No. 9, ...	15 00	
" Waterboro'. No. 8, ...	20 00	
	———	90 00

RESTIGOUCHE COUNTY.

Parish of Colburn and Balmoral, No. 1½, ...	$10 00	
" Durham, No. 10, ...	10 00	
" Durham, No. 11, ...	50 00	
	———	70 00

ST. JOHN COUNTY.

Parish of Lancaster, No. 11, ...	$30 00	
" St. Martins, No. 1, ...	15 00	
" Simonds, No. 7, ...	15 00	
	———	60 00

SUNBURY COUNTY.

rish of Lincoln, No. 4, ...	$15 00	
" Northfield, No. 5, ...	15 00	
	———	30 00

VICTORIA COUNTY.

Parish of Grand Falls, No. No. 4,	$15 00	
" Grand Falls, No. 5,.......	30 00	
		45 00

WESTMORLAND COUNTY.

Parish of Moncton, No. 25, ...	$20 00	
" Moncton, No. 33, ...	25 00	
		45 00

YORK COUNTY.

Parish of Bright, No. 9, ...	$20 00	
" Manners Sutton, No. 9,	20 00	
" Stanley, No. 17, ...	20 00	
		60 00
Total, ...		$945 00

School Libraries.

The total number of volumes reported as having been purchased during the fiscal year for School Libraries was 894 at a cost of $356.75 of which the Province paid $118.90. The total number of volumes reported since 1891 was 13,007, and the money expended $6,335.34. Of this sum the amount contributed from the provincial revenue was $2050.14 and the amount raised by the districts was $4285.20.

Comparatively few teachers or school officials have made the annual report to the Chief Superintendent required by Regulation 34 and Appendix 1, as to the library statistics. No district having a school library will, hereafter, receive any additional bonus until a satisfactory report shall have been made, showing the number and condition of the books on hand, in accordance with instructions given on pages 121 and 122 of the Manual.

Arbor Day Report, 1901.

Inspectoral District.	No. Districts Observing Arbor Day.	No. of Trees Planted.	No. of Shrubs Planted.	No. of Flower Beds.	General Improvement.
No. 1	119	519	75	112	69
" 2	71	292	78	75	66
" 3	117	420	95	166	44
" 4	76	388	45	119	76
" 5	103	208	43	83	103
" 6	89	210	109	121	89
Total	575	2037	445	676	447
For 1900	462	1796	271	510	297
Increase.	113	241	174	166	150

The University of New Brunswick.

The attendance of students at the University is larger than during any former year; but the Freshman Class is considerably less in number than last year's Freshman Class.

The total number enrolled is 116, of whom 30 are women. As a proof of the influence of the Matriculation examinations held under the supervision of the Education Department, and of the more intimate connection maintained between the University and the public schools, it may be stated that about twenty-five per cent of the undergraduates are licensed teachers.

The students are classified as follows :

Seniors,	20	Occasional Students,	
Juniors,	25	" " ...	3
Sophomores,	39	" "	2
Freshmen,	20		7
Undergraduates,	104		12

Of the above 25 are taking the Engineering Course in whole or in part.

The following Degrees were conferred, in course, at the last Encænia : ·helor of Engineering 1 ; B. Sc. 1 ; B. A. 7 ; Ph. D. 1.

The resignation by Professor Stephen M. Dixon, M. A., B. A. I. at the close of the last Academic year, of the Chair of Civil Engineering and Chemistry, was the cause of much regret to the Senate and friends of the University. Prof. Dixon had labored earnestly and successfully since 1892 in the interests of the Department of Civil Engineering, and to his zeal and energy the University is largely indebted for the inauguration and completion of the movement which has placed upon the College grounds the handsome Engineering Building which now provides so much better accommodations than formerly existed for the effective teaching of Applied Science.

The Senate was fortunate in being able to secure without delay the services of Professor Ernest Brydone-Jack, B. A., C. E. Associate Member of the American Society of Civil Engineers. Professor Jack is a graduate of the University of New Brunswick (1891) and son of the late Dr. W. Brydone-Jack who was President of the University from 1861 to 1885.

NOTES ON THE APPENDICES.

Special attention is directed to Part III of this Report which contains: A. The Report of the Principal of the Normal School: B. The Reports of the six School Inspectors: C. The Reports of the School Boards of Fredericton, St. John, Moncton, St. Stephen, Milltown, Woodstock, Campbellton, Chatham and Newcastle: D. The Reports of the School for Deaf Mutes at Fredericton and the School for the Blind, Halifax: E. The Report of the Dominion Educational Association held at Ottawa in September last, a summary of the proceedings of the several County Institutes and a report of the Macdonald Manual Training School at Fredericton by the Director Mr. E. E. MacCready: F. An address delivered before the Dominion Educational Association on Manual Training in Rural Schools, by Professor J. W. Robertson.

I beg to add the following notes and comments on some of these reports.

The Normal School.

The attendance at the Normal School for the year under review was 198 a decrease of 60 as compared with the previous year; but at the present time (1901-2) the enrolment is 270 which is about the average for the past ten years. The difficulty experienced in finding a supply of teachers for the schools indicates that many who receive training at the Normal School teach but a very short time; indeed there is reason to believe that not a few never engage in teaching or drop out of the list of active teachers at the end of a single term. It would appear but reasonable that those who receive the benefit of free tuition and training at considerable expense to the Province should be required to serve in the public schools at least three years.

The attendance at the French Department has proved quite insufficient to provide a supply of teachers for the Acadian Districts. In the County of Madawaska there is a lamentable deficiency of trained teachers. Of the 60 teachers employed in that County during the past year all but three were of the Third Class, and 14 had received no training whatever. So long as the French-speaking teachers aim only to prepare themselves for Licenses of the Third Class, and so long as the rate-payers and trustees are satisfied to employ untrained and imperfectly educated teachers, there is little chance for improvement. Special encouragement has been given to French-speaking candidates to seek for higher classification, and I am not without hope that before long a larger number will be found preparing for the advanced classes. At the present time there are only fourteen French-speaking pupil teachers at the Normal School, and of these five are enrolled in the English Department as candidates for either the Second or First Class.

The temporary withdrawal of Eldon Mullin, Esq., from the principalship of the Normal School, after a period of service of nearly eighteen years, and the appointment of Dr. William Crockett to fill his place, together with the circumstances which led up to the change, demand some notice in this Report, though the principal events occurred after the close of the school year under review.

Educational Assistance for South Africa.

During the summer of 1900 a gentleman giving his name as E. B. Sargant called at the Education Office and presentod a letter of introduction from Lord Strathcona, the Canadian Commissioner in London. The letter stated that Mr. Sargant was an official in the Education Department, London; that he was visiting Canada for the purpose of examining the educational systems of the several provinces of the Dominion, and solicited my assistance in the matter. I was unfortunately preparing to leave Fredericton on the day of Mr. Sargant's call, to meet an engagement in another part of the province; but I spent as much time as possible with him, supplied him with the School Manual, Educational Reports, etc., and gave him a letter of introduction to ıchers and school officials in New Brunswick. Mr. S. had left Fredericton fore my return, and I had almost forgotten the circumstances of his visit ıen I received from him a letter which I hereto append:

EDUCATIONAL DEPARTMENT,
Bloemfontein, March, 20th, 1901.

DEAR DR. INCH,—Perhaps you will remember a visit I paid to you at Fredericton in the summer of last year in connection with some enquiries which I was making unofficially into the educational system of New Brunswick.

Very soon after that time—in fact while I was in the Province of Quebec—I received a cablegram from Sir Alfred Milner asking me to undertake provisionally the education of the new colonies. I have been at work since the beginning of November, but military law has made it difficult to do much as yet. However, there seems a likelihood that by the middle of the year civil administration will have been thoroughly established, and that the important educational buildings, which are now used as hospitals, will have been released by the military.

At Pretoria there is a fine Staats Model School, as well as a Staats Gymnasium and a Staats Meisjes School.

In thinking over various ways of beginning work there, I have come to the conclusion that none would be more satisfactory than to ask for the temporary assistance of experienced teachers from a country which in many ways might provide a model for the new educational system to be introduced here.

New Brunswick is the country which I have in my mind's eye, and there are three of your staff whose work I particularly admired, namely, Mr. Eldon Mullin, Principal of the Normal School; Miss C. E. Bridges, who conducts the kindergarten of the Model School, and Dr. H. S. Bridges, head master of the High School, and superintendent under the St. John School Board. There was also a Miss Nicholson in the York Street School whose method of handling children attracted my attention.

I should like to sound you as to the possibility of the first three, and Miss Nicholson or any teacher whom Miss Bridges preferred to her, coming to South Africa for a year's work and putting the Normal School at Pretoria (perhaps also the Gymnasium) on the right lines. To spare them would, I know, put a strain upon your arrangements; all I can say is that just as in the war, we needed the best soldiers we could find, so now England and her colonies will have to provide the best civil administration.

I do not know what salaries the ladies and gentlemen named are at present receiving, and your Annual Report does not give me the information, but my idea would be that all their travelling expenses as well as their salaries for the time that they were away, should be paid by the Transvaal administration, and that a bonus of (say) a quarter of their salary should be added.

I will not make any more definite proposal than this before I hear from you as to the possibility of the plan being carried out.

If they are willing to come, and you can spare them, perhaps you would mention what salary each is now receiving; then the whole matter could be settled by cable with the assent of the Colonial Secretary and High Commissioner.

I wish it were possible for me to have your advice in many matters of importance which arise for decision every day. I know none to whom I would more readily go. It would help me in my work, if you could let me have your Annual Reports, as they come out, one copy for the Transvaal, and one for the Orange River colony. They should be addressed to me as Acting Director of Education at Bloemfontein and Pretoria respectively. I will, of course, send you my reports in return.

With grateful remembrances,

Believe me,

Yours very truly,

E. B. SARGANT.

After careful deliberation the Board of Education regarded it as a patriotic duty to comply with Mr. Sargant's request, and to aid him as far as possible in organizing the educational work in the Transvaal and Orange River Colonies. Leave of absence was, accordingly, granted to Principal Mullin, of the Normal School, and Miss Bridges, of the Model School, in case they should decide to enter into an agreement with the South African authorities. The prolongation of the war and the consequent unsettled condition of the country delayed the closing of negotiations until a few weeks ago. Mr. Mullin and Miss Bridges carry with them the best wishes of the educational authorities of New Brunswick for their success in their new sphere of labor.

In the cases of Dr. Bridges, Miss Nicholson, and other New Brunswick teachers who are under contract with local School Boards, the Board of Education did not deem it necessary to take any action, other than to obtain such information as might be of interest to any who might desire to offer their services for the South African work.

As a large number of teachers in New Brunswick, Nova Scotia and the United States have applied to me for information in regard to the conditions likely to be met with by teachers in the Transvaal, I append the following as of general interest:

MEMORANDUM WITH REGARD TO THE PROSPECTS OF TEACHERS IN THE ORANGE RIVER COLONY AND IN THE TRANSVAAL FOR THE USE OF APPLICANTS RESIDING BEYOND THE LIMITS OF SOUTH AFRICA.

In considering the question of seeking teaching employment in these colonies, applicants will do well to read carefully the following statement as to the conditions under which they are likely to work:

(1) The cost of living in South Africa, especially at a distance from the coast, is higher than in most other parts of the British dominions. The charges at a good boarding house are from £8 to £10 a month in most towns, and in Bloemfontein, Pretoria and Johannesburg may rise still higher. The charges at hotels are from 12s. 6d. to 15s. a day. Many necessaries of life and nearly all luxuries are proportionally dear.

(2) The climate in the Transvaal and the Orange River Colony is of the "continental" type. The summers are hot and the winters cold, the rains generally falling during the former season. It is, therefore, necessary to be provided with both heavy and light clothing.

(3) Teachers will be for some time at any rate directly under the education department and not responsible to any local committees. This relation, however, may be altered in the future, except in the case of those occupying the higher positions.

(4) The engagement with every teacher from outside the limits of the Colonies is made for three years. Should that engagement be terminated on the part of the teacher before the expiration of the period named, the passage money to the Colony is forfeited and the return fare is not paid by Government. But if the engagement is fulfilled, Government pays the passage money in both directions.

(5) The salaries paid to assistants in elementary schools are from £100 to £200 a year. To head teachers or elementary schools and to the assistants in higher schools from £200 to £400 a year, and to heads of higher schools and inspectors from £400 to £600. There are a few posts carrying larger salaries but these may for practical purposes be disregarded. For the sake of comparison the salaries paid by the leading banks to their junior clerks are here stated: If sent for service up country, they begin at salaries of £250 a year, and are provided with quarters when this is possible, otherwise no allowance is made for lodging.

(6) The medium of instruction in schools is English but it is expected that all teachers (except those in Johannesburg) will learn to speak the "taal" or colloquial Dutch of S. A. Bible instruction is given to Cape Dutch children in Dutch, but, as there will always be plenty of junior assistants able to speak Dutch, no such accurate knowledge of the language, as is required for this purpose, is necessary on the part of those who come from the United Kingdom or the Colonies.

(7) It is expected that all teachers who do not belong to the higher rank will endeavor to raise their scholastic and professional qualifications and the department will endeavor to offer them the opportunity of attendance at courses at one or other of the Normal Colleges for this purpose.

(8 It is considered of the utmost importance that teachers should not be of advanced years.

Teachers wishing to make application for positions in the new Colonies should address their letters to "The Director of Education, Pretoria, South Africa."

THE INSPECTORS' REPORTS.

The details given in the Reports of the Inspectors will be read with interest by all acquainted with the localities mentioned. Taken as a whole they afford encouragement, but at the same time they reveal the difficulties and obstacles which are constantly encountered by those who are working for the best educational interests of the country. The inertia of ignorance is hard to be overcome. It requires more enlightenment and unselfishness than are found in many communities to induce the people to tax themselves for their own benefit or that of their children, and more intelligence than many local school boards possess to manage wisely the business of the schools. But it is satisfactory to note progress in many places which only a few years ago gave little indication of interest in education.

As in former years, most of the Inspectors have found themselves unable to complete the work assigned them by the School Law and Regulations. In July last Inspector Steeves found it necessary to apply for leave of absence for some months on account of impaired health. I am glad to say that he is so far recovered as to be able to resume his duties with his accustomed energy and ty. In September last the Board of Education, in view of the necessities ıe work, appointed an additional Inspector, Mr. Jean Flavien Doucet, who qualified himself for the position by his experience of several years as a successful teacher in the Public Schools, and by passing the prescribed examinations for Grammar School License. It is intended that Mr. Doucet shall, so far as practicable, inspect the schools in the Counties of Madawaska and Gloucester, and as many of the other schools in the French-speaking districts of Northumberland and Kent as his time will permit. This renders necessary a re-distribution of the work of the other Inspectors. The definite boundaries of the several Inspectorates, as re-arranged, will be announced at an early date.

REPORTS OF SCHOOL BOARDS IN CITIES AND INCORPORATED TOWNS.

On account of the change in the beginning of the school year, I gave notice some months ago to the secretaries of the city and town school boards that they need not report for more than the interim term ended June 30, 1901, so that their reports hereafter may be for the school year beginning and ending at mid-summer.

In addition to the usual statistics, which indicate in general satisfactory progress, I beg to call attention to a few facts of more than ordinary educational interest.

Among the prizes to be given hereafter in the Fredericton Grammar School will be a handsome silver medal displaying the profile of the late chairman of the School Board, George E. Courlthard, Esq., M. D., who for many years took an active part in the management and welfare of the city schools and of the Provincial University. The medal is the gift of Mrs. Coulthard. It was won this year by Miss Turner, of Gibson.

The St. John School Board has continued the work of providing proper school accommodation for all parts of the city. A noble building on the West Side, to be known as the La Tour School, is now nearing completion, and will be ready for use at the beginning of the next term. Ground has also been purchased for the erection of a new building for the children now attending the Elm Street School. The estimated value of the school property in the city of Saint John, is about $350,000, on which the Board carries insurance to the amount of $205,730.

In Moncton, the School Board has wisely made provision for a suitable play-ground for the Victoria School. A block of land 230x18I feet adjacent to the building has been purchased for $2,000.

At St. Stephen the graduating exercises of the High School were of mo than ordinary interest. Fully 1,000 people were in attendance. A pup of this school made the highest average of the candidates from th

Maritime Provinces, at the entrance examinations of the Royal Military College at Kingston.

The Milltown Schools maintain their reputation for efficiency. They have long had the distinction of making a very high average of attendance.

The educational event of greatest importance to the eastern part of the province has been the completion and opening of the fine building for the Northumberland County Grammar School at Chatham.

This building was formally opened on Jan. 6th, by interesting exercises. Addresses were made by the Chgirman of the School Board, Mayor W. B. Snowball and by the Hon. J. P. Burchell, M. P. P., C. E. Fish, Esq., M. P. P. Rev. Father McLauchlin, Rev. Canon Forsyth, Rev. W. C. Matthews, His Honor Judge Wilkinson, Trustee J. L. Stewart, and the Principal Dr. Philip Cox.

The building is 103x76½ feet, three stories above the basement. The walls are of rock-face, broken ashler sandstone with cut trimmings; roof, slate and gravel, with galvanized iron cornice, and lead hip-rods, flashings, gutters, etc., and iron cresting.

The three main entrance sections project four feet beyond the general line of the walls and run up the full height of them. That in the front is 35 feet 4 inches wide, and those at the ends, 18 feet wide. They are arched and pillared, reached by stone steps, and vestibuled. The heavy plate glass with which the double doors of all are fitted give the visitor an idea of the substantial character of the materials used in the building and the class to which the work belongs.

The interior is well planned. Nine spacious class rooms with an assembly hall, cloak rooms, teachers' closets, etc., will afford ample accommodation for 450 pupils. The hall ways are wide and airy, the floors and stairs are all of native hardwood finished in natural colors. The sanitary arrangements and the methods of heating, lighting, ventilation, etc., are all in eccordance with the most modern ideas. The cost of the building has been something over $40,000.

THE SCHOOLS FOR DEAF MUTES AND FOR THE BLIND.

The reports from these institutions are so full that I do not think it necessary in this place to say more than to direct attention to the statements of the principals and the boards of directors. The eminently practical work done at School for the Blind is of special importance. To prepare those deprived ght to earn their own living and to become active and productive members dustrial society instead of becoming a charge upon the benevolence of others, is a work which must commend itself to every thoughtful citizen. In a recent letter the Principal, Dr. C. F. Fraser, says: "We have opened a department for manufacturing books in raised print. These books are most advantageous to our pupils. We are looking forward to training some of our pupils as masseurs, and now have one of our graduates in London, G. B., for the purpose of qualifying herself as an instructor. This department will be particularly useful to those boys and girls who are not musical."

TEACHERS' INSTITUTES AND THE SUMMER SCHOOL OF SCIENCE.

In Appendix E will be found an outline of the proceedings of these interesting conventions of teachers. The Summer School of Science of the Atlantic Provinces has been growing rapidly during the last few years not only in membership, but in importance as one of the most effective organizations for enabling teachers during their summer vacation to make themselves better acquainted with certain subjects they are called upon to teach, and especially to keep abreast with the advancement of Natural History and Science. It is found that the teachers who attend the Summer School return to their work with increased enthusiasm and zeal; and their pupils thus gain the benefit.

The legislature of each of the three Atlantic Provinces makes an annual grant towards the expenses of the school. In view of the fact that it met last year at Lunenburg, N. S., the Government of that Province contributed $200, while the other Provinces gave $100 each. Nova Scotia and Prince Edward Island grant also to their teachers who attend an additional vacation of one week. I would be glad to see the same privilege, or its equivalent in some other form, granted to New Brunswick teachers.

The Summer School will meet the last week in July and the first week in August, 1902, at St. Stephen, under the presidency of Professor L. W. Bailey, of the University of New Brunswith. The citizens of St. Stephen and Milltown, with their accustomed hospitality towards teachers, are making special preparations for the reception of those who attend. In view of the meeting of the Summer School at St. Stephen, the Charlotte County Institute will not be convened this year. It is hoped that the membership of the school this year will exceed that of any former year.

The Provincial Institute, which meets bi-ennially is to convene this year at Fredericton, on the 26th of June, and the two days following. A very interesting programme has been prepared. Several prominent educationists fro sister provinces and from the United States are expected to take part in th proceedings. The University Library, Museum and Science building will be open for the inspection of visitors. It is hoped that a very large number of our teachers will enrol as members of the institute.

Manual and Agricultural Instruction in the Public Schools.

The lively and sympathetic interest with which the people of Canada have watched the movement initiated by the generosity of Sir William Macdonald and organized by Professor J. W. Robertson to make Manual Training a part of the Public School Course in every Province of the Dominion, justifies me in giving more space than usual in this report to what has been accomplished in this direction and what is proposed for the future.

During my visit to England, in September last, I took the opportunity of making inquiries in regard to the progress of Manual Training under the direction of the School Boards, and of spending a day in one of the largest central schools in London watching the boys at work, examining the finished articles they had made, and having the system explained to me by the Superintendent.

Manual Training in a few of the Primary Schools was begun in London in 1886. It was found so useful and acceptable that it rapidly extended. In 1890 it was formally recognized by the English Education Department as a school subject, and the funds of the London School Board were thus made available for its support. In the same year Parliament provided liberal grants from the Imperial Exchequer, for its extension throughout the Kingdom. At that time the system had been introduced into less than 50 schools. In 1900 the work had grown to such an extent that provision had been made in Manual Training centres for the instruction in this system of the boys of about 5,000 schools.

In 1897, a Royal Commission was appointed to determine how far, and in what form Manual Instruction should be included in the work of the Primary Schools in Ireland under the direction of the Board of National Education. After a thorough investigation and study of the subject in England, Scotland, Germany, France, Switzerland and Holland, the Commissioners made a most interesting and instructive report. A copy of their last report is before me from which I make the following extracts:

> "We may at once express our strong conviction that Manual and Practical Instruction ..o be introduced, as far as possible, into all schools where it does not at present exist, ..hat, in those schools where it does exist, it ought to be largely developed and extended. ..re satisfied that such a change will not involve any detriment to the literary education of ..pils, while it will contribute largely to develop their faculties, to quicken their intelli-..nd to fit them better for their work in life."

The reasons assigned by the Commissioners for their conclusions are thus summed up:

1. "First, then there are reasons founded on educationsl principles. The present system which consists largely in the study of books, is one-sided in its character , and it leaves some of the most useful faculties of the mind absolutely untrained. We think it important that children should be taught not merely to take in knowledge from books, but to observe with intelligence the material world around them ; that they should be trained in habits of correct reasoning on the facts observed; and that they should even at school acquire some skill in the use of hand and eye to execute the conceptions of the brain. Such a training we regard as valuable to all, but especially valuable to those whose lives are to be mainly devoted to industrial arts and occupations. The great bulk of the pupils attending primary schools under the National Board will have to earn their bread by the work of their hands; it is therefore important that they should be trained, from the beginning, to use their hands with dexterity and intelligence."

2. "Next, we have the practical experience of those schools in England, Scotland, and on the continent of Europe, in which such a system as we recommend has been already introduced and tested. The evidence we have received on this point, is absolutely unanimous and, as we think, entirely conclusive. We have been told, over and over again, that the introduction of manual and practical training has contributed greatly to stimulate the intelligence of the pupils, to increase their interest in school work, and to make school life generally brighter and more pleasant. As a consequence the school attendance is improved ; the children remain at school to a more advanced age ; and much time is gained for the purpose of education.

"We inquired particularly whether the literary side of school studies—reading, writing, arithmetic, grammar, and geography—had suffered any loss by the change ; and the answer was uniform, that no such loss had been observed. In some cases we were assured that the literary studies had been positively improved by the introduction of manual training. This result was accounted for, partly by the increased intelligence of the children, partly by the constant change and variety of their occupations,—many of the most useful exercises being only a kind of organized play, and partly by their increased interest in their work.

"We regard it also as a very significant testimony to the value of manual training, that wherever it has once been introduced, it has, with hardly an exception, been continued and extended. There has been practically no disposition to go back to the old system, which made primary education almost exclusively literary in its character; and after an experience extending over some years, there is a general concensus of managers of schools, inspectors, and parents, that the value of primary education has been greatly enhanced by the change."

3. "Lastly, there is a consideration of a practical character, which seems to us deserving of no little weight. A strong desire exists throughout this country, and it is growing stronger every day, for the introduction of a general system of Technical Education. It is thought that a good system of Technical Education would contribute largely towards the development of arts and industries in Ireland ; and in this opinion we entirely concur. But the present system of primary education is so one-sided in its character that it leaves the pupils quite unprepared for Technical Education. The clever boys trained in the National Schools, if they are disposed to seek for a higher education, may pass with advantage int Intermediate Schools of the kind now general in Ireland ; but they are not fit to enter Technical School, even it they had such a school at their doors. Now it seems to us th changes we recommend would go far to remedy this defect. The system of National Educa tion, modified as we propose, would give an all-round training to the faculties of the childre

and would thus lay a solid foundation for any system of higher education—literary, scientific or technical — which might afterwards be found suitable to their talents and their circumstances."

CONCLUSION.

"In presenting this Report to your Excellency, we venture to express our conviction that, if our recommendations be adopted, the system of education carried out in the Primary Schools of Ireland can be made, within a few years, very thorough and complete. At present, no doubt, it is excellent in some respects; but in other respects it seems to us seriously deficient. Insisting too much, as it does, on the study of books, it leaves the faculty of observation and other important faculties comparatively uncultivated; and it neglects almost entirely that training of the hand and eye which would be so useful to the children in their after life, and which is now regarded both in England and on the Continent of Europe as an element of great importance in primary education.

"The development of Manual and Practical Instruction, on the lines we have pointed out, will remedy these defects, and will not, we are satisfied, inflict any injury on the literary education which is now given. It will quicken the intelligence of the children, brighten the tone of school life, and make school-work generally more interesting and attractive. With the system of National Education modified as we propose, the children will be taught not by means of books only, but also by the more simple and effective agency of things; and they will be better prepared for their work in life, which, for the great bulk of them, must consist mainly of manual occupations.

"It is hardly necessary to say that the changes we have recommended cannot be carried out without a considerable expenditure of money. But we feel confident that the State, which so largely maintains and controls the system of National Education in Ireland, will not hesitate to provide the necessary funds for improving that system within reasonable limits. The progress of the people in wealth and material prosperity must largely depend on the education given in the primary schools; and to make that education thoroughly efficient and fit for its purpose is a task, we submit, which may well be undertaken, in the highest interests of the State, whatever the necessary cost may be."

In reference to the teaching of agriculture in the schools the Commissioners say:

"We do not think that agriculture as an art, that is to say practical farming, is a subject that properly belongs to elementary education. At present the study of what is called the theory of agriculture is compulsory for boys in all rural schools, and is highly encouraged by fees. But our enquiry has shown that this study consists, for the most part, in committing a text-book to memory; and we have come to the conclusion that it has little educational or practical value. We recommend instead that the course of Elementary Science to be taught in rural schools should be so framed as to illustrate the more simple scientific principles that underlie the art and industry of agriculture. We also recommend the maintenance and extension of school gardens, as a means by which these scientific principles may be illustrated and made interesting to the pupils."

The reasons assigned by the Royal Commissioners for the introduction of nual and Practical instruction as part of the public school course in Ireland ,ly with equal, if not greater force, to the conditions obtaining in New unswick. The difficulties to be overcome in grafting these new methods into the stem of the system of public instruction as now established cannot be greater than those which were successfully grappled with in the older lands.

We have as object lessons Macdonald Manual Training Schools in successful operation in Ottawa, Brockville and Toronto, Ontario; in Montreal, Waterloo, Knowlton and Bedford. Quebec; in Winnipeg, Manitoba; in Regina and Calgary, N. W. Territories; in Victoria and Vancouver, British Columbia; in Truro, Nova Scotia, where there is also a special Training School for teachers; in Charlottetown and Summerside, P. E. Island; and in Fredericton, New Brunswick. All these have been established and maintained up to this time without any expense to the several Provinces other than providing the rooms in which the schools are severally located.

For information as to the work of the New Brunswick Manual Training School I direct attention to the Report of Principal MacCredie, found in Appendix E.

But the munificence of Sir William Macdonald has not yet been exhausted. He proposes for the Rural Schools a plan even more comprehensive than that already instituted for towns and cities. This plan has been submitted for the consideration of the educational authorities in the several provinces. I understand that the plan herewith submitted is open to such changes or modifications as observation or experience might suggest for the purpose of adapting it to the conditions of the rural communities in each province.

MEMORANDUM OF A PLAN PROPOSED FOR THE IMPROVEMENT OF EDUCATION AT RURAL SCHOOLS; AND FOR THE ESTABLISHMENT OF COURSES OF INSTRUCTION AND TRAINING IN DOMESTIC ECONOMY OR HOUSEHOLD SCIENCE AT THE ONTARIO AGRICULTURAL COLLEGE.

Having respect to the well known sayings, "Seeing is believing" and, "We learn by doing," the plan which Sir William C. Macdonald offers as one desirable to carry out is presented in four parts — three under the Division of Nature Study, and the fourth under the Division of Domestic Economy or Household Science.

PART I. — THE CONSOLIDATION OF RURAL SCHOOLS.

Part 1 of the plan is intended to give object lessons of improvements in education from the consolidation of five, six or more small rural schools into one central graded school, with a School Garden and a Manual Training room as part of its equipment.

It is proposed to offer financial assistance to one locality in Ontario and one locality in each of the Provinces of Quebec, New Brunswick, Nova Scotia and Prince Edward Island, to induce the people to undertake and carry on object lessons of improvements in education, with School Gardens and Manual Training, all under the control of the regularly-constituted educational authorities.

Notes on Part 1.

(*a*) In our educational progress not much has been done for the girls and boys in rural schools compared with what has been given to and made possible for the children in towns and cities. The difficulties which have hindered progress are said to have been: Want of money, the fact that the time table was already too full, and the fact that teachers are not properly qualified to take up better.mothods.

(*b*) In some districts the area for the rural school is so small that the lack of funds and the isolation of school authorities cause them to let educational matters drift into weakness and inefficiency. If in some district an object lesson could be given of the consolidation of five, six or more weak rural schools into one well-appointed and well-sustained central school, that might lead to general improvement.

(*c*) In some of the United States the consolidation of rural schools has already been carried out to a considerable extent with very great gain in the quality of the education given in the locality, and in most cases with no increase of cost to the ratepayers.

It has not been difficult in Canada to arrange routes for the collecting of milk or cream to one central place; it would not be more difficult to arrange for the collection of children on various routes to one central school; and certainly the children of a neighborhood are best worth the care, thought and spending of anything in the locality.

PART 2.—GROUPS OF RURAL SCHOOLS WITH A TRAVELLING INSTRUCTOR FOR EACH GROUP.

Part 2 of the plan is for the purpose of giving object lessons of the value of School Gardens and Nature Studies, at individual rural schools, as a part of general education, to be begun by means of a travelling instructor, who would visit and spend one-half day per week with the children and teacher at each school of a group, for a term of three years, or until a considerable ..ber of suitably trained and qualified teachers would be available to carry ..h work themselves at rural schools.

t is proposed to offer financial assistance to one group of ten or fewer ls in one locality in Ontario, and to one group in each of the Provinces of

Quebec, New Brunswick, Nova Scotia and Prince Edward Island, to enable the people to provide School Gardens, and to undertake and carry on object lessons and experiments with improvements in education, all under the control of the regularly constituted educational authorities.

Notes on Part 2.

(*a*) A group of ten, or fewer, rural schools in some locality should be chosen in which to give an object lesson or illustration of this better education. If a competent travelling instructor were engaged to spend half a day of every week at each of these schools, he would be able to train teachers and children into methods of Nature Study. The travelling instructor would be a specialist in Nature Study and Nature Knowledge, as well as a good teacher in the subjects which have been common in the schools in the past.

(*b*) It would certainly be of great benefit to the children at any rural school if a School Garden containing plots for every child above the age of eight or nine years could be provided. Those plots would be used (like slates of large size) to put "things" on, to be rubbed off when they had served their educational purpose. The gardens could be used, as they are at a few chools in England, and as they are at many schools on the continent of Europe, for the training of children to habits of close observation, of thoughtfulness, and of carefulness.

(*c*) If one may mention a method which would seem to include the best, it would be that of tracing results back to their causes until that habit of mind is formed in the children. When a child does anything with its own hands, such as planting a seed, pulling up a plant, making examination of the changes which have taken place during its growth, making a drawiug of it, mounting it and putting its name on it, he receives impressions by the sense of touch, he sees, he hears the noise of the movements he makes, and he smells the soil and the part of the plant with which he is dealing. Those impressssons are definite and lasting; they add to the sum of sensuous knowledge; they prepare for the perception of logical knowledge, in a common sense way.

(*d*) For instance, if a child should plant ten grains of wheat in a row, ten grains of Indian corn in another row, ten sets of potatoes in another row, and ten clover seeds in another row; if he should pull up one each of these plants every week, and find out for himself, under the guidance of a competent teacher, what had taken place in the meantime; if, further, he should make drawings of the plants and a written statement of the progress of growth, as he was able to observe it, from week to week, such a course, occupying only half a day per week, would certainly give a boy or girl a great amount of exceedingly useful information, and also habits of investigation, observation, comparison and thoughtfulness, which are immensely desirable. These would quicken the intelligence of the children, and lead them to have both desire and capacity for living happily amid rural surroundings.

(e) Progress in agricultural education would be made by starting Evening Continuation Classes in the rural districts in connection with those groups of schools, or in connection with the consolidated schools mentioned under Part 1. These would provide the true solution for education in agriculture and horticulture of youths in the country at the ages from fourteen to eighteen. One or two central schools of each of these groups might be chosen for Evening Continuation Classes. At these, what the young lad, working on the farm, saw during the day with his uninstructed eye, could be explained to him in such a way as to awaken a new interest in his work, and greatly increase his ability for enjoying it and carrying it on well.

Part 3.—Special Courses of Instruction and Training for Teachers of Rural Schools.

Part 3 of the Plan has for its object to assist in providing short courses of instruction and training for teachers for rural schools, who desire to qualify themselves in these newer subjects and methods of education.

It is proposed to offer to the Province of Ontario at the Ontario Agricultural College at Guelph, a gift of a building, including a Nature Study plant-growing house, and such equipment as may be required, in addition to what is there at present, for the accommodation of teachers while taking short courses in Nature Study for rural schools.

Notes on Part 3.

(a) To make possible such additions and changes in rural schools as have been indicated, and to let them be capable of anything like general adoption and extension, there is need for further preparation of the teachers. No doubt teachers in Canada would be willing to qualify themselves for this better sort of work, if an opportunity were provided. It seems desirable and practical to give such teachers the opportunity which they need.

(b) At several places in England in 1901, short courses of instruction and training in methods were provided for periods of only three weeks, with expectation of doing a good deal towards qualifying teachers to carry on [their] work in a better way. In Canada, it might be possible to arrange for [cour]ses of training for thirty teachers at one place, each course to last for two [or th]ree months. During this course the teachers would carry on 'Nature

Study work as they expected the children to do it at the school afterwards. A plant-growing house for Nature Study work would not be so costly for construction and maintenance that it would be a very difficult accommodation to have for the winter and spring months, when outdoor work would not be practicable.

(*c*) If provision should be made for a class of about thirty teachers at each short course, it is hoped that the Government of each Province concerned would arrange (by providing a substitute or otherwise) to enable approved teachers in rural schools to take the short course without loss of situation or loss of salary.

(*d*) For a period of three years, at least fifteen teachers of rural schools outside the Province of Ontario are to be eligible to receive instruction and training in each short course without any fees.

(*e*) For the first year, it is proposed to make, (1) an allowance at the rate of five cents per mile for the actual distance from the teacher's school to the Ontario Agricultural College, to help in meeting travelling expenses, and (2) an allowance of $25.00 to help in meeting the expenses of board and lodging to every approved teacher who has taken a full course satisfactorily.

PART 4.—DOMESTIC ECONOMY OR HOUSEHOLD SCIENCE.

Part 4 of the Plan is intended to assist in providing courses of instruction and training in Domestic Economy or Household Science for young women from country homes, in order that they may have opportunities for acquiring practical and advanced education not less suitable and helpful to them, than the present courses at the Ontario Agricultural College are beneficial to young men, who take them with earnestness and cheerfulness.

It is proposed to offer to the Province of Ontario at the Ontario Agricultural College at Guelph, (1) a residence building to accommodate not less than 100 female students and teacher-students, daughters of farmers and others, and (2) class rooms, kitchen laboratories and other equipment necessary for courses of instruction and training in Domestic Economy or Household Science.

Notes on Part 4.

(*a*) Suitable courses (long and short) which would include instruction and training in dairying, poultry-keeping, bee-keeping, fruit-growing and general gardening with particular attention to the cultivation of vegetables and flowers would be highly valuable to the young women who were able to take them and through their influence would be of far-reaching benefit to the rural schools, and the rural population generally.

(*b*) Special regard might be given to properly arranged lessons and exercises,—

(1) in the selection, preparation and serving of foods in the most nourishing, wholesome, appetising, and economical manner;

(2) in sewing, dressmaking, and the simpler forms of household art and decoration; and,

(3) in the care and cleansing of rooms, fabrics, sinks, etc.;

All to the end that the pupils might know the relation of those things to health and comfort, and might observe those methods and practices which make for good-living in simple, clean, well-kept and beautiful homes in the country.

I cordially commend the plan above outlined as worthy of the grateful recognition and co-operation of the government and legislature of New Brunswick. The generous promoters of this new departure ask nothing for the present but to be allowed the opportunity to test the merits of their plan. There is of course implied in its acceptance by the educational authorities a moral obligation to render every needed assistance, and to afford every reasonable facility for the selection of a locality for the proposed Model School where it will have the best chances for success; and there is further implied on the part of the Executive Government and Legislative Assembly the obligations to maintain and extend the system when its feasibility and usefulness have been clearly demonstrated by a fair trial.

The important problem of the consolidation of country schools is involved in the proposed scheme. Up to this date, the people in the small districts, with few exceptions, have persistently declined to unite with adjacent districts for the establishment of a central school to which the children of two or more districts might be conveyed. There are, without doubt, many localities in which such a union would be impracticable; but there are scores, if not hundreds of districts in which the centralization of the schools would not only lead to the maintenance of much better schools, with more regular attendance; but would also reduce the educational expenditure. The conditions in many parts of New Brunswick do not materially differ from those of other states and countries in which this system has been successfully introduced.

In my opinion the time is not far distant when it will become the duty of the Board of Education, either under the existing law, or under a more stringent which the legislature may be called upon to enact, to re-adjust the whole ·m of school districts as they exist at present with a view of reducing their ›er and enlarging their area. In the meantime, if the centralization of ¹˥ proposed by Sir William Macdonald's plan be carried into effect, an object lesson as to the advantages of consolidation will aid in removing prejudices and demonstrating the practicability of union in other places.

As to the Macdonald Manual Training School now in operation at Fredericton, it must not be forgotten that two of the three years during which the expenses of its maintenance were to be borne by its founder, have nearly passed. Shall it be closed at the expiration of the three years? Or will the intelligent School Board of the City of Fredericton take up the work when Sir William Macdonald lays it down and establish it on a permanent basis as a constituent part of the school course in Fredericton? And will the intelligent and progressive School Boards of the Cities of St. John and Moncton, and of the incorporated towns and populous centres from Restigouche to Charlotte, having become acquainted with the system and having seen the results of its working in Fredericton, decide in their wisdom to establish and maintain one of these Manual Training departments in each of the several districts under their respective administrations?

At the present time the system has been introduced at the expense of the Macdonald fund into two of our country districts, without detriment in the slightest degree to the ordinary work of the schools. Several of our teachers, after instruction at the Fredericton school, are now taking a six months' course at the Truro Training School to fit themselves more thoroughly for this work. When the proposed Manual Training School shall be opened at Guelph, as outlined in Prof. Robertson's plan, there is no doubt that many more of our teachers will avail themselves of the privileges for instruction it will afford provided suitable financial encouragement is offered.

Frequent inquiries have been addressed to me as to what may be expected from the Board of Education in the way of assistance to School Boards who may decide to introduce the Manual Training work into the schools under their charge, and what encouragement and remuneration may be expected by teachers who shall take the time and incur the expense of making special preparation for this work. These inquiries are reasonable, and the Chief Superintendent should be in a position to answer them definitely.

Recommendations for Grants in Aid of Manual Training.

I recommend, therefore, that at the approaching session of the legislature an Act may be passed authorizing the Board of Education to enlarge its work in the direction indicated; and to expend a reasonable amount for the promotion of Manual Training with its associated branches in the common schools.

Among other provisions of such Act, I venture to make the following suggestions as to the money grants to be provided from the Provincial revenues to aid in the establishment and maintenance of Manual Training instruction:

(a) To any Board of School Trustees, whether in city, town or country district, which shall provide suitable accommodation in connection with the school or schools under its jurisdiction for instruction in Manual Training, there shall be granted a sum not less than one half of the total amount expended for the necessary benches, tools, material and other equipment required.

(b) To any Licensed Teacher who shall obtain from any Manual Training School approved by the Board of Education, a certificate of fitness to teach the system, and who shall in addition to the other regular work of the school under his charge, give instruction in Manual Training in accordance with Regulations to be made by the Board of Education, there shall be granted in addition to the Provincial Grant provided for by the "Schools Act, 1900," the sum of fifty dollars per annum.

(c) To any Certificated Teacher who may be employed in cities, towns or other populous districts to give instruction in Manual Training to the pupils of several schools, and who gives his full time to such instruction under the direction of the local School Board, and in accordance with the Regulations of the Board of Education, there shall be granted a sum of two hundred dollars per annum.

(d) That the provisions of Section 6 of the "Schools Act, 1900" in reference to the travelling expenses of student teachers attending the Provincial Normal School, shall apply to New Brunswick teachers who shall take the course at any Manual Training School approved by the Board of Education, and who shall afterwards actually teach the system in any New Brunswick school.

Before closing my remarks on this proposed new departure, I wish to say a word or two in regard to the relation the subject of Manual Training, if adopted as part of our school course, will hold to the other subjects at present taught in the schools. If I thought its introduction would tend to lessen the attention given by either teacher or pupils to the essential subjects which the wisdom of centuries has placed at the very foundation of all sound education, I would reject it without hesitation. But it is because I am convinced that the spending of two or three hours per week of the child's school life in training his hand and eye, and his intellectual and moral character through the exercise of the hand and eye, will quicken rather than weaken his interest in his reading, writing, arithmetic and other fundamental studies, that I recommend with confidence the adoption of the system.

I have the honor to be

Your Honor's most obedient servant,

JAMES R. INCH,

Chief Superintendent of Education.

PART II.

STATISTICAL TABLES.

E I. PUBLIC SCHOOLS: FOR THE YEAR ENDING JUNE 30TH, 1901. PRELIMINARY.

COUNTIES.	First Term Closed 31st December, 1900. Schools	Teachers and Assistants.	Pupils in attendance at Schools	Second Term Closed 30th June, 1901. Schools.	Teachers and Assistants.	Pupils in attendance at Schools.	New Pupils in attendance this Term, at Schools in operation both Terms.	New Pupils in attendance this Term, at Schools not in operation the previous Term.	Year Ending 30th June, 1901. No. of Districts having Schools in operation during the Dec. Term, that were without Schools in the June Term.	No. of Districts having Schools in operation in the June Term, that were without Schools in the Dec. Term.	Total No. of different Pupils in attendance at Schools within the year.
Albert	76	78	2,217	71	74	2,281	289	113	9	5	2,624
Carleton	152	156	3,941	147	149	4,611	719	252	14	11	4,972
Charlotte	142	144	4,085	144	154	4,579	536	181	5	6	4,802
Gloucester	109	116	4,054	104	109	4,179	629	22	7	2	4,712
Kent	121	123	3,808	112	113	3,860	580	116	14	2	4,509
Kings	158	162	4,026	158	166	4,398	636	204	11	14	4,891
Madawaska	58	62	1,965	55	57	2,140	369	60	6	2	2,394
Northumberland	148	155	4,977	139	146	5,119	576	80	10	1	5,634
Queens	96	96	2,100	91	93	2,299	349	127	12	9	2,576
Restigouche	47	49	1,743	45	46	1,697	166	29	3	1	1,938
Saint John	211	236	8,839	208	239	8,741	483	39	6	4	9,361
Sunbury	40	41	922	40	42	1,051	150	44	3	3	1,122
Victoria	57	58	1,311	52	52	1,592	294	186	10	8	1,791
Westmorland	207	213	7,984	192	203	7,739	746	80	15	5	8,823
York	190	204	5,657	183	198	6,134	837	108	13	6	6,611
New Brunswick	1,812	1,893	57,629	1,741	1,841	60,420	7,419	1,641	138	79	66,760
Cor. Terms, 1899-1900	1,815	1,893	58,925	1,771	1,856	61,444	6,942	1,262	119	61	67,159
Increase	....	....	....	....	....	....	477	379	19	18	....
Decrease	3	....	1,296	30	15	1,024	....	....	....	....	399

TABLE II. PUBLIC SCHOOLS: FOR THE YEAR ENDED 30TH JUNE, 1901.

PART ONE. — The First Term closed 31st December, 1900.

COUNTIES.	No. of Pupils at School this Term.	Proportion of the population at School this Term (Census of 1891).	Age and Sex of Pupils: Number under 6 years of age.	Number between the ages of 6 and 15 years.	Number over 15 years of age.	Boys.	Girls.	Grand total days' attendance made by the Pupils enrolled.	Number daily present on an average during the time the Schools were in Session.	Number daily present on an average for the full Term.	Number daily present on an average during the time in Session per hundred enrolled.	Number daily present on an average for full Term per hundred enrolled.
Albert	2,217	1 in 4.94	7	2,120	90	1,133	1,084	121,414½	1,402	1,302	63.23	58.72
Carleton	3,941	1 in 5.71	19	3,738	184	1,901	2,037	211,381	2,419	2,228	61.38	56.53
Charlotte	4,085	1 in 5.81	9	3,874	202	2,044	2,041	225,455½	2,747	2,425	67.24	59.36
Gloucester	4,054	1 in 6.14	9	3,949	96	2,033	2,021	216,018	2,413	2,348	59.52	57.91
Kent	3,808	1 in 6.26	23	3,717	68	1,927	1,881	196,398	2,150	2,092	56.46	54.93
Kings	4,026	1 in 5.73	12	3,783	231	1,976	2,050	213,491	2,374	2,245	58.96	55.76
Madawaska	1,965	1 in 5.34	37	1,898	30	918	1,047	109,833	1,212	1,183	61.67	60.20
Northumberl'nd	4,977	1 in 5.16	9	4,810	158	2,485	2,492	283,547	3,263	3,179	65.56	63.87
Queens	2,100	1 in 5.78	15	1,947	138	1,045	1,055	106,742⅓	1,185	1,104	56.42	52.57
Restigouche	1,743	1 in 4.76	2	1,683	58	833	910	99,994	1,138	1,131	65.29	64.88
Saint John	8,839	1 in 5.60	2	8,480	357	4,305	4,534	569,356½	6,949	6,823	78.61	77.19
Sunbury	922	1 in 6.24	2	870	50	452	470	45,175½	519	463	56.29	50.21
Victoria	1,311	1 in 5.87	15	1,247	49	671	640	60,087½	648	601	49.42	45.84
Westmorland	7,984	1 in 5.19	28	7,600	356	3,955	4,029	451,189½	5,097	4,993	63.84	62.53
York	5,657	1 in 5.47	36	5,395	226	2,754	2,903	323,124½	3,644	3,539	64.41	62.55
New Brunswick	57,629	1 in 5.57	225	55,111	2,293	28,435	29,194	3,233,208	37,160	35,656	64.48	61.87
Cor. Term, 1899	58,925	1 in 5.45	259	56,116	2,550	29,459	29,466	3,440,002	39,052	36,586	66.27	62.08
Increase	......	......	......	......	......	......	......	......	......	......	......	......
Decrease	1,296	1 in 247.8	34	1,005	257	1,024	272	206,794	1,892	930	1.79	.21

TABLE II. PUBLIC SCHOOLS: FOR THE YEAR ENDED 30TH JUNE, 1901.
PART TWO. — The Second Term closed 30th June, 1901.

COUNTIES.	No. of Pupils at School this Term.	Proportion of the population at School this Term (Census of 1891).	AGE AND SEX OF PUPILS. Number under 6 years of age.	Number between the ages of 6 and 15 years.	Number over 15 years of age.	Boys.	Girls.	Grand total days' attendance made by the Pupils enrolled.	Number daily present on an average during the time the Schools were in Session.	Number daily present on an average for the full Term.	Number daily present on an average during the time in Session per hundred enrolled.	Number daily present on an average for full Term per hundred enrolled.
Albert	2,281	1 in 4.80	2	2,091	188	1,199	1,082	162,835	1,480	1,367	64.88	59.92
Carleton	4,611	1 in 4.88	19	4,181	411	2,386	2,225	300,154½	2,708	2,488	58.72	53.95
Charlotte	4,579	1 in 5.18	3	4,190	386	2,368	2,211	339,697½	3,009	2,698	65.71	58.92
Gloucester	4,179	1 in 5.95	9	4,044	126	2,148	2,031	266,688½	2,322	2,196	55.56	52.54
Kent	3,860	1 in 6.17	31	3,725	104	2,020	1,840	246,021	2,190	2,025	56.73	52.46
Kings	4,398	1 in 5.24	8	4,006	384	2,258	2,140	291,637½	2,508	2,355	57.02	53.54
Madawaska	2,140	1 in 4.91	38	2,065	37	1,066	1,074	137,766½	1,248	1,151	58.31	53.78
Northumberl'nd.	5,119	1 in 5.02	11	4,877	231	2,636	2,483	363,770	3,185	2,993	62.21	58.46
Queens	2,299	1 in 5.28	9	2,039	251	1,204	1,095	141,643½	1,272	1,143	55.32	49.71
Restigouche	1,697	1 in 4.89	4	1,614	79	846	851	114,291	998	954	58.80	56.21
Saint John	8,741	1 in 5.67	5	8,269	467	4,275	4,466	787,395	6,730	6,544	76.99	74.86
Sunbury	1,051	1 in 5.48	4	961	86	565	486	65,401	582	528	55.37	50.23
Victoria	1,592	1 in 4.83	8	1,443	141	844	748	89,067½	804	706	50.50	44.34
Westmorland	7,739	1 in 5.36	9	7,274	456	3,897	3,842	560,631½	4,882	4,694	63.08	60.65
York	6,134	1 in 5.05	27	5,706	401	3,158	2,976	421,235½	3,799	3,409	61.93	55.57
New Brunswick	60,420	1 in 5.31	187	56,485	3,748	30,870	29,550	4,288,235½	37,717	35,251	62.42	58.34
Cor. Term, 1900	61,444	1 in 5.22	312	57,007	4,125	31,550	29,894	4,288,854	37,529	35,343	61.07	57.52
Increase									188		1.35	.82
Decrease	1,024	1 in 313.7	125	522	377	680	344	618½		92		

TABLE III. PUBLIC SCHOOLS: For the Year Ended 30th June, 1901.

Part One. — The First Term Closed 31st December, 1900.

NUMBER OF PUPILS IN THE DIFFERENT BRANCHES OF INSTRUCTION.

COUNTIES.	Physical Exercises. 35	Oral Lessons on Morals, etc. 36	Sewing. (Optional. 37)	Knitting. (Optional. 37)
Albert	1891	2139	.....	.....
Carleton	3334	3573	30	14
Charlotte	3587	3919	3	25
Gloucester	3426	3745	38	9
Kent	2928	3531	52	57
Kings	3401	3793	3	.....
Madawaska	1495	1603	.....	.....
Northumberland	4579	4610	9	.....
Queens	1732	2060	.....	.....
Restigouche	1451	1644	16	.....
Saint John	8279	8434	.....	.....
Sunbury	710	823	.....	.....
Victoria	966	1208	6	6
Westmorland	6122	7001	4	31
York	4556	4996	.....	7
New Brunswick	48457	53079	161	149
Cor. Term, 1899	49580	54557	135	110
Increase			26	39
Decrease	1123	1478	.....	.....

COUNTIES.	Reading–Spelling–Recitation, Etc. 38 — Grade I	II	III	IV	V	VI	VII	VIII
Albert	499	323	398	373	296	78	85	72
Carleton	865	561	652	644	704	176	120	121
Charlotte	766	592	641	742	706	171	173	154
Gloucester	1505	849	655	560	221	89	79	55
Kent	1494	736	628	476	233	70	62	52
Kings	852	626	796	755	634	123	56	79
Madawaska	930	421	317	190	47	30	16	16
Northumberland	1204	947	925	721	568	190	174	146
Queens	482	328	428	389	398	30	11	23
Restigouche	494	317	314	240	198	49	50	34
Saint John	1716	1379	1341	1258	975	791	523	394
Sunbury	239	135	142	179	145	20	6	13
Victoria	411	229	223	191	149	34	20	30
Westmorland	2149	1246	1265	1168	928	347	313	300
York	1380	781	940	982	806	255	160	165
New Brunswick	14986	9470	9665	8868	7008	2433	1848	1654
Cor. Term, 1899	14632	10149	10020	9136	7187	2433	1881	1740
Increase	354	.....	.....	.....	.....	.....	.....	.....
Decrease	.....	679	355	268	179	.....	33	86

COUNTIES.	Grammar and Analysis and Composition. 39 — Grade •III	•IV	V	VI	VII	VIII	History. 40 — Grade •IV	V	VI	VI	VIII
Albert	370	382	289	78	85	72	256	272	80	85	72
Carleton	588	634	697	172	120	121	499	692	175	120	112
Charlotte	545	732	704	171	173	153	525	702	151	173	153
Gloucester	651	553	221	89	79	55	474	201	89	79	55
Kent	570	439	230	65	62	65	160	228	66	62	58
Kings	770	749	631	123	56	79	639	631	123	56	79
Madawaska	273	160	38	30	16	16	155	36	30	6	16
Northumberland	895	719	516	191	174	147	439	555	190	174	147
Queens	424	388	392	30	11	22	378	394	30	11	23
Restigouche	223	240	200	48	50	34	215	200	48	50	34
Saint John	1320	1251	975	791	523	394	1190	976	791	523	394
Sunbury	129	177	138	20	6	13	167	150	23	6	13
Victoria	209	190	145	34	20	30	173	143	34	20	30
Westmorland	1161	1106	868	326	317	306	843	894	317	321	306
York	865	918	810	149	158	156	724	785	222	159	156
New Brunswick	8993	8638	6904	2317	1850	1663	7037	6859	2369	1855	1648
Cor. Term, 1899	9203	8898	6977	2435	1879	1718	7227	7095	2427	1874	1693
Increase	.....	.....	.....	.....	.....	.....	.....	.....	.....	.....	.....
Decrease	210	260	73	118	29	55	190	236	58	19	45

•In Country Districts.

TABLE III. Part One.—Continued.

Form, Color and Industrial Drawing. 41

Counties.	Grade I	II	III	IV	V	VI	VII	VIII
Albert	490	126	398	374	294	78	76	55
Carleton	816	499	644	637	690	174	120	112
Charlotte	761	590	641	749	697	171	173	153
Gloucester	1473	849	657	554	220	89	79	55
Kent	1407	749	614	454	223	66	62	58
Kings	828	631	788	750	626	123	56	79
Madawaska	813	378	306	187	47	30	16	15
Northumberland	1224	930	926	719	568	190	174	146
Queens	465	334	419	388	391	30	11	23
Restigouche	492	317	313	240	199	49	50	34
Saint John	1697	1378	1339	1269	963	791	523	394
Sunbury	226	136	137	172	141	20	6	13
Victoria	394	220	213	191	144	34	20	30
Westmorland	2006	1185	1252	1096	875	326	321	297
York	1346	755	926	977	780	224	151	160
New Brunswick	14438	9277	9573	8757	6858	2395	1838	1625
Cor. Term. 1899	14012	9817	9831	8962	7058	2409	1861	1646
Increase	426	.	....	. ..	......	...	. ..	.....
Decrease	.	540	258	205	200	14	23	21

Print-Script and Writing. 42

Counties.	Grade I	II	III	IV	V	VI	VII	VIII
Albert	493	326	398	374	294	78	85	77
Carleton	865	561	652	644	704	176	120	121
Charlotte	767	592	641	742	704	171	173	154
Gloucester	1501	849	655	560	221	89	79	55
Kent	1452	757	624	487	236	64	64	64
Kings	852	626	786	755	626	120	56	79
Madawaska	906	425	316	187	47	30	16	16
Northumberland	1188	916	826	719	568	190	174	146
Queens	480	336	420	389	399	30	11	23
Restigouche	494	317	313	240	199	49	50	34
Saint John	1716	1378	1341	1258	975	791	523	394
Sunbury	237	129	142	178	142	20	6	13
Victoria	411	229	227	191	149	34	20	30
Westmorland	2126	1248	1265	1163	895	324	321	300
York	1374	774	941	969	801	249	159	161
New Brunswick	14862	9461	9543	8856	6960	2415	1857	1662
Cor. Term. 1899	14549	9922	10011	9145	7121	2424	1878	1723
Increase	313	....	...	....	.....	...		.. .
Decrease	...	461	468	289	161	9	21	61

Singing. (Theory" Optional.) 43

Counties.	Grade I By Rote	II By Rote	III By Rote	IV Rote	IV Note	V Rote	V Note	VI Rote	VI Note	VII Rote	VII Note	VII Rote	VII Note
Albert	248	171	213	175	....	104	....	25	....	23	....	27	....
Carleton	392	283	309	269	.	334	....	128	....	68	.	45	
Charlotte	459	417	372	464	....	436	....	104	....	33	...	5	....
Gloucester	962	570	458	373	...	116	...	61	....	42	....	25	....
Kent	616	328	264	175	....	123	14	45	....	34	6	9	...
Kings	383	271	361	289	....	271	....	96	...	9	...	33	
Madawaska	440	180	168	110	....	29	....	29	..	16	....	16	..
Northumberland	813	643	641	465	26	311	20	130	18	141	12	45	23
Queens	202	108	155	124	...	118	....	6	..	...	....	1	....
Restigouche	295	411	186	178	...	136	.	46	....	33		21	...
Saint John	1532	1271	1198	1138	27	876	80	735	....	470	...	341	....
Sunbury	130	72	57	82	...	55	....	....	..		....	....	
Victoria	192	124	103	84	..	71	...	11	....	6	....	13	....
Westmorland	1142	750	732	618	....	349	...	226	....	218	...	106	....
York	771	450	498	493		429	..	172	....	50	.	74	....
New Brunswick	8577	5849	5715	5037	53	3758	64	1814	18	1121	18	761	23
Cor. Term. 1899	8262	6093	5897	5124	68	3906	40	1739	15	1181	...	917	....
Increase	315	...	...	...		....	24	75	3	....	18	...	23
Decrease	....	244	182	87	15	148	...	....	..	60	..	156	..

TABLE III. Part One—Continued.

COUNTIES.	Number--Arithmetic. 44								Algebra 46		Geography. 47					
	GRADE.								GRADE.		GRADE.					
	I	II	III	IV	V	VI	VII	VIII	VII.	VIII	III	IV	V	VI	VII	VIII
Albert,	493	325	398	371	299	78	85	72	64	74	386	377	305	88	85	72
Carleton,	865	561	651	644	705	156	120	107	114	142	659	642	701	156	120	107
Charlotte,	764	592	648	746	706	171	173	154	270	140	642	740	705	171	173	153
Gloucester,	1,500	850	655	560	221	89	79	55	79	50	657	564	221	89	79	55
Kent,	1,464	756	619	484	231	60	58	58	32	55	624	470	228	66	62	58
Kings,	852	627	794	755	633	123	56	79	82	104	783	733	621	117	56	79
Madawaska,	881	418	316	186	47	30	16	16	10	4	356	163	48	29	16	16
Northumberland,	1,224	938	927	730	565	191	174	147	137	147	907	719	568	190	174	146
Queens,	489	328	421	394	394	30	11	23	94	31	435	385	382	41	6	17
Restigouche,	493	317	313	238	201	45	50	34	70	32	300	240	199	49	50	34
St. John,	1,714	1,372	1,339	1,260	969	791	523	394	242	377	1,354	1,257	977	791	523	394
Sunbury,	237	140	141	178	142	20	6	13	10	22	149	176	145	20	6	13
Victoria,	411	229	220	188	146	34	20	30	7	30	231	191	146	34	20	30
Westmorland,	2,139	1,261	1,251	1,164	891	325	328	301	144	296	1,272	1,154	907	330	318	314
York,	1,387	773	935	979	808	255	160	156	156	152	929	974	804	255	158	156
New Brunswick,	14,913	9,487	9,628	8,877	6,958	2,398	1,859	1,639	1,511	1,656	9,684	8,785	6,957	2,426	1,846	1,644
Cor. Term, 1899	14,543	10,167	10,006	9,129	7,143	2,443	1,866	1,706	1,476	1,760	10,026	9,058	7,168	3,179	1,874	1,700
Increase,	370	.....	.....	.....	.....	.....	.....	.....	35	.....	.....	.....	.....	.....	.....	.....
Decrease,	.....	680	378	252	185	45	7	67	.....	104	342	273	211	753	28	56

TABLE III. Part One.—Continued.

COUNTIES.	Hygiene and Temperance (Health Readers.) 48								Nature Lessons and Agriculture. Minerals—Plant Life—Animal Life. 49								Latin. (Optional.) 50.		French. (Optional.) 51
	Grade.								Grade.								Grade.		Grades.
	I	II	III	IV	V	VI	VII	VIII	I	II	III	IV	V	VI	VII	VIII	VII	VIII	I to VIII
Albert	413	291	375	364	294	78	76	66	415	285	362	355	286	69	71	66	...	27	.....
Carleton	613	450	604	630	687	176	101	74	648	418	586	608	675	165	118	107	80	48	....
Charlotte	686	539	628	737	711	171	173	153	687	524	619	711	638	157	150	147	30	92	
Gloucester	1278	778	654	558	221	89	79	55	1221	723	629	534	198	77	61	46	4	16	1312
Kent	1265	705	564	442	231	56	62	65	1278	698	577	140	222	63	62	6.	1	17	760
Kings	742	551	749	733	618	114	53	73	762	580	740	747	616	120	56	79	18	59	..
Madawaska	96	386	296	153	46	30	16	16	692	314	237	146	43	29	16	16	7	4	617
Northumberland	1112	871	914	716	568	190	174	146	1146	890	916	713	568	190	174	146	50	27	106
Queens	411	303	406	387	381	30	11	20	388	295	395	373	358	27	11	23	..	10	......
Restigouche	463	310	308	240	99	49	50	34	478	311	314	240	199	48	50	34	24	16	207
Saint John	1626	1325	1347	1251	982	791	523	394	1658	1351	1324	1248	938	775	532	374	418	360	.....
Sunbury	129	104	147	178	145	20	6	13	119	103	141	172	135	7	...	13	9	....	.....
Victoria	327	211	219	188	146	34	20	30	370	219	224	187	148	34	20	30	....	...	48
Westmorland	1750	1063	1189	1129	94	347	321	302	1662	1006	1090	1071	849	291	241	243	159	151	847
York	1081	676	868	953	812	254	144	144	992	614	807	886	761	250	164	165	52	55	......
New Brunswick	12592	8563	9268	8649	6945	2429	1809	1585	12516	8337	8961	8431	6634	2302	1726	1550	852	882	3897
Cor. Term, 1899	12273	9115	9552	8891	7092	2420	1846	1598	12173	9058	9351	8650	6775	2278	1828	1669	807	1098	3454
Increase	319	...	...	...	...	9	...	...	343	...	...	...	...	24	...	...	45	....	443
Decrease	...	552	284	242	147	...	37	13	...	721	390	219	141	...	102	119	....	216	......

TABLE III.—Superior, Grammar and Other Schools Having Pupils in Advance of Grade VIII.

PART ONE.—Continued.

COUNTIES.	Language. 52															
	English.				Latin.				Greek.				French.			
	IX	X	XI	XII	IX	X	XI	XII	IX	X	XI	XII	IX	X	XI	XII
lbert	57	35	1	....	46	22	1	....	..	5	1	....	..	..	..	....
arleton	64	25	14	...	33	22	14	....	3	1	9	....	21	12	9	....
harlotte	67	38	38	....	45	29	33	....	4	6	13	....	40	26	20	....
loucester	28	2	-	....	10	1		....	3	..	..	....	3	..	..	....
ent	21	14	..	....	11	2	1	....	1	..	1	....	..	..	..	....
ings	63	13	11	....	46	9	9	....	9	2	5	....	..	..	..	....
adawaska	..	..	..	....	..	..	..	....	..	..	..	....	..	..	..	....
orthumberland	58	36	13	....	45	33	13	....	..	3	..	....	15	21	8	....
ueens	2	10	3	....	6	10	3	....	..	..	3	....	..	..	3	....
estigouche	26	14	4	....	22	13	4	....	10	7	4	....	18	..	..	....
aint John	240	156	65	18	218	147	65	18	22	43	14	5	215	139	65	18
nbury	..	..	..	....	..	..	..	....	..	..	..	....	..	..	..	....
ctoria	12	5	5	....	2	4	4	....	2	2	2	....	1	..	..	....
estmorland	194	77	50	....	128	70	35	....	10	2	4	....	112	49	30	....
ork	100	44	29	....	60	29	17	....	..	12	9	....	14	20	15	....
ew Brunswick	932	469	233	18	662	391	199	18	64	83	65	5	439	267	150	18
r. Term, 1899	918	433	255	17	654	369	236	17	80	87	92	8	473	264	183	16
Increase	14	36	..	1	8	22	..	1	..	..	..	....	..	3	..	2
Decrease	..	..	22	....	..	..	37	....	16	4	27	3	34	..	33	....

COUNTIES.	Mathematics. 53													History and Geography. 54			
	Arithmetic.		Geometry.				Algebra.			Book-Keeping.		Trigonometry.					
	IX	X	IX	X	XI	XII	IX	X	XI	IX	X	XI	XII	IX	X	XI	XII
lbert	57	35	57	34	1	....	50	31	1	42	31	8	....	57	35	1	..
arleton	69	25	39	26	14	....	69	25	14	14	18	14	....	56	25	14	..
harlotte	67	48	70	48	38	....	67	48	38	22	11	17	....	67	48	38	....
loucester	28	..	27	2		....	28	2	..	23	2	..	....	28	2	..	....
ent	27	9	33	3	2	....	21	9	..	40	3	2		21	3	..	...
ings	66	13	68	21	11	....	56	22	11	16	2	..	....	67	13	11	....
adawaska	.	..	3	..	..	....		..	..	..	..	..	....	10	..	..	....
orthumberland	55	36	56	42	13	....	54	36	13	27	17	..	....	54	36	13	....
ueens	7	10	7	10	3	....	7	10	3	7	10	..	....	7	10	3	..
estigouche	25	1	25	14	4	...	25	14	4	3	1	..	....	25	14	4	....
aint John	241	147	233	153	65	18	240	156	65	233	149	5	18	241	156	65	18
nbury	2	..	2	..	..	....	2	..	..	1	..	..	....	2	..	..	-
ctoria	5	..	12	5	8	....	12	5	5	9	5	..	....	12	5	5	....
estmorland	195	85	197	79	44	....	189	80	47	123	44	9	...	194	91	37	....
ork	98	.	59	46	10	....	55	52	29	36	14	..	....	91	8	29	....
ew Brunswick	942	409	888	483	232	18	875	490	230	596	307	55	18	932	446	220	18
r. Term, 1899	948	491	864	448	254	17	900	469	264	509	289	41	15	936	416	254	17
Increase	..	..	24	35	..	1	.	21	..	87	18	14	3	..	30	..	1
Decrease	6	82	..	..	22	...	25	..	34	..	..	..	....	4	..	34	....

COUNTIES.	Drawing. 55	Natural Science. 56								Geology.	German. 57
		Physics.	Physiology & Hygiene.		Chemistry.		Botany.				
	IX	IX	X	XI	X	XI	IX	X	XI	XII	XII
lbert	60	36	25	1	25	1	41	17	1	....	1
arleton	69	47	34	14	20	14	36	18	14	....	
harlotte	58	44	20	14	30	20	47	27	24		..
loucester	28	3	..	..	..	..	22	2	..	....	....
ent	21	21	3	..	..		12	3	..	....	....
ings	45	46	15	11	20	11	63	13	11	....	....
adawaska	..	..	.	..	..	.	..	..	.	....	....
orthumberland	42	48	22	4	16	4	24	35	13	....	....
ueens	7	2	10	3	10	3	7	10	3	....	....
estigouche	25	25	23	..	20	..	3	14	4	....	....
aint John	195	137	156	..	79	15	159	166	37	..	....
nbury	1	2	..	..	2	..	..	..	.	....	....
ctoria	12	12	5	5	..	5	12	5	5	....	....
estmorland	175	129	68	60	50	38	159	91	34	....	....
ork	54	..	47	29	9	.	46	42	29	....	....
ew Brunswick	792	552	428	141	274	111	631	443	175	....	1
r. Term, 1899	732	448	456	153	307	220	836	415	220	4	4
Increase	60	4	.	..	..	..	..	28	..	....	
Decrease	..	.	28	12	33	109	205	.	45	4	

TABLE III. PART TWO.—The Second Term Closed June 30th, 1901.

NUMBER OF PUPILS IN THE DIFFERENT BRANCHES OF INSTRUCTION.

COUNTIES.	Physical Exercises.	Oral Lessons on Morals, Etc.	(Optional) 37		READING—SPELLING—RECITATION, ETC. 38								GRAMMAR AND ANALYSIS AND COMPOSITION. 39						HISTORY. 40				
	35	36	Sewing.	Knitting.	GRADE. I	II	III	IV	V	VI	VII	VIII	GRADE. *III	*IV	V	VI	VII	VIII	GRADE. *IV	V	VI	VII	VIII
Albert,	1893	2093	....	....	455	299	362	398	376	102	95	90	327	390	372	102	95	90	317	353	101	95	90
Carleton,	3765	4413	5	....	1006	578	699	802	982	187	152	121	567	756	951	178	142	128	671	932	185	147	127
Charlotte,	4152	4393	27	27	791	665	708	815	872	212	174	183	619	797	870	209	174	183	569	860	208	172	180
Gloucester,	3755	3917	24	....	1 94	856	675	668	304	118	63	61	668	664	302	118	63	61	559	284	117	63	61
Kent,	3052	3587	40	40	1543	644	616	551	279	79	49	60	581	511	279	79	39	58	460	273	79	39	62
Kings,	3458	4135	11	....	864	676	800	833	852	141	66	71	738	828	845	141	66	71	700	845	134	67	71
Madawaska,	1503	1705	....	....	987	413	345	243	93	17	26	28	334	226	82	17	26	28	194	83	16	26	28
Northumberland,	4615	96	14	1	1254	892	938	807	613	196	181	145	914	807	609	196	170	120	551	595	187	181	145
Queens,	1887	2243	....	....	472	316	99	437	530	32	8	25	459	439	517	32	8	25	420	523	32	8	25
Restigouche,	1201	1382	24	18	445	278	314	250	222	53	59	35	311	250	222	53	59	35	175	222	53	59	35
Saint John,	8125	8298	25	7	1737	1368	1372	1237	945	751	503	385	1353	1244	938	749	502	385	1152	936	748	503	385
Sunbury,	804	933	6	....	264	137	90	224	173	14	5	14	188	221	170	14	5	14	217	170	14	5	14
Victoria,	1256	1420	....	....	450	249	281	266	210	34	20	27	284	261	209	34	20	27	231	189	34	20	27
Westmorland	6228	6970	12	15	1885	1147	1226	1216	984	335	314	314	1107	1121	935	335	331	309	872	956	335	319	306
York,	4472	5266	5	5	1379	803	1054	1048	1059	250	179	162	1021	978	1010	254	177	158	766	1011	254	177	158
New Brunswick,	50166	55661	193	113	14936	9321	10049	9795	8494	2521	1894	1721	9471	9493	8311	2511	1877	1692	7854	8232	2497	1881	1714
Cor. Term, 1900.	50389	56529	105	62	14392	9658	10191	10380	8680	2592	1976	1718	9364	10098	8591	2686	1946	1711	8251	8532	2581	1905	1680
Increase,	....		88	51	544	....	....	....	....	....	....	3	107	..	..	..	..	...	...	..	..	..	34
Decrease,	223	868	....	....	....	337	142	585	186	71	82	....	..	605	280	175	69	19	397	300	84	24	...

*In Country Districts.

TABLE III. PART TWO.—CONTINUED.

Form, Color and Industrial Drawing. 41 — Grade.

OUNTIES	I	II	III	IV	V	VI	VII	VIII
ert,	425	303	367	387	359	102	95	90
leton,	929	592	673	818	957	182	143	128
rlotte,	785	667	708	797	865	209	174	179
ucester,	1381	856	674	669	304	118	63	61
t,	1521	646	620	539	273	79	49	60
gs,	851	662	787	809	836	138	67	71
lawaska,	788	343	323	236	92	17	26	28
thumberland,	1219	891	936	804	602	196	181	145
ens,	465	332	458	436	500	32	8	25
tigouche,	421	274	314	250	222	53	59	35
t John,	1713	1368	1372	1230	940	749	502	385
bury,	260	139	190	221	172	14	5	14
oria,	435	248	262	240	198	34	20	27
stmorland,	1795	1107	1220	1141	944	329	298	290
k,	1390	776	1034	999	978	241	172	154
ew Brunswick	14378	9204	9938	9576	8242	2493	1862	1692
or Term, 1900	13822	9494	10196	10188	8554	2567	1964	1691
ncrease,	556	...	....	....	....	....	....	1
ecrease,	....	290	258	612	312	74	102	....

Print-Script and Writing. 42 — Grade.

OUNTIES	I	II	III	IV	V	VI	VII	VIII
ert,	446	295	364	377	364	101	95	90
leton,	998	608	694	819	980	183	143	128
rlotte,	798	669	700	805	873	209	174	183
ucester,	1397	856	674	669	304	118	63	61
t,	1538	655	619	548	272	79	49	60
gs,	864	676	799	830	851	138	67	71
lawaska,	900	419	364	243	93	17	26	28
thumberland,	1254	892	938	807	613	196	181	145
ens,	476	325	459	442	524	32	8	25
tigouche,	445	278	314	233	197	47	59	35
t John,	1737	1368	1372	1239	943	749	503	385
bury,	264	138	192	221	173	14	5	14
oria,	446	253	281	266	210	34	20	27
stmorland,	1888	1145	1223	1196	999	342	308	307
k,	1374	804	1054	1049	1044	255	179	162
ew Brunswick	14825	9381	10047	9744	8440	2514	1880	1721
or Term, 1900	14145	9613	10282	10334	8662	2578	1887	1700
ncrease,	680	....	....	....	....	....	....	21
ecrease,	....	232	235	590	222	64	7	....

Singing ("Theory" Optional.) 43 — Grade.

OUNTIES	I (By Rote)	II (By Rote)	III (By Rote)	IV Rote	IV Note	V Rote	V Note	VI Rote	VI Note	VII Rote	VII Note	VIII Rote	VIII Note
ert,	269	176	217	218	.	156	.	54		28	.	47	
leton,	377	243	301	327	..	368		120		78		67	
rlotte,	474	465	420	423		533	22	153		110		86	.
ucester,	890	583	459	379	40	160	19	65	..	39		26	
t,	713	329	281	210	.	128		30	.	17		17	
gs,	413	300	392	380		409		75	..	20		38	
lawaska,	618	231	193	149	4	43	5	16	.	26	12	28	6
thumberland,	770	590	619	501	37	372	17	33	54	109	14	11	23
ens,	140	115	154	143	.	124		2		..	..	1	
tigouche,	241	192	206	230		113		45		36		23	
t John,	1547	1248	1262	1102	19	831	25	720	.	448		328	
bury,	139	82	105	110	.	81	..	...	..	..		...	...
oria,	216	117	124	116		101		15		6	.	...	
stmorland,	992	765	731	666		372	..	238	..	235		190	
k,	738	390	459	444	.	482		174		62	..	80	
ew Brunswick	8537	5826	5923	5398	100	4273	88	1740	54	1214	26	922	29
or Term, 1900	8211	5790	5898	5764	23	4403	26	1899	14	1314	15	1030	51
ncrease,	326	36	25	....	77	...	62	..	40	....	11	...	
ecrease,	....	....	......	366		130	...	159	..	100	..	108	22

TABLE III. PART TWO.—CONTINUED

COUNTIES.	Number-Arithmetic. 44 Grade. I	II	III	IV	V	VI	VII	VIII	Algebra. 46 Grade. VII	VIII	Geography. 47 Grade. III	IV	V	VI	VII	VIII
Albert,	455	299	362	398	367	91	87	78	111	83	362	395	372	102	95	88
Carleton,	986	608	695	823	956	180	143	127	257	132	683	811	961	182	143	136
Charlotte,	798	669	711	809	873	209	174	183	324	187	712	813	870	209	174	180
Gloucester,	1404	856	674	669	304	117	63	61	54	49	681	664	312	118	63	61
Kent,	1534	649	621	544	279	79	37	61	37	59	631	538	273	79	39	62
Kings,	849	673	807	833	850	140	67	71	169	89	807	835	850	138	67	71
Madawaska,	915	427	359	242	89	17	26	28	15	14	426	255	95	17	26	28
Northumberland,	1254	892	952	807	613	200	177	145	144	141	923	810	596	196	180	144
Queens	471	310	467	441	525	32	8	25	61	50	474	437	519	32	8	25
Restigouche,	445	278	314	226	204	47	59	35	59	34	318	250	222	53	59	35
Saint John,	1737	1368	1372	1235	947	749	503	383	424	328	1379	1234	948	749	503	385
Sunbury,	264	144	183	224	173	14	5	14	31	19	198	224	172	14	5	14
Victoria,	444	258	271	254	207	34	20	27	37	27	287	267	210	34	20	27
Westmorland,	1868	1153	1239	1213	963	337	298	270	437	296	1219	1158	956	332	318	307
York,	1366	802	1056	1042	1043	260	177	162	284	177	1040	1008	993	241	179	162
New Brunswick,	14790	9386	10083	9760	8393	2506	1844	1670	2444	1685	10140	9699	8349	2496	1879	1725
Cor. Term, 1900,	14287	9659	10311	10271	8691	2588	1904	1692	2371	1704	10281	10236	8591	2567	1960	1702
Increase,	503	....	......	..	......	...	......	......	73	...	......	......	......	......	......	23
Decrease,	...	273	228	511	298	82	60	22	......	19	141	537	242	71	81	....

TABLE III. Part Two.—Continued.

COUNTIES.	Hygiene and Temperance (Health Readers.) 48								Nature Lessons and Agriculture. Minerals—Plant Life—Animal Life. 49								Latin. (Optional.) 50		French. (Optional). 51
	Grade.								Grade.								Grade.		Grades.
	I	II	III	IV	V	VI	VII	VIII	I	II	III	IV	V	VI	VII	VIII	VII	VIII	I to VIII
Albert	404	274	362	393	369	101	95	74	399	276	342	395	363	101	94	88	....	27	......
Carleton,	690	474	637	821	962	182	148	127	756	456	575	774	917	179	143	126	39	10	......
Charlotte,	732	624	708	811	872	209	174	183	750	647	691	797	867	209	174	183	40	82	3
Gloucester,	1215	838	671	662	302	118	63	61	1241	776	649	648	289	118	63	61	4	18	1603
Kent,	1379	610	585	530	170	79	49	60	1341	601	585	532	279	79	49	60	6	26	102
Kings,	758	633	807	832	839	140	67	71	758	598	758	787	828	140	67	71	19	47	......
Madawaska,	750	339	323	225	84	17	26	28	681	301	294	214	71	16	26	28	15	14	506
Northumberland,	1173	850	923	792	610	196	180	144	1196	847	922	800	606	196	180	144	45	61	302
Queens,	400	286	446	422	516	32	8	25	403	282	452	427	513	32	8	24	....	10	......
Restigouche,	392	255	294	221	200	47	59	35	338	261	292	226	199	47	59	35	22	19	139
Saint John,	1663	1340	1372	1234	933	736	502	385	1664	1334	1366	1231	940	749	484	368	381	291	......
Sunbury,	179	114	165	218	172	14	5	14	180	114	164	203	161	....	....	14	....	8	....
Victoria,	329	228	270	256	207	34	20	27	348	246	273	250	206	34	20	27	6	9	8
Westmorland,	1399	965	1126	1168	937	332	318	293	1465	978	1086	1150	731	332	318	296	116	99	561
York,	1064	661	1012	1000	1005	254	177	154	1091	693	957	991	995	251	179	158	79	59	....
New Brunswick,	12527	8491	9701	9585	8178	2491	1891	1681	12611	8410	9406	9425	7965	2483	1864	1682	772	780	3224
Cor. Term, 1900	12166	8795	9783	10177	8498	2685	1849	1691	11963	8586	9610	9807	8353	2533	1926	1693	892	939	3818
Increase,	361	....	....	......	....	....	42	......	648	....	....	....	....	....	....	.....	....	......	....
Decrease,	......	304	82	592	320	194	....	10	......	176	204	382	388	50	62	10	120	159	594

TABLE III.—Superior, Grammar and Other Schools Having Pupils in Advance of Grade VIII.

Part Two.—Continued.

)UNTIES.	Language. 52 English. IX	X	XI	XII	Latin. IX	X	XI	XII	Greek. IX	X	XI	XII	French. IX	X	XI	XII
rt	49	26	10	....	18	10	5	....	2	3	1	....	..	..	..	....
eton	71	31	13	....	35	27	13	....	3	1	4	....	17	12	8	..
rlotte	77	37	39	....	28	26	33	....	2	6	11	....	44	22	26	....
ucester	23	3	..	....	10	1	..	....	2	1	..	....	4	1	..	....
t	34	5	..	....	28	4	1	....	..	1	1	....	..	..	..	....
gs	57	25	10	....	27	12	9	....	7	2	5	....	5	..	..	....
lawaska	..	..	..	....	..	..	..	....	..	..	..	....	..	..	..	....
thumberland	42	27	15	....	40	26	14	....	..	..	3	....	34	19	10	....
ens	8	6	4	....	13	6	4	....	1	..	2	....	..	..	..	....
igouche	19	18	4	...	18	16	4	...	11	7	4	....	15	..	..	....
t John	218	147	62	18	210	133	62	18	18	36	15	5	198	128	51	13
bury	13	..	..	...	1	..	—	....	..	..	..	....	..	..	..	..
oria	17	6	4	...	3	4	4	....	3	2	2	....	..	1	..	....
tmorland	171	83	57	....	99	45	42	....	8	3	4	...	102	38	35	....
k	94	40	28	....	55	28	15	....	10	11	9	...	64	18	17	....
ew Brunswick	893	454	246	18	585	338	206	18	67	73	61	5	483	239	147	13
or. Term, 1900	906	429	209	14	632	325	213	14	86	89	83	6	439	232	144	11
crease	..	25	37	4	..	13	..	4	..	..	..	....	44	7	3	2
crease	13	..	..	....	47	..	7	...	19	16	22	1	..	..	..	....

)UNTIES.	Mathematics. 53 Arithmetic. IX	X	Geometry. IX	X	XI	XII	Algebra. IX	X	XI	Book-Keeping. IX	X	Trigonometry. XI	XII	History and Geography. 54 IX	X	XI	XII	Drawing. 55 IX
rt	54	38	47	34	10	....	40	33	10	49	28	7	...	53	24	10	..	47
eton	78	31	66	31	13	....	76	31	13	42	27	13	...	71	12	..	....	71
rlotte	77	37	90	37	39	....	77	37	39	88	12	20	..	77	37	39	....	45
ucester	23	3	23	2	.	....	23	3	..	20	1	..	....	23	3	..	....	23
t	47	5	34	19	2	...	47	3	2	39	5	2	....	30	5	..	....	16
gs	57	25	51	26	10	....	55	26	10	8	..	..	....	50	23	10	....	50
lawaska	..	..	..	..		....	..	..	..	8	1	..	....	..	..	..	....	..
thumberland	47	27	47	27	15	....	47	27	15	29	27	..	....	47	27	15	....	47
ens	14	8	14	8	3	....	14	8	3	14	8	5	....	14	8	3	...	14
igouche	19	18	19	18	4	....	19	18	4	19	1	..	....	19	18	4	...	19
t John	218	147	218	147	62	18	218	147	62	199	147	5	18	218	147	62	18	215
bury	13	..	10	..	..	....	12	..	..	3	..	..	....	13	..	..	...	13
oria	17	6	17	6	4	....	17	6	4	13	6	..	....	17	6	4	....	17
tmorland	171	95	170	80	47	....	166	83	47	65	65	37	..	167	79	46	....	142
k	94	45	55	34	28	....	94	45	28	28	5	..	....	94	45	28	....	59
ew Brunswick	927	485	861	469	237	18	905	467	237	624	333	89	18	893	434	221	18	778
or. Term, 1900	936	457	874	462	236	33	891	461	241	714	302	50	15	898	438	236	14	808
crease	..	28	..	7	1	....	14	6	..	..	31	39	3	..	..	..	4	..
crease	9	..	13	..	..	15	..	..	4	90	..	..	....	5	4	15	....	30

)UNTIES.	Natural Science. 56 Physics. X	Physiology & Hygiene. X	XI	Chemistry. X	XI	Botany. IX	X	XI	Astronom. XII	Geology. XII	German. 57 XII	Psychology. 58 XII
rt	49	21	7	36	12	47	21	10	...	...	1	....
eton	37	30	24	37	13	73	31	13	...	..	....	....
rlotte	55	26	15	28	34	77	37	33	....	....	....	....
ucester	2	1	..	1	..	19	1	..	....	....	....	....
t	21	3	..	12	2	34	5	.	....	....	....	....
gs	43	27	10	24	10	52	13	..	....	..	....	....
lawaska	..	..	..	..	..	..	..	..	....	....	....	....
thumberland	47	27	15	27	15	40	27	14	....		....	....
ens	14	8	3	13	3	14	8	3	....	....	....	....
igouche	19	18	4	21	5	19	18	..	....	...	....	....
t John	218	147	5	36	74	215	146	53	....	....	....	....
bury	3	13	..	3	..	13	..	..	....	....	....	....
oria	17	6	4	6	4	5	.	.	....	....	....	....
tmorland	161	80	44	85	42	124	63	36	....	....	....	....
k	80	..	28	44	28	49	40	28	....	....	....	....
ew Brunswick	766	407	159	376	242	781	410	190	....	...	1	....
or. Term, 1900	644	461	177	433	189	776	409	104	4	4	....	....
crease	122	..	..	..	53	5	1	86	....	....	1	....
crease	..	54	18	57	..	..	..	..	4	4	....	..

TABLE IV.—PUBLIC SCHOOLS: Teachers Employed During the Year Ended 30th June, 1901.

Part One.—The First Term Closed 31st December, 1900.

COUNTIES.	Grammar Sch'l Teachers.		MALES. Class.			FEMALES. Class.			TOTAL.			Trained.	Untrained.	No of Assistants.		Total number of Teachers employed this Term.
	M.	F.	I	II	III	I	II	III	Male.	Female.	Both.			Male.	Female.	
Albert	1	....	10	1	3	12	39	12	15	63	78	78		.....	.....	78
Carleton	1	1	13	15	3	17	92	14	32	124	156	156	.....	.....	.....	156
Charlotte	1	....	17	8	1	31	70	14	27	115	142	142	.....	.....	2	144
Gloucester	1	....	4	3	33	6	22	44	41	72	113	113	.....	.....	3	116
Kent	1	....	5	3	13	4	32	64	22	100	122	122	.....	.....	1	123
Kings	2	....	12	12	2	26	92	15	28	133	161	161	.....	.....	1	162
Madawaska	....	....	2	....	8	....	1	49	10	50	60	46	14	.....	2	62
Northumberland	1	....	9	5	4	11	95	28	19	134	153	153	.....	.....	2	155
Queens	1	....	4	16	2	9	42	22	23	73	96	96	.....	.....	.....	96
Restigouche	1	....	2	....	1	8	26	10	4	44	48	48	.....	.....	1	49
Saint John	3	2	19	7	1	97	91	7	30	197	227	227	.....	.....	9	236
Sunbury	....	....	2	8	2	2	19	8	12	29	41	41	.....	.....	.....	41
Victoria	1	....	3	4	....	6	22	22	8	50	58	56	2	.....	.....	58
Westmorland	4	....	15	30	16	43	63	41	65	147	212	212	.....	.....	1	213
York	3	....	20	14	2	35	95	33	39	163	203	200	2	.....	2	204
New Brunswick	21	3	137	126	91	307	801	383	375	1494	1869	1851	18	.....	24	1893
Cor. Term, 1899	22	2	145	122	96	300	805	375	385	1482	1867	1848	19	1	25	1893
Increase	....	1	....	4	....	7	....	8	.....	12	2	3	.....	.....	.....	.....
Decrease	1	....	8	....	5	....	4	....	10	....	.....	.....	1	1	1	...

TABLE IV. PART TWO.---SECOND TERM CLOSED 30TH JUNE, 1901.

COUNTIES.	Grammar School Teachers.		MALES. CLASS.			FEMALES. CLASS.			TOTAL.			Trained.	Untrained.	No. of Assistants.		Total number of Teachers employed this Term.
	M.	F	I	II	III	I	II	III	Male.	Female.	Both.			Male.	Female.	
Albert, ...	1	..	9	3	2	9	42	8	15	59	74	74	..	..	..	74
Carleton, ...	1	1	11	16	2	16	84	18	30	119	149	147	2	..	..	149
Charlotte, ...	1	..	14	10	2	34	76	11	27	121	148	148	..	1	5	154
Gloucester, ...	1	..	3	4	34	3	22	39	42	64	106	102	4	1	2	109
Kent, ...	1	..	4	4	12	7	26	58	21	91	112	112	..	..	1	113
Kings, ...	1	..	13	15	2	23	96	15	31	134	165	165	..	..	1	166
Madawaska, ...	..	..	2	..	6	..	1	47	8	48	56	44	12	..	1	57
Northumberland, ...	1	..	10	3	4	9	89	28	18	126	144	141	3	..	2	146
Queens, ...	1	..	5	17	3	7	41	19	26	67	93	90	3	..	..	93
Restigouche, ...	1	..	2	..	1	8	23	10	4	41	45	45	..	..	1	46
Saint John, ...	3	2	20	7	1	97	88	10	31	197	228	228	..	..	11	239
Sunbury, ...	..	..	1	6	3	3	22	7	10	32	42	42	..	..	..	42
Victoria, ...	1	..	3	7	..	4	20	17	11	41	52	51	1	..	..	52
Westmorland, ...	4	..	10	22	11	49	62	41	47	152	199	199	..	..	4	203
York, ...	3	..	17	8	2	36	97	35	30	168	198	193	5	..	..	198
New Brunswick, ...	20	3	124	122	85	305	789	363	351	1460	1811	1781	30	2	28	1841
Cor. Term, 1900, ...	23	2	144	112	91	308	769	381	370	1460	1830	1809	21	1	25	1856
Increase, ...	..	1	..	10	..	..	20	..	..	..	..	.	9	1	3	.. ..
Decrease, ...	3	..	20	..	6	3	..	18	19	..	19	28	..	..	..	15

PART ONE.—THE FIRST TERM CLOSED 31ST DECEMBER, 1900.

COUNTIES.	No. of teachers employed in same District as during previous Term.	No. of teachers removed to a new District.	No. of new teachers this Term.	No. of teachers whose period of service is not reported.	No. of teachers not more than 3 years in the service employed this Term.	PERIOD OF SERVICE OF TEACHERS OF GR., SUP., AND 1ST CLASS. — MALE TEACHERS GR., SUP., AND 1ST CLASS. No. first Term employed.	No. second Term employed.	No. 1 to 2 years.	No. 2 to 3 years.	No. 3 to 5 years.	No. 5 to 7 years.	No. upwards of 7 years.	FEMALE TEACHERS GR., SUP., AND 1ST CLASS. No. first Term employed.	No. second Term employed.	No. 1 to 2 years.	No. 2 to 3 years.	No. 3 to 5 years.	No. 5 to 7 years.	No. upwards of 7 years.
Albert	33	35	9	1	40	1	..	1	2	1	4	2	..	..	2	1	4	3	2
Carleton	89	52	11	4	65	..	..	1	3	5	1	4	..	..	2	3	5	..	8
Charlotte	78	54	10	..	50	..	1	1	3	2	3	8	2	..	1	2	6	7	13
Gloucester	72	25	10	6	40	1	..	..	1	1	..	2	..	..	1	.	2	2	1
Kent	72	40	9	1	52	..	..	..	1	1	.	4	..	..	..	..	..	..	4
Kings	102	38	19	2	69	..	1	3	2	4	1	3	2	1	3	2	8	..	10
Madawaska	30	12	16	2	33	..	..	.	..	2	..	..	.	..	..	..	..	..	..
Northumberland	105	28	15	5	52	..	..	1	..	1	..	8	1	..	1	2	1	3	3
Queens	48	37	11	..	39	1	..	..	1	..	1	2	1	..	..	..	5	1	2
Restigouche	30	13	4	1	15	..	..	..	..	1	..	2	..	1	..	..	2	2	3
St. John	176	23	5	23	35	1	..	..	..	2	..	19	2	3	6	8	9	18	53
Sunbury	26	11	3	1	16	..	..	..	1	..	..	1	..	..	..	..	1	..	1
Victoria	39	11	7	1	26	..	..	..	..	2	..	2	1	..	1	1	..	..	3
Westmorland	139	49	18	6	85	1	..	1	1	2	6	8	.	.	3	2	12	8	18
York	99	66	24	13	88	1	1	3	1	4	1	12	..	2	2	2	5	6	18
New Brunswick	1,138	494	171	66	705	6	3	11	16	28	17	77	9	7	22	23	60	50	139
Cor. Term, 19	1,208	404	191	64	666	10	4	9	17	25	20	82	12	6	26	23	58	47	130
Increase	..	90	..	2	39	..	..	2	..	3	..	..	..	1	..	..	2	3	9
Decrease	70	..	20	..	..	4	1	..	1	..	3	5	3	..	4	..	..	.	..

TABLE V. Part Two—THE SECOND TERM CLOSED 30TH JUNE, 1901.

COUNTIES.	No. of teachers employed in same District as during previous Term.	No. of teachers removed to a new District.	No. of new teachers this Term.	No. of teachers whose period of service is not reported.	No. of teachers not more than 3 years in the service employed this Term.	PERIOD OF SERVICE OF TEACHERS OF GR., SUP. AND 1ST CLASS. — MALE TEACHERS GR., SUP., AND 1ST CLASS. No. first Term employed.	No. second Term employed.	No. 1 to 2 years.	No. 2 to 3 years.	No. 3 to 5 years.	No. 5 to 7 years.	No. upwards of 7 years.	FEMALE TEACHERS GR., SUP., AND 1ST CLASS. No. first Term employed.	No. second Term employed.	No. 1 to 2 years.	No. 2 to 3 years.	No. 3 to 5 years.	No. 5 to 7 years.	No. upwards of 7 years.
Albert	44	25	2	3	31	..	..	1	1	2	1	5	1	..	..	1	2	2	3
Carleton	77	63	8	1	63	..	..	1	3	2	1	5	..	1	2	3	5	1	5
Charlotte	95	47	2	4	48	..	..	1	1	3	2	8	..	2	5	2	2	12	11
Gloucester	67	28	9	2	37	..	..	1	..	1	..	2	.	..	..	..	2	..	1
Kent	70	37	5	..	44	..	..	..	1	1	..	3	..	...	..	..	1	3	3
Kings	81	73	4	7	61	..	1	2	2	3	1	5	..	1	3	1	6	4	8
Madawaska	28	17	10	1	34	..	..	..	..	2	..	..	..	..	..	..	..	-	..
Northumberland	103	30	6	5	48	..	1	1	..	..	2	7	..	..	2	1	..	2	4
Queens	50	40	1	2	31	..	1	..	1	1	1	2	..	..	..	..	4	1	2
Restigouche	34	10	1	..	13	..	..	.	..	..	1	2	..	..	1	1	1	1	4
St. John	180	19	1	28	19	..	1	..	..	2	2	18	..	2	5	5	10	9	68
Sunbury	25	14	1	2	16	..	..	..	1	..	..	..	..	..	..	..	1	1	1
Victoria	33	19	..	..	19	..	..	..	..	2	..	2	..	1	1	..	..	1	1
Westmorland	133	58	1	7	68	..	1	1	1	..	2	9	..	..	6	4	9	9	21
York	101	70	11	16	84	..	..	3	4	1	1	11	1	1	2	3	6	3	20
New Brunswick	1,121	550	62	78	616	..	5	11	15	20	14	79	2	8	27	21	49	49	152
Cor. Term, 900	1,130	534	100	66	636	2	10	13	16	27	21	78	3	13	24	19	53	41	151
Increase	..	16	..	12	..	..	..	..	..	..	..	1	..	..	3	2	..	8	1
Decrease	9	..	38	..	20	2	5	2	1	7	7	..	1	5	..	..	4	..	..

TABLE V.—Continued. PERIOD OF SERVICE OF SECOND CLASS TEACHERS EMPLOYED DURING YEAR ENDED 30TH JUNE, 1901.

COUNTIES.	DURING THE TERM CLOSED 31ST DECEMBER, 1900.														DURING THE TERM CLOSED 30TH JUNE, 1901.													
	MALE TEACHERS, 2ND CLASS.							FEMALE TEACHERS, 2ND CLASS.							MALE TEACHERS, 2ND CLASS.							FEMALE TEACHERS, 2ND CLASS.						
	No. 1st Term employed.	No. 2nd Term employed.	No. from 1 to 2 years.	No. from 2 to 3 years.	No. from 3 to 5 years.	No. from 5 to 7 years.	No. upwards of 7 years.	No. 1st Term employed.	No. 2nd Term employed.	No. from 1 to 2 years.	No. from 2 to 3 years.	No. from 3 to 5 years.	No. from 5 to 7 years.	No. upwards of 7 years.	No. 1st Term employed.	No. 2nd Term employed.	No. from 1 to 2 years.	No. from 2 to 3 years.	No. from 3 to 5 years.	No. from 5 to 7 years.	No upwards of 7 years.	No. 1st Term employed.	No. 2nd Term employed.	No. from 1 to 2 years.	No. from 2 to 3 years.	No. from 3 to 5 years.	No. from 5 to 7 years.	No. upwards of 7 years.
Albert	.	..	1	......	......	......	......	5	3	8	5	9	4	5	......	....	......	1	......	1	1	......	5	12	3	9	9	4
Carleton	3	..	4	3	1	2	2	6	1	13	16	22	19	15	......	2	6	2	1	2	3	2	6	12	12	8	23	21
Charlotte	..	1	4	......	2	......	1	5	4	8	8	13	12	20	......	......	2	3	2	2	1	1	7	11	7	14	13	23
Gloucester	1	..	1	......	......	......	1	1	1	1	3	2	4	10	......	1	......	1	1	......	1	......	2	1	1	3	5	10
Kent	..	1	1	1	......	......	....	4	......	7	2	6	4	9	....	......	1	2	......	1	......	......	3	9	1	4	1	8
Kings	1	..	2	2	3	1	3	15	1	12	9	22	13	20	......	1	3	1	2	2	6	......	13	10	10	19	23	21
Madawaska	..	..	......	......	......	......	......	......	......	......	......	......	......	1	......	......	......	......	......	......	......	......	......	......	1	......	......	......
Northumberland	1	..	......	......	1	......	3	9	......	8	13	11	16	38	......	......	......	......	......	......	3	2	6	7	6	15	18	35
Queens	2	..	......	2	4	1	7	6	1	5	4	12	4	10	......	3	......	......	4	2	8	......	6	6	3	10	5	11
Restigouche	..	..	......	......		......	......	4	......	2	4	4	3	9	......	......	......	......	......	......	......	......	4	1	3	5	1	9
Saint John	1	.	......	......	1	2	3	1	1	5	5	7	17	55	......	1	......	......	......	2	4	......	1	2	10	9	10	56
Sunbury	1	..	2	1	1	2	1	1	2	2	2	5	1	6	......	1	2	1	......	......	2	......	1	3	2	7	1	8
Victoria	..	.	......	......	......	2	2	2	2	2	1	1	4	10	......	1	......	......	2	1	3	......	2	2	1	2	5	8
Westmorland	3	3	9	5	4	1	5	8	1	8	10	11	8	17	......	3	5	5	5	1	3	......	6	6	10	15	7	18
York	7	..	4	2	......	......	1	12	4	17	9	16	15	22	......	3	3	1	......	......	1	2	12	18	13	10	16	26
New Brunswick	20	5	28	16	17	11	29	79	21	98	91	141	124	247	....	16	22	17	17	14	36	7	74	100	83	130	137	258
Cor. Terms 1899 and 90	22	2	17	17	25	11	33	90	14	97	76	149	127	252	2	23	20	9	20	11	27	13	83	86	71	141	123	252
Increase	.	-	11	....	....	....	....	....	7	1	15	....	....	....	....	....	2	8	....	3	9	....	....	14	12	11	14	6
–				1	8	....	4	11	....	....	....	8	3	5	2	7	....	....	3	....	....	6	9	....	....	....	....	....

—PUBLIC SCHOOLS: TIME IN SESSION DURING THE YEAR ENDED 30TH JUNE, 1901.

COUNTIES.	The First Term Closed 31st December, 1900							The Second Term Closed 30th June, 1901.							
	No. of Schools open this Term.	No. of Schools open less than 80 days.	No. in session 80 but less than 94 days.	Total in session less than 94 days.	No. in session the full term of 94 days.*	Av'r'ge days schools in session during the Term.	Aggregate number of days schools open during this Term.	No. of schools open this Term.	No. of schools open less than 80 teaching days.	No. in session 80 but less than 100 days.	No. in session less than 100 days.	No. in session 100 days but less than 120 days	No. in session the full Term or 120 days.**	Av'r'ge days schools in session during the Term.	Aggregate number of days schools open during the Term.
Albert	76	9	30	39	37	87.3	6,638	71	6	3	9	23	39	110.9	7,878½
Carleton	152	28	58	86	66	86.6	13,167½	147	14	7	21	61	65	110.3	16,224½
Charlotte	142	50	56	106	36	83.	11,795	144	20	6	26	67	51	107.6	15,496
Gloucester	109	6	37	43	66	91.5	9,981	104	7	3	10	35	59	113.5	11,811½
Kent	121	6	28	34	87	91.5	11,083½	112	13	1	14	18	80	111.0	12,454
Kings	158	15	80	95	63	88.9	14,051	158	13	2	15	66	77	112.7	17,819
Madawaska	58	1	25	26	32	91.8	5,325½	55	3	7	10	13	32	110.7	6,093½
Northumberland	148	4	93	97	51	91.6	13,560½	139	9	6	15	36	88	112.8	15,691½
Queens	96	15	52	67	29	87.6	8,412	91	13	3	16	39	36	107.9	9,822
Restigouche	47	1	14	15	32	93.5	4,397	45	2	1	3	11	31	114.8	5,168
Saint John	211	8	40	48	163	92.3	19,480	208	6	2	8	24	176	117.2	24,361
Sunbury	40	13	14	27	13	83.9	3,358	40	5	1	6	16	18	109.2	4,368
Victoria	57	8	25	33	24	87.3	4,979	52	10	1	11	13	28	105.4	5,484
Westmorland	207	10	59	69	138	92.1	19,070	192	7	6	13	53	126	115.4	22,160½
York	190	13	76	89	101	91.3	17,361½	183	26	11	37	59	87	107.7	19,726½
New Brunswick	1,812	187	687	874	938	89.7	162,659½	1,741	154	60	214	534	993	111.7	194,578½
Cor. Terms 1899-00	1,815	160	619	779	1,036	88.2	160,132	1,771	134	60	194	595	982	115.4	204,378
Increase	......	27	68	95	......	1.5	2,527½	......	20	......	20	......	11	......	......
Decrease	3	......	......	......	94	......	......	30	......	......	......	61	......	3.7	9,799½

* In the Second Term there were 84 teaching days in the city of Saint John and other incorporated towns. The actual number of days the schools were open in these districts is *raised* to the basis of 94 days.

** In the First Term there were 119 teaching days in St. John and 120 days in other cities and incorporated towns and in other districts. The former is *raised* to the basis of the latter for the purposes of comparison.

TABLE VII. PUBLIC SCHOOLS: Visits—Public Examinations—Prizes: For the Year Ended 30th June, 1901.

THE FIRST TERM CLOSED 31ST DECEMBER, 1900.

COUNTIES.	Visits.						Examinations.		Prizes.	
	No. by the Trustees and Secretary.	No. by the County Inspector.	No. by members of Parliament.	No. by Clergymen.	No. by Teachers.	No. by other visitors.	No. of Schools holding public examinations during the Term.	No. of Schools not holding public examinations during the Term.	No. of prizes given to the pupils.	Value of the prizes.
Albert	188	21	1	28	63	764	70	6	2	$ 1 15
Carleton	242	95	......	40	110	1233	126	26	34	12 88
Charlotte	367	65	11	62	146	1353	122	20	22	7 10
Gloucester	329	46	4	35	173	1163	88	21	6	1 50
Kent	357	43	3	61	86	1220	109	12	23	9 20
Kings	236	89	1	49	105	1289	140	18	42	24 00
Madawaska	180	21	2	33	53	462	57	1	48	8 56
Northumberland	351	80	4	83	95	1715	135	13	24	12 40
Queens	228	33	......	47	70	1010	72	24	3	1 75
Restigouche	129	45	5	24	41	465	43	4	6	2 60
Saint John	142	51	......	32	38	496	205	6	4	1 20
Sunbury	68	19	1	10	13	333	27	13	6	5 05
Victoria	127	51	......	3	24	291	43	14	15	6 05
Westmorland	555	93	6	88	162	2304	187	20	25	11 73
York	243	102	......	56	146	1610	147	43	39	14 49
New Brunswick	3742	854	38	678	1325	15,708	1571	241	209	$119 66
Cor. Terms, 1899-1900	4112	986	50	723	1415	16,962	1639	176	317	125 08
Increase	......	......	......	......	......	....	....	65	......	....
Decrease	370	132	12	45	90	1,254	68	....	18	$ 5 42

THE SECOND TERM CLOSED 30TH JUNE, 1901.

COUNTIES.	Visits.						Examinations.		Prizes.	
	No. by the Trustees and Secretary.	No. by the County Inspector.	No. by members of Parliament.	No. by Clergymen.	No. by Teachers.	No. by other visitors.	No. of Schools holding public examinations during the Term.	No. of Schools not holding public examinations during the Term.	No. of prizes given to the pupils.	Value of the prizes.
Albert	161	41	......	30	53	893	65	6	100	$36 87
Carleton	301	120	5	33	101	1626	110	37	16	39 80
Charlotte	332	110	8	74	107	1579	123	21	10	11 50
Gloucester	362	85	......	41	158	1489	96	8	13	30 00
Kent	436	75	1	74	93	161	101	11	35	14 48
Kings	308	78	......	50	100	1904	136	22	79	40 86
Madawaska	198	42	15	36	68	671	54	1	29	6 70
Northumberland	415	112	4	94	132	1961	131	8	53	51 30
Queens	227	67	......	42	54	1202	71	20	4	1 80
Restigouche	136	......	2	16	26	486	41	4	6	5 80
Saint John	469	116	6	181	135	2533	200	8	8	3 70
Sunbury	80	29	......	15	20	401	28	12	6	13 10
Victoria	158	26	......	14	25	484	39	13	11	3 65
Westmorland	626	133	3	93	128	2177	170	22	5	64 60
York	296	134	4	75	126	1734	138	45	31	12 25
New Brunswick	4505	1168	48	868	1326	20,751	1,503	238	485	$335 81
Cor. Terms, 1899-1900	4798	1177	38	1005	1421	20,614	1,592	179	291	150 45
Increase	......	......	10	......	......	137	....	59	194	$185 36
Decrease	293	9	......	137	95	....	89	....	......	....

BLIC SCHOOLS: AVERAGE SALARIES OF TEACHERS FOR THE YEAR ENDED 30TH JUNE, 1901.

FROM THE RATES PAID IN THE TERM ENDED JUNE 30th, 1901.

COUNTIES.	COMMON SCHOOLS. Average Rate per Year to Male Teachers			COMMON SCHOOLS. Av'ge Rate per Year to Female Teachers			Average Superior Schools.	Average Grammar Schools.
	1st Class.	2nd Class.	3rd Class.	1st Class.	2nd Class.	3rd Class.		
Albert,	$ 372 50	$ 284 66	$ 253 62	$ 256 66	$ 210 82	$ 160 21	$ 550 00	See Table XIII.
Carleton,	435 66	266 18	226 00	278 87	210 68	184 37	500 00	
Charlotte,	472 44	289 20	230 50	303 11	233 64	198 47	680 00	
Gloucester,	......	287 00	222 76	229 00	219 70	177 73	583 33	
Kent,	400 00	283 00	212 83	271 16	216 28	175 63	512 50	
Kings,	361 75	254 60	201 12	253 50	201 31	172 00	500 00	
Madawaska,	255 00	.....	235 00	......	201 00	172 86	500 00	
Northumberland,	505 00	280 33	241 56	258 55	234 06	184 43	688 33	
Queens,	298 75	247 41	180 66	227 96	201 73	164 65	500 00	
Restigouche,	290 00	......	221 00	291 88	219 76	198 37	625 00	
Saint John,	829 11	453 00	201 25	361 24	315 94	182 20	566 66	
Sunbury,	......	256 60	194 41	235 00	205 75	173 14	500 00	
Victoria,	288 00	260 42	......	249 25	218 73	190 48	500 00	
Westmorland,	660 00	268 90	226 09	316 38	254 05	190 34	589 28	
York,	477 07	266 37	229 50	312 11	203 11	175 50	590 00	
New Brunswick,	$ 520 10	$ 276 48	$ 221 41	$ 312 69	$ 226 78	$ 179 34	$ 576 07	......
Average Salaries, 1900,	463 33	278 30	219 62	306.81	228 32	183 81	577 80	......
Increase,	$ 56 77	......	$ 1 79	$ 5 88	......	...	......	......
Decrease,	......	$ 1 82	......	......	$ 1 54	$ 4 47	$ 1 73	...

TABLE IX. PUBLIC SCHOOLS: DISBURSEMENT OF THE PROVINCIAL GRANTS FOR THE YEAR ENDED OCTOBER 31ST.

COUNTIES.	For First Term ended December 31st, 1900.					For Second Term ended June 30th, 1901.					For the Year.	
	Ordinary Grants. 1	Superior Schools. 2	Grammar Schools. 3	Special to those teaching in poor Districts (included in amount in Column 1.)	Total.	Ordinary Grants. 1	Superior Schools. 2	Grammar Schools. 3	Special to those teaching in poor Districts (included in amount in Column 1.)	Total.	Total special aid to those teaching in poor Districts.	Total.
Albert	$2765 67	$52 83	$142 03	$256 02	$3160 53	$3305 59	$429 46	$206 89	$268 71	$3941 94	$524 73	$7,102 47
Carleton	5222 34	420 58	284 06	151 96	5926 98	6408 52	730 73	406 90	78 83	7541 15	230 79	13,468 13
Charlotte	94 23	512 95	142 03	253 62	5599 21	6803 43	728 27	206 89	338 96	7738 59	592 58	13,337 80
Gl ι ester	3829 95	317 47	141 19	464 10	4288 61	4629 95	429 46	206 03	541 09	5265 44	1005 19	9,554 05
Kent	4029 14	419 50	142 03	473 13	4590 67	4684 85	527 53	206 89	5 7 59	5419 27	990 72	10,009 94
Kings	5681 27	512 34	277 30	318 60	6470 91	7477 46	737 67	205 17	421 02	8420 30	739 62	14,891 21
Madawaska	1703 72	108 30	......	89 18	1812 02	1919 31	144 07	......	117 73	2062 38	206 91	3,875 40
Northumberland	52 3 44	513 15	140 34	373 18	5866 93	6229 16	725 02	203 44	411 04	7157 62	784 22	13,024 55
Qeens	3553 45	101 45	129 26	324 79	3784 16	4209 08	147 78	177 34	289 62	4534 20	614 41	8,318 36
Restigouche	1697 20	101 45	142 03	139 27	1940 68	2091 31	147 78	200 00	165 16	2439 09	304 43	4,379 77
Saint John	7930 34	307 73	558 01	122 99	8796 08	10986 95	442 11	795 29	108 00	12224 35	230 99	21,020 43
Sunbury	31 43	108 30	......	160 19	1559 73	1919 95	124 42	......	218 71	2044 37	378 90	3,604 10
Victoria	2006 38	100 84	142 03	269 87	2249 25	2299 38	147 78	197 40	289 39	2644 56	559 26	4,893 81
Westmorland	7333 27	712 96	561 36	243 80	8607 59	8830 95	1025 06	827 56	198 84	10688 57	442 64	19,291 16
York	6938 40	517 48	426 09	376 75	7881 97	8104 18	573 73	620 67	357 42	9298 58	734 17	17,180 55
New Brunswick	$64,300 23	$5007 33	$3227 76	$4017 45	$72,535 32	$79,895 07	$7060 87	$4460 47	$4322 11	$91,416 4	$8339 56	$163,951 73
Cor. Terms 1899 and 1900	65,270 96	5112 44	3242 47	4183 24	73,625 87	82,983 81	6975 32	4639 72	4694 30	94,598 85	8877 54	168,224 72
Increase	....	....	....	....	....	....	$85 55	....	....	....	....	....
Decrease	$970 78	$105 11	$14 71	$ 65 79	$1,090 55	$3,088 74	....	$179 25	$372 19	$3,182 44	$ 537 98	$4,272 99

CHOOLS: Apportionment of County Fund to Trustees for the Year ended June 30th, 1901.

Part One.---First Term ended December 31st, 1900.

Drafts issued by the Chief Superintendent, payable by the respective County Treasurers.

COUNTIES.	Grand Total days' attendance of Pupils; rectified for County Fund Apportionment (Term 94 days.)	In respect of the services of qualified Teachers exclusive of Assistants for the time the Schools were in Session. (1)	Special to Poor Districts (embraced in column 1.)	In respect of the average number of Pupils in attendance, as compared with the whole average number of Pupils attending the Schools in the County and the time in operation. (2)	Special to Poor Districts (included in column 2.)	Total to the Trustees. This Term. Whole amount apportioned this Term. *(3)	Total to the Trustees. This Term. Total special to Poor Districts, (included in column 3).	Rate per Pupil in attendance the full Term per column 2 (4) In Ordinary Districts.	Rate per Pupil in attendance the full Term per column 2 (4) In Poor Districts.
Albert,	131,359	$ 1,186 24	127 52	$ 316 91	$ 21 61	$ 1,503 15	$ 149 13	$ 0 22+	$ 0 30—
Carleton,	222,147	2,192 79	72 69	972 88	15 82	3,165 67	88 51	0 37+	0 49+
Charlotte,	243,434½	2,014 56	132 44	1,443 25	39 27	3,457 80	171 71	0 55+	0 73+
Gloucester,	244,531	1,832 25	241 19	1,902 30	198 10	3,734 55	439 29	0 73+	0 97+
Kent,	220,456	2,009 07	240 47	1,380 18	129 88	3,389 25	370 35	0 58+	0 78—
Kings,	225,930	2,404 13	162 53	833 92	32 88	3,238 05	195 41	0 34+	0 45+
Madawaska,	114,364	883 36	48 73	663 44	26 84	1,546 80	75 57	0 54+	0 72+
Northumberland,	314,318½	2,378 68	192 97	1,410 77	66 78	3,789 45	259 75	0 42+	0 56+
Queens,	115,879½	1,490 69	157 03	302 11	24 34	1,792 80	181 37	0 24+	0 32+
Restigouche,	99,118	721 00	69 15	465 20	30 29	1,186 20	99 44	0 44+	0 59—
Saint John,	580,898½	3,156 25	72 32	4,024 85	22 58	7,181 10	94 90	0 65+	0 86+
Sunbury,	48,946	603 88	77 77	260 42	21 41	864 30	99 18	0 50+	0 67—
Victoria,	68,940½	925 00	131 65	230 75	24 61	1,155 75	156 26	0 31+	0 41+
Westmorland,	479,437½	3,126 10	113 06	2,555 45	41 81	5,681 55	154 87	0 50+	0 67—
York,	253,695½	2,565 60	199 48	998 49	47 34	3,564 09	246 82	0 37+	0 49+
New Brunswick,	3,363,455½	$27,489 59	$ 2,039 00	$17,760 92	$ 743 56	$45,250 51	$ 2,782 56	$ 0 49+	$ 0 65+

*The Balance of the County Fund ($1,963.64) was paid to the School for the Blind, Halifax, and the Institution for the Deaf and Dumb, Fredericton. See Table XI.

TABLE X. PUBLIC SCHOOLS: APPORTIONMENT OF COUNTY FUND TO TRUSTEES FOR THE YEAR ENDED 30TH JUNE, 1901.

PART TWO.—SECOND TERM ENDED JUNE, 1901.

Drafts issued by the Chief Superintendent payable by the respective County Treasurers.

COUNTIES.	Grand total days' attendance of Pupils: rectified for County Fund Apportionment (Term 120 days.)	In respect of the services of qualified Teachers exclusive of Assistants, for the time the Schools were in Session. (1)	Special to Poor Districts (embraced in column 1.)	In respect of the average number of Pupils in attendance, as compared with the whole average number of Pupils attending the Schools in the County and the time in operation. (2)	Special to Poor Districts (included in column 2.)	Total to the Trustees. This Term. *Whole amount apportioned this Term. (3)	Total special to Poor Districts (included in column 3.)	Rate per Pupil in attendance the full Term per column 2. (4) In Ordinary Districts.	In Poor Districts.
Albert,	172,985	$1,089 52	$104 15	$413 63	$24 16	$1,503 15	$128 31	$0 28+	$0 37+
Carleton,	300,463½	2,044 04	31 05	1,140 31	10 15	3,184 35	41 20	0 45+	0 60+
Charlotte,	349,680½	2,074 43	137 62	1,383 37	39 50	3,457 80	177 12	0 47+	0 62+
Gloucester,	292,731½	1,674 54	208 43	2,060 01	200 17	3,734 55	408 60	0 84+	1 12+
Kent,	270,329	1,769 84	213 11	1,619 41	145 62	3,389 25	358 73	0 71+	0 94+
Kings,	300,918	2,372 70	158 36	895 35	36 44	3,268 05	194 80	0 35+	0 46+
Madawaska,	145,403½	813 76	49 04	733 04	37 25	1,546 80	86 29	0 60+	0 80+
Northumberland,	375,574	2,106 23	161 35	1,713 22	78 03	3,819 45	239 38	0 54+	0 72+
Queens,	151,391	1,339 64	118 29	453 16	29 30	1,792 80	147 59	0 36—	0 48—
Restigouche,	133,588½	763 21	72 37	422 99	24 12	1,186 20	96 49	0 38	0 50+
Saint John,	845,452	3,086 39	49 56	4,034 71	14 63	7,121 10	64 19	0 57+	0 76+
Sunbury,	66,719½	622 33	81 95	241 97	20 03	864 30	101 98	0 43+	0 57+
Victoria,	98,756½	792 72	107 37	363 03	35 62	1,155 75	142 99	0 44+	0 58+
Westmorland,	551,420	2,808 37	85 12	2,873 18	45 12	5,681 55	130 24	0 62+	0 82+
York,	322,367½	2,193 74	149 41	1,342 81	52 52	3,536 55	201 93	0 49+	0 65+
New Brunswick	4,377,780	$25,551 46	$1,727 18	$19,690 19	$792 66	$45,241 65	$2,519 84	$0 54—	$0 72—

* The balance of the County Fund ($1,972.50) was paid to the School for the Blind, Halifax, and the Institution for the Deaf and Dumb, Fredericton. See Table XI

AND COUNTY FUND GRANTS TO THE SCHOOL FOR THE BLIND, HALIFAX; AND COUNTY FUND GRANT TO THE INSTITUTION FOR THE DEAF ANE DUMB, FREDERICTON.

Year Ended 30th June, 1901.

COUNTIES.	School for the Blind, Halifax.								Institution for the Deaf and Dumb, Fredericton.					
	Term ended Dec. 31, 1900.			Term ended June 30, 1901.					Term ended Dec. 31, 1900.		Term ended June 30, 1901.			
	No. of Pupils.	Provinc'l Grant, at rate of $75 per pupil per year.	Grant from County fund at rate of $75 per pupil per year.	No. of Pupils.	Provinc'l Grant, at rate of $75 per pupil per year.	Grant from County fund at rate of $75 per pupil per year.	Total Provincial Grant for the year.	Total from County Fund for the year.	No. of Pupils.	Grant from County fund at the rate of $60 per pupil per year.	No. of Pupils.	Grant from County fund at the rate of $60 per pupil per year.	Total for the year.	Total County Fund Grants to both Institutions.
Albert	3	$112 50	$112 50	3	$112 50	$112 50	$225 00	$225 00	1	$30 00	1	$30 00	$60 00	$285 00
Carleton	2	75 00	75 00	2	75 00	75 00	150 00	150 00	5	138 68	4	120 00	258 68	408 68
Charlotte	2	75 00	75 00	2	75 00	75 00	150 00	150 00	1	30 00	1	30 00	60 00	210 00
Gloucester	....	......	......	....	......	......	......	......	....	......	....	......	......	......
Kent	5	187 50	187 50	5	187 50	187 50	375 00	375 00	....	......	....	......	......	375 00
Kings	2	75 00	75 00	2	75 00	75 00	150 00	150 00	5	150 00	4	120 00	270 00	420 00
Madawaska	....	......	......	....	......	......	......	......	1	30 00	1	30 00	60 00	60 00
Northumberl'd	1	37 50	37 50	1	37 50	37 50	75 00	75 00	1	30 00	....	......	30 00	105 00
Queens	....	......	......	....	......	......	......	......	1	30 00	1	30 00	60 00	60 00
Restigouche	....	......	......	....	......	......	......	......	2	60 00	2	60 00	120 00	120 00
Saint John	6	225 00	225 00	6	225 00	225 00	450 00	450 00	1	30 00	3	90 00	120 00	570 00
Westmorland	8	300 00	300 00	8	300 00	300 00	600 00	600 00	8	240 00	8	240 00	480 00	1080 00
York	2	75 00	75 00	2	75 00	75 00	150 00	150 00	2	32 46	2	60 00	92 46	242 46
	31	$1162 50	$1162 50	31	$1162 50	$1162 50	$2325 00	$2325 00	28	$801 14	27	$810 00	$1611 14	$3936 14

TABLE XII.—SUPERIOR SCHOOLS: For the Year ended June 30th, 1901.

Part One.—Term ended December, 1900.

Embodied in Table IX and Foregoing Tables.

No. and Name of District.		Parish.	County.	Teachers.	Provincial Allowance.	Total for County.
Elgin Corner,	No. 2,	Elgin,	Albert,	B. P. Steeves,	$ 108 30	
Hill[illegible]sbo',	" 2,	Hillsboro,	"	L. J. [illegible],	36 23	
[illegible]el Hill,	" 2,	Hopewell,	"	A. C. M. Lawson,	108 30	$ 252 83
Hartland,	" 3,	Brighton,	Carleton,	Jos. E. [illegible]le,	108 30	
Jacksonville,	" 7,	Wakefield,	"	Clinton H. Gray,	102 53	
Centreville,	" 4,	Wilmot and Wicklow,	"	John Barnett, Jr.,	71 26	
				Horace G. Perry,	30 19	
Benton,	" 23 A,	Woodstock & Canterbury,	" and York,	Harry C. Fraser,	108 30	420 58
[illegible]th [illegible]d,	" 1,	Grand Manan,	Charlotte,	Peter G[illegible]wd,	101 45	
St. George,	" 1,	St. George,	"	W. M. [illegible]y,	101 45	
Moore's Mills,	" 1½,	St. James & St. David,	"	H. E. Sinclair,	107 15	
St. [illegible]n, (Town),		St. Stephen,	"	P. G. McFarlane,	101 45	
Mil[illegible]n, (Town),		"	"	J. B. Sutherland,	101 45	512 95
Bathurst Village,	No. 16,	Bathurst,	Gloucester,	E. L. O'Brien,	101 45	
Petit Rocher,	" 4,	[illegible]d,	"	J. Boudreau,	108 30	
Tracadie,	" 3,	Saumarez,	"	Geo. E. Price,	107 72	317 47
Harcourt,	" 5,	[illegible],	Kent,	H. H. [illegible]es,	1[illegible] 45	
Kingston,	" 2,	[illegible]to,	"	R. G. Girvan,	108 30	
Bass River,	" 9,	[illegible]d,	"	Jas. B. Carr,	101 45	
Buctouche,	" 1,	Wel[illegible]gton,	"	Geo. A. [illegible]s,	108 30	419 50
[illegible]enobsquis,	" 1,	Cardwell,	Kings,	G. T. Morton,	101 45	
Hampt[illegible] Station,	" 2,	Hampton,	"	J. W. Howe,	100 84	
Havelock Corner,	" 8,	Havelock,	"	Annie L. T[illegible]r,	107 15	
[illegible]ld Station,	" 2,	Norton,	"	H. A. Wheaton,	101 45	
Apohaqui,	" 25,	Studholm and Sussex,	"	E. H. [illegible]d,	101 45	512 34

[illegible]	Madawaska,	Madawaska,	R. E. Sisson,	$ 108 30	108 30
[illegible], No. [illegible],	Blackville,	Northumberland,	J. C. Carruthers,	107 15	
Doaktown, No. 4,	Blissfield,	"	Geo. A. Wathen,	108 30	
Derby, No. 1,	Derby,	"	J. J. Clarke,	95 41	
Douglastown, No. 6,	Newcastle,	"	M. R. Benn,	101 45	
Newcastle, No. 7,	"	"	F. P. Yorston,	100 84	513 15
Chipman, No. 11,	Chipman	Queens,	H. P. Dole,	101 45	101 45
Dalhousie, No. 1,	Dalhousie,	Restigouche,	R. B. Atkinson,	101 45	101 45
Fairville, No. 2,	Lancaster,	St. John,	S. A. Worrell,	104 83	
Milford, No. 13,	"	"	W. A. Nelson,	101 45	
St. Martins, No. 2,	St. Martins,	"	Flora M. Carson,	101 45	307 73
Fredericton Junction, No. 1,	Gladstone,	Sunbury,	A. H. Barker,	108 30	108 30
Grand Falls, No. 7.	Grand Falls,	Victoria,	M. L. Hayward,	100 84	100 84
Dorchester, No. 2,	Dorchester,	Westmorland,	L. E. Rowley.	101 45	
Sackville, No. 9,	Sackville,	"	F. A. Dixon,	101 45	
Middle Sackville, No. 11,	"	"	A. J. McKnight,	101 45	
Petitcodiac, No. 1,	Salisbury,	"	{ J. H. Crocker,	95 41	
			{ R. D. Hanson,	6 04	
Salisbury, No. 24,	{ " Moncton and	" and Albert,	{ H. F. Alward,	48 96	
	{ Coverdale,		{ C. H. Edgett,	55 30	
Shediac, No. 10,	Shediac,	"	B. H. Webb,	101 45	
Port Elgin, No. 1,	Westmorland and Botsford	" "	H. H. Stuart,	101 45	712 96
Keswick Ridge, No. 1,	Bright	York,	F. C. Jewett,	108 30	
McAdam Junction, No. 9,	McAdam,	"	H. F. Perkins,	101 45	
Harvey Station, No. 2,	Manners Sutton,	"	{ D. T. Belyea,	64 51	
			{ J. B. DeLong,	40 32	
Gibson, No. 2,	St. Marys,	"	M. A. Oulton,	101 45	
Marysville, No. 3.	"	"	W. T. Day,	101 45	517 48
					$5,007 33

TABLE XII.—PART TWO.—TERM ENDED JUNE 30TH, 1901.

No. and Name of District	Parish.	County.	Teacher.	Provincial Allowance.	Total for County.
Elgin Corner, No. 2,	Elgin,	Albert,	B. P. Steeves,	$ 140 84	
Hillsborough, No. 2,	Hillsborough,	"	L. J. [illegible]s,	147 78	
Hopewell Hill, No. 2,	Hopewell,	"	H. H. Stuart,	140 84	$ 429 46
Hartland, No. 3,	Brighton,	Carleton,	Jos. E. [illegible]le,	146 55	
Florenceville, No. 4,	Simonds and Wicklow,	"	E. B. Ross,	147 78	
Jacksonville, No. 7,	Wakefield,	"	C. H. [illegible]y,	147 78	
Centreville, No. 4,	Wilmot and Wicklow,	Carleton,	John Barnett, Jr.,	147 78	
Benton, No. 23 A,	Woodstock & Canterbury,	" and York,	H. C. Fraser,	140 84	730 73
North Head, No. 1,	Grand Manan,	Charlotte,	Peter [illegible]d	147 78	
St. George, No. 1,	St. George,	"	W. M. Veazey,	144 09	
Moore's Mills, No. 1½,	St. James and St. David,	"	H. E. [illegible]ir,	140 84	
St. Stephen, (Town),	St. Stephen,	"	P. G. M[illegible]ane,	147 78	
Milltown, (Town),	"	"	J. B. Sutherland,	147 78	728 27
Bathurst Village, No. 16,	Bathurst	Gloucester,	E. L. O'Brien,	147 78	
Petit Rocher, No. 4,	Beresford,	"	Jerome Boudreau,	140 84	
Tracadie, No. 3,	Saumarez,	"	G. E. I[illegible]de,	140 84	429 56
Harcourt, No. 5,	Harcourt,	Kent,	Miriam Kyle,	91 13	
Rexton, No. 2,	Richibucto,	"	R. G. Gir[illegible]n,	147 78	
Bass River, No. 9,	Weldford,	"	J. B. Carr,	147 78	
Buctouche, No. 1,	Wellington	"	G. A. [illegible],	140 84	527 53
Penobsquis, No. 1,	Cardwell,	Kings,	G. T. M[illegible]n,	147 78	
Hampton Station, No. 2,	Hampton,	"	Rex R. [illegible]r,	147 78	
Havelock Corner, No. 8,	Havelock,	"	R. W. McKenzie,	147 78	
Bloomfield Station, No. 2,	Norton,	"	H. A. [illegible]n,	147 78	
Apohaqui, No. 25,	Studholm and Sussex,	"	E. H. [illegible]d,	146 55	737 67
Edmundston, No. 1,	Madawaska,	Madawaska,	R. E. S[illegible]n,	$ 144 07	144 07
Blackville, No. 6,	Blackville,	Northumberland	J. C. [illegible]s,	140 84	
Doaktown, No. 4,	Blissfield,	"	G. A. [illegible]n,	140 84	
Derby, No. 1,	Derby,	"	E. A. Crocker,	147 78	

[illegible]	Newcastle,	"	M. R. Benn,	147 78	
[illegible]ewcastle, [illegible] 7, ([illegible]own),	"	"	F. P. [illegible],	24 63	
			G. K. [illegible],	123 15	725 02
[illegible]hipm[illegible], [illegible] 11,	Chi[illegible]	Queens,	H. P. [illegible],	147 78	147 78
Dalhousie, [illegible] 1,	Dalhousie,	Restigouche,	R. B. Masterton,	147 78	147 78
Fairville, [illegible] 2,	[illegible],	St. John,	S. A. Worrell,	146 55	
Milford, No. 13,	"	"	W. A. Nelson,	147 78	
St. Martins, [illegible] 2,	St. [illegible],	"	W. L. [illegible]Diarmid,	147 78	442 11
[illegible], No. 1,	[illegible],	Sunbury,	A. H. Barker,	124 42	124 42
Grand Falls, No. 7,	[illegible],	Victoria,	M. L. [illegible],	147 78	147 78
Dorchester, No 2,	Dorchester,	Westmorland	L. E. Rowley,	146 55	
Sackville, No. 9,	Sackville,	"	F. A. Dixon,	147 78	
[illegible], No. 11,	"	"	A. J. McKnight,	147 78	
Petitcodiac, [illegible] 1,	Salisbury,	"	J. H. [illegible],	146 55	
Salisbury, No. 24,	" and Moncton and Coverdale,	" and Albert	A. C. M. Lawson,	140 84	
Shediac, No. 10,	[illegible],	"	B. H. Webb,	147 78	
Port Elgin, No. 1,	Westmorland and Botsford	"	B. R. Field,	147 78	1,025 06
Keswick Ridge, No. 1,	[illegible]ht,	York,	F. C. Jewett,	28 17	
			Annie L. Taylor	110 33	
McAdam Junction, No. 9,	[illegible],	"	H. F. Perkins,	139 67	
Gibson, No. 2	St. M[illegible]ys,	"	J. B. DeLong,	147 78	
Marysville, No. 3,	"	"	W. T. Day,	147 78	573 73
					$7,060 87

TABLE XIII. GRAMMAR SCHOOLS: The Year Ended June 30th, 1901.

(Included in Previous Tables.)

PART ONE.—The Term Closed December 31st, 1900.

Locality.		Names of Principals and other Teachers receiving Grammar School Grants.	Above Grade VIII.							Legally authorized days Department was open.	Provincial Grant, etc., Salaries of the Teachers.		
Counties.	Towns.		No. of Departments.	No of Teachers and Assistants.	Pupils. Grade IX.	Grade X.	Grade XI.	Grade XI'.	Total No.		Provincial aid for the Term.	Salary from Trustees per year.	Rate of Salary for year.
Albert	Alma	T. E. Colpi tt, A. B	1	1	7	9	1	1	18	84	$142 03	$350 00	$[illegible]0
Carleton	Woodstock	G Harrison, A. B	2	2	27	18	14	....	59	84	142 03	650 00	[illegible]00
		Julia Mis								84	142 03	350 00	900
Charlotte	St. [illegible]ws.	J A. Allen, A. B	1	1	13	7	10	....	30	84	142 03	400 00	7[illegible]0
Gloucester	Bathurst	G. K. [illegible]n, A. B	1	1	20	2	....	....	22	83½	141 19	350 00	[illegible]90
Kent	Richibucto	C. H. [illegible]e, A. B	1	1	9	3	....	....	12	84	142 03	350 00	700
Kings	Sussex	GC Crawford	2	3	21	11	11	....	43	82	138 65	375 00	725 00
		G. J. [illegible]Mh.								58	98 07	350 00	700 00
		D. W [illegible]n								24	40 58	350 00	[illegible]0
Northumberland	Chatham	Philip Cx, Ph. D	2	2	21	19	9	....	49	83	140 34	750 00	1[illegible]00
Queens	Gagetown	D. L. [illegible]ll, A. B	1	1	2	10	3	....	15	93½	129 26	300 00	60[illegible]
Restigouche	Campbellton	E. W. Lewis, A. B	1	1	22	13	4	....	39	84	142 03	650 00	1[illegible]00
St. John	St. John	H S. Bridges, Ph D	11	12	196	116	60	18	390	84	....	2000 00	2000 00
		W. J. S. Myles, A. M								84	142 72	850 00	1200 00
		H. S. Bridges, Ph. D								31	52 67	....	....
		Maude M. Narraway, A. B.								84	142 72	550 00	900 00
		Elizabeth [illegible]ug hin								53	77 18	300 00	600 00
		T. E. Powers, A. B.								84	142 72	400 00	750 00
Victoria	Andover	A. [illegible]. Shea, A B.	1	1	7	5	8	....	20	84	142 03	350 00	700 00
Westmorland	Moncton	G. J. Oulton, A. M.	4	5	97	42	34	....	173	84	142 03	850 00	1200 00
		C. H. Acheson								84	142 03	500 00	850 00
		L. R. Hetherington, A. M.								82	138 65	450 00	800 00
		Jos. Mills, A. B.								82	138 65	350 00	700 00
York	Fredericton	B. C. Foster, A. M	4	4	75	42	29	....	146	84	142 03	850 00	1200 00
		H. H. Hagerman, A. M.								84	142 03	650 00	1000 00
		A. S. McFarlane, A. M.								84	142 03	500 00	850 00
New Brunswick			32	35	517	297	183	19	1016	....	$3227 76	$13,825 00	$22,125 00
Cor. Term, 1899			31	34	495	315	204	13	1027	....	3242 47	13,675 00	21,675 00
Increase			1	1	22	....	....	6	....	....	....	$150 00	$450 00
Decrease			....	....	....	18	21	....	11	....	$14 71	....	....

XIII. Part Two.—GRAMMAR SCHOOLS: The Term Ended June 30th, 1901.

(Included in Previous Tables.)

Locality. Counties.	Locality. Towns.	Names of Principals and other Teachers receiving Grammar School Grants.	Above Grade VIII. No. of Departments.	No. of Teachers and Assistants.	Pupils. Grade IX.	Grade X.	Grade XI.	Grade XII.	Total No.	Legally authorized days Department was open.	Provincial Grant, etc.—Salaries of the Teachers. Provincial aid for the Term.	Salary from Trustees per year.	Rate of Salary for year.
Albert	Alma	T. E. Colpitts, A. B.	1	1	4	7	7	......	18	120	$206 89	$350 09	$700 00
Carleton	Woodstock	G H Harrison, A. B.	2	2	29	19	13	......	61	117½	202 59	650 00	1000 00
		Julia Neales								118¼	204 31	350 90	700 00
Charlotte	St. Andrews	J. A. Allen, A. B.	1	1	11	8	9	......	28	120	206 89	450 00	800 00
Gloucester	Bathurst	H. J. Perry	1	1	17	2	......	......	19	119½	206 03	350 00	700 00
Kent	Richibucto	C. H. Cowperthwaite, A. B.	1	1	7	3	......	......	10	120	206 89	350 00	700 00
Kings	Sussex	G C Crawford, A.B.	2	2	17	12	10	......	39	119	205 17	400 00	750 00
Northumberland	Chatham	Philip Cox, Ph. D.	2	2	18	14	11	......	43	118	203 44	750 00	1100 00
Queens	Gagetown	D. L. Mitchell, A. B.	1	1	3	8	8	......	14	120	177 34	300 00	600 00
Restigouche	Campbellton	E. W. Lewis, A. B.	1	1	15	17	4	......	36	116	200 00	650 00	1000 00
St. John	St. John	H S. Bridges, Ph D								119	....	2000 00	2000 00
		W. J. S. Myles A. M								119	206 19	850 00	1200 00
		M Maude Narraway, A. B.	11	13	181	108	57	18	364	119	206 19	550 00	900 00
		Thos. E. Powers, A. B.								119	206 19	600 00	950 00
		Elizabeth McNaughton								119	176 72	300 00	600 00
Victoria	Andover	A. M. Shea, A B.	1	1	12	6	4	......	22	114½	197 40	350 00	700 00
Westmorland	Moncton	G. J. Oulton, A. M.								120	206 89	850 00	1200 00
		C. H. Acheson								120	206 89	650 00	1000 00
		L. R. Hetherington, A. M.	4	4	82	40	32	......	154	120	206 89	550 00	900 00
		D. McLean								120	206 89	450 09	800 00
York	Fredericton	B. C. Foster, A. M								120	206 89	850 00	1200 00
		H. H. Hagerman, A. M.	4	4	73	40	28	......	141	120	206 89	650 00	1000 00
		A. S. McFarlane, A. M.								120	206 89	500 00	850 00
New Brunswick			32	34	469	284	178	18	949	....	$4460 47	$13,750 00	$21,350 00
Cor. Term, 1900			31	35	463	287	186	10	946	....	4639 72	14,475 00	22 825 00
Increase			1	......	6	......	......	8	3	....	....	....	....
Decrease			......	1	......	3	8	......	......	....	$179 25	$725 00	$1475 00

TABLE XIV. PROVINCIAL NORMAL SCHOOL; FOR SESSION ENDED JUNE, 1901.

	NORMAL DEPARTMENT. Students in Attendance.						FRENCH DEPT.			MODEL DEPT. Pupils.		
	No. attended.	Left through various causes.	Failed to Classify.	Eligible for Examination.	Males.	Females.	Males.	Females.	Total.	Boys.	Girls.	Total.
Term ended Dec., 1900	..	..	..	..	..	..	..	..	..	81	114	195
First Term ended Dec., 1900	43	1	..	42	5	19	7	11	42	..	..	..
Session ended June, 1901	136	1	..	135	24	111	..	..	135	..	..	..
Second Term ended May, 1901	19	..	..	19	..	..	5	14	19	.	.	..
Term ended June, 1901	..	..	..	..	..	..	..	..	..	81	111	192
New Brunswick	198	2	..	196	29	130	12	25	196	..	..	..
Cor. Session last year	258	2	..	256	46	158	9	43	256	..	..	..
Increase	..	..	..	..	..	..	3	..	..	..	..	..
Decrease	60	..	..	60	17	28	..	18	60	..	..	..

PROVINCIAL GRANTS TO OCT. 31, 1900.

On Account of Salaries.	Amount.
[illegible]on Mullin, M. A.	$1,400 00
H. C. [illegible]ed, M. A.	1,200 00
John Brittain	1,100 00
G. A. [illegible]ndh, B. A.	1,100 00
Alphée Belli[illegible]eau	1,100 00
M. Allice Clark	800 00
Ed. [illegible]r, B. A.	250 00
Amos O'Blenes	*165 00
Mary E. Phillips	*150 00
M. [illegible]	*183 76
[illegible]ra A. Bridges	*183 76
Total	$7,632 52

*These amounts are paid by the Board of Education in addition to the Provincial Allowance and to Salaries from Trustees.

.—PUBLIC SCHOOLS: Closing Examinations for License; Year Ending June, 1901.

TERMS AND STATIONS.	No. of candidates admitted to the written examination and grounds of admission.						Grammar School Class.				MALE. I Class.					MALE. II Class.				MALE. III Class.			FEMALE. I Class.					FEMALE. II Class.				FEMALE. III Class.			SUMMARY. Males.					SUMMARY. Females.					Tl. Licensed.
	As classified Student-Teachers of the Provincial Normal School.	As holding License from the Board of Education.	As Graduates in Arts.	As having undergone training at a Normal School not in N. B.	As eligible for Examination.	Total No. admitted.	No. examined for this Class.	No. that obtained this Class.	No. obtained 1st Class.	No. obtained 2nd Class.	No. examined for this Class.	No. obtained 1st Class.	No. obtained 2nd Class.	No. obtained 3rd Class.	No. that failed to obtain any Class.	No. examined for this Class.	No. obtained 2nd Class.	No. obtained 3rd Class.	No. that failed to obtain any Class.	No. examined for this Class.	No. obtained 3rd Class.	No. that failed to obtain any Class.	No. examined for this Class.	No. obtained 1st Class.	No. obtained 2nd Class.	No. obtained 3rd Class.	No. that failed to obtain any Class.	No. examined for this Class.	No. obtained 2nd Class.	No. obtained 3rd Class.	No. that failed to obtain any Class.	No. examined for this Class.	No. obtained 3rd Class.	No. that failed to obtain any Class.	No. obtained Grammar Sch. Class.	No. obtained 1st Class.	No. obtained 2nd Class.	No. obtained 3rd Class.	No. that failed to obtain any Class.	No. obtained Grammar Sch. Class.	No. obtained 1st Class.	No. obtained 2nd Class.	No. obtained 3rd Class.	No. that failed to obtain any Class.	Total No. Licensed.
DECEMBER, 1900.																																													
Acadian Teachers	18	....	..	....	2	20	..	..	..	..	..	..	..	..	..	..	..	..	..	7	6	1	..	..	..	..	..	....	....	..	..	13	11	2	..	..	..	6	1	..	..	....	11	2	17
III Class temporary	24	....	..	....		24	..	..	..	..	..	..	..	..	..	..	..	..	..	5	5	..	..	..	..	..	..	....	....	..	..	19	19	..	..	..	..	5	..	..	..	....	19	..	24
MAY, 1901.																																													
Acadian Teachers	19	....	..	....	1	20		..	..	..	..	..	..	..	..	..	..	..	..	5	4	1	..	..	..	..	..	....	....	..	..	15	11	4	..	..	..	4	1	..	..	....	11	4	15
JUNE, 1901.																																													
Fredericton	135	21	7	....	.	163	8	5	3	..	15	6	5	4	..	16	14	2	..	..	..	..	29	23	6	..	..	95	85	10	..	..	..	..	5	9	19	6	..	..	23	91	10	..	163
St. John	..	17	2	....	..	19	3	3	..	..	7	4	1	1	1	1	1	..	..	..	..	..	6	4	2	..	..	2	....	2	..	..	..	..	1	4	2	1	1	2	4	2	2	..	18
Chatham	..	..	..	....	..	....	..	..	..	..	..	..	..	..	..	..	..	..	..	..	..	..	..	..	..	..	..	....	....	..	..	..	..	..	..	..	..	..	..	..	..	....	..	..	....
New Brunswick	196	38	9	....	3	246	11	8	3	..	22	10	6	5	1	17	15	2	..	17	15	2	35	27	8	..	..	97	85	12	..	47	41	6	6	13	21	22	3	2	27	93	53	6	237
Year ending June, 1900	255	54	6	....	8	323	10	8	2	..	20	7	3	7	3	31	29	2	..	20	20	..	42	22	18	2	..	116	102	14	..	84	66	18	7	9	32	29	3	1	22	120	82	18	302
Increase	..	..	3	....	..	....	1	..	1	..	2	3	3	..	..	..	..	..	..	..	..	2		5	..	..	..	....	....	..	..	..	..	..	..	4	..	..	.	1	5	....	..	..	....
Decrease	59	16	..	....	5	77	..	..	..	..	..	..	..	2	2	14	14	..	..	3	5	..	7	..	10	2	..	19	17	2	..	37	25	12	1	..	11	7	..	..	..	27	29	12	65

Of the above, 1 male and 1 female are entitled to Class I., when passed in Reading; 1 female, Class I., when passed in Spelling; 2 females, Class II., when passed in Reading; 1 female, Class II., when the Preliminary Examination is passed. In addition to the above, 6 Candidates at the Fredericton and 4 at the St. John Station, wrote a partial examination for Grammar School Class. Also, 5 Candidates at the Fredericton and 4 at the St. John Station, received Superior, in addition to First Class.

ISSUE OF SCHOOL LICENSES, AWARDED UPON EXAMINATION IN DECEMBER 1900 AND MAY AND JUNE 1901.

The number of applicants for each Class will be seen from the preceding table. The following list contains the names of successful candidates only.

DECEMBER, 1900.

Third Class.—Geo. Ed. Charlton, Chas. N. Gregg, Grant Hawkins, Willey Ernest Leonard, Lorenzo N. Wadlin, Zena Etta Akerley, Annie G. Campbell, Eva B. Culligan, Minnie A. Drost, Bertie E. Faulkner, Maggie T. Flanagan, Jessie R. Gilliland, Mabel Edna Grass, Essie B. Henderson, Sadie B. Hogan, Augusta G. Kelly, Mary J. Kelly, Johannah Elizabeth Maddox, Florence Towers Mahood, Beatrice E. Mitchell, Georgia M. Mitchell, Mary C. Morrisey, Minnie M. Tingley, Ella M. Tompkins, Francois O. Allard, J. Philippe DeGrace, Theodore John DeLaGarde, Elzear Noel, Richard Parise, Jean O. L. Roy, Mary E. Blanchard, Agnes N. Hachey, Agnes Hebert, Lizzie A. Martin, Beatrice A. Melanson, Modeste Michaud, M. Lucie Richard, Clemence Robichaud, Hélène Lapointe, Beatrice Michaud, Suzanne M. Richard.

MAY, 1901.

Third Class.—Joyime W. Cormier, Leonide F. Maillet, Joseph J. Mercure, Jos. Ed. Robichaud, Marie A. Albert, M. Catherine Babineau, Beatrice Cyr, Jeanne P. Doucet, M. A. Lucie LeGresley, M. Catherine P. Losier, Josephine R. Maillet, Marie E. Michaud, Mary A. J. Savoie, Catherine B. Theriault, Marie LeBlanc.

JUNE 1901.

Grammar School..—Maurice D. Coll, Jean F. Doucet, Amos O'Blenes, Frank N. Patterson, Perry B. Perkins, Joseph E. Howe, Mary E. Knowlton, Jessie I. Lawson.

First. Class—C. Jack Mersereau, Baxter B. Barnes, Angus M. Dew--, Ruel E. McClintock, Edward S. McQuaid, Wilford A. Rideout, Brougham . Johnston, George Leonard McCain, Miles F. McCutcheon, Omer L. Northr , Gladys A. Adams, Edna G. Alexander, Harriet L. Irvin, Mary A. Knight, Le a

Maggie Miller, Mary McAuley McInerney, Mabel E. McLeod, Annie L. Pinder, Isabella Reed, Nettie Beairsto, Georgina G. L. Dickson, Alice McKenzie, Mabel McKinney, Lena B. McLeod, Susanna Lamb, Emily S. Crisp, Sadie J. Estey, Helen E. Mullin, Edna L. Golding, Etta Anna M. Cormick, Bertie B. Steeves. Elizabeth F. Hayes, Jennie N. Munro, Lottie L. Weldon, Helena Estabrooks.

Second Class.—Gustave A. Colpitts, *J. Garfield Perry, Geo. Percy Smith, Percy S. Bailey, Willard Brewing, Hugh Allan Carr, Abram Cronkhite, George W. Christie, Walter M. Donahoe, Arthur E. Floyd, H. Murray Lambert, John Law, Jos. Arthur Salter, Ernest W. Sheils, Geo. N. Somers, Will Whitney, Everette S. DeBow, Malcolm J. Hunter, Estella M. Alward, Jennie Parker Alward, Elizabeth C. Anderson, Patience A. Ballentine, Grace Coughlan, Catherine F. Mair, Ada Bonner, †Florence L. Alexander, Grace G. Hamm, *Lavina A. McTaggart, Mabelle B. McKee, Maude W. Bradbury, Annabell Brennan, Mabel K. Burchill, Clara O. Burt, Sarah A. Cameron, Susie E. Carruthers, Mamie F. Cassidy, Cecilia Craig, Pearl Currier, Mary McN. DesBrisay, Blanche W. Dixon, Ivy May Dow, Annie J. Finnigan, Katie J. Fleming, Ada F. Ganong, Elizabeth I. Gleeson, Laura M. Good, Emma E. Goodall, Lottie M. Gregg, Effie M. Hayward, Cecile B. Hewitt, Sadie E. Inch, Eliza A. Ingraham, Eva S. Jacques, Hattie M. Jamieson, Ethel H. Jarvis, Lena M. Kearney, Ida J. Kierstead, Martha J. Lackie, Marguerite G. J. Legere, Maggie R. Loane, Annie M. Loggie, Albina C. London, Ada E. Lutz, Mary A. J. Mahoney, Georgie A. Manzer, Keziah C. Maxwell, Ada A. P. Miller, Annie G. Mitton, Minnie I. Mott, Annie L. Murphy, Ella M. McAdam, Annie G. McAnulty, Georgia H. McCready, Lizzie B. McElwee, Isabella J. McKenzie, Katherine E. McLean, Jessie E. McLean, Parthenia J. O'Leary, Ettawanda A. Palmer, Bessie R. Porter, Louise B. G. Prescott, Florence M. Roberts, Catherine C. Robinson, Mabel G. Schriver, Cora A. Sherwood, Agnes I. Smith, Lulu P. Smith, Winnifred E. Thompson, Bertha L. Tozer, Luella A. True, Victoria R. Turner, Mary N. Turvey, Linda M. Ultican, Annie E. Vallis, Edith B. Wallace, Catherine S. Watling, Frances P. West, Ada I. Wright, Bessie M. Wright, Hariette W. Bolt, Annie M. Briggs, Bertha J. Crealock, Frances N. DeCourcey, Jennie R. Smith, Annie E. Wilson, Maude H. Gerrish, Lisbeth D. Mann.

* First when passed in Reading. † First when passed in Spelling.

Third Class.—Willie B. Dewar. Robert A. Fleming, Annie B. Gallagher, Eliza B. Kelly, Josephine M. Welch, Janie S. R. Cameron, Myrtle A. Keith, Nellie J. Musgrove, Jennie M. Hovey, Lida C. Jewitt, Hulda E. Miller, **Mary E. Barron, †Annie M. Grant, **Maggie N. M. O'Leary, Leila C. Kennedy, Susan V. Price, Clara M. Irving.

Superior Class.—C. Jack Mersereau, Hanson C. B. Allen, Helen E. Mullin, Edna L. Golding, Helena Estabrooks, Eva Keagin, Etta Anna M. Cormick, Bertie Chase.

Passed for Superior Class at the Departmental Examinations held in July, 1901.—Fred. S. James, Charles D. Richards, Alfred H. Schriver, Clarence Sansom, Chas. J. Callaghan, Matthew G. Duffy, B. Hayes Dougan, Baxter Barnes, Angus M. Dewar, Clive M. McCann, Alonzo B. Boyer, Arthur P. Davis, Ruel E. McClintock, Brougham F. Johnston, Alice M. Carleton. Isabella Reed, Ethel I. Emery, Phebe W. Robertson, Clara R. Fullerton, Emily S. Crisp, M. May Howe, Florence M. Foster.

** Second when passed in Reading. ‡ Second when the Preliminary Examination is passed.

TABLE XVI.—PUBLIC SCHOOLS: LIBRARIES.

BONUSES PAID TO DISTRICT SCHOOL LIBRARIES DURING THE YEAR ENDED OCTOBER 31ST, 1901.

Locality.			Dates of Payment.	Value.			Number of Volumes.
County.	Parish.	District.		Local.	Provincial.	Total.	
Albert	Harvey	No. 3	July 12, 1901	$ 15 65	$ 7 82	$ 23 47	38
Carleton	Wicklow	" 2	June 12, 1901	9 51	4 76	14 27	115
"	"	" 2	July 23, 1901	3 10	1 55	4 65	41
"	Wilmot and Wicklow	" 16	Dec. 18, 1900	8 00	4 00	12 00	21
Charlotte	St. Andrews	" 1	April 22, 1901	26 13	13 06	39 19	83
"	St. George	" 1	Dec. 20, 1900	12 36	6 17	18 53	34
"	St. James	" 14	Dec. 31, 1900	4 74	2 37	7 11	38
Kent	Richibucto	" 2	Nov. 1, 1900	12 21	6 10	18 31	59
Kings	Havelock	" 1	May 13, 1901	2 48	1 24	3 72	17
"	Norton	" 2	Nov. 22, 1900	5 35	2 67	8 02	22
"	Rothesay	" 5	Mar. 21, 1901	8 00	4 00	12 00	16
"	Studholm	" 12	June 19, 1901	3 02	1 50	4 52	12
"	Studholm and Sussex	" 25	June 12, 1901	7 42	3 71	11 13	27
"	Upham	" 6	Dec. 12, 1900	1 27	64	1 91	4
Queens	Chipman	" 11	Mar. 13, 1901	2 39	1 19	3 58	7
"	Gagetown	" 6	June 5, 1901	15 50	7 75	23 25	47
Victoria	Gordon	" 8	Feb. 16, 1901	3 94	1 97	5 91	22
Westmorland	Dorchester	" 8	Dec. 12, 1900	22 00	11 00	33 00	80
York	Canterbury & Woodstock	" 23 A	Jan. 15, 1901	28 73	14 37	43 10	111
"	McAdam	" 9	Dec. 12, 1900	15 98	7 99	23 97	48
"	Queensbury	" 7	April 11, 1901	10 00	5 00	15 00	52
"	Stanley	" 3	May 10, 1901	20 07	10 04	30 11	*
				$237 85	$118 90	$356 75	894

* No. not Given.

TABLE XVII.—PUBLIC SCHOOLS.

TRAVELLING EXPENSES PAID TO STUDENT-TEACHERS ATTENDING THE NORMAL SCHOOL DURING THE TERM ENDED JUNE AND MAY, 1900.

(PAID IN 1901.)

(Allowance of Mileage, 3 cents a mile.)

No.	NAME.	COUNTY.	AMOUNT.
1	Callaghan, Chas. J.	Charlotte,	$ 6 84
2	Kirkpatrick, Maurice	Queens,	2 10
3	Wallace, Martin J.	Northumberland,	7 02
4	Sansom, Clarence	York,	0 96
5	Hunter, Jas. M.	Sunbury,	1 02
6	Bartlett, Eunice D.	Charlotte,	5 64
7	Cormack, Etta A. M.	Westmorland,	9 36
8	Emery, Ethel I.	St. John,	4 02
9	Flanders, Gertrude E.	Victoria,	7 80
10	Foster, Florence M.	Albert,	9 90
10½	Howe, Maggie M. W.	Kings,	6 72
11	Keagin, M. Eva	St. John,	4 02
12	McKenzie, Cora E.	Charlotte,	5 70
13	Prichard, Frances P.	Kings,	5 34
14	Taylor, Hazel M.	Westmorland,	9 36
15	Steeves, Bertie B.	Albert,	9 00
16	Floyd, Hannah H.	St. John,	5 40
17	Harmon, Myrtle A.	Carleton,	3 78
18	Hibbard, Elinor C.	Charlotte,	6 30
19	Munroe, Jennie N.	St. John,	4 02
20	Colwell, Burtis L.	Queens,	4 08
21	Crawford, W. Millen	Carleton,	4 50
22	Currier, Walter E.	Queens,	1 44
23	DeGrace, J. Edward	Gloucester,	13 50
24	Duncan, Gustave E.	Restigouche,	13 26
25	Eastman, Arthur E.	Westmorland,	8 04
26	Fraser, Norman S.	York,	1 44
27	Grant, Geo. A.	York,	2 70
28	Henry, John A.	Westmorland,	8 58
29	Hill, John W.	Kings,	5 34
30	Keating, John C.	Westmorland,	9 00
31	Keirstead, Norman McL.	Kings,	6 72
32	Keogh, John P.	Northumberland,	5 28
33	Manuel, Murray H.	York,	2 28

TABLE XVII.—CONTINUED.

No.	Name.	County.	Amount.
34	Maxon, Geo. H.	York,	$ 2 70
35	McCutcheon, Hartley W.	Sunbury,	1 92
36	Perry, Jas. G.	Carleton,	5 34
37	Reid, Perley B.	Carleton,	4 86
38	Robinson, Arthur S.	Westmorland,	13 08
39	Squiers, Fred C.	Carleton,	4 86
40	Stephenson, Arthur F.	Sunbury,	90
41	Wright, Carey P.	Victoria,	6 06
42	Bannister, John A.	Westmorland,	8 34
43	Murphy, Francis P.	Westmorland,	13 20
44	Charters, Lewis F.	Sunbury,	48
45	Mitton, Moses W.	Westmorland,	8 58
46	Anderson, Constance H.	Northumberland,	7 02
47	Annett, Eva H.	Carleton,	4 80
48	Barton, O. Bernice	Queens,	3 90
49	Barton, Hulda	Queens,	3 90
50	Bell, Annie I.	Northumberland,	6 84
51	Brown, Mary M.	Kings,	3 36
52	Campbell, Mary I.	Carleton,	4 20
53	Carvell, Bessie W.	Carleton,	4 80
54	Cassidy, Clara J.	Northumberland,	7 02
55	Colpitts, Celia M.	Albert,	9 00
56	Colpitts, Nellie M.	Westmorland,	9 36
57	Cox, Mary E.	Queens,	3 90
58	Crowhurst, Ella G.	Westmorland,	9 36
59	Curry, Bessie A.	Victoria,	6 06
60	Davis, Mary A.	Sunbury,	1 32
61	DeBow, Florence M.	Kings,	6 72
62	Drum, Christina	Victoria,	6 00
63	Edmunds, Effie A.	Northumberland,	7 02
64	Fenwick, Susie P.	Kings,	6 72
65	Folkins, Sadie M. A.	Kings,	4 80
66	Fowler, Marion W.	Carleton,	4 08
67	Fraser, Marion B.	Northumberland,	7 02
68	Gleeson, Leonora F.	St. John,	3 90
69	Harper, M. Maude	Queens,	4 62
70	Harvey, Ethel M.	Westmorland,	9 36
71	Hood, Frances E.	York,	3 30
72	Irving, Nellie E.	Charlotte,	5 10
73	Jardine, Olive B.	Northumberland,	7 38
74	Jardine, Mina D.	Northumberland,	7 38
75	Kennedy, Fannie H.	Westmorland,	9 36
76	Kinney, Nettie I.	Carleton.	4 50
77	Lackie, Keturah	Kings,	6 00
78	Leishman, Jean C.	Northumberland,	7 02
79	Lucas, Agnes E.	Kings,	6 66
80	Mahoney, Margaret L.	Kings,	7 20

TABLE XVII.—Continued.

No.	Name.	County.	Amount.
81	Malone, Gertrude K.	York,	$ 1 50
82	Marvin, Mabel L.	Kings,	4 20
83	Miller, Marguerite E.	York,	2 10
84	Mitchell, Florence E.	Westmorland,	9 36
85	Murphy, Frances E.	Charlotte,	6 84
86	Murray, Emma V.	Kent,	11 52
87	McCarthy, Mary A.	Northumberland,	7 02
88	McDonald, Mary A.	Northumberland,	6 66
89	McDonald, Elizabeth	Restigouche,	12 48
90	McKenzie, Lizzie M.	Kings,	3 94
91	MacLeod, Emma H.	Westmorland,	9 36
92	Perry, Violet D.	Westmorland,	8 58
93	Pettingell, Grace E.	Kings,	4 74
94	Pickles, Fannie H. L.	Kings,	6 30
95	Poole, Bertha E.	St. John,	4 02
96	Power, Gertrude E.	Gloucester,	9 72
97	Powers, Margaret I. B.	St. John,	4 02
98	Richards, Beatrice	Restigouche,	13 26
99	Robinson, Gertrude M.	Queens,	3 90
100	Ryan, Mary A.	Northumberland,	7 02
101	Shea, Hattie L.	Carleton,	3 84
101½	Thomas, Mabel O.	Westmorland,	9 36
102	Tingley, Mary E.	Albert,	11 34
103	Topham, Lida E.	Victoria,	6 00
104	Troy, Kate L.	Northumberland,	6 84
105	Turney, Annie E.	Carleton,	4 80
106	Weldon, Lottie L.	Westmorland,	9 36
107	Welling, Henrietta	Westmorland,	10 62
108	Wetmore, Ada C.	Kings,	5 70
109	Wilcox, Rosa A.	Kings,	7 20
110	Brewster, Laura B.	Albert,	11 16
111	Fowler, Mary I.	Sunbury,	4 50
112	Marshall, Helen S.	Charlotte,	5 76
113	McBean, Agnes E.	York,	1 14
114	Murphy, Margaret E.	Kings,	6 72
115	Porter, Bell	York,	2 22
116	Polley, Mary Ellen	Charlotte,	5 88
117	Polley, Nettie M.	Charlotte,	5 88
118	Riorden, Angela	Gloucester,	9 60
119	Robinson, Annie E.	Restigouche,	11 82
120	Steeves, Susie E.	Albert,	10 20
121	Wishart Mary A.	Northumberland,	9 30
122	Downing, Florence E.	Westmorland,	8 88
123	Forster, Sarah A.	Kent,	9 78
124	Gerrish, Maude H.	Northumberland,	5 64
125	Hoyt, Myrtle M.	York,	1 50
126	Irving, Clara M.	Charlotte,	5 10

TABLE XVII.—Continued.

No.	Name.	County.	Amount.
127	Kennedy, Leila C.	Queens,	$ 2 40
128	Miller, Hulda E.	York,	2 70
129	McLeod, Mabel E.	Charlotte,	5 76
130	O'Brien, Catherine G.	Northumberland,	6 66
131	Brown, Elinor	St. John,	4 02
132	Crealock, Joyce E.	Queens,	5 10
133	Ellis, Melinda	Gloucester,	9 96
134	Ellison, Maud V.	Kings,	6 66
135	Patterson, Jessie F.	Kings,	7 08
135½	DeBow, Everett S.	Westmorland,	8 34
136	LeBlanc, Jaddus.	Kent,	11 70
137	LeBlanc, Pierre N.	Kent,	11 52
138	Powers, Jos. B.	Victoria,	7 50
139	Robichaud, Dom. T.	Gloucester,	11 40
140	Albert, Odile	Madawaska,	10 20
140½	Bastarache, Octavie	Kent,	11 40
141	Bois, Marie G. A. Z.	Madawaska,	8 10
142	Bourgeois, Marie H. C.	Kent,	10 80
143	Comeau, Marie F. B.	Westmorland,	9 36
144	Cote, Annie L.	Victoria,	7 50
145	Cote, Leona	Madawaska,	7 32
146	Dufour, Annie M.	Victoria,	6 36
147	Gaudet, Albina C.	Westmorland,	10 68
148	Grant, Mary J.	Gloucester,	10 32
149	Hache, M. Georgina	Gloucester,	11 10
150	Landry, Sarah A.	Westmorland,	10 56
151	LeBlanc, Amanda	Westmorland,	10 56
152	Levesque, Lizzie A.	Victoria,	7 50
153	Poirier, Marie T.	Gloucester,	11 16
154	Theriault, Alice O.	Gloucester,	11 10
155	*Cameron, Janie R.	York,	1 14
156	*Gaynor, M. Josephine	Westmorland,	8 58
157	*Milledge, Winifred	Charlotte,	6 12
158	*Gauvin, Jos. L.	Gloucester,	13 50
159	*Robichaud, Ozithe	Northumberland,	8 76
160	*Kelly, Annie M.	St. John,	3 90
161	*Bleakney, Ellen J.	Charlotte,	6 30
162	*Ellis, Muriel	Northumberland,	7 02
163	*Wiggins, Gertrude.	Carleton,	4 86
164	*Graham, Maggie	St. John,	4 02
165	*Keagin, Ida A.	St. John,	4 02
		Govt. War. No. 467.	$1,128 48

*In attendance previous terms, but claims for travelling expenses just matured.

TABLE XVII.—CONTINUED. TERM ENDED DECEMBER, 1900.

No.	NAME.	COUNTY.	AMOUNT.
1	Charlton, Geo. Ed.	St. John,	$7 20
2	Gregg, Charles N.	Kings,	6 72
4	Akerley, Zena Etta	Queens,	3 60
5	Campbell, Annie G.	Carleton,	4 20
6	Culligan, Eva B.	Restigouche,	11 22
7	Drost, Minnie A.	Carleton,	4 86
8	Faulkner, Bertie E.	Carleton,	4 50
9	Flanagan, Maggie T.	Kings,	2 94
10	Gilliland, Jessie R.	Kings,	3 36
11	Grass, Mabel E.	Sunbury,	66
12	Kelly, Augusta G.	Northumberland,	7 50
13	Kelly, Mary J.	Carleton,	4 08
14	Mahood, Florence	Queens,	3 18
15	Mitchell, Beatrice	York,	4 08
16	Mitchell, Georgia M.	Kings,	6 60
17	Morrisey, Mary C.	Kings,	7 68
18	Tingley, Minnie M	Albert,	11 34
19	Tompkins, Ella M.	Carleton,	4 08
19½	*Smith, Annie E.	York,	2 08
20	*Collins, Eva A.	Westmorland,	13 08
21	*Crammond, Estelle	Northumberland,	6 84
22	*McKnight, Margaret	Northumberland,	7 80
23	*Ross, M. Louise	York,	1 50
25	Allard, Francois	Gloucester,	11 40
26	Babin, Amedée	Kent,	10 20
27	DeGrace, Philippe	Gloucester,	13 50
28	DeLaGarde, Theodore	Gloucester,	13 50
28½	Noel, Elzear	Gloucester,	13 50
29	Parise, Richard	Gloucester,	11 58
30	Roy, Jean O. L.	Gloucester,	10 32
31	Blanchard, Mary	Gloucester,	11 40
32	Hachey, Agnes N.	Gloucester,	9 60
33	Hebert, Agnes	Madawaska,	8 40
34	LeBlanc, Marie	Kent,	10 20
35	Martin, Lizzie	Madawaska,	6 84
36	Melanson, Beatrice	Westmorland,	9 84
37	Michaud, Modeste	Madawaska,	8 10
38	Richard, M. Lucie	Kent,	10 20
39	Robichaud, Clemence	Kent,	10 20
40	LaPointe, Helene	Madawaska,	8 10
		Govt. War. No. 1071.	$306 48

*In attendance previous terms, but claims for travelling expenses just matured.

TABLE XVIII.—PUBLIC SCHOOLS: Year Ended 31st October, 1901.

STATEMENT OF CHIEF SUPERINTENDENT'S PROVINCIAL DRAFTS TO TEACHERS, AND OF COUNTY FUND DRAFTS TO TRUSTEES.

(Summarized in Tables IX., X. and XI.)

MEMORANDUM.	Provincial Drafts to Teachers.	County Fund Drafts to Trustees.
For Term ended December 31st, 1900.		
References—Warrants Nos. 464, 465, 466, 515........	$72,535 32	
School for the Blind, Halifax, Warrant No. 468	1,162 50	
Amount County Fund, for term ended December 31st, 1900—Schools		45,250 51
School for the Blind, Halifax		1,162 50
Institution for the Deaf and Dumb, Fredericton....		801 14
For Term ended June 30th, 1901		
References--Warrants Nos. 896, 897, 898, 1070	91,416 41	
School for the Blind, Halifax, Warrant No. 859	1,162 50	
Amount County Fund for Term ended June 30th, 1901—Schools..		
School for the Blind, Halifax		45,241 65
Institution for the Deaf and Dumb, Fredericton..		1,162 50
		810 00
	166,276 73	$94,428 30

TABLE XIX.—SUMMARY OF THE PROVINCIAL GRANTS FOR THE SCHOOL SERVICE FOR THE YEAR ENDED OCTOBER 31ST, 1901

Schools. (See Table IX for details).		
Common, ...	$144,195 30	
Superior, ...	12,068 20	
Grammar, ...	7,688 23	
		$163,951 73
School for the Blind, Halifax, (Table XI), ...		2,325 00
Normal School: Salaries (Table XIV.), ...		7,632 52
Travelling Allowance to Student Teachers, (Table XVII.), ...		1,434 96
Inspectors' Salaries, ...		7,340 00
" Allowance, attending Conferences, ...		600 00
Education Office Salaries:		
Chief Superintendent, ...	$2,000 00	
Chief Clerk, ...	1,000 00	
Clerk, ...	800 00	
Clerk, ...	295 00	
Clerk, ...	190 00	
Clerk, (Temporary), ...	24 44	
		4,309 44
Travelling Allowance to Chief Superintendent, ...		400 00
Incidental expenses:		
Eldon Mullin, M. A., expenses of visit to Normal Schools in United States, ...	$100 00	
Eldon Mullin, M. A.. attending Car. Co. Teachers' Institute, by direction of Cbief Superintendent	6 00	
		106 00
Forward, ...		$188,099 65

Brought forward, ...		$188,099 65
John F. Rogers, work in office, ...	74 00	
Lillian Flewelling, do. do.	12 00	
W. F. P. Stockley, M. A., examining selections for Reader No. V., ...	10 00	
Sergeant Brewer, drilling students at Normal School, ...	15 00	
J. Vroom, examining Book-keeping books, blanks, etc., ...	10 00	
Charles Toner, truckage, ...	14 54	
S. A. Belyea, do.	2 01	
		137 55
Examination Expenses:		
License Examinations, December, 1900, and May and June, 1901, ...		381 07
Departmental Examinations (Normal School Entrance, Matriculation and High School Leaving) June and July, 1901, ...	$821 04	
Less amount received in fees, ...	731 95	
		89 09
High School Entrance Examinations, ...		329 00
School Libraries, (Table XVI.)		118 90
School House Grants (see statement in Chief Superintendent's Report,)		945 00
		$190,100 26

PART III.

APPENDICES.

APPENDIX A.

REPORT OF THE PRINCIPAL OF THE NORMAL SCHOOL FOR THE SESSION ENDED JUNE 30TH, 1901.

FREDERICTON, JAN. 1ST, 1902.

JAMES R. INCH, ESQ., LL. D.,
Chief Supt. of Education,
Fredericton, N. B.

SIR:—I beg leave to submit, for the information of His Honor the Lieutenant Governor and Members of the Honorable the Board of Education, my Annual Report on the workings of the Provincial Normal and Model Schools, for the year ending with June 30th, 1901, and to add such suggestions and observations as may be relevant thereto.

NORMAL DEPARTMENT.

The enrolment for the year was the smallest recorded for many years past amounting only to 199, of which number 43 were young men and 156 young women. I was led to expect a falling off in the attendance from the fact that the standard of age for young women had been raised, as well as from the further fact that the standard of requirement for admission has been gradually made higher. But I feel satisfied that the output of the school made up in quality what it lacked in quantity. We were able on account of the comparatively small number, to give more time to individual instruction and especially so in the professional work. This resulted in our sending out a y of students which, though smaller in numbers than in previous years, was fully prepared to take part in the great work of public instruction in the ols of the Province.

The numbers annually enrolled for the past ten years are given below :

		Young Men.	Young Women.
1891-2	269	38	231
92-3	264	47	214
93-4	320	59	261
94-5	282	56	226
95-6	247	67	180
96-7	266	62	203
97-8	283	57	226
98-9	338	65	273
99-1900	259	56	203
1900-01	199	43	156

The average for the ten-year period is 273. The figures for the current year's enrolment show a rise to about this average. At the present writing the number enrolled for 1901-2 is 270 Last year's comparatively small enrolment was due entirely to the causes stated above, and I should now expect an average of from 250 to 270 students annually to be steadily maintained in the future. All parts of our Educational System were represented in the enrolment, from the common schools to the college. The Secondary Schools continue to send up a large and increasing percentage of our students. This fact shows that the raising of the Standards for Provincial License is devolving upon them their proper share in the preliminary preparation of candidates, especially of those looking toward the higher classes.

The Counties of the Province were represented numerically as follows :

Albert	7
Carleton	22
Charlotte	14
Gloucester	20
Kent	9
Kings	23
Madawaska	9
Northumberland	16
Queens	10
Restigouche	13
St. John	12
Sunbury	6
Victoria	2
Westmorland	13
York	23
	199

By religious denominations, the students enrolled were classified as follows, viz.:—

Baptists	23
Church of England	18
Free Baptists	20
Methodists	36
Presbyterians	31
Roman Catholics	68
Other Denominations	3
	199

At the opening of the Normal Department 138 candidates presented themselves for admission, 23 of whom had passed for Class I., 80 for Class II. and 35 for Class III. 22 of the candidates for Classes I. and II. had passed on the Matriculation Examination, and 101 on the Normal School Entrance.

At the beginning of the Second Term in January, 1901, 22 holders of Provincial License, having passed the required Examination for entrance, were added to the enrolment, 11 for Class I., and the same number for Class II.

At the close of the Term ending December, 1900, and at the close of the year in June, 1901, the students enrolled were recommended or were eligible for Examination for Provincial License as follows :

For Class I	28
" II	107
" III	23
	158

Two candidates who had entered for Class I. withdrew on account of ill health.

The number of students annually recommended for the various Classes of License for the past ten years is given below :

	Class I.	II.	III.
91-2	46	122	85
92-3	46	132	76
93-4	68	129	117
94-5	31	133	106
95-6	35	131	75
96-7	44	137	76
97-8	49	144	88
98-9	45	171	100
99-1900	26	134	109
1900-01	28	107	62

The numbers for Class III., given in the above table include the students of the French Department. The figures for last year show a considerable increase in the percentage of students recommended for Class I and II in the Normal Department and a corresponding reduction of those recommended for Class III., as compared with the preceding years.

During the year a very considerable movement of students from class to class, took place principally in the way of promotion as the following table will show :

Entered for Class		I,	and recommended for Class			I........	26
"	"	I.,	"	"	"	II........	6
"	"	I.,	"	"	"	III........	0
"	"	II.,	"	"	"	I........	2
"	"	II.,	"	"	"	II........	88
"	"	II.,	"	"	"	III........	1
"	"	III.,	"	"	"	II........	13
"	"	III.,	"	"	"	22........	22

FRENCH DEPARTMENT.

The attendance in this department, though above the average, fell off considerably from that reported last year. During the First Term, beginning in August and ending in December, 1900, there were 19 students enrolled, and in the Second Term beginning in January, 1901, and ending in May, 1901, there were 20, making a total enrolment of 39 for the year as against 52 for last year.

The enrolment in this department for the past ten years is exhibited below.

	Total.	Young Men.	Young Women.
1891-2............	30	5	25
92-3............	29	4	25
93-4............	27	7	20
94-5............	21	3	18
95-6............	36	8	28
96-7............	27	9	18
97-8............	35	7	28
98-9............	38	5	33
99-1900.........	52	9	43
1900-01..........	39	13	26

The average attendance for the ten year period is slightly in excess of ;

No efforts should be spared by those more immediately interested in the Acadian Schools and in the intellectual progress of the Acadian element in our population, to direct a larger number of eligible young people qualified to teach in the schools wholly or largely attended by Acadian French children, to attend first the French Department of the Normal School and afterwards to prepare for the higher classes of License by attending the Normal Department. These schools can rise to no higher level of efficiency and progress than that of the teachers.

MODEL DEPARTMENT.

On the retirement of Mr. John F. Rogers, from the Principalship of this Department, Mr. Amos O'Blenes was appointed, and is now in charge. Mr. O'Blenes has shown himself to be an industrious teacher.

Miss M. E. Phillips was in charge of the 3rd department of the school and is gradually bringing it into a very creditable state of efficiency.

Miss Harvey still continues in charge of the 2nd department, and has added another year to her long record of faithful and diligent work for the advancement of her pupils.

Miss Clara E. Bridges has fully maintained her high reputation as a Primary Teacher. Her distinguished ability has brought her an offer from the South African educational authorities, and it is quite probable that the Model School will lose her valuable services in the near future.

GENERAL REMARKS.

During the year considerable additions were made to the equipment of the school. So far as the internal working of the Institution is concerned a good Reference Library is the greatest immediate necessity, and I would strongly recommend that a fixed sum be placed in the estimates for each year to provide for the gradual accumulation of a collection of the standard works of reference, and a good professional library for the use of the students in general. Even so small a sum as $100 a year would give us in a few years a very useful library.

The Sloyd Schools established by Sir William MacDonald for the Normal School and for the City of Fredericton, continues to be largely attended and th students and pupils show much interest in their work.

I would recommend that a building be erected on the Normal School ounds in the rear of the Normal School building, the lower flat to be devoted a gymnasium for the exclusive use of the Normal School students, and the upper flat fitted up to accommodate the Sloyd School, if the same is to be continued after the present arrangements terminate.

The Normal School needs the space now given up to the Sloyd Schools, and it would be much better in every way if these schools were placed in a detached building. The present arrangement was only adopted as a temporary one, and when it is decided to place the Sloyd School on a permanent footing as a part of our Educational System, if such a decision should be made, permanent provision should be made to remove it to a place of its own in a building specially designed for it.

The Public Closing Exercises for the year were held on Friday, June 7th, in the Assembly Hall of the school. His Honor the Lieut. Governor and other members of the Board of Education were on the platform, and the Hall was filled to its utmost capacity by the leading citizens of Fredericton, and the friends of the students. The occasion was a pleasing and interesting one for all present. The vocal and instrumental music by the students was an especial feature.

The silver and bronze medals annually granted by His Excellency the Governor General for highest professional standing was awarded for the year to Miss Isabella Reed of St. Vincent's School, St. John city, in the Senior Division and to Miss Ida J. Kierstead of Albert Co. in the Junior Division respectively. His Honor the Lieut. Governor presented the medals to the successful competitors in a very thoughtful and practical address. The Chief Superintendent of Education, the Chancellor of the University and Dean Partridge also addressed the students during the proceedings.

Miss Kierstead, who won the junior medal entered the school for Class III. and showed such marked progress both in scholarship and in professional ability that she was promoted to Class II. and won the coveted distinction of being announced as the winner of the medal in competition with an exceptionally intelligent body of Class II. students. It was a great sorrow to all who knew her, and recognized her abilities and her promise of future usefulness, to learn of her early death within a few months after leaving the school.

Mr. Fred C. Squiers of Bath, Carleton Co., was elected by his fellow-students as valedictorian for the year and discharged his pleasant duty with great force and spirit, and in excellent taste. Mr. Squiers had, during the year, especially distinguished himself in the Literary and Debating Society.

The school paper, "The Normal Light," was very successfully managed, and added much pleasure and interest to the corporate life of the school.

The Literary and Debating Society, and the Chorus Club, were conducted with energy and interest. A very delightful concert was given to the friends of the students under the auspices of the two organizations in the early spring.

The general health of the school was remarkably good. It is a noteworthy fact in this connection, that we have not had a single death in the school, during the school year, for nearly ten years. In that time over 2,500 students have attended. This fact speaks volumes for the sanitary conditions of the school, and for the healthfulness of the City of Fredericton.

The conduct and deportment of the school was very satisfactory, and the most cordial relations among the students and between instructors and students, prevailed.

In closing my Report for the year, I beg leave respectfully to call the attention of the Honorable, the Board of Education to the recommendations, which I have so often made hitherto, and which will be found in summary form on page 9, Appendix A of the Educational Report for 1900. I am more than ever convinced that these are the main lines of progress along which the future of the Normal School should be developed.

In view of what has taken place since my last Report was written, I may also be pardoned for closing this Report with a personal reference.

It is within the knowledge of the members of the Board of Education, that during the year an invitation has come to me from South Africa to take charge of the organizations and establishment of Normal School work in the Transvaal and Orange River Colonies with headquarters at Pretoria, and in response to this invitation the Board was pleased, in December last, to grant me a year's leave of absence from Feb. 1st, 1902, to enable me to assist the Sister Colonies of the Empire in placing their Normal Schools on an effective basis. In accordance with this patriotic action of the Board, I shall leave for South Africa in the near future.

In laying down my responsibility even for the short time mentioned, I wish to place on record my gratetul sense of the many kindnesses and courtesies extended to me, personally and officially, by the members of the successive Boards of Education since 1883, and in an especial manner to the present Board. Whatever my fortune may be in the future I shall never forget the kindly and public-spirited way in which the Hon. the Premier, the Hon. Attorney General, the Hon. the Chief Commissioner of Public works and other Hon. members of the Board have dealt with all matters relating to the con- ... of the Normal School and to myself as Principal of it.

... r over eighteen years, a much longer period than any one man has ever ... office, it has been my duty to preside over the Normal School and to be responsible for its efficiency. I have laboured strenuously and to the best of my ability and judgment in what I considered to be the interests of the Normal School and of the teaching profession in this Province.

In that time over 5,000 teachers have been trained in the school, many of whom are now among the leaders of educational work in the Province. I have seen progress, often slow, but always sure towards better conditions, and I am glad to say that in all that time, and now more than ever. I had and have a strong and abiding faith in our Public School System, and a confident belief that in the youth of this Province we have as great a measure of life, quality and intelligence, as can be found anywhere.

We have the material out of which to make teachers, what we need now is more and better facilities for doing it, and I earnestly trust that the future will see those facilities provided; for the advance of the public intelligence will only keep pace with the preparation and fitness of the public school teacher, and on the gradual rise of intelligence in the great body of citizens, the future welfare and prosperity of the Province largely depends.

To the Chief Superintendent of Education, to those who have been associated with me in the Normal and Model Schools—to the students of the Normal School, and to my successor in office, I extend my sincerest good wishes and my earnest hope that all their efforts for the advancement of the educational life of the community during the coming year may be abundantly fruitful of the best results.

I am, Sir,

Yours very sincerely,

ELDON MULLIN,

Principal.

APPENDIX B.

INSPECTORS' REPORTS.

INSPECTORAL DISTRICT NO. 1.

Geo. W. Mersereau, M. A., Inspector, Doaktown, N. B.

THIS DISTRICT EMBRACES THE COUNTIES OF RESTIGOUCHE, GLOUCESTER AND NORTHUMBERLAND.

J. R. INCH, ESQ., LL. D.,
Chief Supt. of Education,
Fredericton, N. B.

SIR.—I beg leave to submit the following Report on the condition of Public Schools in Inspectoral District No. 1, for the year ending 31st December, 1901.

During the First Term, I travelled greater distances and visited more schools than ever before in the same time and still there remained about forty schools unvisited. In the Second Term, I spent a large portion of the time, as you suggested, in urging the amalgamation of districts, where such a course seemed advantageous to the schools. However, all my territory (except Rogersville, which I left for Inspector Doucet) was visited once during the year and the greater portion of it for the second time and all the work was as well attended to as could be expected from one man over such an extended field.

I am gratified to be able to report a gradual recovery from the hindrances to advancement noticed in my last Annual Report.

The public meetings which I held during the year, seemed to be highly appreciated by the people, many of whom have badly perverted notions of their duty in the matter of educating their children and worse of what education really is. Much valuable work remains to be done along this line, and in my ...on it would be an advance step for the Board of Education to require of Inspectors a less number of visits per term or year, and a pro...tely greater number of Public Meetings in the less enlightened Districts. A generation ago a propaganda of this kind was carried out and today we notice its effects in the greater knowledge of the School Law and the keener interest in education evinced by the old and middle aged, than by the generations following that have not received this training and who are now exercising local control in educational matters.

This state of affairs probably accounts in large measure for my lack of success in carrying out the Board's policy of amalgamation of districts. There is always some excuse for not joining two districts. Generally the bases of these excuses are narrowness of view, selfishness, jealousy and ignorance. Sometimes one, sometimes another, sometimes all combined. In some cases they consider it merely a scheme of the Inspector's to lessen the number of schools and thus diminish his work regardless of the effect on the schools. This opinion would prevail of course, only in the more densely ignorant districts where they were unable to conceive of an officer being influenced by purely unselfish motives. To give some idea of the difficulties in the way, I shall quote a resolution moved by a County councillor in a district that lies side by side with another district on the opposite side of the river with a bridge between, very nearly in the middle, and their school houses not more than a half a mile apart in a direct line. The districts too are suffering from *inanition* and consequent inferior accomodation, lack of apparatus and want of sympathy of numbers. Their combined enrolment for the last Term was 28 and their combined average 19. If there are two districts in the Province that can be joined to their mutual advantage, these are the two and still this resolution was carried by thirteen to three at the last annual meeting in the larger of the two districts.

" Whereas the School Inspector is trying to induce the Board of Education to coerce the ratepayers of School Districts Nos. — and — to unite their School Districts into one.

" And whereas the ratepayers of District No. — is of the opinion that the amalgamation of the said districts would increase taxation, mar the harmony which now prevails in our School District, and would in no way facilitate or help the children in said districts getting a better education, therefore resolved that the ratepayers of District No — protest against such proposed change and take such steps as they deem necessary to prevent the amalgamation of the respective districts."

I have copied the resolution *verbatim et literatim*, except the numbers of the districts which are omitted for obvious reasons.

In another district which had only three children of school age all belonging to one family, which lived about two miles from the school in the adjoining district, the ratepayers voted $40 to convey the pupils to the school. No one could be found to undertake the job for the money, not even the father of the children, so they remained at home.

Judging from my experience of the past year, the Board need not hope for success in this direction, while it is left to local option. It will be compelled in the interests of the coming generations to take a firm stand and do what is best whether the people agree or not.

New school houses were completed and schools were opened in them for the first time at the beginning of the Second Term, in the following districts: Weldfield, No. 3, Glenelg, Breadalbane, No. 13, Blackville and Little Pass, No. 1, Caraquet.

One new department was opened in September, in each of the Graded Systems of Newcastle, Dalhousie and Campbellton. Thus the number of teachers employed in this Inspectorate has been increased during the year by six.

Two other districts have completed their school houses during the year and it is the intention of their Trustees to open schools in them at the beginning of next year, if the services of teachers can be secured.

The new school house in Wilson's Point, No. 10½, Shippegan, is slowly approaching completion. This district is a very weak one, but the Trustees hope to open school during the coming year.

Gagnon District No. 8, St. Isidore, is now ready to begin to build as soon as the site is determined on. Once a beginning is made the work will be pushed along rapidly.

Gaspereau, District No. 7, Saumarez, was lately erected, but the people wish to have their school opened not later than the beginning of Second Term, 1902.

RESTIGOUCHE COUNTY.

Restigouche, though the smallest, is the banner County in this Inspectorate in everything that relates to Educational progress. All the settlements are erected into districts. Every district is organized, and at the beginning of 1902, all the districts will have schools in operation. In school buildings and appliances it makes a very creditable showing. There are only four or five really poor school houses in the County. On Heron Island the school [illegible]se is small and old-fashioned and not very well provided with apparatus, [illegible] the district is weak numerically, and with the repairs made during the [illegible]r, the school house and equipment, fairly meets the requirements. Dawsonville has a log school house, built in the early days of the settlement which has outgrown it, and though it is comfortable in winter, it will soon have to be replaced by something more pretentious and more in keeping with the other buildings of the district.

The school house at Quinn's Point is not an old building, but it has been allowed to get out of repair by carelessness on the part of the Trustees, (and perhaps of some of the teachers). The furniture and equipment, too, is very inferior and needs an almost wholesale replenishment, which the Trustees and ratepayers seem quite unwilling to provide. In Point La Nim and The Cove, the school houses are old, small, poorly lighted and ventilated, with very unattractive surroundings. I have not urged these districts to rebuild, as the attendance is small in both and I hope at sometime to see the pupils of the former conveyed to Dalhousie and those of the latter to Dalhousie Junction.

While all the other school houses are good, there are some that are superior in construction and arrangement, with good woodhouses and outhouses, and neatly kept and attractive grounds. Among the best may be mentioned those in Upper Charlo, River Charlo, Jacquet River, Dalhousie Junction, New Mills, Black Land, Flat Lands, Riverside, Churchville, Bernard, Balmoral, Mountain Brook and Glencoe.

In many of the schools, the supply of maps and other apparatus is quite satisfactory. A few have slate blackboards any many have hyloplate. Much has been done during the year in adding to the equipment, especially in providing the schools with maps of the empire, flags and flag poles.

In this County is found, too, a large proportion of excellent teachers, industrious, earnest and progressive. Among those deserving special mention are:—Miss Susie B. MacPherson, New Mills; Miss Lizzie Cook, River Charlo; Miss Melissa J. Cook, Point La Nim; Miss Mary J. Crawford, Dalhousie Junction; Miss Mary A. Reid, Tide Head; Miss A. Maude Lachlan, Glencoe; Miss Bertha I. Asker, Flat Lands; Miss Mary Harvie, Black Point; Miss Mary E. Nichol, River Louison; Miss Lena M. Shannon, Upper Charlo; Mr. Antoine Boudreau, Balmoral; and Miss Mary McNair, Summerside.

The graded schools of the County are equally satisfactory. The Campbellton Grammar School is one of the most progressive Institutions of the kind in the Province as its record for the past ten years abundantly proves, and never in its history has it done better work than during the past year. The Trustees take a lively interest in everything that concerns the school a cooperate with the teachers in every way to make it a success. Appointme to the staff are made on merit. The aim is to secure the best and all fut appointees must hold Licenses of the First Class and come otherwise well recommended. Already three of the staff of eight are Graduates in Arts and two of these hold Grammar School Licenses.

Dalhousie Superior School has now four departments. Up to August last it had only three, and this constituted its chief weakness. The Primary Department was very much overcrowded, the pupils' interest could not be kept alive, hence irregular attendance and pupils promoted before they were prepared. Some of the rooms still need better furniture and all need additional apparatus, but the school is better prepared to do effective work than ever before. The Trustees are taking an intelligent interest and are helping the teachers instead of being a hindrance to them, as has sometimes been the case in the past. The staff of teachers is a good one, earnest, experienced and capable.

GLOUCESTER COUNTY.

To give an idea of the condition of schools in this County, it will be necessary for me to give a review of parishes. Progress has not been as rapid as it should have been. The people in many sections do not work together harmoniously. They are much divided and there are many lines of cleavage, such as the social, family, race, religious and political lines. In these sections they do not place a high value on education. Children attend school when not otherwise employed. As soon as they are big enough to work on the farm or at the fishing, the school knows them no more, except perhaps for a haphazard attendance of a month or two in the winter. As a rule the school houses and grounds and outbuildings are not well cared for. Not many are kept well painted, though to this rule there are many notable exceptions, such as at New Bandon, St. Jerome, Green Point, Dumfries, Upper Grand Anse Miscou Harbor, Waugh, Blanchard Settlement, Inkerman, Little River, Upper Paquetville and others, where the school houses and outbuildings and fences are kept well painted and much care is taken with the grounds to have them neat and attractive and a place to which the children like to come.

Beresford No. 1, needs a new school house. The old shed now in use is not fit for people to be shut up in during the cold weather. It is not in the right place to accommodate the people living back of the Railway. In No. 2, the school house is too small, but the people are divided on race lines and ...'t agree on the site for a new building. No. 3 has a fine school ... with grounds and outbuildings well kept. No. 4 has four school ...s that are rapidly falling into decay, through the niggardliness of the ratepayers and the cheeseparing of the Trustees. No. 12 has a school house of which any district might be proud, and an excellent teacher in Miss Melvina J. Godin. Arrangements should be made to convey the pupils of No. 13 and No. 13½ to the big school at Petit Rocher, or those of No. 13½ to the school house in No. 13, thus saving the salary of one teacher and providing better teaching for the children. During the year No. 7 made extensive improvements and provided new furniture through the efforts of the teacher, Miss Mattie H. Renouf. In No. 7½ the school is small, but the work is well done by Miss Agnes Nichol, an excellent teacher of the First Class. Nos. 6 and 6½ have good school houses, but the most disgracefully kept outhouses in the County. Nos. 8½ and 11 need better school buildings. The school house in No. 10 A, was extensively repaired during summer vacation.

BATHURST.—This parish has some fairly good buildings such as the Grammar School building in town and the Superior School building in the village, though the former is getting somewhat out of repair. No. 6 is a very weak district, and has a poor school house, but a good school, with Miss Annie Loggie as teacher. No. 12 rebuilt its school house during the year. No. 3 repaired its school house and provided new furniture. The school in No. 7 is improving slowly. No. 5 made some improvements and promises more. No. 4½ wainscotted school-room and procured hyloplate blackboard. During Second Term, there were only five pupils enrolled in No. 8. The ratepayers of No. 17 will be compelled to build a new school house very soon. The present building is a very poor affair on a poor site not centrally located. No school was operated in No. 9 during the year, as there are only three pupils in the district.

NEW BANDON.—Much needed repairs were made on the school house of No. 9 both inside and outside, and the school was very successfully conducted by Miss Mina D. Plant. In No. 8 the school-room was painted and still needs more blackboard surface. Miss Maggie E. McNair taught the school very acceptably and was a power for good in the district, besides. No. 7 kept its school open during the year and repaired the school house. The school in No. 6 improved very much in tone during the year under Miss Eva B. Culligan. Grand Anse Portage No. 3½, set the best example of zeal in educating the children in my Inspectorate. The district has only eight ratepayers and its total valuation is $2,650. The parents took turns in driving the children to and from school during stormy weather. Needless to say every child attended. In No. 2 the pupils made excellent progress in their own language, but did not care to learn English. No. 1 has a poor school, which is not kept going regularly.

CARAQUET.—For a wealthy Parish, Caraquet has very poor schools. No. 1 was organized late in March, and is now ready to employ a teacher. No. 2 had a kind of graded school of two departments with Grade IV. as the highest Grade and the pupils classified according to size, so that Grades II. and III. were in both departments. No. 2½ was better. and the teacher, Mr. P. P. Murray seemed very zealous and faithful, but the larger pupils attended only a few months in winter. No. 3 was well taught by Mr. Jos. F. Godin. No. 4 was organized late in the year. Nos. 1 and 8 are still dormant as noticed last year.

PAQUETVILLE.—I visited the schools of this parish but once during the year, in the month of March, while a mission was being preached in the Church and all the larger pupils were in almost constant attendance. Nos. 1 and 2 have good school houses and the grounds of No. 2 receive careful attention. No. 3 has a poor school. The pupils have been *told* rather than taught. No. 4 has a good teacher in Miss Josephine M. Godin. No. 5 has a good school house but little in the way of furniture and apparatus.

INKERMAN.—No. 1 has a new school house not yet furnished inside, but warm and comfortable. No. 2 has also a good school house but some of the ratepayers complain that it is not now near the middle of the district, and that it will have to be moved. The school in No. 3, where there is another good school house, improved greatly during the year. The school in No. 5 was reopened after being closed for three Terms. In No. 4 the school house is evidently not in the right place as most of the children live on the opposite side of the River. The Maltumpeque Road Settlement will soon have to be erected into a district with the western end of this district. When that occurs the proper location of this school house can be determined.

SHIPPEGAN.—No. 1 has a graded school of two departments, but the accommodation and equipment are very inferior. The teachers employed this year are two of our brightest young men, Mr. J. Edward De Grace and Mr. Theodore J. De La Garde. Miss Philomène Robichaud achieved success in No. 1½. In No. 2 the pupils never advance beyond Grade IV, and few reach even that. The school in No. 3 was small but was well taught. No. 3½ has n excellent teacher in Mr. Jas. R. Smith, and is building a new school use slowly but steadily. Mr. J. Avila Duguay has given faithful service No. 5 for the past four years. This district has a good school house, but or furniture and little apparatus. No. 4, 4½, and 6, have good school houses, but poor furniture and little apparatus No. 7, has a good building and good furniture, but poorly kept grounds. No. 9 has the best furnished school in the parish and every year sees something added to its equipment. Nos. 9½ and 10 have poor school houses and poor schools. No. 8 will open school at the commencement of the New Year, for the first time in many years. No. 10½ reports progress in building.

SAUMAREZ.—The Superior School House in Tracadie, No. 3, is a plain, substantial, two-story structure that accommodates two departments very comfortably, but the other two buildings in the district are not nearly so creditable. Mr. Geo. E. Price is the Principal of the Superior School and does very faithful work. There is a fair school house and a good school in No. 2, Miss Catherine D. Losier, teacher, but only an apology for either in No. 2½. No. 6 keeps its school open very irregularly. No. 10 A has a very small school house for the number of pupils. I thought some of dividing the district and perhaps this will yet have to be done, though the school has been better taught this year by Miss Alice M. Robichaud and better attended than ever before.

ST. ISIDORE.—This small parish has only three school districts. In No. 7½ there is a good school house, but the most the children have learned for the past five years is reading and that not very understandingly. No. 7 has a miserable school house and a very unsatisfactory school. No. 8 has, at last, decided to build a school house.

NORTHUMBERLAND COUNTY.

This County presents strong contrasts. It has some of the finest school buildings, best equipment and most progressive schools, and also some of the poorest. I shall not have time to do more than to notice very briefly a few of the schools in each parish.

ALNWICK.—Miss Nora Cripps did excellent work in No. 1. The school in No. 1½ is very small and kept open but a part of each year. No. 3 has a fair building, enclosed grounds and a good school under Miss K. Loggie, who was forced by ill health to resign her position. The school in No. 9 is improveing from term to term under Miss Ellen M. Donovan. No. 12 has a good building but only a fair school. The same is true of No. 4. New school houses are being built in Nos. 8½ and 13. The school in No. 5 has been very poorly conducted for the past two years. There are but few pupils in No. 6 so they should be conveyed to the school in No. 7.

NEWCASTLE.—There are but few Ungraded Schools in this parish, only five altogether. No. 2½ has so few pupils that it would be much better to convey them to the school in No. 1, which has not a large enrollment. No. 8 has good buildings and neatly kept grounds and Miss Mabel V. Elliott is the popular teacher.

NORTH ESK.—There is an excellent school house in No. 1, but the school is small. No. 2 has a new, nicely furnished school house. In No. 3 there are very few pupils and it will be difficult to have them conveyed to the next district as some of them are nearly ten miles from the school house. There is a poor school house in No. 4, but it is fairly equipped and the teacher, Miss Stella O'Shea, is an excellent one. No. 5 is a weak district that operates its school very irregularly. The number of pupils in No. 6 is large, but the equipment of the school is poor and the average attendance small. There are about eighty pupils in No. 10 and there is a fair Class-room but the Trustees are very negligent about employing an Assistant. Miss A. Maude Menzies, one of our best teachers, has been employed during the Second Term, but even she could not do satisfactory work under the circumstances.

SOUTH ESK.—The best school in the parish is in No. 9, where the Trustees are interested and attentive to their duties. No. 7 operated school this year for the first time in twenty years. No. 7½, had a very good school during the year. An unfortunate disagreement among the people in No. 13 operates against the school. The attendance is increasing in No. 14, and the school is improving.

DERBY.---The Superior School of two departments is in District No. 1. This district suffered a great loss in the retirement from the Principalship and from the profession, of Mr. J. J. Clark, who had taught here most successfully for eighteen years, at the beginning of the year. Miss Lottie E. Underhill has given excellent satisfaction in No. 3 for the past seven years. She has not only supplied a large amount of apparatus for the school by means of concerts but has offered to raise at least half the funds to build a new school house in the same way.

BLACKVILLE.—The Superior School of three departments is in District No. 6. Mr. J. C. Carruthers, the Principal, has done excellent work and shown himself to be a wide awake, progressive teacher since his appointment to this position. His efforts during the past Term have been ably seconded by his associate teachers, Miss McCarthy and Miss Fairweather. There has been much complaint about the heating of the new building. A new school house [illegible]een built in No. 4, but it is so poor a job that it should not have been [illegible]n off the contractor's hands. At the beginning of the Second Term School [illegible]pened for the first time in District No. 13. The school house in No. 5 [illegible]t yet been moved to the middle of the district.

BLISSFIELD.—The Doaktown Superior School is in No. 4 of this parish. The school house is very inferior and so is the equipment, but the teachers are industrious, skilful and progressive. Mr. Geo. A. Wathen is the Principal and Miss Jessie J. Murray has charge of the Primary Department. The school house in No. 3 has been nicely painted. Miss Beatrice Ellis has done excellent work in No. 3½ under discouraging conditions. No. 1 made some improvements in its house and grounds No. 1½ opened its school at the beginning of the Second Term to continue it for a year at least. No. 2½ has the best kept grounds in the parish.

LUDLOW.—Boiestown, No. 3, has an excellent school house with fair equipment. Mr. W. W. Wright, the teacher, gives satisfaction to all. The school house in No. 5 was ceiled and painted inside during the summer vacation. Nos. 2 and 4 are very weak districts, that it would be well to unite if the people's consent could be gained.

NELSON.—Nelson Village No. 1 has a graded school of two departments but the school house is very inferior for such a district, and not in the centre of the school population. At the last Annual Meeting it was resolved to build more centrally. In No. 5, the school house was shingled throughout and a woodhouse built. No. 6½ has a good school house and No. 8 has well kept grounds. No. 1½ has a good school as usual, neatly painted buildings and well kept grounds.

CHATHAM.—The school in No. 2 has done better than usual under Miss Sophia G. McDonald. Miss Josie M. McNeil has done excellent work in No. 5, where the Trustees are very careless in the performance of their duties. In No. 6½, a new school house was built and school opened in August after being closed for a year and a half after the old building was burnt. No. 6 has a fine new school house and the Trustees are now paying some attention to its surroundings.

GLENELG.—No. 4 has a new school house that should be painted. The school in No. 1 was not quite so successful as usual on account of measles in the district. The school house and outbuildings should be painted. No. 3 opened school in August for the first time in eighteen years. It's new school house is very creditable. Miss Jennie D. Gilliss completed a very successful Term of four years in No. 7. No. 7½ has good buildings and an excellent school.

HARDWICKE.—The schools in Nos. 1 and 2 were closed for a time because of diphtheria. No. 3 has a fine school house in which Miss H. J. Ahern conducted a very successful school. The schools in Nos. 4 and 5 were also satisfactorily conducted by Miss Ruby Noble and Miss Kate McNair. The school house in No. 6 was destroyed by forest fires. A movement is on foot to have a portion of No. 5, called the McDonald Settlement, joined to No. 6, and the school house moved to the middle of the enlarged district. The McDonalds have all petitioned for the change, but the Trustees of No. 5 contend that it will make their district too weak to support a school.

GRADED SCHOOLS.

Of the larger graded systems of schools in the County I shall write but little. Chatham, which has heretofore been behind other towns of the same, or less importance in the matter of High School accommodation and equipment, has opened a new High School building that will place her well in the forefront in these respects.

Since the amalgamation of its three districts the schools of Chatham have continued to grow in efficiency. The improved accommodation will enable Dr. Cox and his staff of capable and earnest teachers to achieve higher degrees of success in their important work. The teaching throughout all the standards aims to be practical, to take nothing for granted that can be verified and to put the pupil in the position of a dicoverer in every subject, in so far as it is posble. In consequence of this the Chatham Schools are well prepared to take up the Manual Training work as illustrated by the Sir Wm. C. McDonald Training Schools. I trust that one of the spare rooms in the new building may be devoted to this purpose before my next report.

The resignation of Mr. F. P. Yorston, M. A., was a great loss to the Newcastle Schools. He was faithful in the performance of his duties and brought to bear upon them exceptional powers of mind. He was succeeded as Principal by Mr. Geo. K. McNaughton, B. A., and if interest in his work and steady application to duty can achieve it, he will win success.

The necessity for some kind of hand work is apparent in all our schools, especially in the miscellaneous ones, something more tangible than Drawing and that would not require too great an outlay for material. I am of the opinion that Cardboard work would meet the requirements, and beg leave to suggest that this subject be added to our Normal School Course.

I have the honor to be, Sir,

Your obedient servant,

GEO. W. MERSEREAU.

INSPECTORAL DISTRICT NO. 2.

George Smith, A. B., Inspector, Shediac, N. B.

THIS DISTRICT COMPRISES THE COUNTIES OF KENT AND WESTMORLAND.

JAMES R. INCH, ESQ., LL D.,
Chief Supt. of Education,
Fredericton, N. B.

SIR:—I have the honor to forward my Report for the year 1901.

The more than usual amount of snow on the ground during the winter months made the work of travelling through my district more difficult than usual and hindered me to some extent in my work. The prevalence of small pox in Westmorland County also interfered to a considerable degree with my plans of inspection, as it became necessary to close for a time some of the schools.

Compulsory vaccination throughout the entire County as a result of the outbreak of smallpox proved more detrimental to the schools than any other cause, as in many cases the children remained home either as the result of vaccination, or from fear of having to undergo vaccination. In one school where the attendance should have been about twenty-five, on the day of my visit I found two pupils present, the result of vaccination, and this school is not less than forty miles from any case of smallpox.

Two new districts have been formed in the parish of Wellington, Saint Michael, No. 17 taken from No. 12, and St. Croix, No. 18, taken from No. 7½.

A new school house has been built in Canaan Station, district No. 25, Moncton. School was in operation in the new house during the term ended the 31st of December. New school houses have also been built in Gallagher Ridge, No. 32, Moncton, Shaw Brook, No. 33, Moncton, and Portage River, No. 10, Carleton, all new districts. In the last two named, school was in operation for the first time during the term closed the 31st of December.

In No. 12 Dundas, where for several years the old school house has been unfit for use, a new house has been built in the centre of the district, and will be occupied the coming term. As the Board of Trustees and a large majority of the rate payers were opposed to building a new house and persistently refused to vote money for the purpose, a new Board of Trustees was appointed by the authority of the Chief Superintendent and an assessment sufficient to build the new house was levied on the district by order of the Board of Education.

The following districts in the parish of Botsford have taken advantage of the act providing for the distribution of school moneys in this parish, and have made extensive repairs in the school houses and improvements in the grounds: Bristol Corner, No. 16, Postage, No. 17, Little Cape, No. 18, Leger Brook, No. 19, Cape Bald, No. 20, and Chapel No. 21. In No. 16, the interior of the school room has been sheathed and painted and new furniture provided. Other districts in the parish contemplate making improvements during the coming year. General improvements have been made as needed throughout the various districts of this Inspectorate.

In the Richibucto Grammar School, Mr. A. E. Pearson was appointed teacher of Grades VII and VIII, beginning in January last. In the Moncton High School, Mr. McNally succeeded Mr. McLean in August. Mr. R. D. Hanson resumed charge of the Petitcodiac Superior School. Mr. H. B. Steeves was appointed Principal of the Dorchester Superior School. and Mr. Charles B. Richards of the Bass River Superior School in August.

GENERAL REMARKS.

Ventilation.—This is a matter which does not hold the place of importance in the minds of teachers, trustees and parents, which its importance demands. In perhaps one-half of the school houses instead of the windows being so that they can be lowered from the top, and thus provide the only proper means of ventilation available, they are securely fastened and in many instances cannot even be raised. Even when provision is made for lowering the top sash, teachers either through ignorance or carelessness do not make a proper use of this means of ventilation. They either close the window entirely or open it five or six inches and thus allow a rush of cold air to blow directly on the pupil. For ventilation in cold weather the upper sashes of two or more opposite windows should be lowered so as to make a very small open space at the top and should be kept in that position during the whole day. This is much better than throwing windows and doors open at short intervals and thus admitting a rush of cold air which will cause a chill on the pupils, especially the smaller ones.

The proper care of the wood is a matter which does not receive the attention it should. As a rule good wood is provided, but instead of being housed it is allowed to remain exposed to the autumn rains and winter snows It ems difficult to convince Trustees and ratepayers that it is good economy to ovide a woodshed. In some instances even where a proper woodshed is pro- ded the wood is allowed to remain exposed to the storms.

It is pleasing to note that an increasing interest is being taken in decorating the interior of the school rooms. As noted in my report of last year few school rooms are entirely void of pictures or some decoration on the walls, some rooms being very tastefully decorated. I wish I could report as favorably of the school grounds. These in many instances are not as well cared for as they should be. A little more effort on the part of the teacher in enlisting the co-operation of the pupils in this matter would be productive of good results.

As a rule the discipline in the schools is all that can be desired. Occasionally however I find a teacher deficient in that most essential qualification, the ability to govern. In all such cases the results show that the lack of this qualification is a very serious drawback and that good work and disorder cannot go together.

Some defects in teaching.—One defect which I have noticed is the habit which some teachers have of dividing their attention between two or even more than two subjects at the same time. I have seen teachers attempt to hear a lesson in reading, correct a slate exercise, and tell pupils who were studying their lessons the pronunciation of words all at the same time. This I need hardly say is not and never can be effective teaching. Another defect is the apparent lack of ability on the part of the teacher to devise new ways of doing things. The same routine in all subjects is followed day after day, and when the results are not so good as might be expected the method is blamed. Children must have variety in order that the interest may be sustained. Lack of punctuality on the part of the teacher is another drawback. The regulation requiring teachers to be in the school room twenty minutes before the time for opening should be strictly enforced by every Board of Trustees. Teachers who complain that they have not time enough to teach all the subjects can save time by making preparation for the lessons before school is opened. Failure to review more frequently is the frequent cause of failure to secure thoroughness and efficiency.

Parents.—As a rule I find parents willing and pleased to give good and faithful teachers their just mead of praise, and where dissatisfaction exists there is generally some fault on both sides. Occasionally, however, the criticisms of the parents seem unfair and unjust.

Trustees.—Some Boards of Trustees do not seem to realize the moral obligation resting upon them to expend to the best advantage the money taken from the ratepayers. In some districts the Trustees will employ and continue in their employ teachers whose inability to properly conduct the school is apparent to all. While this is true in a few cases it is pleasing to know that in most cases an honest effort is made by the Trustees to secure the best teachers available.

While I have referred to some defects in the schools and shortcomings on the part of teachers and Trustees, I do not wish to be understood as implying that these defects are at all general. The great majority of teachers in both graded and ungraded schools manifest a disposition to do the very best work possible and do succeed in very many instances in doiug excellent work.

The good effects of Arbor Day may be observed in many inst:nces, principally in the improvement of the condition of the interior of the school room. Usually the annual scrubbing is done on this day, besides out door improvements of various kinds.

The Kent County Institute met at Harcourt, on the third and fourth of October, and although the weather was unfavorable the attendance was good, and the program was successfully carried out. Too much cannot be said in praise of the citizens of Harcourt for the hospitality extended to the members of the Institute. The Westmorland County Institute met at Shediac on the tenth and eleventh of October. The attendance was large and a good program was carried out.

I have the honor to be, Sir,

Your obedient servant,

GEO. SMITH.

INSPECTORAL DISTRICT, NO. 3

R. P. Steeves, M. A., Inspector, Sussex, K. C.

THIS DISTRICT COMPRISES THE COUNTY OF ALBERT, THE COUNTY OF KINGS EXCEPT THE PARISHES OF WESTFIELD AND GREENWICH, AND THE COUNTY OF QUEENS EXCEPT THE PARISHES OF CANNING, GAGETOWN, HAMPSTEAD AND PETERSVILLE.

J. R. INCH, ESQ., LL D.,
Chief Supt. of Education,
Fredericton, N. B.

SIR:—Following is my Report on the condition of the Public Schools in Inspectoral District, No. 3, for the year ending December 31, 1901.

ALBERT COUNTY.

About the usual number of schools has been in operation this year. Some districts in remote sections customarily keep their schools closed during the severe winter months. Owing to scarcity of teachers many of these had difficulty in securing teachers in early spring, and some schools for this reason were not open at all during the winter term. Generally speaking, the schools are in a progressive and satisfactory condition.

GRADED SCHOOLS.

The Hillsboro' Superior School, in which there are now three departments, has fully demonstrated by increased success, that enlarged accommodation was a necessity. Mr. Lewis J. Folkins, B. A., Principal, Mr. Fred. S. James, B. A., Intermediate, and Miss Beatrice Steeves, Primary, were the teachers employed during the winter term. At the beginning of the summer term Mr. James became Principal, and Miss Deborah Bishop, assumed charge of the Intermediate Department. The school house as repaired and enlarged, presents a creditable and somewhat imposing appearance. The new rooms have been beautifully finished and are very pleasant and attractive. Public interest in the school has been stimulated and it is the wish of the Trustees, I am satisfied, that nothing within reasonable bounds shall be left undone that will contribute to thorough efficiency.

The repairs on the Surrey school house have made it fairly comfortable and pleasant. Material conditions for successful work now exist in a greater degree than for a long time past.

The school house at Dawson Settlement has been arranged for two departments. Both schools exhibit very good work. The primary work which suffered most while the school was ungraded has, with improved accommodation, made rapid strides toward advancement.

The school at Demoiselle Creek continues to prosper. Both departments are fairly efficient. All the above named schools are in the Parish of Hillsboro.

Mr. H. H. Stuart became Principal of the Hopewell Hill Superior School at the beginning of the year. When I visited the school he had been there for so short a time I am scarcely in a position to speak decidedly of his work. The Primary department efficiently conducted by Miss Grace McGorman has a very small enrollment.

The Hopewell Cape School has an advanced department of excellent merit. The Primary department is not for various reasons worthy of such commendation. I understand that Mr. W. C. Jonah, Principal, is now retiring to take up an advanced course of study.

The Riverside graded school is doing the best possible under existing conditions. The interior of the house is not either convenient or satisfactory, but nothing better can be expected until a new building is erected.

During the winter term Mr. J. T. Horsman, B. A., was Principal of the Albert School. On his retirement Mr. W. M. Burns, was appointed for the summer term. Miss Atkinson continues in charge of the Primary department. The school is a large one and steadily growing. If Districts Nos. 2 and 10, Riverside and Albert, could be induced to unite forces and build a central school, there appears no reason why one of the most successful schools in the Province should not be operated at a comparatively small expense.

Harvey Corner, one of the largest graded schools of two departments in this Inspectorate continues to do a very good class of work. The interior of the school house and the school furniture are in a dilapidated and unkempt condition. The supply of apparatus has somewhat increased,

I regret that I have been unable during the year to visit the Alma Grammar School and the Elgin Corner Superior School. The former in charge of Mr. Colpitts, a very capable and experienced teacher, is no doubt being satisfactorily conducted.

UNGRADED SCHOOLS.

There are many large and important ungraded schools in this County, g which may be named those at Point Wolfe, Waterside, Lower Cape, ville, Pleasant Vale, and District No. 1 Coverdale. In most of these a very excellent class of work is being done and the same may also be said of the work in many smaller schools.

It appears to me that the devotion and industry of the teachers and the interest of Trustees and ratepayers in securing the best possible equipment for their schools is every year increasing. Seldom does any unpleasantness occur. The work of inspection is in almost all cases one of pleasure. I am able also to say that almost uniformly, recommendations to school officers have been considered and carried out.

The County Institute convened at Hillsboro' in June. It was a profitable and successful gathering. A well attended public meeting on Thursday evening, was presided over by C. J. Osman, Esq., M. P. P. Addresses were given by the Chairman, Principal J. M. Palmer, of Sackville, Dr. George U. Hay, and others.

KINGS COUNTY.

Perhaps not as large a number of schools has been maintained during the entire year as in some years, but almost all the districts have had schools during some part of the year. Scarcity of teachers and other causes, among which may be mentioned the opinion that prevailed in some sections that small schools would not be recognized by the Board of Education, contributed to cause this state of affairs. In districts where there are but few children to attend school there is usually a number of ratepayers personally interested in having the school closed down. It is thought that if there is no school the assumed extra expense of carrying the children to the next school will deter those rate payers who want a school from demanding and securing their rights to school privileges. Probably in a short time the law will come to be better understood and more pronounced demands by ratepayers, who have children to send to school, will be made. There are some sections in this county where the centralization principle should work with good effect.

GRADED SCHOOLS.

All the graded schools were visited during the year.

Mr. G. C. Crawford, B. A., Principal, and Mr. Guy McAdam, second master of the Sussex Grammar School, retired at the close of the winter term. They were succeeded by Mr. Wm. Brodie, M. A., and Mr. Folkins who taught in Hillsboro' during the winter term. The School Board is to be congratulated upon having a very competent staff of seven teachers. It is to be regrett[illegible] that the attendance of pupils in tenth and eleventh grades has in the last yea[illegible] or so considerably decreased.

In the Superior Schools at Penobsquis, Apohaqui and Bloomfield, the enrollment of pupils in the various classes of the advanced departments has been very small. Under the existing conditions, however, very good work has been done in all of these schools. The Primary department at Bloomfield is also very small. It would appear advisable to annex to Apohaqui the small districts Secord, No. 13, Sussex, and Riverbank, No. 26, Studholm, etc., lying west of Apohaqui on both sides of the Kennebecasis. Perhaps also Penobsquis District might be enlarged by the addition of No. 2, Cardwell. Some districts contiguous to Bloomfield might be added to it.

The Superior School at Hampton, is large and progressive. Mr. Rex Cormier is the Principal and Miss Frances Prichard teacher of the Primary department. The Intermediate department of the Hampton Village School has now somewhat larger accommodation though not what might be desired. It is however, the best that can be done with the present building. Too frequent changes in the Principalship militate against the success of this school. Mr. Kelly, a former Principal, is again in charge.

Owing to overcrowding it was found necessary to grade the Havelock Superior School into three departments. Without doubt better work will be done because of the change. The Intermediate department is located in too small a room to be comfortable or satisfactory. Mr. Aaron Perry, B. A., has been the Principal during the summer term.

Nothing has occurred in the graded school at Norton Station to require comment. The teachers remain as last year. The Primary department has a very large enrollment.

In the school at Sussex Corner the two departments are in enrollment about evenly balanced, At the time of my visit the attendance was very good in both and the work showed that under the present teachers advancement had been made.

UNGRADED SCHOOLS.

There are many large ungraded schools in this County, prominent among which are those at Waterford, Anagance Ridge, Lower Ridge, Newtown, Lower Millstream, Jeffries Corner, Hillsdale, Upham, Hatfield's Point and Nauwigewauk. Much excellent work is done in many of the ungraded schools; but in some, particularly among the large schools, the character of the work is not en-satisfactory. This arises chiefly from the fact that one teacher is required ...ach too many classes and pupils. In many cases it is difficult to lead ...es to see the need of employing assistant teachers. The extra expense is a deterrent factor. Where unfavorable conditions such as the foregoing exist the very best efforts of the teachers have been exerted and the disadvantages have been reduced to a minimum. As I have been unable to visit many of the Ungraded Schools I cannot speak of them with absolute certainty, but from what I do know I feel satisfied that the quality of work done by them is fully up to the usual standard. Without doubt the schools are improving in accommodations, equipment and instruction imparted.

I was unable to be present at the County Institute, held in Sussex, in October. I am told that the sessions were profitable and stimulating. A largely attended public meeting was held in Oddfellow's Hall, on Thursday evening. It was presided over by J. Arthur Freeze, Esq., Secretary to the Sussex School Board. The principal speakers were the Chief Superintendent of Education and Mr. E. E. McCready, Director of the Manual Training School at Fredericton.

QUEENS COUNTY.

My visit to the Chipman Superior School was a very enjoyable one. Both departments are in very good condition. Miss Fairweather, who was quite popular in the Primary department— and deservedly so—retired at the close of the winter term and was succeeded by Miss Cliffie Dobson. Mr. H. P. Dole remains as Principal.

The remaining schools in this Inspectorate in this County are ungraded. Upper Jemseg, Cambridge, Thorntown, Wickham, Cumberland Bay and White's Cove, are among the largest of them. I am able to speak in commendatory terms of very many of the Ungraded Schools. The teachers as a class are painstaking, earnest and industrious men and women. They are doing good work in raising educational standards.

Throughout this Inspectorate about the usual amount of repairing and renovating school buildings, has been done during the summer. A very fair amount of new school furniture has also been procured.

During the year no difficulties of moment have occurred in the administration of the school law.

Many school meetings have been called this year by Inspector's notices, chiefly because the date of the annual school meeting having been changed, the proper parties neglected their duty.

ARBOR DAY.

Arbor Day observance was as general as in former years. The neat and cleanly condition of school houses and grounds attests to the value of work inspired by teachers on this day, though it must be admitted that very much of the time spent in setting out trees is not profitably employed. This is because in many cases school grounds are not enclosed and also because Trustees do not always recognize the value of caring for and protecting school property. Whatever improvements to school grounds are made on Arbor Day are frequently within eight or ten days destroyed by cattle.

Four hundred and twenty trees, ninety-five shrubs and one hundred and sixty-six flower beds were reported from one hundred and thirty-five districts.

Thanking you for your kindness and forbearance towards me during the past year.

I am, your obedient servant,

R. P. STEEVES.

INSPECTORAL DISTRICT, NO. 4.

W. S. Carter, A. M., Inspector, St. John, N. B.

THIS DISTRICT EMBRACES THE COUNTIES OF ST. JOHN AND CHARLOTTE, AND THE PARISHES OF WESTFIELD AND GREENWICH, IN KINGS COUNTY.

J. R. INCH, ESQ., LL. D.,
Chief Supt. of Education,
Fredericton, N. B.

SIR :—I beg to submit the following Report for the year ending December, 1901 :

I have been able to cover my district fairly well during both terms.

The winter term was the most severe in my experience. The month of February and part of March have not been surpassed in many years for storms and depth of snow in the southern part of the Province. It greatly impeded me in my work and seriously affected the school attendance. I was unable to reach a few schools. Some that I did visit had no pupils in attendance and in two or three cases, after coming on the highway opposite to the school house, I was unable to get my horse to it.

During the summer term the smallpox broke out in the City of St. John and later, spread to the vicinity. It resulted in the closing of some of the city schools as well as a number in the country districts, while the attendant scare, caused the attendance to fall off to such an extent, that at one time it seemed to me, they should have all been closed.

These drawbacks coupled with the scarcity of teachers which has prevailed during the year and on account of which some schools remained closed, must have a disastrous effect upon statistics.

As this is my year for reporting each parish, I will make that the most prominent feature. It is difficult to keep in view all the good work done in a year by teachers and Trustees, and any omissions will not be intentional.

LEPREAUX.

Mace's Bay supports a school regularly, The vacations are not as long as formerly. Many improvements have been made, and more are needed. Little Lepreaux, which was closed for some time, has supported a regular schoo. Some good apparatus has been purchased, but outbuildings are much needed. Lepreaux Village has had a school half the year. The number of pupils i small, but as it is again to become a milling centre, I hope the place will improve. The house needs painting.

The school at New River Mills has been operated part of the year. There are now but three or four pupils to attend. The house is kept in good repair.

PENNFIELD.

Miss Mary Hawkins, Teacher in Pennfield Centre for nearly ten years, retired with the good wishes of all in the district. She has been succeeded by Miss Lily Boyd. The house at Beaver Harbor has been painted. In this district the Primary School is kept in regular operation, but owing to the work in the sardine factories, the Advanced Department is closed part of the time, and it is often difficult to get a teacher in the middle of the term.

Coldbrook school is small, but in good condition. Owing to the exertions of the teacher, Miss Laura Boyd, a handsome flag has been procured for the school. Black's Harbor has a large school, but it is very poorly housed. A new school house is needed.

Seely's Cove has also a large attendance with good surroundings. This district has been unable to secure a teacher for the summer term. Pennfield Ridge has supported a regular and satisfactory school.

ST. GEORGE.

The schools in the village are in a healthy condition, the attendance at the High School is very large and beyond the capacity of the room. Mr. W. M. Veazey retired during the year, with the esteem and good wishes of all. He has been succeeded by H. E. St. Clair, a young man with an excellent record as a teacher.

There is need of some good apparatus to replace that which is old or worn out.

Head of L'Etang has had a fair school. Breadalbane has provided new furniture. The school in this district is very small, and I think it would be to the advantage of all concerned if the pupils were conveyed to St. George Red Granite has added some good and necessary apparatus. Bonny River sup--rts an excellent school. Through the exertions of Miss Lucy McKenzie, the -her, a flag, slates, etc., have been added. Second Falls supports a school of the time. Elmcroft, Somerville, Red Rock, Piskahegan and Pomroy -ge, are isolated districts with few children and limited resources. Most of these have kept a school in operation during part of the year. They are too far apart to centralize.

Miss Sadie Carson, teacher at Caithness has been instrumental in procuring for that district a flag pole and slate black boards.

Mascarene and Back Bay have had difficulty in securing teachers for the whole year. The school at Letete has much improved in all respects under the tuition of Miss M. Lizzie Knight. Through her exertions a flag, dictionary, slates and other apparatus, have been added to the school.

Upper L'Etang has had a fair school, the attendance is small. L'Etang has had a good school as usual. Roix has operated a school the usual time. Some improvements are necessary.

ST. PATRICK.

Lower Bocabec has made many improvements of late, and while the same have been well intentioned some of them have not been to the satisfaction of all. Bocabec has had a good school. In no district in the county have more intelligent and praiseworthy efforts been made by ratepayers, Trustees and teachers to improve school grounds and premises, than in McMinn, No. 4. The grounds have been most tastefully laid out and the interior of the house decorated. Some excellent apparatus has been added and it is proposed to provide modern and up to date single sittings and desks. Miss Florence Cunningham, was the teacher in charge, when most of the improvements were made. The school at Elmsville has been intelligently conducted as usual, the attendance is not large. Clarence Ridge has supported a fair school. It is one of the few districts within my knowledge that has a complete set of registers since the school law. At my request the trustees have had them bound, and a most interesting and instructive volume it is. It was regarded with much interest at our last County Institute. McCallum could not procure a teacher during the summer term, which is to be regretted. The grounds have been improved and fenced. The grounds of Digdeguash Mills have been fenced and the energy of Miss Effie Crawley, the teacher, has supplied some excellent apparatus. Owing to the destruction of the bridge at Salt Water, only half of the children were able to attend school during the summer term.

DUMBARTON.

The school in No. 1 is irregularly supported, and little interest seems to be taken in it. The Trustees are very careless about the surroundings.

The house at Flume Ridge has been painted and a fair school maintained.

Provision has been made for a new house at Whittier Ridge, but up to this time the selection of the site has been an obstacle. I hope that it may not prove so long, as the house is badly needed. Through the efforts of the teacher, Miss Mary Hawkins, the school has been supplied with a fine globe and other apparatus. Sorrell Ridge has supported a school as usual and some slate blackboard has been added to the apparatus. Rolling Dam has maintained the excellent reputation of its school under Miss Florence Downing. One young man from this school successfully passed the preliminary for first class and another came within a mark or two of doing so. The house has been painted and through the efforts of the teacher and others a fence in front has been provided for. Greenock has had a good school and through the exertions of Miss Margaret McNabb, many improvements have been made.

The house at Dumbarton has been repaired, the grounds graded and slate blackboards added. Tryon has made the usual effort to maintain a good school.

ST. DAVID.

The school at Tower Hill has been vigorous and regularly maintained. The school in No. 2 is not well attended. Lever has a good school and much interest is taken by the ratepayers. Through the exertions of Miss Priscilla Reid, many improvements have been made. Not much interest is taken in school matters at Meadows and this spirit in the past has probably had much to do with the disposition of the rising generation to commit depredations upon school and other property. Good schools have been operated at Hill's Point and Oak Bay. The first term was a stormy one at Regan's Corner, but not a ripple has disturbed the excellent work of the second. Some repairs have been made in No. 7, and more are needed. The same may be said of No. 8. Bay Road permits too many entertainments to be held in its house for the good of the premises and apparatus. Miss Waldron, the teacher, while in the district, was most active in promoting its interests.

The school at Moore's Mills continues to furnish an excellent opportunity to those desirous of obtaining advanced education, and it is taken advantage of to such an extent, that probably more students are prepared by it than any o[illegible] school in the County. Many improvements have been made during the [illegible] Mr. H. E. St. Clair retired to accept the Principalship of the St. George s[illegible]ols and was succeeded by Miss Bessie Colwell, A. B.—a most successful t[illegible]ner.

ST. ANDREWS.

The schools in the town are efficiently conducted as usual. The attendance is not as large as formerly. Mr. J. A. Allen, the present principal, is performing his duties with much acceptance to all interested.

The school at Chamcook has been operated for a longer time than usual.

ST CROIX.

Lower Bayside supports a good school, but its house and grounds are not up to the importance of the district. The same may be said of Upper Bayside, but in this district, I think, there is a well defined intention to bring about improvement. Bartlett's Mills has greatly improved the interior of its house, but the furniture is still very poor. It is to be regretted that this district could not secure a teacher for the summer term. Waweig, No. 5, has made many improvements since my last report, new furniture has been purchased, the interior of the house most tastefully decorated and by the exertions of the teacher, Miss Fannie Cunningham, some excellent apparatus has been procured. Orr, has new furniture and the teacher, Miss Mabel Jones, has been able to supply an excellent terrestrial globe. The Rev. Hunter Boyd, the Presbyterian clergyman in this locality, takes a deep and intelligent interest in the welfare of the schools, with excellent results.

DUFFERIN.

Crocker Hill has provided new furniture and apparatus. The house at the Ledge has been repaired and excellent outbuildings erected.

ST. JAMES.

DeWolf has built a new house during the year. It was much needed. The school at Baillie is small, but in good order. The same is true of No. 3½. This district might well unite with either Moore's Mills or Old Ridge. No. 4, Anderson, has had a good school. No. 5, Meredith, has experienced much contention during the year. It has caused me much correspondence and a special visit to the district in the interest of harmony, with somewhat doubtful results. There has been a good school at Lynnfield. Miss Bertha Dewar, the teacher, has provided the district with a fine flag and some apparatus. Oak Hill has awakened from its lethargy. It has painted and repaired its house and built fine outbuildings. Miss Mildred McCann, at Lawrence, as in all other districts, has effected great improvement in her school and appliances. I regret her retirement from the service. Basswood Ridge has a small but excellent school and sends out some good pupils.

The schools at Canous and Beaconsfield are small, but fairly efficient, Pomroy Ridge needs a new house and better furniture. There is a good school on the Scotch Ridge. The grounds at Little Ridgeton have been fenced and a fine standard dictionary has been supplied. There was no school at the Lower Little Ridge owing to the inability of the Trustees to obtain a teacher.

ST. STEPHEN (PARISH).

There is a good school at Mayfield, and the exertions of Miss Blanche Nesbitt, the teacher, have provided it with excellent maps of the Dominion and Hemispheres. There is a small school at Barterville which should unite with Mayfield. Moannes has a small school, well housed and furnished. Upper Mills has painted its house. Heathland has rebuilt and enlarged its house. Blacklands and Old Ridge have had excellent schools. There has been no school during the year at Valley Park. There are few pupils.

GRAND MANAN.

The schools in this parish have all been regularly and satisfactorily operated. The few pupils at the Fog Whistle school have been conveyed to the central school at North Head, thus doing away with the necessity of maintaining a school there.

The Superior department at North Head does not in my opinion do the work, that should fairly be expected. The attendance is irregular and pupils do not remain to enter and complete the work of the higher grades. The High School entrance examinations have not been taken. I think there should be greater enthusiasm and interest created in the work and that more advanced pupils should be graduated.

Much interest is taken in Castalia in the improvement of school grounds, and the house and grounds present a very attractive appearance. The practice of maintaining a graded school during part of the year and an ungraded the remaining part has a confusing affect upon the work.

Woodward's Cove has had a fair school, which has been operated more regularly than formerly. There is a disposition in this district to maintain a better school in the future.

Grand Harbor has been as heretofore, one of my most satisfactory districts. 'ell, costing $90.00 has been dug on the school grounds, which have been fenced and much improved. This district obtained first prize in the competition among the Island districts, for the greatest amount of improvement to school grounds and premises during the year. Mr. J. S. Lord and Miss Minnie Ganong were the teachers during the first term, and Mr. R. L. Carson and Miss Katie Wooster, during the second term.

The schools at Whitehead were in better condition than I have ever seen them previously. Seal Cove has a very large school, and has done satisfactory work. Two Islands and Deep Cove do not operate the whole year, but they make the most of their opportunities.

CAMPOBELLO.

The school at Welshpool is still under the efficient management of Mr. A. W. Hickson, who has become a factor in the community. The grounds are easily the best on the Islands, but as all the improvement was not made in one year, they did not rank for the prizes. In this district, the first experiment in centralization in Canada has been successfully inaugurated. The school at Snug Cove has been closed and the pupils conveyed to the central school at Welshpool.

Wilson's Beach has a very large school, with an irregular attendance. At Head Harbor, the house has been painted and many additions made to apparatus and appliances. Much of this is due to the efforts of the teacher, Mrs Myra Lank.

WEST ISLES.

Indian Island has a small school which is kept open only part of the year. The pupils in this district, considering their opportunities, display more than ordinary capacity. Chocolate Cove has had a good school throughout the year. Considerable improvement has been made in the surroundings. Leonardville has had a good school. Miss Ella M. Hay has been most painstaking in her efforts to improve the grounds, and a good fence has been built. The house has also been painted. This district has naturally the best school grounds on the Island. Richardson and Lord's Cove support excellent schools. In both districts many improvements have been made. Lambert Town has added some good apparatus. The house at Lambert's Cove has been enlarged and painted and through the exertions of the teacher, Mr. B. W. Robertson, a fine bookcase has been provided and a good beginning made toward a library.

Fair Haven surpassed all the other districts on the Island in improvement made during the year in school grounds and premises. The initiative in t s was largely due to the teacher, Mr. Louis H. Baldwin.

The school at Northern Harbor was closed at the time of my visit, owing to the illness of the teacher. Bean's Island had a school during the second term.

ST. STEPHEN.

The most notable step in advance in the St. Stephen schools, made recently, has been the introduction of water and sewerage into all the school buildings. I had expected from the sentiment which seemed to prevail in the town a year or two ago, that before this, modern business training would have been introduced into the schools as a substitute for Latin and Greek—nothing has as yet been done in that direction, though I think it has not been lost sight of.

MILLTOWN.

The schools in this town have maintained their usual high standard and regularity of attendance. Much interest is taken in them by trustees and citizens and this is reflected in the work of the teachers. It was my privilege to attend the graduating exercises there in June. They were held in the new and commodious Presbyterian church which was filled by the people of the town on one very warm June afternoon. For enthusiasm, and elaborate detail, I have never seen their closing exercises surpassed.

The enrolment in some of the lower grade rooms was much too large at the time of my visits in April last.

ST. JOHN COUNTY.

MUSQUASH.—Prince of Wales has had a fair school. The Village of Musquash has been the first district in my territory to give encouragement to manual training and at the beginning of next term, Miss Agnes Lucas, the teacher, expects to be equipped with three benches. Chance Harbour maintains an excellent school as usual and it is well equipped in all respects, a library, globe, chemical apparatus and flag have been added by the teachers, Misses McAfee, Norrad and MacVicar. Dipper Harbour house has been improved in appearance and some apparatus provided.

LANCASTER.—Both districts at Pisarinco have large attendance and employ first class teachers. Flags have been presented to both by lodges in the place. No. 12 has added to its apparatus and No. 11 has added a class room and been painted.

:. W. F. Burns has conducted an excellent school at Mahogany. A fi q and pole have been provided and the house has been painted. All regret the resignation of Mr. Burns. Green Head has a well equipped school. Slate blackboards have been added. South Bay and Sutton maintain good schools – the house in the latter needs painting. Beaconsfield has a well equipped school of two departments. The attendance at these departments does not represent the strength of the district as about half of the pupils attend the St. John city schools. The schools in Fairville and Millford are in good order. A new department is required in Fairville and the resources of Milford have been seriously crippled by the burning of two large mills. Mr. J. F. Worrell has retired from the principalship of the Fairville school to the regret of all interested.

SIMONDS.—The schools at Coldbrook, Brookville and the Nail Factory are not as vigorous as they should be. The burning of the Rolling Mills has been a serious loss to them all. It seems curious that in those districts near a large town the same interest in good schools does not exist as in those further removed. The example of the town should prove contagious, but the reverse is the case.

Golden Grove has made decided improvement. The schools at Little River, Red Head and Mispec have been repaired and painted. Silver Falls has repaired its house, put in hard wood floors and the teacher, Miss Ella M. Wetmore, has provided a handsome flag and pole. The flag was raised for the first time on Empire Day. Lakewood has repaired and painted its house This school and those at Coldbrook and Red Head were closed for a time on account of small-pox and the attendance in most of the schools in this parish was affected by the same cause. Loch Lomond has painted its house and Miss Miller has had the grounds fenced at Willow Grove, and made other improvements. Garnet needs a better house. The houses at Black River and Gardiners Creek have been painted. Grove Hill and Otter Lake could not secure teachers for part of the year and Upper Loch Lomond is closed partly owing to small attendance and partly to lack of interest.

ST. MARTINS.—Bain's Corner, through the exertions of the teacher, Miss Katie McPartland, has had its fine grounds fenced. All in the district have willingly assisted and next year it is hoped that some experimental gardening will be done. The house has also been painted. Miss McPartland has left her impress in the way of improvement upon every district in which she has been engaged. In conjunction with Miss Hannah Floyd, teacher, at Fairfield—another progressive district,—a united school concert was given, by which $42 was raised. The proceeds have been divided and are to be devoted toward a school library in each district.

Shanklin needs a better house. Some new furniture has been provided. A teacher could not be procured for the second term.

The schools at Hanford Brook and Hardingville are small. The death of Mr. John Kirkpatrick, who as trustee and secretary in the latter district, ever took an intelligent interest in the school, is much regretted. The school at Wood Lake is closed—the majority of the pupils attending school at the Mountain Miss Mary F. Cremor, the secretary, continues to take a deep interest in the well-being of No. 30 and the house and surroundings are very attractive. The houses at Quaco East, Greer and Salmon River have been painted or improved in other ways.

Something has been done in the way of improvement to the Quaco schools and more is required. Mr. W. L. McDiarmid bids fair to prove a worthy successor to Mr. George J. Trueman. but the work in the advanced department requires an assistant.

City of St. John.—Space will not permit me to give a detailed report of all that has been done in St. John city. The Board has been very active in all that pertains to externals and some very fine buildings have been erected. I have already reported upon the Aberdeen, Alexandra and High School buildings. I have pleasure in reporting another this year, viz: the La Tour, which is located on the West Side and will soon be ready for occupation. I have not visited it recently, but I am informed that it is fully the equal of any of its predecessors. I had hoped this year to be able to report progress in the way of a building to replace the old Madras and I think some steps have been taken in that direction. If one wished to contrast the surroundings of fifty years ago with those of to-day in regard to schools, he would find it suggestive to visit the Madras and the Alexandra schools. I am glad to be able to report that the Douglas Avenue building has been connected with the sewerage system of the city during the year. I think in a city of the importance of St. John, employing 150 teachers, that there should be some organization among them for the purpose of mutual assistance and improvement. Nearly every other profession or trade has such an organization, which gives it strength and standing in the community. In many cities, during the winter, a course of excellent professional lectures is established and supported by the teachers. In St. John the teachers seldom or never meet for any purpose, and are hardly acquainted with each other. Trustees and parents should also take more frequent opportunities of meeting with teachers. It would be a good plan and a profitable the city, if, in two or three of the fine new buildings, a room were set each for a library, reading room and place of meeting for the teachers of that section of the city. I believe if the teachers should ask for this, the request would receive favorable consideration at the hands of the Board.

Time did not permit me to visit the High Schools in St. John during the year.

KINGS COUNTY.

WESTFIELD.—Westfield Beach has painted its house and made other improvements. Public Landing has painted also and built new outbuildings. DeVeber has added to its appointments. Cheyne has been running smoothly.

On the eastern side of the river, Carter's Point, Land's End and Bayswater have had their houses painted, and Sea Dog Cove has made considerable improvement.

GREENWICH.—Considerable very necessary improvements have been made to the house at Upper Greenwich. New furniture has been supplied and many other improvements and repairs have been made at Brown's Flats. In this district and that at Round Hill, teachers could not be procured until late in the second term.

TEACHERS.—Teachers have been very scarce in my district during the year. A few local licenses were issued, but even then ten or a dozen schools could not obtain teachers. The outlook for an increased supply very soon is not bright. Times have been fairly good and the demand for workers in business offices and hospitals has attracted many of our teachers. The higher standard of qualification required necessitates preparation for Normal School at a distance from home in many cases, so that it is becoming more expensive to train for teaching, and fewer are turning their attention in that direction. The only remedy for this is the payment of higher salaries locally and the scarcity is already bringing this about in some degree. In the whole province, there are only three men in the educational service, who are drawing salaries of $2,000 or upwards—an amount that would be considered very moderate by any other successful professional man, and entirely insignificant by those on the highest rungs of the ladder, which is the place of these three in the educational service. Yet in education training and ability, as much, if not more is required of teachers than in any other walk in life. In the face of this it is not surprising that young men and women are not attracted toward teaching, or having entered upon it, do not remain long in the service.

THE SCHOOL DISTRICT.—While I have been able to indicate some of the improvements made in the different districts I have not done so by any means fully. I can only say that as usual my district is indebted for much to the initiative of a very energetic and progressive staff of teachers, who spare no effort to promote the interests of the schools.

There has been the usual crop of difficulties to adjust, but with the exception of the two elsewhere mentioned all have been arranged. It will take a little time to define the exact amount of property belonging to each district under the new plan of assessment.

FORWARD STEPS.—I regard the successful experiment of the Trustees of Walshpool, Campobello, in conveying the pupils from Snug Cove to the central school as a decided step in advance and a useful object lesson for the future. The cost has been little more than half that of supporting the separate school, and in a letter I had from Secretary Mitchell a few days ago, he stated that the plan was giving the utmost satisfaction. The names of the trustees in this district are: J. F. Calder, Silas Mitchell and L. P. Simpson. The teachers are: A. W. Hickson and Miss Mary Mitchell.

If we can combine the advantages of the graded school with the environment of the country district a great good will have been brought about.

It was my privilege to spend a month of the summer vacation as a pupil of the Manual Training School, under the excellent principalship of Mr. E. E. MacCready, and I do not think I have ever derived more profit and pleasure in the same time than from my attendance at this summer school.

There was a large and very attentive and diligent class. The feature that interested me most was a class consisting of fifteen boys from the public schools. Not one of these boys dropped out during the month, though their attendance was purely voluntary. Their hours of work were supposed to be short, but some of them were present early and late, and in attention and interest they were an example to us all. It seems to me that the training of the hands must in the future go along with that of the head, and that this kind of work must become a feature in our education. If we can gain the same, if not better, results in education along utilitarian lines, by all means let us do so. While the St. John authorities did not show as much interest in the work of the school as might have been expected, the general public and the press gave evidence of their hearty approval. It is to be hoped that the school may come to St. John again next summer.

From my observation of her excellent work at this school, I was able to assist the Trustees of Musquash to secure the services of Miss Agnes Lucas. She has awakened such an interest in the district, that with the assistance of Surveyor General Dunn, she will be able to have equipped three benches for work at the beginning of next year. These benches have been contributed by

Prof. Robertson, at the request of Principal MacCready, who has taken a deep interest in the work at Musquash.

The prizes given by Mr. F. A. Holmes, a former teacher, for the greatest amount of improvement during the year, made by schools in the Island Parishes of Charlotte, were won by Grand Harbour and Fair Haven. There was considerable competition, and Mr. Holmes has offered to repeat the prizes of $10 and $5 the coming year. I would be glad to see his example imitated.

COUNTY INSTITUTES.—No County Institute was held in St. John during the year, as there seemed to be sufficient reasons for postponing it.

In Charlotte, it was held in St. Stephen. The enrolment was 117 teachers. There were in addition many former teachers, school officers and parents The meeting was of great practical value. The discussion on "Home Lessons" which followed a very bright and sensible paper written by Mrs. Samuel Johnston, a talented lay woman of St. George, was especially animated and suggestive. Mrs. Irving R. Todd, one of the Trustees of Milltown, presided with tact and dignity.

It has been determined to hold the next session of the Summer School of Science in St. Stephen. It will without doubt be a large and notable gathering and I hope that all my teachers will endeavor to be present at its meetings, as such an opportunity is not likely to present itself again soon, so near their own homes.

Respectfully submitted,

W. S. CARTER.

INSPECTORAL DISTRICT NO. 5.

H. V. B. Bridges, A. M., Fredericton, N. B., Inspector.

THE DISTRICT EMBRACES THE COUNTY OF YORK, EXCEPT THE PARISHES OF CANTERBURY AND NORTH LAKE, THE COUNTY OF SUNBURY, AND THE PARISHES OF CANNING, GAGETOWN, HAMPSTEAD AND PETERSVILLE IN QUEENS COUNTY.

J. R. INCH, ESQ., M. A., LL. D.,
Chief Supt. of Education,
Fredericton, N. B.

I beg leave to submit my Report of the condition of the Public Schools in my Inspectoral District for the twelve months ending 31st Dec., 1901.

In my last Annual Report I made mention of the fact that the supply of teachers was not equal to the demand on the part of District School Boards. I am sorry to say that the present condition of affairs in that respect is not improved, as I have had occasion to recommend several candidates for local licenses in the Counties of Sunbury and York. These teachers in the majority of instances were in possession of an expired 3rd Class License, or had passed the Normal School Entrance Examination, and I am glad to report that they were doing good work. I have found, also, that the number of pupils in preparation at school for the Normal School Entrance Examination is still diminishing and it is not probable that there will be as many candidates presenting themselves for examination in 1902 as in the past, in this Inspectoral District.

New school buildings have been completed and school opened in them in five School Districts, viz: No. 9 Petersville, No. 4 Lincoln, No. 9 Manners Sutton, No. 5 Northfield, and No. 6 Gladstone.

These School Districts are all of low valuation, but the houses erected are very creditable, and fully adapted to the needs of the district.

The building in No. 9 Petersville, is one of the very best school houses in Queens County. and is furnished with slate black boards. Much credit is due Mr. J. A. Fowler, the Secretary of the Board of School Trustees in this district, for the active interest he has displayed in providing the children of the district ...h such a building. The house in No. 4 Lincoln, is also worthy of special ...ntion.

The house in Stanley Village has been remodelled to permit the operation ...wo departments.

A new school house has also been erected at Morrison's Mills, by the Board of School Trustees of the City of Fredericton, in place of the one which was destroyed by fire.

The usual amount of repairing, painting, etc., has taken place during the year, and in many districts through the vote of the ratepayers at the Annual School Meeting there has been expressed the intention of doing something in this direction another year. It takes a good deal of repairing, painting, and improvement, too, in apparatus, to keep pace with the ordinary wear and tear of the school room, and the defacement of the weather.

The improvement in school apparatus has been made largely through the exertions of teachers in getting up entertainments of which I have several times before had cause to report upon.

Modern up-to-date maps of the Dominion of Canada are being provided in many districts as well as maps of the British Empire.

CITY OF FREDERICTON.—The usual state of efficiency has been maintained by the departments of the schools in this city. The principals of the different schools are very enthusiastic in their work, and spare no pains in the discharge of their duties, and the teachers in the elementary grades cannot easily be surpassed in the excellent character of their work in teaching.

The High School under the same teaching staff as I have before reported upon, has again shown the excellent character of the work done by the very high standard which the pupils attained in the University Matriculation Examination.

Miss Mary Phillips was compelled during the year to resign, owing to ill health, and spend the winter elsewhere. Her position in the Model School has been filled by Miss Nicolson who had been teaching the same grades in the Charlotte Street School, Miss Nicolson's position being filled by Miss Annie Taylor, B. A., of the Keswick Ridge Superior School.

GAGETOWN.—Mr. D. L. Mitchell, B. A., has remained in charge of the Grammar School here. Several pupils from this school passed the University Matriculation and others the Normal School entrance in June last.

SUPERIOR SCHOOLS.

MARYSVILLE.—No change has been made in the teaching staff in the different departments of this school. The buildings still remain in much the same condition, and one cannot but hope that in the near future a handsome brick building will replace the several wooden structures now in use. The fine large play-ground is one of the features of this school.

ST. MARY'S AND GIBSON.—Mr. J. DeLong resigned his position as principal in June last, to pursue his college course. The position was filled by the appointment of Mr. A. H. Barker of the Fredericton Junction Superior School. Both of the teachers are earnest workers and the school has been under good discipline. Owing to the case of smallpox in St. Mary's, all the departments remained closed the last three weeks of the Term.

HARVEY STATION.—Mr. Clive McCann has conducted the advance department during the year to the satisfaction of the ratepayers. It is to be regretted that the number of pupils enrolled in this Superior School is not increasing. The Primary department has been successfuly conducted by Miss Emily Hunter.

KESWICK RIDGE. — Mr. Coburn Jewett resigned his position last January, to accept a position at Sudbury in railroad construction. Miss Annie Taylor, B. A., was then placed in charge till November last, when she took charge of a department in the Charlotte Street School. The school is now in charge of Mr. Harry Fraser, a successful teacher, who it is to be hoped will remain in the position for some length of time. There have been upwards of ten teachers in charge of this Superior School in the last six years, notwithstanding the desire of the Trustees to obtain a teacher who might remain in charge for some years.

MCADAM.—Mr. Perkins still remains in charge, there being an Intermediate and a Primary department. A great improvement has been made in the past few years in the educational advantages afforded the children of McAdam.

FREDERICTON JUNCTION.—This is the only graded school in the County of Sunbury. Mr. A. H. Barker under whose control the school made substantial progress, resigned in June last to accept the St. Mary's and Gibson Superior School. His place has been filled by the appointment of Mr. H. H. Bridges, B. A.

STANLEY VILLAGE.—This school though not a Superior School, has been under the principalship of Mr. Clarence Sansom who has been untiring in his efforts to raise the tone of the school, and who has been very successful in this respect. It is to be hoped that before long this department will receive the advantage of the Superior School grant.

THE DISTRICT SCHOOL.

I know of no organized school district in this Inspectoral district where a ' was not maintained at least part of the year, and the troubles incident to the carrying on of the business of the school district have been of a very minor character. The teachers themselves in their daily work are doing the best they know, at least in the majority of instances, and employ the best means they have at hand to assist them in their school work. I think that anybody who saw the large gathering of teachers in Fredericton, last September, must have been pleased with their intelligent appearance, and the keen attention displayed by them at the Institute. The teachers in the district school are in many ways somewhat isolated and it is hardly necessary to add need the hearty co-operation of Trustees and ratepayers in this work, and it is important for the teachers to realize at the start that such co-operation depends largely on the confidence which they are able to inspire in the parents as well as children.

That the intelligent teacher in many instances does not receive this co-operation in a number of our district schools has been painfully impressed upon me frequently, and popular approval cannot be accepted, in the case of teaching, as evidence of genuine merit and success. It is too common, among parents, thoughtlessly to question the wisdom, even the competency of teachers, in the presence of their children and this frequently leads to misconduct and impairs the children's interest and progress in the work of the school.

There is also a growing tendency on the part of some parents in the school district towards an assumption of control, at least, of some of the rights and duties of teachers, particularly where the teacher is young and inexperienced. Teachers are told authoritatively by parents that they *don't* want their children given home lessons, that they *don't* want them to study History, Nature Lessons, Health Reader Lessons, etc., as the case may be, and for this reason there often ensues a sacrifice of efficiency and progress. The teachers, too, are left to the alternative of exercising questioned authority, of permitting the efficiency of the school to be sacrificed, or of procuring another situation.

For such reasons I think we should welcome any movement towards the intelligent co-operation of parents and teachers, and anything that tends, on the part of the parent, towards generously recognizing the authority in the teacher which is requisite for efficient work in the schools.

That the teacher should possess requisite qualifications is of course a necessary condition of success, and there will be greater progress when this condition inspires confidence and hearty co-operation on the part of the parents and Trustees. And yet notwithstanding the many influences which retard progress in the district school, and limit its effiiciency, and the many criticisms that are passed upon it, we must not forget that in these very schools a large proportion of our teachers receive their preparation for Normal School, and attain a standard of proficiency at the entrance examination which compares favorably with that of those prepared in our best graded schools.

SCHOOL VENTILATION.

Complaints have frequently been made to me concerning teachers opening doors and windows for purposes of ventilation during the winter months. It is unfortunate that in the large majority of district school houses there is no other means of ventilating the school room except by the doors and windows, and there is not much to suggest that might afford any relief to teacher and pupils in this connection. I think, however, that competent health authorities are a unit in considering that the open window is doing more harm in our schools than impure air. As one physician aptly expresses it:—"Teachers must not forget though foul air is a slow poison a blast of cold air may slay like a sword." Only a few suggestions can be made toward lessening the evils which attend this method of ventilation. Not to lower the windows on the side from which the wind is blowing, that it is better to open several windows a little than one window wide, to lower windows from the top than raise from the bottom, and if the window must be raised that it is better to have a close fitting board to put under it and allow the air to come in between the sashes, are about all the suggestions the best authorities can make.

THE TEACHING OF THE SUBJECTS OF THE COURSE OF STUDY.

Undoubtedly the quality of the teaching varies in different schools owing to the energy, experience and character of the teachers, but I feel confident that the course is being taken up conscientiously by the large body of teachers and that there is real improvement in the way subjects are presented to the mind of the child. There is certainly more appreciation of the degree of excellence which can be attained by the child in the first steps in Reading and Arithmetic, and in the character of the slatework. And I think experience teaches us that in teaching if a good start has been made, and a proper foundation laid in the elements, the road is thereafter much easier.

COMPOSITION.—More attention is being paid to oral expression as well as written expression of thought, and as a result written work is more easily and naturally performed. Nature lessons, History and Geography are all used in ...ng this subject, and less formal exercises given.

...AMMAR.—I cannot say that much improvement is being made. There ...oo much formal work, and not enough of the practical and incidental.

WRITING.—Some confusion seems to exist owing to the options of copy books, and there does not seem to be enough teaching. The pupil is left to himself too much for improvement.

SPELLING.—I find considerable improvement, particularly in written work.

NATURE LESSONS.—I have noticed, in a number of schools a diary, so to speak, of the observation, of the pupils and teacher with respect to the finding, or seeing, the first plants, birds, etc., and it has seemed to me an admirable way of exciting an interest in this work.

GEOGRAPHY.—Pupils are well drilled at least in this subject, and much of the map drawing is really very good.

DRAWING.—But little object drawing, and yet I have seen some very good work.

SINGING.—Ordinary rote-singing is taken up largely in our district schools; the character of the singing is not always good, but it is usually entered into with spirit and some times one is struck with the clear ringing tones of little children, and it is a pity their advantages are not greater. As an aid in developing the moral tone of a school singing is unequalled.

HISTORY.—The introduction of the new text book will supply to many teachers what they have long felt a necessity.

TEACHERS' INSTITUTES.

The Teachers' Institute for the County of York convened in the Assembly Hall of the High School building, on the 19th September. There were present one hundred and thirty teachers. The Executive Committee of the Queens and Sunbury Co. Institute having experienced grave difficulties in preparing a suitable program, the teachers of these counties were able, through your permission, to attend the sessions of this Institute, and about sixty took advantage of the opportunity.

I do not remember having attended a County Institute where the papers read were of greater practical interest and where the discussions that followed were more animated. The admirable attention given by so large a body of teachers contributed not a little in this respect. The address of the Rev. Wm. Ross, B. A., of Prince William, on the Duties of Parents and Trustees, was very highly appreciated. The concluding session was held in the new Assembly Hall of the University of New Brunswick, through the kind invitation of Chancellor Harrison, and the Museum and new Science Building were opened to the members of the Institute before and after the session.

At a separate meeting of the teachers of Sunbury and Queens the feel of the teachers seemed unanimous in favor of attending County Institutes in Fredericton, as it seems impossible to find a place in either county where the large majority of teachers can assemble without overcoming many difficulties of travel.

ARBOR DAY.

The day was celebrated in the usual manner by a large number of schools. The observance of Arbor Day in recent years has done much to awaken an interest in the planting of trees and shubbery in school grounds, but it is a matter of regret that an interest has not also been awakened in the minds of parents and children to care for and protect these trees and shrubs after they have been planted.

The school house and its surroundings, however, cannot be expected to represent more than the average taste and comfort of the community, and where there is not neatness, taste, and some comfort displayed in the home surroundings of the pupil, the teacher will continue to experience grave difficulties in obtaining proper assistance in celebrating Arbor Day, and protecting the trees and shrubs from the youthful vandals who have but recently been removed from the sphere of the school room. The influence of this day is being seen in many home surroundings. One can only hope that its influence in this direction will rapidly increase.

Much satisfaction is being expressed in many districts of low valuation at the change in the School Act which compels all the real estate situated in a school district to pay taxes in that district.

There are several districts in the Counties of Queens and Sunbury where the number of children of school age falls below that required by law. As the majority of these districts are isolated it would seem a hardship to close their schools particularly as they are endeavouring to comply with the regulation with respect to the average attendance. Indeed the recent change in the Schools Act has made a marked improvement in the average attendance in districts where the enrollment is small.

I have the honor to be, Sir,

Your obedient servant,

HEDLEY V. B. BRIDGES.

INSPECTORAL DISTRICT, NO. 6.

F. B. Meagher, M. A., Woodstock, Carleton Co. Inspector.

THE DISTRICT EMBRACES THE COUNTIES OF CARLETON, VICTORIA AND MADAWASKA, AND THE PARISHES OF CANTERBURY AND NORTH LAKE IN YORK COUNTY.

J. R. INCH, ESQ., LL. D.,
Chief Supt. of Education,
Fredericton, N. B.

SIR:—I beg leave to submit the following Report for the School Terms ended June 30th, and December 31st, 1901:—

Last Term the supply of teachers in my district was not quite equal to the demand. It necessitated the issue of one local license in Carleton County, a thing which has been unheard of in that County for some years past—one in the Parish of Canterbury, and four in the County of Victoria, besides creating some difficulty and embarrassment in other ways. The causes of this scarcity of teachers need not be here discussed, but I trust that no such trouble will arise this year.

THE SCHOOL DISTRICT.

Very few changes were made during the year in the established boundaries of school districts in this Inspectorate. Portions were taken from Nos. 2 and 3 St. Francis, so as to permit of the formation of a new district, No. 2½ opposite Kennedy's Island. A house was erected during the summer holidays in which a school was operated last term. A new district was established in New Denmark, south, which will be a great advantage to a number of people whose isolated position had previously excluded them from school privileges.

A special meeting was recently held in Glassville at which it was resolved to build a house with rooms for two departments near the upper end of the district, where the majority of the people reside, and to hire a conveyance to bring the children from the lower end of the district to and from school. This is the first attempt that has yet been made in my Inspectorate to take advantage of the provisions of Sec. 57 of the Act. No move whatever has been made in the way of combining districts under that section, and yet it is the only way in which the problem of the small country district with its many unsatisfactory features, can ever be satisfactorily solved. It is of course doi good in its way, but if we wish to arrive at better results, we must aim s consolidation, for the best work cannot be done in schools with an average attendance of eight or nine pupils. It is true that in remote and isolated localities such a school is frequently a necessity, but in contiguous districts in a country where good roads abound and where the schools are only two or three miles apart, the reason for its existence has passed away, and it must ultimately give place to the central graded school, where the educational forces at our disposal can be more intelligently and effectively applied.

THE CONSTRUCTION AND VENTILATION OF SCHOOL HOUSES.

The directions in Remark 4, Reg. 7, of the new School Manual in reference to the arrangement and position of windows in school rooms are producing good results. Two handsome and up-to-date houses have been erected in Knoxford and River Bank, in which these directions have been carefully followed, and the pupils there will no longer be obliged to sit between strong cross lights, which are so injurious to the sight. It is here that the average trustee regards the absence of windows in the right side wall of the room and in the rear of the teacher's platform as an unsightly and useless innovation, but its advantages — not only in the saving of wall space, but in the health and comfort of the pupils — are so obvious that this prejudice must be overcome, and the directions referred to be carried out in all districts where new houses are to be erected.

Some reform too is needed in respect to the ventilation of school rooms. Regulation 8, recommends that "in a matter of such vital importance it is better, when practicable, to obtain the services of an experienced architect to provide a plan for a system of heating and ventilation adapted to the size and location of the building, and to the special conditions to be met"; but this is seldom done, and where no such system is provided, the teacher absorbed in his duties is often apt not to notice that the air of the room through lack of ventilation, particularly in the winter, has become vitiated, and no longer fit to breathe. No matter how pressing his other duties may be, the teacher should never neglect the all important one of causing the air in the room to be renewed at frequent intervals during the day, for it is useless to try to create a sound mind in a sound body in an unhealthy atmosphere. Some of the means at the ...er's disposal for securing good ventilation are specified in Reg. 8, a careful ...al of which is recommended to all concerned. The attention of trustees ...thers interested is also called to Regulation 5, in which the minimum ...er of cubic feet of air to be allowed for each sitting provided has been changed from one hundred and fifty to two hundred, and it is even recommended that two hundred and fifty cubic feet of air be provided for each sitting.

THE COURSE OF INSTRUCTION.

READING. — In some districts the teacher's success is to a large extent guaged by the rapidity with which the pupils are advanced from one reader to another, irrespective of their fitness for being thus advanced, or of their other attainments; and though a child who should be in the Second Reader may be stumbling helplessly along in the Third, nothing but praise is bestowed on the teacher who is responsible for this state of affairs. Very few teachers embrace this opportunity of earning a temporary reputation for efficiency, but now and then it is done — particularly during the last term of an engagement in a district — not only to the great detriment of the pupils directly concerned, but to that of the succeeding teacher, who being thus obliged to set the children back in their proper places is apt to incur the ill-will of their parents for so doing, and is otherwise seriously handicapped in his work. Some teachers, too, are not thorough in connection with the reading lesson. There are different degrees of this fault, but when, on visiting a school, one examines a class on the lesson of the preceding day, and finds that the pupils cannot explain the thought of certain passages, or give clearly the meanings of the difficult words, no further evidence is needed of careless and ineffective teaching. And here I might add that every school should be provided with a good dictionary, which the pupils should be constantly encouraged to consult, so that they may be trained to correct habits in using it and referring to it for information.

NATURE LESSONS. — There seems to be a general awakening in reference to the value of Nature Study, and the necessity of giving it more earnest attention. Chiefly through the efforts of the teachers a large number of schools have been provided with natural history cabinets, chemical apparatus, etc., and, judging from present indications, the number will be greatly increased this year. The subject was discussed at the last meeting of the Carleton County Institute, and its practical side dwelt upon at some length. School gardens were referred to, and the object lessons that may be thus afforded the pupils in the study of plants, and the requisites of the soil for plant growth; but, apart from any other consideration, the love of nature that is begotten in the pupils by these studies rightly pursued may do much to check that discontent with their environments and distaste for farm life, which are driving so many from their homes in the country to take up occupations that are frequently unremunerative in the large populous centres. Viewed from both these standpoints the following remarks made on this subject by a high educational authority are worthy of attention: "Our school grounds should be enlarged. They should furnish the opportunity for planting trees and shrubs; for the planting of seeds and growing of flowers; for having a nicely kept lawn, and in time these things with their influences would extend to the homes of children who do not have them, and bring with them those attractions and interest that make a home what it ought to be, pleasant and inviting in its surroundings.

OTHER SUBJECTS.—Lack of space forbids me from here taking up in detail, Geography, History, Grammar and other subjects in the course of instruction The remarks made in my last annual report concerning their mode of treatment are in the main still applicable. More teachers are systematically taking up parsing in connection with the reading lessons and better results are consequently being obtained in Grammar, but there is still great room for improvement. More map drill is needed in Geography. It is to be hoped that the new text-book will give a decided impetus to the study of Canadian History. Something is needed to stimulate the flagging interest of both pupils and teachers in this subject.

LIST OF IMPROVEMENTS FOR THE YEAR, 1901.

Avondale—Schoolroom wainscotted.
Ashland—Minerals and chemical apparatus.
Arthurette—Map of British Empire.
Baker Brook—Schoolroom wainscotted and ceiled.
Benton Ridge—Flag.
Beaconsfield—Teacher's desk,
Blue Bell—Map of Dominion.
Bristol—Primary room wainscotted and ceiled, blackboards slateed.
Bloomfield—Flag.
Benton—Room wainscotted and ceiled.
Bedell Settlement—Map of Maritime Provinces, repairs.
Bon Accord—Map of Dominion.
Black Rock—Map of Dominion.
Bath—Room wainscotted and ceiled.
Borden (No. 15 K. & P.)—New blackboard (hyloplate).
ntreville—Map of Dominion and Map of the World.
arview—Flag.
low—Map of Dominion.

Canterbury Station—House painted.
Digby—Room wainscotted, and other improvements.
Everett—Map of Maritime Brovinces, Map of British Empire, and flag.
East Elorenceville—Room wainscotted.
Fifth Tier (No. 8, St. Basil)—New schoolhouse.
Foley Brook—Map of Dominion, and Map of World.
Ferryville—Flag, Map of British Empire.
Green River Settlement—Map of Dominion.
Grand Falls—House enlarged and painted.
Gould Settlement, (No. 13½, North Lake)—New schoolhouse.
Gillespie—Map of Dominion, and blackboard (hyloplate).
Greenville—Flag.
Greenfield—Map of Dominion, and blackboards (hyloplate).
Gregg Settlement—Map of World.
Green Mountain—Flag and Terrestrial Globe.
Hillandale—Map of Dominion and Natural History cabinet.
Hartford—Room wainscotted and ceiled, new furniture.
Hartland—Minerals and book, amount in all to $32.
Hayward—New blackboard (hyloplate).
Houlton Road—New outhouses.
Havelock—Room wainscotted, and other improvements.
Innishone (No. 8½)—Maps of Dominion and Maritime Provinces.
Kirkland—Dictionary.
Kilburn—Maps of World, Dominion, British Empire and Mar. Provinces.
Knowlton—House repaired.
Lower Wakefield—Map of Maritime Provinces.
Lower Brighton—Map of Maritime Provinces.
Lower Jacksontown—Room wainscotted.
Lindsay—Flag.
Limestone—Minerals, chemical apparatus and flag.
McKenzie Corner—House painted.
Munquart—House repaired and painted.
Mineral—New blackboad (slate).
Maxwell Settlement—Minerals and chemical apparatus.
North View—New desks, blackboard.
New Denmaak (No. 1)—New furniture.
Northfield—Flag.
Northampton (No. 3)—House painted.

New Denmark (No. 2)—New maps and blackboards.
Oakville—Flag.
Plymouth—New blackboard, flag.
Pioneer—Room wainscotted and other improvements.
Perth Valley—Room wainscotted, maps of Dominion and British Empire.
Pembroke—Maps of Dominion and Maritime Provinces; also minerals and chemical apparatus.
Peel Station—Room wainscotted and ceiled, new outhouses.
Portage, (No. 11, St. Francis).—House painted.
River de Chute.—Flag, map of Dominion, blackboard (hyloplate.)
Red Bridge.—Flag.
Riley Brook.—Maps of Dominion and British Empire.
Richmond Corner.—Blackboards, (hyloplate.)
Rockway (4½ St. Basil.)—New school house.
Salmon River Mills.—Maps of British Empire and New Brunswick, other apparatus, blinds, etc., amounting in all to $32.25.
Speerville.—Flag, blinds.
Somerfield.—Maps of Dominion and of Maritime Provinces.
South Knowlesville.—Dictionary, blinds, and room wainscotted.
Sisson Ridge.—New school house.
South Wakefield.—Room wainscotted, map of Maritime Provinces.
Union Corner.—Flag.
Upper Woodstock —Standard dictionary.
" Royalton.—Flag.
" Knoxford.—Blackboard, (hyloplate.)
" Waterville.—Flag.
" Brighton.—Map of Maritime Provinces.
Watson Settlement—Map of British Empire.
Windsor (No. 12, Brighton)—Map of Maritime Provinces.
Windsor (No. 8, Brighton)—Map of Maritime Provinces.
Weston—Flag.
Woodstock (F. A. Goods' Dept)—Minerals, Natural History cabinet.
Wakefield Centre—Flag.

The names of those teachers through whose instrumentality many of these ..ements have been effected are as follows: Leon H. Jewett, Maggie L. Carey Shaw, Ina Semple, Caroline M. Blake, Annie McIntyre, Murray anuel, W. M. Crawford, Nora McIntyre, Katie Dalling, Florence ..llen, Delbert Jones, Maud Hartley, Nettie Hand, Bessie M. Fraser,

Mrs. J. R. H. Simms, Theresa Jamieson, Annie Palmer, Jennie M. Kennedy, Irene Campbell, Charles F. Boone, Alice M. Everett, Joseph Howe, Idella M. Black, F. A. Good, Bessie M. Taylor, Agnes G. O'Brien.

There are, no doubt, many unintentional omissions in this list, which for obvious reasons cannot be a complete one; but this recognition, imperfect though it may be, is only due to those through whose enthusiasm and untiring efforts needed appliances are being procured, and the school environments made more pleasant and attractive.

MISCELLANEOUS NOTES.

The house at Grand Falls has been enlarged in order to make room for another primary department which was operated last term under the charge of Miss Maud Waldron.

The house in Mainstream has been destroyed by fire. Another building will be erected in the spring.

As soon as possible thorough repairs will be made on the houses in Rosedale and Coldstream No. 7. A new house will be erected in Mount Pleasant.

Repairs are greatly needed on the house in Brookville. A new building should be erected in Carrol Ridge.

Miss Ruth Reid, formerly Principal of the graded school at Lakeville, is now in charge of the Superior School at Centreville. Mr. Hamilton has succeeded Mr. Ross at Florenceville, and Mr. Allen, Mr. Fraser at Benton.

In the Andover Grammar School, Mr. Veazey has succeeded Mr. Shea and Miss Baxter has retired from the Primary department to study Sloyd work in the Truro Normal School. Both teachers were popular and will be greatly missed.

Sloyd Work is still being successfully conducted at Inches' Ridge, by Miss O'Brien. This work is exerting a decidedly good influence in that district, not only in causing the pupils to remain longer at school, but in stimulating them to greater zeal in their ordinary studies.

The proceeds of a school picnic have placed the sum of thirty-four dollars at Miss O'Brien's disposal, with which some needed improvements will be made.

The proceeds of a concert, $11.00, in Farmerston, will enable the teacher Miss Bessie Taylor, to procure maps for the school in that district.

Miss Barker (now Mrs. Rideout) and Miss McNally, who did effective work in the Hartland schools have been succeeded in their respective departments by Miss Page and Miss Howe.

ARBOR DAY.

Arbor Day was observed by the usual number of districts during the year just closed. Undoubtedly the observance of the Day is doing good in the way of the improvement of school premises, but the results on the whole are not so appreciable as might be desired. Countless trees and shrubs have been planted which have come to naught, and in this way much time and labor are being yearly expended to no purpose. The trouble is that trustees and ratepayers generally are not interested enough in the matter to give the teacher any active assistance in his Arbor Day work. As soon as this is forthcoming, something more permanent will certainly be accomplished in the way of tree culture, and the improvement and beautifying of school premises. Competition would be a very effective stimulus to public interests in this important question. The County Councils might for example offer prizes each year to be awarded to those districts within their respective Counties which have the best kept and most attractive school premises. I am sure that a number of districts would compete for the prizes thus offered, and that excellent results would be thereby obtained along the desired lines.

TEACHERS' INSTITUTES.

Teachers' Institutes were held during the year at Andover and at Woodstock. Both were well attended, and a number of excellent papers were read. The public meeting at Andover was a particularly good one. It was addressed by several prominent men of that place who take an active interest in educational matters, and are well able to express their views on the public platform.

At Woodstock a musical and literary entertainment was furnished to the Institute on Thursday evening by the Town Board and teaching staff. Those present were addressed by the Chief Superintendent and others.

I have the honor to be,

Your obedient servant,

F. B. MEAGHER.

APPENDIX C.

REPORTS OF BOARDS OF SCHOOL TRUSTEES.

I. CITY OF FREDERICTON.

J. R. INCH, ESQ., LL. D.,
Chief Supt. of Education.

SIR:—Our last Report furnished you with information respecting the schools of Fredericton for the year ending 31st December, 1900. Owing to the subsequent change of the date of the school year we beg to continue our Report so as to include the term ending 30th June, 1901, from which date the new school year begins.

At the beginning of the term several changes occurred in the staff of teachers, Miss O'Reilley having resigned her position as teacher of Brunswick Street School, Miss C. A. McDevitt was appointed to succeed her, Mr. Joseph Mills was appointed to the Principalship of the Charlotte Street School, in succession to Mr. O'Blenes, transterred to the Model School, and Miss Nellie Williamson was placed in charge of the second department of Charlotte Street School to the vacancy caused by the resignation of Miss Ross. Realizing the long years of faithful service given the schools by Miss McAdam the Board ..d her two months' leave of absence and placed her school temporarily in -- of Miss G. R. Porter.

Arbor Day was appropriately observed in all the schools by the introduction of practical talks and experiments bearing upon field work and in other ways calculated to interest the pupils. The only outdoor work of any extent was performed at Charlotte Street School where Principal Mills assembled all the pupils on the lawn and after singing and an appropriate address planted several trees.

The patriotism and loyalty so pronounced by all our people in the early part of the year had its influence upon the minds of the children in the schools. Special preparations were made for a fitting celebration of Empire Day. In the High School and in the Regent Street School the pupils were massed and in each instance suitably prepared programs had been arranged and these included appropriate addresses by prominent citizens.

We are pleased to report very satisfactory results from the faithful work of our excellent staff of teachers. In the High School the members of the staff seem to be well adapted to the various departments over which they preside and we believe are doing excellent work. The name of the late George E. Coulthard, M. D., for many years the respected Chairman of the School Board, through the generosity of Mrs. Coulthard will be kept fresh in the minds of the students. The Coulthard Memorial Medal has been added to the other prizes of the school, and was this year won by Miss Turner, of Gibson.

Appended to this Report you will please notice tabular statements showing names of teachers, attendance of pupils, etc., etc.

Respectfully submitted,

CHAS. A. SAMPSON,

Secretary.

TABLE SHOWING NAMES OF TEACHERS, AGE, SEX, AND NUMBER OF PUPILS FOR TERM ENDING JUNE, 1901.

SCHOOLS.	TEACHER.	Pupils 5 to 15 years.	Over 15 years.	Boys.	Girls.	Total.
Grammar......	B. C. Foster	4	24	12	16	28
	H H. Hagerman....	2	38	20	20	40
	A. S. McFarlane....	22	13	35	..	35
	E. L. Thorne.......	27	11		38	38
York Street....	A. I. Tibbits	30	13	19	24	43
	L. E. VanDine......	52	1	27	26	53
	Kate McCann.......	52	..	28	24	52
	L. A. Burtt	53	..	29	24	53
	I. R. Everett.......	55	..	38	17	55
	L. Nicolson.........	53	..	27	26	53
Model.........	Amos O'Blenes.....	46	3	23	26	49
	M. E. Phillips......	45	..	33	22	45
	M. A. Harvey......	47	..	12	35	47
	C. E. Bridges.......	51	..	23	28	51
Charlotte Street	Jos. Mills..........	44	3	25	22	47
	M. E. S. Nicolson...	53	..	26	27	53
	E. J. Thompson.....	44	..	28	16	44
	N. Williamson......	51	..	29	22	51
	Ida McAdam.......	49	..	22	27	49
Regent Street...	Jas. A. Hughes	27	4	11	20	31
	V. McKenna	32	..	23	9	32
	E. M. Holland......	38	..	12	26	38
	S. G. Duffy	50	..	31	19	50
Brunswick St...	C. A. McDevitt.....	36	..	19	17	36
Morrison's Mill..	S. Thompson	53	..	26	27	53
....	Rose E. G. Davies...	26	..	11	15	26
		1042	110	579	573	1152

CHAS. A. SAMPSON, *Secretary*

TABLE SHOWING NAME AND CLASS OF TEACHER, SALARY AND ATTENDANCE FOR TERM ENDING JUNE, 1901.

SCHOOL.	TEACHER.	Class.	Salary from Trustees.	No. Pupils.	Aver'ge Daily Attendance.	Per Cent. Attendance.
Grammar......	B. C. Foster.......	G. S.	850	28	26.02	93.57
	H. H. Hagerman ...	G. S.	650	40	33.98	84.96
	A. S. McFarlane.....	G. S.	500	35	27.06	78.86
	E. L. Thorne.......	I	400	38	30.48	80.04
York Street....	A. I. Tibbits	G. S.	250	43	30.	70.
	L. E. VanDine......	I	250	53	40.33	76.10
	Kate McCann......	I	250	52	41.42	79.06
	L. A. Burtt........	I	250	53	41.40	78.
	I. R. Everett.......	I	250	55	42.56	77.38
	L. Nicolson	I	250	53	44 03	83.58
Model	Amos O'Blenes	Sup.	650	49	40.04	82.45
	M. E. Phillips......	I	250	45	41.50	92.02
	M. A. Harvey......	I	216	47	44.20	94.02
	C. E. Bridges.... ..	I	216	51	46.06	91.05
Charlotte Street.	Jos. Mills..........	G. S.	600	47	37.73	80.27
	M. E. S. Nicolson ...	II	250	53	41.	78.
	E. J. Thomson......	I	250	44	37.83	85.97
	N. Williamson......	G. S.	250	51	42.45	83.23
	Ida McAdam.......	II	250	49	39.	80.04
Regent Street ..	Jas. A. Hughes......	I	600	31	23.03	75.19
	V. McKenna........	I	250	32	26.53	83.
	E. M. Holland......	I	250	38	32.84	86.42
	S. G. Duffy	I	250	50	39.92	79.80
Brunswick St...	C. A. McDevitt.....	I	250	36	30.97	86.
Morrison's Mill.	S. Thompson.......	G. S.	250	53	43.28	81.66
Doak..........	Rose E. G. Davies...	II	200	26	12.	47.
				1152	36.	81.

CHAS. A. SAMPSON, *Secretary.*

II. CITY OF SAINT JOHN.

To J. R. INCH, ESQ., LL. D.,
Chief Supt. of Education,

SIR.—We have the honor to present for your consideration our Report of the Public Schools of the City of Saint John, for the half year ending June 30th, 1901, being the 30th Report of this Board.

Messrs. Michael Coll and James V. Russell, the members of the Board whose terms expired in December, 1900, were reappointed, so that the *personnel* of the Board remains unchanged.

The Board held twelve meetings during the term, besides several meetings of the Finance and Buildings Committees, under their Chairmen, Dr. White and Mr. Coll, who were again reappointed in January. The official visitors to the different schools, also remain as before and they have carefully attended to the requirements of the buildings. The Lady Trustees have continued to visit all the schools indiscriminately, and have been of great assistance in all departments of the work of the Board.

Dr. Bridges, the City Superintendent, has also continued his afternoon visits of inspection to the schools, encouraging and advising the teachers, observing their methods, and conferirng with the Principals at stated meetings, besides successfully managing the High School.

The largest undertaking of the Board during the term has been the erection of the La Tour School on the West Side, which is expected to be ready for occupation in the spring of 1902. Suitable ground for the erection of a new building to accommodate the children now attending the Elm Street School, has also been purchased. These two new school houses, when completed, will be a great improvement on the unsuitable and crowded quarters at present rented by the Board.

On March 4th, Mr. David P. Chisholm, who as teacher and since as office clerk had done the Board faithful and effective service ever since the inception e Public Schools Act, died. The Board put on record a resolution, mark- their deep regret at the sad occurrence and their sincere appreciation of 'ong services. His place in the office was filled by the appointment of Mr. es Coll.

The following School Debentures fell due at the beginning of 1901:—

St. John First series :

Nos. 248 to 263	....	$35,975 00
265	....	200 00
367 to 374	....	33,334 00
		$69,509 00

To meet this indebtedness, the Board, in accordance with the provisions of the Schools Act 1900, issued on January 2nd, Redemption Bonds to the amount of $69,500 bearing interest at 3½ per cent per annum, running 40 years and numbered St. John 2nd Series, Nos. 272 to 410, which sold as follows: --

$20,000 @ 1-5 of 1 per cent premium.
10,000 @ 1-8 " " "
39,500 at par.

The school attendance during the term was good, and the work generally satisfactory. The following resignations were received:—Mrs. H Henderson, Miss B. Thorne, Miss E. Shaw, Miss J. Jordan, Miss E. I. Yerxa, Miss Z. F. Murray, and Miss G. L. Seeley. Miss Mary Hayes died just at the close of the term. Spar Cove School taught by Mrs. Henderson was closed at the end of the term for want of sufficient attendance.

The appointments during this term were as follows:—Miss Maud Kavanagh at Leinster Street School; Miss Alice Gale at Douglas Avenue; Miss Jenny Drake at Winter Street and Miss F. McInerney at St. Malachi's; Miss Grace Brown and Miss Margaret Graham were appointed on the Reserve Staff.

At the Mid-summer Examinations which closed the year's work, the Corporation Gold Medal for *dux* of the schools, was awarded to Gertrude Lawson; the Parker Silver Medal for Mathematics to May Perkins; and the Governor General's Medal for Highest Standing in Grade X., to William Morrow.

The Chairman continued his Gold Medal for competition among the Grade VIII. Schools, and it was gained by Mary Hansen, of St. Peter's Girls' School.

We have the honor to be, Sir,

Your obedient servants,

EDWARD MANNING, Secretary.

ARTHUR I. TRUEMAN, Chairman.

STATISTICAL TABLES.

TABLE No. I.—General Finance Statement to 30th June, 1901.

ASSETS.

Cash on hand June 30, 1901, ...		$ 8 75		
Furniture, See Table	$ 29,999 34			
Lands and Buildings, No. IV.	318,170 27			
		348,169 61		
Sinking Fund for Debentures issued 1898, ...		7,000 00		
Due from City Corporation for do.		28,000 00		
Water Debenture No. G, 1342, interest to purchase Parker Medal, ...		500 00		
Ground rent balance due, ...		463 00		
On hand:—				
Coal, ...	$512 22			
Medals, ...	55 12			
		567 34		
Due from City Corporation, proportion of Schools Assessment for 1901, ...		53,033 75		
Special deposit Bank of New Brunswick, ...		626 92		
			$438,369 37	
Excess of Liabilities over assets, ...			26,354 81	
			$ 464,724 18	

LIABILITIES.

Debentures due, 1901, ...	$ 700 00	
" " 1902, ...	2,600 00	
" " 1908, ...	6,000 00	
" " 1909, ...	11,500 00	
" " 1910, ...	5,941 00	
" " 1917, ...	20,000 00	
" " 1920, ...	17,000 00	
" " 1921, ...	23,000 00	
" " 1922, ...	35,500 00	
" " 1925, ...	34,500 00	
" " 1926, ...	69,500 00	
" " 1934, ...	10,000 00	
" " 1935, ...	20,000 00	
1936, ...	1,500 00	
" " 1937, ...	34,000 00	
" " 1940, ...	26,500 00	
1940, ...	43,500 00	
		361,741 00

Portland Debentures due Sept. 1901,	400 00		
" " 1906,	7,750 00		
" " 1907,	1,000 00		
		9,150 00	
Debentures issued by consent of Common Council, and by authority of the Legislature, to pay off current indebtedness and in lieu of unpaid assessments, due 1913,..		35,000 00	
Contractors' deposits, ...		471 60	
Coupons not presented, ...		6 00	
Due Bank of New Brunswick, ...		58,355 58	
			$ 464,724 18

TABLE No. 11.—Capital Account for Half Year ending June 30th, 1901.

RECEIPTS.

Sale of Debentures, issue of Jan. 2, 1901.			
Interest at 3½ per cent.,			
Nos. 272 to 276 at Par	$2,500 00		
277 to 280 "	2,000 00		
341 to 410 "	35,000 00		
		$39,500 00	
281 to 300 "	$10,000 00		
1-8 per cent premium ..	12 50		
		$10,012 50	
301 to 340	$20,000 00		
1-5 per cent premium ..	40 00		
		$20,040 00	
		$69,552 50	
Received from Current Account		$15,198 85	
			$84,751 35

EXPENDITURE.

Debentures retired to date:			
Nos. 250 to 255	$26,755 00		
257	1,755 00		
259 to 263	3,435 00		
256 to 258	3,510 00		
367 to 374	33,334 00		
105, 106 (Registered)	200 00		
		$69,009 00	
Furniture purchased, ...		272 75	
Expended on La Tour School			
Purchase of 2 lots	$500 00		
Paid Contractors on Construction Account	8,914 30		
		$9,414 30	
Purchased lots on Elm Street	$5,900 00		
Less, Sale of houses and insurance rebate	261 30		
	$5,638 70		
xpended on the Property	416 60		
		$ 6,055 30	
			$ 84,751 35

TABLE No. III. Current Account for Half Year, ending June 30th, 1901.

RECEIPTS.

Cash on hand, January 1, 1901,..		$ 41 38	
Cash in Bank of New Brunswick, January 1, 1901,..		7,050 71	
			$ 7,092 09
Received for Rent, ...			135 00
" from County Fund, ...			5,586 41
" " Contractors' Deposits, ...			471 60
Inventory January 1, 1901 :			
Coal, ...		$ 2,075 00	
Supplies in office,..		70 00	
Medals, ...		55 12	
			2,200 12
Balance due Bank of New Brunswick, ...			58,355 58
			$73,840 80

EXPENDITURES.

Cost of Schools as per table, ...		$46,305 26	
Incidental expenses,....		150 95	
Advertising and Printing, ...		174 61	
Salaries of Secretary and Clerk,...		766 14	
Special Coupon Interest. Paid Coupons on alleged Bond 277 A, ...	$60 00		
Coupon Interest, ...	8,481 60		
Coupon Interest due 1900, ...	886 03		
Interest on Overdrawn Account at Bank, ..	534 87		
		9,962 50	
Office Expenses, ...		269 03	
Workshop Account,....		54 46	
Supply Account, ...		268 21	
Cash on hand, ...	8 75		
Special Deposit in Bank of New Brunswick,	626 92		
		635 67	
Medals on hand, ...		55 12	
		$ 58,641 95	
Loan to Capital Account, ...		15,198 85	
			73,840 80

COST OF THE SCHOOLS—First Half of 1901.

Schools,	Teachers' Pay.	Care.	Repairs.	Fuel.	Rent.	Insurance.	Supply.	Expense.	Totals.
Spar Cove	$89 36	$9 00	$2 17	$6 20	$5 00	$4 80	.....	.....	$116 53
Sandy Point Road	131 42	13 98	5 30	21 50	.....	10 80	.....	.....	183 00
Millidgeville	208 74	21 00	2 47	21 25	10 00	23 50	.....	.....	286 96
Alexandra	1757 70	199 98	48 13	334 18	75 00	349 48	.....	$14 00	2778 47
Newman Street	924 34	60 00	39 67	20 53	40 00	72 00	.....	.....	1156 54
Douglas Avenue	1107 26	60 00	21 01	132 39	25 00	124 00	.....	11 95	1481 61
Elm Street	1203 63	64 98	28 89	69 74	100 00	9 85	.....	.....	1477 09
St. Peter's (Boys)	1680 83	102 00	224 69	161 50	200 00	20 00	.....	4 80	2393 82
St. Peter's (Girls)	1517 67	81 00	43 87	72 32	200 00	17 00	.....	.....	1931 86
Winter Street	2252 39	199 98	34 72	250 00	.....	271 49	.....	1 00	3009 58
Aberdeen	1490 32	99 96	9 65	191 69	.....	237 14	.....	.....	2028 76
Centennial	1998 57	210 00	37 68	330 20	.....	277 19	$0 48	7 92	2862 04
St. Vincent's	1049 74	102 00	45 85	160 00	150 00	7 80	.....	83	1516 22
High School	4414 42	249 96	80 53	557 24	.....	620 77	.....	41 25	5964 17
St. Malachi's	2534 48	180 00	134 58	196 35	440 31	24 25	.....	13 20	3523 17
Leinster Street	1044 60	100 00	37 26	225 00	175 00	7 80	.....	.....	1581 66
St. Joseph's	1130 91	124 98	159 94	103 00	212 50	11 04	.....	5 25	1747 62
Victoria and Annex	3560 72	299 94	197 47	487 02	.....	514 98	.....	11 78	5071 91
Queen Street	309 90	21 00	10 12	14 50	37 50	2 20	.....	.....	390 97
Britain Street	166 67	.....	109 67	.....	.....	1 65	.....	85	278 84
Albert	2462 21	210 00	42 65	709 34	.....	532 73	.....	2 00	3958 93
Mason Hall	729 97	49 98	10 72	66 18	100 00	.....	.....	.....	956 85
St. Patrick's	1146 12	86 00	46 05	182 68	131 25	16 56	.....	.....	1608 66
	$32,911 97	$2545 74	$1373 09	$4312 81	$1901 56	$3157 03	$0 48	$114 83	$46,305 26

TABLE NO. IV. — Details of Assets in Real Estate and Furniture.

PROPERTY.	LAND AND BUILDINGS.	FURNITURE.	TOTALS.
Sandy Point Road School	$ 597 40	$ 165 84	$ 763 24
Millidgeville	1,236 92	164 05	1,400 97
Alexandra	34,553 04	2,361 33	36,914 37
Spar Cove	355 00	63 90	418 90
Newman Street	2,787 66	498 08	3,285 74
Douglas Avenue	7,034 31	708 09	7,742 40
Elm Street	6,055 30	919 91	6,975 21
St. Peter's (Boys)	....	1,280 92	1,280 92
St. Peter's (Girls)	....	1,092 98	1,092 98
Winter Street	33,439 96	2,147 40	35,587 36
Centennial	34,175 11	2,355 37	36,530 48
St. Vincent's	....	885 42	885 42
Leinster Street	....	823 35	823 35
St. Malachi's	....	1,722 05	1,722 05
St. Joseph's	....	1,188 57	1,188 57
St. Patrick's	....	663 60	663 60
Mason Hall	....	330 80	330 80
Britain Street	....	95 77	95 77
Queen Street	....	136 80	136 80
Victoria	54,289 03	2,892 47	57,181 50
Victoria Annex	9,230 52	1,201 91	10,432 43
Aberdeen	20,247 41	1,069 25	21,316 66
High	52,352 50	4,121 56	56,474 06
Office	....	1,327 33	1,327 33
Shop	1,330 98	60 00	1,390 98
Weldon Lot	3,000 00	....	3,000 00
St. Malachi's Addition	668 67	....	668 67
Grammar School Lots	13,000 00	....	13,000 00
St. Patrick's Improvements	283 90	....	283 90
LaTour School (in process of erection)	10,394 70	....	10,394 70
Albert	33,137 86	1,722 59	34,860 45
	$318,170 27	$29,999 34	$348,169 61

TABLE V.- Public School Insurance in Force to June 27th, 1904.

COMPANIES.	AMOUNT.
North British and Mercantile	$11,000 00
Guardian	11,000 00
Liverpool and London, and Globe	11,000 00
Phœnix of London	11,000 00
Imperial	11,000 00
Connecticut	11,000 00
Royal	11,000 00
Commercial Union	9,000 00
Northern	8,000 00
Caledonian,	8,000 00
Norwich Union	6,000 00
British America	6,000 00
Manchester	6,000 00
Sun	6,000 00
Keystone	6,000 00
Phœnix of Hartford	6,000 00
Scottish Union	5,000 00
Queen	4,000 00
Atlas	4,000 00
Insurance Co. of North America	4,000 00
London Assurance	4,000 00
Western	4,000 00
National of Ireland	4,000 00
Hartford	4,000 00
Aetna	4,000 00
London and Lancashire	4,000 00
Quebec	3,000 00
Ottawa	3,000 00
Union Assurance	3,000 00
Alliance	2,000 00
Phœnix of Brooklyn	2,000 00
Canadian	2,000 00
Law, Union, and Crown	2,000 00
Mercantile	2,000 00
American	2,000 00
Boiler Insurance Co, 1 year	5,000 00
Law, Union, and Crown, 1 year	730 00
	$105,730 00

TABLE VI — Details of Fire Insurance in Force to June 27, 1904.

SCHOOLS.	Buildings.	On Furniture.	On Improvem'ts.	Total.
Sandy Point Road	$ 400	$ 140	......	$ 540
Millidgeville	800	140	......	940
Spar Cove	160	....	......	160
Alexandra	21,300	2,000	......	23,300
Newman Street	2,000	400	......	2,400
Douglas Avenue	5,600	600	......	6,200
St. Peter's (Boys)	....	1,000	......	1,000
St. Peter's (Girls)	....	850	......	850
Winter Street	21,000	1,500	......	22,500
Aberdeen	13,000	850	......	13,850
Centennial	21,000	1,800	......	22,800
St. Vincent's	....	650	......	650
High School	30,600	3,000	......	33,600
Leinster Street	....	650	......	650
St. Malachi's	....	1,325	$475	1,800
St. Joseph's	....	920	......	920
Victoria	35,000	2,400	......	37,400
Victoria Annex	5,600	850	......	6,450
Queen Street	....	110	......	110
Britain Street	....	150	......	150
Albert	20,000	1,310	......	21,310
St. Patrick's	....	500	220	720
Shop	850	250	......	1,100
Office	....	600	......	600
	$177,310	$21,995	$695	$200,000

SPECIAL INSURANCE — ANNUAL.

Elm Street		$730
Albert, 2 Boilers	$2,000	
Victoria, 1 Boiler	1,000	
High, 1 "	1,000	
Centennial, 1 Boiler	1,000	

TABLE VII.—Estimates for the Year 1901.

1. Salaries of Teachers and Superintendent, ...			$55,950 00
2. Salaries of Officers, ...			1,600 00
3. Fuel, Water and Light, ...			6,500 00
4. Care of Buildings, ...			5,130 00
5. Rent of Buildings and Land, ...			4.250 00
6. Insurance of Buildings and Furniture, ...			3,180 00
7. Printing and Advertising, ...			300 00
8. Repairs, ...			5,000 00
9. Incidental Expenses, ...			1,000 00
10. School Supplies and Apparatus, ...			500 00
			$83,410 00
Less County Fund, say	$11,000 00		
Ground Rent and Interest, ..	500 00		
			11,500 00
			$71,910 00
Additional Debenture Interest:			
On $28,250 at 6 p. c.		$ 1,695 00	
69,509 at 6 p. c., one coupon....		2,085 27	
6,941 at 5 p. c.		347 05	
204,000 at 4 p. c.....		8,160 00	
96,500 at 3½ p. c.....		3,377 50	
69,500 at 3½ p. c., one coupon...		1.216 25	
		$16,881 07	
Sinking Fund, ...		2,123 00	
			19,005 00
			$90,915 00

TABLE VIII.—Ground Rent Statement, January to June, 1901.

Lessee and Time.	Amounts.	Rent Due.	Rent Paid.	Balance Due.
Mr. Hugh H. McLean :				
Half year's rent to May 1, 1901	$40 00	$40 00	$40 00	
Mrs. C. D. McAlpine :				
Balance due Jan. 1, 1901......	30 00			
Six months' rent to May 1, 1901	30 00	60 00		$60 00
Mrs. F. Gregory :				
Balance due to Jan. 1, 1901....	100 00			
Six months' rent to May 1, 1901	20 00	120 00	20 00	100 00
Mr. James Pullen :				
Balance due to Jan. 1, 1901....	60 00			
Six months' rent to May 1, 1901	30 00	90 00		90 00
Mr. Chas. A. Clark :				
Balance due to Jan. 1, 1901....	123 00			
Six months' rent to May 1, 1901	40 00	163 00	50 00	113 00
Mr. F. S. Thompson :				
Balance due to Jan. 1, 1901....	25 00			
Six months' rent to May 1, 1901	25 00	50 00		50 00
Mrs. L. E. Sprague :				
Six months' rent to May 1, 1901	25 00	25 00	25 00	
Dr. Jas. Manning :				
Balance due Jan. 1, 1901......	25 00			
Six months' rent to May 1, 1901	25 00	50 00		50 00
Total..................	......	......	......	$463 00

TABLE IX.—Bonds Issued by Board of School Trustees of St. John, N. B.

Series.	Numbers.	Denominations.	Amount.	When Due.	Rate.
St. John First Series,	277	$ 2,000	$2,000	July, 1902	6 per cent.
" " "	278	600	600	"	" "
" " "	279 to 290	500	6,000	Jan., 1908	" "
" " "	291 to 313	500	11,500	July, 1909	" "
" " "	314 to 324	500	5,500	Jan. 1910	5 " "
" " "	325	441	441	"	" "
" " "	327 to 366	500	20,000	July, 1917	4 " "
" " "	375 to 408	500	17,000	Sept., 1920	" "
" " "	409 to 421	500	6,500	Mar., 1921	" "
" " "	422 to 454	500	16,500	Aug., 1921	" "
" " "	455 to 479	1,000	25,000	" 1922	3½ "
" " "	480 to 500	500	10,500	" 1922	" "
" " "	501 to 535	1,000	*35,000	May, 1913	4 " "
" " "	536 to 604	500	34,500	" 1925	3½ "
Portland First Series,	63	400	400	Sept., 1901	6 " "
" " "	64, 65,	500	1,000	Aug. 1907	5 " "
Portland Second Series	1 to 14	500	7,000	Sept. 1906	6 " "
" " "	15	750	750	"	" "
St. John Second Series	1 to 20	500	10,000	Nov., 1934	4 " "
(Redemption Bonds)	21 to 60	500	20,000	May, 1935	" "
" " "	61 to 31	500	1,500	Mar., 1936	" "
" " "	64 to 131	500	34,000	Jan., 1937	" "
" " "	132 to 218	500	43,500	May, 1940	" "
" " "	219 to 271	500	26,500	July, "	3½ "
" " "	272 to 410	500	69,500	Jan. 1941	" "

* With Sinking Fund.

REDEEMED: Nos. 1-100, 201-247, 250-264, 266-276, 326 St. John 1st Series.
Nos. 101-120 registered. From 120-200, never issued.
Nos. 1-62 Portland 1st Series.

DUE, BUT NOT PRESENTED FOR PAYMENT: Nos. 248, 249 and 265 St. John 1st Series. Total $700.

TABLE X.—Summary of Work of the Term.

Number of Buildings occupied as Schools	24
" " " owned	12
" " " rented	11
" " " occupied without rent	1
" " Rooms rented	61
" " " owned	92
" " " occupied without rent	1
" " High School Departments, Grades XII-IX	13
" " Advanced " " VIII-V	44
" " Advanced and Primary Departments, Grades VII-I	11
" of Primary Departments, Grades IV-1	85
Number of Pupils enrolled	6,947
" " Boys	3,339
" " Girls	3,508
" " Pupils over 15 years of age	408
" " " under 15 years of age	6,539
" " " reduced by transfer	6,902
Grand Total Days' Attendance	716,431½
Number daily present on an average	5,590
Percentage of enrolment daily present	87
Number attending High Schools	408
" " Advanced "	2,083
" " Primary "	4,456
" of pupils to each teacher	45
Percentage of whole number attending High Schools ..	5⅞
" " " " Advanced " ..	30
" " " " Primary " ..	64⅛
Average number of days each pupil attended	103

TABLE XI.—Particulars of School Attendance by Grades.

SCHOOL.	TEACHERS' NAMES.	Class of License.	1st Term ending June 30.			
			Grades. Taught.	Enrolled.	Attendance.	Per Cent.
Sandy Point Road..	M. Eva Keagin........	I	B&G 5-1	16	9	56
Milledgeville.......	J. Vernon Keirstead.,..	I	B&G 5-1	36	25	70
Spar Cove.........	H. Henderson	III	B&G 3-1	10	5	50
Alexandra	Hedley V. Hayes......	I	B&G 8	35	28	80
	Jean Scott............	Sup.	" 6	48	40	83
	Ada Cowan	I	" 6	52	45	86
	Grace Murphy.........	I	" 5	58	47	81
	Ella McAlary..........	II	" 4	48	40	83
	Bertha E. Forbes......	I	" 3	52	46	88
	Emma Colwell........	II	" 2	5[illegible]	42	84
	Bessie J. Stevenson....	I	" 1	68	82	77
Newman Street.....	Malcolm D. Brown....	I	" 7	46	37	80
	P. W. Livingstone.....	II	" 4, 3	48	41	85
	Edna G. Powers.......	I	" 2	54	44	81
	Jane H. Mowry......	II	" 1	51	44	86
Douglas Avenue	Geo. W. Dill...	I	" 8, 7	44	36	84
	Blanche J. Thorne	I	" 6, 5	45	35	78
	Louise C. Brown......	II	" 4, 3	47	40	85
	Helen M. Dale........	II	" 3, 2	44	38	87
	Ella J. Connell.........	II	" 1	64	57	90
Elm Street.........	Kate A. Kerr..........	I	" 5, 4	55	44	80
	Minnie S. Fowler.....	I	" 4	55	44	80
	Mary C. Evans........	I	" 3	51	37	72
	Margaret I. Strang....	II	" 3, 2	53	39	73
	Sarah Gray..	II	" 2	53	42	79
	Violet C. Roberts.....	II	" 2, 1	44	31	70
	Mary J. Morrow..... .	I	" 1	71	35	50

PARTICULARS OF SCHOOL ATTENDANCE BY GRADES. — Continued.

SCHOOL.	TEACHERS' NAMES.	Class of License.	1st Term ending June 30.			
			Grade Taught.	Enrolled.	Attendance.	Per Cent.
St. Peters (Boys)....	Joseph Harrington.....	I	B 8-6	43	35	81
	M. D. Sweeny........	II	" ,4	47	34	73
	Josephine Quinn.......	I	" 5,3	51	40	80
	M. L. McMillan.......	II	" 3	58	47	81
	A. B. McInnes........	II	" 2	52	40	78
	K. S. Buckley.........	II	" 2, 1	52	41	78
	A. McCarron	II	" 1	53	40	76
St. Peters (Girls)....	Joanna Carney........	I	G 8-7	36	33	91
	M. H. McCluskey	I	" 6	43	32	74
	Kate Haggerty	II	" 5	40	36	89
	Sarah Smith..........	II	" 4	40	32	80
	M. E. Kelly	II	" 4, 3	38	28	74
	M. R. Corkery........	II	" 3, 2	43	38	88
	Sarah Boudreau.......	II	" 2, 1	46	36	79
	Ellen Marry	II	" 1	44	33	75
Winter Street......	Thomas Stothart......	I	B&G 8	38	29	76
	Amy M. Iddles........	I	" 7	48	39	81
	J. K. Sutherland.......	II	" 6	48	39	81
	Jenny S. Drake.	I	" 6, 5	42	34	81
	A. A. McLeod.........	I	" 5	53	45	85
	Maud Gibson	I	" 4	52	43	82
	Sarah Taylor..........	I	" 3	47	40	86
	Gertrude Webb	I	" 3	55	44	80
	Lilian Simpson........	II	" 2	56	46	82
	M. R. Gray...........	II	" 2, 1	61	47	77
	Etta Barlow	I	" 1	59	47	80
	M. R. Graham	I	" 1	44	27	62
Aberdeen..........	W. M. McLean	G. S.	B&G 8,7	18	16	88
	E. G. Corbet..	I	" 6,5	52	41	80
	A. B. Honeywill.......	I	" 4	54	42	78
	Mary Anderson........	I	" 3	48	39	
	Jessie Caird	II	" 3	51	39	
	A. L. Page	II	" 2,1	48	37	
	M. V. Lawrence.......	II	" 1	59	38	

PARTICULARS OF SCHOOL ATTENDANCE BY GRADES. — Continued.

SCHOOL.	TEACHERS' NAMES	Class of License.	1st Term ending June 30. Grades Taught.	Enrolled	Attendance	Per Cent.
Centennial....	Henry Town..........	I	B 7, 6	42	34	81
	J. M. Rowan..........	II	" 4	41	33	80
	L. M. Clark..........	I	" 3	50	42	84
	J. Estabrook..........	I	" 2	52	39	75
	A. B. Allen..........	II	" 1	69	56	81
	A. M. Hea..........	I	G 5	39	29	74
	Ethel Shaw..........	I	" 4	42	32	76
	M. J. Campbell........	II	" 3	51	41	80
	Jessie Milligan.... ...	I	" 2	51	42	82
	L. K. Mackay.........	I	" 1	63	49	78
St. Vincent's.......	M. McDonald.........	Sup.	G 11, 10	25	22	90
	M. E. Carey..........	I	" 9, 8	33	27	82
	H. A. Kirke..........	I	" 5, 4	43	37	86
	Mary Legère..........	I	" 3, 2	57	45	79
	Anne Cassidy.........	I	" 1	44	34	77
	Bridget Cosgrove......	II	" 6-1	52	51	98
High School.......	H. S. Bridges.........	G. S.	B&G 12	18	16	89
	W. J. Myles..........	S. S.	B 11	25	22	88
	M. M. Narraway......	G. S.	G 11	32	29	90
	K. R. Bartlett........	I	G 10	34	29	85
	M. E. Knowlton.......	I	G 10	42	33	79
	T. E. Powers.........	G. S.	B 10	32	27	84
	B. H. Wilson..	I	G 9	41	37	90
	H. May Ward........	I	B 9	36	32	89
	P. K Vanwart.......	I	B 9	39	34	87
	E. McNaughton.......	G. S.	G 9	37	32	86
	J. S. Lawson.........	Sup.	B&G 9	28	22	78
	A. K. Lingley.........	I	B 8	39	32	81
	L. H. Yandall	I	G 8	40	37	91
	F. Ida Thorne.........	I	G 7	48	37	77

PARTICULARS OF SCHOOL ATTENDANCE BY GRADES. — Continued.

SCHOOL.	TEACHERS' NAMES.	Class of License.	1st Term ending June 30. Grades Taught.		Enrolled.	Attendance	Per Cent.
Leinster Street	John Mackinnon	I	B	7	48	41	85
	L. M. Kavanagh	I	"	6	48	37	77
	E. W. Gilmour	Sup.	"	5	52	43	83
	E. Kate Turner	I	"	5	50	41	82
	F. L. Dieuaide	I	"	4	48	41	85
St. Malachi's	James Barry	I	B	8	24	22	90
	M. R. Carlyn	I	"	7, 6	36	32	89
	M. C. Coughlan	II	"	6, 5	44	37	83
	A. B. Harrington	II	"	5	33	26	79
	M. E. Gallivan	II	"	4	41	34	83
	F. E. McManus	II	"	4	41	35	85
	M. E. Hayes	I	"	3	40	33	83
	J. R. Sugrue	II	"	3	38	30	79
	Kate A. Cotter	II	"	2	51	42	82
	C. M. Hogan	II	"	2, 1	38	30	79
	Kate E. Lawlor	II	"	1	68	44	66
St. Joseph's	Sarah Burchill	I	G	8, 7	33	29	87
	Mary Walsh	I	"	6	36	32	88
	Kate O'Neill	II	"	6, 5	45	34	75
	R. B. Gallagher	II	"	5, 4	43	31	73
	Françoise Bourgeois	II	"	4, 3	54	38	70
	G. Fitzgerald	II	"	2	44	36	81
	A. P. Delaney	II	"	1	40	28	70
Victoria	W. H. Parlee	I	G	8	35	29	82
	E. A. Godard	I	"	7	49	39	80
	M. L. Lingley	I	"	6	55	46	83
	M. C. Sharpe	II	"	6	53	43	81
	June W. Estey	I	"	5	52	45	87
	Annie D. Robb	I	"	5, 4	55	42	76
	L. G. Ingraham	I	"	4	59	48	81
	S. T. Payson	I	"	3	47	39	83
	F. E. Henderson	I	"	3, 2	47	36	77
	B. G. Thompson	I	"	2	49	42	85
	M. H. Shaw	II	"	1	50	31	72
	H. D. Gregg	I	"	1	50	38	76

PARTICULARS OF SCHOOL ATTENDANCE BY GRADES. — Continued.

SCHOOL.	TEACHERS' NAMES.	Class of License.	1st Term ending June 30.			
			Grades Taught.	Enrolled.	Attendance.	Per Cent.
Victoria Annex	A. L. Dykeman	I	B 6, 5	46	39	84
	Louise Wetmore	I	" 5	46	37	80
	L. L. Salter	I	" 3	55	47	85
	Grace B. Brown	Sup.	" 2	47	40	85
	Mary G. Carr	II	" 2	51	43	84
	Harriet Howard.......	II	" 1	47	37	78
Albert.............	John Montgomery	I	B&G 8	30	22	73
	C. R. Fullerton	I	" 7	36	29	80
	G. L. Seely	II	" 6, 5	51	29	86
	Enoch Thompson......	I	" 6, 5	56	44	78
	M. G. Emerson	I	" 5, 4	53	44	82
	L. J. Fullerton........	I	" 4	57	46	81
	H. N. Thompson.......	I	" 3	50	42	84
	A. M. Carleton........	I	" 3	48	38	79
	H. A. Smith..........	I	" 2	61	53	88
	B. A. Brittain	I	" 2, 1	60	51	85
	Lily Belyea	I	" 1	66	52	79
Mason Hall........	Geo. E. Armstrong	I	B&G 5, 4	35	28	80
	Annie Emerson........	II	" 3, 2	39	31	80
	Mary A. Nannary......	II	" 1	39	27	70
St. Patrick's.......	J. F. Owens	G. S.	B 7, , 4	41	33	80
	F. M. Quinn..........	II	" 6, 2	34	26	77
	Margaret McKenna....	I	G 7-5	40	33	82
	Mary A. Farrel........	I	" 4-2	41	34	83
	Mary J. Doherty	II	B&G 1	49	31	63
een Street.....	I. T. Richardson......	II	B&G 5-1	33	22	67
ain Street	Helen Adam.....	I	" 6-1	19	16	83

TABLE XII — Enrolment, Daily Average Attendance, Percentage of Enrolment, Daily Present, Etc., 1872 to 1901, Inclusive.

Year.	Term.	No. of Pupils Enrolled.	Average Daily Attendance.	Percentage of Enrolment Daily Present.	No. of Departments.	Average No. Pupils to Each Teacher.
1872	First	5214	3445	66	92	57
	Second	6477	3473	55	106	61
1873	First	5972	3842	58	106	56
	Second	5884	3517	61	112	52
1874	First	6109	3814	62	121	50
	Second	5925	3838	65	119	50
1875	First	6044	3873	64	122	50
	Second	6085	3895	64	120	51
1876*	First	5988	4050	65	122	49
	Second	6098	3996	65	110	55
1879	First	7489	4875	65	137	55
	Second	7339	4920	67	136	54
1880	First	6356	4522	71	121	53
	Second	6488	4356	67	115	56
1881	First	5924	4182	71	116	51
	Second	6212	4341	70	115	54
1882	First	5657	4063	70	155	49
	Second	6067	4339	71	117	52
1883	First	5715	4247	74	117	49
	Second	6339	4360	70	121	52
1884	First	6021	4316	70	121	50
	Second	6669	4822	72	125	54
1885	First	6802	4656	68	129	53
	Second	6624	4864	74	125	53
1886	First	6577	4580	70	124	53
	Second	6530	5025	77	125	52
1887	First	6338	4658	73	125	51
	Second	6426	4847	76	129	50
1888	First	6414	4598	72	129	50
	Second	6470	4468	70	132	49
1889	First	6531	4408	67	132	49
	Second	6735	5316	79	132	49
1890	First	6789	4732	72	142	48
	Second	6786	5097	76	135	50
1891	First	6818	4969	73	140	49
	Second	6780	5353	79	144	47
1892	First	6661	4891	73	143	47
	Second	6651	5432	81	142	47
1893	First	6681	4923	75	142	47
	Second	6672	5433	82	143	47
1894	First	6440	5059	79	144	45
	Second	6742	5557	83	143	47
1895	First	6580	5261	80	143	46
	Second	6636	5332	81	143	46
1896	First	6391	4853	76	146	44
	Second	6584	5466	83	146	45
1897	First	6557	4934	76	146	44
	Second	6821	5572	82	148	45
1898	First	6531	5153	79	148	44
	Second	7000	5629	80	151	45
1899	First	6832	5268	77	149	
	Second	6941	5743	83	155	
1900	First	6753	5783	78	150	
	Second	7160	5849	82	153	
1901	First	6902	5590	87	153	

* The loss of records by the great fire of 1877, and the unsettled state of the Schools for months afterw… rendered the figures attainable of little value in a comparative table like this. They are therefore omitted.

TABLE XIII.—Detailed Statement of Pupils in the Several Subjects.

SUBJECTS.	Primary School Grades.				Advanced School Grades.				High School Grades.			
	I	II	III	IV	V	VI	VII	VIII	IX	X	XI	XII
Reading and Spelling, . .	1304	1065	1121	966	713	655	441	318	200	128	62	18
Arithmetic, ...	1304	1065	1121	966	713	655	441	318	200	128	62	18
Form, Color & Drawing	1304	1065	1121	966	713	655	441	318	200	128	62	18
Writing, ...	1304	1065	1121	966	713	655	441	318	200	128	62	18
Singing, ...	1304	1065	1121	966	713	655	441	318	200	128	62	18
Geography, ...	1304	1065	1121	966	713	655	441	318	200	128	62	18
Animals, Plants and Minerals. .	1304	1065	1121	966	713	655	441	318	. . .	. . .	. . .	. . .
Hygiene and Physiology	1304	1065	1121	966	713	655	441	318	200	128	62	18
History, ...	. . .	. . .	. . .	. . .	713	655	441	318	200	128	62	18
Grammar and Composition, .	1304	1065	1121	966	713	655	441	318	200	128	62	18
Algebra, ...	. . .	.	. . .	. . .	. . .	. .	371	293	200	128	62	18
Geometry, ...	. . .	. . .	. . .	. . .	. . .	. . .	. . .	. . .	200	128	62	18
Latin, ...	. . .	. . .	. . .	. . .	. . .	. . .	. . .	. . .	200	128	62	18
French, ...	. . .	. . .	. . .	. . .	. . .	. . .	. . .	. . .	198	128	51	13
Greek, ...	. . .	. . .	. . .	. . .	. . .	. . .	. . .	. . .	18	36	15	5
Bookkeeping, ...	. . .	. . .	. . .	. . .	. . .	. . .	. . .	. . .	181	128	. . .	. . .
Chemistry, ...	. . .	. . .	. . .	. . .	. . .	. . .	. . .	. . .	. . .	20	62	. . .
Botany and Agriculture, .	. . .	. . .	. . .	. . .	. . .	. . .	. . .	. . .	200	127	53	. . .
Trigonometry, ...	. . .	. . .	. . .	. . .	. . .	. . .	. . .	. . .	. . .	. . .	5	18
Physics, ...	. . .	. . .	. . .	. . .	. . .	. . .	. . .	. . .	200	. . .	. . .	. . .

TABLE XIV.—Medalists in the Public Schools of Saint John.

Year.	Corporation, Gold, *Dux* of Schools.	Parker Silver, Mathematics.	Governor-General's Silver, English.	Governor-General's Bronze, Science.	Alexandra, Silver.*	Alexandra, Bronze* Various.
1872	John Hale.	James [illegible]	.. ..	.. ..	.. ..	Kate Barlett.
1873	Richard McGivern.	James Trueman.	.. ..	.. ..	.. ..	Annie Everett.
1874	James R. Mace.	G. Fred. [illegible]	Maggie Underhill.	Mary W. Hart.	Alexander Rankine.	Annie Steeves.
					Charlotte Olive.	Mary McAfee.
1875	James Trueman.	Alban F. Emery.	Frank Millidge.	James Trueman.	Lizzie Thomas.	
			Mary Humphrey.	Annie Everett.	Frank Millidge.	
1876	William A. Ewing.	William Sewall.	William A. Ewing.	James Seely.	Elmer Spiller.	*Silver, A. C. Smith.*
			Annie Everett.	Kate R. Bartlett.	.. ..	K. Bartlett.
1877	J. Twining Hart.	James S. Clark.				*Gold, J. Ellis.*
1878	Elmer Spiller.	Colin Livingston.	.. ..	.. ..	.. ..	Annie Hunter.
1879	John McIntosh.	Wilmer A. Duff.	.. ..	.. ..	.. ..	Martha McKilligan.
						Silver, Wm. Elder.
1880	Wilmer V. Duff.	Martin A. Henderson.	Lilian [illegible]	Herman Peil[illegible]	.. ..	Walter Taylor.
						Silver, S. Jones.
1881	Howard D. Fritz.	W. F. Ganong.	L. Eliz. Narraway.	Samuel W. Kain.	Christina McLaren,	Sophia McLaren.
						Emma Purvis.
1882	Herman Peiler.	Herman Peiler.	Sophia [illegible]	George E. Keator.	.. ..	Annie Robb.
1883	John W. Gallivan.	Arthur Richardson.	[illegible] R. Hall	William C. [illegible]	.. ..	Frank Hartley.
1884	William D. Matthews.	William C. [illegible]	Sarah Shenton.	Thomas [illegible]	.. ..	Ellen Coholan.
1885	Alex. O. Macrae.	[illegible]	Alice Rainnie.	Charles J. Milligan.		
			Jennie [illegible]			
1886	Ed. D. Johnson.	William A. Vanwart.	Annie D. Robb.	[illegible] J. Mildon.		
1887	William McFarlane.	Allan Wilson.	Mary Evans.	Percy Hanington.		
1888	Francis Walker.	John McKnight.	[illegible]	Ernest Ruel.		
			Gertrude Hanington.			
1889	Cyrus H. [illegible]	[illegible]	Carrie M. Sulis.	George Milligan.		
1890	Frank [illegible]	William [illegible]	[illegible] Morrow.	Charles M. Manning.		
1891	Kate Travers.	Herman Peck.	[illegible]	Kate [illegible]		
1892	H. May Ward.	Oscar Ring.	[illegible] Hanington.	[illegible] Hannah.		
1893	Hattie A. Smith.	H. A. Smith.	Helen G. [illegible]	[illegible] G. [illegible]		
1894	Muriel B. Carr.	Muriel B. Carr.	Francis Coll.	Maud [illegible]		*Gold. C. W. Weldon.*
1895	Jessie Lawson,	[illegible] Clark.	Walter J. Wilson.	Thomas Lunney.	.. ..	Chas. Montgomery.
1896	Walter J. R. Wilson.	W. J. E. Wilson.	Harry Devlin.	Emily [illegible]	.. ..	Marian Belyea.
1897	Wallace Bagnall.	Harry Devlin.	Emily [illegible]	Charles Lawson.		
						Gold, D. R. Jack.
		[illegible] Martin.	Charles Lawson.	Frederic Jordan.		Ethel Fanjoy.

* The Alexandra Medals were given by J. Boyd, Esq.

TABLE XIV. — Medalists in the Public Schools of Saint John. — (*Continued.*)

Year.	Corporation Gold *Dux* of Schools.	Parker Silver, Mathematics.	Governor-General's Silver, Grade IX.	Various.
1899	Charles Lawson.	Charles Lawson.	Ella M. Smith.	.. ..
1900	Ella M. Smtth.	Ella M Smith.	May Perkins.	1, W. Morrow; 2, I. McGerrigle; 3, M. Coggar
1901	Gertrude Lawson.	May Perkins.	William Morrow.	2, Mary Hanson.

1. Gold Medal for Grade IX, given by Lady Trustees.
2. 2 Gold Medals for Grade VIII, given by A. I. Trueman, Chairman.
3. Gold Medal for 2nd in Grade VIII, given by C. N. Skinner.

III. CITY OF MONCTON.

Staff of Grammar School, 1901.

GEORGE J. OULTON, M. A., Principal, Teacher of Science, and Geometry.

CYRUS ACHESON, { Teacher of English Literature, Grammar, Analysis, Essay Work, French.

G. FRED MCNALLY, B. A., { Teacher of Latin, Greek, General History, Civics, Book-keeping, British History.

LUTHER R. HETHERINGTON, B A. { Teacher of Mathematics and Canadian History and Geography.

To J. R. INCH, ESQ., LL. D.,
Chief Supt. of Education.

SIR :—The Board of School Trustees for the City of Moncton, have the honor to present for your consideration the annual Report of the Public Schools in the City of Moncton, for the year 1901.

During the year some changes have taken place in the constitution of the Board. Mr. G. B. Willet, much to the regret of the Board resigned his position as Trustee early in the year, his position was filled by the City Council appointing Mr. John H. Hanis in his stead. The term of office of Mr. W. D. Martin having expired Mr. H. S. Bell was appointed by the City Council on the 22nd of March last. Messrs Willet and Martin for years have given very effective service as Trustees, and the interests of the schools were actively promoted by both gentlemen. During the year there have been no change in the *personnel* of Trustees appointed by the Lieutenant-Governor-in-Coun. The grand total number of pupils in attendance at various schools at close December, 1901 was 1778.

ABERDEEN SCHOOL.

During the year there were sixteen schools conducted in this building, the Grades running from I. to XI. inclusive, in which 802 pupils were enrolled. Grades IX., X. and XI. of which there were two classes in Grade IX., constitute the High School, and the Grammar School for the County of Westmorland. There were 152 pupils in the High School.

The Staff of the High School has undergone some changes during the year. In June last, Mr. McLean's term of contract having expired, the position of Classical Instructor was given to Mr. G. Fred McNally, B. A., formerly Instructor in Classics in Stanstead College, Quebec. Mr. McNally came highly recommended as a good disciplinarian and an excellent teacher. The Board has not been disappointed. One department of Grade IX., in the High School has not in the judgment of the majority of the Board been conducted in a satisfactory manner. The Board have therefore readjusted the Four Departments of the High School for the coming year under three teachers instead of four as formerly.

MATRICULANTS.

The following were successful candidates from the High School in passing the examination held this year for Matriculation in the University of New Brunswick: Harry Ayer, Louise Copp.

ENTRANCE EXAMINATION.

In June last, examinations for entrance into the High School were held in the Aberdeen Building under the supervision of Principal Oulton of the High School, Principal Irons of Victoria School and the secretary. 85 candidates presented themselves of whom 22 passed in the first division, 43 in the second division, and 20 in the third division. Of the number presenting themselves for examination 76 were admitted to the High School for Grade IX. The one making the highest marks in this examination was Miss Beatrice Bourque of Wesley Street School, who made a total of 863. She won the Silver Medal for 1901 donated by His Honor the Lieutenant Governor.

GRADUATION EXERCISES.

In June last the closing exercises of the High School were held in the ›embly Hall of the Aberdeen Building. The Hall was crowded with visitors, ›ncipal Oulton of the High School presiding.

The following constitutes the graduating class for 1901, who received diplomas in order of merit.

Louise Copp, Harry Ayer, Joanna Moore,	1st Division.
James Barnett, Alice Marks, John Charters, Julia Flanagan, Edith Cameron,	2nd Division.
Jules Girouard, Wanda Sullivan, Alva Lockhart, James Pitfield, Agnes Marks, Maggie Buchanan Mary Peters, Maud Gibson,	3rd Division.

After which the following program was successfully carried out:
Selection—Orchestra.
March—To music of High School Class, headed by graduates.
High School Call.
Chorus—The Land of the Maple, High School.
Recitation—Canadian Born, Miss Ida Bishop.
Original Essay—Dominion of Canada, Miss Alva Lockhart.
Solo—The Dear Home Land, Miss Mary Peters.
Recitation—"How Reuben Played," Miss Eva McCracken.
Chorus—The Brook, High School.
Essay—Duke of Wellington, Lincoln Crowsen.
Selection—Orchestra.
Recitation—The School Master Beaten, Miss Edith Nugent.
Essay—"Victorian Era," Miss Louise Copp.
Prophecy—Miss Jennie Rippey, Prophetess.
Recitation—Brown's Steam Chair, Miss Mamie Chapman.
Chorus—Down by the River Side, High School.
Valedictorian—John Charters.
Class Song—Grade XI.

PRIZES AND MEDALS.

The following prizes were awarded:

Gold Medal for the best general average in Grade XI, given by Mr. J. T. Hawke, won by Miss Louise Copp.

Course in Shorthand and Typewriting, highest in Final English, Grade XI, given by Miss Johnston, won by Harry Ayer.

Gold Medal, English and French, Grade XI, given by Mr. H. H. Ayer, won by Harry Ayer.

Books, General average in Science Grade XI, given by Mr. F. A. McCully, won by Harry Ayer.

Books, Best home-made apparatus, Grade XI, given by Mr. F. A. McCully, won by James Pitfield.

$5.00 Gold, Highest average, Grade X, given by Mr. E. C. Cole, won by Miss Margaret Wilson.

Governor General's medal, highest general average Grade IX, won by Miss Lizzie McBeath.

$5.00 Gold, Highest in Health Reader, Grade VIII, won by Herbert Clark, donated by His Worship, Mayor Atkinson.

$5.00 Gold, Highest in Health Reader, Grade VIII. won by Miss Mary Willett and Arthur Eddington, donated by His Worship, Mayor Atkinson.

Silver Medal, average Entrance Examination, donated by His Honor Lieutenant Governor, won by Miss Beatrice Bourque.

VICTORIA SCHOOL.

This school has suffered somewhat by reason of changes in the staff which have taken place during the year. In April last, Miss Margaret Simpson resigned her position on account of ill-health, and Miss Hazel Taylor was appointed in her stead. Miss Simpson has been a successful teacher in this building for many years, and the Board expressed regret at her resignation. At the close of the term in July, Miss Bailey who was in charge of Grade VI, in this school resigned her position. The Board endeavoured to secure the most competent teacher available for this position and Miss Cora L. Simpson, M. L. A. a graduate of Mount Allison University, Ladies' College, was engaged.

Miss Bailey has long been one of the most successful teachers in the Moncton Schools. The Board passed a resolution expressing their appreciation er services rendered while a teacher in Moncton. Notwithstanding the culties experienced by frequent changes of the staff in this school the k has been successfully carried on during the year. There were enrolled pupils.

WESLEY STREET SCHOOL.

There are seven teachers on the staff in this school. The reputation of this school has been fully sustained during the year. A pupil from this school, Miss Beatrice Bourque, led all others in the city in the Examination for Entrance to High School, and secured the Medal which had been donated by the Lieutenant Governor to the student making the highest average in this examination.

The Principal of this school who is a very successful teacher, is to be congratulated on this result.

The Primary Departments in charge of Misses Elodie and Evangeline Bourque, are very much overcrowded, and it is expected that another department in the Primary Grades will be opened at the beginning of the school year in August next.

The Board have made provision in the estimates for such a contingency. There are enrolled in this school 413 pupils.

INSPECTOR'S REPORT.

Early in the year written reports upon the condition of the various schools in the City of Moncton were submitted by the Inspector of Schools for the County of Westmorland, and the Secretary.

A PLAY GROUND FOR VICTORIA SCHOOL.

About the Victoria Building the Trustees do not control any land to be used as playground for the children attending that school. The Board deemed it wise at the present time to secure a block of land lying to the east of the School Building between Park and Princess Streets, 230 feet by 184 feet. Accordingly it was resolved to purchase this land from the Moncton Land Co., Ltd., for the sum of $2000.00, for which sum the Company agreed to accept School Debentures for the amount, bearing interest at 5 per cent and running 10 years. It is proposed to secure legislation to carry out this agreement.

BONDS.

School Bonds Number 32 and 33, issued July 1881 for $500.00 each at 6 per cent interest, fell due during 1901. One Bond $500.00 the Board paid out of Current Account. Legislation will be secured to reissue these Bonds at 4 per cent. Attached to this report are a number of tabular and comparative statements relating to the City Schools. All of which is respectfully submitted.

F. A. McCULLY, Secretary.

JOHN T. HAWKE, Chairman.

Moncton, December 31, 1901.

RECAPITULATION OF VOUCHERS, 1901.

January	$ 91 02
February	2,126 97
March	1,928 11
April	1,903 94
May	1,303 84
June	3,341 91
July	960 89
August	283 67
September	1,334 36
October	1,570 42
November	1,335 61
December	3,867 77
	$20,048 51
To Balance due the Bank January 1, 1901, ...	1,499 51
	$ 21,548 02

SCHOOL TRUSTEES' RECEIPTS FOR 1901.

Tuition Fees, Miss Weldon	$	5 00
Cash from City		1,158 80
Cash from County Fund		1,192 32
Cash for Sale of Desks		1 75
Cash from City		2,714 62
Cash from City		1,301 29
Cash from City		2,472 50
Tuition Fees, J. H. Lockhart		3 00
Cash from City		1,452 49
Cash from A. Leaman, (Ashes)		11 90
Cash for Ashes		2 10
Cash from City		3,695 59
Cash from County Fund		1,333 96
Tuition Fees, J. H. Lockhart		6 00
Cash from City		1,933 93
Cash from City		4,163 79
Balance		98 98
	$	21,548 02

EXPENDITURES, 1901.

Dec. 31	By Salaries, Teachers and Officers	$ 12,123	26
"	Janitors' Salaries	1,216	00
"	General Repairs	129	81
	Expenses	265	06
	Interest	3,558	20
	Insurance	223	00
	Fuel, Wood	681	75
	" Coal	933	86
	Water	75	00
	School Supplies	111	64
	Furniture	7	88
	Rent, Wesley Street	12	00
	Fuel, Wesley Street	200	00
	Real Estate	11	00
Total expenditure for 1901		$19,548	51
6 per cent. Bond No. 3½ paid and to be issued at 4 p. c.		500	00
		$20,048	51

ESTIMATES MONCTON SCHOOL, 1902.

By Salaries, Teachers and Officers..................		$ 12,300
" " Janitors...........................		1,316
" General Repairs...........................		200
" Expenses.................		250
" Interest................................		4,000
" Insurance................................		308
" Fuel, Wood		600
" " Coal................................		900
" Water....................................		75
" School Supplies...........................		120
" Furniture		
" Rent.....................................		12
" Electric Light...........................		
" Real Estate..............................		
" Fuel, Wesley Street School..................		200
		$20,281 00
Less Co Fund, Estimated...............	$2,281 00	
Bond No. 33 re-issued.................	500 00	2,781 00
Total amount required for 1902.........		$17,500 00

Passed January 9, 1902.

STATEMENT NO. 1.

TERM ENDING JUNE 30, 1901. TEACHERS AND ACTUAL ATTENDANCE RETURNS.

SCHOOLS.	TEACHERS.	Salaries.	Days of Session.	Pupils Enrolled.	Boys.	Girls.	Gross Days Pupils Attended.	Gross Days Lost.	Av'ge Days Pupils Attended.	Percentage of Attendance.
Aberdeen	Geo. J. [illegible]lton	$850	117	32	16	16	2556½	441	23.05	72.03
	C. H. Acheson	650	120	40	7	33	3631½	569	31.04	78 5
	L. R. [illegible]	550	120	41	20	21	3691½	592	31.66	77
	D. McLean	450	120	41	22	19	3734	680½	32	81
	S. B. [illegible]n,	480	120	54	23	31	4810½	520½	41.32	76.53
	Ethel Murphy	275	120	45	20	25	4059½	780½	35	78
	Alice Lea	265	120	59	34	25	5749½	642½	49.275	83.5
	Agnes McSweeney	275	120	55	29	26	5121	1413	44.2	80
	Ella J. [illegible]ay	275	120	57	28	29	5360	919½	46	80.7
	Amelia I. Smith	240	120	57	30	27	5711½	762½	48.8	85.6
	Emma Condon	275	118½	55	27	28	4903	1653½	[illegible]	80.89
	Maggie Gross	275	120	58	33	25	5436	1196½	46	79
	Elspeth Charters	275	120	51	31	20	4790	1060	41	80.9
	[illegible]ary A. M[illegible]	225	120	46	15	31	4307	848	36.5	79.3
	Mrs. M. P. [illegible]ion,	275	118	52	27	25	4721	910½	41	79
	Eva Sullivan	240	120	44	22	22	4292	626	36.6	83.18
Victoria	S. W. Irons	850	120	38	14	24	3561	539	30.207	79.5
	Catherine Barton	275	120	33	17	16	2872	432½	24.72	75
	Mary L. F. Bailey	275	120	34	14	20	3077	338	26.125	76.83
	Harriet Willis	265	120	60	25	35	5722½	635	48.97	81 6
	Hazel Taylor	200	120	60	31	29	5943	815½	50.5	83.1
	Fannie McLaren	265	120	63	29	34	6128	1087	51.82	82.25

..	Eunice Brown	275	120	50	32	18	5071	805	42.8	85.6
	G. May Forge	225	120	57	28	29	5641	1098	47	62.5
	Edith Mitchell	240	120	62	38	24	6051½	783	51.34	82.8
	Ella Stevens	275	120	61	29	32	5767	846	49.33	79.22
.terloo	Florence Murphy	240	120	25	14	11	2266	457	19	77.5
St. Bernard's	Agnes Quirk	100	120	35	9	26	3519	367	29.78	85.08
	Kate Hamilton	240	119	55	28	27	5243½	691½	45.08	81.94
	Natalie Allain	275	120	49	19	30	4803½	802	42.75	87.24
	Eli zbth Richard	240	120	50	24	26	4945	480	42.25	84.5
	Catherine Hennessy	275	120	59	28	31	5429½	1013½	45.4	77
	Evangeline Bourque	240	120	59	33	26	4894	1128½	42	71.7
	Elodie Bourque	225	120	56	19	37	4366½	1061½	37.7	67.4

STATEMENT NO. 2.

TERM ENDING JUNE 30, 1901. NO. OF PUPILS IN THE SEVERAL STANDARDS OF INSTRUCTION.

SUBJECTS.	I	II	III	IV	V	VI	VII	VIII	IX	X	XI	TOTALS.
Reading, Spelling and Recitation	245	277	219	213	297	150	131	108	..	..	..	1640
Composition	..	..	167	169	196	150	131	108	..	.	..	921
[illegible]ar and Analysis.	..	..	167	169	196	150	131	108	..	..	..	921
History	..	..	..	..	196	150	131	108	82	40	32	739
Form	245	277	219	169	196	150	131	108	..	..	..	1495
Industrial Drawing	245	277	219	169	196	150	131	108	82	..	..	1577
Print Script	245	277	219	213	197	150	131	108	..	..	..	1540
Writing	245	277	219	213	197	150	131	108	..	..	..	1540
[illegible]tic.	245	277	219	213	197	150	131	108	82	40	..	1662
[illegible]ry	..	..	..	..	..	..	..	87	82	40	32	241
Algebra	..	..	..	..	55	..	147	107	82	40	32	463
Geography	..	..	219	213	196	150	131	108	82	40	32	1171
Mineral, Plant and Animal Life	220	245	219	213	23	150	131	54	..	..	..	1255
[illegible]lor	245	277	219	169	196	150	131	108	..	..	..	1495
Objects	..	..	..	..	..	..	..	..	..	..	..	....
Temperance Teachings of Science	245	277	219	213	196	150	131	108	..	..	..	1539
Physics	..	..	..	..	..	..	..	..	82	..	..	82
Physiology	..	..	..	..	..	..	..	..	..	40	29	69
Latin	..	..	..	..	..	..	105	48	..	..	..	153
French	..	.	..	..	..	..	25	25	82	38	29	249
Bookkeeping	..	..	..	..	..	..	..	..	..	40	..	40
Greek	..	..	..	..	..	..	..	..	..	..	4	4
Trigonometry	..	..	..	..	..	..	..	..	..	..	29	29
Agriculture and Botany	..	..	..	..	..	..	..	..	..	..	32	32
Chemistry	..	..	..	..	..	..	..	..	..	..	32	33

STATEMENT NO. 3.

TERM ENDING DECEMBER 31, 1901. TEACHERS AND ACTUAL ATTENDANCE RETURNS.

SCHOOLS.	TEACHERS.	Salaries.	Days of Session.	Pupils Enrolled.	Boys.	Girls.	Gross Days Pupils Attended.	Gross Days Lost.	Av'ge Days Pupils Attended.	Percentage of Attendance.
Aberdeen	Geo. J. Oulton	$850	80	25	6	19	1591½	239	20.54	82.16
	C. H. Acheson	650	80	51	22	29	3481	474	44.67	87.6
	L. R. Hetherington	550	80	38	10	28	2408½	312	30.63	80
	G. Fred McNally	500	80	38	13	25	2639	294	33.62	88.4
	S. B. Anderson	480	80	48	22	26	3091½	450½	40	83.5
	Ethel Murphy	275	80	46	24	22	3068½	459½	39	85
	Alice Lea	275	80	46	31	15	3271½	296	41.15	89.45
	Agnes McSweeney	275	80	47	23	24	2864½	883½	37	78
	Mame I. Smith	265	80	60	34	26	4040½	534	51.84	86.4
	Ella J. McKay	275	80	54	28	26	3455	478½	44	81.6
	Emma Condon	275	80	59	24	35	3633½	1186½	46.34	76.76
	Maggie Gross	275	80	63	27	36	4164½	554½	52.9	83.9
	Elspeth Charters	275	80	55	31	24	3300½	646	42	76
	Mary A. Moore	225	80	55	21	34	3632	650½	45.5	82.7
	Mrs. M. P. Simpson	275	80	57	38	19	3871	512½	49	86
	Eva Sullivan	240	80	60	24	36	3707½	586½	47.4	79
Victoria	S. W. Irons	850	80	49	21	28	3102	413½	39.59	80.8
	Catherine Barton	275	80	61	21	40	3622½	97	46.42	76
	Eva L. Simpson	240	80	52	22	30	3484½	374½	44.5	85.5
	Harriet Willis	275	80	66	31	35	4181	740	53.9	81.6
	Hazel Taylor	225	80	55	27	28	3445½	65	43.3	78.7
	Fannie McLaren	275	80	57	24	33	3714½	450	47.46	83.26

STATEMENT NO. 3—Continued

TERM ENDING DECEMBER 31, 1901. TEACHERS AND ACTUAL ATTENDANCE RETURNS.

SCHOOLS.	TEACHERS.	Salaries.	Days of Session.	Pupils Enrolled.	Boys.	Girls.	Gross Days Pupils Attended.	Gross Days Lost.	Av'ge Days Pupils Attended.	Percentage of Attendance.
Victoria...	Eunice Brown	275	80	51	29	22	3395	283	42.73	83.68
	G. May Forge...........	225	80	55	36	19	3650	490	46.5	84.5
	Edith L. Mitchell........	240	80	60	37	23	4020½	523½	51.2	85.3
	Ella Stevens.............	275	80	57	31	26	3808½	440½	48.50	85.08
Wesley Street....	Agnes Quirk	400	81½	38	11	27	2716½	212	33.90	89,21
	Kate Hamilton	240	81½	60	32	28	3818	464	47.9	79.83
	Elizabeth Richard........	275	81½	56	34	22	3773	398	47.66	85.1
	Natalie Allain............	275	81½	57	21	36	3667	607½	46.39	81
	Evangeline Bourque......	240	79½	69	26	43	3577½	418½	46.1	66.8
	Elodie Bourque..........	225	79½	68	32	36	3758	756	49.5	72.7
	Catherine Hennessy	275	81½	65	32	33	4041	890½	50.51	77.7
		......	.....	1778	845	933	113,995½	16,177	43.98	81.91

STATEMENT NO. 4.

ENDING DECEMBER 31, 1901. NO. OF PUPILS IN THE SEVERAL STANDARDS OF INSTRUCTION.

SUBJECTS.	I	II	III	IV	V	VI	VII	VIII	IX	X	XI	TOTALS.
Reading, Spelling and Recitation	286	212	284	215	219	168	129	113	....	....	....	1626
Composition	....	....	271	168	219	168	129	113	....	....	....	1068
Grammar and Analysis	....	....	271	168	219	168	129	113	....	....	....	1068
History	....	....	....	....	122	168	129	113	75	51	25	683
Form	286	212	284	200	194	208	129	113	....	....	....	1626
Industrial Drawing	286	212	284	200	194	208	129	113	....	....	....	1626
Print Script	286	212	284	215	219	168	129	113	....	....	....	1626
Writing	286	212	284	215	219	168	129	113	....	....	....	1626
Arithmetic	286	212	284	215	219	168	129	113	76	51	....	1753
Geometry	....	....	....	....	....	....	....	....	76	51	25	152
Algebra	....	....	....	....	....	....	22	113	76	51	24	286
Geography	....	....	284	215	219	168	129	113	75	51	25	1279
Natural, Plant and Animal Life	123	121	284	275	122	98	129	113	....	....	....	1265
Color	....	....	....	....	....	....	....	....	....	....	....	....
Objects	....	....	....	....	....	....	....	....	76	51	25	152
Temperance and Things of Science	286	212	284	215	219	168	129	113	....	....	....	1626
Physics	....	....	....	....	....	....	....	....	75	....	....	75
Physiology	....	....	....	....	....	....	....	....	....	51	25	76
Latin	....	....	....	....	....	....	107	106	65	49	21	348
French	....	....	....	....	....	....	....	....	75	44	23	142
Bookkeeping	....	....	....	....	....	....	....	....	76	50	....	126
Greek	....	....	....	....	....	....	....	....	....	7	....	7
Chemistry	....	....	....	....	....	....	....	....	51	25	....	76
Agriculture and Botany	....	....	....	....	....	....	....	....	75	51	25	151
Drawing	....	....	....	....	....	....	....	....	75	....	....	75

IV. TOWN OF ST. STEPHEN.

To JAMES R. INCH, LL. D.,
Chief Supt. of Education.

SIR :—I have the honor to present for your consideration the Report of the Board of School Trustees of the Town of Saint Stephen for the second term of the school year ending June 30th, 1901.

The term of office of John Black, Esq., as a member of the Board having expired on the 31st of December, 1900, he was re-appointed by the Town Council.

Mr. Frank A. Duston resigned his position as teacher of Grades IX, X, and XI at the end of the school year as did also Miss H. D. Hanson who taught Grades III and IV in the King Street building. Mr. Duston was a very efficient instructor, but after a year's service with the Board he decided to accept a more renumerative position with the Saint Stephen's Bank. Miss Hanson who had been a member of the teaching staff for many years was one of the most successful teachers ever engaged by the Board. Her resignation was received with much regret by trustees, parents and pupils.

On Friday evening, June 28th, the graduation exercises of the High School were held in the Rink. Each year the interest in these exercises increases. This is very gratifying to the Board as well as to the Principal and his pupils. Fully one thousand people were in attendance to hear the essays of the graduates. The class consisted of five boys and eight girls. Several prizes which had been offered at the beginning of the year were awarded, t presentations being made by Mrs. Mary D. McGibbon and G. W. Ganoı M. P. In connection with graduates of our High School it is very satisfacto to know that Ernest Hill a graduate of 1900 made the highest average of any of the Maritime Province applicants for admission to the Royal Military College at Kington, and he is now a student of that College.

You will notice by the Statement of Receipts and Expenditures which goes forward with this report that there is an over draft of $2757.50 which amount was due the St. Stephen's Bank on June 30th. The cause of this large over draft was the unusually large expenditure of funds in payment of bills contracted on account of sanitary arrangements, and the fact that to June 30th only $1000 00 had been received from the Town owing to the assessment not having been collected at that time.

Respectfully submitted

LEWIS A. MILLS, Secretary.

June 30th, 1901.

TABULAR STATEMENT.

Showing Names of Teachers, Class, Salary, Etc., for the Term Ending June 30th, 1901.

School.	Name of Teacher.	Class.	Salary.	Pupils. Boys.	Pupils. Girls.	Aver'ge Daily Attendance.	Per Cent. Attendance.	Standards Taught.
High School ..	P. G. McFarlane.........	I	$700	15	13	22 54	80.50	IX., X., XI,
"	Frank A. Duston.........	I	260	8	17	21.89	87.56	IX., X., XI.
Marks Street...	F. O. Sullivan............	I	665	46	35	67.35	83.14	VII., VIII.
"	Etta E. DeWolfe, Assistant	I	320	....	....	.....	.....	
"	M. Flora Boyd...........	I	260	27	26	45.20	85.28	V., VI.
"	May B. Carter	I	320	22	32	45.75	84.72	V., VI.
"	Jessie D. Henry..........	I	260	28	24	46.	89.96	IV., V.
"	Mercy Murray.....	I	260	59	29	43.91	91.49	I., II.
King Street ...	H. D. Hanson............	I	320	29	28	50.00	88.00	III., IV.
"	Jessie H. Whitlock	I	320	27	18	38.5	85.5	I, II.
Cove	Charles H. Murray.......	I	300	34	24	50.38	86.86	III,, IV,
"	Ella M. Veazey..........	I	320	18	23	35.61	86.85	I.. II,

RECEIPTS AND EXPENDITURES OF BOARD OF SCHOOL TRUSTEES OF THE TOWN OF SAINT STEPHEN, FOR THE TERM ENDED JUNE 30TH, 1901.

1900.			
Dec. 31.	To amount in St. Stephen Bank, ...	$450 00	
1901.			
Feb. 10.	" County Fund, ...	408 99	
"	" Town Treasurer, ...	1,000 00	
		———	$1,858 99

1901	CR.		
June 30.	By Amount paid for Teachers' Salaries, ...	$ 2,186 19	
"	" " " Repairs, ...	1,954 91	
"	" " " Care of Rooms, ...	302 39	
"	" " " Contingencies, ...	173 00	
		———	4,616 49
	Balance, ...		$2,757 50

V. TOWN OF MILLTOWN.

J. R. INCH, LL. D., Chief Superintendent.

Report to June 30, 1901.

The schools of Milltown have consisted of the same number of departments as before, being nine; conducted by the same teachers as last year reported, save that Miss Gale retired and Miss Osborne joined the staff. The graduation exercises took place in the Presbyterian Church. Mr. Inspector Carter accepted an invitation and by his wise and helpful address added much to the inteiest of the occasion.

STATEMENT TERM ENDING JUNE 30TH, 1901.

School.	Teacher.	No. Boys.	No. Girls.	Total.	Present Average.	Per Cent. Average.	Standard.
Superior	J. B. Sutherland...	10	19	29	24.86	85.74	IX., X., XI.
"	I. J. Caie. ..	7	16	23	20.54	89.31	VIII.
Intermediate......	M. C. Osborne....	13	21	34	30.18	88.76	VII.
"	Bessie A. Young..	10	19	29	23.40	80.60	VI.
"	C. M. Caswell.....	37	19	56	46.24	82.57	IV.
"	M. E. Connolly....	11	28	39	34.33	87.3	V.
Primary	A. D. Young......	32	30	62	53.67	86.4	II-III.
"	T. S. Kirk.........	16	10	26	23.30	89.61	I-II-III.
"	M. A. Sutherland..	34	31	65	55.42	85.3	I-II.

STATEMENT OF EXPENDITURE.

For Teachers' Salaries	$ 1,565 20
" Construction Account	25 37
" Care of Rooms	159 00
" Fuel, $56.87; Insurance, $7.50	64 37
" Expense Account	101 69
Total	$1,915 63

Respectfully Submitted,

E. H. BALKAM,

Secretary.

Milltown, December 11, 1901.

VI. TOWN OF WOODSTOCK.

Board of School Trustees.

J. R. INCH, ESQ., LL. D.
Chief Supt. of Education.

SIR:—The Board of School Trustees for the Town of Woodstock, submit the following statement of their receipts and expenditure for the School Term ending June 30th, 1901.

RECEIVED.

From Town Treasurer, ...	$2,900 00
" County Fund, ...	425 50
" Interest, ...	1 87
	$ 3,327 37

PAID OUT.

Balance due Treasurer, ...	$ 69 95	
Teachers, ...	1,997 00	
Janitor,....	198 00	
Secretary, ...	50 00	
Insurance, ...	26 00	
School Supplies, ...	118 51	
Fuel, ...	358 01	
Incidentals, ...	38 35	
Interest on Debentures, ...	100 50	
Balance in Treasurer's hands, ...	371 05	
		$3,327

The following is a statement of the schools under their care with the attendance, etc., during the same term :

TEACHER.	Standards Taught.	Per Cent. Pupils Daily Present.	No. of Pupils.
Minnie Carman	I and II	82 29	60
Ella Smith	"	76.78	56
Mary Milmore	"	86.98	44
Frances Peters	III and IV	79.25	62
Mary Baker	"	84.75	33
Elizabeth J. Cupple	"	88.23	34
Katherine Clark	I and VII	77.14	47
Helena Mulherrin	V and VI.	73.57	61
Kate Appleby	"	80.09	51
Alexandra Comben	"	75.8	43
N. F. Thorne	VII and VIII	80	56
Frank A. Good	"	79.5	44
Julia Neales	IX	64.09	29
G. H. Harrison	X and XI	77.44	32
			652

Respectfully submitted,

A. B. CONNELL,

Secretary.

July 6th 1901.

VII TOWN OF CHATHAM.

To JAMES R. INCH, LL. D.,
Chief Supt. of Education.

SIR:—I beg to submit statements of our schools for half year ending June 30th, 1901.

Mrs. Minnie R. Loggie was appointed by the Town Council to fill vacancy made by the death of Miss M. R. Tweedie.

In April owing to illness Miss Bessie M. Creighton was granted leave of absence to end of term and Miss Grace Henderson appointed to the vacancy.

The contractor is making good progress with new building and we are looking forward to occupy it in November.

GEORGE STOTHART, Secretary.

Financial Statement for Half Year Ending June 30th, 1901.

EXPENDITURE.

For salaries	$3,007 50
" Rent	160 00
" Fuel	231 30
" Interest	180 85
" Paid on account debt	250 00
" Incidentals	38 53
	$3,868 18

RECEIPTS.

County School Fund	$ 634 51	
Town Treasurer	3,144 15	
		$ 3,778 66
Balance		$ 89 52

NAMES OF TEACHERS, NUMBER OF PUPILS AND GRADES TAUGHT FOR TERM ENDED JUNE 30, 1901.

Teachers.	Salaries.	Boys.	Girls.	Total.	Grades Taught
Philip Cox, Ph. D.	$750	11	14	25	X., XI.
James McIntosh	500	9	9	18	IX.
R. W. Alward	375	20	17	37	VIII.
Miss Maggie Mowatt	280	22	18	40	VII., VI.
" Ida J. Haviland	200	30	11	41	V.
" K. Maude Lawlor	200	37	20	57	IV., III.
" Laula S. Smith	200	41	11	52	II., I.
" Bessie N. Creighton. } " Grace Henderson. }	200	26	12	38	II., I.
" K. J. B. Maclean	200	26	14	40	IV., III.
Sister Ellen Walsh	200		60	60	II., I.
" E. O. Keeffe	200		41	41	III., II.
" S. Jane Curry	200		60	60	VI., V., IV.
" Margaret Barden	280		36	36	VIII., VII.
Miss Anna G. McIntosh	280	21	11	32	VII.
" Mary C. Edgar	200	25	20	45	VI., IV.
" Essie L. Keoughan	200	20	24	44	V.
" V. C. Wright	200	44	13	57	IV.
" Mabel J. Flood	200	28	19	47	III.
" Katie A. McDonald	200	30	17	47	III., II.
" M. C. Sutherland	200	35	29	64	I.
" Annie M. Curran	200	35	18	53	II.
Totals		460	474	934	

NUMBER OF PUPILS IN GRADES.

I.	II.	III.	IV.	V.	VI.	VII.	VIII.	IX.	X.	X
145	105	142	141	102	69	65	62	18	14	1

IX. — TOWN OF NEWCASTLE

TO J. R. INCH, ESQ., LL. D.,
Chief Supt. of Education.

SIR :— As requested, I have the honor to present for your consideration, the Report of the Board of School Trustees, of the Town of Newcastle, for the Winter Term, school year ending 30th June, 1901.

EXPENDITURES.

For Teachers' Salaries,	$ 1555 21
Janitors' "	131 00
Secretary,	50 00
Insurance,	12 00
Printing,	28 60
Furniture,	75 55
Rent for 1 year,	200 00
Repairs,	16 95
Fuel,	104 75
School Supplies,	13 46
Incidentals,	6 00
Total,	$ 2193 52

The following table shows the number of schools, pupils, teachers, etc. :

WINTER TERM.

TEACHER.	No. Boys.	No. Girls.	Total.	Av'g'e Daily Attendance.	Per Cent. Attendance.	GRADES TAUGHT.
M. J. Dunnet	32	17	49	35.54	72.53	V.
I. H. Falconer	23	21	44	34	78.5	III and IV.
M. J. Wallace	37	29	66	50	76	VII and VIII.
S. M. Harriman	40	17	57	43.24	75.86	I and II.
E. McLachlan	25	21	46	38.46	83.6	VI.
P. F. Morrissy	7	11	18	14.34	79.33	II, III, IV, V, VII.
F. P. Yorston / G. K. McNaughton	15	18	33	23.31	70.63	IX, X, XI.
B. M. Reid	19	18	37	24.3	65.9	I, II, III, IV, VI, VII.
L. B. Troy	37	18	55	45.98	81.8	III and IV.
B. M. Bell	48	22	70	54	77	I and II.
	283	192	475			

Respectfully submitted,

R. NICHOLSON, Chairman.

P. F. MORRISSY, Secretary.

Newcastle, N. B., 13th December, 1901.

VIII. TOWN OF CAMPBELLTON.

J. R. INCH, ESQ., LL. D.,
Chief Supt. of Education.

SIR.—The Board of School Trustees for the Town of Campbellton herewith submit a statement of the receipts and expenditures of the Board, together with statistical tables in connection with the various departments under its charge for the Special Term ending June 30th, 1901.

WORKING ACCOUNTS STATEMENT.

RECEIPTS.

Cash on hand January 1, 1901,	$ 496 92	
Tuition Fees,	17 00	
Town Treasurer	1,100 00	
County Treasurer	240 54	
Bank Nova Scotia (overdraft)	444 92	
		$ 2,299 38

EXPENDITURES.

Teachers' salaries	1,215 00	
Interest on debentures	400 00	
Exchange on drafts	1 48	
Contingencies	5 00	
Repairs	13 57	
Fuel	182 22	
Supplies	5 92	
Water Rates	10 84	
Printing	2 15	
Insurance Premiums	208 00	
Discount on drafts	30	
[illegible]niture	12 90	
[illegible]etary's salary	50 00	
[illegible]itor's salary	175 00	
[illegible]n hand, secretary	17 00	
		$ 2,299 38

NAMES OF TEACHERS, NUMBER OF PUPILS, GRADES TAUGHT ETC., DURING TERM ENDING JUNE 30TH, 1901.

	Teachers.	Departments.	Class.	* Yearly Salary.	Boys.	Girls.	Total.	Grades Taught.
1	E. W. Lewis, B. A..	Grammar...	G. Class.	$650	15	21	36	IX., X., XI
2	E. M. Downey, B.A.	Intermediate.	" "	350	21	20	41	VII., VIII.
3	Mary McRae.......	"	II. "	200	37	26	63	V., VI.
4	Kate E. Currie......	"	I. "	200	37	27	64	IV., V.
5	Clara E. Shannon...	"	II. "	200	33	31	64	III.
6	Amanda Doyle......	Primary.....	I. "	200	30	20	50	I., II.
7	Martha G. Barnes...	"	I. "	225	30	28	58	I., II.
				2025	203	173	376	

* Exclusive of Government Allowance.

Respectfully submitted,

WM. F. COMEAU,
Secretary.

D. MURRAY, M. D
Chairman.

Campbellton, N. B., June 30th, 1901.

APPENDIX D.

REPORTS OF THE INSTITUTION FOR THE DEAF AND DUMB AT FREDERICTON, AND OF THE SCHOOL FOR THE BLIND, HALIFAX.

I.—Fredericton Institution for the Education of the Deaf and Dumb.

MANAGING COMMITTEE.

MR. J. W. SPURDEN, *Chairman.*

MR. H. C. CREED,
REV. J. MCLEOD, D. D.,
REV. WILLARD MCDONALD,
MR. CHAS. FISHER, K. C.,
HIS HONOR JUDGE GREGORY,
REV. J. D. FREEMAN,
MR. HENRY CHESTNUT, *Treasurer.*
MR. G. T. WHELPLEY,
W. C. CROCKET, M. D.,
MR. ARTHUR R. SLIPP,
REV. H. HARTLEY,
REV. J. J. TEASDALE,
MR. HAVELOCK COY,
REV. CANON ROBERTS, D. D., *Secretary.*

MR. ALBERT F. WOODBRIDGE, *Principal.*

ASSISTANTS.

MR. G. ERNEST POWERS,
MR. E. E. PRINCE,
MR. JAMES L. NEVILLE.

TEACHER OF ARTICULATION.

MISS IRENE WOODBRIDGE.

DR. MCLEARN, Royal Canadian Regt., *Physician.* DR. TORRENS, *Dentist.*

J. R INCH, ESQ., LL. D.,
Chief Superintendent of Education.

SIR: In accordance with your request I beg to forward a brief report of the work for the period from January Ist to June 30th, 1901.

It is a pleasure to be able to report that during this period the work of the Institution was carried on harmoniously and that nothing serious occurred to mar or interrupt its progress.

The principal and most interesting event of the half year was the annual closing exercises held in June, which were very largely attended.

The excellent showing made by the pupils in the different classes was most gratifying to the committee and to the officers of the Institution who had labored earnestly through the long winter months, that marked improvement might be seen by the numerous visitors who usually attend our annual closing examinations.

The warm words of approval by many of those present and by the press whose representatives were also here, were fully appreciated by the Principal and his staff whose sole desire is to bring enlightenment and education to the deaf children throughout the Province.

A number of our pupils attended the Sloyd School, established in the city through the liberality of Sir Wm. C. Macdonald and the Instructor, Mr. Macredie reported that our boys made good progress, their work comparing very favorably with that of the hearing and speaking students.

ome of the results of the work at the Sloyd School were exhibited at the Annual closing exercises.

While rendering our sincere thanks to our Local Government and the Legislature for the aid which has been extended to the Institution in the past we would make an earnest appeal for increased support.

Many of our subscribers throughout the Province have urged us to circulate a petition for signature asking for an increased government appropriation and without doubt such a petition would be freely signed as there is a growing feeling among the friends of the Institution that the work should be more liberally supported from the Provincial Treasury.

A deputation consisting of some members of our Managing Committee waited upon the Government last session, their object being to urge the claims of the Institution to increased Government support. The deputation had reason to hope that these claims would be more fully recognized and a larger grant made.

It was urged by the deputation that our Provincial Institution for the Deaf should be placed on the same financial basis and given the same liberal measure of support as is extended to the Nova Scotia Institutions for the Blind and Deaf.

It was believed that after eighteen years of steady and unremitting continuance of the work it was but a just and reasonable request and a claim that would have met with ready acquiescence and approval and especially at a time when the status of the Province had been marked by great social and commercial progress.

Some little disappointment was naturally felt by the Directors and officers of the Institution when, after the cordial manner in which the deputation had been received, the House prorogued without making provision for an increase to the usual annual grant of $500.

It is earnestly hoped however, that at the forthcoming session of the House, this omission will be cheerfully rectified and an increase made in our yearly appropriation, as the education of the Deaf is a work now generally recognized as part of that liberal educational system which has won for the Province the warm appreciation and high encomiums of other lands.

ATTENDANCE.

The following has been the attendance.

NAMES AND ADDRESSES — BOYS.

No.	Name.	Age.	Address.
1	Warren Allen	17	Westmorland County.
2	Edward B. Allen	14	" "
3	Harold McManus	13	Kings "
4	Russell Dobson	13	Westmorland "
5	Geo. D. Crain	22	Carleton
6	Melbourne Bleakney	11	York
7	Purdy C. T. Rogers	12	Westmorland "
8	Achille St. Onge	12	Madawaska "
9	Willie Matthews	9	Prince Edward Island.
10	Anoley Andrew Green	11	Charlotte County.
11	Willie Olsen Trenholm	11	Westmorland County.
12	John Arthur Wiley	10	Carleton "
13	Oscar Haines	10	" "
14	Clarence S. Nicholls	12	Restigouche "
15	Ernest Gordon Rogers	9	Westmorland "
16	Jno. Francis Patterson	11	St. John
17	Clyde Dow	13	York
18	Abe Levine	11	St. John
19	David Samuel Ferguson	8	York "
20	Isaac Hawkes	16	Kings "

NAMES AND ADDRESSES — GIRLS.

No.	Name.	Age.	Address.
1	Della Maud Green	19	St. John County.
2	Viva H. Wasson	16	Queens "
3	Nellie H. Dixon	10	Kings "
4	Edna Isabel McKenzie	16	Albert "
5	Muriel Morrison	17	Carleton "
6	Ellen Robinson	14	Kings "
7	Helen J. Bowland	26	" "
8	Essie May Haines	13	Carleton "
9	Grace McFarlane	9	Westmorland Connty.
10	Martha Eva Dickie	19	Restigouche "
11	Melissa J. Watson	14	Queens "
12	Clara Bell Mitton	8	Westmorland "
13	Emma Scott	14	St. John "

The total attendance for the half year has been thirty-three, viz., twenty boys and thirteen girls representing the following counties.

Albert	1	Queens	2
Carleton	5	Restigouche	2
Charlotte	1	St. John	4
Kings	5	Westmorland	8
Madawaska	1	York	3
Prince Edward Island	1		

The closing exercises illustrating the work of the session were held at the Institution and considerable interest was manifested in the proceedings, the house being filled to overflowing with distinguished and appreciative visitors from Fredericton, Gibson, Marysville, St. John, Moncton, Florenceville, Digby, Winnipeg and other places.

The Hon. Judge Gregory presided and among the visitors were the Very Rev. Dean Partridge, D. D., Canon Roberts, D. D., the genial Secretary of the Institution, J. D. Phinney, K. C., Messrs. Havelock Coy, H. C. Creed and other members of the Committee.

The afternoon's program was received with much appreciation and all expressed themselves as delighted with evidences of careful instruction shown by the pupils.

The exercises were held in the school-rooms, the folding doors between which were opened making one large audience room. About the walls of the room were arranged specimens of the work of the pupils in free hand drawing, map making and water color painting, while upon a large table was displayed the work done by the boys who attended the Sloyd School during the term. They took pleasure in pointing out to the visitors the specimens of their own manufacture and all had just reason for being proud of their work.

The exercises opened with the pupils reciting the Lord's Prayer which was followed by the Principal's address.

A cordial welcome was extended to all on behalf of the Institution. Most of the advanced pupils having left the previous June to enter on their life avocations, a younger class had been taken to supply their places and while less experienced had done fairly well and the results were shown in their examination.

Neither death nor serious sickness occurred during the session and the whole year had been a profitable one to the pupils and a pleasure and satisfaction to the teachers.

he financial position of the Institution was referred to and thankfulness ssed that all obligations resting upon it had been met.

A few practical points regarding the deaf were then touched upon to give the visitors a clearer understanding of the condition in which they are placed by the deprivation of hearing and some of the difficulties with which they have to contend in attaining a knowledge of language and other subjects.

In speaking of the condition of the deaf previous to education he said:

"About sixty per cent. of our pupils are born deaf. Let us try to realize what hereditary deafness means We all know of cases of friends or relatives who have become hard of hearing as it is called or entirely deaf in mature age, but this, while serious enough, is but a minor affliction in comparison with the state of these children. If everyone of us in this room were to become stone deaf this afternoon we should no doubt consider it a heavy affliction, but it would not place or lower us to the plane of those who are born deaf. It would gradually deprive us of vocal speech but not affect our written language nor the ability to read the thoughts of others."

The methods of teaching were then described. The problem confronting the teacher was how can a knowledge of written language be conveyed to them so that they can assimilate it and use it as a means of communication in the struggle of life?

Thousands of earnest men and women were devoting their lives to the elucidation of this problem. They had taxed their minds and patience for years to restore the deaf as far as possible to society and lay the basis for useful, honest, responsible and self-supporting citizens.

Efforts had been made for the restoration of their hearing, medical experts had used their utmost skill in this direction, but all in vain. Instruments had been devised to improve their hearing but with little success.

Failing in this, attention was then given to a system of oral training or articulation and lip reading, the idea being that they should be taught to read the lips of others and use their vocal organs without hearing, depending only on the sense of sight.

Another method was to adopt a language, a silent language which would appeal wholly to the sight and be totally independent of the ear.

Both these methods had been largely adopted and were the principal method of teaching the deaf at the present day. The advantages derived from the use of both methods were then referred to and he gave a number of illustrations of the difficulties arising in teaching the deaf, the shades in meaning of words spelled differently and also of words similarly spelled. He appealed to his hearers to persist in the use of only good English, to avoid slang and glory in their birthright of the English tongue.

The examination of the pupils then took place and the rapt attention of the audience showed the great interest which this part of the program elicited.

Miss Woodbridge then brought forward her pupils in the lip reading and articulation department and the proficiency which they had acquired testified to the tact and patience shown by their instructress.

The presentation of prizes followed, the presentations with suitable addresses being made by some of the gentlemen present.

A pleasing feature was the presentation by the pupils of a gold mounted ebony cane to Canon Roberts who had been secretary of the Institution since its formation eighteen years ago.

Miss Della Green (one of the pupils of Miss Woodbridge's class) first wrote her address upon the blackboard and then spoke the words orally as she presented the cane.

Dr. Roberts made a feeling and happy reply. The program closed with remarks from the chairman who expressed the pleasure he and all had derived from witnessing the bright happy demeanour of the children and the successful results of the training they had received.

In Conclusion—cheered by the fact that the session had been a successful one and thankful that the work was making headway and prospering, the teachers joined with the pupils in anticipating with considerable pleasure the long midsummer holidays which now lay before them.

ALBERT F. WOODBRIDGE, Superintendent.

II.—Thirty-First Annual Report of the Board of Managers of the School for the Blind, Halifax, Nova Scotia.

INTRODUCTION.

The Board of Managers of the School for the Blind have great pleasure in submitting to the members of the Corporation, to the Provincial Governments and Legislatures interested, and to the friends of the institution, the 31st annual report. In so doing they desire to express their grateful thanks for the Legislative grants which have been so liberally made by the several provinces and to the support given to the work by the many friends of the blind throughout Eastern Canada. Under the blessing of Almighty God the work of educating and training the blind has been successfully and satisfactorily carried on and the usefulness of the school has been steadily developed.

SUPERINTENDENT'S REPORT.

As will be seen by the report of the Superintendent, the several departments of the school are thoroughly equipped and in a high state of efficiency. The members of the teaching staff have shown commendable zeal, and their devotion to their chosen work well merits approval.

It is a matter of satisfaction to your Board to find that the course of instruction in the school is well abreast of the times and that the youthful blind of the Maritime Provinces and Newfoundland have within their reach an education of such an eminently practical character. The school keeps close in touch with its graduates and it is gratifying to note that the great majority of them are meeting with success, are respected in the communities in which they reside, and are living happy and useful lives.

DOMESTIC DEPARTMENT.

The former matron of the school, Miss Fraser, owing to family bereavement resigned her position at the commencement of the present school ye[illegible]. After some consideration it was decided to combine the positions of mat[illegible] and housekeeper and to appoint a second assistant matron. This has b[illegible] done and so far the arrangement works admirably. Mrs. Chisholm, now acti[illegible] matron, supervises the entire domestic work of the school and still finds ti[illegible] to discharge her duties as housekeeper in superintending the work in the kitchen, dining rooms and laundry, and in taking charge of the food supplies. Mrs. Chisholm has been given two assistants, the one to act as matron of the girls' department, to be responsible for the scrupulous cleanliness of the girls' wing and the repairing of the girls' clothing. The boys' assistant matron has been assigned similar duties in the boys' department. We believe that this arrangement will prove most satisfactory and that Mrs. Chisholm, who is deeply interested in the pupils, will discharge her duties with characteristic energy and efficiency.

BUILDINGS AND GROUNDS.

During the summar the roofs of the main building and east wing were re-covered and several alterations and improvements in the interior of the buildings were carried out. The buildings, although extensive and well adapted for their purpose, are nevertheless too small to meet the present needs of the school. It must be remembered that our household, including officers, members of the teaching staff, the domestic staff, and pupils numbers 144 persons and that to provide dormitories, schoolrooms, music rooms, sitting rooms, dining rooms and other requisite accommodation, is under present circumstances no easy matter. We have utilized every available space, have used our music rooms at night for bed rooms, have turned our hallways and reading rooms into practice rooms, and our sitting rooms into class rooms. In fact we have done everything that can be done to keep the doors of the school wide open to those for whom it is intended. We fully realize that in the very near future an effort must be made to provide increased accommodation, and we believe that when the friends of the school appreciate the fact that such increased accommodation is absolutely essential they will, as hitherto, gladly aid us with their subscriptions, and will do all in their power to help us in extending the grand educational work which is being carried on.

As the means at our command would allow, we have, from time to time, improved the grounds of the school and arranged them so as to meet the requirements of the pupils. In the lower square we have constructed an artificial pond 120 feet in length by 60 feet in breadth. Owing to the nature ~ ground it was necessary to lay the bottom in concrete and to build the ..nding wall in a most substantial way. In this connection we desire to ..owledge the indebtedness of the Board to Mr. F. W. W. Doane, who ..y supervised the construction of the pond, and who has heretofore advised the laying out of the grounds. The pond will be a source of pleasure to the pupil throughout the school year, but it will be more particularly appreciated during the winter season, when it can be used for skating. We hope at no distant day to be able to asphalt the paths so as to make them clean and dry and fit for use at all times excepting for a short time in winter. This would obviate the necessity of constructing balconies or piazzas where the pupils might exercise, and would make the grounds much more available during the early spring and late autumn months.

The actual cost of educating a blind boy or girl in this school, considering capital expenditure, is $225 per annum. Through the bequests of its benefactors and the subscriptions of its friends this association or corporation is fortunately able to meet one-third of this cost, or $75 per pupil. The Acts provide that for each pupil from Nova Scotia or New Brunswick the school should receive $75 from the respective Provincial Governments and a like sum from the municipality to which the child belongs. The cost of education is thus equally divided between our own association, the Provincial Governments and the municipalities.

NOVA SCOTIA.

There are now pupils attending the school from seventeen of the eighteen counties in Nova Scotia, making in all seventy-one pupils from this province. From two of these counties we have at present seven pupils, while three other counties have but one pupil in attendance. This disproportion in attendance is somewhat difficult to explain, but in a cycle of years it will be found that any given section of the country will probably have no more or no less than its proportion of schoolable blind children, although at one time it may have more and at another time less. During the first fifteen years in which the school was in operation we had five pupils in all from the Musquodoboit Valley, while during the past fifteen years we have had but one pupil from that section of the County of Halifax.

NEW BRUNSWICK.

There are at present thirty-two pupils in attendance from the Province of New Brunswick. These are drawn from ten of the fifteen counties, leaving five counties unrepresented. Taking into consideration the respective populations of the provinces of Nova Scotia and New Brunswick, and the number of blind children from each province now under training, it would appear th there are at present from fifteen to eighteen young blind persons in Ne Brunswick who are growing up without receiving an education. We woul earnestly request those interested in the education of the blind to send in to th

Superintendent of the school the names, ages and addresses of all blind persons under twenty-one years of age. In this matter the co-operation of clergymen and medical men would be most advantageous.

PRINCE EDWARD ISLAND.

In the matter of the education of the blind the Government and Legislature of P. E. Island have not yet placed themselves fully in line with the other provinces, but it may at least be said that their position in this respect has somewhat improved during the past two years, and it is earnestly to be hoped that before long the statutes of P. E. Island will contain an Act making education free to the blind of that province. At the present time the school receives a grant from the Legislature of $450 per annum for the six pupils in attendance, and a further grant of $150 from the city of Charlottetown. This makes in all $600. The actual cost per annum of educating these six pupils is $1350, of which the school voluntarily assumes one-third, or $450, and asks the Government and Legislature to provide the balance of $900. We commend these figures to the kind and thoughtful consideration of the public-spirited men and women in P. E. Island, and respectfully urge the government to introduce such legislation as will place the education of the blind upon a footing honorable to the province and equitable to the school.

NEWFOUNDLAND.

We have at present eight pupils from the Colony of Newfoundland for the tuition of whom the Legislature makes an annual grant to the school of $1,200.00. Hitherto the Government of Newfoundland has limited the number of beneficeries to eight, but we have the assurance of the Premier, Hon. Sir Robert Bond, that during the coming session of the Legislature he will see if something cannot be done to secure an increased grant so as to provide for the admission of a larger number of pupils.

The Superintendent:

The following is an extract from the minutes of a meeting of the Board of Managers, held on May 1st, 1901.

"The Board of Managers desires to place on record its appreciation of the action of the Senate of Dalhousie College in conferring upon the Superintendent the School, Mr. C. F. Fraser, the degree of LL. D. The Board has on many asions expressed its high estimate of the services rendered to the Blind of Maritime Provinces by Dr. Fraser, and it feels that the public recognition which these services have received reflects great credit upon the school and upon the teaching staff as well as upon the Superintendent. In presenting Mr. Fraser to the President of the University, Dr. MacMechan on behalf of Senate said, " Mr. Charles Frederick Fraser, M. M, has been Principal of the School for the Blind twenty-eight years. Through his personal exertions the number of pupils in that period has risen from less than ten to more than one hundred, and the methods employed for their education have been of the most modern and scientific kind. Mr. Fraser has led the way in an important reform. Through his untiring efforts the education of the blind has ceased, in this province, to be regarded as a charity, and is looked upon as a necessary public charge. The Government of this Province was the first on this continent to recognize its duty in this respect, and to grant to the blind and deaf a free education. As a teacher Mr. Fraser has been very successful in developing in his pupils a self-reliant and hopeful spirit. They have been made to feel that success in almost any calling is within their reach. This spirit, called out and strengthened by sound practical courses of training, is proving efficient in making those who, under less happy circumstances, were doomed to life-long dependence, into successful and useful members of the community. In this, the direct outcome of Mr. Fraser's gifted and buoyant personality, and of his unceasing efforts, our Halifax school is recognized as one of the very best Schools for the Blind to be found anywhere. Mr. Fraser's efforts are not confined to the work of the school. For the benefit of the blind who, through age or other causes cannot attend the school, he has organized a staff of itinerant teachers and a circulating library. The beneficent plan which Nova Scotia had the honor of originating has been adopted in several places elsewhere."

ACKNOWLEDGEMENTS.

In addition to the donations elsewhere noted, your Board gratefully acknowledges the following bequests: Estate of John S. McLean, Halifax, $1000.00; estate of George H. Starr, Halifax, $500.00; estate of C. C. West, Halifax, $418.57; estate of Patrick O'Mullin, Halifax, $100 00; estate of H. P. Archibald, Halifax, $25.00; estate of Peter Coffin, Halifax, $10.00; estate of Gilbert Pugsley, Amherst, N. S. $100.00; estate of Mrs. Elizabeth, New Glasgow, N. S. $51.60; estate of C. E. Stanfield, Truro, N. S. $50.00. These bequests which amount to $2455.17, have been carefully invested and now form part of the endowment fund of the school. The income from this fund is used further the education of the blind, and it is a great satisfaction to your Bo to find that the friends of the institution are thus numbering its needs that the income from the endowment fund is slowly and steadily increasing.

The thanks of the Board of Managers are due Doctors Lindsay, Kirkpatrick and Cogswell. These gentlemen are ever ready when called upon to attend the pupils, and their professional services are generously given free of charge. The Board of Managers also desires to express its thanks to Mr. H. B. Clark, Mr. J. D. Medcalf, the Weil School of Music, the Halifax Symphony Orchestra, and other individuals and organizations, for kindly admitting the pupils to lectures, concerts, etc, under their respective managements. The value to the pupils of these entertainments from an educational standpoint cannot be overestimated in addition, to which they are a great source of enjoyment.

The railways and other transportation companies have our thanks for the special rates granted and for the uniform kindness and care shown to the pupils while travelling to and from their homes.

All of which is respectfully submitted.

W. C. SILVER,
President of the Board of Managers.

Superintendent's Report.

To the President and Board of Managers of the School for the Blind :

GENTLEMEN :—The table of attendance herewith submitted shows that 135 blind persons have been under instruction during the past year, of which 80 were males and 55 females. Of these 18 have since graduated or remained at home, making the total number registered December 1st, 1901, 117, of whom 70 are males and 47 females, Of these 71 are from the Province of Nova Scotia, 32 from New Brunswick, 6 from P. E. Island and 8 from Newfoundland.

TABLE OF ATTENDANCE.

	Boys.	Girls.	Adults	Total.
Registered Dec., 1st, 1900	64	48	5	117
Entered during the year, ...	9	7	2	18
Graduated or remained at home, ...	8	8	2	18
Registered Dec. 1st, 1901	65	47	5	117

TEACHING STAFF.

After five years of faithful and satisfactory work as a teacher in the literary department, Miss Bessie Cumming resigned her situation at the close of the last school year. Miss Cumming, now Mrs. Robb, has gone with her husband to the mission field of Corea, where she hopes to turn to practical account the experience gained while here. The vacancy caused by the retirement of Miss Cumming has been filled by Miss Elma Baker, a graduate of Dalhousie College and a teacher of high standing in the public schools. An assistant teacher of modern languages being required, the position was given to Miss Bowes, an advanced pupil of Prof. Lanos. With the foregoing exceptions our staff of teachers remains the same as at this date last year. This is a matter for congratulation, as it is of importance that our pupils should receive their training from teachers of skill and experience and of broad education. In the literary department Miss C. R. Frame, Miss Baker, Mr. S. R. Hussey, Prof. Lanos, Miss Bowes and two assistants have faithfully performed their work, and have sought in every way to develop their pupils and make them strong and self-reliant men and women.

The Kindergarten pupils have continued to enjoy the thoughtful care and admirable training imparted by Miss Josie Howe and her assistants, Miss Campbell and Miss Callanan.

In the boys' and girls' musical departments Prof. A. M. Chisholm has been assisted by Miss B. Studd and Mr. T. A. Hubley, as piano-forte teachers; Miss Corbin, vocal teacher, and Messrs. Hanson, Covey and Ivimey as teachers respectively of the clarionet, cornet and mandolin. The work of the departments has been progressive and up-to-date in all respects, and has been carried forward with zeal and energy.

Mr. D. M. Reid, teacher of piano-forte tuning; Mr. D. A. Baird, trade instructor; M. J. S. Scrimgeour, physical instructor, and Miss Allison, teacher of the girls' work, have been steadily at their posts, and have been deeply interested in the success of their pupils.

We have in past years been very fortunate in securing as teachers men and women of character and marked ability, but without disparaging the excellent work done by them, I may safely say that never in the history of the school have we had a stronger or more effective teaching staff, and never have the results been more satisfactory or more gratifying. This is due in part to the long experience in this special work which the majority of the teachers have enjoyed, and in part to the more careful grading of the pupils which the larger school makes possible, and also to the improved equipment of our several departments.

COURSE OF INSTRUCTION.

In most respects the course of instruction in this school is similar to that followed in the more advanced institutions for the blind in Great Britain and the United States. It is based upon the idea that our pupils, notwithstanding their lack of sight, are to be educated with the view of becoming self-supporting men and women. Were it possible for blind persons to perform ordinary labour, or to market hand made articles in competition with the output of mills and factories equipped with steam and machinery, we might be justified in limiting their education to the rudimentary branches of learning and be satisfied with the results. We have, however, to face the fact that the blind cannot perform ordinary labour to advantage and cannot hope to become so skilled in manual work as to be able to undersell machine-made products. It is therefore a fundamental principle with the best educators of the blind that every effort should be made to train and develop the mental faculties of their pupils -- -- to prepare them for such professions and occupations as call for intellect- acumen. To the educated blind person the loss of sight is a handicap but barrier to success. His trained senses of touch and hearing and even of make up to him in a great measure for his loss of sight, while his intellectual powers are none the less strong, keen and effective, because he is deprived of vision. Bearing the foregoing facts in mind our course of study has been carefully arranged so as to place within reach of our pupils a broad and liberal education which is in all respects equal to that imparted in the best public schools of Canada. This education is supplemented by a careful training in music, pianoforte tuning and such other branches as the pupils can turn to practical account when they graduate from the school.

APPLIANCES.

It is a great satisfaction to note that the appliances used in the education of the blind have of late years been greatly improved. The old arithmetic board with its ten distinct raised type has given place to a board with star-shaped holes and one type by which sixteen separate characters can be represented. This, in my opinion, although an improvement, is not yet an ideal arithmetic board. We use the Braille Point characters in both reading and writing and should, I believe, use the same system in the study of arithmetic. This idea I have suggested to the manufacturers of appliances for the blind.

In the making of raised maps the British and Foreign Blind Association of London have scored a distinct success and well merit the gratitude of the instructors of the blind. The political as well as the physical maps made by the association are wonderfully perfect in their execution and accurate in detail. Their cheapness makes it possible to supply each pupil with a map of the country to be studied, and the teacher is thus enabled to keep the attention of the entire class apon the work in hand.

In the manufacture of point print books the advance has been phenomenal. A few years since books for the blind were embossed only on one side of the leaf. The first great saving of space was secured by the method known as interlining, that is, the lines on one side of the leaf were embossed between the lines upon the opposite side. Still more recently it has been found that space might be economised by embossing the points on one side of the sheet between the points upon the opposite side, thus completely filling with reading or other matter both sides of the page.

The latest invention comes from Birmingham, England, where a system of shorthand has been devised and a machine for rapidly embossing the Braille characters has been invented. With this machine, one of which has b ordered for the school, a pupil can be trained to take notes of a public meet or even make a verbatim report of a speech and then reproduce the same typewritrng from an ordinary machine. This invention will unquestionably make it possible for the blind to become newspaper reporters and correspondence clerks.

HEALTH.

The health of the pupils throughout the year has been most satisfactory, and the work of the several departments of the school has been but slightly interrupted by the carrying out of a general vaccination. Such cases of sickness as have occured have been promptly and carefully looked after by the attending physician, Dr. A. H. Lindsay, and by the matron in charge.

PHYSICAL TRAINING.

The physical training of the pupils, which is recognized to be of first importance, has received careful attention. The pupils spend forty-five minutes daily in the gymnasium under the instruction of Mr. James Scrimgeour, and are taught to march, to use dumb-bells and wands, and to freely and easily perform exercises upon the overhead ladder, the rings, the parallel bars and the German horse. Contests in walking and running in the open air, and participation in out-of-door sports are also encouraged and are keenly enjoyed by the pupils. Now that the artificial pond in our grounds has been completed, we anticipate that the majority of the boys and girls will learn to skate during the winter season, and that they will derive a great deal of pleasure from this healthful exercise.

GRADUATES.

At the close of the school year in June last a number of young men and women received their graduating diplomas. Among these may be mentoined the following : T. B. Fletcher, of DeBert, N. S., received first class certificate as a teacher of music, and has since settled in Truro, where he has secured a number of music pupils. Charles Kaulback, of New Germany. N. S., and Hiram Colby, of Bear River, N. S., received first class certificates as piano-forte tuners, and are finding employment in the counties in which they respectively reside. Daniel Morrison, of Black Brook, C. B., was awarded a certificate as a willow basket and brush maker, and has established himself in the vicinity of Sydney. C. B. Miss Nellie Taylor, of Halifax, N. S., received a certificate as a teacher of vocal and instrumental music. Miss Taylor went ...gby, N. S., for the purpose of securing a class of music pupils, but finding ...t popular summer resort that she could turn to advantage the knowledge ...mposing she has gained while here she followed that occupation during the summer months, and proved it to be a remunerative employment, and one that could be satisfactorily followed by a person deprived of sight.

In August last Mr. Frank McLean, who graduated from the school nineteen years ago died at his home in Truro much to the regret of his many friends and his fellow citizens. The obituary notices which appeared in the Truro newspapers bore testimony to the high character of Mr. McLean, to the esteem in which he was held, and to the success which attended his efforts in connection with the founding and carrying on of the Truro Conservatory of Music. After referring to Mr. McLean's early training in this school and to the four years spent by him in the study of music in Germany, the Truro Weekly News says, "in 1894 Mr. McLean opened the Truro Conservatory of Music, in the Queen Building, Prince Street. To the success of this worthy institution, Mr. McLean bent all his energies, and though labouring under blindness, this remarkable man, with the assistanee of his talented wife, built up a successful business, and the name "Truro Conservatory of Music" is now widely and favorably known. The late Mr. McLean was, by his kindly, happy and gentlemanly bearing, highly respected and beloved by all who had the pleasure of his acquaintance." In reference to the funeral of Mr. McLean we find the following:—"there were many friends assembled to do honor to the respected dead and to pay the last tribute to the memory of one who, though afflicted with blindness, was an active and untiring worker in life's busy hive." The foregoing tribute to the memory and work of one of our most successful graduates will be appreciated by the friends and supporters of the school and by the educated blind in all parts of this country.

LIBRARY.

In another part of this Report will be found the names of the new point print books, which during the year, have been added to our circulating library and also an acknowledgment of our deep indebtedness to the gentlemen and ladies and to the young people who assisted in the production of the Spectacle Opera of Zephra under the management of Mr. R. W. Averill. From the proceeds of this entertainment we received for our library fund the sum of $415.60 a portion of which amount has been placed on deposit and the balance used in purchasing and manufacturing new books. This edition to our circulating library will be keenly appreciated by those who enjoy the privileges o reading, free of charge, the many instructive and interesting volumns listed ir its catalogue.

NEW PUBLICATIONS.

We have issued during the year a number of new publications stereotyped and printed on the machines presented to the school by Mr. H. M. Whitney. These publications are for the use of our pupils and graduates and are of the greatest advantage to them in their school work and in the teaching of music. The Braille musical notation and the ordinary Braille point print can be stereotyped upon the same machine and hence we have the facilities for printing music in tangible form as well as for printing ordinary books.

Among the recent publications may be mentioned, Zobansky's Gallin Paris Cheve method of sight singing, volumes, two, three and four; the Practical Speller in one volume; the Multiplication Tables, Euclid's Definitions, Practical Method for the Piano-forte, by Louis Kohler, a Selection of Easy Pianoforte Pieces for Young Beginners in the First Grade, Hymns, Choruses, etc.

THE EDUCATION OF THE BLIND IN GREAT BRITAIN.

During the summer holidays I had the pleasure of making an extended tour in England and Scotland and of visiting many of the schools and institutions for the blind in the Old Country. I was accompanied by Mrs. Fraser and Miss C. R. Frame, principal of our girls' department, both of whom were deeply interested in the education of the blind. It is impossible in a brief report to refer in detail to the institutions we inspected, or to give a succinct account of the relative standing of the various schools. Speaking generally, the most noticeable feature was the great advancement that had been made in the education of the blind since my visit to the institutions in 1888. This is due in great measure to the enactment of laws by the British parliament making provision for the free education of the blind incumbent upon the board-school authorities instead of the poor-law guardians, upon whom the obligation previously rested. This change in the status of the education of the blind has infused new life into the schools, and as they are now periodically examined by government inspectors, the standard of education has been raised and is now more uniform in its character and more effective in its results. British methods in education, as in other matters, are distinctly conservative, and while I noted with pleasure the progress referred to in educating the blind, I could not help regretting that the bright school boys and girls with whom I talked were unnecessarily handicapped by their surroundings, by class distinc-[illegible] and the traditional pauperism which their condition implies. In the [illegible]teenth and in the early part of the nineteenth centuries, the blind in poor [illegible]stances were gathered into asylums, where they were fed, clothed and lodged at the expense of the charitable public. At a later date the inmates of these asylums were taught light handicrafts, and the workers, some of whom resided outside, were paid a small weekly wage for their labor. These asylums have, owing to numerous bequests, become very wealthy, and many of them undertake to give employment to all blind persons needing work. The workers no longer dwell within the walls of the asylum, but live in their own homes or board themselves. They receive a weekly wage far beyond the value of their labor. The committee in charge of these asylums, having ample funds at their command, distribute the same as remuneration for work done, or grant pensions to those who by age or infirmity are unable to work. The schools for the youthful blind have, in the majority of cases, been attached to these asylums, and the children have grown up with the idea that come what would they would be looked after and cared for by the institution. One can readily imagine the baneful influence that such a system would necessarily have upon the children of poor parents. There is no incentive to effort, no desire to rise above the circumstances by which they are surrounded. The result is, that after obtaining a somewhat limited education, these boys and girls naturally become workers in the asylum and live and die as recipients of its charity and oversight.

In speaking of this matter to a kind-hearted and thoughtful superintendent, I expressed my regret that such a system should be in vogue and told him that in Canada such methods would not be deemed expedient or in the best interests of the blind. He replied, "in our country we do not believe in educating the blind beyond the class to which they belong" and he added "the asylums look after those who are deprived of sight, literally from the cradle to the grave."

Many of these asylums in addition to their endowments are supported by annual subscriptions and in their reports make special mention of the generosity of the subscribers and give details as to the number of men and women that the committee has been enabled to employ. As a consequence the British public are constantly imbued with the idea that the blind as a class, are mendicants and this impression makes it all the more difficult for one of the poorer class to work independently of the asylum with which he has been associated.

In the limited work that is being done for the higher education of the blind, the Royal Normal College at Upper Norwood stands in the very front rank. It is in many respects an ideal institution, with ideal surroundings. In this college from 150 to 200 boys and girls are receiving a really first cla education and it may be hoped that when the educational authorities reali the excellent work it is doing, an effort will be made to disassociate all schools from asylums and at once raise the status of the schools and of the education imparted in them. To the late Doctor T. R. Armitage, the blind of Great Britain owe a deep debt of gratitude for the progress that has already been made; and to Doctor F. J. Campbell, the practical and energetic principal of the Royal Normal College, are due the thanks of the blind of that country for his untiring efforts to place them on a level with persons with sight.

During my visit I learned much that will be most helpful to me in this school and which cannot fail to be advantageous to the blind of Eastern Canada. Our own Institution is not in every way all that I would desire to see it, but it is in so many respects in advance of the majority of the institutions on the other side of the Atlantic that we should have no reason to feel discouraged in our work, and we should in fact be thankful that the blind of the Maritime Provinces and Newfoundland have within their reach an education of such a broad and eminently practical character.

CONCLUSION.

In conclusion, gentlemen, I again tender you my sincere thanks for the warm interest you have evinced in the school, and for the hearty co-operation you have ever extended to me in the conduct of its affairs.

All of which is respectfully submitted.

C. F. FRASER, *Superintendent.*

APPENDIX E.

REPORT OF THE DOMINION EDUCATIONAL ASSOCIATION, OF THE COUNTY INSTITUTES, OF THE SUMMER SCHOOL OF SCIENCE AND OF THE MACDONALD MANUAL TRAINING SCHOOL.

1.—The Dominion Educational Association.

The Fourth Convention of the Dominion Educational Association met in the Normal School, in the City of Ottawa, on the 14th, 15th and 16th of August, 1901. Dr. J. B. McCabe, of the Ottawa Normal School, presided. The following was the program :

GENERAL.

WEDNESDAY, 14TH AUGUST.

8 P. M.—Addresses of Welcome by the Mayor of Ottawa, and the Very Reverend H. A. Constantineau, D.D., O. M. I., President, University of Ottawa.

Responses by Dr. J. A. MacCabe; the Hon. G. W. Ross, LL. D.; Hon. Richard Harcourt; Hon. Boucher de la Bruere; D. J. Goggin, M. A.; Alex. Robinson, Esq.; D. J. McLeod, Esq.

THURSDAY, 15TH AUGUST.

8 P. M.—"The Desirability of Dominion Registration of Trained Teachers." S. P. Robins. LL, D., Principal McGill Norman School.

"Patriotism in Schools." Mrs. Clark Murray, Montreal.

"Comment cultiver le Sentiment National a l'Ecole Primaire." Prof. C. J. Magnan, Laval Normal School.

Address by Prof. Robertson, of the Department of Agriculture.

FRIDAY, 16TH AUGUST.

8 P. M.—"Art Education." A. F. Newlands, Esq., Buffalo, N. Y.

"Dominion Educational Bureau." Dr. J. M. Harper, Inspector of Superior Schools, Quebec.

"Educational Exhibit at Paris." S. B. Sinclair, Ph. D., Vice-Principal Ottawa Mormal School.

KINDERGARTEN.

President.—Miss E. Bolton, Normal School, Ottawa.

WEDNESDAY, 14TH AUGUST.

9.30 A. M.—Reception of Delegates.

President's Address of Welcome.

"Educational Value of Music." Mrs. F. M. S. Jenkins, Organist Saint George's Church, Ottawa.

Discussion and Illustration of Method.

Songs by Kindergartners.

2 P. M.—Round Table Conference.

Subjects :—Songs, Games, Programmes, Discipline.

THURSDAY, 15TH AUGUST.

9.30 A. M.—Opening Talk and Prayer.

Address to Mothers, Mrs. Ada M. Hughes, Toronto.

"Some Phases of Infant Mind, from a Mother's Point of View." Mrs. (Rev.) C. E. Bolton.

Discussion.

"The Parents' Responsibility to the State." The Hon. Justice Burbidge, Ottawa.

2 P. M.—Games, Led by Miss MacIntyre, Normal Kgt., Toronto, assisted by Miss Emma Duff, Toronto. Pianist, Miss Maud Lyon, Ottawa.

Social Gathering.—Hostesses, Kindergartners, Ottawa.

FRIDAY, 16TH AUGUST.

9.30 A. M.—Opening Talk and Prayer.

"Art in the Kindergarten." A. F. Newlands, Esq. Buffalo, N. Y.

Discussion and Illustrations.

"The Play Method of Teaching Music." Miss Jean Stocks, Ottawa. An illustration of her original system of teaching notation (staff), time, etc., to beginners.

ELEMENTARY SECTION.

President.—J. B. Calkin, M. A., Truro, N. S.

WEDNESDAY, 14TH AUGUST.

9.30 A. M.—President's Address

"Independent Work by Pupils." Principal MacIntyre, Winnipeg, Man., and Principal Reid, Owen Sound, Ont.

"The Relation of Phonics to the Public School Course." Principal Ward, Collingwood, Ont.

"Current Criticisms on the Ontario Educational System." Principal Edwards, Napanee, Ont.

2 P. M.—"English Grammar as a Culture Subject." Principal Meldrum, Morrisburg, Ont.

"The School and the Home—Co-Workers." Principal Masten, Odelltown, Que.

"Education and Crime."

THURSDAY, 15TH, AUGUST.

9·30 A. M.—"What the Teacher can do for the Farmer." Principal Marshall, Halifax, N. S.

" "Who Shall Prepare Public School Text Books." Principal Moore, Dundas, Ont.

"Drawing in the Public School." J. A. Dobbie, Normal School, Ottawa.

"Child Study" Principal Spence, Clinton Street School, Toronto.

2 P. M.—"The School as a Preparation for Practical Life." Ernest Smith, Esq., Westmount, Quebec.

"Science in the Public School." A. E. Atwood, M. A., Principal of Waller Street School, Ottawa.

FRIDAY, 16TH AUGUST.

9.30 A. M.—"Comparison of the Common School Curricula of the various Provinces." Principal Robbins, McGill Normal School.

"Manual Training." Principal Kidner, MacDonald Training School, Truro, N. S.

"Religion in the Public School."

2 P. M—"Education in Nova Scotia." Inspector Creighton, Halifax, N. S

"Education in New Brunswick." Prof. John Brittain, Fredericton, N. B.

"Education in Prince Edward Island."

"Education in Quebec.

"Education in Ontario." Principal F. C. Powell, Kincardine, Ont.

"Education in Monitoba." Principal MacIntyre, Winnipeg.

"Education in North West." D. J. Goggin, Esq., M. A., Superintendent of Education, N. W. T.

"Education in British Columbia." Alex. Robinson, Esq., Superintendent of Education, Victoria, B. C.

HIGHER EDUCATION.

President—D. J. Goggin, M. A., D. C. L., Supt. of Education, N. W.

WEDNESDAY, 14TH AUGUST.

9.30 A. M.—President's Address.

"Some Phases of Secondary Work in Europe and America." W. Packenham, B. A., Chairman Board of Examiners for Ontario Education Department.

"Modifications of High School Courses Demanded by Conditions of To-Day." W. J. Robertson, B A., LL. B., Collegiate Institute, St. Catherine's, Ont.

2 P. M.—"Entrance Requirements to High Schools and Universities." John Squair, B. A., Associate Professor of French, University College, Toronto,

"Should Greek and Latin be Retained as Snbjects in our Secondary School?" J. Henderson, M. A., Principal Collegiate Institute, St. Catherine's, Ont.

THURSDAY, 15TH AUGUST.

9 A. M.—"Modern Geometry." N F. Dupuis, M. A., F. R. S. C., Professor of Mathematics, Queen's University, Kingston, Ont.

"History in the High School." A. Stevenson, B. A., Collegiate Institute, Woodstock, Ont.

2 P. M.—"Literature in the High School." John Marshall, M. A., Assistant Professor of English, Queen's University, Kingston, Ont.

"What a Pupil has a Right to Expect as a Result of His High School Training in French or German." A. H. Young, M. A., Professor of Modern Languages, Trinity University, Toronto, Ont.

FRIDAY, 16TH AUGUST.

9.30 A. M.—"Ecology *vs.* Morphology." G. U. Hay, D. Sc., F. R. S. C., Editor *Educational Review*, St. John, New Brunswick.

"The Educational and Industrial significance of the Later Developments of School Work in Kindergarten, Nature Study and Manual Training." W. S. Ellis, B. A., Principal Collegiate Institute, Kingston, Ont.

2 P. M.—"The Educational Demands of Democracy." John Miller, B. A., Deputy Minister of Education, Toronto, Ont.

"Geometry in Secondary Schools." A. H. McDougall, B. A., Collegiate Institute, Ottawa.

INSPECTION AND TRAINING.

President—H. V. B. Bridges, M. A., Fredericton, N. B.

WEDNESDAY, 14TH AUGUST.

9.30 A. M.—President's Address.

"What Child Study has Done for Education." Principal Scott, M. A., Normal School, Toronto.

"Methods in Arithmetic." W. J. Summerby, Esq., Inspector of Public Schools, Russell, Ont.

2 P. M.—"The Third Element in Education" Dr. J. M. Harper, Inspector of Superior Schools, Quebec.

"County Model Schools in Ontario." Principal Jordan, Prescott, Ont.

THURSDAY, 15TH AUGUST.

9.30.—"Duties of the School Inspector, Outside the Schoolroom." John Parker, B. A., Inspector of Schools, Leeds, Quebec.

"Duties of the School Inspector, Inside the Schoolroom." J. W. McOuat, B. A., Inspector of Schools, Lachute, Quebec.

"The Teaching of French." Principal Truell, Lachute Academy.

"Some Problems of our Rural Schools." Colin W. Roscoe, M. A., Inspector of Schools, Kentville, N. S.

2 P. M.—"Attention. How it Can be Secured in the Schoolroom." Dr. H. S. Bridges, St. John, N. B.

"The Psychology of Nature Study." Sidney Silcox, B. A., B. Paed, Inspector of Public Schools, St. Thomas, Ont.

"Dominion Certificates." Rev. W. H. G. Colles, Inspector of Public Schools, Chatham, Ont.

The attendance was small — less than 100 having enrolled; but the papers read and the discussions which followed the reading of the papers were of the deepest interest.

A visit to the Dominion Experimental Farm, to the library, museum and parliament buildings, and an excursion to Britannia on the Bay were pleasant features of the meeting.

One of the most important features of the Association was the proposal made by Prof. Robertson, of the Department of Agriculture, to establish a number of experimental schools in rural sections throughout the dominion to effect improvements along the following lines: To establish well-equipped schools with the best available teachers, and thus bring about the centralization of several scattered districts into one; to make provision for school gardens and the best possible sanitary arrangements for rural schools; to exemplify the best methods of teaching nature subjects and manual training; to so handle the subjects in the curriculum of studies for each province that the schools shall deserve the usual local and provincial support, and at the same time be object lessons in education for governments and communities. Prof. Robertson said that the money for the experiment would be forthcoming as soon as a competent committee, to be appointed by the Association, had decided upon the details of the scheme. The Association approved heartily, and the following committee was appointed: Dr. Goggin (Regina), Dr. S. B. Sinclair (Ottawa), Supt. McIntyre (Winnipeg), Principal Scott (Toronto), R. H. Cowley (Ottawa), Dr. McKay (Halifax), Dr. Inch, Inspector Carter, J. Brittain (New Brunswick), Dr. Anderson, Prof. Robertson (P. E. Island), Inspector Parker, C. J. Magnan (Quebec). Prof. Robertson, of Ottawa, was invited to act with the committee.

The following are the officers of the Association: President, Dr. D. J. Goggin, Regina, Superintendent of Education for the N. W. T.; Vice-Presidents, the heads of education for the different provinces; Directors, Principal Scott, Toronto; F. H. Schofield, Winnipeg; Dr. S. P. Robbins, Montreal; G. W. Parmelee, Quebec; G. U. Hay, St. John, N. B.; Dr. J. B. Hall, Truro; Prof. Robertson, Charlottetown; F. H. Cowperthwaite, Vancouver; Secretary, W. A. McIntyre, Winnipeg; Treasurer J. T. Bowerman, Ottawa.

Winnipeg was chosen as the next place of meeting, the time to be early in July, 1903.

II.—Reports of the County Institutes.

ALBERT COUNTY.

[From the Educational Review June, 1901.]

The twenty-fourth annual meeting of the teachers of Albert County, N. B., took place at Hillsboro on Thursday and Friday, the 6th and 7th inst. President T. E. Colpitts, of the County Grammar School, presided. About fifty teachers were in attendance, and Dr. B. A. Marven, secretary of the School Board, welcomed them to the hospitalities of the town in a warm address. Miss E. A. Swanson gave a practical lesson to a primary class, illustrating in a very excellent manner how color, number and paper-folding may be taught to primary grades.

On Thursday afternoon the members of the Institute enjoyed a natural history excursion to the Plaster Quarries under the guidance of Manager C. J. Osman, M. P. P., who placed his time and conveyances unreservedly at the disposal of the teachers. The plaster caves were visited, and modes of quarrying the plaster seen. Afterwards the visitors gathered in groups around the summer house of Mr. Osman, when a talk on plants was given by Mr. G. U. Hay, and Mr. Osman explained the qualities and uses of the gypsum, which forms such an important industry at Hillsboro. After refreshments, and a hearty vote of thanks to their kind host and hostess, the party returned to town.

On Thursday evening a largely attended educational meeting was held in the public hall at Hillsboro, presided over by C. J. Osman, Esq. Much regret was expressed at the unavoidable absence of Chief Superintendent, Dr. Inch. A fine band, of which the townspeople are justly proud, and an excellent choir, enlivened the proceedings with appropriate music. Addresses were delivered by Inspector Steeves, Mr. G. U. Hay, Principal J. M. Palmer and Rev. C. W. Townsend. References were made at this meeting and during the sesions of the Institute to the fine position, well-kept surroundings, and clean, airy and well-appointed rooms of the Hillsboro school building. It is a credit to the people.

On Friday an interesting nature lesson on Indian Corn was given to a class by Miss Helena Atkinson. A paper which aroused considerable discussion was The Teacher as a Factor in Politics, by J. T. Horsman, A. B. The views of the writer were quite warmly discussed by H. H. Stuart, J. M. Palmer and others. An excellent lesson on British History was taught to a class of Grade Seven pupils by Miss Agnes E. Reynolds.

The following officers were chosen: President, T. Colpitts (re-elected); Vice-President, Miss Beatrice Steeves; Secretary-Treasurer, A. D. Jonah (re-elected). Additional members of the executive committee: Misses Ella Smith and Martha Avard. The next meeting of the Institute will be held at Hopewell Hill.

CARLETON COUNTY.

[From the *Educational Review*, January, 1902.]

The twenty-fourth annual session of the Carleton County Teachers' Institute was held at Woodstock, on Thursday and Friday, Dec. 19th and 20th, President G. H. Harrison, in the chair. Eighty-five teachers enrolled. In interest and excellence of the papers and discussions the meeting was one of the most successful ever held in the county. Chief Supt. Dr. Inch and Inspector Meagher were present and contributed very largely to the interest of the proceedings. The following papers were read: On the Teaching of History and Geography, by Mr. Joseph Howe; the History of Education in Carleton County, by Mr. D. W. Hamilton, A. B.; On Nature and Science, touching on the study of agriculture, birds, plants, minerals and chemistry, by Mr. Leon H. Jewett; Our Schools from the Standpoint of the Parent, by Rev. James Crisp; The Teaching of Fractions, by Mr. A. P. Davis. The discussions on these papers were practical and spirited. The teachers, trustees and citizens of Woodstock were excellent hosts and entertained the visiting teachers at a conversazione on Thursday evening, at which music, addresses, refreshments, helped to while away a few very pleasant hours. The following officers of the Institute were elected for the current year; President, N. F. Thorne; Vice-President, Miss Helen Page; Secretary, G. U. Harrison; Additional members, D. W. Hamilton and Miss Nettie Bearisto.

Woodstock was decided upon as the next place of meeting to be held about the last of September, if the teachers of Victoria County join with the Carleton Institute.

CHARLOTTE COUNTY.

From the Educational Review, October, 1901.]

The twenty-second annual meeting of the Charlotte County Teachers' Institute met in St. Stephen on the last Thursday and Friday in September. Mrs. Irving R. Todd, of the Milltown School Board, presided in the absence of the president, Mr. W. M. Veasey. The total enrolment was

113 out of a possible 120—the total number of teachers in the county. This justified the remark of Inspector Carter, that the Charlotte County Institute was the best attended in the province. Papers and addresses were given as follows: The President's Address (read by the secretary); Prof. E. E. MacCready, of the MacDonald Manual Training School, Fredericton; J. A. Allen, B. A., of St. Andrews, a paper on literature; one on home study and over-pressure in schools, prepared by Mrs. Samuel Johnson, St. George, was read by Mrs. W. J. Graham, Milltown; a paper on school libraries was read by Mr. J. Vroom; and an address on drawing by Mr. F. O. Sullivan. The subject of nature study occupied the attention of the Institute on Friday afternoon. Papers were read by G. U. Hay, P. G. McFarlane, and an address given by Dr. L. W. Bailey.

The public meeting on Tuesday evening was presided over by J. D. Chipman, of the St. Stephen School Board. An interesting program of addresses, interspersed with music, was carried out.

The excellence of the papers read at the Institute, and the spirited discussions which followed, made the meeting one of the most interesting that has taken place in the county, the fine autumnal weather adding much to the enjoyment of those who attended. The officers for the coming year are: Mrs. I. R. Todd, President; Henry E. Sinclair, Vice-President; James Vroom, Secretary; Ernest F. A. Towers, J. B. Sutherland and Margaret Kerr, additional members of the executive.

GLOUCESTER COUNTY.

[Reported by Edward L L. O'Brien, President.]

The Gloucester County Teachers' Institute was held at Caraquet, on the 17th and 18th of October. President Edward L O'Brien in the chair. Thirty-seven teachers enrolled. Two addresses of welcome were given, one in French by Mr. F. O. Allard, and one in English by Mr. A. J. Witzel. These called forth a happy response by Miss Laura J. Eddie.

After the transaction of the necessary routine business, a paper was read by Mr. P. P. Morais, Secretary of the Institute, on the "Phonic Method of Teaching French Reading" which was warmlv discussed by many of the teachers present. Next a very excellent paper was read by Mr. C. J. Mersereau on "Attention in Education." This paper was carefully prepared by Mr. Mersereau, and was commented upon in very favorable terms by E. L. O'Brien and M. R. Tuttle who took part in the discussion. This was followed by a lively discussion on "Home Lessons" participated in by E. L. O'Brien, M. R. Tuttle, A. J. Witzell and others

A public meeting was held in the evening, at which President O'Brien and Revs. Fathers Le Bastard and Morin spoke to a large and appreciative audience. An excellent musical program was carried out during the evening which added much to the enjoyment of all.

On Friday morning an excellent paper was read by Miss Eugene Hachey, on "Geography," and was discussed at length by a number of teachers.

In the afternoon, Mr. J. E. DeGrace, of Shippegan, read a very carefully prepared paper on "Patriotism," which was warmly discussed by several members of the Institute.

The officers elected for next year are President, A. J. Witzel; Vice-President, Miss Eugene Hachey; Secretary, F. V. Allard; Members of the Executive Committee, J. E. DeGrace and Jos. A. Salter.

The next meeting of the Institute will be held at Tracadie.

KENT COUNTY.

[From the Educational Review, October, 1901.]

The Kent County Teachers met in the Superior School, Harcourt, on Thursday and Friday, October 3rd and 4th, Principal Geo. A. Coates, of the Superior School, Buctouche, presiding. The people of Harcourt showed their interest by entertaining the visiting teachers, by their presence at the sessions of the Institute, and by attending a very enthusiastic and well conducted public meeting on Thursday evening. Much credit is due to the trustees, Messrs, Dunn and Delaney, to Miss Miriam Kyle, and her associate teacher, Miss Minnie Buckley, and others, for the local arrangements which contributed to make this institute one of the most successful ever held in the county. Papers were read by Miss M. Mazeroll, on School Government; Mr. A. E. Pearson on Everybody and the School; Mr. Charles Richards, on History, and Mr. G. U: Hay, on Nature Study. An excellent lesson on grammar was given to a class of Grade Seven pupils by Miss Miriam Kyle, and President Coates introduced the subject of The Teacher in a practical address. The discussion of the subjects and papers throughout the meeting was marked by earnestness and directness that speaks well for the teaching spirit in the county.

KINGS COUNTY.

[From the Educational Review, November, 1901.]

The sixteenth annual meeting of the Kings County Teachers' Institute held at Sussex on the 24th and 25th October, President H. R. Keith in the chair. The excellence of the papers and addresses, the spirited discussions, and the cordial welcome extended by the citizens and teachers of Sussex, rendered this one of the most interesting gatherings of teachers ever held in the county.

The absence of Inspector R. P. Steeves through illness was a matter of general regret. The presence of Chief Supt. Dr. Inch at the first Institute he has been able to attend since his return from England was a great source of help. There were papers and addresses as follows: Matthew G. Duffy on discipline; D. P. Kirkpatrick on history; E. E. MacCready, drawing and manual work, followed by an exhibition of designs, etc., from the Manual Training School, Fredericton; Miss A. Peck, mental arithmetic; Miss Laura E. Mace and Susan P. Fenwick, local history papers; Miss Mabel Folkins, time table difficulties; Weldon Pickle, literature; J. T. Horsman, arithmetic.

The election of officers resulted as follows: President, Wm. Brodie; Vice-President, Margaret Stewart; Secretaay-Treasurer, C. M. Kelly.

Hampton Station was decided on for the next place of meeting.

After adjournment the teachers of Sussex Grammar School served the members ot the Institute with refreshments.

The public meeting on the evening of the 24th was largely attended. Addresses were given by J. A. Freeze, Secretary of the School Board; Dr. Inch, G. U. Hay and E. E. MacCready, Principal of the Macdonald Training School Fredericton.

NORTHUMBERLAND COUNTY.

[Reported by Mr. R. W. Alward, Secretary.]

The twenty-fifth annual meeting of the Northumberland County Teachers' Institute was held in the Council Chamber of the Town Hall, Chatham, on Thursday and Friday, October 10th and 11th. The meeting was called to order by Mr. Geo. Wathen, Doaktown, President, and ninety-five teachers were enrolled as members. A paper on "Attention in Education," written by J. C. Mersereau, Bathurst, was read at the first session. On Thursday afternoon, Dr. Cox gave a lecture on "Methods of Education." On Friday morning, an interesting lesson on "Botany," was given by Mr. James McIntosh, Chatham, the Institute being transformed into a class for that purpose. Other papers read and discussed were — "School Discipline," by Miss Beatrice Ellis, of Doaktown; "School Devices," by Mr. Geo. K. McNaughton, of Newcastle; "Nature Work in Grades III and IV." by Miss L. B. Troy, of Newcastle. On Thursday evening, a well attended public meeting was held in the Town Hall, at which Mayor Snowball addressed the teachers reviewing their work from the point of view of a business man, drawing attention to the lack of practical teaching in the schools as evidenced by the ignorance of business principles and business arithmetic displayed by the ordinary common school graduate. He was followed by Rev. M. MacLean and Canon Forsyth, who discussed the teacher and his responsibilities as a factor in the moral life of the community. Dr. Cox discussed the educational institutions of the Province — in particular the Normal School which he thought should do less academic and more professional work.

A very successful meeting of the Institute was brought to a close on Friday afternoon.

The officer selected for the ensuing year were: Mr. Geo. K. McNaughton, President; Miss Maggie Mowatt, Vice-President; Mr. R. W. Alward, Secretary-Treasury; Miss Beatrice Ellis and Miss Kate J. B. MacLean, additional members of executive.

VICTORIA COUNTY.

[Reported by Wm M. Veazey, President.]

Victoria County Teachers' Institute was held October 24th and 25th, at Andover. The number of teachers enrolled was twenty-nine. An interesting program was carried out with ability and profit to the teachers. The public meeting held on Thursday evening, was well attended, and was considered one of the best held for some time.

WESTMORLAND COUNTY.

[From the Educational Review, November, 1901.]

The twenty-fourth annual meeting of the Westmorland Teachers' Institute was held at Shediac, on the 10th and 11th October, the President, C. H. Acheson in the chair. The attendance was about one hundred. Mr. Acheson made an excellent President keeping the Institute well to the work. The discussions were spirited and practical, especially those on Principal Dixon's paper on Bird Life and Miss Bourque's on Manual Training and its Effect on Character Building. Principal H. B. Steeves read a thoughtful paper on The School and Citizens. The public meeting on the evening of the 10th was largely attended and interesting addresses by Rev. Messrs. Burt and Pierce, Principal Oulton and G. U. Hay were given, interspersed by a fine musical program.

The next meeting of the Institute will be held at Port Elgin. The following officers were elected: President, R. L. Hetherington, Moncton;

Vice-President, Miss Ella Copp, Sackville; Secretary-Treasurer, S. W. Irons, Moncton.

THE COUNTIES OF YORK, QUEENS AND SUNBURY.

[From the Educational Review, October, 1901.]

A meeting of the united institutes of York, Queens and Sunbury was held at Fredericton on the 19th and 20th of September The enrolment of teachers showed 119 present from York County and 46 from Queens and Sunbury. At the first session each institute met for organization, with President O'Blenes, of York, and President Mitchell, of the Queens and Sunbury Institute.

President O'Blenes before the united institute read a suggestive paper, in which he advocated the formation of a teachers' union, and pointed out the need of a law for compulsory attendance at schools. Miss Maggie Parker read a paper on The Defects of the District School, dealing with some of the difficulties met with. An interesting discussion followed, during which parish school boards and centralization of schools were favored, and the practice of teachers underbidding each other to gain positions was strongly condemned.

Papers were read by the Rev. Mr. Harvey and Rev. Mr. Ross. By invitation of Chancellor Harrison, the last session of the Institute was held in the University library, which has recently been enlarged and improved. The following are the officers elected for the ensuing year: For York County—President, J. Hughes; Vice-President, Miss Maggie Parker, Secretary-Treasurer, Miss Thorne. Additional members of Executive, Messrs. Foster, Mills Sansom. For Queens and Sunbury—President, D. L. Mitchell; Vice-President, Miss Hoar; Secretary-Treasurer, Miss Purdy. Members of Executive, Messrs. Stephenson, Johnson, and Miss Flora White.

III—Report of the Summer School of Science.

To J. R. INCH, ESQ., LL. D.,
Chief Supt. of Education
Fredericton, N. B.

SIR: I have the honor to submit the following Report of the Fifteenth Annual Session of the Summer School of Science for the Atlantic Provinces of Canada, which was held at Lunenburg, N. S, July 23, to August 9, 1901.

In January the announcement of the school was issued and sent to the teachers of the Maritime Provinces and others interested in educational matters. In this way the advantages of the school were brought to the notice of those likely to be interested in it.

The opening meeting was largely attended, filling the spacious drill shed, in which it was held. A most cordial welcome was extended to the school by Mayor Rudolf, Mr. Kaulbeck, M. P., and others. The words of welcome, spoken by their representatives were emphasized by the enthusiastic applause of the people.

Classes met each day from 9 o'clock, a. m., to 1 p. m., in the Lunenburg Academy. This admirable building on its commanding site, is creditable to the public spirit and interest in educational matters of the citizens of Lunenburg.

The work of the class-room was marked by diligent application on the part of the students, and intelligent and enthusiastic effort on the part of the instructors. Much interest was taken in the Field Work, for which Lunenburg, afforded excellent opportunities. On the afternoons of alternate days, enthusiastic groups of Natural History students under the guidance of Drs. Bailey Mackay, Hay and Andrews and Messrs. Nelson and Dixon were to be found exploring meadow and brook, hill and vale, for specimens to be used in their class work. Not less enthusiastic was the laboratory work as conducted in chemistry by Drs. Andrews and Magee, on physiology by Mr. Starrett and in zoology by Mr. Dixon.

An exceedingly pleasant feature of the session was the hospitality extended to the school by the citizens of Lunenburg, who by excursions and entertainment caused the time to pass very quickly and agreeably. The neighboring n of Bridgewater treated the school to a most enjoyable excursion up the H..ve and entertained the members.

The enrollment surpassed that of any previous session, being from provinces as follows:

From Nova Scotia	346
" New Brunswick	14
" Prince Edward Island	6
" Ontario	1
" Newfoundland	1
" United States of America	4
Total	372

The large attendance from Nova Scotia was largely due to the efforts put forth by Inspector McIntosh, Principal McKittrick, and Mr. Love the Local Secretary, all of whom both before the meeting of the school, and during the time it was in session were untiring in their endeavors to promote the interests of the school. Another factor that adds in inducing the teachers of Nova Scotia to attend the Summer School is the liberal policy of the Council of Public Instruction for that province, in that it recognizes the efforts of teachers for self-improvement by granting an additional week's holidays to those who attend an educational gathering.

The session held this year at Lunenburg was the most successful in the history of the school.

The next session of the school will be held at St. Stephen, N. B., July 22, to August 8, 1902.

Appended find a list of the Officers and Faculty for the ensuing year, also the financial statement.

I have the honor to be,

Yours respectfully,

J. D. SEAMAN, Secretary
Summer School of Science.

OFFICERS.

PRESIDENT.

L. W. Bailey, LL. D., University of New Brunswick, Fredericton, N. B.

VICE-PRESIDENTS.

B. McKittrick, B. A., County Academy, Lunenburg, N. S.
J. Vroom, Esq., St. Stephen, N. B.
J. G. McCormick, Esq., Inspector of Schools, Charlottetown, P. E. I.

SECRETARY-TREASURER.

J. D. Seaman, Esq., Prince Street School, Charlottetown, P. E. I.

LOCAL SECRETARY.

F. O. Sullivan, Esq., St. Stephen, N. B.

BOARD OF DIRECTORS.

The President, the Secretary-Treasurer, G. J. Oulton, M. A., W. R. Campbell, M. A., S. A. Sterratt, Esq., J. B. Hill, Ph. D.

FACULTY.

BOTANY.

G. U. Hay, Ph. D. .... St. John, N. B.
J. Vroom, Esq. .... St. Stephen, N. B.

ANHYDROUS CHEMISTRY.

W. W. Andrews, LL. D. .... Sackville, N. B.

CHEMISTRY.

W. H. Magee, Ph. D. .... Parsboro, N. S.

DRAWING.

G. Matthews, Esq. .... Truro, N. S.

ENGLISH LITERATURE.

MISS ELEANOR ROBINSON........St. John, N. B.

GEOLOGY.

L. W. BAILEY, LL. D........Fredericton, N. B.

KINDERGARTEN.

MRS. S. B. PATTERSON........Truro, N. S.

MUSIC (Tonic Sol-Fa)

MISS ADA F. RYAN........Halifax, N. S.

PEDAGOGICS.

J. B. HALL, Ph. D........Truro, N. S.

PHYSICS.

W. R. CAMPBELL, M. A........Truro, N. S.

PHYSIOLOGY AND HYGIENE.

S. A. STARRATT, ESQ........Yarmouth, N. S.

ZOOLOGY.

G. J. OULTON, M. A........Moncton, N. B.

ECONOMIC ENTOMOLOGY.

F. A. DIXON, M. A........Sackville, N. B.

Financial Statement.

RECEIPTS.

Balance from 1900	$ 2 81
Grant from Government of Nova Scotia	200 00
" " " " New Brunswick	100 00
" " Town of Lunenburg	100 00
Registration Fees	398 00
Proceeds of Entertainment	24 00
Advertisements in Calendar	97 50
	$922 31

EXPENDITURES.

Printing, Advertising, and Stationery	$ 87 51	
Calendars	82 44	
Postage, Freight, Expressage	51 61	
Class Expenses	60 85	
Sundries	108 41	
Instructors and Officers	490 00	
Balance	41 49	
		$922 31

IV—Report of Macdonald Manual Training School.

E. E. MACCREADY, DIRECTOR FOR NEW BRUNSWICK.

J. R. INCH, LL. D.,
Chief Superindent oi Education.

SIR: In compliance with your request I beg to submit the following Report of Manual Training in New Brunswick for the past year, carried on by the generosity of Sir William Macdonald.

In my last Report (1900) I spoke of the equipment provided at Fredericton and of the various classes attending the school here.

During the summer vacation (1901) the second session of the "Summer School of Manual Training" was held in the City of St. John, that place being more central than Frederteton, and cooler. The large hall, with two adjoining rooms, in the Centennial School building were granted by the St. John School authorities for the purpose and the equipment for the work was moved from Fredericton and returned after the session ended.

There were forty teachers in attendance at this school; also sixteen boys. Applications to attend were received from other teachers after the work had begun and many times the number of boys taken wished to attend; but we were unable to accommodate more.

Courses of instruction were given in Mechanical Drawing and Woodworking and in Cardboard Construction Work. Advanced work was given to sixteen of the teachers who had previously taken the courses at Fredericton.

All seemed impressed with the educational value of the work and it would be difficult to find a more earnest and interested school. It was no unusual sight to see a large number at work long before the time of opening. Applications are already being received to attend the school next summer, provided another session is to be held there.

The school at Fredericton reopened in September with the students of the Normal School and the boys of the city schools in attendance.

The class for the teachers of Fredericton and vicinity, which was esta lished when the school began, still continues — with twenty teachers attendin ; and a class of boys from the "Deaf and Dumb School" is doing good worl The interest of the students in this work is so great that two classes have be formed outside of school time to accommodate those who wish to devote more time to the study than is regularly given and often some have to be turned away for lack of accommodation.

This report would certainly be incomplete if I failed to speak of the manual training work now being done in one of the ungraded, rural schools of New Brunswick.

The equipment—consisting of three benches well supplied with tools, ten drawing kits, ten Sloyd knives and ten sets of carving tools for chip-carving—was placed in the regular class-room. During three afternoons of each week the very small children are allowed to go home at three o'clock thus leaving about ten older boys and girls to take the manual training work with the teacher who is thus free to give all her attention to them. A course of models was arranged to be made, largely with the knife, and a good deal of chip-carving introduced; and this can all be done at the school desk or at least without the use of a bench.

The benches are in constant use, during the time devoted to manual training, each student being able to get about one hour of work at a bench, each week; and here the models of the regular course are constructed; so that the knife work and the carving at the desk do not supersede but merely supplement the bench work.

Miss A. Gertrude O'Brien, who is the teacher at the school just described, situated at Inches' Ridge, York Co., N. B., was a member of the first Summer Manual Training School held at Fredericton, and has since taken additional courses.

The manual training work was started at Inches' Ridge, in October, 1900, as an experiment, and it has proved eminently successful. Parents and children are alike enthusiastic and the results show a larger attendance, and greater regularity of attendance as well as more interest and better work in the other subjects studied.

Manual training is now about to be started at Musquash, with a similar equipment and in the same way as at Inches' Ridge. Miss A. E. Lucas, the teacher at Musquash, has spent over six months at Fredericton in preparation to teach manual training.

We have received inquiries from teachers in towns and country districts asking if the Provincial School Board would give any financial assistance to establish manual training in their districts. In the Provinces of Nova Scotia and Ontario special grants have been provided to aid districts in establishing manual training. If something of a similar nature could be provided in New Brunswick we feel sure that it would aid greatly in a more general introduction of this subject into our schools and make them of greater efficiency.

Respectfully submitted,

E. E MACCREADY.

Macdonald Manual Training Room, No. 1, Fredericton, N. B.

APPENDIX F.

IMPROVEMENT OF EDUCATION IN RURAL SCHOOLS.

Address Delivered at the Meeting of the Dominion Educational Association, August 1901.

BY PROFESSOR JAMES W. ROBERTSON.

Mr. President, Ladies and Gentlemen,—I desire to thank you for the honour of an invitation to address the convention of the Dominion Educational Association. In expressing my thanks, I must beg your indulgence while I speak of something which may be attempted towards the improvement of rural schools in Canada. The eloquence and fervor of those who have addressed the convention to-night and at previous sessions have been such as to nourish national sentiment or the sentiment which finds its expression in patriotic displays in connection with national movements. National life of a worthy sort for us rests on the labours of teachers; and whatever helps to make them effective, strengthens the national life. Any national greatness, which we may have or attain to, must come from an intelligent, God-fearing and capable population. To ensure these qualities in our people, it will be admitted by every one, that in the rural schools we need the best education.

THE DOMINION EDUCATIONAL ASSOCIATION.

I take it that this organization, like all other organizations, comes from the life and activity of the individual members who compose it; and that as an organization, it is meant for real use, that is to bring something to pass, besides the passing of resolutions. At a convention of teachers, one may look for a frank and unhesitating intellectual hospitality. More even than other people with open minds, those engaged in educational work should have no prejudice against information, or suggestions, even if these should come from unexpected quarters. I have observed in the discussions that teachers are fearless and even lavish in their criticisms of the educational systems in the various provinces from which they hail. They speak with a vehemence of adjectives which I would not venture to imitate. Such words of a descriptive sort as "vicious," "pernicious," "preposterous," are tossed about with a freedom from responsibility which I would not dare claim. However, out of the information, the suggestions and the criticisms should come some inspiration to be directed into definite practical action after these meetings are over.

An organization or convention which does not do anything except make or listen to speeches, pass or record resolutions, makes but little use of the intellectual ammunition of those who take part in its discussions. My own contribution to the proceedings will have value only in so far as it leads to practical action afterwards.

THE MANUAL TRAINING MOVEMENT.

My name has been connected with Manual Training in the public schools since I have the honour to administer the Macdonald Manual Training Fund for Canada.

It is rather unfortunate that this reform in the methods of education should have come to us under the name of "Manual Training." There are in this newer education three forms of expression which are used interchangeably. I am sorry for that; it leads to much confusion. The three are: Manual Training, Industrial Education, Technical Education. I see them in the newspapers, read them everywhere, and hear people talking about them; and the one means the other to most people. Now, they are not the same thing at all —not at all the same sort of thing. The spirit of the thing determines its nature. The spirit is quite different in those things I have named.

Manual Training is that part of general education which seeks its result in the boy himself or in the girl herself, seeks the result there and nowhere else, without regard to the particular occupation to be followed afterwards. The things made by a child in Manual Training may as well go into the stove or into the waste-paper basket; but the things made by a boy in an industrial school, under a system of Industrial Education, are made for the sake of the things and made for the sake of the ability to make the same or similar things that will sell. I do not say that is a poor part or an unnecessary part of education, but it is not Manual Training.

Industrial education imparts information and gives training for the particular purpose of fitting a boy or girl, or man or woman, to be capable, expert and skillful in some industrial occupation.

Technical Education has some manual training in it, but the manual training in technical education has a price in it and on it for the worth of its products. It is looking to the effect of the training on the craft and on the product, and not on the person. Technical Education is to prepare a boy or girl, or man or woman, for following successfully a trade or profession. Manual Training in a technical school is pursued as an end in itself; the idea behind it is utilitarian only. There is a differance — a tremendous differenee — and Manual Training is not so valuable after a boy is past fifteen. It then becomes technical education and craftsmanship, which have their value in dollars and cents, but which are not essential as part of an elementary school system. On heother hand, Manual Training is a means for developing the faculties and giving the boy that all-round training which he is entitled to in a country like ours.

Any attempt to impart a purely utilitarian character to the education of young children is bound to defeat its own object. A child is one and indivisible. After reading books on the subject one is almost persuaded that a child is not one - that a child is like the wooden puzzle we used to have as boys. You pulled out one peg, and that was one part; you continued, and laid all the parts in separate places. After a while you tried to put them together, and when it was finished it was a man. So we speak of the body, and we have gymnastics for the body; we speak of the mind, and we have intellectual training for the mind; we have the emotions, and we have music and all such nice things for the emotions; and then we have the will, and we make a boy do disagreeable things, and refrain from doing pleasant things, to train his will. The disagreeable has been counted a necessary element in mental and moral training of high discipline. That is my old wooden puzzle over again; you take the boy all apart and scatter him about, and then try to put him together again — and you find that you haven't the boy. The boy is not that sort of thing; the division is not real, and the making of the divisions for clearness of explanation, is at too great a cost.

EDUCATION IN RURAL DISTRICTS.

The improvement of the rural schools is one of the important public questions in Canada to-day. In our educational progress not much has been done for the boys and girls in rural schools compared with what has been given to and made possible for the children in towns and cities.

The after-life of the boy who leaves the country school, to follow some occupation in the locality, does not readily join itself to the school life which he then leaves behind. In nearly every case the school life has been an experience apart from, different from, and only in a very remote way leading up to, the mental or bodily labours and social duties which are to occupy him afterwards. It becomes necessary, since the school house absorbs so much of the time of the boys and girls, to adapt rural schools to rural life.

In educational Manual Training the advance has been one from books to benches as a means of mental culture. In rural schools the advance should be from books to benches, and from both to plots of ground and various objects as a means of mental culture. This sort of thing is being carried on most successly, particularly in the schools of Nova Scotia and those of the North West rritories. A piece of ground attached to a rural school should be utilized, h child having his own small plot, which he can use like his slate, putting ıgs in it and on it, and rubbing them off again—not for the sake of the ıngs, but for the sake of the child's growth in knowledge and mental ability.

I hope that ere long we shall have many schools in Canada, where boys and girls will have an opportunity of getting this better sort of education. For instance, suppose a boy should plant ten grains of wheat in a row, ten grains of Indian corn in another row, ten sets of potatoes in another row, and ten clover plants in another row. Suppose, further, that he should pull up one of these plants every week, and find out for himself, under the guidance of a competent teacher, all that had happened in the meantime. Suppose, further, that as far as he was able he should make drawings of the plants and a written statement of the progress of growth as he was able to observe it from week to week, would not such a course for ten weeks, occupying only half a day per week, give an intelligent boy or girl not only a great amount of exceedingly useful information, but also habits of investigation, observation, comparison and thoughtfulness, which are so desirable?

In this matter, as in Manual Training, the course of studies and exercises should be graduated to the abilities of the children. Such courses have been followed with great success for many years in European countries, and of late years they have become part of the school system in some places of our own country, under the name of Nature Studies. Perhaps what is needed most is the help of experienced teachers, who know the true educational plan to put below such work and study by the children, that it might not degenerate into only a means of giving them a mass of scrappy and disconnected information about a great number of things. Books do that well enough, or badly enough now. The purpose below this newer method should be to train the faculties of the children in natural ways, and to make the objects, the exercises, and the information acquired, all strictly serviceable to that end.

The difficulties which have hindered progress in the past are said to have been: Want of money, the fact that the time table was already too full, and the fact that teachers are not properly qualified to take up fully these better methods.

Reforms of a permanent sort must necessarily be brought about little by little. The teacher and the school trustees, without substantial outside help at the beginning, can go only a little further than they are followed and supported by local opinion.

ABOUT SUBJECTS AND METHODS.

In considering the subjects which should be to the very front in the scho-' course, one is warranted in saying that those which deal with nature shou' come first, and perhaps those which deal with human nature should follow. seems to me that a great deal of nonsense has been talked about the cultur value of the subjects, which have been grouped under the name of Humaniti for children in the elementary schools. In the elementary schools, the childr are very much children, and it is obvious that their faculties can be called out into activity, and trained better, on what they can see and handle and even make for themselves, than on subjects more or less (and usually a great deal more) theoretical.

The matter of all subjects should itself be suggestive and not artificial. It should certainly be full of purpose for the awakening and sustaining of the interest of the child and the training of his mind.

If one may mention a method which would seem to include the best, it would be that of tracing results back to their causes until that habit of mind is formed in the children. In Nature Studies, those who have experience say that the beginning should be made with what is solid and obviously practical, and that then the child should proceed to book lessons when his own observation is exhausted.

It will certainly be of great benefit to the children at any rural school if a school garden containing plots for every child above the age of eight or nine years could be provided. These gardens could be used, as they are at a few schools in England and as they are in many schools on the continent of Europe for the training of children to habits of close observation, of thoughtfulness, of reflection and of carefulness.

It is certainly most desirable to cultivate in the child a love of labour, of even the sort of labour by which the child is to live, in order that he may be trained to ability therein. It is most desirable to cultivate a love of study and to incline the children towards becoming lovers of ideas as well as lovers of labour.

To start and nourish ideas the teachers use methods, processes and devices Children get ideas and ideals far better from things and from life than from symbols and words and books. We have six avenues for taking in impressions before we are educated; after that, we have many more. We have six to start with: tasting, smelling, hearing, seeing, feeling and the sense of temperature,—that even a baby has. Those are six avenues for impressions. Now, if an impression reaches a boy's consciousness by all these channels at one time, don't you think he has the impression a good deal more clearly and distinctly and lastingly than if it came to him by only one of them?

When a child does anything with its own hands, such as planting a seed ...lling up a plant, making examination of the changes which have taken place ...g its growth, making a drawing of it, mounting it and putting its name on ... receives impressions by the sense of touch, he sees, he hears the noise of ...movements he makes, and he smells the soil and the part of the plant with ...h he is dealing. Do you not remember the smell of the woods and fields ...ing, and the lingering odour of the leaves in Autumn; and do they not, bring back to you every voice and every sound, every bird and every twig that contributed to your impressions at the time?

Six avenues for impressions and only two avenues for expression — the tongue and the hands; a little in the countenance when you are angry or pleased, but otherwise the two avenues, the tongue to say and the hands to do things. Now, if we get clean-cut impressions along all those lines of sense, we ought to give them a chance of getting out as expressions by both lines, and not only by one line. We ought to do that for the sake of the ideas, and for the sake of the boys. Both may thus be of use and benefit to each other — the ideas and the children. Children would become lovers of ideas, and ideas would nourish their minds.

SOME SUGGESTIONS FOR ADVANCE.

No doubt teachers in Canada would be willing to qualify themselves for this better sort of work in schools, if an opportunity were provided. It seems desirable and practicable to give such teachers the opportunity which they need.

I would suggest four ways in which beginnings towards improvement in the right direction might be made. Might not a group of ten rural schools in some locality be chosen in which to give an object lesson or illustration of this better education to which I have been alluding? If a competent travelling instructor were engaged, who would spend half a day of every week at each of these ten schools, would he not soon be able to train teachers and children into these better methods of nature study and give practical illustration of training these faculties of the children which too often are altogether neglected? In some other locality could not a group of five schools be arranged under the care of one travelling instructor, who would be a specialist in nature study and nature knowledge as well as a good teacher in the subjects which have been common in the schools in the past? Such a travelling instructor could then visit each of these five schools two half days per week and give the teachers and children together lessons in the school garden, and other object lessons, which would train their observation, quicken their intelligence and lead them to have desire and capacity for living happily amid rural surroundings.

Another way in which I would suggest progress would be to start evening continuation classes in the rural districts. These would provide the true solution for education in agriculture of youths in the country at the ages from fourteen to eighteen. One or two central schools of each of these grc might be chosen for evening continuation classes. At these, what the yo. lad working on the farm saw during the day with his uninstructed eye, coı be explained to him in such a way as to awaken a new interest in his w and greatly increase his ability for enjoying it and carrying it on well.

Moreover, in some districts, the area for the rural school is so small that the need of funds and the isolation of school authorities from contact with others, cause them to let educational matters drift into still greater weakness and helplessness. If in some district an object lesson could be given of the consolidation of five or six rural schools and of the establishment of one well appointed and well sustained central school instead of five or six weak ones, that might lead to a general improvement in that direction. In some of the United States the consolidation of rural schools has already been carried out to a considerable extent, and in most cases with a very great gain in the quality of the education given in the locality and with no increase of cost to the rate-payers. It has not been difficult to arrange routes for the collecting of milk or cream to one central place; it would not be more difficult to arrange for the collection of children on various routes to one central school, and certainly the children of a neighbourhood are worth the best care and thought and spending of anything in the locality.

To make possible such work as I have hinted at and to let it be capable of anything like general adoption and extension, there is need for further preparation of the teachers. At several places in England this year, short courses have been provided for periods of only three weeks, with the expectation of doing a good deal towards qualifying teachers to carry on their work in a better way. In Canada it might be possible to arrange for courses of training for say twenty-five teachers at one place, each course to last for two months. During this course the teachers should carry on nature study as they expected the children to do it at the school afterwards. A plant house is not so costly for construction and maintenance that this would be a very difficult accommodation to have for the winter and spring months.

RECOMMENDING AND SUPPOSING.

I recommend these four matters to your most sympathetic consideration (1) the possibility of giving an illustration of the best method of carrying on educational work in rural schools in groups of five or ten schools; (2) the carrying on of evening continuation classes for boys and girls of from fourteen or fifteen to eighteen years of age; (3) the consolidation of rural schools in one or two districts: and (4) the establishment of training schools for teachers, at one or more places. These would all be in a measure experimental. I think t[illegible] would serve for education a purpose somewhat similar to that which i[illegible]tration stations, dairy stations and experimental farms have served for a[illegible]lture in Canada.

[illegible]ow, *supposing* a committee of this Association should be appointed to t[illegible] these matters into consideration, do you not think that such a committe could bring something to pass and have an amount of exceedingly valuable information to present to the convention of this Association to be held two years hence. *Supposing*, but you may say, what is the use of *supposing* when the want of funds and the want of time put the matter beyond the ability of the Association or its members? Mr. President, I have a great regard for the habit of *supposing*. Let me give you an illustration. One night with my feet on the fender, I sat musing and *supposing* what would happen if a thousand boys on Canadian farms could be led to take up the systematic study of the selection of seed grain, if they would each grow a special plot on their father's farm and discover for themselves what improvement would result by systematic and continued selection for several years. *Supposing* that were possible, what a great gain to the agriculture of the Dominion and to the intellectual life of the people on farms would result. *Supposing* ten thousand dollars should become available in the shape of prizes to encourage these boys to take up this work; *supposing* that could be done, what then? Well, the illustration of *supposing* I have given you, led to the sum of ten thousand dollars being put into the Bank of Montreal by Sir William C. Macdonald to do the very thing which I began *supposing* might be done, and which if done would be of great benefit to the people of Canada.

Now let me go back again to the matter of the committee of this Dominion Educational Association. *Supposing* a committee should be appointed to take up the matter of the improvement of rural schools; and *supposing* the committee out of its collective wisdom decided that suggestions such as I have made, or others better than them, should be attempted in the way of object lessons, illustrations or experiments, in educational matters; and *supposing* further that such a committee would undertake to supervise these object lessons, illustrations and experiments, if the money actually needed were provided; do you not *suppose* that such a committee would do exceedingly valuable work in Canada? Now, Mr. President, if I may drop the *supposing*, I think I am able to say that if this Association appoints such a committee I know where the funds for such work could likely be obtained to enable the committee to render such a great service to the Dominion of Canada as only trained, experienced, capable and unselfish educators could render to it, when assisted by sufficient money provided by one or more of the generous friends of education in our Dominion.

Such a committee could approach the Departments of Education in the various provinces with suggestions and recommendations and offers of co-operation, which would doubtless be welcomed. Their knowledge, zeal and enthusiasm could carry forward educational work in wise ways with due regard to the varied and manifold needs of the people of Canada. I am sure that out of such efforts might grow what would be of the greatest possible benefit to this country; and I am confident that one of my friends will make good whatever I have intimated to the Association in my supposing, if such a committee is appointed and takes up the matter of the improvement of rural schools.

ANNUAL REPORT

OF THE

SCHOOLS

OF

NEW BRUNSWICK

1902.

BY THE CHIEF SUPERINTENDENT OF EDUCATION.

FREDERICTON, N. B.
1903.

[illegible]

Superintendent of Documents.

EDUCATION OFFICE.

FREDERICTON, N. B., March 15th, 1903.

SIR,—

I have the honor to transmit to you, to be laid before His Honor the Lieutenant Governor, the Annual Report on the Common Schools of the Province for the School year, 1901–2.

I have the honor to be, Sir,

Your obedient servant,

J. R. INCH,
Chief Supt. of Education.

TO THE HON. L. J. TWEEDIE,
Provincial Secretary.

CONTENTS.

Part I.—General Report.

Part II.—Statistical Tables.

PART III.—Appendices.

Appendix A.

Appendix B.

Appendix C.

Appendix D.

Appendix E.

Appendix F.

PART I.

GENERAL REPORT

LaTOUR SCHOOL,
ST. JOHN WEST.

ANNUAL REPORT

OF THE

Schools of New Brunswick

SCHOOL YEAR 1902.

PART I.—GENERAL REPORT.

To His Honor, the Honorable Jabez Bunting Snowball, Lieutenant Governor of the Province of New Brunswick.

MAY IT PLEASE YOUR HONOR :—

I beg to submit, as required by law, my report on the public schools of the Province for the school year 1901-02.

By the Provisions of "The Schools' Act, 1900," the school year now begins on the first day of July and ends on the thirtieth day of June in each year.

The tabular statements given in Part II. are for the school year ending June 30th, 1902. The Inspectors' reports cover the whole of the Calendar year, 1902.

The following summary of the statistical tables (see part II) presents a general comparison of the work of the two terms under review, with that of the corresponding terms of the previous twelve months:—

STATISTICAL ABSTACT.

Table I. Number of Schools, Teachers, Pupils, Etc.

	First Term. 1901.		Second Term. 1902.
Number of Schools, ...	1795	....	1736
Decrease, ...	17	Decrease,	5
Number of Teachers, ...	1869	....	1825
Decrease, ...	24	Decrease,	16
Number of Pupils, ...	58,575	....	60,477
Increase, ...	946	Increase,	57

TABLE II.—PROPORTION OF POPULATION AT SCHOOL AGE AND SEX OF PUPILS, PERCENTAGE OF ATTENDANCE.

	First Term, 1901.		Second Term, 1902.
Proportion of population at school	1 in 5.65	....	1 in 5.47
Increase on corresponding term last year,....	1 in 350	....	1 in 5809
Number of Pupils under six years of age, ...	1645	....	1522
Number between 6 and 15...	54628	....	55350
Number over 15 years, ...	2302	....	3605
Number of boys....	28906	....	30767
Increase	471	Decrease	103
Number of Girls....	29,669	....	29,710
Increase	475	Increase	160
Grand total number of days made by pupils eurolled, ...	3.284,754½	....	4,360,797½
Increase	51,546½	Increase	72,562
Average number of pupils daily present during time schools were in session, ...	38,571	....	38.736
Increase, ...	1411	Increase	1019

Average number daily present for the full term,....	36,787	....	36,058
Increase, ...	1131	Increase	807
Percentage daily present during time schools were in session	65.84	....	64.05
Increase, ...	1.36	....	1.63
Percentage daily present during full term	62.80	....	59.62
Increase, ...	.93		1.28

The following table shows the enrolment and percentage of average attendance for the Province for full term, from 1890 to 1902, inclusive:

Year.	Enrolment.		Percentage of Attendance for Full Term.	
	June.	December.	June.	December.
1890	58,570	55,622	50.96	57.36
1891	59,568	56,217	52.40	59.82
1892	60,786	56,547	53.45	62.38
1893	60,154	57,195	54.58	61.89
1894	61,280	57,282	56.04	63.36
1895	62,518	57,889	57.62	62.93
1896	61,918	57,200	55.64	62.63
1897	61,908	58,174	55.94	64.16
898	63,333	59,457	57.03	61.12
899	63,536	58,925	55.69	62.08
900	61,444	57,629	57 52	61.87
901	60,420	58,575	58.34	62.80
902	60,477	......	59.62	.....

The following Table shows the Enrolment in Cities and Incorporated Towns since 1894.

	1894.		1895.		1896.		1897.		1898.		1899.		1900.		1901.		1902.
	June.	Dec.	June.	Dec.	June.	Dec.	June.	Dec.	June.	Dec.	June.	Dec.	June.	Dec.	June.	Dec.	June.
St. John..........	6412	6721	6543	6606	6326	6566	6413	6709	6711	6986	6792	6952	6753	7160	6991	7297	6928
Fredericton......	1160	1227	1213	1225	1212	1243	1225	1209	1181	1203	1169	1231	1184	1214	1152	1196	1174
Moncton..........	1571	1632	1663	1708	1660	1716	1680	1749	1678	1741	1682	1825	1736	1718	1693	1809	1712
St. Stephen......	585	595	592	592	581	580	565	581	560	583	545	555	541	545	542	544	542
Milltown...	354	370	362	369	379	381	385	389	377	370	371	371	362	368	363	338	335
Woodstock........	643	680	656	638	643	678	688	713	712	719	674	662	644	652	652	655	639
Marysville.......	246	281	276	301	300	324	314	338	300	316	304	322	319	305	302	307	303
Campbellton....	324	348	353	378	343	388	382	370	355	373	367	407	416	401	376	506	426
Chatham.........	....	....	....	....	941	942	973	980	1019	1024	1004	1018	989	933	934	970	972
Newcastle.......	....	....	....	....	....	....	....	....	....	....	....	....	478	497	475	502	503

TABLE III.—Subjects of Instruction.

The following summary of Table III, shows the number of pupils receiving instruction in each subject, both in the Common Schools and in the Superior and Grammar Schools:

COMMON SCHOOL GRADES, I. TO VIII. INCLUSIVE.—YEAR ENDED JUNE 30TH, 1902.

	Dec. Term. 1901.	June Term 1902.
Reading and Spelling, etc.	56,581	58,369
Writing and Print Script	56,391	58,220
Number and Arithmetic	56,370	58,178
Drawing	55,290	57,062
Health Lessons	52,879	54,508
Nature Lessons	51,632	53,985
Lessons in Morals, etc.	54,309	56,240
Physical Exercises	49,396	50,073
Singing	34,301	34,464
Geography	32,165	34,881
English Grammar, etc.	31,306	34,119
History	20,032	22,496
Algebra	2,756	3,305
French (Optional)	5,185	6,218
Latin (Optional)	1,774	1,828
Sewing, etc. (Optional)	258	241

HIGH SCHOOL GRADES, IX. TO XII. INCLUSIVE.—YEAR ENDED JUNE 30TH, 1901.

	Dec. Term. 1901.	June Term. 1902.
English Language and Literature	1,834	1,751
Latin	1,404	1,273
Greek	229	212
French	976	982
Arithmetic	1,578	1,536
Geometry	1,708	1,641
Algebra	1,779	1,694
Trigonometry	64	106
Book-keeping	994	1,142
History and Geography	1,849	1,721
Industrial Drawing	1,003	866
Botany	1,564	1,545
Chemistry	451	666
Physiology and Hygiene	546	534
Physics	672	879

Table IV.—Number and Class of Teachers Employed.

The growing difficulty of finding trained teachers for many of the rural districts was discussed at some length in my last annual report. I regret to say that the difficulty continues. Schools have been closed for want of teachers notwithstanding the fact that local licenses were granted to 36 untrained teachers for the first term and to 52 for the second term, and that the expired licenses of a number of Third Class Teachers were renewed for a fourth year. During each of the terms the decrease in the number of trained teachers employed was 37. During the last two years the number of trained teachers employed has decreased by 65.

Tables V, VI, VII and VIII show the period of service of the teachers employed; the time in session of the schools; the interest shown by school officials and the general public in the work of the schools as indicated by visits and the offering of prizes; the number of public examinations, and the average salaries of the teachers. An examination of these tables will show but little variation in comparison with the corresponding statistics of recent years.

Table IX.—Disbursement of Provincial Grants.

The total provincial grants to the Common, Superior and Grammar schools for the year 1901-2 amounted to $162,227.19, a decrease of $1,724.-54 on the disbursement of the previous year and of nearly $6000 on that of the year 1899-1900. This decrease is accounted for by the smaller number of schools in operation, and the employment of a larger proportion of untrained and Third Class teachers in country schools.

The following statement shows the annual expenditure from the provincial revenues since 1891, the number of schools open during the term ending June 30th, and the number of teachers of each class employed.

YEAR.	Schools. No. of	TEACHERS OF EACH CLASS.					PROVINCIAL GRANT.
		Grammar School.	Sup. and Class I.	Class II.	Class III.	Totals.	
1891	1536	14	274	765	579	1632	$ 137,679 03
1892	1585	14	304	783	568	1669	142,681 21
1893	1614	14	345	787	547	1693	147,669 71
1894	1653	14	360	786	589	1749	150,882 20
1895	1695	13	382	827	568	1790	156,341 65
1896	1720	13	423	839	554	1829	158,135 23
1897	1737	17	440	840	534	1831	161,445 94
1998	1778	20	427	904	513	1864	163.021 86
1899	1806	25	464	894	529	1912	167,988 40
1900	1771	25	452	881	498	1856	168,224 72
1901	1741	23	429	911	478	1841	163,951 73
1902	1736	22	423	889	514	1825	162,227 19

The total expenditure during the year 1901-2 for the maintenance of the Grammar, Superior and Common Schools is approximately as follows:

District Assessments (approximate)..........	$341,475.12
County Fund.............................	92,095.29
Provincial Grants........................	162,227.19
Total..................................	$595,797.60

Amount per pupil enrolled nearly $9.00.

TABLES X. AND XI.—The County Fund.

The total amount of the County Fund for the term ended December, 1901 (levied on the basis of the census of 1891) was $47,214.15, and for the term ended June 1902 (levied on the basis of the census of 1901) was $48,585.57, making a total for the school year of $95,799.72. This amount was apportioned as follows:

To Trustees of the Public Schools....	$ 92 080 41	
" The School for the Blind..	2,193 41	
" The School for the Deaf and Dumb, ...	1,525 90	
		$ 95,799 72

The appropriations to the School for the Blind were as follows:

Albert County, 3 pupils, ...	$ 225 00	
Carleton County, 2 pupils, ...	150 00	
Charlotte County, 2 pupils, ...	150 00	
Kent County, 4 pupils, ...	262 50	
Kings County, 3 pupils, ...	225 00	
Northumberland County, 2 pupils, ...	130 91	
Queens County, 1 pupil, ...	75 00	
St. John County. 5 pupils, ...	375 00	
Westmorland County, 8 pupils,..	600 00	
		$ 2,193 41

The appropriations to the School for the Deaf and Dumb were as follows:

Albert County, 4 pupils, ...	$ 228 44	
Carleton County, 4 pupils, ...	194 99	
Charlotte County, 1 pupil, ...	60 00	
Gloucester County, 2 pupils,....	90 48	
Kings County, 3 pupils, ...	165 54	
Madawaska County, 1 pupil,....	10 11	
Northumberland County, 1 pupil, ...	53 36	
Restigouche County, 1 pupil,...	60 00	
St. John County, 3 pupils, ...	168 70	
stmorland County, 7 pupils,..	401 80	
k County, 3 pupils, ...	92 48	
		$ 1,525 90

The amount ($814.29) apportioned to the School for the Deaf and Dumb the term ended in June last is still in the hands of the County Secretaries.

TABLES XII AND XIII.—SUPERIOR AND GRAMMAR SCHOOLS.

There were 51 Superior and 13 Grammar schools in operation during the year. Twenty-two teachers received the Grammar School provincial grant. The total number of pupils enrolled in the High School Grades (IX-XII) was 1834 for the first term and 1751 for the second term. Of these numbers 1066 and 982 respectively, belonged to the Grammar Schools, and 768 and 769 to the Superior Schools.

The following table shows the Superior Schools which had 10 pupils or more above Grade VIII:

	First Term.	Second Term.
St. Stephen High School	71	69
Harkins' Academy, Newcastle	27	28
Superior School, Dorchester	38	38
" " Milltown	32	33
" " Sackville	38	32
" " Petitcodiac	14	14
" " Havelock Corner	23	23
" " St. Martins.	23	19
" " Rexton	15	12
" " Shediac	16	15
" " St. George	15	17
" " Middle Sackville	21	21
" " Hillsboro	22	20
" " Hartland	19	24
" " Centreville	15	19
" " Moore's Mills	11	11
" " Penobsquis	..	11
" " Buctouche	10	16
" " Elgin Corner	15	10
" " Derby	12	12
" " Dalhousie	10	12
" " Grand Falls	12	..
" " Florenceville	11	16
" " North Head Grand Manan	..	13
" " Bathurst Village	15	12

The growth of our High School work since 1890 is shown in the following statement:

No. of Pupils in Grades IX. to XII. in Grammar and Superior Schools.

	Term Ended December.	Term Ended June.
1890-1	574	610
1891-2	701	694
1892-3	782	724
1893-4	738	806
1894-5	1155	1060
1895-6	1093	1099
1896-7	1220	1228
1897-8	1469	1523
1898-9	1495	1510
1899-1900	1565	1545
1900-1	1543	1528
1901-2	1834	1751

DEPARTMENTAL EXAMINATIONS.

These examinations consist of:

(1) The High School Entrance Examinations (See Regulation 46, School Manual) held during the month of June at the several Grammar Schools, and such of the Superior Schools as apply for the same. They cover the work of Grades I. to VIII. inclusive, or the Common School Grades. Those who successfully pass these examinations receive a certificate which is intended to serve a two-fold purpose; for pupils who do not intend to continue longer at school it serves as a diploma given under the authority of the Education Department, testifying that the holder has completed satisfactorily the course of studies of the Common Schools; for pupils who intend to continue their studies it serves as a certificate of admittance to the High School classes.

(2) The High School Leaving Examinations (See Regulation 45, School Manual) held the first week in July at different examination stations throughout the province. They cover the work of Grades IX., X. and XI. (ne Grammar Schools. Diplomas are granted to those who successfully [illegible] these examinations.

(3) The University Matriculation Examinations held at the same time [illegible] stations as the Leaving Examinations.

(4) The Normal School Entrance Examinations held at the same time and places as the two former. Candidates for admittance to the Normal School and Licensed Teachers seeking for advance of Class are required to pass these examinations.

(5) The Normal School Closing Examinations, held at the Normal School, Fredericton, and at St. John and Chatham, beginning on the second Tuesday of June, and for Third Class Candidates in December and May of each year.

The following were the results of these several examinations during the past year:

High School Entrance Examinations.

I.—Grammar Schools.

Name of School.	No. of Candidates.	Passed Division I.	Passed Division II.	Passed Division III.	Failed.
Albert County Grammar School..........	11	5	5	1	...
Carleton " " "	61	8	31	21	1
Charlotte " " "	25	2	15	4	4
Gloucester County Grammar School.........	13	..	5	8	..
Kent " " "	10	4	6	..	..
Kings " " "	9	..	..	6	3
Northumberland County Grammar School......	46	9	30	5	2
Queens " " "	5	2	..	2	1
Restigouche " " "	23	2	7	12	2
St. John " " "	227	98	85	30	14
Victoria " " "	9	2	5	1	1
Westmorland " " "	79	11	42	21	5
York " " "	94	13	32	40	9
	612	156	263	151	42

II. SUPERIOR SCHOOLS.

Name of School	Number Entered for Examination.	Passed Division I.	Passed Division II.	Passed Division III.	Failed.
Hopewell Hill	9		3	5	1
Florenceville	8	2	2	4	
Grand Manan	11	7	4		
St. George	14	1	5	7	1
St. Stephen	32	8	20	3	1
Milltown	23	11	10	2	
Rexton	6	2		4	
Hampton	12	6	5	1	
Havelock	5	1	3	1	
Bloomfield	8	2	3	2	1
Doaktown	12	3	4	4	1
Douglastown	15	5	2	6	2
Newcastle	27	8	11	6	2
Dalhousie	15	1	2	7	5
Fairville	15	3	10	2	
St. Martins	19	4	8	7	
Fredericton Jct.	4	1	1	2	
Grand Falls	7			3	4
Dorchester	16	7	8	1	
Sackville	17	2	9	4	2
Salisbury	4	2	2		
Shediac	7	6	1		
McAdam Jct	7	1	5	1	
Superior Schools	293	83	118	72	20
Grammar Schools	612	156	263	151	42
Total 1901-2	905	239	381	223	62
Total 1900-1	931	303	394	181	53
rease	....	....	....	42	9
crease	26	64	13	....	....

University Matriculation and High School Leaving Examinations.

Examiners:

Professor W. T. Raymond, B. A., University of New Brunswick.
" S. W. Hunton, M. A., " Mount Allison.
" A. M. Scott, M. A., Ph. D., " New Brunswick.
" John Brittain, Normal School.

Eighty-three candidates presented themselves for Matriculation Examinations and three for High School Leaving Examinations.

Of the candidates for Matriculation 5 passed in Division I; 27 in Division II; 26 in Division III; 16 others are classed in Division III on condition of passing supplementary examinations in one or two subjects; 9 failed to be classified.

Of the three candidates for the Leaving Examinations 2 passed in Division III and one failed.

The following are the names of the candidates who passed in Divisions I and II (arranged in the order of the highest marks):

Matriculation.

Division I.

Margaret M. Belyea	Fredericton Grammar School.
William Morrow	St. John Grammar School.
J. Arthur Estey	Fredericton Grammar School,
A. Winifred Turner	Fredericton Grammar School.
Ruth E. Everett	Fredericton Grammar School.

Division II.

Osburn N. Brown	Harkins Academy, Newcastle.
Sarah L. B. Waycott	Fredericton Grammar School.
Annie McGuiggan	St. Vincent's School, St John.
Wm. T. Denham	St John Grammar School.
Pearl Yerxa	Fredericton Grammar School.
C. W Clark	Fredericton Grammar School.
Hart Green,	St. John Grammar School.
Lena Graham,	Campbellton Grammar School.
Geo. H. Burnett,	Sussex Grammar School
Fred. W. Fowler,	St John Grammar School.
Bessie B. Wisdom,	St. John Grammar School

Jessie E. Fowlie, ... Chatham Grammar School.
W. Everett Gray, ... Campbellton Grammar School.
A. Veronica Osborne, ... Milltown Superior School.
Florence M. Bird, ... Fredericton Grammar School.
Hazel Millican, ... Fredericton Grammar School.
Gilbert B. Peat, ... Andover Grammar School.
John H. Allingham, ... Gagetown Grammar School.
Malcolm L. Orchard, ... Fredericton Grammar School.
Edith Hazen Allen, ... Fredericton Grammar School.
Wilmot G Miller, ... Fredericton Grammar Schoel.
John Connors, ... Chatham Grammar School.
Ernest E. Clawson, ... St. John Grammar School.
Eva M. Irving, ... Chatham Grammar School.
W. Spencer Fverett, ... Fredericton Grammar School.
Chester M. Mowatt, ... Chatham Grammar School.
Mary E. Wetmore, ... Woodstock Grammar School.

JUNIOR LEAVING.

Frank Henderson, ... Chatham Grammar School.
Gertrude M. McKinnon, ... Fredericton Grammar School.

THE NORMAL SCHOOL.

Final Examinations for Teachers' License, held December, 1901, and May and June, 1902.

EXAMINERS:

Mathematics—CHANCELLOR HARRISON.
English Language and Literature—H. S. Bridges, M. A., Ph. D.
Latin and Greek—H. S. BRIDGES, M. A., Ph. D.
Physiology and Botany—PROF. L. W. BAILEY, M.A., Ph. D., F. R. S. C
Physics and Chemistry—PROF. A. M. SCOTT, Ph. D.
School System—G. W. MERSEREAU, M. A.
Teaching and School Management, etc.—G. U. HAY, M. A., D. Sc.
Industrial Drawing, Book-keeping, etc.—MR. VROOM.
French and General History—PROF. W. T. RAYMOND, B. A.

The full details of the final Examinations for License held in December, 1901, and May, 1902, for the French Department and for the Third Class Candidates of the English Department, and the closing examinations for the higher classes held at Fredericton and St. John in June, 1902, are given in Table XV., page A 35, to which reference is directed.

The total number admitted to these examinations (including those who were examined for advance of class) was 312. The following is a summary of results:

	No. Examined.	No. Passed.
Grammar School Class......	10	7
Class I..................	89	63
Class II..................	163	177
Class III..................	50	59
Failed to be classed........		6
	312	312

Twenty-one other candidates stood a partial examination for Grammar School Class, and five of those who gained Class I, or had previously held a First Class License, qualified for Superior School License. At the July examinations 16 other First Class Teachers received the Superior School Certificate.

The names of the successful candidates for Grammar School and Superior School Licenses are given on pages A 36, A 37 and A 38, Part II.

CLASS I.

The following candidates made 70 per cent, and upwards at the Closing Examinations for Provincial License (arranged in order of the highest marks):

Mildred M. Black....................Fairville, St. John Co.
Maud L. Cuming,....................St. John.
Florence C. Estabrooks,..............Carleton.
Josephine R. Cormier, ... St. John.
Annie H. Whittaker,................St. John.
John S. Smiley,....................Milltown.
Margaret Wilson,....................Moncton.
Arthur W. Barbour,..................Cape Enrage, Albert Co.
Annie M. Loggie,.....................Chatham.
Percy S. Bailey,......................Oak Bay, Charlotte Co.
Sarah L. Brown,.......................Snider Mountain, Kings Co.
Violet E. Goldsmith,..................Bathurst.
W. Orton Gray,.......................Hampton Village.
F. Arnold Jewett,.....................Waterville, Carleton Co.
John M. Clindinin,...................Moores Mills. Charlotte Co.
Marjorie F. Mair,....................Campbellton.
Evangeline LeBlanc,.................St. John.
Arthur E. Eastman,..................Petitcodiac.
Clara G. Turner,....................Gibson, York Co.
Grace B. Campbell,..................St. John.
Sadie Sterling,.......................Fredericton.
Addie M. Hartt,......................Fredericton Junction.

CLASS II.

The following (arranged in the order of the highest marks) made an average of 70 per cent. or upwards on Second Class papers:

Louise R. Copp.......................Baie Verte. Westmorland Co.
R. Gertrude Parlee..................Apohaqui, Kings Co.
Jessie H. Brown.....................Quaco, St John Co.
Ida M. McGerigle...................Nerepis Station, Kings Co.
Arthur Graham......................Dumfries, York Co.
Grace H. Waring....................Milford, St. John Co.
E. Stanley Cox ....Briggs Corner, Queens Co.
Percy A. Fitzpatrick................Port Elgin, Westmorland Co.

A. Laura Moore	Petitcodiac.
Pearl E Babbitt	Fredericton.
Jessie McD McKnight	Lower Napan, North'mb'rl'nd Co.
Ralph McKinney	Rolling Dam, Charlotte Co.
Beatrice M. Newman	Millerton, Northumberland Co.
Bernadette Cormier	Caraquet, Gloucester Co.
Lizzie M. Holmes	Florenceville. Carleton Co.
Ethel W. L. Good	Millstream, Kings Co.
Mabel R Saunders	Jubilee, Kings Co.
M. Kathleen Kelly	Fredericton.
William J. Young	Havelock, Kings Co.
A. M. Evelyn Cook	Oak Bay, Charlotte Co.
Medley F. Miller	Grand View, York Co.
Sadie B. Hogan	Newcastle.
Bertie H. Plummer	Upper Gagetown.
Alice M. Nickerson	Hibernia, Queens Co.
M. Bella Eddy	Clifton, Gloucester Co.
Florence G. DeMille	Goshen, Albert Co.
Arthur E. Mitchell	Welchpool, Charlotte Co.
Jessie R. Gilliland	Westfield Centre, Kings Co.

NORMAL SCHOOL ENTRANCE EXAMINATIONS AND PRELIMINARY EXAMINATIONS FOR ADVANCE OF CLASS, JULY 1902.

The total number of candidates entered for these examinations was **488**, distributed as follows:—Fredericton, 80; St. John, 70; Moncton, **60**; Chatham, 58; Woodstock, 57; Bathurst; 37; Hil'sborough, 36; Sussex, **33**; St. Stephen, 30; Andover, 18; Campbellton, 9.

Of the total number, 161 presented themselves for Class I; 306 for **Class** II. and 21 for Class III.

The results are as follows:

Gained Class I	42
" " II	158
" " III	147
Failed	141
Total	488

CLASS I.

The following candidates for Class I. made an average of 70 per cent. and upwards.

(Arranged in order of highest marks)

Annie Gosnell,	St. John.
Laura A. Moore,	Petitcodiac, Westmorland Co.
Gaynell E Long,	Good Corner, Carleton Co.
Harry A. Prebble,	Butternut Ridge, Kings Co.
Paulina Fox,	Lower Gagetown, Queens Co.
Auguste E. Daigle,	Cocagne, Kent Co.
Lona J. Belyea	Lower Windsor, Carleton Co.
R. Gertrude Parlee,	Apohaqui, Kings Co.
Margaret A. Gillman,	Milltown, Charlotte Co.
A. Zella Alward,	Havelock, Kings Co.
Nellie B. Harmon,	Peel, Carleton Co.
Maggie N. Briggs,	Springfield, Kings Co.

CLASS II.

The following candidates for Class II made an average of 60 per cent. and upwards on Second Class papers (arranged in order of highest marks):

Jean G. Robichaud	Shippegan, Gloucester Co.
Rheta N. Allingham	Welshpool, Charlotte Co.
William A. R. Archer	Sheila, Gloucester Co.
H. Nellie Blake	Black Point, Restigouche Co.
Melbourne R. Smith	Oak Bay, Charlotte Co.
Lewis King	Buctouche, Kent Co.
Mabel E. Perkins	Scribner, Kings Co.
Francis J. Kinney	Florenceville, Carleton Co.
E Murray Burtt	Jacksonville, Carleton Co.
Fred L. Bowser	Upper Point de Bute, West'd Co.
Otty J. Fraser	Lower Prince William, York Co.
Mabel A. Estabrooks	Chester, Carleton Co.
Jos. Cronkhite	Campbell Settlement, York Co.
Chas. G. Crawford	Debec, Carleton Co.
Katie L. Colpitts	Petitcodiac, Westmorland Co.
Ethel A. Sears	Moncton.
G. Foster Camp	Upper Sheffield, Sunbury Co
M. Edith Weade	Royalton, Carleton Co.
Harry E. Hayward,	Ashland, Carleton Co.

Bertha M. Wilbur,....................	Shediac Cape, Westmorland Co.
Annie L. Wilson,....................	Clones, Queens Co.
Bertha B. Bateman,..................	Shediac Cape, Westmorland Co.
Ethel L. Steeves,....................	O'Neills, Westmorland Co.
D. F. Robichaud,....................	Lower Caraquet, Gloucester Co.
Robt. H. Flewelling,................	Chipman, Queens Co.
Reuben Getchell,....................	Scotch Ridge, Charlotte Co.

The following tabular statement gives the details for each examining station:

NORMAL SCHOOL ENTRANCE EXAMINATIONS, AND PRELIMINARY EXAMINATIONS FOR ADVANCE OF CLASS, 1902.

STATIONS.	No. Presented at Each Station for Examination.	Number of Candidates Presented for the Various Classes with Results.												SUMMARY.			
		Class I.					Class II.				Class III.			Total Results for Each Class.			
		No. Examined for this Class.	No. Obtained 1st Class.	No. Obtained 2nd Class.	No. Obtained 3rd Class.	No. that Failed to Obtain any Class.	No. Examined for this Class.	No. Obtained 2nd Class.	No. Obtained 3rd Class.	No. that Failed to Obtain any Class.	No. Examined for this Class.	No. Obtained 3rd Class.	No. that Failed to Obtain any Class.	No. Obtained 1st Class.	No. Obtained 2nd Class.	No. Obtained 3rd Class.	No. that Failed to Obtain any Class.
No. 1, Fredericton	80	16	6	5	4	1	60	20	24	16	4	2	2	6	25	30	19
" 2, St. John	70	30	5	11	10	4	38	10	15	13	2	1	1	5	21	26	18
" 3, Moncton	60	26	9	9	8	..	31	14	11	6	3	1	2	9	23	20	8
" 4, St. Stephen	30	14	4	5	3	2	16	3	3	10	..	..	..	4	8	6	12
" 5, Woodstock	57	15	3	7	2	3	40	16	7	17	2	..	2	3	23	9	22
" 6, Chatham	58	20	5	8	6	1	35	9	10	16	3	2	1	5	17	18	18
" 7, Sussex	33	9	4	3	2	.	23	8	5	10	1	..	1	4	11	7	11
" 8, Campbellton	9	3	..	1	1	1	6	4	2	..	..	..	..	..	5	3	1
" 9, Bathurst	37	7	1	4	.	2	24	4	9	11	6	..	6	1	8	9	19
" 10, Hillsboro	36	16	2	7	6	1	20	6	8	6	..	..	..	2	13	14	7
" 11, Andover	18	5	3	1	..	1	13	3	5	5	..	..	..	3	4	5	6
Total	488	161	42	61	42	16	306	97	99	110	21	6	15	42	158	147	141
1901	515	172	57	74	29	12	335	132	105	98	8	1	7	57	206	135	117
Increase	...	...	..	..	13	4	..	..	..	12	13	5	8	..	..	12	24
Decrease	27	11	15	13	..	..	29	35	6	..	..	..	..	15	48	..	..

The dates at which the next Departmental Examinations will begin are as follows:

High School Entrance, Monday, June 22nd, 1903.
High School Leaving, Tuesday, July 7th, 1903.
University Matriculation, Tuesday, July 7th, 1903.
Normal School Entrance, etc., Tuesday, July 7th, 1903.
Normal School Closing, Tuesday, June 9th, 1903.
Normal School Closing for French Department, Tuesday, May 26th, 1903.
Normal School Closing for Third Class, Tuesday, Dec. 15th, 1903.

The stations at which the University Matriculation, the High School Leaving and the Normal School Entrance examinations will be held are:

Fredericton, St. John, Moncton, St. Stephen, Woodstock, Chatham, Sussex, Campbellton, Bathurst, Hillsborough and Andover.

Candidates for Superior Class Certificates may be examined either during the Closing examinations in June or the Entrance examinations in July.

TABLE XVI.—School Libraries.

The total number of new volumes purchased for School Libraries during the year was 898, at a cost of $378, of which the Province paid $125.77.

TABLE XVII.—Travelling Expenses of Student Teachers.

The sum of $1138.50 was paid during the year as travelling expenses to student teachers attending the Normal School, a decrease of $296.46 as compared with the same account for the preceding year.

TABLES XVIII and XIX.

These tables give a summary of all moneys disbursed by the Chief Superintendent for the School Service, for the fiscal year ended October 31st, 1902.

ARBOR DAY REPORT, 1902.

Inspectoral District.	No. Districts Observing Arbor Day.	No. of Trees Planted.	No. of Shrubs Planted.	No. of Flower Beds.	General Improvement.
No. 1	69	309	76	67	51
" 2	62	222	146	59	60
" 3	92	402	143	135	92
" 4	65	470	39	126	65
" 5	84	210	27	50	81
" 6	94	203	67	111	87
" 7	39	234	55	42	39
Total	505	2050	553	590	475
For 1901	575	2037	445	676	447
Increase	....	13	108	....	28
Decrease	70	....	....	86	....

POOR DISTRICTS.

School districts which have an assessable valuation of $12,000 or less, receive from 25 to 33⅓ per cent. additional grants from the provincial revenues and the County Fund. It has been hoped from year to year that the number of these districts would decrease, but the tendency has been in the opposite direction. The organization of districts in new settlements, the division of some old districts and, in some cases, the successful efforts made by interested parties to keep the assessable valuation as given upon the district lists at a figure much lower than the actual value of the assessable property, have all contributed to increase rather than diminish the number of districts demanding this special aid. The operation of the change in the Schools Act, making the property within the boundaries of any school district taxable for the benefit of such district, without regard to the place of residence of the owner, has been for the advantage of the poorer districts, and will tend in that direction more and more. The total special aid granted to the Poor Districts during the year has been $7,947 23 from the Provincial revenues and $5,155 77 from the County Fund, or $13,103 from both sources.

The total number of Poor Districts for the calendar year 1903 are as follows:

ALBERT COUNTY.

Parish of Alma,	Nos. 3, 6, 7, 8 (and Harvey), 9	5
" Coverdale	" 6, 7 (and Hillsboro), *8, 9, 11, 12 15 (and Salisbury)	7
Elgin,	" 4, 5, *6, 7, *9, *13, 15, 17, 18, 19 20, ...	11
Harvey,	" 6, 7 (and Alma), *8, *10, ...	4
" Hillsboro,	" 8, *9, *11 (and Elgin), 12, 13 (and Elgin), 15, ...	6
" Hopewell,	" *4, 5 (and Hillsboro), 9, ...	3
		36

CARLETON COUNTY.

Parish of Aberdeen,	Nos. 2, 7, 8, 9, 10, 11, 13 (and Kent),	7
" Brighton,	" 11, 17, 18, 19, 19½, ...	5
" Kent,	" *1½ (and Peel), *9, 19, ...	3
" Northampton,	" *8, 11 (and Southampton)	2
" Peel,	" 5, ...	1
" Wicklow	" *8, ...	1
Wilmot,	" *14, 17, ...	2
" Woodstock,	" 11, 13, ...	2
		23

CHARLOTTE COUNTY.

Parish of Clarendon,	Nos. 1, 3, 9 (and Blissville)	3
" Dumbarton,	" 1, 4, 5, *7, *7½, ...	5
" Grand Manan,	" 7, *9, ...	2
" Lepreaux,	" 1, *2 (and Musquash), 5, ...	3
" Pennfield,	" *6	1
" St. David,	" *2, *7, ...	2
" St. George,	" 7, 8, 8½ (and Dumbarton), 9, 10, 11, *15	7
" St. James,	" *4, *4½ (and St.David), *5, 8, *10 11, *13, *19, ...	8
" St. Patrick,	" *4, *6, *9 (and St. George), *10	4

CHARLOTTE COUNTY.—Continued.

"	St. Stephen,	" *2, 7½ (and St. James), ...	2
"	West Isles,	" 1, *5½, 6½. 8, ...	4
			41

GLOUCESTER COUNTY.

Parish of	Bathurst,	Nos. 3, 4, 6, 7, *8, 10, 11, ...	7
"	Beresford,	" *7 (and Bathurst), 7½ (and Bath), 8,*8½, 9, *10A (and Bathurst), 11, 12, 13, 13½, 14, 15, 16, ...	13
"	Caraquet,	" 1, 3, 4, 4½	4
"	Inkerman,	" 1, 4, 5, 7, *8, ...	5
"	New Bandon,	" 1, 3, 3½, 4½, 5½, 7, 10,	7
"	Paquetville,	" 1, 2, *4, 5, ...	4
"	Saumarez,	" 2, *2½, *4, 7	4
"	St. Isidore,	" *8, ...	1
"	Shippegan,	" 1½, *3, *3½, 5, *6½, 8, 8½, 9, 9½, 10, 10½, ...	11
			56

KENT COUTY.

Parish of	Acadieville,	Nos. 1, 2, 3, 4, *5, 7, 8, 9, ...	8
"	Carleton,	" 2, 4, 6, 8, 9, 10	6
"	Dundas,	" *5, 5½, 6A (and Moncton) *10A (and Moncton), 14, ...	5
"	Harcourt,	" 1, 6, 7, 7½, 10, 11, ...	6
"	Richibucto,	" 3, 5, 7, 9, 9A, 11, 13, ...	7
"	St. Louis,	" 1, *5, *8, *9 (and Ricibucto), 10, 11,...	6
"	St. Mary's,	" 5, 7, 7½, *14,..	4
"	St. Paul,	" 1, 2, 3, *4, 5, 6, 7 (and St. Mary's) 9,....	8
"	Weldford,	" 2½, 4, 5½ (and St. Mary's), 7, 11, 12, 13, 17, 18, *20, 21, 22, 23, 24,	14
"	Wellington,	" *7½, *12½, 13, 15, 16, 17, 18,....	7
			71

KINGS COUNTY.

Parish of	Cardwell,	Nos. 4, *8, 9, 10 (and Sussex), ...	4
"	Hammond,	" 1 (and Waterford), 2, *3, *5, 8 (and Sussex),..	5
"	Havelock,	" *5, 6, 11, 15,..	4
	Kars.	" 4, 6,..	2
"	Kingston,	" 8, 9, 14, *15,..	4
	Norton,	" 9, *11 (and Sussex), ...	2
"	Rothesay,	" *6,...	1
"	Springfield,	" *4, *5, *6 (and Johnston), *13, 14, 18, 21, ...	7
"	Studholm,	" 1, 2, *5, *6, *19, *26, ...	6
"	Sussex,	" 4 (and Waterford), *8, 11, 12, 14, 15,....	6
	Upham,	" 25 (and St. Martins)....	1
"	Waterford,	" 1, 3, 4 (and Cardwell), *6, 7, 9,..	6
"	Westfield,	" 5 (and Greenwich), *8, 9, *10, *12, *13,...	6
			54

MADAWASKA COUNTY.

Parish of	Madawaska,	Nos. 3, 4, 4½, 5, 6,..	5
"	St. Anne,	" *2, 5, 6, 7,....	4
"	St. Basil,	" 2, 5, 8, 9, 10,..	5
"	St. Francis,	" *5, 6, 7, 8, 9, 10, 11, 13, 14, ...	9
"	St. Hilaire,	" 5, 6, 7, 8, 9,...	5
"	St. Jacques.	" 2, 3, 4, 5, ...	4
"	St. Leonard,	" 7, 8...	2
			34

NORTHUMBERLAND COUNTY.

Parish of	Alnwick,	Nos. *1, *2, 8½, *12, 14, ...	5
"	Blackville,	" 1½, 3, 3½, 9, 12, 13, ...	6
"	Blissfield,	" 1, *1½ (and Blackville), *2, *2½, 3,	5
	Glenelg,	" *3, 5, 6, 8, 8½, 9	6
"	Hardwicke,	" 3, 6,..	2
"	Ludlow,	" 1, *1½, 2, 4, 5,...	5
	Nelson,	" 6, *6½, 7, ...	3

NORTHUMBERLAND COUNTY.—Continued.

" Newcastle,	" *2½, ...	1
" Northesk,	" *1, 3, 11½, ...	3
" Rogersville	" 1, 2, 3A (and Acadieville), 5, 10½, *11, *13, *14, *15, 16 (and Acadieville), ...	10
" Southesk,	" 7, *7½, ...	2
		48

QUEENS COUNTY.

Parish of Brunswick	Nos. *3, 4, 5, 7, 23 (and Salisbury),	5
" Cambridge,	" *6 (and Waterboro), *7, *9, ...	3
" Canning,	" 3, 4, *6, ...	3
" Chipman,	" 2, 3, 7, *9, 12, 13 (and Waterboro), 14 (and Waterboro), 16 (and Harcourt), ...	8
" Gagetown,	" *1, ...	1
" Hampstead,	" 3 (and Gagetown), 10, ...	2
" Johnston,	" 2, 6, *6 (and Springfield), 8, *9 *11 (and Wickham), *12, 13, *15 (and Springfield), 17, ...	10
" Petersville,	" 2, *13, 16, ...	3
" Waterboro,	" *2, 3, *5, *8 (and Johnson), 9,	5
" Wickham,	" *10, *12 (and Johnston), ...	2
		42

RESTIGOUCHE COUNTY.

Parish of Addington	Nos. *2½, 3, ...	2
" Balmoral,	" 1, 4, 5, 6 (and Addington), ...	4
" Colborne,	" 1½ (and Balmoral), 4,	2
" Dalhousie,	" 4, ...	1
" Durham,	" 1½, *5, 9, 10, 11, ...	5
Eldon,	" *1, ...	1
		15

ST. JOHN COUNTY.

·ish of Musquash,	Nos. *7, *8, 9	3

ST. JOHN COUNTY.—Continued.

"	St. Martins,	" 1, *3, *3½, *4, 9, *11, *12, *23 (and Simonds), 30, ...	9
"	Simonds,	" *14, *15, *16, *20, *21 (Bdr), 22 (Bdr), ...	6
			18

SUNBURY COUNTY.

Parish of	Blissville,	Nos. *5, *6, 7, 8, 9 (and Clarendon),	5
"	Burton,	" 6, *8, 9, 10, 11, 12, 13, ...	7
"	Gladstone,	" *2, *3, 5, 6, 8, 9 (and New Maryland), ...	6
"	Lincoln,	" 6, ...	1
"	Maugerville,	" 4 (and St. Mary's), ...	1
"	Northfield,	" 1, 2. *3, 5, ...	4
"	Sheffield,	" 1A (and Canning), 3, 6, *7, ...	4
			28

VICTORIA COUNTY.

Parish of	Andover,	Nos. 6, 8, ...	2
"	Drummond,	" 1½, 2, 3, 5, 6, 8½, 9, 11, 12, 13, 14,	11
"	Gordon,	" *2, 3, 7, *8, 9 (and Lorne), ...	5
"	Grand Falls,	" *2, 3, *4, 5, 8, 10, *11, ...	7
	Lorne,	" 1, 2, 5, 8, ...	4
	Perth,	" 3, 5, 6, 7, *8 (and Drummond), 10, *11, *12, *13, ...	9
			38

WESTMORLAND COUNTY.

Parish of	Botsford,	Nos. *4, 20, 22, 23,.	4
"	Dorchester,	" *4 (and Sackville), 15, 26, ...	3
"	Moncton,	" *6A (and Dundas), *20, *21, 22, *24, 25, 26, *30, 32, 33, ...	10
"	Sackville,	" 1, 3, 4, 15, 17, 18, ...	6
"	Salisbury,	" 9, 14, 23,(and Hav. and Bruns.), 25,	4
"	Shediac,	" 22, 23, 24, 26, ...	4
"	Westmorland,	" 11 (and Sackville), ...	1
			32

YORK COUNTY.

Parish of Bright,	Nos.	*6½ 7½. 9, *11 (and Southampton)	4
" Canterbury,	"	*5, 10, 10½, 12, 20, 22, 24, ...	7
" Douglas,	"	12, 14, *16, 20, ...	4
" Kingsclear,	"	*7, *8. 9, 12, ...	4
" Manners Sutton,	"	7, 9, 10, 11, ...	4
" McAdam,	"	*7, ...	1
" New Maryland,	"	1A, *3, ...	2
" North Lake,	"	*13½, 17, 18, 19½, ...	4
" Prince William,	"	6, ...	1
" St. Mary's,	"	9, 10, 11, 14, 15, ...	5
" Southampton,	"	*8, *10, 13, 14, 15, *16, 17, 18, 19,	9
Stanley,	"	*1½, *2, 4, 6½, *9, 14, *16, 17, ...	8
			53
		Total for 1903, ...	590
		Increase, ...	5

*Districts marked * to receive one-quarter rate.

School House Grants to Poor Districts.

By vote of the Legislature the sum of $1000 was appropriated at the last session to assist Poor Districts in building and furnishing school houses.

The following grants from this appropriation were made during the year ending October 31st, 1902:

ALBERT COUNTY.

District No. 3, Hopewell, ...	$25 00	
" 3, Alma, ...	15 00	
		$40 00

CARLETON COUNTY.

District No. 19, Brighton, ...		30 00

CHARLOTTE COUNTY.

District No. 2½, Dumbarton and St. Patrick, ...		70 00

GLOUCESTER COUNTY.

District No. 12, Bathurst, ...	$20 00	
" 4, Caraquet, ...	20 00	
" 4½, Caraquet, ...	20 00	
		60 00

KENT COUNTY.

District No. 12, Dundas, ...	$20 00	
" 6, Harcourt, ...	15 00	
" 7, St. Paul, ...	15 00	
" 17, Wellington, ...	15 00	
" 18, Wellington, ...	15 00	
		80 00

KING'S COUNTY.

District No. 19, Rothesay and Simonds, ...		25 00

MADAWASKA COUNTY.

District No. 2½, St. Francis, ...	$10 00	
" 9, St. Leonard, ...	20 00	
		30 00

NORTHUMBERLAND COUNTY.

District No. 8½, Alnwick,	....	$25 00	
" 1, Blissfield,	....	15 00	
" 9, Glenelg, ...	....	10 00	
" 6, Hardwicke,	....	25 00	
" 2, North Esk,	....	25 00	
" 16, Rogersville,	....	15 00	
			$115 00

QUEENS COUNTY.

District No 3, Canning, ...	....	$15 00	
" 5, Canning, ...	....	20 00	
" 6, Canning, ...	....	10 00	
" 3, Waterborough.	....	20 00	
			65 00

RESTIGOUCHE COUNTY.

District No 1½, Colborne and Balmoral,	....	$10 00	
" 11, Durham, ...	....	10 00	
" 1 A., Beresford and Durham,	....	30 00	
			50 00

ST. JOHN COUNTY.

District No. 5, Musquash,	... .	....	70 00

SUNBURY COUNTY.

District No. 6, Gladstone,	....	$40 00	
" 4, Lincoln, ...	....	10 00	
			50 00

VICTORIA COUNTY.

District No. 6, Gordon, ...	....	$25 00	
" 7, Gordon	....	35 00	
			60 00

WESTMORLAND COUNTY.

District No. 32, Moncton,	....	$30 00	
" 26, Shediac,	....	15 00	
			45 00

York County.

District No. 7, Manners-Sutton, ...	....	$25 00	
" 1 A, New Maryland and Lincoln,	....	15 00	
" 13½, North Lake, ...	....	15 00	
" 3, St. Marys, ...	....	10 00	
			65 00
Total, ...	....	....	$855 00

THE UNIVERSITY OF NEW BRUNSWICK.

The attendance of students at the University during the last year has been the largest in its history. At present there are enrolled 121, of whom 40 belong to the Engineering School and the rest are taking the Arts course in whole or in part. Of the total number 23 are licensed teachers. There are students in attendance from every county in the Province except Gloucester and Madawaska.

The following Degrees in Course were conferred at the last Encœnia:

Bachelor of Arts	14
Bachelor of Science	1
Bachelor of Engineering	5
Master of Arts	1
Doctor of Philosophy	1
Total,	22

Two important changes have taken place in the Academic Faculty. Professor W. F. P. Stockley, at the close of the Academic year, vacated the chair of English and French which he had occupied for sixteen years. The Senate accepted Prof Stockley's resignation with regret. and in doing so entered upon its minutes a resolution highly appreciative of the faithful and eminent services which he has rendered to the University and to the Province.

Prof. Davidson who for the last ten years has filled the chair of Mental and Moral Philosophy and Political Economy asked and obtained leave of absence for one year for the purpose of pursuing special studies in Europe. Though Prof. Davidson's health has been somewhat impaired since leaving New Brunswick it is hoped that he will be able to resume the duties of his professorship at the University in September next.

Mr. W. H. Clawson who after a distinguished course at the University of New Brunswick, from which he graduated with high honors in 1900, received the degree of B. A. from Harvard in 1901, and subsequently spent some time in Europe in further preparation for his professional duties, was appointed to the chair of English and French language and literature vacated by Prof. Stockley.

Mr. Isaac Woodbridge Riley, Ph. D., of Yale University, was appointed to the chair of Philosophy and Political Economy as *locum tenens* during the absence of Prof. Davidson.

While the educational condition of the University, within its present limitations, is highly satisfactory, and the attendance of students, especially in the Engineering department, is annually increasing, its financial resources are found insufficient to maintain efficiently the chairs already established, much less to provide for normal growth by the founding of additional professorships, however much needed.

The Annual Provincial grant of $8,844.48 does not provide for the salaries of the seven professors, small and inadequate as most of these salaries are. Other sources of revenue are very limited, while the addition of the new Science building has materially increased the annual expenditure.

The fact that the University is a public provincial institution and non-denominational seems to turn aside from it the streams of private benevolence which during recent years have tended to enrich other Colleges and Universities, both in Canada and the United States. There is no sound reason why this should be so. The State Universities in the American Republic have shared with the denominational Colleges the many millions contributed by private citizens in support of the higher education. Indeed within the last two years these private contributions have reached such an enormous magnitude that Congress has found it expedient to incorporate a General Education Board, whose special function is to receive and administer the immense sums of money placed at its disposal by wealthy citizens for educational purposes.

It is to be hoped that the time is not far distant when the increasing wealth and liberality of the patrons and alumni of our University will supplement its resources by generous gifts; but under existing conditions the senate has no other recourse than an appeal for an increased annual ---nt from the provincial revenues. If the province is to maintain a Uni-sity worthy of the name, provision must be made not only to increase salaries of the present staff of professors, but to establish additional ...irs as the industrial and educational development of the country may ...and.

The establishment of a chair of Agricultural Chemistry would supply a long felt want. A School of Forestry and Mines for the Atlantic Provinces in affiliation with the University of New Brunswick would prove of great economic importance. An immense loss to the country is sustained every year through ignorance of the best methods which science and experience have discovered for the preservation and enlargement of our forest resources. We should certainly, in view of the importance of our lumber interests, spare no reasonable pains or expense to preserve and increase the value of the timber lands of the province. Our mineral resources are also attracting increased attention. A united effort of the governments of New Brunswick and Nova Scotia could establish a School of Forestry and Mining, which would be of untold benefit to both provinces. There is reason to hope that with proper effort such a school could be established in affiliation with the University of New Brunswick.

Gift of Senator Wark.

A very pleasing incident connected with the last Encœnia at the University was the announcement of a gift by the Hon. Senator Wark of one thousand dollars to be placed at the disposal of the Senate for such purposes as seemed most urgent. The Senate subsequently placed upon record its warm appreciation of the generous act of the venerable Senator.

The Rhodes Scholarships.

Probably the most notable educational event of the year has been the provision by the will of the late Right Hon. Cecil John Rhodes for the endowment of over two hundred scholarships in the Colleges of Oxford University, to be given to young men in the British Colonies, the United States and Germany. The value of each scholarship is £300 sterling a year, tenable for three years. The list of colonial scholarships as enumerated in the will included for Canada the Provinces of Ontario and Quebec only; but as the omission of the other provinces was manifestly an oversight steps were promptly taken by both the Board of Education and the Senate, of the University of New Brunswick, acting jointly with the educational authorities of Nova Scotia and Prince Edward Island, to call the attention of Mr. Rhodes' trustees to the omission of the other Canadian Provinces. The result has been that to each of the Maritime Provinces has been allotted an annual scholarship.

For the information of prospective candidates and others interested in this important matter, I append extracts from the testamentary dispositions of Mr. Rhodes in so far as they reveal the purposes of the testator and indicate his views as to the qualifications and the grounds of selection of the beneficiaries:

EXTRACTS FROM THE WILL OF THE RIGHT HON. CECIL JOHN RHODES.

Whereas, I consider that the education of young Colonists at one of the Universities in the United Kingdom is of great advantage to them for giving breadth to their views for their instruction in life and manners and for instilling into their minds the advantage to the Colonies as well as to the United Kingdom of the retention of the Unity of the Empire, and whereas in the case of young Colonists studying at a University in the United Kingdom I attach very great importance to the University having a residential system such as is in force at the Universities of Oxford and Cambridge, for without it those students are at the most critical period of their lives left without any supervision, and whereas there are at the present time 50 or more students from South Africa studying at the University of Edinburgh, many of whom are attracted there by its excellent medical school, and I should like to establish some of the Scholarships hereinafter mentioned in that University, but owing to its not having such a residential system as aforesaid I feel obliged to refrain from doing so; and whereas my own University, the University of Oxford, has such a system, and I suggest that it should try and extend its scope so as if possible to make its medical school at least as good as that at the University of Edinburgh, and whereas I also desire to encourage and foster an appreciation of the advantages which I implicitly believe will result from the union of the English-speaking peoples throughout the world and to encourage in the students from the United States of North America who will benefit from the American Scholarships to be established for the reason above given at the University of Oxford under this my will, an attachment to the country from which they have sprung but without, I hope, withdrawing them or their sympathies from the land of their adoption or birth: Now therefore I direct my Trustees as soon as may be after my death, and either simultaneously or gradually as they shall find convenient, and if gradually then in such order as they shall think fit to establish for male students the Scholarships hereinafter directed to be established each of which shall be of the yearly value of £300 and be tenable at any College in the University of Oxford for three consecutive academical years.

My desire being that the students who shall be elected to the scholarships shall not be merely bookworms, I direct that in the election of a student to a scholarship regard shall be had to (i) his literary and scholastic attainments; (ii) his fondness of and success in manly outdoor sports, such as cricket, football and the like; (iii) his qualities of manhood, truth, courage, devotion to duty, sympathy for the protection of the weak, kindliness, unselfishness and fellowship; and (iv) his exhibition during school days of moral force of character and of instincts to lead and to take an interest in his schoolmates; for those latter attributes will be likely in after life to guide him to esteem the performance of public duties as his highest aim. As mere suggestions for the guidance of those who will have the choice of students for the scholarships I record that (i) my ideal qualified student would combine these four qualifications in the proportions of three tenths for the first, two tenths for the second, three tenths for the third, and two tenths for the fourth qualification, so that according to my ideas if the maximum number of marks for any scholarship were 200 they would be apportioned as follows: 60 to each of the first and third qualifications and 40 to each of the second and fourth qualifications; (ii) the marks for the several qualifications would be awarded independently as follows (that is to say) the marks for the first qualification by examination, for the second and third qualifications respectively by ballot by the fellow-students of the candidates, and for the fourth qualification by the head master of the candidate's school; and (iii) the results of the awards (that is to say the marks obtained by each candidate for each qualification) would be sent as soon as possible for consideration to the trustees or to some person or persons appointed to receive the same and the person or persons so appointed would ascertain by averaging the marks in blocks of 20 marks each of all candidates the best ideal qualified students.

No student shall be qualified or disqualified for election to a scholarship on account of his race or religious opinions. The election to scholarships shall be by the trustees after such (if any) consultation as they shall think fit with the minister having the control of education in such colony, province, state or territory.

A qualified student who has been elected as aforesaid shall within six calendar months after his election or as soon thereafter as he can be admitted into residence, or within such extended time as my trustees shall allow, commence residence as an undergraduate at some college in the University of Oxford.

The scholarships shall be payable to him from the time when he shall commence such residence.

The trustees are the Earl of Rosebery, Earl Grey, Lord Milner, M Alfred Beit, Dr. Leander Starr Jameson, Mr. Lewis Loyd Mitchell and M Bourchier Francis Hawksley.

In July last the Trustees, through Lord Strathcona and the Secretary of State for Canada, brought to the notice of the Governments of the various Provinces the Scholarship provisions of Mr. Rhodes' will with the view of eliciting the opinions of the Education department of each Province with respect generally to the election of qualifying students.

Subsequently the Trustees appointed George R. Parkin, C. M. G., LL. D.,Principal of Upper Canada College of Toronto, as their agent and commissioner to make all necessary arrangements for carrying out at the earliest possible date the testamentary disposition of Mr. Rhodes. From Dr.Parkin's widely extended acquaintance with the educational conditions of all parts of the Empire as well as because of his energy, enthusiasm and high standing as an educationist, his appointment has been universally regarded with marked approval both in Great Britain and the Colonies. To New Brunswickers especially it is a matter of pardonable pride that a native of our own Province, a graduate of our University and a teacher who has had a distinguished record both at home and abroad, has been selected for the discharge of the delicate and difficult task of advising the Trustees as to the best methods of administering Mr. Rhodes' will and accomplishing his purpose in endowing these scholarships.

In October Dr. Parkin visited England and held a consultation with the authorities of Oxford University as to the conditions on which the Rhodes' scholars would be admitted to the several Colleges. Immediately on his return from England, a conference was held at Sackville with the Superintendents of Education and representatives of the degree conferring colleges and universities of the Maritime Provinces.

There were present at the conference Dr. Parkin ; Dr. Inch, Chief Superintendent of Education for New Brunswick ; Dr. McKay, Supt. of Education for Nova Scotia ; Dr. Anderson, Supt. of Education for Prince Edward Island; Dr. Allison, of Mount Allison University ; Dr. Guertin of St. Joseph's ; Dr. Scott, of the University of New Brunswick ; Dr. Chisholm, of St. Francis Xavier ; Dr. Keirstead, of Acadia ; Dr. Willets, of Kings ; and Prof. Walter Murray, of Dalhousie.

After prolonged discussions the following resolutions were passed :

1st. That one Scholarship be allotted to candidates from each of the -inces of Nova Scotia, New Brunswick and Prince Edward Island.

2nd. That the competition for these Scholarships shall be open only to luates or undergraduates of at least two years standing of a degree coning College or University.

3rd. That the ordinary age limit of candidates shall be 23 years, provided, however, that in exceptional circumstances a candidate whose age does not exceed 25 years may be nominated.

4th. A system of selecting candidates by College Nomination was also unanimously approved. The following summary was officially published:

"Scholars being British subjects shall be selected by the trustees on the nomination of the college within the territory to which the scholarship is assigned. Colleges entitled to make nominations must be equipped to give adequate literary preparation up to the standard of Oxford Responsions, which is the minimum on which scholars will be admitted. These colleges shall nominate in a rotation fixed by the number of undergraduates in each. Each nomination shall be accompanied by a full statement of the school and college qualifications on which the nomination is based, in compliance with the terms of the Rhodes bequest."

The conference was indebted to Prof. Walter C. Murray, who acted as Secretary, for preparing the following statement of the reasons which influenced its members in determining the method of the selection of candidates and for suggesting the scheme of rotation among the several colleges, in accordance with the principles embodied in the fourth resolution given above:

A METHOD FOR THE SELECTION OF THE RHODES SCHOLARS FOR THE MARITIME PROVINCES.

There are at least two possible methods:—The College Nomination and the Competitive Examination.

The College Nomination System provides that the trustees or their representatives select the scholars on the nomination of the teaching bodies or staffs of the colleges, each nomination being accompanied by a full statement of the school and college records of the candidates, including all the evidence that influenced the college in recommending the nominee.

This system has been adopted for the award of the Science Research Scholarships given to the Colonies and Great Britain by the commissioners of the 1851 exhibition.

The principal advantages of the College Nomination System are;

1. It permits the different qualifications specified in the will being given the importance in the selection of the scholar suggested by Mr. Rhodes. This is possible when the moral and social qualifications of the candidates for any scholarship are estimated by the same authorities according to the same standards.

2 It will permit the different colleges and universities to develop without interference along the lines suitable to their conditions.

There will be neither inducement nor necessity for any college to become a coaching institution for candidates for these scholarships.

It will interfere with the college courses of the unsuccessful as well as the successful candidates much less than the Competitive Examination System.

3. The examinations of the Competitive System must be highly diversified to meet the conditions of the different localities to which the scholarships are assigned. Consequently they will lack the uniformity that is usually regarded as the excellence of the examination test.

Only in examinations of an elementary character is uniformity possible, but such elementary examinations are entirely unsuited to the candidates from the larger universities. Such was the case with the Gilchrist Scholarships, which were awarded on the results of the London University Matriculation Examination.

4. It avoids the elaborate organization and expense of a system of Competitive Examinations.

The difficulties of the College Nomination System are:—

A. Making provision for provinces or territories without degree conferring colleges.

B. The selection of nominating institutions.

(A) In Canada the first difficulty presents itself in Prince Edward Island and British Columbia.

In each of these provinces there is an excellent College or High Scoool which by a self denying ordinance has refused to ask for or accept degree conferring powers.

Vancouver College in British Columbia, however, is affiliated with McGill so that students taking the full course in the British Columbia institution are admitted to the third year in McGill and are thus the equals of undergraduates of at least two years standing of a degree conferring college.

Prince of Wales College in Prince Edward Island can secure the same privileges from any or all of the Maritime colleges. Students who have completed the full course there may be deemed undergraduates of at least —— years standing.

(B) In selecting the nominating colleges the following conditions ·ld be observed:—

1. The degree conferring colleges within the territory to which the ··larship is assigned are to be grouped together.

2. To receive the privilege of nominating a college must satisfy certain requirements, such as :—

(a) It must not exclude any student because of race or creed.

(b) Its staff and course of study must be such that students who have completed its second year are well qualified to enter Oxford or pass the Responsions Examinations.

(c) It must have at least a Faculty of Arts (it may have other faculties) well organized and equipped with a staff of not less than four or five professors devoting all their time to the work of that Faculty.

3. The colleges possessing the above qualifications within each political unit shall nominate in rotation. The system of rotation may be determined by the number of possible candidates for these Scholarships within each college—that is practically by the number of undergraduates of the different faculties of the College or University.

The application of this system to the Maritime Provinces;

1. The nominating body in Prince Edward Island shall be the Prince of Wales College. Its nominees may be either

(a) Students who have completed its course of study and are entitled to become undergraduates of at least two years standing of a degree conferring college, or,

(b) Young men from Prince Edward Island who are studying in any Canadian University or College. Students from Prince Edward Island shall not be eligible for nomination by other institutions in Canada.

2. Each qualified college for every 50 (or fraction thereof) undergraduates may have one nomination in the period of rotation.

Thus in New Brunswick, if the University of New Brunswick have 120 undergraduates, Mount Allison 110, and St. Joseph's 40, the University of New Brunswick shall have 3 nominations, Mount Allison 3, and St. Joseph's 1 in a period of 7 years.

In Nova Scotia, if Kings have 40, St. Francis 80, Acadia 130, and Dalhousie 320, undergraduates, then Kings shall have 1 nomination, St. Francis 2, Acadia 3, and Dalhousie 7 in a period of 13 years.

3. In each period of rotation the nominations given to any one college shall be distributed as evenly as possible over the period. Thus in New Brunsick the nominations may be made in the following order:

1904	University of New Brunswick.
1905	Mount Allison.
1906	University of New Brunswick.
1907	St. Joseph's.
1908	Mount Allison.
1909	University of New Brunswick.
1910	Mount Allison.

And in Nova Scotia:

1904	Dalhousie.
1905	Acadia.
1906	Dalhousie.
1907	St. Francis.
1908	Dalhousie.
1909	Acadia.
1910	Dalhousie.
1911	Kings.
1912	Dalhousie.
1913	St. Francis.
1914	Dalhousie.
1915	Acadia.
1916	Dalhousie.

4. Should a college not be ready to nominate the year assigned to it, the privilege of nominating shall be be held over one year for it.

5. At the completion of the period of rotation the cycle may be revised so as to meet changes in the nominating colleges.

It will be understood, of course, that the action and decisions of the Conference as above reported will have no effect until submitted to and approved of by the trustees of the Rhodes scholarships; but it is highly probable that the scheme in its essential features will receive the approval of the trustees. The Conference at Sackville was the first held by Dr. Parkin after his return from England. Since that date he has consulted the edu- .onal authorities of Quebec and Ontario and of several of the United tes. It is gratifying to know that he has met with no insuperable diffi- :ies in formulating plans adapted to the several local conditions; and that ıll essential particulars the principles adopted by the Conference of the -itime Provinces have been followed by the others.

Notes on the Appendices.

I beg to direct attention to Part III. of this Report which contains (a) The Report of the Principal of the Normal School; (b) The Reports of the Seven School Inspectors; (c) The Reports of the School Boards of Fredericton, St. John, Moncton, St. Stephen, Milltown, Woodstock, Chatham, Newcastle and Campbellton; (d) The Reports of the Board of Directors and the Principal of the School for the Blind, Halifax; (e) The Report of the Provincial Educational Institute held at Fredericton in June, 1902; (f) Addresses delivered before the Provincial Educational Institute by Professor John Davidson and Inspector W. S Carter.

I beg to add the following notes and comments on some of these Reports:

THE NORMAL SCHOOL.

The attendance of pupil-teachers for the year under review was 273, an increase of 75 over the enrolment of the previous year. At the present time (Feb. 1903) the enrolment is 177 in the English Department, and 14 in the French Department. To these may be added 47 candidates for Third Class (including 13 in the French Department) who, after examination in December, left the school. The above shows an aggregate enrolment for the current year of 238 of whom 24, now holders of Second Class License, entered in January as candidates for First Class.

The withdrawal of Professor John Brittain in October last from the Natural Science Department was a cause of great regret, not only to his colleagues in the Normal School, but to the hundreds of teachers throughout the province who for the last thirteen years have had the benefit of his teaching and the inspiration of his enthusiasm in the study of Botany, Chemistry and Natural History. It is gratifying to know that the valuable services of Mr. Brittain in his own department are not to be lost to the province. Since his withdrawal from the Normal School, he has been taking special courses of study at the University of Chicago and at Cornell University, in preparation for entering upon new and important duties in New Brunswick as organizer and director of one branch of the plan proposed by Sir William Macdonald and Prof. J. W. Robertson for the purpose of giving object lessons of the value of school gardens and nature studies at rural schools, as described in my last Annual Report. No better man than Prof. Brittain could have been selected for this purpose.

H. H. Hagerman, M. A., teacher of Natural Science in the Fredericton Grammar School, was appointed to the position in the Normal School vacated by Prof. Brittain.

DEATH OF ELDON MULLIN, M A., LL. D., LATE PRINCIPAL OF THE NORMAL SCHOOL.

My last Annual Report referred to the temporary withdrawal of Mr. Mullin from the principalship of the Normal School, under leave of absence from the Board of Education for one year, for the purpose of enabling him to proceed to South Africa to assist in organizing the educational work in the Transvaal and Orange River Colonies. Mr. Mullin left New Brunswick in February, 1902, and on arriving in South Africa entered upon his work in Pretoria and afterwards at Johannesburg with every prospect of success. In January last, having decided to remain in South Africa for several years, he addressed a letter to the Board of Education definitely tendering his resignation as principal of the New Brunswick Normal School. This letter of resignation was laid before the Board on Feb. 4th, 1903, and the following resolution was unanimously passed:

"The Board of Education of the Province of New Brunswick having granted to Dr. Eldon Mullin, who for many years filled the office of principal of the Normal School of this province leave of absence for the purpose of enabling him to go to South Africa with a view to assuming an important position in connection with educational work in that country, and having now received his resignation to take effect at the expiration of his leave of absence, desire to place on record their appreciation of the zeal and ability which Dr. Mullin brought to the discharge of the duties of his position while connected with this Board, and express their regret that the Province of New Brunswick is likely to be permanently deprived of his services, and earnestly hope he may long be spared to devote his talents and his energy to the advancement of education in South Africa."

The hope expressed by the Board in the closing sentence of the above resolution was doomed to early disappointment, for in little more than a week afterwards the sad tidings of Dr. Mullin's death at Johannesburg reached Fredericton, on the anniversary of the day (Feb. 13th) on which he had set out from the city, a year before, on his long journey to the field s anticipated labors and new responsibilities.

It is needless to say that among the numerous friends and co-workers Dr. Mullin in New Brunswick the news of his premature death evoked strongest expressions of sorrow, and of sympathy for his bereaved wife and ily.

Mr. Mullin was associated with educational work in this Province for nearly 30 years. He received his first Teacher's License (Class I) in 1872 and a Grammar School License in 1879. He graduated from the University of New Brunswick (B. A.) in 1881, M. A. in 1884, and received the honorary degree of LL. D. in 1902. He was appointed Inspector of Schools in 1879 and Principal of the Normal School in 1883, which position he held up to the date of his leaving for South Africa in 1902.

Upon the acceptance of Dr. Mullin's resignation on Feb. 4th, 1902, William Crocket, M. A., LL. D., who had been filling the vacancy during Mr. Mullin's leave of absence, was regularly appointed as Principal of the Normal School.

The Inspectors' Reports.

An analysis and comparison of these reports show a unanimity of opinion in regard to many matters bearing on the conditions of the rural schools throughout the province.

It is gratifying to note that all bear testimony to growing improvement in school buildings and equipments as well as to better teaching in many of the ungraded schools.

On the other hand all speak of the serious loss and embarrassment that have resulted from the scarcity of properly qualified teachers, and the consequent necessity of placing untrained and poorly qualified persons in charge of the schools, or of leaving them closed indefinitely. In my last Annual Report I discussed at some length the causes of this unfortunate state of affairs, and do not think it necessary to repeat the statements and arguments which I then used. I beg, however, to quote a passage from Inspector Carter's report, bearing on this question:

Teachers are scarce and this state of affairs will continue so long as other vocations offer stronger inducements to our young men and women. Business offices and hospitals continue to attract our best teachers and lately they have been in demand not only in South Africa, but in our own North West and the United States.

I have rather given up the expectation that our most intelligent school boards would endeavour to stem this tide by offering stronger inducements to good teachers but where College graduates are appraised at $150 per year in a city and experienced teachers are placed upon the same footing as inexperienced, and allowed to retire because of a request for a paltry increase of salary after years of faithful service what are the inducements for teachers?

The United States are getting our most highly cultured teachers at a great cost to us. The graded schools will be the last to feel the pinch, but to them it will surely come later, in the form of inferior qualifications. People have to pay more for everything than formerly, except education, and the expenditure for that, in as far as teachers are concerned, remains stationary or has become less. The cost of living has increased to them as to everyone else, and the towns should set the example and give their teachers a substantial increase of pay. Some deserved increases have been given during the year to the higher grade teachers, which is a healthy sign and is a tendency which I hope will extend downward without delay. The only sure remedy is the fixing of a minimum salary for all classes of teachers, for, as long as country districts can get local licensed teachers, many of them will be indifferent to the class or quality.

The failure to obtain trained teachers in many districts may be traced to the reluctance of fairly educated young men and women to subject themselves to the primitive conditions of living which obtain in remote settlements, but in many more cases to the ignorance, the indifference and the parsimony of those who are appointed as school trustees. Inspector Bridges says:

"In some school districts the trustees will not make any exertion to obtain a teacher, and if no application is made by a teacher to them personally, the school is allowed to remain vacant during the term or at least a greater part of it. This only serves to emphasize the fact that greater care should be exercised by the ratepayers at the annual school meeting, in electing to the office of school trustee only those who have a direct, vital interest in maintaining a good school."

Unfortunately, however, the ratepayers in many cases will not even attend the annual school meetings, and of those who do attend the majority are more anxious to cut down expenses than to maintain a good school.

In another part of this report I will discuss what I conceive to be the best remedy for the evils referred to.

Reports of School Boards in Cities and Incorporated Towns.

The three cities and six incorporated towns organized under the provisions of section 105 of the Schools Act, having School Boards appointed in part by the Governor in Council and in part by the City or Town Councils, trol in the aggregate 287 schools, attended by over 14,000 pupils. In er words the School Boards of these cities and towns have the manage- it of nearly one-sixth of the total number of schools in the Province at- led by nearly one-fourth of the total number of pupils enrolled in all the

public schools. The educational expenditure in these cities and towns disbursed by the School Boards during the past year aggregated more than $270,000.

The magnitude and importance of the trust committed to these Boards can scarcely be over.estimated. The time, attention and labour devoted to the discharge of their duties is given gratuitously. Though assisted by paid secretaries, the full responsibility of the proper administration of the funds, the employment of teachers and the efficiency of the schools rest absolutely upon the trustees.

During recent years most of these cities and towns have expended large sums in the erection and equipment of school buildings of the finest class. This is especially true of Campbellton, Chatham, Moncton, Fredericton and St. John. In the latter city a splendid edifice known as the Latour school, a full description of which is given in the Board's report, was opened during the year in St. John West, and it is intended to complete during the coming year in St. John North another building of equally fine proportions and architecture. Our largest city will then compare very favorably, as to the housing of its school children, with any city of its size elsewhere.

The public interest manifested in the schools of the cities and towns is indicated by the number of prizes awarded to the children, and by the enthusiasm of the citizens who in large numbers attend their public closing exercises.

The excellent report of Dr. H. S. Bridges, Superintendent of the St. John City schools, is well worthy of careful perusal.

THE SCHOOL FOR THE BLIND.

As we have 32 New Brunswick children attending the School for the Blind in Halifax, the report of its Board of Directors and of its accomplished Principal will be read with special interest.

In November last I visited the school and had the opportunity of examining all its departments and noting the characteristic features of its management. I was more than pleased with what I observed. The teachers were earnest, enthusiastic and thorough, evidently expending their best energies as a labor of love for the training of their pupils. The children were bright and intelligent and seemed very happy in their intercourse with their teachers, and in the comforts of their commodious and well-managed home.

The course of study includes most of the subjects taught in the public schools and in addition manual training and such mechanical work as will in most cases prepare the pupils to carn their own livelihood when they leave the institution. The intellectual quickness and manual dexterity of many of these blind students seemed to me scarcely less than marvellous. The music department, under the direction of Prof. H. B. Campbell and his assistants, has attained a degree of efficiency rarely equalled. A fine orchestra composed of pupils from six to sixteen years of age played their several instruments in almost perfect harmony, while an immense chorus class, comprising nearly the whole school, rendered some really difficult pieces with a verve and accuracy which would have done credit to professionals.

A very valuable addition to the equipment of the school is a circulating library of point print books for the use not only of the pupils in residence but of those who have left the school and are now located in various parts of the Provinces. The Post Office department allows these books to be forwarded free of postage through the mails. Many of these publications have been stereotyped and printed at the school on machines presented by Mr. H. M. Whitney.

The Directors are now engaged in the erection of a new building 131 x 71 ft. and four stories high which will cost with its furnishings and equipment over $60,000. The new building will be used for school-rooms, recreation rooms, etc., leaving the present buildings to be used for residence purposes only. The Nova Scotia Legislature has contributed $20,000 towards the cost of the new building, and about $12,000 more up to the present time has been contributed by private subscription. The Principal, Dr. C. F. Fraser, accompanied by a number of his pupils will visit Fredericton, St John and other places in New Brunswick during the month of April, for the purpose of awakening renewed interest in the School for the Blind, and of soliciting aid towards the completion of the new building. I bespeak for him and his pupils a cordial and sympathetic reception.

SCHOOL FOR THE DEAF AND DUMB.

The deplorable circumstances which have led to the closing of the School for the Deaf and Dumb in the City of Fredericton need not be referred to here further than to point out the necessity which now exists for prompt action in making other provision for the education of the unfortunate s of our children deprived of the power of hearing and speech. We not be indifferent to their claims on our sympathy and benevolence, as l as to their right to a free education in common with the other children the Province.

Two plans have been proposed to meet the exigency which has arisen. The first suggests the establishment of a school at Fredericton, or elsewhere in the Province, under the direct control of the Education Department and largely maintained by Provincial and County Funds. The alternative plan is to avail ourselves of the advantages of the Institution for the Deaf and Dumb at Halifax, with the Directors of which arrangements could be made for the care and education of our deaf and dumb children similar to those which have proved so satisfactory in the case of the blind.

The principal objections to the former plan are the considerable expense involved in providing and maintaining suitable buildings and grounds with the necessary equipments; the difficulty and risk involved in providing, as soon as required, for a competent staff of trained teachers, and for the judicious and economical management of such an establishment under government control; and the almost certain result that the assumption of the management and expense of the institution by the government will tend to dry up the springs of private benevolence which have hitherto been almost universally the chief source of revenue to such institutions.

The latter plan enables us to make provision without delay, and without serious interruption, for the continued education of the children who were in attendance at the Fredericton school up to June last, and of the other deaf mutes who are now ready to enter upon their course of training; it would give us the advantage of sharing in the results of the experience in the management of such schools acquired by the Directors of the Halifax Institution over a period of 45 years, and would place our children at once under the instruction of a staff of twelve trained teachers; it would practically make us partners on more than equal terms in the benefits of a very valuable property and endowments The annual income of the school from various sources for the year 1901 was over $20,000.

For the reasons above stated and because, in my opinion, such a school as the province of New Brunswick alone would be able to maintain could not for many years to come furnish to our deaf mute children advantages to be compared with those provided by the larger school, I confidently recommend the latter plan.

Teachers' Institutes and Summer School of Science,

The Provincial Institute of New Brunswick meets biennially. The last meeting was held at Fredericton on the 26th of June and two following days. There was a very large attendance of teachers. The total number enrolled as members was 446. In the report given in Appendix E. the secretary gives a general outline of the proceedings. These were full of interest and marked by able and earnest discussions. It was the intention to publish the full proceedings for distribution among the teachers of the Province, but the secretary, Mr. Brittain, upon whom rested the responsibility of compiling and editing the work, having been called away from the Province, the publication was abandoned. In Appendix F. to this report I have given in full two important papers read before the Institute—the first written by Prof. John Davidson of the University of New Brunswick, on "Teachers Wages"; and the second by Inspector W. S. Carter, on "The Centralization of Rural Schools." As both these papers treat of matters of vital importance to the stability and progress of our schools, I commend their perusal to all interested in educational affairs.

The Summer School of Science is growing in interest and importance from year to year. The last meeting was held at St.Stephen from July 22nd to Aug. 8th and was attended by 259 teachers and others from the three Maritime Provinces and from Ontario, Quebec and the United States.

The next meeting of the summer school will be held at Chatham in July and August next.

Reports of the County Institutes will be found on pp. 168 to 173 of part III. of this Report.

Macdonald Manual Training Schools.

I hereto append the report of Edwin E. McCready, Director of the Macdonald Manual Training Schools in New Brunswick:

J. R. Inch, LL. D.,
Chief Superintendent of Education.

Sir,—In compliance with your request I beg to submit the following report on Manual Training in New Brunswick.

Since my last report was handed to you a decided advance has been made in the introduction of manual training in the schools of the Province.

The Act which was passed at the last session of the Legislature aiding all districts establishing manual training in their schools has been of great assistance.

The Board of School Trustees of the town of Saint Andrews established during January last a department of manual training and engaged Miss Agnes E. Lucas as teacher. Miss Lucas had for the year and a half previous been teaching in Musquash where she introduced manual training and was most successful in teaching it. Miss Sadie Inch has taken the place of Miss Lucas at Musquash.

The Board of School Trustees of the town of Campbellton established during January a department of manual training and engaged as teacher Miss Ethel I. Morsereau, who was graduated recently from the training course at Truro, N. S.

The school trustees of the village of Mascarene, Charlotte County, have also introduced manual training into their school. Miss Harriette Bolt, the teacher, deserves much credit for arousing interest in the subject and for raising a large part of the necessary funds.

The Boards of School Trustees of the towns of Saint Stephen and Milltown have voted to establish departments of manual training in connection with their schools and preparations are now being made to start the work next September. Doubtless there will be other districts to take up this work next term.

At Inches Ridge manual training, which was started more than two years ago, is now taught by Miss Bessie Kelly. The interest of pupils, parents and trustees seems to be as great there as ever. A new hardwood floor has greatly improved the school room and there is now a prospect of slate blackboards being added, so great interest is taken in school matters.

Manual training will be taught in the Central School to be built by Sir Wm. Macdonald at Kingston; also in the group of schools in Carleton County which are to be under the charge of Mr. Brittain.

At Fredericton during the past year the work has been carried on as heretofore. All the student teachers at the Normal School have two hours per week instruction in either woodwork and mechanical drawing or cardboard construction and mechanical drawing. All the boys in the city schools from grades six to nine, inclusive, have had the work as usual.

During the summer vacation a session was held for four weeks Fredericton with forty (40) teachers in attendance; some of whom h previously had some instruction at the summer school held in Saint Jo the previous summer; and at the Normal School. To those who had sp time equivalent to three months in this study an examination was given, and to those who passed this satisfactorily certificates of qualification to teach manual training in rural schools were granted.

Three New Brunswick teachers have been graduated from the Truro training course, and three more are in attendance there this year.

On April 10, 1903 will expire the three years for which Sir Wm. Macdonald arranged to carry on the manual training work at Fredericton. During this time there have been 1,315 persons taking courses in manual training at Fredericton (and at summer school held in St. John).

Boys of Fredericton (some of whom have attended during the entire three years)	298
Boys from Deaf and Dumb School	15
Boys at summer school (St. John)	16
Teachers at summer courses	88
Teachers' class, Fredericton and vicinity	34
Student teachers at Normal School, Woodwork	661
Student teachers at Normal School, Cardboard	203
Total	1315

In our course of woodwork for the student teachers some models have been added which will be of value in teaching certain science problems.

Because of the educational and practical value of manual training it is important that it be continued in connection with the Provincial Normal School; further, that special three months' courses be arranged for rural school teachers to prepare them to teach this subject in their schools.

Respectfully submitted,

EDWIN E. MACCREADY.

As stated in the above report the three years during which Sir Wm. Macdonald has made provision for carrying on the Manual Training work at Fredericton will end in April. I am informed that the work will be continued at his expense until the close of the school year on June 30th. The experiment has been an unqualified success. The possibility of adding this ·k to the public school course without detriment to the studies which ·st always be regarded as the basis of a sound education has been demon-·ted. The duty of continuing and developing the work now devolves ·n School Boards and the Provincial authorities.

It is confidently anticipated that the School Boards of cities, towns and many country districts will avail themselves of the liberal encouragement o r this work provided by the Legislature in the Act passed on the 10th of April, 1902; which is as follows:

Whereas it is desirable to encourage manual training and instruction in the public schools of the Province ;

Be it therefore enacted by the Lieutenant Governor and Legislative Assembly, as follows :—

1. "The Lieutenant Governor in Council is hereby authorized to make the following grants from the provincial revenues to aid in the establishment and maintenance of manual training and instruction :

"(a) To any Board of School Trustees, whether in a city, town or rural district, which shall provide suitable accommodation in connection with the school or schools under its jurisdiction, for instruction in manual training, there shall be granted a sum not less than one-half of the total amount expended for the necessary benches, tools, material and other equipment required.

"(b) To any licensed teacher who shall obtain from any Manual Training School approved by the Board of Education a certificate of fitness to teach the system, aud who shall, in addition to the other regular work of the school under his charge, give instruction in manual training in accordance with the regulations to be made by the Board of Education, there shall be granted, in addition to the provincial grant provided for by the said Act, the sum of fifty dollars per annum.

"(c) To any certified teacher who may be employed in cities, towns or other populous districts, to give instruction in manual training to the pupils of the several schools, and who gives his full time to such instruction, under the direction of tha Local School Board, and in accordance with the regulations of the Board of Education, there shall be granted the sum of two hnndred dollars per annum.

"(d) The provisions of Section 6 of the Schools Act, 1900, in reference to the travelling expenses of student teachers attending the Provincial Normal School, shall apply to New Brunswick teachers who shall take the course of any manual training school approved by the Board of Education, and who shall afterwards actually teach the system in any New Brunswick School."

The term "Manual Training" as used in the Act above quoted is, in m opinion, sufficiently comprehensive to include Domestic Science or Hon Economics. If there be any doubt as to the correctness of this view, would suggest that the Act be amended by pl[illegible] the words "and Domest Science" after the words "Manual Training." It is fitting that the girls

our public schools should have some instruction and training in the special duties which will devolve upon them as home makers; and that the same encouragement and assistance shall be offered to School Boards to provide for instruction in Domestic Science for the girls, as is offered by the Act for instruction in Manual Training for the boys. The two branches can be carried on simultaneously.

TEACHERS OF MANUAL TRAINING AND DOMESTIC SCIENCE.

The preparation and training of teachers of these subjects in our schools is a matter of importance. How are we to find a supply of properly qualified teachers? If the system is to be introduced into the rural as well as the city schools, it would appear desirable that a shorter and less expensive course of instruction should be provided for the former, whose duties would require only three or four hours per week devoted to these special subjects; while in the towns and cities there would be required thoroughly trained and expert teachers who would give their whole time to the work in central schools to which would come at stated hours all the children of certain grades in attendance at the other public schools.

For the training of these expert teachers we will have to depend for the present at least upon schools outside of the limits of our own province. Fortunately two such schools will be available in sister provinces; the Macdonald Manual Training School at Truro, N. S., which offers a six month's course for teachers, and the magnificent Macdonald Institute in connection with the Agricultural College at Guelph, Ontario. Two noble buildings are now in process of erection at Guelph at a cost to Sir William Macdonald of $170,000. One of these is a residence for the women while in attendance at the Institute, and the other is devoted to the work of instruction in manual training, domestic science and nature study, with commodious class rooms, laboratories, green-houses, library, reading-room, and every appliance for carrying on the work in its various branches. Courses covering from one to three years will be provided under expert teachers, the best that can be found in Great Britain and America. The advantages offered at this Institute will be free to a limited number of teachers from w Brunswick, and I have no doubt that many will avail themselves of the ortunity of thus fitting themselves for taking charge of the central mantraining schools in our towns and cities.

For preparing teachers of these subjects in rural schools I think it er to make provision at our own Provincial Normal School. With this object in view I recommend that instruction in wood-work, card-board work, etc., similar to that which has been provided for by the Macdonald fund for the last three years shall be continued at the Normal School for the benefit of the student-teachers undergoing training there, and that in addition special courses of three months' duration shall be provided for licensed teachers to enable them to qualify for such work as is now carried on successfully in several country districts. This work will require the services of two instructors.

There will be required, further, the appointment of a Director of Manual Training for the province whose duties shall be:

(a) To supervise all manual training work in the public schools, for which purpose he shall visit at least twice each year every department of manual training, and report thereon annually to the Chief Superintendent.

(b) To confer with Boards of School Trustees in regard to the establishing of manual training in their respective schools, and to render such advice and assistance as may be needed.

(c) To give instruction at the Normal School to teachers attending the special courses in the theory of manual training, the management of classes, the arrangement of rooms, etc.

(d) To examine the work and the qualifications of the teachers who shall have completed the special course of training at the Normal School, and to recommend to the Board of Education for certificates those whom he shall find properly prepared for giving instruction in manual training in the rural schools.

The Macdonald Consolidated School at Kingston, Kings County.

In my last Annual Report I gave an outline of the plans proposed by Prof. J. W. Robertson for the improvement of education at rural schools, and the establishing and maintenance for three years, at the expense of the Macdonald fund, of a model consolidated school in some country district. I have now to report progress in the carrying out of these plans.

After visiting several localities in the province and consulting local School Boards, Prof. Robertson finally selected Kingston, the old county town of Kings County, as the site of the proposed consolidated school.

Six school districts will be united as the constituency of the new school. The work of erecting the building will be commenced in the course of a few weeks and, it is hoped, will be completed in time for the opening of the schools in September next. The building will contain six class rooms, a laboratory, a room for mechanic science and a room for domestic science. A spacious school garden will be attached.

Comfortable covered vans for the conveyance of the children will be provided. These vans will carry from 15 to 25 children each, and will be placed in charge of responsible drivers who shall enter into bonds for the faithful discharge of their duties. The vans will arrive at the school 15 minutes before the hour of opening and will be promptly on hand at the closing hour for the conveyance of the children to their homes in the afternoon.

Under the provisions of section 57(2), one half the actual expense incurred for the conveyance of the children to and from school will be chargeable to the provincial revenues, the regularly licensed teachers who may be employed will receive the usual grants, the school will share in the County Fund grants. A sum not exceeding in the aggregate the amounts levied annually upon the several districts during recent years will be levied upon the united district; all other expenses, including the cost, furnishing and equipment of the building, will be provided by Sir William Macdonald.

Groups of Schools with Travelling Instructor.

Another of Professor Robertson's plans is the grouping of a number of contiguous schools and placing each group under the charge of a travelling instructor. A model school garden will be provided for each school of the group. It will be the duty of the travelling instructor not only to supervise the teaching of nature lessons and the care and management of the school gardens in connection with these schools, but also so to correlate the several subjects taught as to prevent any neglect of the other studies of the course.

The first group of schools selected for this interesting experiment will be located in Carleton County and will include districts on the St. John river from Hartland or Florenceville extending up the river as far as may be found practicable.

As mentioned elsewhere, Mr. John Brittain, so well and favorably known throughout the province as the enthusiastic and successful teacher of natural science in the Normal School for many years, will have the organization and supervision of this group of schools, and will devote his full time and energies to make the experiment successful.

D. W. Hamilton, B. A., a graduate of the University of New Brunswick, who has already proved his ability as a teacher in the public schools, will have the principalship of the consolidated school at Kingston.

Both the above named gentlemen, under the direction of Professor Robertson, have been making special preparation for the important duties they are soon to undertake. They have completed courses at the University of Chicago and at Cornell University and are now finishing their course at the Teachers' College of the University of Columbia in New York.

The country is certainly under a great debt of gratitude to Sir William Macdonald for the large expenditure already made in connection with the manual training schools throughout Canada during the last three years, and for the immense expenditure to be incurred for at least three years more in connection with the several educational enterprises he has initiated.

To Professor J. W. Robertson the country is scarcely less indebted for the energy, zeal and practical wisdom he has brought to bear on the difficult problems which have confronted him in administering the trust committed to him. With Professor Robertson it has been a labor of love, for no educational interest appeals to him in vain.

The duty of effecting such legislation as may be found necessary to encourage and legalize, as part of the public school system, the various educational movements outlined above will devolve upon the government and legislature during the approaching session.

Amendments to the School Law Suggested.

In my annual report for 1899 I strongly recommended the increase of the County Fund from 30 cents per head to 40 or 50 cents. As anticipated the proposal met with determined opposition even from those whose best interests would have been served by the change. Nevertheless I am convinced that the increase of the fund is eminently reasonable, and almost essential to the continuance of schools in some of the poorer districts.

There are more than 1000 districts in the province with a taxable valuation of less than $20000 each; over 500 having a taxable valuation of less than $10000. each; nearly 200 having a taxable valuation of less than $5000 each.

To maintain a poor school for a part of each year in the poorest districts even with the help of the provincial and county poor aid, requires an assessment of from $1.50 to $2.00 on each $100 of valuation. In the wealthier districts the assessment is from 20 cents to 60 cents (rarely higher) on $100 of valuation, to maintain for the whole year graded schools of the highest class.

An increase of the county fund will tend to relieve the poorer districts; the districts with average valuation will receive from the fund as much as they contribute to it, and if their county tax be higher their district tax will be proportionately lower. To the wealthy districts the increase will be scarcely perceptible, and it is quite in harmony with the spirit of the school law that the rich shall contribute of their abundance to the educational necessities of their poorer fellow-citizens.

There is another aspect of the case that I beg to present. The amount of the county school fund remains practically the same as when the law came into force in 1872. As the number of schools has increased from year to year, while the amount to be distributed remains the same, each recurring distribution shows a diminution of the sum granted to each school. The grants from this fund since 1892 to the school for the Deaf and Dumb and to the school for the Blind lessens still further the sums allotted to the public schools. The average allowance to each of the schools in the province is nearly 25 per cent. less than in 1875. In some of the counties the loss is very much greater.

If the county fund were raised to 40cents per head of the population it would place the schools about in the same position in relation to this source of income as they were 30 years ago.

Parish Instead of District School Boards.

After a trial of nearly 30 years of our present system of school districts it must be admitted by those best acquainted with the facts that the results in a majority of the country districts have been very unsatisfactory.

In 1876 the province was divided into 1426 school districts. Since the first division the number of districts has increased to 1662. More than one third of these are poor districts, some of them having a taxable valuation of s than $5000 and a very small enrolment of pupils. It is impossible der these conditions to maintain efficient schools.

It ought not to excite surprise to be told that in many of these districts is impossible to find men capable of discharging properly the duties of ool trustees. Some who are elected to this responsible office are unable write their own names in attesting to the alleged correctness of the school urns. It occurs, occasionally, that the man appointed as school secretary, on whom devolves the responsibility of attending to the financial affairs he district, is obliged to make his mark instead of writing his name in signing school contracts and returns. Under such control what hope is there for the maintenance of a school worthy of the name?

Further, in these small and isolated communities the educational and other higher interests of the people are often sacrificed to the local jealousies and petty disputes which divide the ratepayers into cliques and factions contending with each other or with the teacher about some trivial matter to the utter demoralization of the school, or to its closing for an indefinite period. It is difficult to remedy these evils, for under the law each district is a free and independent republic electing its own school board.

The school board, when elected, has large powers. If disposed to neglect their duties or to act in an arbitrary or obstructive way, school trustees may block for a considerable time all educational progress in the district.

The present system tends to perpetuate and increase the evil complained of. Parents who live at the extreme ends of districts see no reason why their children should be obliged to travel farther to school than the children of their neighbours have to travel, and they forthwith begin an agitation for the division of the district. When disputes arise as to the location of a new school house, the opposing parties will often clamor for the division of the district and the opening of two schools where one would amply accommodate all the children within a radius of two miles. For reasons like these, and others more ingenious and plausible, persistent pressure for the multiplication of districts is brought to bear upon the Board of Education which it is sometimes difficult to resist.

Any proposal for the consolidation of two or more of these weak districts is met by most strenuous opposition. The proposed conveyance of children to a central school, however advantageous to the interests of all concerned the plan might prove to be, will never be brought about so long as the present district system obtains. While the narrow local ideas fostered by the district system are allowed to prevail, the weak rural school will be intermittently maintained, poorly housed, imperfectly organized, scantily equipped and taught by the cheapest teacher that it is possible to obtain.

After a careful study of existing conditions in the country schools have reached the conclusion that a radical change in the school law is desirable.

I recommend, therefore, that the plan of small school districts be abolished, and that each parish shall constitute a single district under the contro of a parish school Board consisting of not less than seven persons appoint in part by the Governor in Council and in part by the County Municipalit

The duties and powers of the Parish School Boards would be similar to those of the city and town school Boards in so far as the conditions and requirements of the parish district would be analogous to those of the town district. Provision would have to be made for estimating the amount of money required annually for school purposes, and for levying and assessing the same upon the parish, for determining the number and locality of the schools to be maintained and the class of teachers to be employed in each and generally for discharging the duties and exercising the powers in relation to the schools and the school property of the parish now vested in the trustees of the districts in relation to the schools and property of the district.

Each school Board should have the assistance of a paid secretary who would act as their executive officer, and have general supervision of all the educational interests of the parish under their direction. Much of the success of the work would depend upon the intelligence, the energy and educational zeal of this officer, who should, if possible, be selected from among those in the parish best acquainted with schools and school requirements.

The adjustment of the general provisions of the schools act to the changes suggested would not be difficult. The essential principles of the law would remain unchanged. If the Government and Legislature accept the general plan outlined, the details as to local supervision and other incidental matters could be easily worked out.

Some of the advantages I anticipate as likely to result from the proposed change are:

(a) A more intelligent and effective administration of the law because of the character and ability of the trustees;

(b) Better salaries paid to good teachers, and a more permanent tenure of office;

(c) The consolidation of weak schools and the conveyance of children to central graded schools wherever the conditions will permit, thus affording to a large number of country children educational advantages equal to those enjoyed by children in the towns;

(d) Better, more economic and more permanent school privileges for lated sections now too poor to maintain schools except for a few months the year;

(e) The more equal distribution of the burden of school support oughout the parish;

(f) The lessening of the dissensions and factious disturbances in the nagement of school affairs and in the conducting of school meetings. The erness and intensity of these disturbances are often in inverse ratio to numbers and intelligence of the school community in which they occur,

The management of public schools by parish school Boards is nothing new. Until the enactment of the Common Schools Law of 1871, the schools were under the control of trustees elected by the parish or appointed by the sessions. The late Dr. Theodore Rand, who had a larger part than any other man in the organization and first administration of the schools under the Act of 1871, advises in his Annual Report of 1876 "the gradual abolition of district lines within the several parishes."

The township (or parish) system prevails in nearly all the New England states and has been found eminently satisfactory.

It may be that the changes above advocated involve too important a departure from the long established system to justify the legislature in enacting a law on the subject during the coming session. It is probably expedient to give the country sufficient time to weigh carefully the issues likely to arise if the changes should be made. In the meantime I commend the matter to the thoughtful consideration of all interested in the educational welfare of the country.

All of which is respectfully submitted.

I have the honor to be

Your Honor's most obedient servant,

JAMES R. INCH,

Chief Superintendent of Education.

PART II.

STATISTICAL TABLES.

i 5

TABLE 1. PUBLIC SCHOOLS: For the Year Ended June 30th, 1902.

Counties	Second Term Closed 31st December, 1901.			First Term Closed 30th June, 1902.					Year Ended 30th June, 1902.		
	Schools.	Teachers and Assistants.	Pupils in Attendance at Schools.	Schools.	Teachers and Assistants.	Pupils in Attendance at Schools.	New pupils in attendance this term, at Schools in operation both Terms.	New pupils in attendance this term, at Schools not in operation the previous Term.	No. of Districts having Schools in operation in the June Term, that were without sch'ls in Dec. term	No. of Dis. having Sch'ls in operation in the Dec. term, that were without Schools in the June term.	Total No. of different Pupils in attendance at Schools within the year.
Albert	72	72	2,155	63	67	2,098	275	83	4	10	2,513
Carleton	149	155	4,039	147	153	4,423	652	355	14	15	5,056
Charlotte	134	137	3,924	136	144	4 429	352	205	11	9	4,492
Gloucester	109	111	4,267	107	109	4 298	537	59	6	5	4,894
Kent	120	121	3.805	114	116	3,967	508	174	6	10	4,515
Kings	154	160	3,966	152	157	4,265	580	264	15	15	4,843
Madawaska	57	57	2,048	59	60	2,262	294	168	5	4	2 530
Northumberland	149	158	5,094	143	154	5,253	534	53	3	9	5,695
Queens	100	102	2,184	91	92	2,287	332	145	7	14	2,681
Restigouche	48	51	1,815	45	48	1,734	184	73	2	4	2,077
Saint John	208	228	8,950	208	235	8,618	436	53	4	3	9,441
Sunbury	39	39	935	40	40	1,036	124	80	4	3	1,154
Victoria	59	59	1,476	59	59	1.707	308	184	7	6	1,976
Westmorland	208	218	8,181	197	206	8,200	881	92	4	13	9,181
York	189	201	5.736	175	185	5,900	691	174	15	19	6,633
New Brunswick	1,795	1,869	58,575	1,736	1,825	60,477	6,688	2,162	107	139	67,681
Cor. Terms, 1900-1901	1,812	1,893	57,629	1,741	1,841	60,420	7,419	1,641	138	79	66,760
Increase			946			57		521		60	921
Decrease	17	24		5	16		731		31		

TABLE II. PUBLIC SCHOOLS: FOR THE YEAR ENDED 30TH JUNE, 1902.

PART ONE.—The First Term Closed 30th December, 1901.

COUNTIES.	No. of pupils at School this Term.	Proportion of the population at School this Term (Census of 1901)	AGE AND SEX OF PUPILS.					Grand total days' attendance made by the Pupils enrolled.	Number daily present on an average during the time the Schools were in Session.	Number daily present on an average for the full Term.	Number daily present on an average during the time in Session per hundred enrolled.	Number daily present on an average for full Term per hundred enrolled
			Number under 6 years of age.	Number between the ages of 6 and 15 years.	Number over 15 years of age.	Boys.	Girls.					
Albert	2,155	1 in 5 06	55	2,012	88	1,095	1,060	124,711½	1,425	1,347	66.12	62.50
Carleton	4.039	1 in 5 35	143	3,683	213	1,936	2,103	211.092½	2.496	2,278	61.79	56.40
Charlotte	3,924	1 in 5 71	75	3,664	185	1,938	1,986	242 389½	2,779	2.476	70.82	63.09
Gloucester	4,267	1 in 6 54	96	4 057	114	2,140	2,127	227,022	2.617	2,548	61.33	59.71
Kent	3 805	1 in 6 29	147	3,571	87	1,955	1,850	213,220½	2 377	2 330	62 47	61.23
Kings	3,966	1 in 5 46	110	3,633	223	1,953	2,013	215.261	2,477	2 326	62.45	58.64
Madawaska	2,048	1 in 6.01	210	1,805	33	961	1,087	113,661½	1,308	1,261	63.86	61.57
Northumberland	5,094	1 in 5.60	86	4.852	156	2,546	2,548	294.921	3,440	3,290	67.53	64.58
Queens	2,184	1 in 5.11	94	1,959	131	1,055	1,129	111.732	1,358	1,237	62 17	56.63
Restigouche	1,815	1 in 5.83	52	1,711	52	907	908	94,127½	1,137	1 081	62.64	59 55
Saint John	8,950	1 in 5.78	70	8,489	391	4,370	4,580	517,407	[illegible],409	[illegible]	[illegible]	70 04
Sunbury	935	1 in 6.12	39	850	46	465	470	47,946½	591	539	63 20	57.64
Victoria	1,476	1 in 5.97	68	1.367	41	747	729	68,094	837	762	56 70	51 62
Westmorland	8,181	1 in 5.14	187	7.683	311	4 033	4,148	469,097½	5.533	5,388	67.63	65 86
York	5,736	1 in 5.51	213	5,292	231	2 805	2,931	334,070½	3,787	3,655	66.02	63.72
New Brunswick	58,575	1 in 5.65	1,645	54,628	2,302	28,906	29,669	3,284,754½	38,571	36,787	65.84	62.80
Cor. Term, 1900	57,629	1 in 5.74				28,435	29,194	3,233,208	37,160	35,656	64 48	61.87
Increase	946	1 in 350.0				471	475	51,546½	1,411	1,131	1.36	.93
Decrease												

TABLE II. PUBLIC SCHOOLS: For the Year Ended 30th June, 1902.

Part Two.—The Second Term closed 30th June, 1902.

COUNTIES.	No. of pupils at School this Term.	Proportion of the population at School this Term (Census of 1901)	AGE AND SEX OF PUPILS. Number under 6 years of age.	Number between the ages of 6 and 15 years.	Number over 15 years of age	Boys	Girls.	Grand total days' attendance made by the Pupils enrolled.	Number daily present on an average during the time the Schools were in Session.	Number daily present on an average for the full Term.	Number daily present on an average during the time in Session per hundred enrolled.	Number daily present on an average for full Term per hundred enrolled
Albert	2,098	1 in 5.20	55	1,886	157	1,080	1,018	154,123½	1,367	1,262	65.15	60.15
Carleton	4,423	1 in 4.88	145	3,900	378	2,268	2,155	311,970½	2,678	2,458	60.54	55.57
Charlotte	4,429	1 in 5.06	77	3,967	385	2,303	2,126	330,927½	2,942	2,592	66.42	58.52
Gloucester	4,298	1 in 6.50	76	4,056	166	2,237	2,061	292,562½	2,510	2,403	58.39	55.90
Kent	3,967	1 in 6.03	167	3,677	123	2,074	1,893	273,581½	2,368	2,220	59.69	55.96
Kings	4,265	1 in 5.07	88	3,839	338	2,161	2,104	300,378½	2,578	2,389	60.32	56.01
Madawaska	2,262	1 in 5.44	216	1,995	51	1,104	1,158	163,917½	1,402	1,321	61.98	58.40
Northumberland	5,253	1 in 5.43	89	4,915	249	2,706	2,547	385,015½	3,363	3,095	64.02	58.91
Queens	2,287	1 in 4.88	72	2,025	190	1,141	1,146	143,340½	1,316	1,164	57.54	50.89
Restigouche	1,734	1 in 6.10	32	1,600	102	889	845	123,224½	1,068	986	61.59	56.86
Saint John	8,618	1 in 6.00	48	8,172	398	4,246	4,372	773,501	6,613	6,396	76.73	74.21
Sunbury	1,036	1 in 5.52	32	927	77	534	502	66,993¼	609	564	58.78	54.44
Victoria	1,707	1 in 5.16	65	1,528	114	896	811	99,205	942	782	55.18	45.81
Westmorland	8,200	1 in 5.12	199	7,561	440	4,125	4,075	615,312	5,324	5,105	64.92	62.25
York	5,900	1 in 5.35	161	5,302	437	3,003	2,897	326,744	3,661	3,321	62.05	56.28
New Brunswick	60,477	1 in 5.47	1,522	55,350	3,605	30,767	29,710	4,360,797½	8,336	36,058	64.05	59.62
Cor. Term, 1901	60,420	1 in 5.48				30,870	29,550	4,288,235½	37,717	35,251	62.42	58.34
Increase	57	1 in 5809					160	72,562	1,019	807	1.63	1.28
Decrease						103						

TABLE III. PUBLIC SCHOOLS: FOR THE YEAR ENDED 30TH JUNE, 1902.

PART ONE.—The First Term closed 31st December, 1901.

NUMBER OF PUPILS IN THE DIFFERENT BRANCHES OF INSTRUCTION.

COUNTIES.	Physical Exercises 35	Oral Lessons on Morals, etc. 36	[Optional.] 37 Sewing.	Knitting.	Reading—Spelling—Recitation, Etc. 38 Grade I	II	III	IV	V	VI	VII	VIII	Grammar and Analysis and Composition. 39 Grade III*	IV*	V	VI	VII	VIII	History. 40 Grade IV*	V	VI	VII	VIII
Albert	1660	2007	...	...	465	352	316	363	294	96	56	84	294	372	266	75	51	73	252	287	91	56	83
Carleton	3487	3680	41	...	837	562	713	711	686	183	100	144	644	685	681	180	100	144	536	677	180	99	143
Charlotte	3561	3782	3	3	659	552	654	678	681	213	132	150	627	668	680	220	132	150	484	685	214	132	150
Gloucester	3842	4061	15	5	1594	882	657	590	271	99	62	71	643	590	261	99	62	71	508	267	99	62	44
Kent	3099	3630	29	23	1533	710	621	461	259	41	63	62	594	449	244	37	63	59	359	236	37	62	61
Kings	3309	3763	18	...	816	597	751	766	646	148	89	61	742	764	635	144	88	52	670	628	121	68	41
Madawaska	1609	1902	...	...	899	450	323	220	78	24	21	27	283	197	65	22	24	27	184	61	27	24	27
Northumberland	4405	4754	...	10	1308	824	987	750	553	246	168	141	977	736	552	246	168	141	546	553	220	168	141
Queens	1761	2104	...	...	474	374	428	432	355	52	22	11	416	424	338	48	22	11	385	338	55	22	11
Restigouche	1376	1652	...	...	473	317	304	274	217	96	54	34	301	274	217	96	54	34	225	217	96	54	34
Saint John	8261	8392	82	125	1791	1249	1363	1220	1116	709	569	394	1348	1220	1115	709	560	394	1148	1114	709	569	394
Sunbury	755	871	7	...	265	144	170	160	117	14	17	7	163	159	116	14	17	7	159	119	14	17	7
Victoria	1105	1224	3	7	416	243	282	212	171	29	28	17	256	212	168	24	28	17	186	162	24	28	17
Westmorland	6535	7315	16	20	2185	1181	1321	1185	1040	363	328	274	1178	1112	1021	369	316	274	785	893	355	324	275
York	4628	5172	...	...	1375	799	932	980	886	219	161	179	829	942	866	217	161	173	655	840	184	161	173
New Brunswick	49396	54309	214	193	15090	9236	9822	9002	7370	2532	1873	1656	9295	8804	7225	2500	1855	1627	7082	7077	2426	1846	1601
Cor. Terms, 1900	48457	53079	161	149	14986	9470	9665	8868	7008	2433	1848	1654	8993	8638	6904	2317	1850	1663	7037	6859	2369	1855	1648
Increase	939	1230	53	44	104	...	157	134	362	99	25	2	302	166	321	183	5	...	45	218	57	...	...
Decrease	...	...	...	...	...	234	...	...	...	...	...	...	...	...	...	...	...	36	...	...	...	9	47

TABLE III. PART ONE.—Continued.

COUNTIES.	Form, Color and Industrial Drawing. 41 — Grade. I	II	III	IV	V	VI	VII	VIII
Albert	446	344	306	373	292	95	56	83
Carleton	800	550	706	690	654	179	97	187
Charlotte	639	521	654	671	679	213	132	150
Gloucester	1592	882	657	590	271	99	62	71
Kent	1468	680	588	460	233	87	63	62
Kings	814	600	742	741	620	148	88	61
Madawaska	775	417	316	218	66	22	24	27
Northumberland	1296	821	974	744	548	246	168	14
Queens	465	371	419	437	839	46	22	11
Restigouche	468	310	307	274	167	74	54	34
Saint John	1781	1249	13 3	1220	1116	709	5 9	394
Sunbury	264	144	170	157	116	14	17	7
Victoria	365	207	267	194	160	24	28	17
Westmorland	2089	1162	1279	1185	999	348	324	271
York	1350	793	924	954	867	214	150	167
New Brunswick	14571	9051	9672	8908	7124	2468	1863	1633
Cor. Term, 1900	14438	9277	9573	8757	6858	2805	1838	1625
Increase	133	....	99	151	266	78	25	8
Decrease	....	226	....	....	....	....	....	....

COUNTIES.	Print-Script and Writing. 42 — Grade. I	II	III	IV	V	VI	VII	VIII
Albert	459	341	316	366	298	96	56	83
Carleton	829	562	713	711	684	182	104	142
Charlotte	655	554	664	678	481	218	132	150
Gloucester	15 5	864	657	500	271	99	62	71
Kent	1545	718	621	458	249	87	63	66
Kings	816	508	750	750	641	147	88	61
Madawaska	864	440	832	216	65	22	24	27
Northumberland	1307	825	987	750	552	246	168	141
Queens	474	374	429	434	357	47	24	11
Restigouche	463	315	302	279	217	96	54	84
Saint John	1791	1249	1363	1220	1116	709	569	394
Sunbury	265	144	170	160	117	14	17	7
Victoria	416	243	282	212	171	24	28	17
Westmorland	2183	1193	1317	1193	1096	353	328	275
York	1872	803	932	977	886	219	161	172
New Brunswick	14974	9228	9825	9001	7336	2504	1877	1651
Cor. Term, 1900	14862	9461	9543	8856	6960	2415	1857	1662
Increase	112	....	282	145	376	89	20	....
Decrease	....	233	....	....	....	....	....	11

COUNTIES.	Singing ["Theory" Optional] 43 — Grade. By Rote. I	By Rote. II	By Rote. III	IV Rote.	IV Note.	V Rote.	V Note.	VI Rote.	VI Note.	VII Rote.	VII Note.	VIII Rote.	VIII Note.
Albert	224	175	192	180	....	104	....	39	....	16	....	13	....
Carleton	306	240	294	293	....	300	....	113	....	32	....	36	....
Charlotte	392	384	373	366	....	428	....	168	....	50	....	34	....
Gloucester	1063	714	491	354	23	114	25	39	30	22	14	52	....
Kent	676	357	278	221	....	111	....	11	....	27	....	2	....
Kings	399	335	349	328	....	286	....	40	....	32	....	9	....
Madawaska	507	280	172	117	2	23	....	12	....	15	....	6	....
Northumberland	799	493	682	480	....	329	....	114	....	36	....	16	....
Queens	121	98	124	120	....	91	....	10	....	....	....	2	....
Restigouche	267	198	171	164	7	119	2	58	41	41	....	22	....
Saint John	1640	1141	1252	1112	....	1021	....	692	....	529	....	342	....
Sunbury	94	67	80	70	....	58	....	....	....	3	....	....	....
Victoria	135	93	98	101	3	83	8	19	....	9	....	....	....
Westmorland	1180	706	811	611	....	440	15	257	....	229	....	97	....
York	770	488	507	538	....	490	....	177	....	56	....	76	....
New Brunswick	8573	5749	5874	5055	35	3996	45	1744	71	1097	14	726	....
Cor. Term, 1900	8577	5849	5715	5037	53	3758	64	1814	18	1121	18	761	23
Increase	....	....	159	18	....	238	....	....	53	....	....	....	....
Decrease	4	100	....	....	18	....	19	70	....	24	4	35	23

TABLE III. Part One—Continued.

COUNTIES.	NUMBER—ARITHMETIC. 44								ALGEBRA. 46		GEOGRAPHY. 47					
	GRADE.								GRADE.		GRADE.					
	I	II	III	IV	V	VI	VII	VIII	VII	VIII	III	IV	V	VI	VII	VIII
Albert	459	343	315	370	288	96	56	84	47	65	319	366	293	96	56	84
Carleton	828	560	720	716	668	182	104	142	99	143	716	695	675	172	97	137
Charlotte	658	558	645	656	685	216	132	150	221	132	659	675	685	216	132	150
Gloucester	1594	882	657	590	271	99	62	71	40	44	669	582	268	99	62	71
Kent	1531	721	628	461	248	37	63	62	17	62	611	447	245	37	63	66
Kings	802	602	767	765	627	144	89	52	139	81	771	761	637	149	94	52
Madawaska	879	436	334	211	71	22	24	27	15	19	344	226	67	22	24	27
Northumberland	1302	820	985	750	552	246	168	141	106	134	987	750	553	241	168	141
Queens	472	381	425	434	349	52	23	11	84	15	429	421	354	47	22	11
Restigouche	473	315	302	275	217	96	54	34	49	43	296	274	217	96	54	34
St. John	1791	1249	1363	1220	1116	709	569	394	132	342	1373	1220	1116	709	569	394
Sunbury	264	144	170	163	115	14	17	7	43	7	176	157	119	14	17	7
Victoria	388	231	272	212	169	24	28	17	12	17	275	211	164	24	28	17
Westmorland	2179	1186	1328	1176	1035	356	328	275	110	267	1341	1231	1030	338	328	275
York	1366	810	933	981	874	219	162	179	108	163	922	966	874	218	161	179
New Brunswick	14,986	9238	9844	8980	7285	2512	1879	1646	1222	1534	9888	8982	7297	2478	1875	1645
Cor. Term, 1900	14,913	9487	9628	8877	6958	2398	1859	1639	1511	1656	9684	8785	6957	2426	1846	1644
Increase	73		216	103	327	114	20	7			204	197	340	52	29	1
Decrease		249							289	122						

TABLE III. PART ONE.—Continued.

COUNTIES.	HYGIENE AND TEMPERANCE (Health Readers). 48								NATURE LESSONS AND AGRICULTURE. MINERALS—PLANT LIFE—ANIMAL LIFE. 49								LATIN. (Optional.) 50		FRENCH. (Optional.) 51
	GRADE.								GRADE.								GRADE		GRADES.
	I	II	III	IV	V	VI	VII	VIII	I	II	III	IV	V	VI	VII	VIII	VII	VIII	I to VIII
Albert	414	325	306	364	298	96	56	84	389	313	297	348	283	90	46	78		13	3
Carleton	570	497	649	696	675	178	100	144	589	465	628	655	683	166	78	102	77	96	
Charlotte	587	499	648	677	685	216	132	150	590	58	566	674	668	198	115	150	8	79	
Gloucester	1402	805	638	591	270	99	62	44	1377	793	621	583	269	99	62	71	1	6	1487
Kent	1324	639	577	434	238	37	63	66	1334	652	590	436	236	37	62	66	14	25	1130
Kings	760	575	747	714	638	142	81	49	750	552	704	714	623	140	78	61	31	31	21
Madawaska	709	399	303	186	63	22	24	24	660	345	282	174	54	22	24	27		4	1665
Northumberland	1202	769	976	747	553	246	168	141	1225	775	955	746	532	209	160	139	13	76	256
Queens	385	328	371	432	337	46	20	11	390	347	373	420	321	43	22	11	6	5	
Restigouche	400	293	300	274	217	96	54	29	377	269	281	253	206	96	54	34	32	22	140
Saint John	1763	1239	1367	1220	1116	709	569	394	1683	1235	1321	[illegible]	1113	709	569	394	414	322	
Sunbury	218	133	160	163	115	14	17	7	214	135	151	156	111	12	17	7			
Victoria	330	200	262	206	166	24	28	17	294	197	246	183	150	15	19	17	6		
Westmorland	1747	1038	1316	1132	1000	332	327	274	1809	1043	1204	1123	960	314	325	275	142	156	483
York	1053	685	888	948	937	218	161	172	1216	721	837	907	824	167	161	172	111	84	
New Brunswick	12864	8424	9506	8834	7308	2475	1862	1606	12897	8360	9056	8573	7033	2317	1792	1604	855	919	5185
Cor. Term, 1900	12592	8563	9268	8649	6945	2429	1809	1585	12516	8337	8961	8431	6634	2302	1726	1550	852	882	3897
Increase	272		238	185	363	46	53	21	381	23	95	142	399	15	66	54	3	37	1288
Decrease		139																	

TABLE III.—Superior, Grammar and other Schools Having Pupils in Advance of Grade VIII.

PART I.—Continued.

COUNTIES.	Language. 52 — English. IX	X	XI	XII	Latin. IX	X	XI	XII	Greek. IX	X	XI	XII	French. IX	X	XI	XII
Albert	71	40	5	...	21	20	7	..			4	..	..	..	.	...
Carleton	64	31	13	..	40	20	13	..	4	1	.	..	21	10	10	...
Charlotte	118	38	29	...	81	30	22	..	15	2	6	..	61	32	22	...
Gloucester	31	7	...	...	8	5	...	...	.		.	...	17	..	.	..
Kent	39	8	2	...	27	2	2	..				...	...	..	.	..
Kings	61	32	6	...	32	20	4	..	6	16	2	..	1	9	1	...
Madawaska	...	...	.	...	...	...	.	..	..	..		..	.	...	.	..
North'd	73	25	12	3	55	24	11	3	3	...	1	...	32	24	7	3
Queens	17	9	..	...	12	8	...	..		1		..	..	..	..	...
Restigouche	31	15	5	...	29	13	5	..	14	7	5	..	10	4	.	.
St. John	266	154	104	10	252	153	104	10	50	24	31	6	248	142	91	7
Sunbury	8		...	...	4	...	...	..	..	..	..	...	...	..	..	..
Victoria	20	10	3	...	8	8	3	..	..	...	...	..	9	..	..	..
West'd	173	96	30	...	116	73	22	..	2	7	..	..	87	54	23	...
York	88	51	36	...	59	47	30	..	..	10	12	..	..	35	16	..
N. B.	1060	516	245	13	744	424	223	13	94	68	61	6	486	310	170	10
Cor. t'm, 1900	932	469	233	18	662	391	199	18	64	83	65	5	439	267	150	18
Increase	128	47	12	...	82	33	24	..	30	..	..	1	47	48	20	..
Decrease	...	..	...	5	..	...	...	5	..	15	4	..	..	...	..	8

COUNTIES.	Mathematics. 53 — Arithmetic. IX	X	Geometry. IX	X	XI	XII	Algebra. IX	X	XI	Book-Keeping. IX	X	Trigonometry. XI	XII
Albert	71	40	58	37	7	...	67	37	5	26	25	10	.
Carleton	69	31	61	31	13	...	69	31	13	5	13	13	..
Charlotte	118	28	114	38	29	...	111	38	29	75	5	10	...
Gloucester	30	..	26	6	.	...	23	..	..	6	2	..	..
Kent	37	14	40	14	2		37	14	2	43	8	..	...
Kings	50	32	62	32	6	...	52	32	6	27	3	..	...
Madawaska	..	..	..		..	...	...		..		..	..	...
North'd	78	25	71	25	12	3	78	25	12	28	..	1	..
Queens	21	9	29	12	..	...	17	9	.	15	8	..	..
Restigouche	31	15	31	15	5	...	31	15	5	31	..	..	..
St. John	265	154	266	15[illegible]	104	10	266	151	104	65	154	18	10
Sunbury	8	..	8	..	..	...	8			8	..	.	..
Victoria	20	10	..	.	...	...	19	10	8	18	8	1	...
West'd	177	92	175	90	30	...	16[illegible]	89	29	113	70	1	..
York	88	51	7	5	35		88	51	36	29	14	..	...
N. B.	1067	511	948	504	243	13	1030	505	244	684	310	54	10
Cor. t'm, 1900	942	409	888	483	232	18	875	490	230	596	307	55	18
Increase	125	102	60	21	11	...	155	15	14	88	8	..	..
Decrease	...	...	...	...	..	5	...	..		..	..	1	8

COUNTIES.	History and Geography. 54 — IX	X	XI	XII	Drawing. 55 — IX	Natural science. 56 — Physics. IX	Physiology & Hygiene. X	XI	Chemistry. X	XI	Botany. IX	X	XI	Geology. XII	German. 57 — XII
Albert	71	40	5	..	68	23	35	8	38	3	34	28	5	13	...
Carleton	69	31	13	..	77	50	27	13	18	14	31	31	13	...	...
Charlotte	118	38	20	..	78	50	9	9	24	22	97	29	25	...	...
Gloucester	30	7	...	..	85	1		..	..	..	22	3		...	...
Kent	45	8	2	..	39	29	15	2	8		33	12	2	...	...
Kings	59	32	6	..	50	11	25	11	15	6	47	29	6	..	..
Madawaska	.	.	..	..	...	...		..	..	..			..	...	...
North'd	7	25	11	8	79	40	10	..	..	..	67	25	11	...	...
Queens	17	9	..	..	17	21	13	..	12	..	21	9	..	...	...
Restigouche	31	15	5	..	81	23	15	5	18	5	31	15	5	...	.
St. John	266	158	104	10	264	281	148	18	21	104	234	153	91	8	8
Sunbury	8		..	...	8	8	..	..	..	..	..	..	..	...	...
Victoria	24	10	3	..	20	9	14	3	10	3	20	10	3	...	...
West'd	179	89	30	..	154	176	90	26	73	29	143	76	30	...	..
York	88	51	36	..	88	...	57		...	34	88	51	34	...	...
N. B.	1084	508	244	13	1003	672	453	93	232	219	868	471	225	16	3
Cor. t'm, 1900	932	446	220	18	792	552	428	141	274	111	631	443	175	...	1
Increase	152	62	24	..	211	120	25			108	237	28	50	16	2
Decrease	...	..	..	5	...	..	..	48	42	..	...	..	..	...	...

TABLE III. PART TWO.—The Second Term Closed June 30th, 1902.

NUMBER OF PUPILS IN THE DIFFERENT BRANCHES OF INSTRUCTION.

COUNTIES.	Physical Exercises. 35	Oral Lessons on Morals, &c. 36	Optional. 37		Reading—Spelling—Recitation, Etc. 38								Grammar and Analysis and Composition. 39						History. 40				
			Sewing.	Knitting.	Grade I	II	III	IV	V	VI	VII	VIII	Grade *III	*IV	V	VI	VII	VIII	Grade *IV	V	VI	VII	VIII
Albert	1727	1923	..	..	409	308	320	353	322	102	57	101	316	349	332	102	56	100	261	326	102	56	100
Carleton	3900	4295	..	..	819	589	730	855	872	252	111	146	668	850	858	232	111	145	702	831	234	103	143
Charlotte	3552	4078	..	..	735	588	649	840	887	226	140	165	625	824	884	226	140	165	639	873	224	140	165
Gloucester	3771	4093	12	..	1332	920	799	657	324	108	53	65	775	658	332	108	53	65	506	320	108	53	65
Kent	3149	3735	26	18	1506	742	655	546	294	57	62	57	644	523	288	57	62	50	469	289	57	62	59
Kings	3248	3978	25	..	768	606	785	875	833	106	90	65	763	855	827	106	90	55	764	827	106	90	55
Madawaska	1740	2066	4	2	805	465	435	324	119	24	27	26	396	287	120	24	27	26	268	107	24	27	26
Northumberl'd.	4889	5074	..	16	1322	831	968	847	621	226	185	152	943	819	616	226	185	152	529	616	226	185	152
Queens	1849	2216	..	..	459	360	422	490	460	35	27	6	406	500	451	35	27	6	428	460	32	27	6
Restigouche	1183	1307	..	..	417	256	332	275	231	66	50	55	256	271	291	63	50	55	217	229	63	50	55
Saint John	8008	8201	89	..	1628	1259	1354	1211	1068	681	563	372	1351	1211	1068	681	563	372	1141	1068	681	563	370
Sunbury	766	931	..	..	236	158	180	194	181	21	12	7	172	193	180	21	12	7	192	178	21	12	7
Victoria	1150	1450	2	3	474	252	333	287	217	26	30	14	320	283	216	26	31	20	262	216	26	31	22
Westmorland	6319	7382	10	24	2022	1166	1365	1220	1100	368	338	276	1238	1202	987	357	344	266	820	1057	349	346	268
York	4813	5412	5	5	1183	789	879	1080	985	229	175	183	868	1058	946	234	175	182	794	937	233	175	181
N. Brunswick	50073	56240	173	68	14113	9349	10212	10054	8524	2507	1920	1690	9741	9883	8306	2498	1926	1675	8082	8334	2486	1920	1674
Cor. Term, 1901	50166	55661	193	113	14936	9321	10049	9795	8494	2521	1894	1721	9471	9493	8311	2511	1877	1692	7854	8232	2497	1881	1714
Increase	....	579	...	...	....	28	163	259	30	....	26	....	270	390	85	....	49	....	228	102	....	39	....
Decrease	93	....	20	45	823	....	....	....	....	14	....	31	....	....	....	13	....	17	....	....	11	....	40

TABLE III. PART TWO.—Continued.

COUNTIES.	Form, Color and Industrial Drawing. 41 — Grade I	II	III	IV	V	VI	VII	VIII
Albert	390	289	308	353	332	102	56	100
Carleton	802	586	722	836	854	232	110	143
Charlotte	695	551	644	830	860	214	140	165
Gloucester	1308	920	798	658	334	108	53	65
Kent	1475	723	650	539	284	57	61	57
Kings	757	656	769	845	821	106	90	65
Madawaska	766	399	407	281	104	23	27	26
Northumberl'd	1261	802	953	821	618	226	185	152
Queens	437	350	417	470	451	26	27	6
Restigouche	304	252	325	272	231	66	50	55
Saint John	1626	1259	1354	1214	1065	681	563	372
Sunbury	243	170	180	191	177	21	12	7
Victoria	430	219	322	274	211	26	31	22
Westmorland	1853	1177	1363	1194	1036	364	330	270
York	1159	788	878	1080	940	230	170	167
N. Brunswick	13596	9141	10090	9858	8318	2482	1905	1672
Cor. Term, 1901	14378	9204	9938	9576	8242	2493	1862	1692
Increase	....	....	152	282	76	....	43	....
Decrease	782	63	....	....	....	11	....	20

COUNTIES.	Print-Script and Writing. 42 — Grade I	II	III	IV	V	VI	VII	VIII
Albert	409	308	320	352	328	106	56	101
Carleton	823	590	725	801	873	232	111	144
Charlotte	735	[illegible]	649	840	884	226	140	165
Gloucester	1332	920	798	658	334	108	53	65
Kent	1490	745	652	550	294	57	62	59
Kings	767	664	786	856	827	106	90	65
Madawaska	816	442	433	312	120	24	27	26
Northumberl'd	1317	830	966	855	619	226	177	150
Queens	457	362	419	496	458	26	27	6
Restigouche	407	256	333	264	231	66	50	52
Saint John	1628	1259	1354	1211	1068	681	503	372
Sunbury	233	163	182	189	179	21	12	7
Victoria	431	222	333	346	214	23	21	22
Westmorland	2006	1162	1364	1238	1068	353	328	264
York	1175	790	976	989	1010	238	177	185
N. Brunswick	14035	9301	10290	10017	8507	2493	1894	1683
Cor. Term, 1901	14825	9381	10047	9744	8440	2514	1880	1721
Increase	....	....	243	273	67	....	14	....
Decrease	790	80	....	....	....	21	....	38

COUNTIES.	Singing ("Theory" Optional.) 43 — By Rote. I	II	III	IV Rote.	IV Note.	V Rote.	V Note.	VI Rote.	VI Note.	VII Rote.	VII Note.	VIII Rote.	VIII Note.
Albert	222	166	105	184	...	128	..	47	..	19	..	17	..
Carleton	352	280	307	365	...	415	..	103	..	38	..	53	..
Charlotte	387	356	360	371	...	420	..	161	..	66	..	64	..
Gloucester	854	629	554	390	10	187	..	78	..	31	..	20	..
Kent	697	316	321	200	4	144	2	8	5	20	..	23	..
Kings	410	357	401	407	...	384	..	43	..	43	..	19	..
Madawaska	483	243	274	130	38	50	37	13	7	18	5	6	3
Northumberl'd	800	592	604	557	...	438	..	167	..	38	..	66	..
Queens	210	124	198	219	...	170	..	5	..	5	..	....	..
Restigouche	263	187	170	117	50	124	..	64	..	43	..	33	..
Saint John	1325	1175	1248	1130	...	975	..	673	..	549	..	348	..
Sunbury	106	65	89	66	4	65	6	9	..	....	..	....	..
Victoria	161	104	137	121	6	100	10	10	..	....	..	....	..
Westmorland	1168	715	826	588	13	488	30	238	10	226	24	80	..
York	682	501	533	572	2	531	2	160	..	59	..	59	..
N. Brunswick	8210	5810	6277	5486	127	4628	87	1839	22	1153	29	792	3
Cor. Term, 1901	8537	5826	5923	5308	100	4273	88	1740	54	1214	26	922	29
Increase	....	....	354	88	27	353	..	99	..	....	3	....	..
Decrease	327	16	....	....	....	....	1	....	32	61	..	130	26

TABLE III. PART TWO.—Continued.

COUNTIES.	Number—Arithmetic. 44								Algebra. 46		Geography. 47					
	Grade.								Grade.		Grade.					
	I	II	III	IV	V	VI	VII	VIII	VII	VIII	III	IV	V	VI	VII	VIII
Albert	409	308	320	354	332	102	57	101	50	81	322	350	334	102	56	100
Carleton	813	592	735	851	883	232	111	146	195	160	744	844	868	232	111	143
Charlotte	735	587	649	842	886	226	140	165	248	152	665	833	872	226	140	165
Gloucester	1332	920	798	658	334	108	52	65	59	72	790	657	329	105	52	65
Kent	1504	742	655	547	293	57	62	57	61	52	670	533	291	57	62	57
Kings	767	662	795	870	831	96	80	65	172	89	778	872	834	96	80	65
Madawaska	832	445	439	308	120	24	27	26	16	13	442	293	115	24	27	26
Northumberland	1311	831	968	844	621	226	185	152	163	137	950	842	616	226	185	152
Queens	449	362	420	493	461	36	27	6	99	29	437	494	437	31	27	6
Restigouche	411	256	325	276	221	66	50	55	60	52	337	265	230	63	50	55
Saint John	1428	1259	1354	1210	1068	681	563	372	59	55	1362	1212	1068	681	563	372
Sunbury	229	164	193	192	173	21	12	7	55	13	187	193	181	21	12	7
Victoria	447	245	331	283	217	26	31	22	44	25	330	282	217	26	31	22
Westmorland	2010	1197	1403	1230	1037	361	348	226	365	272	1393	1228	1028	379	325	277
York	1182	791	969	1094	997	242	178	186	268	189	960	1097	991	239	181	186
New Brunswick	13859	9361	10354	10052	8474	2504	1923	1651	1914	1391	10367	9995	8411	2508	1902	1698
Cor. Term, 1901	14790	9386	10083	9760	8393	2506	1844	1670	2444	1685	10140	9699	8349	2496	1879	1725
Increase			271	292	81		79				227	296	62	12	23	
Decrease	931	25				2		19	530	294						27

TABLE III. PART TWO.—Continued.

COUNTIES.	Hygiene and Temperance (Health Readers.) 48 — Grade.								Nature Lessons and Agriculture. Minerals—Plant Life—Animal Life. 49 — Grade.								Latin. (Optional) 50 — Grade		French. (Optional). 51 — Grades
	I	II	III	IV	V	VI	VII	VIII	I	II	III	IV	V	VI	VII	VIII	VII	VIII	I to VIII
Albert	358	283	314	346	336	102	56	100	382	289	301	351	323	101	56	100	8	21	4
Carleton	616	518	672	841	855	227	103	143	680	517	653	817	851	238	111	144	69	103	
Charlotte	606	496	635	845	883	226	140	165	627	510	625	830	874	225	140	165	17	73	
Gloucester	1143	882	798	658	334	108	52	65	1119	814	748	643	334	108	52	65	15	6	2,227
Kent	1324	673	626	518	293	57	62	59	1361	688	626	524	292	57	59	57	26	25	1,340
Kings	656	599	770	867	829	96	80	65	693	633	765	740	819	96	80	65	47	35	
Madawaska	716	375	382	284	114	24	27	26	662	358	372	261	110	24	27	26		4	1 652
Northumberland	1165	779	955	836	611	126	185	152	1197	772	926	830	616	226	185	152	72	78	358
Queens	366	328	409	471	450	29	27	6	373	319	407	456	447	29	27	6	9	4	
Restigouche	332	207	319	261	231	66	50	55	341	222	320	262	176	66	50	54	34	23	109
Saint John	1390	1250	1348	1211	1068	681	563	372	1398	1255	1354	1205	1068	681	563	372	457	324	
Sunbury	184	145	154	180	187	24	12	7	203	147	173	188	178	21	12	7	1		
Victoria	370	208	322	283	217	26	31	22	340	214	283	263	199	26	31	22	4	4	45
Westmorland	1617	1018	1349	1155	1030	363	336	283	1667	1044	1292	1090	862	336	309	275	160	151	483
York	995	677	949	1091	961	235	178	172	1006	701	911	1051	953	224	191	193	27	31	
New Brunswick	11838	8438	10002	9847	8399	2390	1902	1692	12049	8513	9756	9511	8102	2458	1893	1703	946	882	6,218
Cor. Term, 1901	12527	8491	9701	9585	8178	2491	1891	1681	12611	8410	9406	9425	7965	2483	1864	1683	772	780	2,224
Increase	....	....	301	262	221	....	11	11	....	103	350	86	137	....	29	20	174	102	3,994
Decrease	689	53	....	....	....	101	....	....	562	....	....	....	....	25	....	....	....	....	....

I.—Superior, Grammar and Other Schools Having Pupils in Advance of Grade VIII.

Part Two.—Continued.

COUNTIES.	Language. 52. English IX	X	XI	XII	Latin. IX	X	XI	XII	Greek. IX	X	XI	XII	French. IX	X	XI	XII
Albert......	48	40	7	....	38	18	5	....	....	..	2	....	3	...	...	....
Carleton....	71	40	12	...	43	16	12	....	4	1	..	...	34	10	11	....
Charlotte..	126	39	32	....	76	36	24	...	17	3	5	....	54	32	25	....
Gloucester..	25	4	..	..	4	2	...	....	....	...	....	....	9	2	..	....
Kent.......	34	15	..	....	26	8	..	....	....	..	...	....	.	...	...	....
Kings......	59	36	5	....	32	26	3	....	....	12	1	....	20	8	1	....
Madawaska	..		..	....	....	.	...	....	....	..	...	....	.	..	..	..
North'd......	72	28	13	2	58	24	11	2	3	..	1	....	43	15	7	2
Queens.....	13	7	1	...	7	6	1	....	....	.	1	....	...	...	...	....
Restigouche	34	12	5	....	29	12	6	....	12	8	6	...	10	4		.
Saint John..	234	141	98	9	213	140	97	9	17	26	29	6	221	131	86	6
Sunbury....	..	...	...	..	5	..	....	....	..	...	....	....	.	..	...	....
Victoria.....	18	10	5	....	5	8	5	....	2	1	4	....	5	..	..	....
West'd......	176	82	27	....	99	69	19	....	2	7	...	....	100	47	22	....
York.......	86	51	34	....	25	29	30	...	9	10	11	....	32	23	14	....
N. B........	996	505	239	11	660	389	213	11	66	68	60	6	536	272	166	8
Cor. t'm 1901	888	454	246	18	585	338	206	18	67	73	61	5	483	239	147	13
Increase....	108	51	..	....	75	51	7	....	...	..	...	1	53	33	19	....
Decrease...	....	...	7	7	....	.	..	7	1	5	1	....	...	...	...	5

COUNTIES.	Mathematics. 53. Arithmetic IX	X	Geometry IX	X	XI	XII	Algebra IX	X	XI	Book-Keeping IX	X	Trigonometry XI	XII
Albert......	63	42	47	39	8	....	55	39	7	37	39	14	...
Carleton....	71	38	64	38	12	...	71	30	12	62	18	12	...
Charlotte..	127	38	127	39	32	....	127	39	32	104	15	11	...
Gloucester..	25	4	25	4		....	25	4	..	18	2	..	....
Kent.......	28	21	28	21	..	....	28	21	..	31	13	...	.
Kings......	59	36	56	48	5	....	50	36	5	30	17	3	35
Madawaska	....	..	....			..	...	.	.	..	...	..	...
North'd......	73	28	72	28	13	2	73	28	13	67	..	.	2
Queens.....	13	7	13	7	1	....	11	7	1	6	1	...	...
Restigouche	34	12	34	12	6	....	34	12	6	34	..		....
Saint John..	234	141	234	141	98	9	234	141	98	234	141	17	9
Sunbury....	9	..	6	..	...	....	6	...	..	9	...	..	...
Victoria.....	18	10	18	8	7	...	6	3	..	..	..	..	...
West'd......	184	82	193	79	27	.....	188	81	27	181	66	...	..
York.......	91	49	56	1	34	....	58	2	34	14	..	..	...
N. B........	1028	508	975	465	243	11	963	443	235	830	312	60	46
Cor. t'm 1901	927	485	86[illegible]	409	237	18	905	467	237	624	333	89	1[illegible]
Increase....	101	23	114	..	6	...	58	...	...	206	..	...	28
Decrease...	....		...	4	...	7	....	24	2	..	21	29	....

COUNTIES.	History and Geography 54. IX	X	XI	XII	Drawing 55. IX	Natural Science 56. Physics IX	Physiology & Hygiene X	XI	Chemistry X	XI	Botany IX	X	XI	Geology XII	German 57. XII
Albert......	58	40	7	...	54	37	42	5	50	7	57	40	7	...	......
Carleton....	71	40	13	....	71	50	30	12	49	12	70	40	12	.....	.....
Charlotte..	124	39	82	.....	82	73	45	10	42	82	103	30	18	....	....
Gloucester..	25	4	...	....	23	20	2	.	4	..	21	4	...	.....	....
Kent.......	28	21	...	....	12	21	18	..	9	..	31	15	..	.....	....
Kings......	39	11	...	.....	50	46	17	..	28	17	50	30	5	.....	...
Madawaska		..		..	.....	..	...	..	...		..	..	..	.....	....
North'd......	73	18	12	2	86	86	42	12	26	34	65	20	12	....	....
Queens.....	13	7	1	......	13	13	6	1	1	1	9	7	1	....	.....
Restigouche	34	12	6	....	84	34	12	6	12	6	34	12	6	....	.....
Saint John..	234	141	98	9	234	240	146	21	9	81	233	141	86	3	3
Sunbury....	9		.	....	9	9	...	..		.		..	..	.....	...
Victoria.....	18	10	5	.....	8	3	10	5	10	5	18	10	5	.....	...
West'd......	176	82	27	.....	108	161	31	27	92	27	173	47	22	.....	......
York.......	90	49	34	......	90	86	12	34	78	31	37	44	24	.....	.....
N. B........	992	484	234	11	806	879	416	136	410	256	901	446	198	3	3
Cor. t'm 1901	893	434	221	18	778	766	407	159	376	242	781	410	190	......	1
Increase....	99	50	13	....	88	113	..	..	34	14	120	3[illegible]	8	3	2
Decrease...	...	..	..	7	...	...	9	23	..	.	...	..	.	......	......

TABLE IV. PUBLIC SCHOOLS: Teachers Employed During the year Ended 30th June 1902

Part One.—The First Term closed 31st December, 1901.

COUNTIES.	Grammar School Teachers.		MALES.			FEMALES.			TOTAL.			Trained.	Untrained.	No. of Assistants.		Total Number of Teachers Employed this Term.
			Class.			Class.										
	M.	F.	I	II	III	I	II	III	Male	Female.	Both.			Male.	Female.	
Albert	1		9	6		9	40	7	16	56	72	72				72
Carleton	1	1	12	13	2	20	87	19	28	127	155	154	1			155
Charlotte	1		14	7	1	31	70	10	23	111	134	131	3		3	137
Gloucester	1		3	3	34	2	23	43	41	68	109	107	2		2	111
Kent	1		4	3	18	7	28	59	26	94	120	120			1	121
Kings	1		16	15	2	23	87	15	34	125	159	158	1		1	160
Madawaska			2		8		1	46	10	47	57	47	10			57
Northumberland	1		12	5	6	12	93	27	24	132	156	150	6		2	158
Queens	1		4	20	3	7	48	19	28	74	102	102				102
Restigouche	1		2	1	1	6	29	10	5	45	50	50			1	51
Saint John	3	2	20	7	1	100	85	5	31	192	223	222	1		6	229
Sunbury			1	4		5	20	9	5	34	39	38	1			39
Victoria	1		2	7	3	6	20	20	13	46	59	54	5			59
Westmorland	4		15	22	13	49	67	45	54	161	215	213	2		3	218
York	3		17	10	2	33	103	32	32	168	200	196	4		1	201
New Brunswick	20	3	133	123	94	310	801	366	370	1480	1850	1814	36		20	1870
Cor. Term, 1900	21	3	137	126	91	307	801	383	375	1494	1869	1851	18		24	1893
Increase					3	3							18			
Decrease	1		4	3				17	5	14	19	37			4	23

TABLE IV. PART TWO—SECOND TERM CLOSED 30TH JUNE, 1902.

COUNTIES.	Grammar School Teachers.		MALES.			FEMALES.			TOTAL.			Trained.	Untrained.	No. of Assistants.		Total number of Teachers employed this Term.
			CLASS.			CLASS.										
	M	F	I	II	III	I	II	III	Male.	Female.	Both.			Male.	Female.	
Albert	1	......	9	7	......	8	36	4	17	48	65	64	1	1	1	67
Carleton	1	1	11	13	1	24	85	17	26	127	153	151	2	....	....	153
Charlotte	1	......	15	5	1	31	67	18	22	116	138	133	5	1	5	144
Gloucester	1	......	3	4	34	2	22	41	42	65	107	106	1	....	2	109
Kent	1	......	5	3	14	6	24	62	23	92	115	113	2	....	1	116
Kings	1	......	14	14	1	22	88	16	30	126	156	156	....	....	1	157
Madawaska	......	......	2	......	7	......	1	50	9	51	60	47	13	....	....	60
Northumberland	1	......	10	4	6	9	93	29	21	131	152	146	6	....	2	154
Queens	1	......	2	14	5	6	46	18	22	70	92	91	1	....	....	92
Restigouche	1	......	2	1	1	6	29	7	5	42	47	45	2	....	1	48
Saint John	3	2	20	6	1	97	85	10	30	194	224	219	5	....	11	235
Sunbury	......	......	1	5	......	5	19	10	6	34	40	38	2	....	....	40
Victoria	1	......	3	3	2	6	22	22	9	50	59	54	5	....	....	59
Westmorland	3	......	15	24	12	43	68	39	54	150	204	202	2	....	2	208
York	3	......	15	8	4	31	93	30	30	154	184	179	5	....	1	185
New Brunswick	19	3	127	111	89	296	778	373	346	1450	1796	1744	52	2	27	1825
Cor. Term, 1901	20	3	124	122	85	305	789	363	351	1460	1811	1781	30	2	28	1841
Increase	......	......	3	......	4	......	......	10	....	....	....	....	22	....	....	....
Decrease	1	......	......	11	......	9	11	......	5	10	15	37	....	....	1	16

TABLE V. PUBLIC SCHOOLS. PERIOD OF SERVICE OF TEACHERS EMPLOYED DURING YEAR ENDED 30TH JUNE, 1902.

PART ONE.—THE FIRST TERM CLOSED 31ST DECEMBER, 1901.

COUNTIES	No of teachers employed in same District as during previous Term.	No of teachers removed to a new District.	No. of new teachers this Term.	No. of teachers whose period of service is not reported.	No of teachers not more than 3 years in the service employed this Term.	PERIOD OF SERVICE OF TEACHERS OF GR., SUP., AND 1ST. CLASS.													
						MALE TEACHERS GR., SUP., AND 1ST CLASS							FEMALE TEACHERS GR., SUP., AND 1ST CLASS						
						No. first Term employed.	No. second Term employed.	No. 1 to 2 years.	No. 2 to 3 years.	No. 3 to 5 years	No. 5 to 7 years.	No. upwards of 7 years.	No. first Term employed.	No. second Term employed.	No 1 to 2 years.	No. 2 to 3 years.	No. 3 to 5 years.	No. 5 to 7 years.	No upwards of 7 years.
Albert	34	30	7	1	31	1		2	1		3	3			2	1	2	2	2
Carleton	75	62	10	8	50	1			1	4	3	4			1	3	7	4	6
Charlotte	79	44	11		44				2	3	2	8			4	1	6	7	13
Gloucester	58	35	16		45	1				1		2					1		1
Kent	67	43	10		43					2		3	1					2	4
Kings	83	59	12	5	56			1	1	3	5	7			3	2	5	6	7
Madawaska	24	21	11	1	35					2									
Northumberland	106	30	13	7	50			1	1	3	1	[illegible]	1		1	1	1	3	5
Queens	44	48	9	1	41					2		3	1				1	2	3
Restigouche	31	8	9	2	18							3		1			1		4
St. John	178	17	5	23	27			1	1	3	1	17			6	6	12	16	62
Sunbury	19	13	6	1	19							1	1		1	1		1	1
Victoria	24	30	4	1	24						1	2			1	1		1	3
Westmorland	127	70	11	7	70	1		1		2	3	12	1		2	5	9	13	19
York	106	55	24	15	85			2	4	1	1	12	1	1			8	4	19
New Brunswick	1055	565	158	72	638	4		8	11	26	20	84	6	2	21	21	53	61	149
Gr. Term 1900	1138	494	171	66	705	6	3	11	16	28	17	77	9	7	22	23	60	50	139
Increase		71		6							3	7						11	10
Decrease	83		13		67	2	3	3	5	2			3	5	1	2	7		

TABLE V. PART TWO—THE SECOND TERM CLOSED 30TH JUNE, 1902.

COUNTIES.	No. of teachers employed in same District as during previous Term.	No. of teachers removed to a new District.	No. of new teachers this Term.	No. of teachers whose period of service is not reported.	No. of teachers not more than 3 years in the service employed this Term.	PERIOD OF SERVICE OF TEACHERS OF GRAM. SUP. AND 1ST CLASS. — MALE TEACHERS GRAM. SUP. AND 1ST CLASS — No. First Term employed.	No. Second Term employed.	No. 1 to 2 years.	No. 2 to 3 years.	No. 3 to 5 years.	No. 5 to 7 years.	No. upwards of 7 years	FEMALE TEACHERS, GRAM. SUP. AND 1ST CLASS — No. Frst Term employed.	No. second Term employed.	No. 1 to 2 years	No. 2 to 3 years.	No. 3 to 5 years.	No. 5 to 7 years.	No. upwards of 7 years.
Albert,	43	18	2	2	27	......	......	2	2	......	1	5	......	......	1	1	2	3	1
Carleton,	77	66	4	6	42	......	1	......	......	4	3	4	......	......	1	2	10	4	8
Charlotte,	76	50	9	3	43	......	......	......	2	4	2	8	......	......	3	1	5	10	12
Gloucester,	82	19	6	..	42	......	1	......	......	1	......	2	......	......	......	......	......	1	1
Kent,	81	28	5	1	36	......	......	......	1	......	2	3	......	1	......	......	......	1	4
Kings,	95	32	6	3	50	......	1	......	2	2	2	8	......	......	1	2	2	7	10
Madawaska,	40	8	11	1	83	......	......	......	......	2	......	......	......	......	......	......	......	......	......
Northumberland,	102	35	6	9	46	......	......	1	1	1	2	6	......	1	1	1	1	1	4
Queens,	47	33	8	1	27	......	......	......	......	1	......	2	......	1	......	......	1	2	2
Restigouche,	31	13	3	..	12	......	......	......	......	......	......	3	......	......	......	......	1	......	5
Saint John,	183	16	5	20	26	......	1	1	......	......	4	17	......	......	1	7	12	7	72
Sunbury,	24	14	2	..	18	......	......	......	......	......	......	1	......	......	......	1	2	1	1
Victoria,	23	26	5	..	21	......	......	......	......	1	......	3	......	......	1	1	......	1	3
Westmorland,	118	44	5	7	60	......	1	2	......	1	4	10	......	......	3	4	7	7	22
York,	105	54	13	12	70	......	......	2	3	3	3	7	2	......	2	......	8	4	15
New Brunswick,	1162	479	90	65	553	......	5	8	11	20	23	79	2	3	14	20	51	49	160
Cor. Term, 1901,	1121	550	62	78	616	......	5	11	15	20	14	79	2	8	27	21	49	49	152
Increase,	41	......	24	......	......	......	......	......	......	......	9	......	......	......	......	......	2	......	8
Decrease,	......	71	......	13	63	......	......	3	4	......	......	......	......	5	13	1	......	......	......

TABLE V.—Continued. PERIOD OF SERVICE OF SECOND-CLASS TEACHERS EMPLOYED DURING YEAR ENDED 30TH JUNE, 1902.

DURING THE TERM CLOSED 31ST DECEMBER, 1901.

COUNTIES.	Male Teachers, 2nd Class.							Female Teachers, 2nd Caass.						
	No. 1st Term employed.	No. 2nd Term employed.	No. from 1 to 2 years.	No. from 2 to 3 years.	No. from 3 to 5 years.	No. from 5 to 7 years.	No. 7 years and upwards.	No. 1st Term employed.	No. 2nd Term employed.	No. from 1 to 2 years.	No. from 2 to 3 years.	No. from 3 to 5 years.	No. from 5 to 7 years.	No. upwards of 7 years.
Albert	2	....	1	1	1	...	1	4	....	6	5	9	7	9
Carleton	....	....	2	1	4	2	4	5	1	9	10	25	16	21
Charlotte	4	....	1	....	1	1	....	4	1	9	11	12	13	20
Gloucester	1	....	....	1	....	1	....	4	1	2	....	2	4	10
Kent	1	....	1	....	1	....	....	2	....	4	5	4	4	9
Kings	3	....	1	2	2	3	4	8	....	13	12	13	15	23
Madawaska	....	....	....	....	....	....	....	....	....	....	....	1	....	....
Northumberland	....	....	2	....	....	....	3	4	4	7	7	17	18	36
Queens	....	1	4	1	3	4	7	7	....	9	5	10	8	9
Restigouche	1	....	....	....	....	....	....	6	....	2	3	7	1	10
St. John	....	1	1	....	....	1	4	4	1	2	2	10	12	54
Sunbury	....	....	1	1	1	....	1	2	....	4	4	2	2	6
Victoria	....	....	2	1	1	1	2	....	1	4	1	2	6	6
Westmorland	1	1	2	9	3	3	3	4	....	8	7	15	11	22
York	2	....	3	4	....	....	1	17	1	17	15	13	12	28
New Brunswick	15	3	21	21	17	16	30	71	10	96	87	142	129	266
Cor. yr., 1900-1901	20	5	28	16	17	11	29	79	21	98	91	141	124	247
Increase	....	....	....	5	....	5	1	....	....	....	....	1	5	19
Decrease	5	2	7	....	....	....	....	8	11	2	4	....	....	....

DURING THE TERM CLOSED 30TH JUNE, 1902.

COUNTIES.	Male Teachers, 2nd Class.							Female Teachers, 2nd Class.						
	No. 1st Term employed.	No. 2nd Term employed.	No. from 1 to 2 years.	No. from 2 to 3 years.	No. from 3 to 5 years.	No. from 5 to 7 years.	No. upwards of 7 years.	No. 1st Term employed.	No. 2nd Term employed.	No. from 1 to 2 years.	No. from 2 to 3 years.	No. from 3 to 5 years.	No. from 5 to 7 years.	No. upwards of 7 years.
Albert	....	3	1	....	....	1	2	....	2	3	8	5	8	10
Carleton	....	....	1	1	4	2	5	....	7	8	10	21	14	25
Charlotte	....	3	....	1	1	....	....	....	4	4	12	17	12	18
Gloucester	....	....	2	....	1	1	....	....	3	2	1	2	5	9
Kent	....	....	1	....	1	....	1	....	2	3	4	2	3	10
Kings	....	2	....	3	2	2	5	1	7	9	11	15	14	31
Madawaska	....	....	....	....	....	....	....	....	....	....	....	1	....	....
Northumberland	....	....	....	....	....	....	4	1	2	10	11	14	16	39
Queens	....	....	2	....	1	1	10	....	3	8	6	11	9	9
Restigouche	....	....	....	....	1	....	....	....	8	1	1	6	3	10
St. John	....	....	2	....	....	....	4	....	1	2	1	10	7	64
Sunbury	....	....	1	1	1	1	1	....	3	2	4	2	4	4
Victoria	....	....	....	....	....	1	2	....	1	4	3	4	3	7
Westmorland	1	2	2	5	5	4	5	1	5	5	9	13	10	25
York	....	....	3	3	2	....	....	....	15	13	12	13	14	26
New Brunswick	1	10	15	14	19	13	39	3	63	74	93	136	122	287
Cor. yr., 1900-1901	....	16	22	17	17	14	36	7	74	100	83	130	137	258
Increase	1	....	....	....	2	....	3	....	....	....	10	6	....	29
Decrease	....	6	7	3	....	1	....	4	11	26	....	....	15	....

3 VI.—PUBLIC SCHOOLS: TIME IN SESSION DURING THE YEAR ENDED 30TH JUNE, 1902.

COUNTIES.	The First Term Closed 31st Dec., 1901.							The Second Term Closed 30th June, 1902.							
	No. of Schools open this Term.	No. of Schools open less than 80 days.	No. in session 80 but less than 92 days.	Total in session less than 92 days.	No. in session the full Term of 92 days.*	Average days schools in session during the Term.	Aggregate number of days schools open during this Term.	No. of Schools open this term.	No. of Schools open less than 80 days.	No. in session 80 but less than 100 days.	No. in session less than 100 days.	No. in session 100 days but less than 122 days.	No. in session the full Term of 122 days.**	Average days schools in session during the Term.	Aggregate number of days Schools open during the Term.
Albert	72	9	16	25	47	87.	6,279	63	6	3	9	21	30	112.7	7,103½
Carleton	149	33	49	82	67	84.	12,596	147	12	6	18	63	66	112.	16,718½
Charlotte	134	51	34	85	49	82.	11,048	136	20	9	29	72	35	107.5	14,626½
Gloucester	109	6	33	39	70	89.6	9,773	107	4	4	8	77	22	116.8	12,498½
Kent	120	7	22	29	91	90.2	10,831	114	9	2	11	61	42	114.4	13,051
Kings	154	20	54	74	80	86.4	13,300½	152	11	6	17	67	68	113.3	17,235
Madawaska	57	5	21	26	31	88.7	5,061	50	4	2	6	47	6	115.	6,785
Northumberland	149	12	52	64	85	88.	13,192	143	16	5	21	76	46	112.3	16,073
Queens	100	23	42	65	35	83.8	8,387½	91	12	6	18	43	30	108.	9,834
Restigouche	48	5	9	14	34	87.5	4,201½	45	5	2	7	16	22	112.7	5,072
Saint John	208	5	36	41	167	90.	18,813	208	5	3	8	127	73	118.	24,402
Sunbury	39	11	13	24	15	84.	3,287	40	4	1	5	13	22	113.	4,520½
Victoria	59	14	22	36	23	83.8	4,945½	59	14	4	18	26	15	101.4	5,983½
Westmorland	208	10	61	71	137	89.6	18,650½	197	8	7	15	75	107	117.	23,049
York	189	17	77	94	95	88.8	16,789½	175	21	7	28	62	85	110.7	19,386
New Brunswick	1,795	228	541	769	1,026	87.5	157,164	1,736	151	67	218	819	699	113.	196,338
Cor. Terms 1901-02	1,812	187	687	874	938	89.7	162,659½	1,741	151	60	214	534	993	111.7	194,578½
Increase	......	41	......	......	88	......	....	......	......	7	4	315	......	......	1,759½
Decrease	17	......	146	105	......	2.2	5,495½	5	3	......	......	......	321	1.3	......

* In the First Term there were 82 teaching days in Cities, Towns and other Districts, having eight weeks vacation; in all other districts there were 92 teaching days. The actual number of days the schools in the former were open is raised to the basis of 92 days for the purposes of comparison.

** In the Second Term there were 121 teaching days in St. John City, and 122 days in all other districts. The former is raised to the basis of the latter for purposes of comparison.

TABLE VII.—PUBLIC SCHOOLS: VISITS—PUBLIC EXAMINATIONS—PRIZES: FOR THE YEAR ENDED 30TH JUNE, 1902.

COUNTIES.	THE FIRST TERM CLOSED 31ST DECEMBER, 1901.										THE SECOND TERM CLOSED 30TH JUNE, 1902.									
	VISITS.						EXAMINATIONS.		PRIZES.		VISITS.						EXAMINATIONS.		PRIZES.	
	No. by the Trustees and Secretary.	No. by the County Inspector.	No. by members of Parliament.	No. by Clergymen.	No. by Teachers.	No. by other visitors.	No. of Schools holding public examinations during the term.	No. of Schools not holding public examinations during the term.	No. of Prizes given to the pupils.	Value of the Prizes.	No. by the Trustees and Secretary.	No. by the County Inspector.	No. by members of Parliament.	No. by Clergymen.	No. by Teachers.	No. by other visitors.	No. of Schools holding public examinations during the term.	No. of Schools not holding public examinations during term.	No. of prizes given to the pupils.	Value of the prizes.
Albert	164	2	2	28	76	906	67	5	......	$......	129	59	......	32	43	767	59	4	5	$ 4 00
Carleton	247	99	......	20	103	1,105	124	25	39	18 24	312	143	1	58	90	1,296	125	22	42	30 05
Charlotte	303	70	4	50	82	1,104	109	25	13	4 25	318	109	9	44	114	1,358	111	25	17	7 45
Gloucester	370	35	......	52	124	1,327	87	22	4	1 90	387	99	......	52	188	1,733	97	10	20	33 00
Kent	427	54	3	51	98	1,474	111	9	25	15 04	474	90	......	79	94	1,738	103	11	22	6 20
Kings	256	19	......	40	125	1,426	136	18	43	23 20	273	136	1	49	103	1,648	125	27	59	32 06
Madawaska	217	55	8	48	49	762	55	2	43	8 32	215	27	12	37	57	807	59	......	8	4 20
Northumberland	391	53	4	97	110	1,531	136	13	10	5 45	374	122	3	128	131	2,150	132	11	94	67 85
Queens	191	38	......	24	68	947	72	28	1	1 00	225	69	11	33	69	1,176	75	16	......	......
Restigouche	109	44	2	29	32	496	44	4	1	1 00	107	5	......	16	34	479	42	3	......	......
Saint John	284	111	4	91	148	548	201	7	21	9 70	544	111	1	125	155	2,268	206	2	33	13 05
Sunbury	69	28	......	8	17	292	26	13	8	4 70	52	42	......	4	16	36	32	8	......	......
Victoria	120	43	1	11	18	316	46	13	23	6 37	158	43	2	18	20	473	44	15	17	4 00
Westmorland	554	96	8	104	186	2,350	196	12	25	7 55	651	180	4	104	120	2 801	174	23	83	117 78
York	256	94	1	69	151	1,908	143	46	45	26 23	302	127	7	70	138	1,506	132	43	17	21 25
New Brunswick	3958	841	37	725	1378	16,492	1,553	242	301	$132 95	4521	1362	51	849	1372	20,236	1516	220	417	$340 89
Cor. Terms 1901 02	3742	854	38	678	1325	15,708	1,571	241	299	119 66	4505	1168	48	868	1326	20,751	1503	238	485	335 81
Increase	216	......	......	47	53	784	......	1	2	$ 13 29	16	194	3	......	46	......	13	......	......	$ 5 08
Decrease	......	13	1	......	......	......	18	......	......	......	......	......	......	19	......	515	......	18	68	......

PUBLIC SCHOOLS: AVERAGE SALARIES OF TEACHERS FOR THE YEAR ENDED 30TH JUNE, 1902 FROM THE RATES PAID IN THE TERM ENDED JUNE 30TH, 1902.

COUNTIES.	COMMON SCHOOLS. Av'ge Rate per Year to Male Teachers			COMMON SCHOOLS. Av'ge rate per Year to Female Teachers			Average Superior Schools.	Average Grammar Schoo's.
	1st Class.	2nd Class.	3rd Class.	1st Class.	2nd Class.	3rd Class.		
Albert,	$408 33	$277 57	....	$257 00	$222 82	$154 19	$550 00	See Table XIII.
Carleton,	387 30	274 33	$231 00	264 70	213 49	191 86	500 00	
Charlotte,	452 90	323 40	233 00	316 23	246 06	183 14	660 00	
Gloucester,	....	293 50	221 53	243 50	221 86	183 64	583 33	
Kent,	359 50	258 00	212 82	267 80	221 66	175 58	512 50	
Kings,	377 33	255 35	204 00	266 14	207 82	171 32	530 00	
Madawaska,	255 00	...	227 71	....	201 00	170 53	500 00	
Northumberland,	470 00	328 25	211 92	256 33	232 83	180 64	623 00	
Queens,	275 00	255 57	216 85	254 54	208 21	176 96	500 00	
Restigouche	305 00	308 00	231 00	306 66	227 54	189 14	625 00	
Saint John,	839 41	479 66	251 25	365 30	315 64	173 88	566 66	
Sunbury,	....	270 00	....	246 00	211 30	167 12	500 00	
Victoria,	265 50	263 33	224 50	252 83	223 77	193 14	500 00	
Westmorland,	464 37	277 54	226 33	321 88	231 11	196 06	600 00	
York,	486 44	283 00	219 81	304 58	216 51	180 60	583 33	
New Brunswick,	$510 59	$286 39	$220 85	$315 25	$232 38	$180 51	$569 41	$954 54
Average Salaries, 1901,	520 10	276 48	221 41	312 69	226 78	179 34	576 07	928 26
Increase,	....	$9 91	....	$2 56	$5 60	$1 17	....	$26 28
Decrease,	$9 51	....	$0 56	....	....	....	$6 66	....

TABLE IX.—PUBLIC SCHOOLS: DISBURSEMENT OF THE PROVINCIAL GRANTS, FOR THE YEAR ENDED JUNE 30TH, 1902.

COUNTIES.	For First Term ended December 31st, 1901.					For Second Term ended June 30th, 1902.					For the Year.	
	Ordinary Grants. (1)	Superior Grants. (2)	Grammar Schools. (3)	Special to those teaching in poor Districts, [included in amt. in col'm 1]	Total.	Ordinary Grants. (1)	Superior Schools. (2)	Grammar Schools. (3)	Special to those teaching in poor Districts [included in amt. in Col'm 1]	Total.	Total special aid to those teaching in poor Districts.	Total.
Albert	$ 2,714 21	$300 60	$140 69	$255 55	$ 3,164 50	$3,031 05	$434 55	$209 31	$194 68	$3,674 91	$450 23	$ 6,839 41
Carleton	4,897 30	499 19	281 38	119 27	5,677 87	6,652 32	709 92	418 62	158 11	7,780 86	277 71	13,458 73
Charlotte	4,611 04	488 24	140 69	225 19	5,239 97	6,200 42	718 36	198 17	212 88	7,176 95	438 07	12,416 92
Gloucester	3,711 48	313 06	140 69	476 96	4,165 23	4,880 20	432 80	209 31	607 57	5,522 31	1,084 53	9,687 54
Kent	4,042 55	405 27	140 69	481 84	4,588 51	4,825 39	591 17	210 34	551 73	5,626 90	1,033 57	10,215 41
Kings	5,587 36	493 86	140 69	340 12	6,221 91	7,233 17	744 48	209 31	393 81	8,186 96	733 93	14,408 87
Madawaska	1,572 41	99 26	....	109 70	1,671 67	2,236 35	148 28	....	105 56	2,384 63	215 26	4,056 30
Northumberland	5,083 53	515 20	140 69	324 93	5,739 42	6,260 75	733 57	199 02	382 33	7,193 34	707 26	12,932 76
Queens	3,586 76	96 81	122 66	322 25	3,806 23	4,031 37	149 51	168 22	236 76	4,349 10	559 01	8,155 33
Restigouche	1,644 16	100 49	140 69	106 08	1,885 34	1,998 93	149 51	209 31	85 37	2,357 78	191 45	4,243 12
Saint John	7,788 47	300 86	536 70	96 99	8,626 03	11,064 86	446 81	796 81	109 24	12,308 48	206 23	20,934 51
Sunbury	1,357 83	103 98	....	119 70	1,461 81	1,868 72	137 85	....	179 29	2,006 57	298 99	3,468 38
Victoria	2,042 37	100 49	140 69	252 28	2,283 55	2,484 38	148 28	209 31	321 67	2,841 97	573 95	5,125 52
Westmorland	7,196 49	707 97	562 76	219 10	8,467 22	9,323 95	1,038 35	627 93	283 37	10,990 23	502 47	19,457 45
York	6,716 52	521 10	422 07	367 63	7,659 69	7,817 48	721 84	627 93	306 94	9,167 25	674 57	16,826 94
New Brunswick	$62,552 48	5,055 38	3,051 09	3,817 59	70,658 95	79,969 37	7,305 28	4,293 59	4,129 64	91,568 24	7,947 23	162,227 19
Cor. Terms 1900-1901	64,300 23	5,007 33	3,227 76	4,017 45	72,535 32	79,895 07	7,060 87	4,460 47	4,322 11	91,416 41	8,339 56	163,951 73
Increase	....	48 05	....	....	....	74 30	244 41	....	....	151 83	....	....
Decrease	$ 1,747 75	....	176 67	199 86	1,876 37	....	....	166 88	192 47	....	392 33	1,724 54

—PUBLIC SCHOOLS: APPORTIONMENT OF COUNTY FUND TO TRUSTEES FOR THE YEAR ENDED JUNE 30th, 1902.——PART ONE.—First Term ended December 31st 1901.

Drafts issued by the Chief Superintendent, payable by the respective County Treasurers.

COUNTIES.	Grand Total days' attendance of pupils; rectified for County Fund Apportionment (Term 92 days)	In respect of the services of qualified teachers, exclusive of assistants for the time the schools were in session. (1)	Special to poor districts (included in Column 1).	In respect of the average number of pupils in attendance, as compared with the whole average number of pupils attending the schools in the County and the time in operation. (2)	Special to poor districts (included in column 2)	Total to the Trustees this term. Whole amount apportioned this term. * (3)	Total to the Trustees this term. Total special to poor districts (included in column 3)	Rate per pupil in attendance the full term per column 2. 4 In ordinary districts.	Rate per pupil in attendance the full term per column 2. 4 In Poor districts
Albert	135,313	$1,147 38	$123 73	$ 277 33	$ 18 51	$1,424 71	$142 24	$0 19—	$0 25—
Carleton	222,515	2,100 19	52 80	1,099 17	17 71	3,199 36	70 51	0 45+	0 60+
Charlotte	261,963½	1,916 52	115 81	1,541 28	37 49	3,457 80	153 30	0 54+	0 72+
Gloucester	259,455½	1,830 58	237 01	1,873 49	189 70	3,704 07	426 71	0 66+	0 88+
Kent	240,361½	2,020 22	257 17	1,406 53	137 81	3,424 75	394 98	0 53+	0 70+
Kings	233,425½	2,355 69	172 98	916 66	41 71	3,272 35	214 69	0 36+	0 48+
Madawaska	123,768½	895 96	59 19	680 84	37 73	1,576 80	96 92	0 50+	0 67—
Northumberland	326,875	2,358 12	176 78	1,419 56	58 63	3,777 68	235 41	0 39+	0 52+
Queens	122,318½	1,536 72	162 64	248 58	18 68	1,785 30	181 32	0 18+	0 24+
Restigouche	102,464½	735 84	53 59	480 36	17 58	1,216 20	71 17	0 43+	0 57+
Saint John	578,558½	3,131 17	52 97	4,033 09	22 90	7,164 26	75 87	0 64+	0 85+
Sunbury	55,503½	612 86	60 24	251 44	14 03	864 30	74 27	0 42—	0 56—
Victoria	77,154	929 58	125 03	226 17	21 60	1,155 75	146 63	0 27—	0 36—
Westmorland	521,935	3,232 34	114 80	2,497 41	46 34	5,729 75	161 14	0 44+	0 59—
York	268,614	2,569 71	195 55	1,071 84	48 57	3,641 55	244 12	0 37—	0 49—
New Brunswick	3,530,225½	$27,372 88	$1,960 29	$18,023 75	$728 99	$45,396 63	$2,689 28	$0 47—	$0 63—

*The Balance of the County Fund (1,817.52) was paid to the School for the Blind, Halifax, and to the Institution for the Deaf and Dumb, Fredericton. See Table XI.

TABLE X.—PUBLIC SCHOOLS: APPORTIONMENT OF COUNTY FUND TO TRUSTEES FOR THE YEAR ENDED 30TH, JUNE, 1902. PART TWO.—SECOND TERM ENDED JUNE 30TH, 1902.

Drafts issued by the Chief Superintendent payable by the respective County Treasurers.

COUNTIES.	Grand total days attendance of Pupils; rectified for County Fund Apportionment (Term 122 days)	In respect of the services of qualified Teachers exclusive of Assistants, for the time the Schools were in Session. [1]	Special to Poor Districts (included in column 1.)	In respect of the average number of pupils in attendance as compared with the whole average number pupils attending the schools in the County and the time in operation. [2]	Special to Poor Districts [included in column 2.]	Total to the Trustees, This Term, *Whole amount apportioned this Term. [3]	Total to the Trustees, This Term, Total special to poor districts [included in column 3]	Rate per Pupil in attendance the full Term per column 2. In ordinary Districts.	Rate per Pupil in attendance the full Term per column 2. In Poor Districts. [4]
Albert	161 322½	$ 945 17	$ 71 78	$ 461 08	$ 20 57	$1,406 25	$ 92 35	$0 34+	$0 45+
Carleton	313,218	2,122 09	60 25	956 06	14 77	3 078 15	75 02	0 37+	0 49+
Charlotte	335,793½	1,870 59	83 09	1,386 66	27 09	3 257 25	110 18	0 50+	0 67—
Gloucester	325,016½	1,772 77	235 99	2,357 63	235 42	4 140 40	471 41	0 88+	1 17+
Kent	301,394½	1,826 08	220 99	1,655 12	152 31	3 481 20	373 30	0 67+	0 89+
Kings	312 525½	2,267 37	148 16	781 04	30 35	3 048 41	178 51	0 30+	0 40+
Madawaska	171,938½	886 71	52 39	949 83	44 31	1,836 54	96 70	0 67+	0 89+
Northumberland	400 829½	2,130 36	153 18	2,046 09	80 11	4,176 45	233 29	0 62+	0 83—
Queens	151 237½	1,310 45	92 11	328 60	15 94	1,639 05	108 05	0 26+	0 35—
Restigouche	127.210½	663 43	35 41	894 47	27 01	1 557 90	62 42	0 85+	1 13+
Saint John	782,081	3,071 17	52 53	4,420 82	18 84	7,491 99	71 37	0 68+	0 91—
Sunbury	72 224	625 95	70 53	233 40	18 18	859 35	88 71	0 40+	0 53+
Victoria	110.714½	873 93	122 54	434 94	47 73	† 1,308 87	170 27	0 49+	0 65+
Westmorland	619,634½	2.912 76	108 72	2,886 24	55 85	5 799 00	164 57	0 57—	0 76—
York	326,089	2,125 53	122 95	1,487 44	47 39	3,612 97	170 34	0 55+	0 73+
New Brunswick	4 511,229½	$25,404 86	$1,630 62	$21 279 42	$835 87	$46 683 78	$2 466 49	$0 57+	$0 76+

*The balance of the County Fund ($1,901.79) was apportioned to the School for the Blind, Halifax, and the Institution for the Deaf and Dumb, Fredericton. See Table XI.

†... rtioned in February, 1903, not included in this amount.

—PROVINCIAL AND COUNTY FUND GRANTS TO THE SCHOOL FOR THE BLIND, HALIFAX; AND COUNTY FUND GRANT TO THE INSTITUTION FOR THE DEAF AND DUMB, FREDERICTON.

Year ended 30th June, 1902.

COUNTIES.	School for the Blind, Halifax.								Institution for the Deaf and Dumb, Fredericton.					Total County Fund Grants to both Institutions.
	Term ended Dec 31, 1901			Term ended June 30, 1902.					Term ended Dec. 31, 1901		Term ended June 30 1902			
	No. of Pupils.	Provincial Grant, at rate of $75 per pupil per year.	Grant from County fund at rate of $75 per pupil per year.	No. of Pupils.	Provincial Grant, at rate of $75 per pupil per year.	Grant from County fund at rate of $75 per pupil per year.	Total Provincial Grant for the year.	Total from County Fund for the year.	No. of Pupils.	Grant from County Fund at the rate of $60 per pupil per year.	No. of Pupils.	Grant from County fund at the rate of $60 per pupil per year.	Total for the year.	
Albert	3	$112 50	$112 50	3	$112 50	$112 50	$225 00	$225 00	4	$108 44	4	$120 00	$228 44	$453 44
Carleton	2	75 00	75 00	2	75 00	75 00	150 00	150 00	4	104 99	3	90 00	194 99	344 99
Charlotte	2	75 00	75 00	2	75 00	75 00	150 00	150 00	1	30 00	1	30 00	60 00	210 00
Gloucester	—								2	30 48	2	60 00	90 48	90 48
Kent	4	150 00	150 00	3	112 50	112 50	262 50	262 50						262 50
Kings	3	112 50	112 50	3	112 50	112 50	225 00	225 00	3	78 20	3	87 34	165 54	390 54
Madawaska	—										1	10 11	10 11	10 11
Northumberland	2	55 91	55 91	2	75 00	75 00	130 91	130 91	1	23 36	1	30 00	53 36	184 27
Queens	1	37 50	37 50	1	37 50	37 50	75 00	75 00						75 00
Restigouche	—								1	30 00	1	30 00	60 00	60 00
Saint John	5	187 50	187 50	5	187 50	187 50	375 00	375 00	3	84 34	3	84 36	168 70	543 70
Sunbury	—													
Victoria	—													
Westmorland	8	300 00	300 00	8	300 00	300 00	600 00	600 00	7	191 80	7	210 00	401 80	1001 80
York	—								1	30 00	3	62 48	92 48	92 48
	30	$1105 91	$1105 91	29	$1087 50	$1087 50	$2193 41	$2193 41	27	$711 61	29	$814 29	$1525 90	$3719 31

TABLE XII.—SUPERIOR SCHOOLS; For the Year ended June 30th 1902.

Part One.—term ended december, 1901.

Embodied in Table IX, and Foregoing Tables.

No and Name of District.	Parish.	County.	Teachers.	Provincial Allowance.	Total to County.
Elgin Corner, No. 2,	Elgin	Albert	J. H. Crocker	$ 101 63	
Hillsborough, No. 2,	Hillsborough	"	Fred. S. James	100 49	
Hopewell Hill, No. 2,	Hopewell	"	H. H Stuart	107 48	309 60
Hartland, No. 3,	Brighton	Carleton	Jos E. Howe	102 22	
Florenceville, No. 4,	Simonds and Wicklow	"	D. W. Hamilton	100 49	
Jacksonville, No. 7,	Wakefield	"	Clinton H. Gray	100 49	
Centreville, No. 4,	Wilmot and Wicklow	"	Ruth L. Reid	94 35	397 55
North Head, No. 1,	Grand Manan	Charlotte	Peter Girdwood	100 49	
St. George, No. 1,	St. George	"	H. E. Sinclair	100 49	
Moore's Mills, No. 1½	St. James and St. David	"	Elizabeth S. Colwell	89 96	
St. Stephen, (Town)	St. Stephen	"	P. G. McFarlane	96 81	
Milltown, (Town),	"	"	J. B. Sutherland	100 49	488 24
Bathurst Village, No. 16,	Bathurst	Gloucester	C. J. Mersereau	99 27	
Petit Rocher, No. 4,	Beresford	"	Jerome Boudreau	107 48	
Tracadie, No. 3,	Saumarez,	"	Geo. E. Price	106 31	313 06
Harcourt, No. 5,	Harcourt	Kent	Miriam Kyle	100 49	
Rexton, No. 2,	Richibucto	"	R. G. Girvan	100 49	
Bass River, No. 9,	Weldford	"	Chas. D. Richards	96 81	
Buctouche, No. 1,	Wellington	"	G. A. Coates	107 48	405 27
Penobsquis, No. 1,	Cardwell	Kings	G. T. Morton	93 13	
Hampton, No. 2,	Hampton	"	Rex. R. Cormier	100 49	
			Forward		$1913 72

TABLE XII.—Part One—*Continued.*

No. and Name of District.	Parish.	County.	Teachers.	Provincial Allowance.	Total to County.
			Brought forward...	....	$1913 72
Havelock Corner, No. 8,...	Havelock........ ...	Kings.......	Aaron Perry.........	99 26	
Bloomfield Station, No. 2,..	Norton......	"	H. A. Wheaton.....	12 25	
			B. P. Steeves......	88 24	
Apohaqui, No. 25,........	Studholm and Sussex...	"	J. T. Horsman.......	100 49	493 86
Edmundston, No. 1,......	Madawaska,..........	Madawaska ...	J. F. Worrell.........	99 26	99 26
Blackville, No. 6,.........	Blackville............	North'd	J. C. Carruthers......	107 48	
Doaktown, No. 4,........	Blissfield............	"	G. A. Wathen........	107 48	
Derby, No. 1,.....	Derby....	"	E. A. Crocker.........	99 26	
Douglastown, No. 6,......	Newcastle............	"	M. R. Benn..........	100 49	
Newcastle, (Town)........	"	"	G. K. McNaughton....	100 49	515 20
Chipman, No. 11,........	Chipman............	Queens.	H. P. Dole..........	96 81	96 81
Dalhousie, No. 1,.........	Dalhousie............	Restigouche..	R. B. Masterton......	100 49	100 49
Fairville, No. 2,..........	Lancaster............	St. John......	S. A. Worrell........	99 88	
Milford, No. 13,.........	"	"	W. A. Nelson.........	100 49	
St. Martins, No. 2,......	St. Martins.........	"	W. L. McDiarmid....	100 49	300 86
Fredericton Junction, No. 1,	Gladstone............	Sunbury.....	H. H. Bridges........	103 98	103 98
Grand Falls, No. 7,.......	Grand Falls....	Victoria......	M. L. Hayward......	100 49	100 49
Dorchester, No. 2,.... ...	Dorchester..........	West'd......	H. B. Steeves........	100 49	
Sackville, No. 9,........	Sackville............	"	F. A. Dixon.........	100 49	
Middle Sackville, No. 11,	"	"	A. J. McKnight......	100 49	
Petitcodiac, No. 1, ...	Salisbury............	"	R. D. Hanson.........	100 49	
Salisbury, No. 24,......	Salisbury, Monct, & Cover.	" & Albert	A. C. M. Lawson.....	107 48	
Shediac, No. 10,..........	Shediac.............	"	B. H. Webb.........	100 49	
			Forward......	....	$3724 67

TABLE XII.—PART ONE—*Continued.*

No. and Name of District.	Parish.	County.	Teachers.	Provincial Allowance.	Total to County.
			Brought forward...	....	$3724 67
Port Elgin, No. 1,........	West'd and Botsford..	West'd......	B. R. Field..........	98 04	707 97
Keswick Ridge, No. 1,....	Bright............	York........	Harry C. Fraser....	31 54	
			Annie L. Taylor....	73 61	
Benton, No. 23, A,.......	Canterbury and Woodstock.........	" & Carleton..	H. C. B. Allen....	60 75	
			M. A. Oulton......	40 89	
McAdam Junction, No. 9,	McAdam.............	"	H. F. Perkins.......	107 48	
Harvey Station, No. 2,	Manners Sutton......	"	C. M. McCann.......	107 48	
Gibson, No. 2,............	St. Marys...........	"	A. H. Barker........	100 49	
Marysville, No. 3,........	"	"	W. T. Day..........	100 50	622 74
					$5055 38

TABLE XII.—Part Two—Term ended June 30th, 1902.

No. and Name of District.	Parish.	County.	Teacher.	Provincial Allowance.	Total for County.
Elgin Corner, No. 2,	Elgin	Albert	Clive M McCann	$84 11	
			J Howard Crocker	58 41	
Hillsborough, No. 2,	Hillsborough	"	F S James	149 51	
Hopewell Hill, No. 2,	Hopewell	"	H H Stuart	142 52	$434 55
Hartland, No. 3,	Brighton	Carleton	J E Howe	149 51	
Florenceville, No. 4,	Simonds and Wicklow	"	D W Hamilton	120 10	
Jacksonville, No. 4,	Wakefield	"	C H Gray	149 51	
Centreville, No. 4,	Wilmot and Wicklow	"	Ruth L Reid	148 28	
Benton, No. 23, A,	Woodstock and Canter.	"	H C B Allen	142 52	709 92
North Head, No. 1,	Grand Manan	Charlotte	B F McLeod	149 51	
St. George, No. 1,	St. George	"	H E Sinclair	149 51	
Moore's Mills, No. 1½	St. James and St. David	"	Elizabeth S Colwell	120 32	
St. Stephen, (Town),	St. Stephen	"	P G McFarlane	149 51	
Milltown, (Town),	"	"	J B Sutherland	149 51	718 36
Bathurst Village, No. 16,	Bathurst	Gloucester	C J Mersereau	149 51	
Petit Rocher, No. 4,	Beresford	"	J Boudreau	142 52	
Tracadie, No. 3,	Saumarez	"	George E Price	140 77	432 80
Harcourt, No. 5,	Harcourt	Kent	M Miriam Kyle	148 90	
Rexton, No. 2,	Richibucto	"	R G Girvan	149 51	
			" " June 1901	73	
Bass River, No. 9,	Weldford	"	A B Boyer	149 51	
Buctouche, No. 1,	Wellington	"	G A Coates	142 52	591 17
Penobsquis, No. I,	Cardwell	Kings	G T Morton	149 51	
			Forward		$2886 80

TABLE XII.—PART TWO—*Continued*

No. and Name of District.	Parish.	County.	Teacher	Provincia Allowance.	Total for County.
			Brought forward	....	$2886 80
Hampton Station, No. 2,	Hampton	Kings	R R Cormier	$147 66	
Havelock Corner, No. 8,	Havelock	"	A Perry	148 29	
Bloomfield Station, No. 2,	Norton	"	B P Steeves	149 51	
Apohaqui, No. 25,	Studholm and Sussex	"	J T Horsman	149 51	744 48
Edmundston, No. 1,	Madawaska	Madawaska	J F Worrell	148 28	148 28
Blackville, No. 6,	Blackville	North'd	J C Carruthers	142 52	
Doaktown, No. 4,	Blissfield	"	G A Wathen	142 52	
Derby, No. 1,	Derby	"	E A Crocker	149 51	
Douglastown, No. 6,	Newcastle	"	M R Benn	149 51	
Newcastle, No. 7,	"	"	G K McNaughton	149 51	733 57
Chipman, No. 11,	Chipman	Queens	H P Dole	149 51	149 51
Dalhousie, No. 1,	Dalhousie	Restigouche	R B Masterton	149 51	149 51
Fairville, No. 2,	Lancaster	St. John	A M DeWar	149 51	
Milford, No. 13,	"	"	W A Nelson	149 51	
St. Martins, No. 2,	St. Martins	"	{ W L McDiarmid	147 06	
			{ " " June 1901	73	446 81
Fredericton Junction, No. 1,	Gladstone	Sunbury	H H Bridges	137 85	137 85
Grand Falls, No. 7,	Grand Falls	Victoria	M L Hayward	148 28	148 28
Dorchester, No. 2,	Dorchester	West'd	H B Steeves	148 28	
Sackville, No. 9,	Sackville	"	F A Dixon	149 51	
Middle Sackville, No. 11,	"	"	A J McKnight	149 51	
Petitcodiac, No. 1,	Salisbury	"	R D Hanson	149 51	
Salisbury, No. 24,	Salisbury, Monct. & Cover.	"	A C M Lawson	142 52	
			Forward	....	$5545 09

TABLE XII —PART TWO—*Continued*,

No. and Name of District.	Parish.	County	Teachers	Provincial Allowance.	Total for County.
			Brought forward...	....	$5545 09
Shediac, No. 10,..........	Shediac	West'd......	B H Webb...........	$149 51	
Port Elgin, No. 1,.......	West'd and Botsfod...	"	B R Field...........	149 51	1038 35
Keswick Ridge, No. 1,....	Bright	York.......	H C Fraser..........	142 52	
McAdam Junction, No. 9,	McAdam	"	H F Perkins.........	142 52	
Harvey Station, No. 2,....	Manners Sutton......	"	J P Bulyea.........	139 02	
Gibson, No. 2,...........	St. Marys..........	"	J B Delong........	30 64	
			A H Barker........	117 64	
Marysville, No. 3,.......	"	"	W T Day...........	149 50	721 84
					$7305 28

i 7

TABLE XIII.—GRAMMAR SCHOOLS: THE YEAR ENDED JUNE 30TH, 1902.

(INCLUDED IN PREVIOUS TABLES)

PART ONE.—THE TERM CLOSED DECEMBER 31ST, 1901.

LOCALITY.		NAMES OF PRINCIPALS AND OTHER TEACHERS RECEIVING GRAMMAR SCHOOL GRANTS.	ABOVE GRADE VIII.								PROVINCIAL GRANT, ETC.—SALARIES OF THE TEACHERS.		
					PUPILS.								
COUNTIES.	TOWNS.		No of Dep'tments	No. of Teachers and Assistants.	Grade IX.	Grade X.	Grade XI.	Grade XII.	Total No.	Legally authorized days department was open.	Provincial aid for the Term.	Salary from trustees per year.	Rate of Salary for year.
Albert	Alma	T. E. Colpitts, A. B.	1	1	9	7	3	......	19	82	$ 140 69	$ 350 00	$ 700 00
Carleton	Woodstock	G. H. Harrison, A. B.	2	2	35	12	13	......	60	82	140 69	650 00	1000 00
		Julia Neales								82	140 69	350 00	700 00
Charlotte	St. Andrews	J. A. Allen, A. B.	1	1	28	9	4	......	41	82	140 69	450 00	800 00
Gloucester	Bathurst	M. R. Tuttle, A. B.	1	1	8	7	......	......	15	82	140 69	350 00	700 00
Kent	Richibucto	C. H. Cowperthwaite, A. B.	1	1	11	4	2	......	17	82	140 69	350 00	700 00
Kings	Sussex	Wm. Brodie, A. B.	2	2	23	12	6	......	41	82	140 69	500 00	850 00
Northumberland	Chatham	Philip Cox, Ph. D.	2	2	21	17	8	3	52	82	140 69	750 00	1100 00
Queens	Gagetown	D. L. Mitchell, A. B.	1	1	9	8	......	......	17	92	122 66	300 00	600 00
Restigouche	Campbellton	E. W. Lewis, A. B.	1	1	23	13	5	......	41	82	140 69	650 00	1000 00
St. John	St. John	H. S. Bridges, Ph. D.	11	13	216	130	86	7	439	82	......	2000 00	2000 00
		W. J. S. Myles, M. A.								82	141 38	850 00	1200 00
		T. E. Powers, B. A.								82	141 38	600 00	950 00
		M. Maud Narraway, B. A								77	132 76	500 00	850 00
		Elizabeth McNaughton								82	121 18	300 00	600 00
Victoria	Andover	W. M. Veazey, B. A.	1	1	11	8	2	......	21	82	140 69	350 00	700 00
Westmorland	Moncton	Geo. J. Oulton, M. A.	4	4	70	45	22	......	137	82	140 69	850 00	1200 00
		C. H. Acheson								82	140 69	650 00	1000 00
		L. R. Hetherington								82	140 69	550 00	900 00
		G. F. McNally, B. A.								82	140 69	500 00	850 00
York	Fredericton	B. C. Foster, M. A.	4	4	79	51	36	......	166	82	140 69	850 00	1200 00
		H. H. Hagerman, M. A.								82	140 69	650 00	1000 00
		A. S. McFarlane, M. A.								82	140 69	500 00	850 00
New Brunswick			32	34	546	323	187	10	1066	......	$3051 09	13850 00	21450 00
Cor. Term, 1900			32	35	517	297	183	19	1016	......	$3227 76	13825 00	22125 00
Increase			......	......	29	26	4	......	50	......	......	$ 25 00	......
Decrease			......	1	......	......	......	9	......	......	$ 176 67	......	$ 675 00

TABLE XIII.—Part Two.—GRAMMAR SCHOOLS: The Term Ended June 30th, 1902.

(Included in Previous Tables)

Locality: Counties.	Locality: Towns.	Names of Principals and other Teachers receiving Grammar School Grants.	Above Grade VIII: No. of Departments.	No. of Teachers and Assistants.	Pupils: Grade IX.	Grade X.	Grade XI.	Grade XII.	Total No.	Legally authorized days department was open.	Provincial Grant, etc.—Salaries of the Teachers: Provincial aid for the Term.	Salary from trustees per year.	Rate of Salary for year.
Albert	Alma	T. E. Colpitts, A. B.	1	1	9	8	4	......	21	122	$ 209 31	$ 350 00	$ 700 00
Carleton	Woodstock	G. H. Harrison, A. B.	2	2	31	11	12	......	54	122	209 31	650 00	1000 00
		Julia Neales								122	209 31	350 00	700 00
Charlotte	St. Andrews	J. A. Allen, A. B.	2	2	23	9	4	......	36	115½	198 17	450 00	800 00
Gloucester	Bathurst	M. R. Tuttle, A. B.	1	1	6	2	......	......	8	122	209 31	350 00	700 00
Kent	Richibucto	C. H. Cowperthwaite, A. B.	1	1	8	4	......	......	12	122	209 31 *1 03	350 00	700 00
Kings	Sussex	Wm. Brodie, A. B.	2	2	24	13	5	......	42	122	209 31	500 00	850 00
Northumberland	Chatham	Philip Cox, Ph. D.	2	2	22	15	8	2	47	116	199 02	750 00	1100 00
Queens	Gagetown	D. L. Mitchell, A. B.	1	1	7	6	1	......	14	120	168 22	300 00	600 00
Restigouche	Campbellton	E. W. Lewis, A. B.	1	1	22	12	6	......	40	122	209 31	650 00	1000 00
St. John	St. John	H. S. Bridges, Ph. D.	11	14	188	119	81	6	394	121	....	2400 00	2400 00
		W. J. S. Myles, M. A.								121	208 62	850 00	1200 00
		T. E. Powers, B. A.								121	208 62	600 00	950 00
		M. Maud Narraway B. A.								119	205 18	550 00	900 00
		Elizabeth McNaughton.								118	174 39	300 00	600 00
Victoria	Andover	W. M. Veazey, B. A.	1	1	12	7	5	......	24	122	209 31	350 00	700 00
Westmorland	Moncton	Geo. J. Oulton, M. A.	3	3	70	45	22	......	137	122	209 31	850 00	1200 00
		C. H. Acheson								122	209 31	650 00	1000 00
		G. Fred McNally, B. A.								122	209 31	500 00	850 00
York	Fredericton	B. C. Foster, M. A.	4	4	72	47	34	......	153	122	209 31	850 00	1200 00
		H. H. Hagerman, M. A.								122	209 31	650 00	1000 00
		A. S. McFarlane, M. A.								122	209 31	500 00	850 00
New Brunswick			32	35	494	298	182	8	982	.....	4293 59	13750 00	21000 00
Cor. Term, 1901			32	34	469	284	178	18	949	.....	4460 47	13750 00	21350 00
Increase			.....	1	25	14	4	.....	33	.....	....	....	....
Decrease			.....	.....	.....	.....	.....	10	.....	.....	$ 166 88	....	$ 350 00

* Balance for June, 1901.

TABLE XIV.—PROVINCIAL NORMAL SCHOOL; FOR SESSION ENDED JUNE, 1902.

NORMAL DEPARTMENT. Students in Attendance.	No. attended.	Left through various causes	Failed to Classify.	Eligible for Examination	Males.	Females.	French Dept. Males.	French Dept. Females.	Total.	Model Dept. Pupils. Boys.	Model Dept. Pupils. Girls.	Model Dept. Pupils. Total.
Term ended Dec., 1901										75	115	190
First term ended Dec., 1901	39			39	5	30	1	3	39			
Session ended June, 1902	221			221	62	159			221			
Second term ended May, 1902	9			9				9	9			
Term ended June, 1902										72	118	190
New Brunswick	269			269	67	189	1	12	269			
Cor. Session last year	198	2		196	29	130	12	25	196			
Increase	71			73	38	59			73			
Decrease		2					11	13				

PROVINCIAL GRANTS TO OCTOBER 31, 1902.

On Account of Salaries.	Amount.
Eldon Mullin, M. A.	$ 566 6
W. Crocket, M. A., LL D.	1,200 00
H. C. Creed, M. A., D. Lit	1,200 00
John Brittain	1,054 15
G. A. Inch, B. A.	1,100 00
Alphee Belliveau	1,100 00
M. Alice Clark	800 00
Ed. Cadwallader, B. A.	250 00
Amos O'Blenes	*165 00
Mary E. Phillips	* 4 07
Mary E. Nicholson	*145 93
M. Annie Harvey	*183 76
Clara Bridges	* 67 09
Lillian Nicolson	*126 33
Total	$7,962 99

*These amounts are paid by the Board of Education in addition to the Provincial Allowance and to Salaries from Trustees.

TABLE XV.—PUBLIC SCHOOLS: Closing Examinations for License; Year Ending June, 30, 1902.

TERMS AND STATIONS.	No. of candidates admitted to the written examination and grounds of admission.						Grammar School Class.				MALE. I Class.					MALE. II Class.				MALE. III Class.			FEMALE. I Class.					FEMALE. II Class.				FEMALE. III Class.			SUMMARY. Males.					SUMMARY. Females.					Total Licensed.
	As classified Student-Teachers of the Provincial Normal School.	As holding License from the Board of Education.	As Graduates in Arts.	As having undergone training at a Normal School not in N. B.	As eligible for examination.	Total No. admitted.	No. examined for this Class.	No. that obtained this Class.	No. obtained 1st Class.	No. obtained 2nd Class.	No. examined for this Class.	No. obtained 1st Class.	No. obtained 2nd Class.	No. obtained 3rd Class.	No. that failed to obtain any Class.	No. examined for this Class.	No. obtained 2nd Class.	No. obtained 3rd Class.	No. that failed to obtain any Class.	No. examined for this Class.	No. obtained 3rd Class.	No. that failed to obtain any Class.	No. examined for this Class.	No. obtained 1st Class.	No. obtained 2nd Class.	No. obtained 3rd Class.	No. that failed to obtain any Class.	No. examined for this Class.	No. obtained 2nd Class.	No. obtained 3rd Class.	No. that failed to obtain any Class.	No. examined for this Class.	No. obtained 3rd Class.	No. that failed to obtain any Class.	No. obtained Grammar Sch. Class.	No. obtained 1st Class.	No. obtained 2nd Class.	No. obtained 3rd Class.	No. that failed to obtain any Class.	No. obtained Grammar Sch. Class.	No. obtained 1st Class.	No. obtained 2nd Class.	No. obtained 3rd Class.	No. that failed to obtain any Class.	Total No. Licensed.
DECEMBER, 1901.																																													
Acadian Teachers	4	...	..	....	2	6	..	..	..	..	..	..	..	..	..	..	..	..	..	2	1	1	..	..	..	..	..	....	...	...	..	4	3	1	..	...	...	1	1	..	.	..	3	1	4
III Class temporary	34	...	..	....	..	34	..	..	..	..	..	..	..	..	..	..	..	..	...	5	5	...	..	.	.	..	.	....	....	.	..	29	29	..	..	...	.	5	.	..	...	...	29	...	34
May, 1902.																																													
Acadian Teachers	9	...	..	....	1	10	..	..	..	..	..	..	..	..	..	..	..	..	..	..	..	...	..	...	.	..	...	....	....	...	..	10	6	4	...	.	.	...	...	...	..	....	6	4	6
JUNE 1902																																													
Fredericton	216	20	9	....	..	245	7	4	2	1	31	23	8	..	...	38	36	2	...	..	.	.	47	33	12	2		122	113	9	...	..	.	..	4	25	45	2	..	..	33	125	11	..	245
St. John	....	14	..	....	..	14	2	2	.	...	2	..	2	..		..	..	.	..	..	..	...	7	3	2	2	..	3	3	..	.	..	.	..	...	.	2	...	...	2	3	5	2	..	14
Chatham	..	1	2	...	..	3	1	1		..	1	1	..	..		.	.	.			...	...	1	1	..	.	.	....	....	..		.	...		1	1		...	..	..	1	....	..	..	3
New Brunswick	263	35	11	....	3	312	10	7	2	1	34	24	10	..	...	38	36	2	.	7	6	1	55	37	14	4	...	125	116	9	...	43	38	5	5	26	47	8	1	2	37	130	51	5	306
Year ending June, 1901	196	38	9	....	3	246	11	8	3	..	22	10	6	5	1	17	15	2	...	17	15	2	35	27	8	..	..	97	85	12	..	47	41	6	6	13	21	24	3	2	27	98	53	6	237
Increase	67	...	2	....	..	66	..	..	.	1	12	14	4	..	..	21	21	...	...		..	...	20	10	6	..	...	28	31	...	.	..	...	...	..	13	26	..	...		10	37	.	..	69
Decrease	...	3	..	....	..	....	1	1	1	..	..	..	..	5	1			...	...	10	9	1	..	...	.	4	...	....	...	3	..	4	3	1	1	.		14	2	...	..	....	2	1	....

In addition to the above, 15 candidates at Fredericton, 5 at St. John and 1 at Chatham wrote a partial examination for Grammar School Class. Also 5 candidates at the Fredericton station received Superior in addition to Class 2.

Issue of School Licenses, awarded upon Examination in December, 1901, and May and June, 1902.

The number of applicants for each Class will be seen from the preceding table. The following list contains the names of successful candidates only.

DECEMBER, 1901.

Third Class.—Howard B. Johnson, Willard B. Kay, Elmer T. Kennedy, Leslie Murray, Samuel K. Nason, Annie P. Armstrong, Maude E. Brophy, Sarah J. Bryson, Angelina Clowes, E. Hope Crandall, Anna M. Dibblee, Emma J. Dougherty, Eva M. W. Duke, Martha L. Elliott, Alice G. Gallagher, Georgia B. Gunter, Mary B. Harrington, Lizzie J. R. Harvey, H. Milliken Henderson, Ethel May Hurley, Greta M. Jones, Clara B. McCullough, Mary W. McDiarmid, Minnie H. McDonald, Rosanna G. McNabb, S. Kathleen Marcy, Mary M. H. Mooney, Mary L. Murphy, Hannah M. O'Donnell, Olive H. Reid, A. Bertie Richardson, Margaret Riedle, Ethel E. Swanson, Mary A. Wilson, Abraham Vienneau, M. E. Cecile Landry, Jane Genevieve Legere, Lizzie A. Levesque.

MAY, 1902.

Third Class,—Jennie Sara Babin, Rosalie Barrieau, Philomene Chiasson, Marie M. Cyr, Azilda B. Daigle, Amelia L. Gagnon, Margaret Anderson.

JUNE, 1902.

Grammar School.—John Howard Crocker, Charles D. Hébert, Chalmers Jack Mersereau, A. Ernest G. McKenzie, Raleigh Trites, Katharine R. Bartlett, Bessie Harrison Wilson.

First Class.—Percy S. Bailey, *Arthur W. Barbour, *Allan A. Barter, *Frank H. Blake, George W. Burton, John M. Clindinnin, Harry C. Cody, Gustavus A. Colpitts, *Wm. Millen Crawford, *Abram M. Cronkhite, Arthur E. Eastman, Warren Orton Gray, Frederick A. Jewett, Lynus D. Jones, Goldwin S. Lord, James Simpson Lord, Wm. W. K. Maxwell, Wm. F. McKnight, Holland R. McGill, Walter B. O'Regan, Allan R. Reid, *Clarence Shannon, Fred C. Squiers, John Stanley Smiley, E. C. Weyman, A. J. Witzell,

*First Class when passed in reading.

Florence J. Alexander, Lena Gertrude Babbitt, Glendine Yolinda Brewster, Sarah Lavinia Brown, Mildred Melissa Black, Mabel K. Burchill, *Grace A. Campbell, Susie E. Carruthers, Muriel M. T. Colpitts, Maude Louise Cuming, *Edith Gertrude Cummings. Josephine R. Cormier, Florence C. Estabrooks, Blanche Marion Fraser, *Mary E. Gillman, Violet E. Goldsmith, Mary A. Gillen. Addie M. Hartt, Ethel H. Jarvis, Annie M. Loggie, Evangeline LeBlanc, Marjorie F. Mair, Catherine F. Mair, Jessie E MacLean, Augusta E. Smith, Sadie Sterling, Janie E. G. Strong, Winifred E. Thompson, Mary E. Tingley, *Clara G. Turner, Jessie G. Vince, Annie Hunter Whittaker, Margaret Wilson, Ada I. Wright, Nellie Young, *Mary Hill McBeath.

Second Class.—George Hazen Adair, Dexter W. Allen, Oscar J. McC. Allen, Artemas Allen, **William A. R. Archer, Nathan Tupper Blakeney, Fred L. Bowser, Frederick Roy Branscombe, Max D. Cormier, James Watson Crocker, C. Bradley Dalton, William P. Day, Percy Alex. Fitzpatrick, Martin G. Fox, Arlis T. Ganong, Louis LeB. Godard, Arthur E. Graham, Chas. Nelson Gregg, Hazen W. Hall, Grant Hawkins, John M. Keefe, **Albert P. Jewett, Walter S. Jones, E. Stanley Knox, Medley F. Miller, Arthur E. Mitchell, Donald L. McCain, Ralph McKinney, Milton A. McLeod. John D. McMillan, Goldwin I. Nugent, Asael W. Peck, Frank L. Shaw, Robert A. Simpson, Sydney B. Smith, Robert A. Taylor, Aaron E. Tower, Lorenzo N. Wadlin, Wm John Young, Verna Pearl Alexander, Cora B. Allen, Pearl E. Babbitt, Della A. Brown, Christina J. Blake, Daisy Alice Bowser, Thirza E. Branscombe, Clara M. Brown, Harriet E. Brown, Jessie H. Brown, Maud Brown, Gertrude A. Cameron, Estella Y. Coburn, **Minnie E. Colpitts, May Evelyn Cook, Louise R. Copp, Rhoda J. Corbett, Bernadette Cormier, Mary Gertrude Creaghan, Lulu A Cronkhite, S. Janie R. Cameron, Alice T. Day, Elizabeth I. Daye, Florence O. Demille, Pearl Vinetta Dennison, Fannie F. Doyle, Seraph Elizabeth Dysart, Belle M. Eddy, Daisy B. M Farnham, Mabel I. Finn, Lena M. Firlotte, Annie M. Forsey, Evelyn E. Gallagher, Ella M. Gartley, Delia M. Gauvin, Jessie R. Gilliland, Annie G. Gillis, Lila L. Gillis, Ethel McL. Good, Ethel M. Graham, Mary E. Haining, Annie M. B. Harding, **Margaret Anne Harper. Annie J. Harrison, Patience N. Hawkes, Mary M. Hayes, Sadie B Hogan, Lizzie M. Holmes, Lizzie E. James, Lydia A. Jewett, **Augusta G. Kelly, Mary Kathleen Kelley, Elizabeth B. Kelly, Myrtle A. Keith, Agnes A. LeBlanc, Hermeline T. LeBlanc, Isadora P. Leighton, Helen M. Lunnin, Mildred Pearl Milton, Mary G. Mitchell, Clara L Moore, Annie L. Moore, Verna Blanche Murch, Lily Agnes Murdock,

*First Class when passed in reading.

**Second Class when passed in reading.

Nellie J. Musgrove, Flora H. McCallum, Marguerite E. McCormack. L. Ethel McCrea, Jennie Beatrice McCutcheon, Beatrice A. McEwen, Rachel McEwen, Emily I McFee, Ida M. I. McGerigle, Sarah C. McKenzie, Jessie McD. McKnight, Nellie M. McNaughton, Beatrice M. M. Newman, Sadie V. Newman, Alice Maude Nickerson, Minnie E. O'Brien, Alma L. Ogden, Mary Belle Page, Ruth G. Parlee, Minnie I. F. Pedolin, Verna R. Perkins, Bertie Harding Plummer, Jessie F. S. Patterson, Grace A. Peters, Margaret J. Phelan, †Maggie B. Pond, Susie V. Price, Emma J. Read, Selena M. Reynolds, Madge J. Ricketson, †Gertie Rosengren, Mabel R. Saunders, Mary A. B. Saunders, Ethel A. Sears, Minnie L. Seely, Ethel E Sharpe, Beula Maude Shaw, Georgia A. Sherwood, Mabelle C. Sherwood, **Ruby V. Sinnett, Hester G. L. Sleep, Myrtle A. Slipp, Minnie P. Spragg, Mabel Muriel Steeves, Violet M. Steeves, Helena J. Tamlyn, Louise Tomilson, Ella M. Tompkins, Louisa V. Traill, Emma Walker, Grace H. Waring, Mary Weldon, Fannie E. J. Wetmore, Glenna Faye White, Annie W. Williston, Emily J. Williston, Bessie M. Wilson, **Effie J. Young.

Third Class.—Harry Sterling Heustis, C. Frank Rideout, Margaret Alberta Barton, Agnes T. Cummings, Sarah Alice Jones, Alice Grace Kay, Myrtle A. C. Libbey, Annie Sophia Mowatt, Inez E. Murphy, Mary Gertrude McGrand, Josephine M. Welsh.

Superior Class.—Edward C. Weyman, Holland R. McGill, John S. Smiley, Fred S. James, Mildred M. Black, Maude Louise Cuming, Sadie Sterling, Annie H. Whittaker, Marjorie Ferguson Mair.

Passed for Superior Class in the Departmental Examinations held in July, 1902.—W. C. Anderson, Fred J. Carruthers, John M. Clindinnin, Gustavus A. Colpitts, W. Orton Gray, Jas. Simpson Lord, George P. McCrea, Fred C. Squiers, Susie E Carruthers, Florence C. Estabrooks, B. Marion Fraser, Myrtle A. Harmon, Annie M. Loggie, Mabel Shaw.

†The Preliminary Examinations for this Class to be passed.

**Second Class when passed in Reading.

TABLE XVI.—PUBLIC SCHOOLS: LIBRARIES.

BONUSES PAID TO DISTRICT SCHOOL LIBRARIES DURING THE YEAR ENDED OCTOBER 31ST, 1902.

LOCALITY.			Dates of Payment.	Value.			Number of Volumes.
COUNTY.	PARISH.	Dist'ict		Local.	Provincial	Total.	
Albert	Hopewell	No. 2	June 7th, 1902	$ 8 83	$ 4 42	$ 13 25	10
"	"	" 10	Dec. 24th, 1901	11 45	5 72	17 17	?
Carleton	Brighton	" 3	Dec. 14th, 1901	22 35	11 17	33 52	?
"	Kent	" 2	June 25th, 1902	8 44	4 22	12 66	26
"	Simonds and Wicklow	" 4	Mar. 17th, 1902	29 07	14 54	43 61	223
Charlotte	Dumbarton	" 7½	Nov. 18th, 1901	20 29	10 14	30 43	66
"	St. Croix and St. Andrews	" 2	April 12th, 1902	7 01	3 51	10 52	23
"	St. Patrick	" 2	Mar. 19th, 1902	20 00	10 00	30 00	54
Kings	Hammond	" 4	Dec. 9th, 1901	4 34	2 17	6 51	26
"	Kars	" 1	April 11th, 1902	6 03	3 02	9 05	28
"	Kingston	" 5	Nov. 2nd, 1901	8 20	4 10	12 30	47
"	Rothesay	" 2	June 7th, 1902	2 98	1 50	4 48	9
"	Sussex	" 2	April 14th, 1902	30 08	15 03	45 11	44
Victoria	Andover	" 2	June 24th, 1902	6 56	3 27	9 83	31
Westmorland	Moncton	" 2	Sept. 24th, 1902	15 48	7 74	23 22	61
"	Shediac	" 12	Feb. 24th, 1902	11 70	5 85	17 55	85
York	McAdam	" 9	June 25th, 1902	18 73	9 37	28 10	56
"	Manners Sutton	" 5	June 25th, 1902	20 70	10 00	30 70	109
				$252 24	$125 77	$378 01	898

TABLE XVII.—PUBLIC SCHOOLS.

Travelling Expenses Paid to Student Teachers Attending the Normal School During the Terms Ended June and May, 1901.

(Paid in 1902.)

(Allowance of Mileage, 3 cents a mile.)

No.	Name.	County.	Amount.
1	Baxter B. Barnes,	Westmorland,	$ 11 88
2	Gustavus A. Colpitts,	Albert,	9 12
3	Angus M. Dewar,	Charlotte,	5 88
4	Ruel E. McClintock,	Carleton,	4 86
5	Gustavus E. Duncan,	Restigouche,	13 26
6	Ed. S. McQuaid,	Albert,	9 90
7	Wilford A. Rideout,	Carleton,	4 08
8	Fred E. Squiers,	Carleton,	4 86
10	Edna G. Alexander,	Sunbury,	1 32
11	Florence L. Alexander,	Sunbury,	1 32
12	Mary A. Knight,	Northumberland,	2 88
13	Lena M. Miller,	Restigouche,	13 14
14	M. Caulie McInerny,	Kent,	9 78
15	Mabel E. McLeod,	Kings,	7 08
16	Lavinia A. McTaggart,	Restigouche,	12 12
17	Isabelle Reed,	St. John,	4 02
18	Nettie Beairsto,	Carleton,	4 80
19	Georgina G. Dickson,	Northumberland,	7 02
20	Alice McKenzie,	Restigouche,	13 26
21	Mabel McKinney,	Charlotte,	5 04
22	Lena B. McLeod,	Carleton,	4 50
23	Lottie L. Weldon,	Westmorland,	9 36
24	Percey S. Bailey,	Charlotte,	6 12
25	Willard Brewing,	Kings,	6 78
26	Hugh A. Carr,	Restigouche,	13 26
27	Abram M. Cronkhite,	York,	2 94
		Forward........	$188 58

TABLE XVII.—Continued.

No.	NAME.	NAME	AMOUNT.
		Brought forward	$188 58
28	George W. Christie,	Charlotte,	5 70
29	William B. Deware,	Carleton,	4 86
30	Walter M. Donahoe,	York,	2 58
31	Arthur S. Floyd,	Kings,	6 66
32	Howard M Lambert,	Charlotte,	5 76
33	John Law,	Queens,	1 92
34	Joseph A. Salter,	Gloucester,	10 98
35	Ernest W. Sheils,	Queens,	1 92
36	George N. Somers,	Westmorland,	13 08
37	Will Whitney,	Charlotte,	5 88
38	Estella M. Alward,	Kings,	8 76
39	Jennie P. Alward,	Kings,	8 76
40	Patience Ballentine,	York,	1 80
41	Mary E. Barron,	Northumberland,	6 48
42	Maude W. Bradbury,	York,	2 70
43	Clara O. Burtt,	York,	1 08
44	Sarah A. Cameron,	Northumberland,	5 28
45	Susie E. Carruthers,	Northumberland,	7 02
46	Mary F. Cassidy,	Northumberland,	7 02
47	Cecilia A. Craig,	Charlotte,	5 76
48	Pearl L. Currier,	Queens,	1 50
49	Mary M. Desbrisay,	Restigouche,	12 12
50	Blanche W. Dixon,	St. John,	4 02
51	Ivy M. Dow,	York,	4 50
52	Annie Finnigan,	Kent.	9 78
53	Kate J. Flemming,	Northumberland,	6 84
54	Anna C. Gallagher,	Kings,	4 74
55	Ada F. Ganong,	Kings,	6 72
56	Elizabeth Gleeson,	St. John,	3 90
57	Lana M. Good,	York,	84
58	Anna E. Goodall,	Albert,	9 18
59	Lottie M. Gregg,	Kings,	6 42
60	Effie M. Hayward,	Sunbury,	60
61	Cecilia B. Hewitt,	Charlotte,	6 30
62	Eliza A. Ingraham,	York,	2 70
63	Eva S. Jacques,	Carleton,	3 78
		Forward.......	$386 52

TABLE XVII.—Continued.

No.	NAME.	COUNTY.	AMOUNT.
		Brought forward	$386 52
64	Hattie Jamieson,	Carleton,	4 20
65	Lena M. Kearney,	Carleton,	3 66
66	Bessie B. Kelly,	Queens,	2 40
67	Ida J. Kierstead,	Albert,	9 48
68	Martha J. Lackie,	Kings,	6 00
69	Marguerite G. Legere,	St. John,	4 02
70	Maggie R. Loane,	Gloucester,	10 68
71	Annie M. Loggie,	Northumberland,	7 02
72	Albina C. London,	Carleton,	4 74
73	Ada L. Lutz,	Westmorland,	9 36
74	Georgia A. Manzer,	Charlotte,	5 76
75	Kezia C. Maxwell,	Charlotte,	5 22
76	Annie G. Mitton,	Albert,	9 36
77	Minnie I. Mott,	Sunbury,	1 14
78	Annie L. Murphy,	Restigouche,	11 22
79	Ella M. McAdam,	Carleton,	3 78
80	Annie G. McAnulty,	Albert,	11 52
81	Georgia H. McCready,	Charlotte,	5 52
82	Lizzie B. McElwee,	Northumberland,	7 50
83	Isabella J. McKenzie,	Restigouche,	13 26
84	Katherine E. McLean,	Restigouche,	12 12
85	Jessie E. McLean,	St. John,	4 02
86	Perthenia O'Leary,	Kings,	7 68
87	Ettawanda Palmer,	Queens,	2 40
88	Bessie R. Porter,	Victoria,	6 60
90	Florence M. Roberts,	Queens,	4 20
91	Catherine Robinson,	Kings,	5 46
92	Mabel E. Schriver,	York,	2 94
93	Cora A. Sherwood,	Kings,	4 20
94	Agnes I. Smith,	York,	3 12
95	Winifred Thompson,	Westmorland,	12 00
96	Bertha L. Tozer,	Northumberland,	6 66
97	Luella A. True,	Carleton,	3 78
98	Victoria R. Turner,	Westmorland,	12 9[illegible]
99	Mary E. Turvey,	Restigouche,	11 2[illegible]
100	Linda M. Ultican,	Restigouche,	11 2[illegible]
		Forward......	$632 86

TABLE XVII.—Continued.

No.	Name.	County.	Amount.
		Brought forward	$632 88
101	Annie E. Vallis,	Queens,	3 54
102	Edith B. Wallace,	Victoria,	6 60
103	Kate S. Watling,	Northumberland,	7 80
104	Josephine M. Welch,	Carleton,	4 50
105	Francis P. West,	Carleton,	4 86
106	Ada I. Wright,	St. John,	4 02
107	Bessie M. Wright,	Restigouche,	12 60
108	Harriet W. Bo't,	St. John,	4 02
109	Annie M. Briggs,	York,	2 58
110	Janie S. Cameron,	York,	1 44
111	Bertha J. Crealock,	St. John,	4 02
112	Frances N. De Courcey,	Kings,	6 66
113	Myrtle A. Keith,	Westmorland,	9 00
114	Nellie J. Musgrove,	Kings,	6 42
115	Maggie N. O'Leary,	Kings,	7 20
116	Jennie R. Smith,	Sunbury,	1 50
117	Annie E. Wilson,	Kings,	6 66
118	*Grant Hawkins,	Carleton,	4 86
119	*Sadie B. Hogan,	Northumberland,	6 84
120	*Ella M. Gartley,	Carleton,	4 50
121	*Mary E. McMurray	St. John,	4 02
122	Joyime Cormier,	Madawaska,	6 84
123	Leonide Maillett,	Kent,	11 40
124	Jos. J. Mercure,	Madawaska,	8 10
125	J. Ed. Robichaud,	Northumberland,	8 76
126	M. Angele Albert,	Gloucester,	11 58
127	M. Catherine Babineau,	Kent,	10 20
128	Beatrice Cyr,	Madawaska,	9 00
129	Jeanne Doucett,	Gloucester,	10 32
130	Rose J. Doucett,	Gloucester,	11 58
131	Amanda M. Gaudet,	Westmorland,	10 56
132	M. A. Lucie LeGresley,	Gloucester,	11 16
133	M. Catherine Losier,	Gloucester,	10 20
133½	Josephine R. Maillet,	Kent,	9 90
		Forward......	$876 12

*In attendance previous term but claims for travelling expenses just matured.

TABLE XVII.—Continued.

No.	Name.	County.	Amount.
		Brought forward	$876 12
134	E. Helen Martin,	Madawaska,	8 10
135	Marie Michaud,	Madawaska,	9 96
136	M. A. Josephine Savoie,	Northumberland,	8 76
137	Marie Savoie,	Gloucester,	10 20
138	Catherine Theriault,	Gloucester,	11 40
		In Gov. War. No. 379.	$ 924 54

TABLE XVII.—CONTINUED. TERM ENDED DECEMBER, 1901.

No.	Name.	County.	Amount.
1	Howard B. Johnson,	Kings,	6 72
2	Elmor T. Kennedy,	Queens,	3 30
3	Leslie Murray,	Westmorland,	13 50
4	Samuel K. Nason,	York,	1 98
5	Annie P. Armstrong,	Victoria,	6 00
6	Maude E. Brophy,	St. John,	3 90
7	Sarah J. Bryson,	Sunbury,	66
8	E. Hope Crandall,	Carleton,	4 68
9	Anna M. Dibblee,	Carleton,	3 84
10	Emma J. Dougherty,	Carleton,	4 92
11	Eva M. W. Duke,	Kings,	5 34
12	Martha Elliott,	Kings,	7 68
13	Georgia B. Gunter,	York,	1 44
14	Mary Harrington,	St. John,	4 02
15	Lizzie J. R. Harvey,	York,	1 50
16	Ethel M. Hurley,	Gloucester,	10 98
17	Greta M. Jones,	Westmorland.	12 00
18	Mary W. McDiarmiad,	Northumberland,	7 50
18½	Minnie McDonald,	Northumberland,	5 28
18¾	Rosanna McNabb,	York,	4 08
19	Kathleen S. Marcy,	Carleton,	5 16
20	Mary M. H. Mooney,	Queens,	1 98
21	Mary L. Murphy,	Gloucester,	9 96
22	Hannah O'Donnell,	Carleton,	4 50
23	Olive H. Reid,	Queens,	3 90
24	A. Bertie Richardson,	Charlotte,	6 72
25	Margaret Riedle,	Kings,	6 42
26	Mary A. Wilson,	Charlotte,	5 22
27	Mary A. Mahoney,	St. John,	4 02
28	Louise G. B. Prescott,	Westmorland,	12 90
29	Abraham Vienneau,	Gloucester,	11 28
30	M. E. Cecile Landry,	Gloucester,	13 50
31	Jane G. Legere,	Gloucester,	11 58
32	Lizzie A. Levesque,	Madawaska,	7 50
		Gov. War. No. 963.	$ 213 96

TABLE XVIII.—PUBLIC SCHOOLS: YEAR ENDED 31ST OCTOBER, 1902.

Statement of Chief Superintendent's Provincial Drafts to Teachers and of County Fund Drafts to Trustees.

(Summarized in Tables IX., X. and XI.)

MEMORANDUM.	Provincial Drafts To Teachers.	County Fund Drafts To Trustees.
For Term Ended December 31st, 1901.		
References—In Warrants Nos. 379, 960	$70,658 95	
School for the Blind, Halifax, Warrant No. 379	1,105 91	
Amount County Fund, for term ended December 31st, 1901—Schools.		$45,396 63
School for the Blind, Halifax..........		1,105 91
Institution for the Deaf and Dumb, Fredericton..........		711 61
For Term Ended June 30th, 1902		
References—In Warrants Nos. 960, 961, 962.	91,568 24	
School for the Blind, Halifax, Warrant No. 967..........	1,087 50	
Amount County Fund, for term ended June 30th, 1902, Schools..........		46,683 78
School for the Blind, Halifax..........		1,087 50
Institution for the Deaf and Dumb, Fredericton..........		814 29
	$164,420 60	$95,799 72

TABLE XIX — SUMMARY OF THE PROVINCIAL GRANTS FOR THE SCHOOL SERVICE FOR THE YEAR ENDED OCTOBER 31ST, 1902.

Schools (See Table IX for details):		
Common, ...	$142,521 85	
Superior, ...	12,360 66	
Grammar, ...	7 344 68	
		$162,227 19
School for the Blind, Halifax, (Table XI), ...		2,193 41
Normal School: Salaries (Table XIV), ...		7,962 99
Travelling Allowance to Student Teachers, (Table XVII), ...		1,138 50
Inspectors' Salaries, ...		9 207 77
" Allowance, attending Conferences, ...		700 00
Education Office Salaries:		
Chief Superintendent, ...	$2,000 00	
Chief Clerk, ...	1,000 00	
Clerk.	800 00	
Clerk, ...	300 00	
Clerk, ...	54 00	
Clerks, (temporary)	127 67	
		4 281 67
Travelling Allowance to Chief Superintendent, ...		400 00
Incidental expenses:		
H. V. B Bridges, work on Course of Instruction, ...	$ 6 00	
John Brittain, part payment of expense of publishing proceedings of Educational Institute,	64 00	
Jos. McPeake, stenography, ...	3 50	
Charles Toner, trucking	5 10	
		78 60
Forward..............		$188,190 13

Brought forward		$188,190 13
Examination Expenses :		
License Examinations, December, 1901, and May and June 1902,		462 92
Departmental Examinations (Normal School Entrance, Matriculation and High School Leaving) June and July, 1902, ...	$803 57	
Less amount received in fees, ...	714 22	
		89 35
High School Entrance Examinations, ...		558 50
School Libraries, (Table XVI), ...		125 77
School House Grants (see statement in Chief Superintendent's Report,).		855 00
Conveyance of school children, ...		100 00
		$190,381 67

PART III.

APPENDICES.

APPENDIX A.

REPORT ON THE PROVINCIAL NORMAL SCHOOL FOR THE YEAR ENDED JUNE, 1902.

J. R. INCH, ESQ, LL., D.,
Chief Supt. of Education.

SIR: I have the honour to submit the following report on the Provincial Normal School for the year ended June, 1902.

As I did not enter upon duty till February, when nearly two-thirds of the session had passed, the report will lack completeness in some details.

From the official register it appears that the total enrolment for the year was 273, of which number 70 were young men. Of this total, 230 entered at the beginning of the session in September and 43 in January, the beginning of the second term. These numbers include the students attending the French Department of whom there were 4 during the first term and 9 the second—one of the former being a young man.

The Counties of the Province were severally represented as follows:—

Albert	14	Queens	17
Carleton	35	Restigouche	7
Charlotte	19	St. John	21
Gloucester	10	Sunbury	9
Kent	3	Victoria	2
Kings	25	Westmorland	37
Northumberland	28	York	38
Madawaska	7	Temiscouata (Quebec)	1

And the religious denominations as below:—

Baptist	66	Presbyterian	37
Ch. of England	35	R. Catholic	47
F. Baptist	26	Other Denominations	4
Methodist	58		

At the close of the first term in December, 40 of the enrolled number are recorded as recommended for examination for License of Class III. This recommendation implies that each of these candidates had received professional classification, but the recorded estimates on the scholarship of several of them do not warrant a recommendation for any class.

When the session closed in June, 208 were presented for examination for License as follows:—

For Class I.......................... 61
For Class II,......................... 157

Classification of the above according to "Teaching ability and Skill was:—

Superior, 0: Good, 100; Fair, 111; Not Classed, 7; and the classification in Vocal Music was:—Rote Singing and Theory, 10; Rote Singing, 16.

GENERAL INSTRUCTION.

The course of instruction as prescribed by the Board of Education for the Institution was for the most part faithfully and effectively carried out. One of these subjects, Book Keeping, has never received, and cannot, without serious loss to vastly more important work, receive much attention. If the subject is to be retained in the course, the most that can be done is to give the student some instruction in general principles through methods that may prove helpful, should he afterwards be called upon to teach it. There is another requirement in the course which has, without any valid reason, been largely overlooked. This is the recent regulation of the Board which requires each Instructor to discuss and illustrate the methods of teaching the special subjects assigned to him, and which also provides that he shall examine his class by written papers at least once in each term in the instruction he has thus given, and estimate the answers and that these estimates shall form an element in determining the students professional standing. The requirement is one which must greatly enhance the importance of method and ensure in a higher degree skilful work in the public schools. It also gives each member of the Faculty an interest and a responsibility in connection with the special work of the Institution and as a consequence their joint estimates of this work will be accepted with confidence. So far as the records show, however, it does not appear that the regulation has been complied with during the session under review.

PROFESSIONAL INSTRUCTION.

As no record or memo was left of the work that had been overtaken before I assumed duty, it was deemed advisable to give as complete a course on the subject as was practicable within the limited period. The course embraced principles and methods of teaching and school management, illustrative lessons, practice and criticism. The principles upon which all successful methods are based, were discussed. The study of psychology as a subject *in se* was deemed out of place in an institution which provides only one session of nine months for training the teacher. The established results of mental science were accepted as a basis and methods arising out of them were considered. School management embraced such subjects as organization, principles, and construction of time-tables, discipline, &c. The Model School affords illustrative lessons in the several subjects of the course. . The students had opportunities for practice both in the Model and Normal Departments. The lessons given in their own classroom were perhaps in one sense the most serviceable. Here a lesson is given in any grade of the course by a student to his own classmates who must for the time being assume to be of the same age as the pupils of the grade. The advantages are that the Teacher has to modify his methods to suit the assumed conditions. and the students are compelled to look at the subject from the children's standpoint and to answer the questions accordingly. One of the greatest needs of an inexperienced teacher is to look at things as children look at them and perhaps one of the best means of supplying this need is to accustom him to do so through such exercises. The criticisms which followed the practice lessons were often the means of bringing out in a practical way the fuller significance of a principle and of confirming or rectifying the student's knowledge. Outlines of lessons or lesson plans were occasionally required as were also written exercises in professional subjects. In addition to the above the senior class had lectures on the principles and practice of some of the earlier educational reformers as Comenius, Pestalozze, Froebel.

The Governor General's Medals for the highest professional standing in the Senior and the Junior class were awarded respectively to Miss Florence C. Estabrooks of St. John and Miss Bell M Eddy of Clifton, Gloucester Co.

With the large number of students and the comparatively limited staff it is impossible to give them that amount of practice which is needed. Sometimes criticisms, notes of lessons, &c., have to be accepted in lieu of practice. Each student should have an opportunity of regular or special practice three times at least during the session.

MODEL DEPARTMENT.

This department provides instruction in the first eight grades of the prescribed public school .course, and has a staff of four regularly licensed teachers. The schools practically form a part of the city school system, the Board of School Trustees under agreement with the Board of Education supplying the pupils to the number of about 200 and paying a part of the Teacher's salaries. The Teachers are, however, the appointees of the Board of Education and are under its control, and the schools are arranged and conducted so as to secure to the student-teachers facilities for observation and practice. There are therefore large demands made upon each of these schools but they need not and do not, under proper arrangements, interfere with the regular work. The illustrative lessons are such as should be given in any case, and the practice lessons which are given in the presence of the regular Teachers may be made helpful towards securing on the part of the pupil the valuable habit of testing the extent and accuracy of his knowledge. Moreover these demands are of great advantage to the school. They keep alive proper methods—a result which will prove of more value to the pupil than the instruction itself—and they act as incentives upon the Teachers to put forth their best work. Were all the city schools efficient as they are, subject to the same visitations, no school interest would suffer in any way.

SLOYD.

Instruction was given in this subject to all the student-teachers two hours per week. All without exception were much interested in the work, so much so indeed that they seemed as if they had awoke for the first time to the conscious possession of a new power. There is in the subject an educative value which far outweighs what is called its practical utility and and which would fully justify its introduction as an integral part of the school course. I sincerely hope that the Board of Education will make such provision for continuing this instruction as will give to the future student-teachers the same privileges as their predecessors have enjoyed for the last three years through the wise munificence of Sir William MacDonald.

PROFESSIONAL TRAINING FOR UNIVERSITY GRADUATES.

I have long been convinced of the importance of making some professional training obligatory on graduates in Arts, who propose to engage in teaching and who have never attended a Normal School. The service needs more men with that culture and breadth of view which a University supplies not only to maintain the scholarly character of our secondary education but to diffuse their broadening influence amongst those who have been less favoured and who have a tendency to fall into rote and routine. But these same gentlemen labour under considerable disadvantage when as Principals of graded schools, they find themselves incapable of judging of the real character of the work of their primary teachers or of giving them counsel as to suitable methods in varying circumstances. A course of one term's training suitable to graduates, or to undergraduates of the fourth year would benefit the whole service and bridge the gap in our otherwise complete system of training. Coming and going as many of the undergraduates have heretofore done as observers, just when it suited them, was useless to themselves, unsatisfactory to the Institution and not respectful to the Profession.

I have to thank the Instructors and Teachers of the whole Institution for their good service and cheerful co-operation in the work of the school, and yourself for introducing me in so kindly a manner to the student-teachers and for the interest you take in the Institution.

I have the honour to be, Sir,

Your obedient servant,

WM. CROCKET
Principal.

APPENDIX B.

INSPECTORS' REPORTS.

INSPECTORAL DISTRICT No. 1.

GEO. W. MERSEREAU, M.A., Inspector, Doaktown, N. B.

This District Embraces the County of Restigouche except the Parish of Balmoral and Districts No. 1½ Colborn and Balmoral and No. 3 Addington ; The County of Northumberland except the Parish of Rogersville and Districts 4, 5, 12, 13, 14 and 15 in the Parish of Alnwick : in the County of Kent the Parishes of Harcourt and Weldford, and Districts 1, 2, 5, 9, 10 and 13 in the Parish of Stanley in the County of York.

JAMES R. INCH, ESQ., LL. D.,
Chief Supt. of Education,
Fredericton, N. B.

SIR : I beg leave to submit my Annual Roport for 1902. As I have dealt so minutely with all the schools in my monthly reports, I shall do no more in this than notice briefly some of the salient features of the work as they presented themselves to me in daily rounds among the schools.

I am gratified to be able to report that owing to the revision of the Inspectorates on the appointment of the seventh Inspector it has been made possible for me to visit each ungraded school twice during the year. During the second term of this year I visited, with one exception, all the ungraded schools of my inspectorate that were kept open the full school hours on the days my arrangements were made to visit them. This is the first time in seventeen years that I have been able to do this, so for the future I hope to be able to have a closer supervision over the schools under my charge and to give more time to the professional aspects of my work than for many years. The distances I have to travel are just as great as ever, and to drive from one detached portion of my Inspectorate to another takes time that could be profitably spent in the schools were the several parts of my district continuous.

Teachers have been so scarce during the year that I have been compelled to recommend a greater number of Local Licenses than is good for the schools or the profession.

Though the Trustees of all the better class of districts appreciate the value of trained and experienced teachers and will engage none without testimonials of competency from some qualified authority, there are still some benighted districts that regard the keeping down of expense as of more importance than anything else. These latter are those that invariably fail to secure trained teachers and seem very willing to engage Local Licensees. In my opinion it would be better in such cases to allow the schools to remain closed than to issue Local Licenses. In that way the ordinary law of supply and demand would in course of time advance the salaries to a paying rate and thus induce many of our clever young people to remain in the profession.

There is in this Inspectorate a number of weak schools in remote and isolated communities that cannot afford salaries that would attract the better class of teachers. In times of scarcity Local Licenses might still be issued for these. I have been trying to confine the issue of Local Licenses to such districts and have met with a fair degree of success.

New school houses were built during the year in Nelson Village, No. 1, Nelson, and in Indiantown No. 3, Derby. I have not seen the former since its completion, but it is said to be a neat commodious structure, well suited to the requirements of the district and much nearer the centre of the district than the old one. It will accommodate three departments and thus do away with the overcrowding of the Primary Department about which I have frequently reported. The funds for the latter were raised by the Teacher, Miss Lottie E. Underhill, and the ladies of the district, by means of concerts, pie socials and the like.

The school house at Sevogle, No. 4, North Esk, has been extensively repaired, in fact, rebuilt, at a cost to the district that would have about built a new one.

These are about the largest outlays ; but much has been done in all the parishes in the way of ceiling, wainscotting, painting and repairs, supplying blackboards, maps, flags and flagpoles, blinds, and building fences, woodhouses, etc., to add to the usefulness and utility of the schools.

In Northumberland and Restigouche Counties the people value their schools, and an attempt to close one for a term, or part of a term meets with determined opposition. They may not have the true concept of what education is but they are firmly convinced of its desirability and thoroughly persuaded as to its utility in their children's life-equipment and readily assume financial burdens for its acquisition. They show this by not only keeping their schools open the year round, but in enclosing and beautifying the grounds, in providing apparatus, etc. In the Parishes of Kent County added to my Inspectorate by the last revision this is not so, at least to the same extent. The school houses are not painted, or in good repair, they are ill supplied with maps, blackboards, and other apparatus, the grounds are rarely enclosed and everything about the schools has an air of neglect and decay. There are some notable exceptions to this rule such as at Galloway, Grangeville and Mundleville and in the towns of Richibucto and Rexton. The cause of this is want of interest on the part of the people. As an illustration of this lack of interest I would say that when I made my first visit to the Parish of Weldford, in February, 1902, *ten* of the twenty-two schools of the Parish were closed and all but two of them remained closed till the end of the term, no effort being made to open them so far as I know. It is only fair to say that all these schools were opened the Second Term, but what value can be attached to education by these people and what must be the state of public opinion in these districts, many of them with twenty-five to thirty children, when such a state of affairs is allowed to exist.

It is to be deplored that there are so many parents even in the most progressive districts that always keep their schools open, who do not send their children to school, or send them so intermittently that they receive little benefit. Some penalty should be attached to such negligence which rightly regarded is a crime. As a rule the people who sin in this way are themselves lamentably ignorant and boast that they have got along well enough without education and their children can do the same. To their neighbors they seeem to be poor creatures, eking out a miserable existence by occasional "odd jobs" and in more questionable undertakings, and this dependence, wretchedness and misery they are leaving as a legacy to their children who thus become a source of weakness and danger rather than of strength and security to the state.

GRAMMAR SCHOOLS.

There are three Grammar Schools in this Inspectorate, at Chatham, Campbellton and Richibucto, and they are all doing a high grade of work when the conditions are taken into account. The Chatham School is the best equipped for advanced work in the number of teachers on its staff and in its accommodation and appliances. It has, however, but *one* Grammar School teacher when by its enrollment in the High School Grades it is entitled to *two*. The Trustees are alive to their privileges in this respect, and will, in the near future, arrange for departmental work in their High School, with teachers specially qualified for each group of subjects in the Collegiate Course. This is very essential in the Classical and Natural Science subjects especially. The Campbellton School has but one teacher for its High School work and it is marvellous how he can obtain the results he does. He has not the time to give a thoroughly practical course in the Natural Science subjects while he has all the work of Grades IX, X and XI. This school has the most progressive Board of Trustees of my Inspectorate, if not of the Province, and it will not be long before they will employ for Grade IX a teacher qualified to take a group of subjects throughout the High School Grades. The Richibucto School does not get the support from the town and county that it deserves. The parents are tinctured with the prevailing lack of interest already noticed as being a feature of the county. The enrollment at the time of my visit was twenty-two, a sufficient number if they came regularly. This large and populous county could surely supply a larger attendance to the only Public School within its borders qualified to prepare students for matriculation into the University of New Brunswick. Only *four* of the twenty-two were in Standard X, the highest standard in the school. Two of the four were studying Classics and Mathematics of the 11th Standard but the Principal did not think it wise to advance them to Grade XI and I quite agreed with him.

SUPERIOR SCHOOLS.

There are nine of these schools in my Inspectorate, viz., at Dalhousie, Newcastle, Douglastown, Blackville, Derby, Doaktown, Rexton, Harcourt and Bass River. They are for the most part doing fairly well the work for which they are intended. In a comparative estimate of their work I would rate Newcastle and Dalhousie among the best and Blackville and Douglastown among the poorest of these schools. As a matter of fact, Blackville can scarcely be ranked as a Superior School, so poorly do the pupils attend and so little interest is taken in the advanced work by anyone in the district. If better results are not shown at my next visit I shall be compelled to recommend that the Superior Grant be suspended, if not withdrawn from this school.

GRADED SCHOOLS.

For the most part the Graded Schools of this section do very satisfactory ork. The exceptions to this rule have been mentioned in my monthly ports. In the larger towns where there is but one grade in a room and where one would naturally expect to find perfect work, the surroundings afford many distractions to draw the pupils' minds away from their studies. Here the teacher's hardest task is to keep up the interest so as to stimulate the pupils to self exertion. Some fail to do this and their work degenerates into "grind" and "cram" of the worst description in which the pupil becomes merely a passive recipient. Hence the failures that have been noticed. In such rooms the discipline is notoriously bad and order is preserved by frequent resort to corporal punishment, a thing unknown in the best taught schools. In the smaller villages the outside attractions are not so great but the teacher has four grades to teach, and to do this so as to keep all constantly employed at interesting and educative work requires ability of a high order, perfected by years of experience. Appointments to these positions are not always decided by merit.

UNGRADED SCHOOLS.

I can assert with confidence that these schools are doing better work than ever before, that the school houses are more comfortable, more attractive and better supplied with apparatus, that the teachers are better educated have greater skill and are more devoted than at any time in the history of our free schools, and still they are not giving the satisfaction they gave years ago when they were much less efficient. The demands made upon this class of schools are much greater than they were. Many parents living in the rural districts are ambitious to have their children acquire as good an education as the town schools afford. They have neither the means nor the inclination to send their children away from home. They look to the district school for what they require. The consequence is that while in former years it was unusual to find in these schools pupils in advance of grade IV, now it is not unusual to find one or more classes in advance of Grade V. To this add the fact that the course is fuller than formerly and it will be readily seen that there are now demands made upon the country teacher not thought of in former times and that call for a combination of almost superhuman qualities to ensure success. That success is attained in the majority of cases proves the possession of these qualities by a majority of the teachers of rural schools

I shall give a brief review by Parishes of the portions of Restigouche and Kent counties which belong to my Inspectorate.

Durham —Lorne Settlement was unable to secure the services of a teacher for the second term. The Doyle Settlement School is increasing in size. The school in Sunnyside was closed during first term. Quinn's Point School House was repaired but it is still in great need of better furniture.

Colborne.—The four schools of this small but wealthy Parish were kept in operation during the year and were more than ordinarily satisfactorily conducted. On Heron Island some much needed repairs were made to the school house.

Dalhousie.—The attendance at Shannon Vale School has fallen off considerably the last year or two. At Summerside the attendance is on the increase. The school at Dalhousie Junction made some needed improvement. At Richardsville the school accommodation was taxed to its limit.

Addington—Glencoe has a very small but well conducted school. Glen Levit school had such a mixture of old and new readers in its classes that the teacher found it impossible to do good work in this subject. The Flat Lands school has two classes (Grades VI and VII) in advance of Grade V.

Eldon—There are four schools in this Parish, all small except at Churchville from which the teacher was absent on business the day of my visit.

Harcourt—District No. 5 has the Superior school of two departments, and a small miscellaneous school a couple of miles away from the superior school. It would be better in every way to have the pupils of this small school conveyed to the Superior school building. Adamsville and Adamsville West have very inferior schools, though the enrollment at the former is quite respectable. Grangeville had the best school in the Parish at the time of my visit in September.

Weldford—There are far too many schools in this Parish closed in the winter, for good results to be expected. All the schools opened second term but the smallpox broke out while I was making my tour among them and many of them were closed by order of the Board of Health. Brown's Yard keeps its school open during the summer only. If it continues this practice I shall recommend that it be joined to Bass River district. The upper Main River school house is sadly out of repair. The school at Bass River Point improved considerably during the year. Main River school should be one of the best in the Parish and should not be closed a single school day in the year. The Mundleville school was closed during first term. East Branch was open only second term and the same is true of Brown's Yard, Harley Road, Upper Main River, Smith's Corner and East Branch. Some repairs were made in South Branch school house. St. Norbert keeps school egularly but the pupils advance little beyond Grade II. Louisbourg repaired ıe inside of its school house during summer vacation. Maple Ridge is a ›w district. Beersville has a large enrollment and should never be closed ɜ it was first term. Bend Road had no school for over two years till near he middle of second term.

Richibucto—East Galloway had not operated a school for a year before the begining of second term. Mill Creek and Upper Mill Creek should be joined. The two would make one good district that could keep a school continuously and could afford decent school accommodation and appliances The trustees of the town of Richibucto made extensive repairs on the outside of the Grammar School building and will repaint and refurnish the rooms as funds permit. The school house at Jardine's Yard is a very poor affair and should be replaced by a new building.

ARBOR DAY.

Arbor Day was observed by about the usual number of schools in about the usual manner—part house cleaning and part holiday, with some crude attempt at tree planting, not a whit more skilful than on the first Arbor Day now many years ago.

I had hoped that the yearly observance of Arbor Day in the schools would lead to an interest being taken throughout the country, not only in tree-planting and care of trees but in the whole subject of Forestry, and that in a few years when the school grounds had become plentifully supplied with trees, the roads and byways would receive attention, and finally that each waste place would receive similar treatment and thus become "a thing of beauty and a joy forever." Greater progress would undoubtedly be made in our schools could we have districts large enough to embrace Parishes or even larger areas, with the Boards of Trustees partly appointed by the Board of Education and partly appointed by the County Council or elected at the Parish meeting. We would thus get quit of the narrowness and petty jealousies that now hamper our advance.

MANUAL TRAINING.

The School Boards in several of the towns of this Inspectorate are seriously considering the advisability of opening departments of manual training. The Campbellton Board, always foremost in everything that gives promise of advantage to its schools, has arranged to open a manual training department at the beginning of next school year, the first so far as I can ascertain, to be opened in the Province under the Act passed last session of the legislature.

I have the honor to be, Sir,

Your obedient servant,

GEO. W. MERSEREAU.

INSPECTORAL DISTRICT No. 2.

GEO. SMITH, A. B., Inspector, Sackville, N. B.

This District comprises the County of Westmorland and the Parishes of Coverdale, Hillsborough, Hopewell and Harvey in Albert County.

JAMES R. INCH, ESQ., LL. D.,
Chief Supt. of Education,
Fredericton, N. B.

SIR:—I have the honor to forward my Report for 1902.

The usual number of schools were in operation during the year. A few districts have not a sufficient number of pupils to maintain a school. These are Taylor Village, No. 22, Dorchester, which has only one child of school age, Second Westcock, No. 1, Sackville, and Coles Island, No. 8, Sackville. Some of the pupils of this district attend the school in No. 9, Middleton. No. 3, Dorchester, ran a school last term with an enrolment of four pupils. The pupils of this district are within reach of the Dorchester School and attended there for one term.

New school houses have been built during the year in Murray Road district, No. 13, Botsford, and in Long Lake, No. 23, Botsford. In Forest Glen district, No. 2, Salisbury, the school house has been moved to a more suitable location and an additional department built, so that this is now a graded school of two departments, and the school accommodation is much better suited to the needs of the district. The credit of this improved accommodation is largely due to the efforts of Mr. T. W. Colpitts. The usual amount of general improvements have been made in the various districts during the year. A new school house is needed in Hicksville, No. 15, Salisbury and Havelock.

WESTMORLAND COUNTY.

SUPERIOR SCHOOLS.

At the end of the year Mr. R. D. Hanson, M. A., resigned his position principal of the school at Petitcodiac to accept the principalship of the athurst Grammar School. Mr. Harry Burns, B. A., was appointed to the etitcodiac School. Mr. Burnett and Miss Laura Fowler continued to do :ood work in the Intermediate and Primary departments. Mr. A. C. M.

Lawson was followed by Mr. M. J. Wallace, in the Salisbury school at the beginning of the year. This school which for several years has been a school of three departments was at the first of the year reduced to two departments. I understand, however, that the Board of Trustees contemplate again establishing the third department. Mr. H. B. Steeves, B. SC., who very successfully filled the position of principal of the Dorchester School for the year ended 30th June, resigned to accept a position on the High School staff in Moncton city. Mr. B. P. Steeves followed him as principal of this school. The other teachers are Mr. T. T. Goodwin, Miss Nichol, Miss Alice Alward, and Miss Chambers, Mr. F. A. Dixon, M. A. remains principal of the school in No. 9, Sackville. He has for associate teachers Mr. Barnes, Miss Ramsay, and Miss Brownell. Mr. Fred. S. James followed Mr. McKnight in the School in No. 11, Sackville, and Mr. J. T. Allen followed Mr. Field in the Port Elgin School at the beginning of the year. Mr. Fitzpatrick and Miss Birdie Doyle are Mr. Allen's associate teachers. Mr. Webb remains principal of the Shediac School. He has associated with him Miss Jessie MacDougall, and Miss Nesbit.

OTHER GRADED SCHOOLS.

Besides the Superior Schools there are in this county graded schools of two departments each, in Fox Creek, No. 3, Moncton; Mill, No. 9, Moncton; Lewisville, No. 10, Moncton; Lutz Mountain, No. 16, Moncton; Forest Glen, No. 2, Salisbury, and Baie Verte, No. 2, Westmorland.

In many of the ungraded schools work beyond the requirements of Grade V is done, and as many of these schools have a large enrolment especially during the winter months the work for one teacher becomes very heavy. More of these schools should have class-rooms and employ regular assistants.

ALBERT COUNTY.

SUPERIOR SCHOOLS.

Mr. Wm. M. Burns was appointed principal of the Hillsboro school on the retirement of Mr. Fred S. James at the end of the year. Miss Deborah Bishop and Miss Beatrice Steeves remain in the Intermediate and Primary departments. Mr. H. H. Stuart remains principal of the Hopewell Hill School with Miss Grace McGorman in the Primary department.

OTHER GRADED SCHOOLS.

Besides the Superior schools there are in my Inspectorate in this county schools of two departments in Harvey Corner district, No. 3, Harvey; Riverside No. 1, Hopewell; Hopewell Cape, No. 7, Hopewell; Albert No. 10, Hopewell; Surrey, No. 3, Hillsboro'; and Demorselle Creek, No. 5, Hillsboro'. The Dawson Settlement School is now being operated with a teacher and an assistant.

The work done throughout the year has been on the whole quite satisfactory. The work in the Superior and other graded schools very satisfactory.

MONCTON CITY.

The High School staff suffered a loss in the retirement of Mr. Acheson who received an appointment in South Africa. Mr. W. A. Cowperthwaite, M. A., was appointed to fill the vacancy. The schools throughout the city continue to maintain their high standard of efficiency. A careful and judicious oversight is exercised over the schools by the painstaking and competent Superintendent, Mr. F. A. McCully, M. A., LL. B., who possesses in a high degree the happy faculty of adjusting any difficulty that may arise.

Should the principle of centralization which is being now advocated be adopted, and I hope it will be, there will be ample opportunity for carrying out the principle in this Inspectorate, as there are many populous and wealthy districts with school houses at very short distances apart. This is especially true of certain sections of Albert County where this plan could be carried out to the advantage of all concerned.

The Westmorland County Institute met at Port Elgin, and the Albert County Institute at Hopewell Hill. As it was not my privilege to attend either I cannot speak from personal knowledge, but from reports received I learn that both Institutes were as usual successful in a high degree.

The usual amount of improvements, external and internal, were made on Arbor Day.

I have the honour to be, Sir,

Your obedient servant,

GEO. SMITH.

INSPECTORAL DISTRICT No. 3.

R. P. STEEVES, M. A., Inspector, Sussex, K. C.

This District comprises the Parishes of Elgin and Alma in the County of Albert, the County of Kings, East of the St. John River, aud the County of Queens except the Parishes of Canning, Gagetown, Hampstead, Petersville and Chipman

J. R. INCH, ESQ., LL D.,
Chief Supt. of Education,
Fredericton, N. B.

SIR:—I beg to submit the following report on the condition of the public schools in Inspectoral district No. 3, for the year ending Dec. 31, 1902.

A scarcity in the supply of teachers has existed throughout the year. During the winter term I felt it advisable to recommend granting a few local licenses. The schools in districts in which such local licensed teachers were employed, were for the most part very inefficient, and therefore unsatisfactory to me. I find also that many rate payers disapprove of untrained teachers being employed. Accordingly, I have recommended no one for local license during the summer term, although many districts have for this reason been without schools.

The practice of not opening school in the summer term until about the first of September appears to be growing in country districts. The services of the larger children are needed at home, and parents are not desirous that the younger children should go to school until the days of the greatest summer heat are gone.

I am able to say that the number of schools in which a very good class of work is being done, is increasing. Perhaps more than the usual amount of attention has been given to the care of school property, and a corresponding improvement in the appearance of school houses, premises, furniture and apparatus is the result.

GRADED SCHOOLS.

The Alma grammar school continues in charge of T. E. Colpitts, Esq., B. A. The primary department is taught by Miss Evelyn Bennett. Both departments have a large number of pupils. Mr. Colpitt's room needs refurnishing. The work of this school would be more efficient if another department were established, as the principal has far too many grades to teach.

The frequent changes in the principalship of the Sussex grammar school necessarily affect to a considerable extent the thoroughness of the work done. Mr. A. B. Maggs, M. A. (Harv.), and Mr. W. C. Jonah, two very competent teachers, are now in charge of the grammar department. It is to be hoped, in the best interest of the school, that these gentlemen may be induced to remain in charge for a lengthened period. The enrollment of pupils in all the schools of the town is increasing each year. Before long the trustees and people will find themselves face to face with a problem of supplying enlarged accommodation.

Mr. Rex Cormier continues in charge of the Hampton superior school, with good success. At the time of my visit last spring I was able to note a marked improvement in both departments. Miss Frances Prichard is the primary teacher.

The Bloomfield superior school has a very small attendance of pupils in both departments. Mr. B. P. Steeves, B. A. and Miss Ada Wetmore were the teachers for the winter term. Since that time there has been a change in the principalship. It is my opinion that district No. 6, Norton, which has a considerable child population, and in which there has been no school for a number of years, should be united with district No. 2, in which is the superior school of the parish, and I intend to recommend the same to the Board at an early date.

The Apohaqui superior school had a complete change of teachers at the begining of the summer term. Mr. Geo. McCrea and Miss Ada Northup assuming charge at that time. The enrollment in this school is also quite small, but I think not quite so small as it was a year ago. There is besides a feeling of confidence in the efficiency of the school which augurs well for its future success.

The work of the Penobsquis superior school I found at my last visit to be highly satisfactory, in both departments. Quite extensive repairs have since been made to the principal's room and new black-boards have been supplied. Principal G. T. Morton has resigned his position, and retires from the profession after many years of successful work.

Since the re-arrangement of grades in Havelock superior school, more satisfactory work has been shown, but there are far too many changes in the teachers, especially of principal, for the best results to be attained in the school.

The Elgin superior school has a very large enrollment of pupils. Another department should be opened. The assessable valuation of the district however, is not very large, and it seems difficult to convince the people of the present in-efficient service.

There is little of special interest to report of the Hampton Village school (three departments). Mr. Orton Grey is the principal, Miss Margaret M. Stewart successfully conducts the primary department. I have strong hope that before long, Hampton Village and Hampton Station districts will unite and have a central school, which will also be able to accommodate two other outlying districts. Many of the rate payers are in favor of such a union, which, I think, could not fail to be beneficial in a very high degree.

I hope that the trustees of Norton Station district No. 1. Norton, will, before long see their way clear to the erection of a good school building which is much needed. The number of children in the district is large. With a new house and a good staff of teachers there is an opportunity to have one of the best schools in the country.

A very efficient school is maintained at Sussex Corner. Both teachers have been in charge for some time. A supply of very excellent furniture has recently been provided.

UNGRADED SCHOOLS.

Albert Co.—Nos. 2, 3, and 6, Alma have had schools both terms this year. In No. 2 the school did not open in the summer term until quite late, as a teacher could not be procured. Hastings, No. 3 has procured some new furniture and some apparatus. In Sinclair Hill, No. 6, the school is very small. Hebron, No. 8, has a larger number of pupils than for some time past. Kerry, No. 7, has had no school because a teacher could not be obtained.

No. 4, Elgin, has had a school during a portion of the summer term. Collier, No. 6, Elgin, is sadly in need of a new school house. I have brought the matter to the attention of the trustees, and trust that a new school house will be built next summer. Mullins, No. 8, has a school house in very poor condition. Steps are being taken to repair it. New furniture has been provided. Pleasant Vale, No. 11, has a very good school indeed. It ranks among the best ungraded schools in this Inspectorate. Graves Settlement No. 18, had a school during the summer term—the first in several years. Nos. 7, 19 and 15, in the parish of Elgin were unable to get teachers.

Queens Co—At the time of my visit to the parish of Brunswick, there were but two schools in operation, Nos. 1 and 3. Other districts were seeking teachers but with little prospect of success.

District No. 4, Cambridge, has repaired its school house, so that the inside now presents quite a respectable appearance and it must be quite comfortable. New furnitu1e is needed. Mill Cove, No. 6, had no school during the summer term. Trustees found it difficult to find a teacher. The house has been supplied with new furniture.

Thorne Town, No 3, Johnston, has a very poor equipment of maps and apparatus. The attention of the trustees has been frequently called to the needs of the school. I should regret if I am compelled to recommend sterner measures. Lower Rapids, No. 6, was without a school the summer term. The probabilities are, that before very long, No. 7, Johnston, must have a school. There has been no school in this district for ten or eleven years. Upper Salmon Creek, No. 13, Johnston, has provided new furniture. Nos. 2, 7 and 11, are the only districts in the parish of Johnston in which there has been no school some time during the year.

No. 3, Waterboro, has very well repaired the school house and provided new furniture. Nos. 5 and 6 have not yet been united. Both have had schools some time during the year. In both, the attendance is quite small. A union is most desirable. I hope, when I visit Young's Cove, No. 7 and Wiggin's Cove, No. 10, to find the school property in better condition than at my last visit.

The only district in the parish of Wickham not having school the summer term was Lewis' Cove, No. 8. The enrollment in Carpenter, No. 2, is very small.

Kings Co.—Goshen, No 4, Cardwell, has made some repairs to school house, and is again operating a school. Portage, No. 6, had no school during the summer term. The number of children in the district is quite small. The school house in Moore's Mills, No. 7, needs painting, as does also the school house in No. 8, after repairs have been made.

Saddleback, No. 5, has ceased to operate a school, as has also Londonderry No. 3, Hammond. Cause—very few or no children. No. 2 has again no school. The enrollment the last term the school was in operation was small. Martin's Head Road No. 7 is mostly wilderness land and should be made a part of Hammond Vale, district No. 4. os. 4 and 6 have the largest schools in Hammond parish.

Groom's Cove, No. 8, Hampton, has made thorough repairs to the school house. It is now a comfortable and respectable building. District No. 4, has had no school for about three years. In No. 7 the school house is dilapidated and presents a forsaken appearance. Through the efforts of a former teacher, new furniture has been procured. Nos. 5, and 9, offer an excellent opportunity for centralization—both schools are quite small.

Elmwood No. 23, Havelock, has at present so few children to attend school, that none can be maintained. Canaan Road, No. 10, has provided new furniture, a hard-wood floor, and considerable apparatus. Springhill, No. 9, does not keep the school fence and grounds in good condition. They are untidy. Elm Corner, No. 7, on account of the large number of pupils in the district, has consented to grade the school, and two teachers will hereafter be employed. There has been no school in Perry Settlement, No. 3, throughout the year. The school in Anagance Ridge, No. 1, is very large. The capacity of the new school house is over-taxed. A gradual improvement in the school and school property in Corn Hill, No. 2, is taking place. There was no school in White's Mountains, No. 4, during the winter term.

There are six districts in the Parish of Kars. Four of them at least should be united, and a good school house built at Downeyville. Such a school would have no more than fifty or sixty pupils. Eastern Kars has a smaller attendance than any school in the Parish. It is however so remotely situated, it would be very difficult to unite the district with any other.

At Kingston Village, in the Parish of Kingston, the McDonald centralized school is expected to be in operation in September next. Five districts, I believe, are to unite, and the experiment of centralizing schools on an extended scale, so far at least as this Province is concerned, will be given a fair trial. Walton Lake, No. 14, which for some time has been without a school, had school during the summer term.

There was no school in Lower Norton, No. 4, Norton, during the winter term. A teacher was engaged who taught only a few days. A good school was in operation the summer term. At the time of my visit to District No. 5, Norton, the school had not been opened. Miss Mabel Chapman was in charge of the school throughout the year. There has been no school in Middleton, No. 11, for some time past.

Forrester's Cove, No. 6, Rothesay, has procured by means of a social, good school furniture. Much credit is due to Miss Gallagher, the teacher, for her efforts on behalf of the school. The school house is becoming dilapitated. I have called the Trustees' attention to the necessity for repairs at once. All the working districts in this Parish have had school during the year. Westmorland Road, No. 1, is defunct.

Pascobac, No. 16, Springfield, has not sufficient room accommodation for the number of pupils attending school. The furniture is also poor. Brunswick, District No. 7, has thoroughly repaired its school house inside and out, but owing to difficulties in the district, there was no school during the summer term. Kiersteadville, No. 8, has again a school in operation. District No. 1, is lacking some needful apparatus. The school is not as satisfactory as I should like. East Scotch Settlement, No. 5, has now good furniture and a very good school room. In District No. 2, the enrollment is very small, but the school has been very efficiently conducted.

All districts in the parish of Studholm, with the exception of Nos. 1, 2 and 22, have had school some portion of the year, most of them throughout the year. New furniture is needed in the school at Lower Millstream, District No. 13. This District has a large number of children, and consequently a class-room assistant, holding a regular provincial license, is employed. The apparatus in the school is indifferent. In Summerfield, No. 5, some repairs have been made to school property, and a supply of apparatus obtained. Sheck, No. 2, has, I understand, on my recommendation, enlarged the school house. Carsonville, No. 4, is steadily improving its school, and the condition of its school property. A very good class of work is being done at Newtown, No. 8. Some needful apparatus should be procured in Collina School, District No. 15, but as their new school house is not yet paid for, I have not urged them too strongly. Improvements have been made to the school house in Fenwick District, No. 17. It looks better and is more comfortable. District No. 16, lacks a good deal of necessary apparatus for an efficient school. I have called the Trustees' attention to the needs, but have, as yet, received no intimation of compliance with my request.

New furniture and black-boards have been supplied for the school in Ward's Creek, District No. 7, Sussex. The school in Ratter's Corner, No. 11, is very small. It is doubtful whether the school can be continued. Very satisfactory work indeed continues to be done in Drury's Cove, No. 16. The same teacher has been in charge for over seven years.

Primrose, Border District, No. 2, Upham, which has had no school for some time, has under pressure again opened its school house doors to the children. Connor Settlement, No. 25, had a school during a part of the winter term. The Titusville School, District No. 3, is in need of new furniture. New furniture has recently been provided for the school in Barnesville, No. 1.

In Wallace, No. 9, Waterford, there has been no school throughout the year. Trustees say they could not find a teacher. Donegal, No. 4, has had no school for a similar reason.

Kennebecasis Island, No. 9, Westfield, has a very poor school house. I have recommended that a new one be built.

During the year, I have visited 404 schools and districts—230 during the winter term and 174 the summer term. I have made more than the usual number of written reports to Trustees, and have held several public meetings of rate-payers. I have endeavored to impress upon the people the advantanges to be derived from uniting weak and sparsely settled districts. It is quite easy to convince them of the greater efficiency that would result n school work, but the fear of increased expense delays action.

The annual meeting of the Kings County Institute was held at Hampton in September. A public meeting, largely attended, was held in the hall at Hampton Village. Interesting and instructive addresses were delivered by the Chief Superintendent of Education, Prof. W. T. Raymond, and others.

I have the honor to be,

Your obedient servant,

R. P. STEEVES.

Dec. 31, 1902.

INSPECTORAL DISTRICT, NO. 4.

W. S. CARTER, A. M., Inspector, St. John, N. B.

This District embraces the Counties of St. John and Charlotte.

J. R. INCH, ESQ., LL. D.
Chief Supt. of Education,
Fredericton, N. B.

SIR:—I beg to submit the following report for the year ended December 31st. 1902.

I have been able to overtake my work during both terms and not more than three schools in operation at the time of my visits have not been inspected.

Since my last report I have been relieved from the work in the parishes of Westfield, Greenwich and Clarendon, embracing in all about seventeen organized districts.

While having as much or more than I can do well, without these parishes, I feel regret leaving them as they contained very satisfactory schools and I had many pleasant associations with the people.

As I reported by parishes last year I will follow my usual plan and report more generally this year.

The School District.—There is an increase in the number of graded schools each year and possibly a small shrinkage in the number of ungraded. The city of St. John now employs about one hundred and sixty teachers—at the time of the union there were in the vicinity of one hundred and forty.

During both terms there were a few schools that were unable to obtain teachers.

There are a number of districts in which the attendance does not come up to the legal requirement and some of these could with great advantage unite with adjacent ones.

Centralization is becoming better understood, though there are yet many who are fearful of its results. As I have stated before, some object lessons are needed, and it would be of the greatest benefit if some circulars giving results in other places and explaining the general advantages of the plan were issued for general circulation. This has been done with excellent results in several states to the south of us.

The most instructive object lesson in this province will be that furnished by the Sir William Macdonald central school at Kingston which Prof. Robertson expects to open in September next. The experiment will prove the more educative as the group of schools will be entirely rural and ungraded.

Centralization on Campobello continues to give the utmost satisfaction.

I am still most strongly of the opinion that before any general or successful scheme of centralization can be carried out, that district school boards will have to give place to parish or, as they are styled in other places, township school boards.

Such boards would be better able to overcome the petty local feelings that often interfere now to prevent consolidation. There would be much more sentiment favourable to centralization if every man could be sure that the central school would be in his own district. From the wider field for selection, such boards should be more progressive and intelligent and as in the towns some of the members should be appointed by the Board of Education. It would ensure independent action as to the location of the schools, greater permanency and I believe, better salaries for the teachers.

In matters relating to assessment the change would be greatly advantageous.

It seems desirable that some change should be made in the manner of appointing assessors as considerable dissatisfaction is caused by their unequal valuations.

Being at present the appointees of parish councillors, their work seems rather in the direction, in too many cases, of pleasing the powers that be, than of arriving at a just and true valuation. The whole tendency is in the direction of lower values, and the estimates in different parishes vary greatly. This results in a large number of poor districts.

There has been fully as much improvement in building and renovating school buildings as in other years.

In St. John City, West, the La Tour, a very fine new building, has been occupied.

In the North End of the city, the Dufferin is in course of erection. It is to take the place of the old Madras building and will provide ten rooms and an exhibition hall. It promises to be the equal if not the superior of any school building in the city.

The new school house at Dewolf, Charlotte Co. was occupied at the beginning of the year, and is well suited to the needs of the district. A fine new house has, during the year, been built at Whittier's Ridge, Charlotte Co. It will be opened at the beginning of 1903.

Prince of Wales, St. John Co., has almost completely rebuilt its house,

The following districts have made improvements of various kinds during the year.

Charlotte Co.—Seely's Cove, Beaver Harbour, Head of Letang Mascarene, Basswood Ridge, Lawrence, Hill's Point, Young Dist., Ledge, Crocker Hill. Bartlett's Mills Bay Road, Waweig, Orr, Levar, Oak Bay, Old Ridge, Valley Park, Lower Bocabec, Bocabec Ridge, McCallum, St. Andrews, Indian Island, Fair Haven, Wilson's Beach, Welshpool, Seal Cove, Two Islands, Roix, Clarence Ridge, Letete, Back Bay, Burns, Greenock, Baillie, Anderson, Central Tower Hill, Gleason Road, Pomroy Ridge, Upper Mills, Pennfield Ridge and North Head.

St. John Co—Musquash, Coldbrook, Golden Grove, Red Head, Mispec, Little River, Pisarinco E, Handford Brook, Bains Cor., Fairfield, Coldbrook (nail factory), Green Head, Greer, Lorne Hill, Milford and Quaco.

New or enlarged accommodation is required in Blacks Harbour, Bu-- and Pomroy Ridge in Charlotte County, and in Fairville and Garnett in John County.

There has been the usual interest taken in libraries, pictures and proved apparatus.

Teachers.—Teachers are scarce and this state of affairs will continue so long as other vocations offer stronger inducements to our young men and women. Business offices and hospitals continue to attract our best teachers and lately they have been in demand not only in South Africa, but in our own North West and the United States.

I have rather given up the expectation that our most intelligent school boards would endeavour to stem this tide by offering stronger inducements to good teachers, but where College graduates are appraised at $150 per year in a city and experienced teachers are placed upon the same footing as inexperienced, and allowed to retire because of a request for a paltry increase of salary after years of faithful service, what are the inducements for teachers?

The United States are getting our most highly cultured teachers at a great cost to us. The graded schools will be the last to feel the pinch, but to them it will surely come later, in the form of inferior qualifications. People have to pay more for every thing than formerly, except education, and the expenditure for that, in as far as teachers are concerned, remains stationary or has become less. The cost of living has increased to them as to everyone else, and the towns should set the example and give their teachers a substantial increase of pay. Some deserved increases have been given during the year to the higher grade teachers, which is a healthy sign and is a tendency which I hope will extend downward without delay. The only sure remedy is the fixing of a minimum salary for all classes of teachers, for, as long as country districts can get local licensed teachers, many of them will be indifferent to the class or quality.

I have recommended more local licenses this year than for a long time.

Space will not permit a reference to all the excellent teachers who have left the service during the year. Miss Maud Narraway of the St. John High School Staff retired to the regret of all interested in the school. Few teachers have enjoyed the confidence and esteem of the citizens to a greater degree than Miss Narraway. Miss Jessie Whitlock, one of St. Stephen's best primary teachers also retired, followed by the best wishes of all. Mr. Angus Dewar, after a very successful year's service in Fairville, resigned as l also Miss Annie Simpson, who had successfully conducted the inter- .ediate department in the same place for several years. Both teachers joyed the esteem of the community and their resignation was caused by refusal of the Board to grant them an increase in salary.

The St. John Board has been so fortunate as to secure the services of Mr. William Brodie, a post graduate of Harvard and a gentleman of the best culture and excellent reputation as a teacher.

My teachers have been active as usual in promoting the material interests in their districts and much improvement in the way of libraries, school decoration, flags, apparatus, school grounds and premises has been the result. While I have not room to particularize in the case of each teacher I give the names with apologies for any omissions.

Charlotte County —M. Lizzie Knight, Mary Hawkins, Mildred McCann, Will Whitney, Louise Milliken, Mary W. Finlay, Cecilia Craig, Florence Cunningham, Mabel Jones, Annie L. Adams, Jennie McIntire, Evelyn Boone, J. A. Allen, Agnes Cummings, Margaret S. McNabb, Jas. A. Edmonds, Harriet Bolt, John Clindinnin, Georgia McCready, Cecil Hewitt, Nellie Polley, Margaret Hyslop.

St. John County.—Isabelle Patchell, May Watters, Kate Girdwood, Alice M. Dohaney, Katie McPartland, Hannah Floyd, Sadie Turner, Florence Debow, W. . McDiarmid.

Pupils.—The attendance in both St. John and Charlotte Counties was greatly curtailed by the outbreak of smallpox during the winter. Several schools were closed altogether and in all the fear of contagion kept many pupils from school. In the western part of Charlotte County there was almost a panic for a time. There were great numbers of children vaccinated with no ill affects, and the Boards of Health have notified teachers not to admit pupils who have not been vaccinated. There has arisen an unreasoning opposition in some localities to such a very proper safeguard and some districts are threatening to close their schools preferring ignorance to vaccination.

The boy question has been much in evidence in St. John City especially, during the year. There is no doubt that non-attendance at school and truancy exist in the cities. Parental control is often weak and there is at present no means but it, to check these evils. Public sentiment has been quickened by the recent occurrences in our midst, but it is doubtful if it is as yet sufficiently pronounced to vigorously enforce a compulsory law. It is rather peculiar that in Ontario and Nova Scotia, where the enforceme of attendance is optional with districts, and must be voted upon each yeai that they always vote in favour of it and with equal unanimity fail to carr out its provisions.

It seems to me that if in each city the police officers had power to summon idle boys before the magistrate, who might have power to order them to school or to go to the reformatory for a term, that a good effect would be had.

The evil of employing young children in factories, while not extensive at present in my district is yet a growing one and should be looked to. In some districts in the vicinity of sardine and other factories, the schools are either closed in the packing season or their attendance is very small. Numbers of children from the Island districts go each year to work in the factories at Eastport and Lubec. The effect is very demoralizing, but there seems no remedy for this.

Course of Instruction.—There have been few changes during the year. It would be difficult to devise a course of study that would give rise to no criticism and the teachers display much divergence in opinion on many points. The new history meets with approval but the geography is not so satisfactory. I find it difficult to induce teachers to become less mechanical and to devote more attention to oral and mental arithmetic. I think it would be well to assign a mental arithmetic paper for license as was done some years ago. Much intelligent attention is given to spelling and writing and the results are good.

The teachers in country districts are rather disposed to put off the teaching of the Natural Science subjects, and to neglect them for the others. There is not great enthusiasm in the pursuit of these subjects among city teachers.

With grammar as arithmetic there is too much attention to text book. Our pupils do not generally express themselves well either orally or in writing.

Modern Education.—A great awakening is taking place as to the value of Manual Training, Domestic Science, Experimental Gardening and Commercial Training as factors in education.

Sir William MacDonald's foresight and generosity are beginning to bear fruit in this Province as it has done in others.

Each teacher who has come out from the school in Fredericton has done more or less missionary work, with the result that preparations have been r--d- or will be made soon to introduce Manual Training in many places.

ı my own district Musquash School under the tuition of Miss Agnes .ɟ has had three benches in operation for the year.

'Iascarene has through the exertions of the teacher, Miss Harriet Bolt, equipped to begin work at the beginning of the next term.

St. Andrews will provide Manual Training at the same time. It has been one of the first, if not the first town in the Province to inaugurate this work.

I am informed that St. Stephen and Milltown have agreed to unite to employ a teacher for this work in September next.

I regret that nothing tangible in this direction has been done in St. John, which many looked to, to take the lead.

I think in order to give proper balance that Domestic Science should be introduced where possible.

I have pleasure in reporting that by the exertions of Miss Katie McPartland, teacher at Bain's Corner, St. John Co., interest was aroused in the district and all assisted to fence, plough, and grade the very commodious school ground there. Many trees were planted, a beautiful flower garden laid out, and seeds of various kinds were obtained from Ottawa and planted. The result—the work of teachers and pupils—was a fine crop of excellent vegetables. This is the first example of experimental gardening in my district.

The Trustees of St. Stephen and Milltown have not as yet availed themselves of the permission obtained from the Board of Education two years ago to introduce Modern Commercial Training into their schools.

The indications are that such will soon be introduced into the schools of St. John. Mayor White, who is also a school trustee, has taken the matter in hand and I hope his efforts may be successful. The St. John High School with its facilities and large staff of teachers should be well able to grapple successfully with the work and give the training that students have now to seek at Business Colleges.

School Grounds.—Mr. F. A. Holmes, renewed his offer of prizes for the greatest amount of improvement to school grounds during the year in the Island districts.

North Head, Grand Manan, won first prize and Welshpool, Campobello, second prize.

The school grounds of Little Ridgeton and Basswood Ridge, Charlotte County, and Bain's Corner, Fairfield and Quaco, St. John Co., are worthy of special mention.

I regret to report that no special provision has been made in any of th town schools for systematic instruction in music.

In St. John County a very largely attended and excellent Count Institute was held in September.

No meeting of the Charlotte County Institute was held during the year owing to the meeting of the Summer School of Science in St. Stephen in July and August. The Summer School was well attended and its officers state that it was one of the best meetings in its history.

Respectfully submitted,

W. S. CARTER.

INSPECTORAL DISTRICT No. 5.

H. V. B. BRIDGES, M. A. Inspector, Fredericton.

This District embraces the County of Kings, west of St John River; the Parishes of Gagetown Petersville, Hampstead, Canning and Chipman, in Queens County; the County of Sunbury; the County of York, except the Parishes of North Lake, Canterbury. McAdam and Southampton, and School Districts Nos 9, 10, 11, 12A and 13 in the Parish of Stanley

JAMES R. INCH, ESQ., LL. D.,
Chief Supt. of Education,
Fredericton, N. B.

SIR,—I beg leave to submit my report for the year closing 31st December, 1902.

I again have to report that the supply of regularly licensed teachers has not been equal to the demand. The demand for teachers of local license merely has been greater than in the preceding year, not confined to one county but uniform throughout the Inspectoral district. I am glad to be able to report, however, that local licenses were very largely confined to those teachers whose 3rd class licenses had expired and pupils who had creditably passed the Normal School Entrance examinations. In this way the efficiency of the School work was interfered with in a very slight degree.

In some school districts the trustees will not make any exertion to obtain a teacher, and if no application is made by a teacher to them personally, the school is allowed to remain vacant during the term or at least a greater part of it. This only serves to emphasize the fact that greater care should be exercised by the ratepayers, at the annual school meeting, in electing to the office of school Trustee only those who have a direct, vital interest in maintaining a good school.

Two districts in which no schools have been operated previously have been properly organized, and buildings have been completed during the year—in No. 8, Gladstone, and No. 7, Manners Sutton, and there is no doubt hereafter schools will be regularly maintained in each.

At Enniskillen Station there are now about twenty children situated at least two and a half miles from any school, and I consider this fact actually retards the growth of the place. Some means will have to be taken in the near future to provide some better school privilege, than is at present afforded these children.

It was my intention to take up each parish in detail and make some report upon the educational condition of each, but as there have been changes recently made in the limits of the Inspectoral district, I have thought best to defer a detailed report until I may become better acquainted with those parishes in which I have only recently commenced the work of supervision.

I have prepared a statement of the number of districts, all of which are at least either organized or capable of organization, and the number of schools and departments which have been maintained during both terms of the year.

The number of schools is somewhat less than last year owing to the fact already mentioned, that great difficulty was met with in obtaining regularly licensed teachers.

It will be noticed that schools are maintained more uniformly in the County of York than in Sunbury and Queens. This is largely owing to the fact that the number of pupils per school district is very much larger than in the last mentioned counties.

PARISHES.	No. Schools and Departments in Operation	No. in operation during First Term.	No. in operation during Second Term
York Co.			
Bright	13	11	13
Douglas	19	17	17
Dumfries	5	4	5
City of Fredericton	26	26	26
Kingsclear	12	10	11
Manners Sutton	12	11	11
New Maryland	5	3	4
Prince William	9	8	8
Queensbury	10	10	10
Saint Marys	24	22	23
Stanley	16	16	16
Sunbury Co.			
Blissville	8	5	6
Burton	13	11	9
Gladstone	10	7	9
Lincoln	6	5	5
Northfield	5	4	3
Maugerville	4	4	3
Sheffield	7	5	6
Queens Co.			
Canning	8	5	6
Chipman	17	14	13
Gagetown	8	7	8
Hampstead	11	11	9
Petersville	15	14	14
Kings Co.			
Greenwich	5	5	4
Westfield	6	6	5
Charlotte Co.			
Clarendon	3	0	2
	277	241	246

New school houses were erected in No. 2, New Maryland, and No. [illegible] New Maryland and Lincoln. A school building has also been provided in No. 7, Manners Sutton. This is the first school house there has been in this district and it is needless to say the necessity was great. In No. 8, Gladstone, a house which had been started years ago was completed and a school opened.

In No. 6, Hampstead and Greenwich, the school house was burned down, undoubtedly the work of an incendiary. A new building will be erected next year.

Substantial improvements have been made in the school houses in many districts, also in the way of painting and providing new desks and apparatus. I mention those districts that I have made note of, possibly there may be some others:

No. 10, Bright; Nos. 8, 10, 11 and 12, Douglas; No. 1, Dumfries; Nos. 8, 9 and 11, Kingsclear; No. 11, Manners Sutton; No. 6, Prince William; Nos. 5 and 10, Queensbury; No 1½, Saint Marys; Nos. 5½ and 16, Stanley; Nos. 2, 5 and 8, Blissville; No. 3, Lincoln; No. 1, Maugerville; No. 1A, Sheffield and Canning; Nos. 3 and 5 Canning; No. 1A, 3 and 8, Chipman; No. 5, Gagetown; Nos. 1, 10 and 11, Petersville.

GRADED SCHOOLS—YORK CO.

City of Fredericton.—Some changes have been made in the staff of teachers. Miss Bridges who for several years had taught the primary department of the Model School left for South Africa to assume charge of the School of Practice in Pretoria, a position for which she had been personally selected by the Director of Education for the new Colonies, Mr. E. B. Sargent. Her position was filled by Miss Lillian Nicholson of the York St. school.

Miss Sarah Duffy who had for many years charge of one of the departments of the Regent St. school resigned at the end of June last. Miss Annie Tibbits, B. A., who had conducted successfully the VII. and VIII. grades in the York St. school, also resigned her position at the end of the first term, and her situation was filled by Miss Sadie Thompson, M. A., then in charge of the school at Morrison's Mills. In the High School a change was made by the appointment of Mr. H. H. Hagerman, M. A., to the vacancy in the Provincial Normal School caused by the resignation of Mr. Brittain. Mr. Hagerman's position was a difficult one to fill. Mr. Frank N. Patterson, B. A. a recent graduate of the University of New Brunswick, and a teacher of some experience, was appointed to the vacancy.

The general character of efficiency has been maintained in the different departments throughout the past year and the graduates of the High School have been singularly successful in the Departmental Examinations.

Truancy, which is now termed "a prolific source of crime," is but seldom met with in the departments of the schools in this city.

Marysville.—Some improvements have been made in connection with the wood shed and outbuildings, but the condition of school houses remains the same and they are not all that can be desired. Mr. W. T. Day is still the efficient principal of the six departments. The efficiency of the primary departments is much interfered with by irregularity of attendance, as the school is so far from the residents of the opposite side of the stream that it is hardly possible for little children to walk so far in cold winter weather.

St. Marys and Gibson.—Mr. A. H. Barker, who conducted successfully the Superior School for the first term, resigned to pursue his studies at the Provincial University. Miss Ida Myles, who has for some time taught the V. and VI. grades, was promoted to the principalship. Miss Maud Ashfield, who for several years was in charge of the ungraded school at Tay Creek, received an appointment on the staff, and I have no doubt will meet with the same success as in her former position.

The interior of the different rooms of this school building received thorough improvements during the summer vacation. New floors were laid and new black boards prepared.

Harvey Station—The Superior School has been in charge of Mr. Jno. P. Belyea, and the trustees have retained his services for another year, as well as those of Miss Emily Hunter in the Primary Department.

Keswick Ridge.—It is a matter of regret that the trustees have still been unable to retain the services of a teacher for the superior school for a full year. The enrollment in both departments is decreasing, and it is doubtful if the superior school requirements will be fulfilled many years longer.

Stanley Village.—Though there is not a superior school in Stanley the enrollment is much larger than in some graded schools that are receiving the grant, and the work that is being done compares very favourably with the avarage so called superior school. In this modern, thriving village there should be a school which would prepare pupils at least for the University, and it is to be hoped that a superior school grant will be obtained before long.

QUEENS COUNTY.

Gagetown.—The County grammar school continues under the charge of Mr. D. L. Mitchell, B. A. and is doing good work, pupils being prepared for the University and the Provincial Normal School. Mr. Geo. Dingee who taught the primary department for a number of years was compelled on account of his eyesight to give up the work of teaching. Miss Laura Chase is now teaching this department.

Chipman.—The rate payers at the last annual meeting showed their active interest in maintaining an efficient school by voting more money for the teachers' salary and manifesting a disposition to erect a new school building in the near future. Mr. Harvey P. Dole who had charge of the superior school for several years resigned to attend the University of New Brunswick, and the school is now conducted by Mr. A. C. M. Lawson who has entered upon the work earnestly, and brings with him the prestige of a number of years successful experience in the work of teaching.

The rapid increase in population which is already noticeable in the village of Newcastle, and the probability of its being the centre in the development of the coal area in that vicinity, will no doubt raise the village school to the rank of a graded, and eventually a superior school.

SUNBURY COUNTY.

The only graded and superior school in this County is F'ton Junction, and it is one of the best in this Inspectoral district. The pupils in the Normal School entrance examination have always taken a high stand, and the general character of the work of the pupils is excellent. Mr. H. H. Bridges was principal the first term, and during the remainder of the year Mr. F. N. Patterson B. A., and Mr. Chas. L. Richards. The primary department is taught by Miss Addie Hartt.

UNGRADED SCHOOLS.

The large majority of schools in this Inspectoral district are included under this heading, and in a report of this length it is of course impossible to make anything like a statement in detail of their actual condition. Undoubtedly what retards the educational progress of these schools is the continual march of teachers from one school to another, and the short period of service during which so many teachers are engaged in the actual work of teaching. During one term a supervising officer may be quite satisfied with the educational progress in a whole parish, and yet in the very next term the good work may be almost obliterated by the inexperience and inefficiency of those in control,

The average school trustee is slow also, to appreciate the value of experience; indeed it is not uncommon to find the idea prevailing that the teacher fresh from Normal School is like the proverbial new broom which sweeps clean.

There certainly has been a marked improvement in the character of the interior decorations of our school rooms. In no place has a beautiful picture more influence for good than on the walls of an elementary school. Of course it is easy to disfigure a school room with daubs of colour that lend no charm and do not cultivate taste. But it is now easy for the earnest teacher to procure pictures for this purpose which have both beauty and story as they are within easy reach of nearly every school in the country, and the providing of suitable frames is not beyond the skill of pupils with occassional assistance from the teacher. The beneficient influence of a beautiful school room is not easily over estimated, while on the other hand a dingy and dilapidated school house is a frequent cause of disorder and low aims, and it is not an exceptional experience of a supervising officer to note that the removal of a school from an old building to a new has caused a transformation in the school itself. It is with pleasure therefore that I report an improvement in this direction.

There has also been improvement in school discipline. An Inspector may still find some teachers attributing their failure in this regard to external conditions such as school surroundings and home training, when he knows that there are other teachers who could step into their places and easily change discord into harmony.

Yet improved scholarship, special training, combined with greater natural aptitude, and more cheerful manner among our teachers, have produced more practical wisdom in dealing with the little affairs that make up school life, and a very important feature in the large majority of our schools today is the cheerful, even happy response to all that is required of them by the teacher.

The number of school districts in which the average attendance falls actually below that required by law is somewhat increasing, particularly in the Counties of Sunbury and Queens. The enrollment of a number of schools is so small, however, that the removal of one family from one district to another may change the conditions of both, and as there is a continual moving from one district to another, districts that now do not come up to the requirement may in a year or two more than fulfil the conditions. Two years ago many of the school districts bordering on the proposed railroad line from Chipman to Fredericton hardly fulfilled the conditions of the law. Since then there has been quite a change for the better.

ARBOR DAY.

I have reported about the same number of districts as in former years from which I have received an account of what has been done on this day. From personal examination I am satisfied that much has been done in schools from which I have received no report. It is customary with some teachers to call the roll in the afternoon and then spend the rest of the day in working with the pupils on the school grounds. It seems very little use, however, in attempting to set out trees or shrubs, or make flower beds, unless the grounds are properly fenced and even then much damage is done in vacation in those districts where cattle are allowed to wander at will on the roads, as gates will occasionally be left open.

No County Institute was held in this important district during the year. The Provincial Teachers Institute was held in Fredericton the last week in June, and as the large majority of teachers were present at its session it was thought advisable by the executive committee to postpone the County Institute till the long term. Arrangements have been made to hold the York County Institute on the Thursday and Friday preceding the 24th May. The teachers of Sunbury County will probably convene with them. An Institute will also be held in Gagetown probably in June. In Queens County it is not possible to select a place for holding a Teachers' Institute which is easy of access to even the majority of the teachers of that County, and for that reason the attendance at County Institutes in that County has always been proportionately small.

I have the honor to be, Sir,

Your obedient servant,

H. V. B. BRIDGES.

INSPECTORAL DISTRICT No. 6.

F. B. Meagher, M. A., Woodstock, Carleton Co., Inspector.

The District embraces the Counties of Carleton and Victoria except the Parish of Drummond; and the Parishes of Canterbury, North Lake, McAdam and Southampton in York County.

James R. Inch, Esq., LL. D.,
Chief Supt. of Education,
Fredericton, N. B.

Sir,—I beg leave to submit the following report for the year ending December 31st, 1902.

Some noteworthy features in connection with the year's work in this Inspectorate are: extensive improvements in the externals of education, detailed elsewhere in this report; an increased interest in nature study and its more effective treatment in the schools generally; and the proposed establishment of manual training schools to be provided for by Sir William McDonald. This last named feature deserves further mention. In order to encourage the training of the hand and eye as well as of the mind, and to facilitate the consolidation of rural schools, Sir William McDonald has made provision for the establishment of manual training schools at Florenceville and Andover, and such other places as may be subsequently determined upon. The lumber and tools used in connection with the manual work will be provided free, and an acre or more of land will be purchased in the vicinity of each school where the work is being carried on, so that the pupils may be enabled, under competent supervision, to cultivate their own plots of ground, and to observe in a practical and intelligent way the conditions of plant life and the requisites of the soil for plant growth, as soon as the advantages that will thus be extended to children in the places selected, become apparent to the people in the surrounding districts, it is expected that they will desire to have their children enjoy the same advantages, and will avail themselves of the provisions of section 57 (2) of the School Manual. This section provides for the combination of contiguous districts into one district, and the conveyance of the children to and from a central school, one half of the cost of conveyance to be borne by the entire district, and the other half by the Provincial Government. As the central school will require to have several graded departments in consequence of the number of pupils thus brought in, not only will special advantages be afforded in the way of manual training and nature study, but the other subjects embraced in the course of instruction can be treated far more effectively than in the ungraded schools of the country district.

Provision is also made by Sir William McDonald for the appointment and support of a travelling instructor, whose duty, as nearly as I can learn, will be to place the scheme on a practical working basis; to proceed from school to school and supervise the manual and field work; to give lessons in natural science; to encourage and aid the consolidation of districts; and in general to see that the intentions of Sir Wm. McDonald in establishing these schools are properly fulfilled. This will be strenuous work for some years to come and on the ability and energy displayed in its prosecution the success of the scheme will mainly depend. All will be pleased to learn that Mr. John Brittain has been appointed to the position of Travelling Instructor, and all will unite in saying that the right man has been chosen for the right place.

I have dwelt upon this subject at some length, but not longer, perhaps than its importance demands, for I regard the establishment of these schools as a very decided gain in the way of educational progress and a promise of better things for the country district which will thus obtain benefits and privileges not now within its reach, and which might otherwise be indefinitely postponed.

Appended are some notes on the educational condition of each parish in my Inspectorate.

Aberdeen.—A handsome and up-to date schoolhouse has been erected in Glassville. There are no strong cross lights in the schoolroom to injure the sight of the pupils, the windows being placed chiefly on the south side of the house. On the north side several small windows about a foot square are placed near the ceiling for the purpose of ventilation. The children living in the lower end of this district are conveyed to and from school in accordance with the provisions of Section 57 of the School Manual. The people living in Ketchum Ridge are anxious to have a school district established there. As there are only six families (representing fifteen children) it will be hard for them to successfully maintain a school.

This is one of the many hardships connected with pioneer life in isolated localities. Every effort will be made however to carry out their wishes, if it be possible.

Northfield No. 13 comes under the head of Section 121 of the Act.

LAKEVILLE SCHOOL No. 6, WILMOT, CARLETON CO.
Empire Day, 1902.

Brighton.—At the close of the last school year Mr. John Page succeeded Mr. Jos. Howe as Principal of the Superior School at Hartland. This school has three graded departments. The school in Hayward, No. 13, was closed this term. East Cloverdale, No. 19, after a long period of inaction is now operating a school continuously. Highgate, No. 18, has less than twelve children of school age, and it will be necessary to have them conveyed to Ashland, No. 10. The school in No. 15 was in operation this term.

Kent.—The house in Egypt, No. 1½, has been repaired and painted. A new house will probably be erected next year in Moose Mountain, No. 5. It is very much needed. In the locality commonly known as "The Gore," there are a number of children to whom school privileges should be extended. The people are poor, and scattered over quite an extent of territory, but I believe they could support a school by making a strong effort, and I hope to have a district established and a school in operation there in the near future.

The tide of affairs is flowing quite smoothly now in the De Merchant Settlement, and school is kept in constant operation.

Northampton—After being in operation about a month of the present term, the school in No. 3 was closed on account of the illness of the teacher, Miss Ethel Bourne.

Grafton is now operating an ungraded school. The enrolment at the time of my last visit was forty. The removal of several families from Kilmarnock, No. 11, has rendered it impossible for the few remaining ratepayers to support a school, and the district is nowdisorganized.

Peel.—The new school house in Mt. Pleasant, No. 4, is nearly completed and will shortly be ready for occupancy. The arrangements for ventilation and the admission of light are not quite modern, as the trustees were averse to having the windows placed principally on one side of the house, but in other respects it is a handsome and serviceable building. The school in this district was closed last term, but it was reopened this term in the old school house under the management of Mr. John Guy. With this exception all the schools of the parish were in constant operation during the year.

Richmond.—The house in Debec, No. 3, has been repaired and new out-buildings have been erected. Repairs are greatly needed on the house in Monument, No. 11 A. Greenville, No. 13, has barely the prescribed number of pupils for the operation of a school, and it is probable that they will be conveyed to the school at McKenzie Corner.

Simonds.—Mr. Fred Squiers has succeeded Mr. D. W. Hamilton, B. A., as Principal of the Superior School at Florenceville. During the time that Mr. Hamilton was in charge, he not only greatly improved the efficiency of the school, but by his personal efforts succeeded in procuring much needed apparatus. In the latter work he was assisted by Mrs. H. L. Ross, the teacher of the primary department. The same dilapidated school house still remains in St. Thomas, No. 6. The school there was closed this term.

Wilmot.—There are two graded schools in this parish; the one (a Superior School) at Centreville, and the other at Lakeville. Their respective Principals are Miss Ruth Reed and Miss Lena B. McLeod, both of whom are faithful teachers. The school in Deerville, No. 8, was closed this term, as repairs were being made on the house. The house in No. 17, has been thoroughly repaired, and will no longer be uncomfortable for the pupils during the winter months.

Wicklow.—Of the sixteen districts of this parish all with the exception of No. 8, operated their schools continuously during the year. After a long period of inaction, No. 8 reopened its school this term, Miss Lizzie Holmes being placed in charge. An application has been made for the establishment of a new district between Upper Knoxford and River De Chute, adjoining the American boundary. It is claimed that there are seventeen ratepayers and thirty-two children in the proposed district. This matter will receive my attention when I resume work next term.

Wakefield.—The school in Rosedale, No. 4, was closed during the present term to admit of repairs being made on the house. There being less than twelve children in Third Tier, No. 6, they are conveyed to the school in an adjoining district. Jacksonville, No. 7, has a Superior School the principalship of which has been satisfactorily filled by Mr. C. H. Gray for ten years. The schools in Hartford and Wakefield Centre were closed this term, presumably, for the reason that no teachers could be procured.

Woodstock.—There are fourteen districts in this parish. Upper Woodstock, No. 6, will operate a graded school next term. The present teacher, Mr. I. N. Draper, will act as principal. Porton, No. 11, has less than twelve resident children, In Springfield, the adjoining district, the enrolment during the present term was seven, and it was necessary for the trustees to obtain your permission to operate their school. Some time ago a proposition was made to combine these two districts, but it was found to be impracticable.

Town of Woodstock.—The schools of the town of Woodstock contain in all fourteen departments under the principalship of Mr. G. H. Harrison, M. A. There is evidence of an increasing interest being taken in the school work both by trustees and parents, which cannot but serve as an encouragement to the teachers. The present large enrolment in Grades IX, X, and XI of the Grammar School departments—the greatest within the past ten years or more—is an indication that the schools in general are prospering under their present management. Miss Ella Smith, the teacher of one of the primary departments of the College Schools, has retired after a number of years of faithful and efficient service. Miss Smith's resignation will be greatly regretted by all concerned. Her successor is Miss Maud McAdam. I understand that the School Board has had under consideration the advisability of establishing a department for manual training. It is the general opinion amongst those qualified to judge that manual training in connection with our schools has come to stay, not only on account of its direct practical value, but also of the increased stimulus that it gives to the school work in general, and it is to be hoped that the Board will consider the matter favourably, particularly when it is borne in mind that one half of the cost of the equipment for the manual work will be paid by the Provincial Government and the sum of fifty dollars awarded yearly to each teacher in charge from the same source.

VICTORIA COUNTY.

Andover.—A falling off in the attendance at the Grammar School in Andover has caused the primary department to be dispensed with. It is now combined with the intermediate department, under the control of Miss Bessie E. Scott. The principal is Mr. W. M. Veazey, B. A. This district contains a handsome school house with large airy and well lighted rooms. Flush closets have been placed in the basement, and every provision made for the health and comfort of the pupils.

In Carlingford there are so many children living at a remote distance from the school house that they should be conveyed there by teams. The present agitation to have the house moved, even if it succeed, would only partially settle the difficulty.

The school in Tomlinson, No. 6, was closed last term, but this term all the schools of the parish were in operation.

The school in Bairdsville was conducted by Miss Iva Baxter, a graduate of the Manual Training School at Truro.

Drummond.—This parish is now included in Inspector Doucet's district.

Gordon.—At the time of my last visit to Arthurette, the school was closed, and everything in the school room had a battered and neglected appearance. The trustees then promised to set things to rights, and I presume they have done so, though I have not since heard from them. There is a well equipped school in the new district at Plaster Rock, No. 4. The school in Sisson Ridge was closed at the time of my visit in September last.

Grand Falls.—Mr. J. C. Carruthers has succeeded Mr. M. L. Hayward as principal of the Superior School at Grand Falls, which now contains four graded departments. The school in Silver Beach, No. 5, was reopened this term, an unlicensed teacher being placed in charge. The two schools in the California Settlement are operated in a very unsatisfactory way. The house in South California has outlived its usefulness for school purposes, and should be replaced by a new one.

Lorne.—There is a good school in Riley Brook, No. 4. The teacher is Mr. H. M. Manzer. Nictau, No. 5, is about sixty miles up the Tobique river, and on account of its remote situation finds it very difficult to procure a teacher. Owing to the energy of the Secretary, Mr. W. M. Miller, this difficulty has generally been surmounted, but no teacher was available this term, and the school could not be reopened. The remaining districts of the parish succeeded in obtaining teachers.

Perth.—Repairs are needed on the house in Forest Glen, No. 4, and better apparatus should be provided. This district is small and barely contains twelve children. The Scotch Colony in this parish contains four districts, namely, Upper Kintore, No. 9; Lower Kintore, No. 10; Bon Accord, No. 11; and Lower Kincardine, No. 12. A new house is needed in Lower Kintore. No school was operated there this term. The house in Upper Kintore is beginning to wear a very dilapidated appearance. The schools in Bon Accord and Lower Kincardine are very well equipped, but the enrolment in both districts is small.

YORK CO.

Canterbury and North Lake:—Mr. Maurice Coll is now the Principal of the Graded School at Canterbury Station, and is giving good satisfaction in that position. The schools in Pocawagomis and Dorrington Hill were re-opened this term. Repairs have been made on the house in California Settlement, No. 10½. The school in Inch's Ridge, No. 24, where the Sloyd Work is being carried on, is now conducted by Miss Bessie Kelly.

McAdam:—My first tour of visitation to the schools and districts in this Parish was made in the month of December. The Superior School at the Junction has three graded departments, in all of which good work is being done. The Principal is Mr. H. F. Perkins. St. Croix, No. 7, has been disorganized for some time, but a general meeting will be held on the 10th day of January next at which trustees will be elected and provision made for school purposes. St. Croix South, No. 8, will have less than an enrolment of twelve when the school in No. 7 will be re-opened, and if these two districts should elect to combine under the Provisions of Sec. 57 (2) of the Act it would be much to their advantage.

Southampton:—This Parish contains eighteen districts, to nearly all of which I paid my first official visits during the month of October last. The school in Waterville for unavoidable reasons was closed this term. The school in Norton Dale was closed at the time of my visit, but was subsequently re-opened under the charge of an unlicensed teacher. There is great room for improvement in Norton Dale, Centre Waterville and West Waterville in so far as their houses and school equipment are concerned. The house in Millville is entirely too small to accommodate the large number of resident children, the school having an enrolment of seventy pupils this term. I called a meeting of the trustees, and pointed out the necessity of having a new building erected in which a graded school with two departments could be operated. A general meeting was to have been held shortly after to consider this recommendation, but as it was thought best to postpone it until a later and more favorable date, the notices will not be issued until February or March next.

LIST OF IMPROVEMENTS FOR THE YEAR 1902.

North Glassville, room wainscotted and ceiled, hardwood floor, and new furniture. Palmer, Settlement, map of British Empire. Argyle, Highlands, and Foreston, school flags. East Coldstream, map of Maritime Provinces and flag Dow Settlement, room wainscotted. Benton Ridge, house painted Ruther Glen, maps of the World and Dominion of Canada. Debec, new desks, hardwood floor and new outhouses. Meductic, new outhouses, maps of the World and Dominion of Canada. Central Newburg, room wainscotted and ceiled, new desks. Irish Settlement, room painted, hardwood floor, new desks and flag. Victoria Corner, map of the Dominion. Biggar Ridge, map of Maritime Provinces, and flag. Lower Southampton, maps of the World and North America. Temperance Vale, maps of World and Dominion of Canada. Hawkinsville, new desks. Bull Lake, map of World. Kirkland, blackboards (hyloplate). Rapides des Femmes, room wainscotted and ceiled. Wakefield Centre, maps of N. B., Dominion of Canada and World. Lower Kincardine, map of Dominion. Lower Northampton, chemical apparatus and flag. Plymouth, room wainscotted and ceiled, dictionary. Upper Kent, new porch, stone wall under house, and other improvements. Monquart, room wainscotted and ceiled, new outhouses. Bristol, room wainscotted and ceiled. Bath, Standard dictionary and other books. Lower Wicklow, map of British Empire, new outhouses. DeMerchant Settlement, blackboards (hyloplate). Perth Centre, dictionary. Andover, maps and other apparatus. Three Brooks, house painted. Red Rapids, new outhouses. South Wakefield, minerals and flag. Temple, maps and flag. Jacksonville, map of British Empire. Golden Ridge, flag. Grenville, globe. Pemberton Ridge, map of Dominion. Knowlesville, flag, map of British Empire, new outhouses. West Glassville, maps of the World and Dominion of Canada, new outbuilding. Canterbury (No. 3), chemical apparatus and minerals. Lakeville, globe and other apparatus, flag. East Florenceville and Middle Simonds, maps of British Empire and Maritime Provinces. Gould Settlement, flag. Green Mountain, map of Dominion. Plaster Rock, dictionary ($10), minerals, cabinet, and flag. Florenceville, rooms wainscotted and ceiled, new blackboards (hyloplate), maps and flag. Many of these improvements have been effected through the efforts of teachers. Their names, with apologies for omissions are as follows:

Mildred Jones, Re. Agatha Carpenter, Albina London, Mrs. Cassie Wheeler, Hattie Jamieson, Edith M. O'Brien, W. M. Veazey, B A., Bessie E. Scott, Annetta Bradley, Maggie M. McLeod, Georgia Parent, Eva Annett, Myrtle I. Fowler, Nettie Bearisto, Mrs. J. R. H. Simms, Mabel Shaw, Maud McAdam, Malcom Hunter, Blanche Plumer, Elvya E Manual, Annie Palmer, Iva Semple, Mrs. H. L. Ross, D. W. Hamilton, B. A., Jennie P. Cro hite.

FLAG RAISINGS.

Flag raisings were held in a number of districts, amongst which mig be mentioned: Lakeville, East Coldstream, Irish Settlement, Temple, Argyle, Rosedale, Silverdale, Foreston, Golden Ridge, Biggar Ridge and Lower Northampton (No. 1).

ARBOR DAY.

If a list were given of those districts in which the results of the observance of Arbor Day are plainly to be seen, I am afraid it would not be a long one. Of course, we cannot measure these results by merely external indications, for undoubtedly much has been done on this day to cultivate in the pupils a love of nature, but I shall look for better and more intelligent efforts being made in both directions as soon as the groups of rural schools are established and systematic lessons are given by the Travelling Instructor in tree planting and nature study. His influence will, undoubtedly, also awaken a public interest, which is now almost entirely lacking, in the observance of the day.

TEACHERS' INSTITUTES.

The Victoria Co. Institute was held in September last at Andover. The enrolment was small, but the proceedings were quite interesting and instructive. A number of excellent papers were read, amongst which might be mentioned one by Miss Iva Baxter on Manual Training. On Friday morning a botanical excursion was held under the direction of Mr. John Britain. The weather was delightful and all the teachers derived much pleasure and profit from this outing. The Institute at Woodstock was the most successful of all that I have yet attended in Carleton County. A number of visitors were present, some of whom took part in the discussions. The following papers were read: Discipline, by I. N. Draper; Something About Birds, by Frank A. Good; The First Steps in the Teaching of Geometry, by Miss Lena B. McLeod; Fungi (illustrated by specimens) by Dr. G. U. Hay; Drawing, by E. J. Branscombe. The public meeting on Thursday evening was addressed by the Mayor, the chairman of the Board of School Trustees, Dr. G. U. Hay and others.

I have the honor to be

Your obedient servant,

F. B. MEAGHER.

INSPECTORAL DISTRICT No. 7.

J. F. DOUCET, INSPECTOR, Richibucto, N. B.

This District embraces the Counties of Gloucester and Madawaska; the County of Kent, except the Parishes of Weldford and Harcourt and the English Schools in the Parish of Richibucto; the Parish of Rogerville and School Districts Nos. 4, 5, 10A, 12, 13, 14 and 15 in the Parish of Alnwick, in the County of Northumberland; the Parish of Drummond in the County of Victoria; the Parish of Balmoral, District No. 3 *in the Parish of Addington, and District No.* 1 1-2, *in the Parishes of Colborne and Balmoral in the County of Restigouche.*

J. R. INCH, ESQ., LL. D.
Chief Supt. of Education,
Fredericton, N. B.

SIR,—I have the honor to submit to you my annual report on the condition of the Public Schools in my Inspectoral District, for the year ended December 31st, 1902. In this report is included the second term of the year 1901, for the Parish of Rogerville, Acadieville, St. Louis and Carleton, and the County of Madawaska.

This being my first experience as an Inspector, I cannot make any comparison with former years. I shall, therefore, limit my remarks to actual facts, as noted in the course of my inspection.

There are 311 School Districts in this Inspectorate, viz: 107 in the County of Gloucester, 88 in the County of Kent, 72 in the County of Madawaska, 19 in the County of Northumberland, 17 in the County of Victoria, and 8 in the County of Restigouche. Of these, 27 are unorganized and 16 are in an encouraging state of organization. Of graded schools, there are in the County of Gloucester, 10 districts with 32 departments; in the County of Kent, 1 district with 4 departments; in the County of Madawaska, 3 districts with 11 departments; and in the County of Northumberland, 1 district with 2 departments. This makes in all, 305 schools and departments in this Inspectoral Division.

GLOUCESTER COUNTY.

Bathurst.—The several departments of the Town and Village school, Districts Nos. 2 and 16, have good supplies of apparatus, excellent equipments, and are giving entire satisfaction. On the retirement of Mr. M. F.

Tuttle, B. A., in June last, Mr. R. D. Hanson, B. A., was appointed principal of the Grammar School. Mr. C. J. Mersereau, B.A., has had charge of the Superior School in the Village for a year and a half, and has attracted many pupils from the neighbouring parishes. The schools in Nos. 3, 6 and 12 which were closed during the winter term, were re-opened in the month of August. There are only three children of school age in No. 9, and about eight in No. 8. I found it necessary to recommend untrained teachers for the schools in Nos. 4 and 11. Maps of the Maritime Provinces and of the British Empire were provided in No. 17. Steps must soon be taken to erect a new building in this District, as the present one is rather dilapidated. Good work is being done in Nos. 7 and 10. No. 5 procured hyloplate blackboards.

Beresford.—There are seventeen organized Districts in this Parish. I have not been able to locate No. 14, St. Lawrence, and no one seems to know where it is. No. 16, Lugar, is not yet organized. A new school house is in course of construction in No. 1. No. 2 needs a larger school house. The one now in use is altogether inadequate for the number of pupils in the District. The school was closed during the first term owing to the Trustees' inability (?) to find a second class French and English teacher. The school house in No. 3 has been extensively repaired. The Superior school at Petit Rocher has been under the constant direction of Mr. Jerome Boudreau, since its organization. This school is a very important feeder for the French department of the Normal School. District No. 15 engaged a local licensee during the first term of the year, and No. 6 during the second term. No. 11 needs a better school house. No. 12 has the finest school house of the Parish, and a very good school. Nos. 7½ and 8½ should be united, as there is not a sufficient number of children in the former District to maintain a school. The two districts together are no more than three miles in length. A map of the Dominion of Canada has been procured in No. 13½.

Caraquet.—This parish has ten organized Districts. Nos. 1½ and 8 remain unorganized. No. 2 has been in operation for the first year, and No. 4, for the first term. No. 4½ will open at the commencement of the year. New furniture has been provided in No. 7, and the school house painted inside. No. 6 procured new school desks. No. 2½ needs a larger school house. The graded school in No. 10 is under the management of Mr. Alf. J. Witzell, a skillful teacher of the first class.

Inkerman.—There is only one unorganized District in this Parish, No. 6. The other seven Districts maintained schools during the whole year.

No. 2 has a good school house and a good school. There is also a good school in No. 7, but the inside of the school house is unfinished. The Maltampeque Road settlement should be organized into a school District. This will be a part of my work on my next tour of inspection in this Parish.

New Bandon.—All the schools of this Parish were in operation during the whole year. No. 3 has been without a school for a long number of years. A general meeting of the ratepayers of the District was held in the month of September and provision made for the building of a school house. The school house in No. 4 has been finished inside, and a hyloplate blackboard procured. The trustees have also ordered lately a complete set of modern school desks. Nos. 1, 5 1-2, 6 and 7 have poor school houses. An application has been made for the formation of a new district by cutting off a portion from No. 5, St. Joseph, and No. 7, Black Rock. As District No. 7 would have been greatly weakened, with little prospect of having a respectable school in either of them, the request was not granted. There is a good school in No. 9. No. 11 has a good school also, but there is not sufficient accommodation.

Paquetville:—No. 6, Georgeville, is not yet organized. The other five districts have fair schools and school buildings. The house in No. 2, has been thoroughly painted during the summer vacations.

St. Isidore:—No. 7 has a most miserable school house, and the attendance is so irregular that the pupils know hardly anything well. The new school building in No. 8, is now ready for occupancy.

Saumarez:—The Superior School at Tracadie, No. 3, is doing satisfactory work. Mr. Geo. E. Price, who for five terms, has been its principal, resigned in the month of June, and has been succeeded by Mr. Ed. L. O'Brien, M. A., whom I have not yet visited. The school in No. 6, was re-opened after being closed for three terms. The house in 2 1-2 badly needs repairing. The school house in No. 4, was destroyed by fire, early in August, supposed to have been by the hand of an incendiary.

Shippegan:—There have been during some portion of the year, sixteen schools in operation in this parish. No. 8 has been opened for the firr year. Owing to an attack of la grippe at the time of my first visit to th parish, I could not visit the three schools on the eastern side of the Shi pegan Island. At my second visit to Shippegan, in October, such hign winds prevailed, that I would not risk to cross over to the Island. Tl graded school in Shippegan Village is efficiently conducted under the principalship of Mr. J. Edouard DeGrace.

KENT COUNTY.

Acadieville has now six schools in operation. New school houses are being built in Districts No. 1, McInnis Brook, No. 2, Acadieville, and No. 7, St. Athanase. School has been opened in No. 9, for the first term, and in No. 8, for the third term. The inside of the school house in No. 4, has been finished, which makes it warm and comfortable.

Carleton:—This parish operated five schools. A new school house was erected in No. 4, during last summer to replace the one destroyed by fire a few years ago. New furniture has been provided in No. 10. There has been no school in No. 2 for many years. No. 1 is the best school of the parish.

Dundas:—Fifteen schools were in operation in this parish at the time of my visit in April. The school at Cocagne Village, was admirably conducted by Mr. Auguste E. Daigle. A new school house has been constructed in No. 12, in the centre of the district. With the exception of No. 1, the schools of this parish are poorly equipped and furnished.

Richibucto:—Only six schools in this parish are under my supervision, Nos. 3, 6, 7, 8, 11 and 12. The school houses are for the most part, kept unsatisfactorily. The school house at Richibucto Village is much too small for the number of pupils in this thriving village. An amount was voted at the last annual meeting for the purpose of providing more accommodation.

St. Louis:—The schools of this parish are among the best conducted in the County of Kent. I must make special mention of the school at McLeod's Mill, conducted with marked success by Miss Marguerite M. Richard. No. 9 has also a good school, taught by Mr. Honore Maillet. There were eleven schools in operation during the year.

St. Mary's:—The outbreak of Small Pox in this parish and the neighboring sections has had a disastrous effect on the working of these schools. ine schools were operated during some portion of the year. No. 3 has een closed for over two years. The old school house was not centrally ocated and the great majority of the children could not attend. The rustees petitioned to have the site of the school changed to a more centra place, which petition I sanctioned. A new school has been built, and is now ready for the reception of the pupils. The boundaries between districts No. 1 and No. 3 will now have to be revised.

St. Paul:—Of the nine organized districts, eight operated schools during the year. A new school house has been erected in No.7, McLean Settlement. The attendance is very irregular in No. 4. No. 3 is very deficient in apparatus. There is a very poor school house in No. 1.

Wellington:—No. 1, Buctouche Village, has two buildings with five departments. The superior school is under the principalship of Mr. Geo. A. Coates, a most enthusiastic and successful teacher. The departments in the convent buildings are very efficiently conducted. The school house in No. 18, St. Croix, is a new building, and the school has been in operation for the first term. The school house in No. 17, St. Michael, is being built slowly but steadily. There is a good school in No. 12½, Upper Chockpish. The other schools in this parish are giving but fair satisfaction, most of them not being provided with the necessary maps and apparatus. No. 3½ is a noted exception. A map of the British Empire was procured in this district and one of the world in No. 2.

MADAWASKA COUNTY.

Madawaska:—At the time of my visit in November, there were 250 pupils enrolled in the six departments of the superior school at Edmundston. Mr. John Barnett, Jr., has succeeded Mr. J. F. Worrell, as principal. Extensive repairs have been made on the school house in No. 2. There has been no school in No. 4 for a number of years. No. 3 engaged an untrained teacher during last term, and No. 5 during the whole year.

Ste. Ann:—Ste. Ann comprises six districts and operates five schools. No. 3 engaged a local licensee during the first term. This district needs a better school house. The eastern part of district No. 7 will have to be organized into a new district, as many families are evidently out of reach of school.

St. Basil:—The parish of St. Basil contains the most successful educ- tional institution of the County of Madawaska. With but few exceptions, the teachers of this county have been prepared at St. Basil Convent. has now five departments and an enrolment of one hundred and ninety-t pupils. In No. 4, a map of the Maritime Provinces has been procured. No

4½, 5, 7, 8, 9, in charge of untrained teachers, have inferior school houses and unsatisfactory schools. Nos. 1 and 2 are up to the standard of miscellaneous schools.

St. Francis:—School districts Nos. 1, 2, 10, 11, 12, 13, and 14 are situated in the new parish of Clair; Nos. 9 and 15 are partly in the parish of Clair and partly in the parish of St. Francis; the remaining districts belong to the Parish of St. Francis. A new district, under the popular name of St. Norbert, has been created back of District No. 9. It has a sufficient number of children of school age to maintain a school, and the people are able and seem willing to support one. A fine school house has been completed in No. 2 1-2, Island Vale. The school house in No. 2 has been thoroughly repaired. The school in No. 1 is under the management of Mr. Theodore Paillard, who holds a Superior School license. No. 14 has been in operation for one term only. Nos. 5, 5 1-2, 7, 10, 11, 12, 13, 14, were taught by untrained teachers for some portion of the year.

St. Hilaire:—The inhabitants of District No. 1 are justly proud of their new and pretty school house. Miss Osilie Richard did good work in No. 2. Four other schools were in operation.

St. Jacques:—No. 1 has a good school. Mr. J. Amedee Charest is the teacher. No. 2, which has been closed for a year, was re-opened last term. Nos 3 and 5 were taught by local licensees.

St. Leonard:—The graded school at St. Leonard's station is in charge of Mr. Maximilien D. Cormier, B. A. A new school house has been built in No. 1. Nine of the seventeen districts in this parish operated schools. The school house in No. 8 was burned in the summer of 1901. In No. 6, Byram, at a meeting of the rate-payers in October, 1901, money was voted to erect a school house, but since, things have remained at a standstill. I visited No. 9, Combe's Road Settlement, and No. 15, Comeau Ridge, in the fall of 1901. No. 9 is being organized. No. 15 is a hopeless case.

NORTHUMBERLAND COUNTY.

Alnwick:—Mr. William L. Allain, a teacher of the first class, is achieving success in No. 4. A new house has been erected in No. 13, Upper eguac. No. 14 has a very poor school house and a poor school.

Rogersville is divided into twelve districts and operates eleven schools, very creditable showing of the good-will, intelligence and energy of the people of this new and progressive parish. A new district has been formed back of District No. 14. It is known under the name of Rogersville West, No. 5. The graded school at Rogersville Village has improved in tone and management since Mr. J. Phileas Laplante has had charge of it. Miss Marie Flore Comeau is doing good work in the primary department. No. 11 provided new furniture. Needed repairs were made on the house in No. 16. All the schools in this parish except No. 13 were closed during the latter part of the year on account of smallpox.

RESTIGOUCHE COUNTY.

Balmoral:—The school houses in this parish are, for the most part, good. No. 2 has the best school. No. 3, Addington, has been closed during the whole year for want of a teacher.

VICTORIA COUNTY.

Drummond:—There are in this parish seventeen organized districts. Inspector Meagher visited most of the schools of this parish shortly before they were assigned to me. I have not been able to visit the whole of that parish since.

The necessity of employing untrained teachers is still felt to a great extent in the County of Madawaska. During the term just closed, fourteen local licenses were issued for this county only, and during the previous term, fifteen. This is a serious drawback to educational progress, and as long as this necessity exists, the best interests of the people living in these sections, must suffer. In many cases, I have refused to grant permission to teach to an applicant for local license, until I was assured that he was reasonably remunerated by the trustees. I have no doubt that this will induce the inhabitants of these sections where local licensees are employed to assess themselves to give better salaries to their teachers and thus encourage a larger attendance from this county at the French Department, and as a consequence—better teaching and better schools.

ARBOR DAY.

Arbor Day was observed on the 2nd day of May by fifty-three schools. Two hundred and thirty-four trees and fifty-five shrubs were planted, and forty-two flower beds made. Very few districts in Madawaska celebrated Arbor Day.

TEACHERS' INSTITUTE.

The Gloucester County Teacher's Institute convened at Tracadie on the 8th and 9th of November. The attendance was not large, but the exercises were interesting and practical. The Institute was much indebted to Dr. Geo. U. Hay, Editor of the "Educational Review," for practical lessons on "Nature" and for many valuable suggestions. The public meeting in the evening was well attended, and addresses were delivered by Dr. Hay, Mr. P. P. Murray, Principal O'Brien, C. J. Mersereau, B. A., the President, Mr. Witzell, and the Inspector.

In concluding this report, I beg to tender my thanks to my numerous friends, particularly the clergymen, who have aided me during the first year of my inspectoral career, and to you, Sir, for valuable assistance at all times.

I have the honor to be,
Your obedient servant,
J. F. DOUCET.

APPENDIX C.

REPORTS OF BOARDS OF SCHOOL TRUSTEES.

I. CITY OF FREDERICTON.

BOARD OF SCHOOL TRUSTEE.

J. R. Inch, LL. D.,
Chief Supt. of Education

Sir,—We beg to submit for your consideration the following report of the schools in this city for the year ended 30th June, 1902.

The work of the year just closed has, in many respects, been highly satisfactory, yet we feel that with the thorough equipment of our schools and the experience of our teaching staff, the advantages to be derived from regular attendance are not yet fully appreciated by the public. As is usual, several changes occurred in the teaching staff. Miss Holland (Sr. Catherine) of Regent Street School, whose health was indifferent for some time, was granted leave of absence for the first term and her school was placed in charge of Miss Isabel Reid. Miss Holland resumed her duties at the beginning of last term and struggled faithfully with her work, which most reluctantly she was obliged to relinquish before the year closed. Miss Mary E. Phillips, who had been doing most excellent work in the third department of the Model School, felt the need of rest last fall and obtained leave of absence. This department, as you are aware, has since been in charge of

Miss Nicolson of the Charlotte Street School staff, and the latter school is since in charge of Miss Annie L. Taylor, a young lady of some experience and the holder of a G. S. license. Another change in the teaching staff of the Model School was occasioned in February by the call of Miss Clara E. Bridges to South Africa. The loss of the services of one of our most popular and successful teachers, as well as the loss of the counsel of the Board's Examiner, Mr. Eldon Mullin, were of considerable significance from the standpoint of our own schools, but the honor thus conferred upon members of the profession in Fredericton as well as the Province is in some measure a compensation for any temporary inconvenience resulting therefrom. The leave taking of Miss Bridges by her pupils was interesting and affecting and evidenced the firm grasp she had upon them. The vacancy created in this department was filled by the transfer of Miss Lillian Nicolson from the York Street School. This arrangement necessitated a disturbance in the staff of the latter school. Miss L. A. Burtt was transferred from the third to the first department and Miss Katherine E. Currie was appointed on the staff and assigned to the charge of the department vacated by Miss Burtt. The close of the year brought further changes in our staff. Miss S. G Duffy, for more than twenty years an industrious and hard working member of the teaching staff in Regent Street School, has resigned her position. Miss A. I. Tibbits, for several years one of our most successful teachers and lately in charge of Grades VII and VIII in York Street School, has also resigned her position and withdrawn from the service.

Although it is the policy of the Board to retain the services of teachers with experience, whose work has been satisfactory, it will be seen by the foregoing that frequent changes are liable to occur year after year The equipment of our schools is being steadily increased, and with the necessary supply of apparatus maintained we naturally anticipate good results. Our pupils continue to take a deep interest in the work of the Sloyd School and many of them show marked ability in the use of the hand and eye. Much credit is due to Prof. Macready and his associates for the success already attained. They are well skilled in the art themselves and possess the necessary qualifications for training the most stupid lad to be careful and exact. The exhibition of manual work shown at the recent Provincial Institute formed a most pleasing attraction to teachers from every section of the Province. Samples of every day school work, including printing, drawing, and composition, from the city schools, were also on exhibition and no doubt received kind criticism from the profession.

Arbor Day was appropriately observed in the schools by lessons suited to the occasion and by practical illustrations of the growth of plants. Empire Day also received attention, although the actual date did not fall on a teaching day. With the prospect of an extensive celebration of the King's Coronation in June the scholars were full of patriotism and British history was a favorite theme.

Teachers and scholars alike very much appreciated the formal visit to all the city schools of His Honor Lieut.-Governor Snowball, early in May, accompanied by the Chief Supt. of Education. His Honor pleasantly conversed with each teacher in her class room, administering sympathy or encouragement as occasion required, and in a happy manner addressed the pupils in their respective departments, urging them to foster ambition and to have a high ideal in life. Perhaps to the children the most interesting feature of His Honor's address was when he authorized a holiday on a subsequent day which he named. Vociferous applause followed the announcement in every instance.

Considerable interest is manifested in our schools by the general public, but if this were true of all parents and guardians a stimulus would come to the pupil and the teacher would experience greater encouragement in his work. At the regular semi-annual public examinations visitors in large numbers throng the schools, but they are thus enabled to form but a slight conception of the character of the work performed. At the close of each term certificates are given by the Board to the pupils in each department showing the highest general standing, and this plan of recognition is much appreciated by the pupils. Excellent work continues to be accomplished in the High School and the closing exercises this year were very interesting and were witnessed by a large gathering of friends. After the classes had been convened in the Assembly Hall the following medals and prizes were distributed:

The Douglas Silver Medal for Classics was awarded to Miss Ruth E. Everett, and the presentation was made by the Chief Superintendent of Education. In recognition of his standing a second prize, a book, was given to A. J. Estey.

The Governor-General's bronze medal for English was awarded to Miss Ada W. Turner, and was presented by Dr. H. C. Creed.

The Coulthard memorial medal for Natural science was awarded to Miss Margaret M. Belyea, and the presentation was made by Sheriff Sterling.

Miss Belyea also won the Class '01 prize for French and received the prize at the hands of Dr. Scott.

The Mathematical prize, given by Chancellor Harrison, was awarded to A. J. Estey and the presentation was made by Principal Crocket.

The Class '01 prize for highest general average among those not win ning a prize was awarded ro Miss Sarah L. B. Waycot, and the presentation was made by Canon Roberts.

A prize was awarded to Miss R. B. Watson for highest general average in Class B. and the presentation was made by Dean Partridge. A second prize in this class was given to Ralph Sherman.

Miss Clara G. Orr was awarded a prize for highest general average in Class C. and the presentation was made by Rev. E. C. Turner, of Gibson.

The following were the members of the graduating class this year :

Division I.—Margaret May Belyea, Sarah Louisa Bowden Waycot, Ruth Elizabeth Everitt, Florence Mabel Bird, James Arthur Estey, Wilmot Guion Miller, Ada Winifred Turner, Edith Hazen Allen, Charles Walter Clarke.

Division II.—Kate Haws Miles, Franklin M. Bonner, Pearl Yerxa, Spencer William Everett, Minnie Isabel Bustin, James Hugh McLean, Hazel Millican, Sadie Emack, Eden Maunsell Stopford, Mabel Jean McLenahan, Francis Winslow Johnson.

Omitted Latin or French.—Gertrude May McKinnon, VanBuren Keith, Grover Carleton Torrens, Sarah Viola Drucilla Butler, Robert Napier Winslow, Byron H. Kinghorn, Idella May Ingraham, Theodore Rand McNally.

Richard Alexander Malloy and William Franklin Smith omitted the Classical Course, and Miss Nina Clements was a special student.

As the report of this year's High School entrance examinations will show, the size of the new class will probably equal that of previous years, an indication that the supply is not exhausted.

In his annual report to the Board, Mr. Mullin, City Superintendent, takes a hopeful view of the outlook. After a statement in detail of all the schools he remarks that they have held their own and in some directions there has been marked progress.

We beg to refer you to the accompanying statements giving particulars of expenditure, names of teachers, attendance of pupils, etc.

I have the honor to be

Your obedient servant,

CHAS. A. SAMPSON,

Secretary.

STATEMENT A.

Receipts and Expenditures for 1901.

On What Account.	Amount	Amount	On What Account.	Amount
Permanent Expenditure—			By Taxes from City Treasurer	16,000 00
Apparatus	39 72		Tuition fees,	67 00
Furniture and Furnishing,	432 80		Interest	34 12
Mill School,	1174 00	1646 52	Insurance,	865 50
			Debentures	2,650 00
Annual Expenditure—			Contingent,	17 80
			Unpaid Cheques,	132 20
Auditors	10 00		Bal. Jan. '01	5,566 31
Office	23 30			
Printing,	55 68			
Fuel	829 30			
Insurance,	148 40			
Debentures	2800 00			
Interest	2837 61			
Contingent,	211 43			
Rent,	200 00			
Repairs,	242 84			
Indigent Pupils,	1 88			
Salaries,	9889 21			
Janitors	924 50			
Unpaid Cheques Jan. '01	5 11			
Balance	5507 15	23,686 41		$25,332 93
		25 332 93		

CHAS. A. SAMPSON, *Secretary*.

STATEMENT B.

Names of Teachers, age, sex, and Number of Pupils for Term ended 31st December, 1901.

SCHOOL.	Teacher.	Pupils 6 to 15 years.	Over 15 years,	Boys.	Girls.	Total.
High School....	B. C. Foster......	...	36	19	17	36
	H. H. Hagerman..	5	6	22	29	51
	A. S. McFarlane..	24	5	29	..	29
	Ella L. Thorne....	33	17	...	50	50
York Street....	A. I. Tibbits......	40	8	19	29	48
	L. E. Vandine....	54	..	28	26	54
	Kate McCann.....	58	..	33	25	58
	L. A. Burtt.......	60	..	38	22	60
	I. R. Everett.....	54	..	28	26	54
	L. Nicolson.......	53	..	24	29	53
Model...........	Amos O'Blenes....	46	..	16	30	46
	M. E. S. Nicolson.	48	..	18	30	48
	M. A. Harvey....	47	..	20	27	47
	C. E. Bridges.....	49	..	21	28	49
Charlotte Street.	Jos. Mills........	48	..	27	21	48
	A. L. Taylor.....	50	..	30	20	50
	E. J. Thompson:...	55	..	36	19	55
	N. Williamson.....	51	..	27	24	51
	Ida McAdam......	47	..	14	33	47
Regent Street...	J. A. Hughes....	29	2	16	15	31
	V. McKenna......	33	..	19	14	33
	Isabel Reid.......	34	..	13	21	34
	S. G. Duffy......	50	..	28	22	50
Brunswick Street	C. McDevitt......	29	...	15	14	29
Mill............	S. Thompson.....	59	..	24	35	59
Doak	R. E. G. Davies...	26	..	12	14	26
		1,082	114	576	620	1,196

CHAS. A. SAMPSON,
Secretary.

STATEMENT C.

Names of Teachers, age, sex, and number of Pupils for Term ended 30th June, 1902.

SCHOOL.	TEACHER	Pupils 6 to 15 Years.	Over 15 yrs.	Boys	Girls	Total
High School.....	B. C. Foster......	3	31	17	17	34
	H. H. Hagerman..	......	47	21	26	47
	A. S. McFarlane..	18	10	28	......	28
	Ella L. Thorne....	......	44	......	44	44
York Street.	A. I. Tibbits......	36	8	19	25	44
	L. E. VanDine	51	1	23	29	52
	K. McCann..	62	......	34	28	62
	K. E. Currie.....	61	......	37	24	61
	I. R. Everett......	55	......	29	26	55
	L. A. Burtt.......	51	......	24	27	51
Model....	Amos O'Bleues.....	44	......	16	28	44
	M. E. S. Nicolson .	46	......	16	30	46
	M. A. Harvey.....	50	......	19	31	50
	L. Nicolson..	50	......	21	29	50
Charlotte Street..	Jos. Mills.........	48	......	28	20	48
	A. L. Taylor......	48	......	30	18	48
	E. J. Thompson. ..	55	1	36	20	56
	N. Williamson.....	54	......	28	26	54
	Ida NcAdam.......	48	......	15	33	48
Regent Street.. .	J. A. Hughes.. ...	25	......	12	13	25
	V. McKenna..	32	......	18	14	32
	E. M. Holland.....	35	......	22	13	35
	S. G. Duffy.......	49	......	26	23	49
Brunswick Street.	C. McDevitt.... ..	28	......	13	15	28
Mill	S. Thompson..... ..	56	1	27	30	57
Doak	R. E. G. Davies. ..	26	......	15	11	26
		1031	143	574	600	1174

CHAS. A. SAMPSON, *Secretary*.

STATEMENT D.

Name and class of teacher, salary and attendance for term ended 31st December, 1901.

SCHOOL.	Teacher.	Class.	Salary from Trustees.	No. Pupils.	Average Daily Attendance.	Per cent. Attendance.
High.	B. C. Foster......	G. S.	850	36	33.67	93.53
	H. H. Hagerman..	G. S.	650	51	45.35	88.92
	A. S. McFarlane...	G. S.	500	29	26.32	90.42
	E. L. Thorne.....	I.	400	50	43.05	87.
York St.........	A. I. Tibbits......	G. S.	250	48	39.13	83.
	L. E. Vandine....	I.	250	54	46.02	85.05
	K. McCann	I.	250	58	49.17	84.07
	L. A. Burtt	I.	250	60	44.06	74.
	I. R. Everett.....	I.	250	54	43.88	81.26
	L. Nicolson	I.	250	53	44.	83.
Model...........	A. O'Blenes	G. S.	650	46	40.13	87.25
	M. E. S. Nicolson.	II.	250	48	41.	85.
	M. A. Harvey	I.	216	47	42.11	89.59
	C. E. Bridges.....	I.	216	49	44.33	90.05
Charlotte St......	Jos. Mills........	G. S.	600	48	31.08	82.09
	A. L. Taylor.	G. S.	250	50	40.12	80.25
	E. J. Thompson..	I.	250	55	46.07	83.76
	N. Williamson ...	G. S.	250	51	44.11	86.49
	Ida McAdam.	II.	250	47	38.06	82.
Regent St...	J. A. Hughes....	I.	600	31	24.96	80.52
	V. McKenna.....	I.	250	33	28.98	87.81
	Isabel Reid	Sup.	250	34	29.81	87.67
	S. G. Duffy.....	I.	250	50	42.87	85.
Brunswick St.....	C. McDevitt......	I.	250	29	23.	78.25
Mill....	S. Thompson.....	G. S.	250	59	42.	71.49
Doak.	R. E. G. Davies..	II.	200	26	13.09	53.
				1196	37.93	83.17

CHAS. A. SAMPSON, *Secretary.*

STATEMENT E.

Name and Class of Teacher, Salary and Attendance for Term ended 30th June, 1902.

SCHOOL.	Teacher.	Class.	Salary from Trustees.	No. Pupils.	Average Daily Attendance.	Per cent. Attendance.
High............	B. C. Foster ...	G. S.	$850	34	31.47	92.55
	H. H. Hagerman.	G. S.	650	47	41.24	87.73
	A. S. McFarlane.	G. S.	500	28	23.29	83.18
	E. L. Thorne.....	I.	500	44	35.04	80.
York Street......	A. I. Tibbits.....	G. S.	350	44	33.83	76.
	L. E. Vandine...	I.	250	52	44.56	85.69
	K. McCann.......	I.	250	62	49.83	80.
	K. E. Currie	I.	250	61	47.	73.
	I. R. Everett....	I.	250	55	45.65	83.
	L. A. Burtt......	I.	250	51	44.47	87.
Model......... ...	A. O'Blenes	G. S.	650	44	36.11	82.06
	M. E. S. Nicolson.	II.	250	46	41.	89.
	M. A. Harvey....	I.	216	50	46.75	93.50
	L. Nicolson......	I.	216	50	44.	89.
Charlotte St.....	Jos. Mills........	G. S.	600	48	41.07	87.04
	A. L. Taylor....	G. S.	250	48	38.14	79.05
	E. J. Thompson..	I.	250	56	46.51	83.05
	N. Williamson ...	G. S.	250	54	46.66	86.04
	Ida McAdam	II.	250	48	39.52	82.33
Regent St	J. A. Hughes ...	I.	600	25	20.84	83.36
	V. McKenna.....	I.	250	32	26.17	84.09
	F. M. Holland...	I.	250	35	28.88	82.05
	S. G. Duffy.....	I.	250	49	42.96	87.
Brunswick St....	C. McDevitt.....	I.	250	28	22.	72.
Mill.............	S. Thompson ...	G. S.	250	57	45.93	80.52
Doak............	R. E. G. Davies.	II.	200	26	14.	57.
				1174	37.56	82.50

CHAS. A. SAMPSON, *Secretary.*

II. CITY OF ST. JOHN.

BOARD OF SCHOOL TRUSTEES.

APPOINTED BY LIEUT. GOVERNOR IN COUNCIL.	Retire.	APPOINTED BY COMMON COUNCIL.	Retire.
ARTHUR I TRUEMAN, *Chairman*,	1906	HERBERT J. OLIVE,	1902
MRS. E. C. SKINNER,	1902	WALTER W. WHITE, M. D.	1903
JAMES V. RUSSEL,	1903	MRS. M. DEVER,	1904
W. C. RUDMAN ALLAN,	1904	DAVID H. NASE,	1905
JOHN KEEFE,	1905	MICHAEL COLL,	1906
		ROBERT MAXWELL,	1907

Committees.

REAL ESTATE AND BUILDINGS.	SCHOOLS AND TEACHERS.	FINANCE.
M. COLL, *Chairman*,	A. I. TRUEMAN, *Chr'm*,	W. W. WHITE, *Chr'm*
D. H. NASE,	M. COLL,	W. C. R. ALLAN,
R. MAXWELL,	D H NASE,	R. MAXWELL,
H. J. OLIVE,	W. C. R. ALLAN,	H. J. OLIVE,
J. V. RUSSELL,	W. W. WHITE, M. D.	J. KEEFE,
Mrs. E. C. SKINNER,	R. MAXWELL,	
Mrs. M. DEVER,	H. J. OLIVE,	
	J. V. RUSSELL,	
	J. KEEFE,	
	Mrs. M. DEVER,	
	MRS. E. C. SKINNER,	

HENRY S. BRIDGES, M. A., PH. D.
Superintendent.

EDWARD MANNING, A. M.,
Secretary.

JAMES COLL, *Clerk.*

J. R. INCH, ESQ., LL. D.
Chief Supt. of Education.

SIR:—We have the honor to present for your consideration our report of the Public Schools of the City of St. John for the year ending June 30th, 1902, being the 31st report of this board.

At the begining of the school year the chairman was re-appointed by the Lieutenant Governor in Council, and Robert Maxwell, Esq., by the Common Council of the city, so that the membership of the Board remains unchanged.

The Board held twenty-six meetings during the year. In addition to this the committees and sub-committees held numerous meetings as required The chairman re-appointed Dr. W. W. White and Mr. M. Coll as chairman of the finance and building committees respectively.

THE PLAN OF VISITATION TO THE SCHOOLS WAS AS FOLLOWS.

Buildings.	Departments.	Official Visitors.
Sandy Point Road (1), Milledgeville (1), Alexandra (8), Newman Street (4), Douglas Avenue (5), Elm St. (7), St. Peters (15)...	41	M. Coll, D. H. Nase.
Victoria (12), Victoria Annex (6)................	18	Dr. White, J. V. Russell.
High School	14	A. I. Trueman, Dr. White.
St. Vincent's................	7	A. I. Trueman, J. Keefe.
Winter Street................	12	H. J. Olive, R. Maxwell.
Centennial	10	J. V. Russell, R. Maxwell.
Aberdeen................	7	R. Maxwell, J. Keefe.
St. Joseph's................	7	J. Keefe, W. C. R. Allan.
St. Malachi's................	11	A. I. Trueman, J. Keefe.
Queen St. (1), Brittain St. (1)	2	W. C. R. Allan.
Albert (11), Latour (3), St. Patrick's (5), Leinster St. (5)................	24	W. C. R. Allan, H. J. Olive.
	152	

THE CHANGES IN THE TEACHING STAFF DURING THE YEAR WERE AS FOLLOWS.

Resigned.	School.		Appointed.
Annie L. Page,.........	Aberdeen	Grade II,	B. Alward.
Violet Roberts,.........	Elm St.	" II,	Isabel Donaldson.
Lily H. Clark,.........	Centenniel,	" IV,	Edith McBeath.
Gertrude Seely,.........	Albert,	" VI,	Edith Comben.
Agnes Harrington,.....	St. Malachi's	V,	Emily Bardsley.
Florence McManus,.....	"	V, IV,	Mary T. Sugrue.
Maud M. Narraway, .	High S.	" XI,	Wm. Brodie, A. M.
Francoise Bourgeois,....	S. Josephs,	" II	Josephine Cormier.
Mary Farrell,...........	S. Patrick's	IV II,	Mary Gillen.
R. H. Estabrooks,......	Assistant V. Annex,	III,	Grace B. Brown,

As several of these appointments were made by advancing assistants to the permanent staff the following new assistants were appointed:

Lottie Fullerton, Jennie Munro, Effie McDougall, Minnie Maguire, Isabella Reed and Elizabeth Hayes,

Miss Narraway, whose retirement was regretted by the Board, had performed for some time most valuable work in the Victoria and High School.

At the closing examinations of the High School at midsummer the following medals were won:

Corporation Gold Medal for *dux* of the school .... William Morrow
Parker Silver Medal for *dux* in Mathematics .... William Morrow
Governor Generals' Silver Medal for Grade X .... William Woods
Chairman's Gold Medal for Grades VIII (whole city)....Alice Kelly
of S. Peters' Girls.

The schools heartily participated in the welcome given to the Duke and Duchess of York, on the occasion of their visit to the city of St. John in Oct. 1901. By arrangement with the Provincial Government a chorus of 700 pupils under the direction of Prof. Collinson sang the "National Anthem" and "My Own Canadian Home" at the reception given in the Exhibition Building. The singing of the children was greatly appreciated by all who were present.

The lady trustees, as they have done since the time of their appointment have visited all the schools, and a general inspection of all the schools by the entire Board was made in June, according to the annual custom.

The Superintendent, Dr. H. S. Bridges, has continued the inspection of the schools efficiently, as well as acting as principal of the High School. In November 1901, he received the high compliment of an offer from the Colonial Office in England, to assist in the establishment of a system of education in the Transvaal in South Africa, on the lines of the New Brunswick system; but declined the offer at the request of this Board which felt that the city could not afford to loose his valuable services. His salary was increased by $400 per annum.

The following bonds matured during the year and were paid:

St. John School	Board	No.	277	$2000 00
"	"	"	278	600 00
Portland	"	"	63	400 00

The Board also paid $2,333.32 on the sinking fund account, making the amount to its credit $9,333.32.

To meet the expense of building the Latour School just built in Carleton, the Board obtained the following authorization of a new issue of $25,000 of School Bonds:

Minutes of Council passed and approved by His Honor the Lieutenant-Governor on the 4th of June, 1901:—

The Honorable the Provincial Secretary, reports that the Board of School Trustees of the City of Saint John have petitioned, setting forth in detail the several issues of Debentures made by the said Board under and by virtue of Chapter 65 of the Consolidated Statutes, and with the consent of the Governor in Council; and also the purposes to which the proceeds thereof had been devoted, by which it appears that the total issue of debentures to date amounts to Three Hundred and Sixty-Nine Thousand, Seven Hundred and Ninety-One Dollars; that for several years they have rented for school purposes three rooms in the lower flat of the Masonic Hall in Carleton (West End), which have never been and cannot possibly be made suitable for such purposes, owing to the construction of said hall; that the increase of the number of scholars in the West End has rendered it necessary that additional school accomodation be provided in that part of the City of Saint John; that the said Board after careful consideration decided to erect a brick building of sufficient seating capacity to accommodate the increased number of pupils, together with those who have been hitherto occupying the Masonic Hall Building—the building to be furnished and equipped in every way with the requirements of a modern school building; that in order to complete and equip such new building, the Board required the sum of Twenty-Five Thousand dollars, which amount, under the provisions of the Schools' Act, can only be raised by the issue of debentures; that the said Board of School Trustees, by their said petition, respectfully request that the consent of His Honor the Lieutenant-Governor in Council may be given to the said Board for the issue of additional School Debentures to the amount of Twenty-Five Thousand Dollars.

The Committee of Council concurring in the prayer of the said petition of the said Board of School Trustees, and under and by virtue of the Act of Assembly in such case made and provided, recommends that it be ordered that the said Board of School Trustees have leave to issue, in the usual form, debentures to the amount of Twenty-Five Thousand Dollars, for the erection and equipment of the said school building.

And His Honor the Lieutenant Governor concurring therein,

It is accordingly so ordered.

Certified (Signed) A. R. McCLELAN.

R. W. L. TIBBITS,
Deputy Provincial Secretary.

The Board accordingly issued the amount mentioned, which sold as follows:

$24,000 at 99¾ p. c.
1,000 at par.

The issue was in bonds of $500 each, running 25 years, and bearing interest at 3½ per cent.

The Latour School, which is designed to accommodate pupils in the southern half of Carleton, faces on St. John Street, the school lot running back to St. George Street. It is built of brick with stone trimmings, measuring 80 by 90 feet, and contains two stories and basement, with high roof. There are three entrances, one at the front and two at the side.

The basement is airy and well lighted, with a good height of ceiling. Its outer walls are built hollow and the interior ones of solid brick. the plastering is cement work directly on the brick, there being no woodwork in this part of the building except the doors and window finish. Here are the boys' and girls' lavatories, 28 x 32 feet each, situated at each side, separated by the furnace and coal room, which run from front to rear. Here also are the play rooms with asphalt floor. The boys' lavatory is fitted up with slate urinals and enamelled W. C. range, the girls' with double W. C. range —besides which are four teachers' W. C.'s with marble wash basins and cement floor.

On the ground floor are four class rooms, each 32 x 28 feet, also four cloak rooms and a well lighted centre and cross hall, 12 feet wide. The Principal's room is at the right of the main entrance. There are two flights of wide stairs from ground floor to second floor, neatly framed in birch.

The second floor has two class rooms of the same size as those on the ground floor and a fine Assembly Hall 88 x 32 feet, also two cloak rooms. Each class room is fitted up with a teacher's room and each room contains a cabinet.

The floors above the basement are of the best quality of birch, and the walls of the class rooms and corridors are wainscotted 3 or 4 feet from the floor with the same wood. The rest of the interior finish is of white wood. The partitions between the cloak rooms and corridor are of wire work.

The plastering above the basement is of Windsor cement. Each room is fitted up with ventilating boxes connected with a heated ventilation flue.

The entrance steps are of granite, the vestibule of cast iron, the cornices and covering of the high roof of galvanized iron, the deck of gravel roofing.

The building is heated throughout with hot water, supplied by two Dowy boilers with twin connection, is well lighted and in every respect thoroughly modern and convenient. The architect was H. H. Mott, Esq., the builders B. Mooney & Sons, with Andrew Myles as sub-contractor for carpentering, Jas. McDade for galvanized iron work, Jas. Pullen for painting, J. Fitzgerald for heating, and P. Campbell for plumbing.

The Board has also made some needed improvments of a permanent nature as follows:—At winter Street School, by substituting a hot water heating system for the hot air system, which had been found unsatisfactory; at the High School, by placing additional radiators at the north side where they were required; and by taking advantage of the new street sewer just laid in Douglas Avenue to establish a fine series of sanitaries there. The cost was;

At Winter Street School	2,457.00
High School	1,371.71
Douglas Avenue	2,092.23
	$5,920.94

Besides these expenditures on capital account, the year's repairs amounted to $3365.14, the chief of which were :—

Miscellaneous repairs to Albert both exterior and interior, as well as yards and fences. New floors in St. Patrick's. Repairs to roof and furniture of Douglas Avenue. Repairs to fence, windows, desks and yard of Victoria. Kalsomining and wall slates in Victoria Annex. New desks and basement whitewashed in St. Joseph's. Wall slates in St. Malachi's, Repairs to desks and walls in Leinster Street. Retaining wall rebuilt, wall slates and new desks in Centennial. Additional radiators in out room of Aberdeen and yard levelled and raised. Wall slates and new desks in one room in Winter Street. New desks in one room in St. Peters' Girls. High School entrance improved.

New maps, globes and dictionaries were supplied to the amount of about $288 by the committee on school aparatus.

The year opened with the largest enrolment on record, but the attendance was afterwards sadly lessened by an epidemic of small pox, which appeared in the city in October. The attendance gradually went down to little over 50 per cent of those on the rolls, ahd one school, the Aberdeen, seemed exposed to so much danger that it had to be temporarily closed and thoroughly disinfected. Soon after the Christmas holidays, however, the epidemic was effectually controlled, but the rate of attendance was materially affected till midsummer.

The Board contemplates erecting during the coming year a large school building in the centre of that portion of the city formerly called Portland, to accommodate the children now attending the Elm Street school and to relieve other over crowded buildings. On the completion of this building all the children of the city will be provided with commodious and well ventilated schoolrooms in modern and properly equipped buildings, of which any community might well feel proud. The questions of manual training and domestic science will no doubt receive the careful consideration of the Board at an early date.

We have the honor to be, Sir,

Your obedient servants,

ARTHUR I. TUEMAN, *Chairman.*

E. MANNING, *Secretary.*

STATISTICAL TABLES.

TABLE I—GENERAL FINANCIAL STATEMENT.

Assets.

Cash on hand June 30, 1902		$ 22 64
Furniture (See Table)	$ 31,315 46	
Lands and Buildings	343,373 92	
		$ 374,689 38
Sinking Funds for Debentures issued 1898....		9,333 32
Due from City Corporation for same		25,666 68
Water Bond No. G. 1342		500 00
Ground Rent, balance due		422 00
Due from City Corporation, proportion of School Assessment for 1902....		44,720 50
On hand, Wood and Coal	229 00	
Supplies in Office	66 01	
Medals	55 12	
		350 13
		455,704 65
Excess of Liabilities over Assets		27,975 21
		$ 483,679 86

LIABILITIES.

Debentures due	1901,	Paid	$ 700 00	
" "	1902,	"	2,600 00	
" "	1908,	"	6,000 00	
" "	1909,	"	11,500 00	
" "	1910,	"	5,941 00	
" "	1917,	"	20,000 00	
" "	1920,	"	17,000 00	
" "	1921,	"	23,000 00	
" "	1922,	"	35,500 00	
" "	1925,	"	34,500 00	
" "	1926,	"	69,500 00	
" "	1926,	"	25,000 00	
" "	1934,	"	10,000 00	
" "	1935.	"	20,000 00	
" "	1936,	"	1,500 00	
" "	1937,	"	34,000 00	
" "	1940,	"	26,500 00	
" "	1940,	"	43,500 00	
Portland debt.	1906,	"	7,750 00	
" "	1907,	"	1,000 00	
			————	$ 395,491 00
Debentures issued by consent of Common Council and by authority of Legislature to pay off current indebtedness and in lieu of unpaid assessments due 1913				35,000 00
Coupons not presented, 36.				
Due Bank of New Brunswick				53,152 86

Table II—CAPITAL ACCOUNT FOR YEAR ENDING 30TH JUNE 1902.

RECEIPTS.

Sale of Debentures		
Issue August 1st. 1901, interest		
$3\frac{1}{2}$ p. c. Nos. 605 to 606 $1000		
at par	1,000 00	
607, 654, $24000, at $99\frac{3}{4}$	23,940 00	
Received from Current account	1,984 77	
		26,924 77

EXPENDITURE.

Debentures Retired		
No. 63 Town of Portland	400 00	
Furniture purchased	1,321 12	
LaTour school property on construction		
account	18,972 96	
Elm St. Property	309 75	
Douglas Avenue improvements	2,092 23	
Winter St. improvements	2,457 00	
High Schools	1,371 71	
		26,924 77

Table III.—RECEIPTS ON CURRENT ACCOUNT, 1902.

Cash on hand June 30th 1901, ...	$ 8 75	
Special deposit Bank of N. B., ...	629 92	
		$ 635 67
Received from Ground Rent, ...		511 00
Assessment, 1901, ...		90,915 06
County Fund, "		11,276 22
For Medals, "		125 00
Coal, ...	$ 512 22	
Medals, ...	55 12	
		567 34
Balance due Bank of New Brunswick, ...		53,152 86
		$157,183 15

EXPENDITURE, 1902.

Cash of Schools per Table IV., ...	$ 74,912 39	
Incidental Expenses, ...	760 29	
Salary of Secretary and Clerk, ...	1,400 00	
Expenses of Office, ...	397 80	
Advertising and Printing,....	128 09	
Work Shop Account, ...	60 20	
La Tour School Water Rate, ...	2 60	
Weldon Lot, ...	3 60	
		77,664 97
Coupon Interest, ...		14,856 11
Special Coupon Interest Bond 277, ...		120 00
Bank of New Brunswick, on Overdrafts, ...		1,246 90
Cash on hand, ...		22 64
Sinking Fund Account, ...		2,110 45
Repaid Contractors Deposits, ...		471 60
Paid Bank of New Brunswick, Loan, Balance due 1901, ...		58,355 58
Supplies on hand, ...	66 01	
Fuel, Wood and Coal, ...	229 00	
Medals, ...	55 12	
		350 13
To Capital Account, ...		1,984 77
		$157,183 15

TABLE IV.—Cost of the Schools for the Year Ending June 30th, 1902.

SCHOOLS.	Teachers.	Care.	Repairs.	Fuel, Water & Light.	Rent.	Insurance	Supply.	Expense.	Totals.
Spar Cove	$	$	3 65	$	$ 10 00	$	$ 12	$	13 77
Sandy Point Road	245 43	28 00	2 00	24 00	....	....	32	5 00	304 75
Millidgeville	347 15	42 00	22 44	21 25	20 00	....	55	4 00	457 39
Alexandra	2,927 36	400 00	102 83	500 47	150 00	....	35 04	1 00	4,116 70
Newman Street	1,593 81	120 00	28 54	150 14	80 00	....	2 26	....	1,974 75
Douglas Avenue	1,839 53	120 00	178 84	199 35	50 00	....	5 54	7 50	2 400 76
Elm Street	1,725 36	130 00	53 36	182 19	200 00	....	8 78	80	2 300 49
St. Peter's, Boys	2,812 09	204 00	80 67	230 34	400 00	....	36 85	1 00	3,764 95
St. Peter's, Girls	2,467 42	192 00	287 96	178 12	400 00	....	10 45	4 00	3,539 95
Winter Street	3,808 01	400 00	354 02	470 00	....	....	9 51	....	5,041 54
Aberdeen	2,406 66	200 00	271 85	325 99	....	....	18 96	8 50	3 231 96
Centennial	3,507 81	420 00	224 46	591 05	....	10 00	21 15	3 25	4 777 72
St. Vincent	2 028 79	204 00	80 82	160 00	300 00	....	24 63	....	2 798 24
High School	7,943 04	500 00	204 11	1,042 07	....	10 00	33 06	75	9,769 03
Leinster Street	1,802 89	200 00	241 57	274 65	350 00	....	6 99	....	2 876 10
St Malachi's	4,097 23	362 00	104 33	316 57	880 62	....	15 21	3 25	5,779 20
St. Joseph's	2,062 57	250 00	186 18	212 31	425 00	....	34 34	2 50	3,172 90
Victoria and Annex	6,124 13	623 30	232 72	779 65	....	10 00	41 65	13 60	7,825 05
Albert	4,238 46	376 66	554 02	180 84	....	20 00	36 32	90	5,407 20
Latour (and Mason's Hall)	1,238 88	135 34	47 46	46 14	300 00	153 55	3 20	....	1,924 57
St. Patrick's	1,890 37	192 00	61 71	57 90	262 50	....	14 51	....	2,478 99
Queen Street	518 00	42 00	5 60	21 39	75 00	....	8 56	....	670 55
Brittain Street	281 85	....	....	....	....	....	3 98	....	285 83
	$ 55,906 83	$ 5,141 30	$ 3,365 14	$ 5 964 42	$ 3,903 12	$ 203 55	$ 371 98	$ 56 05	$74,912 39

Table V.—DETAILS OF ASSETS OF REAL ESTATE AND FURNITURE.

Property.	Land and Buildings.	Furniture.	Totals.
Sandy Point Road School........	$597 40	$165 84	$ 763 24
Milliidgeville "	1,236 92	164 05	1,400 97
Spar Cove "	355 00	....	355 00
Alexandra "	34 553 04	2,358 83	36.911 87
Newman Street "	2.787 66	498 08	3,285 74
Douglas Avenue "	9.126 54	708 09	9.834 63
Elm Street "	6,365 05	919 91	7,284 96
St. Peters', Boys' "	....	1,280 92	1,280 92
St. Peters', Girls' "	....	1,092 98	1.092 98
Winter Street "	35.896 96	2,187 50	38,084 46
Aberdeen	20 247 41	1,066 75	21.314 16
Centennial	34,175 11	2 360 37	36,535 48
St Vincent's	....	910 42	910 42
High "	53,724 21	4,198 76	57.922 97
Leinster Street "	....	823 35	823 35
St. Malachi's "	....	1,765 17	1,765 17
St. Joseph's "	....	1,188 57	1,188 57
Victoria "	54.289 03	2,932 57	57,221 60
Victoria Annex "	9,230 52	1,242 01	10.472 53
Albert	33.137 86	1,762 69	34 900 55
Latour	29,367 66	1,341 19	30,708 85
St. Patrick's	....	663 60	663 60
Queen Street "	....	136 80	136 80
Brittain Street "	....	95 77	95 77
Office	....	1,327 34	1,327 34
Shop	1,330 98	123 90	1,454 88
Weldon lot	3,000 00	....	3,000 00
Grammar School lots	13,000 00	....	13,000 00
St. Malachi's addition	668 67	....	668 67
St. Patrick's addition	283 90	....	283 90
	$343,373 92	$31.315 46	$374,689 38

TABLE VI.--PUBLIC SCHOOL INSURANCE IN FORCE TO JUNE 27, 1904.

Companies.	Amount.	Period.	Represented by
North British & Mercantile..	$ 11,000	3 years	D. R. Jack.
Guardian..................	11,000	do	Weldon V. McLean.
Liverpool & London & Globe	11,000	do	Wm. M. Jarvis.
Phoenix (of London)......	11,000	do	S. S. Hall.
Imperial.................	11,000	do	E. L. Whittaker.
Connecticut..............	11,000	do	Vroom & Arnold.
Royal....................	11,000	do	J. S. Kaye, J. M. Grant.
Commercial Union.........	9,000	do	H. C. Fairweather.
Northern.................	10,000	do	P. Clinch.
Caledonian...............	9,000	do	Cowie & Edwards.
Norwich Union............	8,000	do	F. B. & H. B. Robinson
British America..........	6,000	do	Knowlton & Gilchrist.
Manchester...............	8,000	do	W. H. White.
Sun......................	8,000	do	H. C. Tilley.
Keystone.................	8,000	do	A. G. Leavitt.
Phoenix of Hartford......	6,000	do	Knowlton & Gilchrist.
Scottish Union...........	5,000	do	J. M. & C. H. Grant.
Queen....................	4,000	do	C. E. L. Jarvis.
Atlas....................	4,000	do	H. Chubb & Co.
Insurance Co. of N. America	4,000	do	C. E. L. Jarvis.
London Assurance.........	4,000	do	R. W. W. Frink.
Western..................	5,000	do	do do
National (of Ireland).......	4,000	do	F. B. & H. B. Robinson
Hartford.................	4,000	do	G. E. Fairweather.
Aetna....................	4,000	do	do do
London & Lancashire......	4,000	do	do do
Quebec...................	3,000	do	Edwin Mackay.
Ottawa...................	4,000	do	T. Dunning.
Union Assurance..........	3,000	do	G. O. D. Otty.
Alliance.................	2,000	do	F. B. & H. B. Robinson
Phoenix (of Brooklyn)......	2,000	do	A. C. Fairweather.
Canadian.................	3,000	do	P. Clark.
Law, Union & Crown......	2,000	do	E. Machum.
Mercantile...............	2,000	do	W. H. White.
American.................	2,000	do	H. Chubb & Co.
Anglo American...........	2,000	do	J. F. Sullivan.
Boiler Insurance Co........	5,000	1 year	R. W. W. Frink.
Law, Union & Crown......	730	do	E. Machum.
Total................	221,730		

TABLE VII.—Details of Fire Insurance in Force to June 27, 1904.

SCHOOLS.	Buildings	On Furniture	On Improvements.	Total.
Sandy Point Road	$ 400	$ 140	$	$ 540
Millidgeville	800	140	......	940
Spar Cove	160	....	......	160
Alexandra	21,300	2,000	......	23,300
Newman Street	2,000	400	......	2,400
Douglas Avenue	5,600	600	......	6,200
St. Peter's (Boys)	......	1,000	......	1,000
St. Peter's (Girls)	......	850	......	850
Winter Street	21,000	1,500	......	22,500
Aberdeen	13,000	850	......	13,850
Centennial	21,000	1,800	......	22,800
St. Vincent's	......	650	......	650
High School	30,600	3,000	......	33,600
Leinster Street	......	650	......	650
St. Malachi's	......	1,325	475	1,800
St. Joseph's	......	920	......	920
Victoria	35,000	2,400	......	37,400
Victoria Annex	5,600	850	......	6,450
Queen Street	......	110	.....	110
Britain Street	......	150	......	150
Albert	20,000	1,310	......	21,310
St. Patrick's	......	500	220	720
Latour	15,000	1,000	......	16,000
Shop	850	250	......	1,100
Office	......	600	......	600
	$192,310	$ 22,995	$695	$216,000

SPECIAL INSURANCE—ANNUAL.

Elm Street, Furniture			$730
Albert, 2 Boilers	$2,000		
Victoria, 1 Boiler	1,000		
High, 1 Boiler	1,000		
Centennial, 1 Boiler	1,000	—$5,000	—$5,730
Total			$221,730

TABLE VIII.—School Estimates for 1902.

1. Salaries of Teachers and Superintendent			$56,070
2. Salaries of Officers,			1,400
3. Fuel, Water and Light,			6,500
4. Care of Buildings			5,392
5. Rent and Insurance			4,403
6. Printing, Advertising and Binding			300
7. Repairs			5,000
8. Incidental Expenses			1,500
9. School Apparatus			500
10. Interest on Bank Overdraw			1,200
			$82,265
Less—County Fund, say,		$11,000	
Ground Rent and Interest		500	
			11,500
			$70,765
Add Debenture Interest:—On $ 27,850 @ 6 p. c.	$1,671 00		
" 6,941 @ 5 p. c.	347 05		
" 240,000 @ 4 p. c.	8,160 00		
" 187,000 @ 3½ p.c.	6,545 00		
Sinking Fund	2,053 00		
			18,776
			$89,541

TABLE IX.—Ground Rent Statement, Year Ending June 30th, 1902.

	AMOUNTS	RENT DUE.	RENT P'D.	BALANCE.
Mr. Hugh H. McLean,				
Year's rent to May 1, 1902,	$ 80 00	$ 80 00	$ 80 00	....
Mrs. C. D. McAlpine,				
Balance due..................	60 00	....	....	....
Year's rent to May 1, 1902,........	60 00	120 00	46 00	$74 00
Mrs. Fred. Gregory,				
Balance due,....................	100 00	....	....	....
Year's rent to May 1, 1902,........	40 00	140 00	40 00	100 00
Mr. Jas. Parken,				
Balance due,....................	90 00	....	....	....
Year's rent to May 1, 1902,........	60 00	150 00	120 00	30 00
Mr. Chas. A. Clark,				
Balance due,....................	113 00	....	....	....
Year's rent to May 1, 1902,........	80 00	193 00	75 00	118 00
Mr. Fred S. Thompson,				
Balance due,....................	50 00	....	....	....
Year's rent to May 1, 1902,........	50 00	100 00	750 00	250 00
Dr. Jas Manning,				
Balance due,....................	50 00	....	....	....
Year's rent to May 1, 1902,........	50 00	100 00	25 00	75 00
Mrs. L. E. Sprague,				
Year's rent to May 1, 1902	50 00	50 00	50 00	....
Total of balances due,..............	....	....	......	$422 00

Table X.—BONDS ISSUED BY BOARD OF SCHOOL TRUSTEES, ST. JOHN.

Series.		Numbers.	Denominations	Amount	When Due.	Rate of Int'rst.
St. John, First Series		277	$ 2,000	$ 2,000	July, 1902	6 p. c.
do	do	278	600	600	" "	6 "
do	do	279 to 290	500	6,000	January, 1908	6 "
do	do	291 to 313	500	11,500	July, 1909	6 "
do	do	314 to 324	500	5,500	January, 1910	5 "
do	do	325	441	441	" "	5 "
do	do	327 to 366	500	20,000	July, 1917	4 "
do	do	375 to 408	500	17,000	Sept. 1020	4 "
do	do	409 to 421	500	6,500	March, 1921	4 "
do	do	422 to 454	500	16,500	August, 1921	4 "
do	do	455 to 479	1,000	25,000	" 1922	3½ "
do	do	480 to 500	500	10,500	" "	3½ "
do	do	501 to 535	1,000	*35.000	May, 1913	4 "
do	do	536 to 604	500	34,500	" 1925	3½ "
do	do	605 to 654	500	25,000	August, 1926	3½ "
Portland, First Series		64. 65	500	1,000	" 1907	5 "
do	Second Series	1 to 14	500	7,000	Sept., 1906	6 "
do	do	15	750	750	" "	6 "
St. John, Second series		1 to 20	500	10,000	Nov., 1934	4 "
(Redemption Bonds)		21 to 60	500	20,000	May, 1935	4 "
do	do	61 to 63	500	1,500	March, 1936	4 "
do	do	64 to 131	500	34,000	January, 1937	4 "
do	do	132 to 218	500	43,500	May, 1940	4 "
do	do	219 to 271	500	26,500	July, 1940	3½ "
do	do	272 to 410	500	69,500	January, 1941	3½ "
			Total	$429,791		

Redeemed Nos. 1—100, 201 to 276, 326, 367 to 374, St. John 1st series.
Nos. 101—120 registered. From 120 to 200 never issued.
Nos. 1—63 Portland, 1st series.

*With sinking fund.

TABLE XI.—Summary of the Year's Work.

I. BUILDINGS.	First Term.	Second Term.
Number of Buildings Occupied as Schools	23	24
" " Owned	12	13
" " Rented	10	10
" " Occupied without Rent	1	1
" Rooms owned	88	94
" Rented	60	57
" Occupied without Rent	1	1
" High School Departments Grades XII.—IX.	13	13
" Advanced Departments, Grades VIII.—	46	43
" Advanced and Primary Depart. Grade VII —I	16	16
" Primary Departments Grade IX.—I	77	80

II. PUPILS.	First Term.	Second Term.
Number of Pupils enrolled	7,297	6,928
" Boys "	3,519	3,367
" Girls "	3,778	3,561
" Pupils over 15 yrs. of age	346	338
" " under 15 yrs. of age	6,951	6,593
" " Reduced by transfer	7,279	6,859
" Daily present on an average	5,549	5,495
Percentage of enrolled, daily present, Fall term	76.5	80
Grand Total Days' Attendance	443,951	637,828
Number attending High Schools	505	459
" " Advanced Schools	2,368	2,246
" " Primary "	4,408	4,223
" of Pupils to each Teacher, (average)	40 nearly	45
" Reported new to Schools	1,056	232
Percentage whole number attending High Schools	7	6.7
" " " " Advanced Schools.	32.5	33.02
" " " " Primary Schools	60.5	60.28

III. THE SCHOOL YEAR.	
Number of Teaching Days in the School Year	201
Total Number of Pupils enrolled	7,529
Grand Total Days Attendance for the Year	1,081,779
Average Number of Days each Pupil attended	143.7

TABLE XII.—Particulars of School Attendance. Year Ended June 30th, 1902.

SCHOOLS.	TEACHERS.	Class of License.	Grades Taught. 1st Term.	Grades Taught. 2d Term.	1st Term. Enrolled.	1st Term. Attended.	1st Term. Per cent.	2nd Term. Enrolled	2nd Term. Attended.	2nd Term. Per cent.
Sdy. Pt. Road	M. Eva Keagin	Sup.	B & G 5,1	B & G 5-1	14	9	62	19	9	47
Millidgeville	J. V. Kierstead	I	B & G 5,1	B & G 5-1	33	24	73	30	22	74
Alexandra	H. V. Hayes	I	B & G 8	B & G 8	41	33	79	36	29	82
	Jean Scott	Sup.	" 7, 6	" 7, 6	55	44	80	53	41	81
	Ada Cowan	I	" 6	" 6	57	47	82	56	49	88
	Grace Murphy	I	" 5	" 5	58	46	80	58	49	86
	E. McAlary	II	" 5, 4	" 5, 4	58	45	78	65	52	81
	B. E Forbes	I	" 4, 3	" 4, 3	64	52	81	65	56	86
	E. L. Colwell	II	" 2	" 2	58	46	78	62	49	81
	B. I. Stevenson	I	" 1	" 1	63	48	76	68	52	77
Newman St	M. D. Brown	I	B & G 7	B & G 7	48	40	83	48	40	84
	P. W. Livingstone	II	" 4, 3	" 4, 3	54	41	76	52	43	86
	E. G. Powers	I	" 2	" 2	46	38	82	48	41	85
	J. H. Mowry	II	" 1	" 1	55	37	66	50	36	78
Douglas Av	Geo. W. Dill	I	B & G 8, 7	B & G 8, 7	37	32	88	37	30	81
	A. G. Gale	I	" 6, 5	" 6, 5	49	36	74	47	37	78
	L. C. Brown	II	" 4, 3	" 4, 3	47	38	81	45	37	83
	H. M. Dale	II	" 3, 2	" 3, 2	52	40	76	54	41	80
	E. J. Connell	I	" 1	" 1	58	43	73	53	59	75
Elm St	Kate A. Kerr	I	B & G 5	B & G 5	57	45	78	52	43	83
	I. Donaldson	I	" 4	" 4	53	40	75	48	38	79
	G. P. Sharp	II	" 4, 3	....	56	40	71	...	...	...
	B. A. Alward	I	....	" 4, 3	...	...	...	54	49	81
	Sarah Gray	II	" 2	" 2	59	40	75	50	38	79
	M. I. Strang	II	" 3, 2	" 3, 2	52	46	78	50	39	81
	J. N. Munro	I	" 2, 1	" 2, 1	43	29	66	38	28	73
	M. I. Morrow	I	" 1	" 1	74	48	65	59	44	74
St. Peter's Boys	J. Harrington	I	B 8, 6	B 8, 6	39	30	76	35	28	79
	M. D. Sweeney	II	" 5, 4	" 5, 4	58	41	70	52	40	78
	E. J. Quinn	I	" 4	" 4	56	48	85	55	45	82
	M. L. McMillin	II	" 3	" 3	60	48	80	59	48	82
	A. B. McInnis	II	" 2	" 2	44	35	79	42	36	85
	K. S Buckley	II	" 2, 1	" 2, 1	58	41	71	55	41	75
	A. F. McCarron	II	" 1	" 1	74	45	60	56	41	74
St. Peter's Girls	J. Carney	I	G 8, 7	G 8, 7	35	31	89	32	27	84
	M. H. McClaskey	I	" 6	" 6	42	32	76	40	31	78
	A. Cassidy	I	" 5	" 5	40	27	68	35	27	76
	F. M. Quinn	II	" 5, 4	" 5, 4	40	29	73	40	30	75
	M. E. Kelly	II	" 4, 3	" 4, 3	41	30	74	41	32	78
	M. R. Corkery	II	" 3	" 3	45	38	84	46	39	86
	S. Boudrean	II	" 2	" 2	57	41	72	49	39	79
	E. Marry	II	" 1	" 1	59	39	67	60	42	70

PARTICULARS OF SCHOOL ATTENDANCE. YEAR ENDED JUNE 30TH, 1902. CONTINUED.

SCHOOLS.	TEACHERS.	Class of License.	Grades Taught. 1st term	Grades Taught. 2d term	1st term. Enrolled.	1st term. Attended.	1st term. Per. Cent.	2nd term. Enrlledo.	2nd term. Attended.	2nd term. Per. Cent.
Winter St...	T. Stothart........	I	B & G 8	B & G 8	36	25	69	33	26	80
	A. M. Iaddles.....	I	" 7	" 7	47	36	76	45	37	70
	J. K. Sutherland..	II	" 6	" 6	46	34	74	43	34	78
	J. S. Drake........	I	" 6, 5	" 6, 5	37	23	64	43	32	74
	A. A. McLeod.....	I	" 5	" 5	49	34	70	49	43	86
	M. Gibson.........	I	" 4	" 4	50	33	66	48	39	80
	S. Taylor	I	" 4, 3	" 4, 3	41	31	77	38	33	86
	Gertrude Webb...	I	" 3	" 3	60	41	67	56	46	81
	L. I. Simpson.....	II	" 2	" 2	60	39	66	50	40	81
	M. R. Gray........	II	" 2, 1	" 2, 1	60	44	73	59	46	79
	E. Barlow..........	I	" 1	" 1	58	39	68	52	39	80
	M. R. Graham.....	I	" 1	" 1	41	25	62	40	22	67
Aberdeen ...	W. M. McLean....	G. S.	B & G 8, 7	B & G 8, 7	32	24	75	29	20	68
	E. G. Corbet.......	I	" 6, 5	" 6, [illegible]	50	35	69	41	32	78
	A. B. Honeywill...	I	" 5, 4	" 5,	50	35	66	45	31	68
	M. Anderson......	I	" 4	"	44	30	65	41	30	75
	Jessie Caird.......	II	" 3	"	52	36	69	50	39	78
	A. L. Page.........	II	" 2	....	48	32	66	....	....	....
	M. S. Fowler......	I	....	" 2	....	....	....	45	33	74
	M. V. Lawrence...	II	" 1	" 1	56	35	62	53	40	76
Centennial ..	Henry Town.......	I	B 7	B 7	38	27	70	37	29	78
	J. M. Rowan......	II	" 4	" [illegible]	41	29	71	40	36	89
	M. C. Evans.......	I	" 3	"	47	31	65	41	32	78
	I. Estabrook......	I	" 2	"	60	43	71	62	52	83
	A. B. Allen........	II	" 1	"	70	43	61	68	49	72
	A. M. Hea..........	I	G 5	G	44	29	65	40	35	82
	E. McBeath.......	I	" 4	"	55	33	61	55	44	81
	M. I. Campbell....	II	" 3	"	42	26	59	39	30	79
	J. Milligan.........	I	" 2	"	44	26	59	42	33	87
	L. K. Mackay.....	I	B & G 1	"	70	35	56	60	43	73
St. Vincent's	M. McDonald.. ...	Sup.	G 12, 10	G 12, 10	34	26	76	33	29	87
	M. E. Carey.......	I	" 9	" 9	32	23	72	32	26	80
	H. M. Kirke.......	I	" 5, 4	" 5, 4	43	26	60	41	35	84
	M. A. Legere......	I	" 3, 2	" 3, 2	55	32	58	51	42	83
	R. B. Gallagher...	II	" 1	" 1	58	34	58	54	40	74
	B. Cosgrove.......	II	" 6, 1	" 5, 1	56	54	96	55	54	98
High School	H. S. Bridges......	G. S.	B & G 12	B & G 12	7	6	84	6	5	86
	W. J. S. Myles....	G. S.	" 11	" 11	43	39	90	40	35	88
	M. M. Narraway..	G. S.	G 11	G 11	43	38	88	41	35	85
	T. E. Powers... ..	G. S.	B 10	B 10	41	36	87	42	34	81
	M. E. Knowlton...	G. S.	B & G 10	G 10	45	36	79	35	30	85
	K. R. Bartlett.....	I	G 10	" 10	44	38	81	42	36	85
	E. McNaughton....	G. S.	" 9	" 9	44	34	78	40	33	83
	H. M. Ward.......	I	B 9	B 9	43	34	80	41	31	77
	P. K. VanWart...	I	" 9	" 9	44	38	86	36	31	87
	B. H. Wilson......	I	G 9	G 9	45	34	75	38	30	80
	J. I. Lawson.......	G. S.	B & G [illegible]	B & G 9	40	32	81	33	26	80
	A. K. Lingley.....	I	B	B 8	44	36	81	43	38	89
	L. H. Yandall.....	I	G	G 8	36	27	75	35	29	84
	F. I. Thorne.......	I	"	G 7	43	33	76	39	31	79
inster St..	J. McKinnon......	I	B 7	B 7	45	33	74	46	40	87
	L. M. Kavanagh...	I	" 6	" 6	48	39	82	46	36	80

PARTICULARS OF SCHOOL ATTENDANCE. YEAR ENDED JUNE 30TH, 1902.—CONTINUED.

SCHOOLS.	TEACHERS.	Class of License.	Grades Taught.		1st term.			2nd term.		
			1st term	2d term.	Enrolled.	Attended.	Per. Cent.	Enrolled.	Attended.	Per. Cent.
Leinster St..	E. W. Gilmore.....	Sup.	B 5	B 5	52	35	68	50	41	81
	E. K. Turner.....	I	" 5	" 5	49	38	78	48	41	86
	F. J. Dieuaide.....	I	" , 4	" 5, 4	46	30	65	39	31	80
St. Malachi's	James Barry......	I	B 8	B 8	31	25	81	29	23	80
	M. R. Carlyn......	I	" 7	" 7, 6	40	28	71	39	33	84
	M. C. Coughlan....	II	" 6, 5	" 6	37	27	73	33	27	82
	A. B. Harrington..	II	" 5	" 5	38	23	61	35	28	79
	F. E. McManus....	II	" 5, 4	" 5, 4	49	34	70	46	37	81
	M. E. Gallivan.....	II	" 4	" 4	50	33	67	47	39	82
	E. F McInerney..	I	" 3	" 3	45	31	70	42	36	86
	Jas. R. Sugrue...	II	" 3	" 3	37	24	67	38	30	78
	K. A. Cotter.......	II	" 2	" 2	51	34	66	47	36	77
	C. M. Hogan.......	II	" 2, 1	" 2, 1	41	22	57	35	27	76
	K. E. Lawlor.....	II	" 1	" 1	71	44	62	64	40	63
St. Joseph's.	S. Burchill.........	I	G 8, 6	G 8, 6	31	21	69	30	23	77
	M. E. Walsh......	I	" 7	" 7	42	33	79	40	35	88
	K. O'Neill.........	II	" 6	" 6	50	36	72	47	38	81
	K. Haggerty.......	II	" 5, 4	" 5, 4	50	35	70	44	37	83
	F. Bourgeois......	II	" 4, 3	" 4, 3	53	36	69	51	44	86
	G. Fitzgerald......	II	" 2	" 2	44	29	66	41	35	84
	A. P. Delaney.....	II	" 1	" 1	48	29	62	44	33	76
Victoria......	W. H. Parlee.......	I	G 8	G 8	41	31	76	36	31	85
	E. A. Godard......	I	" 7	" 7	50	36	72	46	34	75
	M. L. Lingley......	I	" 6	" 6	48	34	70	48	42	87
	M. G. Sharpe....	II	" 6	" 6	48	35	73	48	40	83
	J. W. Estey.......	I	" 5	" 5	54	35	65	48	37	77
	A. D. Robb........	I	" 5, 4	" 5, 4	47	31	66	48	33	81
	L. G. Ingraham....	I	" 4	" 4	53	36	68	51	41	82
	S. T. Payson..	I	" 4, 3	" 4, 3	53	39	73	51	43	84
	F. E. Henderson...	I	" 3	" 3	53	:9	73	51	44	88
	B. G. Thompson...	I	" 2	" 2	55	39	71	53	42	81
	M. H. Shaw......	II	" 2, 1	" 2, 1	51	30	58	48	35	73
	H. D. Gregg.......	I	" 1	" 1	56	36	64	49	45	76
Victoria Annex....	A. L. Dykeman....	Sup.	B 6	B 6	48	37	76	45	39	90
	L. Wetmore.......	I	" 4	" 4	49	38	77	50	45	89
	L. L. Slater.....	I	" 3	" 3	51	38	74	50	43	85
	G. B. Brown.......	Sup.	" 3	" 3	53	30	72	46	40	86
	M. G. Gunn........	II	" 2	" 2	57	41	73	56	49	87
	H. O. Howard.....	II	" 1	" 1	63	39	61	65	45	70
Queen Street	I. T. Richardson..	II	B & G 4, 1	B & G 4, 1	30	20	68	28	20	70
Brittain......	Helen Adam.....	I	B & G 6, 1	B & G 6, 1	20	17	84	29	23	79
Albert.......	J. Montgomery....	I	B & G 8, 7	B & G 8, 7	45	36	80	40	39	[illegible]
	C. R. Fullerton....	Sup.	" 7	" 7	45	35	77	43	34	[illegible]
	E. A. Comben......	I	" 6, 5	" 6, 5	46	34	74	38	29	[illegible]
	Enoch Thompson..	I	" 6, 5	" 6, 5	45	31	69	39	30	[illegible]
	M. G. Emerson....	II	" 6, 5	" 6, 5	39	31	80	36	29	8
	A. M. Carleton....	Sup.	" 4	" 4	61	47	79	52	40	[illegible]
	L. J. Fullerton....	I	" 4, 3	" 4, 3	51	39	76	61	49	[illegible]
	H. M. Thompson..	I	" 3	" 3	50	41	82	52	44	[illegible]
	H. A. Smith.......	I	" 3, 2	" 3, 2	61	48	79	61	51	[illegible]

PARTICULARS OF SCHOOL ATTENDANCE. YEAR ENDING JUNE 30TH, 1902.—CONTINUED.

SCHOOL.	TEACHERS.	Class of License.	Grades Taught.		1st term.			2nd term.		
			1st term	2nd term	Enrolled.	Attended.	Per Cent.	Enrolled.	Attended.	Per Cent.
Albert.......	B. A. Brittain.....	I	B & G 2, 1	B & G 2, 1	68	55	81	63	53	85
	L. A. Belyea.......	I	" 1	" 1	77	53	69	80	37	71
Mason Hall..	G. E. Armstrong..	I	B & G 6, 4	B & G 6, 4	36	28	79	38	30	79
	A. Emerson........	II	" 4, 2	" 4, 2	40	31	77	48	34	70
	M. A. Nannary.....	II	" 1	" 1	32	23	70	35	22	65
St. Patricks'.	J. F. Owens........	G. S.	B 7, 5, 4	B 7, 5, 4	39	31	81	37	29	78
	Sarah Smith.......	II	" 3, 2	" 3, 2	34	25	72	32	24	76
	M. McKenna......	I	G 7, 5	G 7, 5	42	34	81	39	33	83
	M. A. Farrel.......	I	" 4, 2	" 4, 2	45	34	76	40	29	74
	M. J. Doherty.....	II	B & G 1	B & G 1	45	30	67	40	22	55

Table XIII.—Enrolment, Daily Average Attendance, Percentage of Enrolment, Daily Present, Etc. 1872 to 1902, Inclusive.

YEAR.	TERM.	No. of Pupils Enrolled.	Average Daily Attendance.	Percentage of Enrolment Daily Present	No. of Departments.	Average No. Pupils to Each Teacher.
1872	First	5214	3445	66	92	57
	Second	6477	3473	55	106	61
1873	First	5072	3842	58	106	56
	Second	5884	3517	61	112	52
1874	First	6109	3814	62	121	50
	Second	5925	3838	65	119	50
1875	First	6044	3873	64	122	50
	Second	6085	3895	64	120	51
1876*	First	5988	4050	65	122	49
	Second	6098	3996	65	110	55
1879	First	7489	4875	65	137	55
	Second	7339	4920	67	136	54
1880	First	6356	4522	71	121	53
	Second	6488	4356	67	115	56
1881	First	5924	4182	71	116	51
	Second	6212	4341	70	115	54
1882	First	5657	4063	70	155	49
	Second	6067	4339	71	117	52
1883	First	5715	4247	74	117	49
	Second	6339	4360	70	121	52
1884	First	6021	4316	70	121	50
	Second	6669	4822	72	125	54
1885	First	6802	4656	68	129	53
	Second	6624	4864	74	125	53
1886	First	6577	4580	70	124	53
	Second	6530	5025	77	125	52
1887	First	6338	4658	73	125	51
	Second	6426	4847	76	129	50
1888	First	6414	4598	72	129	50
	Second	6470	4468	70	132	49
1889	First	6531	4408	67	132	49
	Second	6735	5316	79	132	49
1890	First	6789	4732	72	142	48
	Second	6786	5097	76	135	50
1891	First	6818	4969	73	140	49
	Second	6780	5353	79	144	47
1892	First	6061	4891	73	143	47
	Second	6651	5432	81	142	47
1893	First	6681	4923	75	142	47
	Second	6672	5433	82	143	47
1894	First	6440	5059	79	144	45
	Second	6742	5557	83	143	47
1895	First	6580	5261	80	143	46
	Second	6636	5332	81	143	46
1896	First	6391	4853	76	146	44
	Second	6584	5466	83	146	45
1897	First	6557	4934	76	146	44
	Second	6821	5572	82	148	45
1898	First	6531	5153	79	148	44
	Second	7000	5629	80	151	45
1899	First	6832	5268	77	149	46
	Second	6941	5743	83	155	46
1900	First	6753	5783	78	150	45
	Second	7160	5849	82	153	47
1901	Half year	6947	5590	87	153	45
1901-2	First	7297	5549	77	152	48
	Second	6928	5495	80	152	45

* The loss of records by the great fire of 1877 and the nsettled state of the Schools for months afterwards rendered the figures attainable of litt : value in a comparative table like this. They are therefore omitted.

TABLE XIV.—Pupils Studying in the Several Subjects, Jan., 1901, to June, 1902.—Three Terms.

SUBJECTS.	PRIMARY GRADES.												ADVANCED GRADES.												HIGH SCHOOL GRADES.											
	I.			II.			III.			IV.			V.			VI.			VII.			VIII.			IX.			X.			XI.			XII.		
Physical Culture	1327	1343	1278	1081	1003	964	1045	1077	1020	1009	984	961	773	890	823	694	634	605	456	513	508	338	331	310												
Mor'ls & Man'rs.	"	"	"	"	"	"	"	"	"	"	"	"	"	"	"	"	"	"	"	"	"	"	"	"												
Singing	"	"	"	"	"	"	"	"	"	"	"	"	"	"	"	"	"	"	"	"	"	"	"	"												
Sewing & Knit'g			59					27		21	76	24		22																						
Reading & Spell'g	1327	1343	1278	1081	1003	964	1045	1077	1020	1009	984	961	773	890	823	694	634	605	456	513	508	338	331	310	215	248	220	139	143	132	65	104	98	18	10	9
Gram'r & Comp'n				"			"	"	"	"	"	"	"	"	"	"	"	"	"	"	"	"	"	"	"	"	"	"	"	"	"	"	"	"	"	"
Form, Col'r, Draw	1327	1343	1278	"	1003	964	"	"	"	"	"	"	"	"	"	"	"	"	"	"	"	"	"	"	"	"	"	"	"	"	"	"	"	"	"	"
W't'g, print script	"	"	"	"	"	"	"	"	"	"	"	"	"	"	"	"	"	"	"	"	"	"	"	"	"	"	"	"	"	"	"	"	"	"	"	"
Arithmetic	"	"	"	"	"	"	"	"	"	"	"	"	"	"	"	"	"	"	"	"	"	"	"	"	"	"	"	"	"	"	"	"	"	"	"	"
Hyg'ne & Phys'y	"	"	"	"	"	"	"	"	"	"	"	"	"	"	"	"	"	"	"	"	"	"	"	"	"	"	"	"	"	"	"	"	81			
Animls, plts, mins	"	"	"	"	"	"	"	"	"	"	"	"	"	"	"	"	"	"	"	"	"	"	"	"												
History										"	"	"	"	"	"	"	"	"	"	"	"	"	"	"	245	248	220	139	143	132	65	104	98	18	10	9
Geography	1327	1343	1278	1081	1003	964	1045	1077	1020	"	"	"	"	"	"	"	"	"	"	"	"	"	"	"	"	"	"	"	"	"	"	"		"	"	"
Latin																			404	408	440	265	297	301	"	234	207	"	143	131	"	"	97	"	"	"
Greek																									22	50	16	43	24	24	14	31	20	5	6	6
French																									215	248	220	139	142	131	56	91	86	18	7	6
Algebra																			97	82	433	338	290	310	"	"	"	"	143	132	65	104	98	"	10	9
Geometry																						150			"	"	"	"	"	"	"	"	"	"	"	"
Book Keeping																									"	"	"	"	"	"						
Trigonometry																															5	18	17	18	10	9
Chemistry																												139	143	132	65	104		18	10	"
Physics																									119	216	220							18	7	6
Botany & Agric.																									200	216		139	143	132	65	91		18	10	9
Astron'y & Geol'y																																			3	

REPORT OF SUPERINTENDENT.

The Chairman and Board of School Trustees Saint John, N. B.

LADIES AND GENTLEMEN: I have the honor to submit for your consideration the following report on the condition of the schools under your administration. This report covers the period of the last eighteen months. If the work of the educational department is regarded from a purely business standpoint, it will be seen that its transactions are not exceeded in importance by those of any other department of the city, for these transactions involve in the first place the care of property which cannot be valued at much less than $400,000, and in the second place an annual expenditure of about $100,000. They thus represent what is ordinarily considered a pretty large business. But when citizens consider the object of these transactions, and reflect that this large expenditure is not made for the ordinary commodities of life, but concerns the preparation of fully 7,000 young people for success in life and honourable citizenship, they will be compelled to acknowledge the great importance of such a work.

Two things have contributed to make this important work successful in a very high degree — first, the faithfulness of the School Board in performing its official duties; second, the zeal and professional ability of the great majority of teachers in your employ. It is a pleasure for me to state that both principals and teachers are, as a rule, loyally devoting themselves to the best interests of the pupils. It seems to me that professional ability and study are slowly but gradually on the increase, while I am pleased to note a disposition and a desire to keep fully abreast with what is latest both in the theory and practice of education. Of course there are some teachers who do not seem to comprehend their responsibilities, and a few who are actually incapable, but by far the larger number realize that capable and faithful work is the surest guarantee to permanence and success in their positions. A teacher who does not make a study of education generally, and who neglects that daily preparation which is so essential to the successful carrying out of the work of the school, is no longer fit to be placed in charge of pupils. Indeed it may with truth be said that if the position of such a teacher and his pupils were reversed the pupil might take the book in hand and carry on the instruction with about as much ability and spirit as the teacher now does. Neither should the energies of teachers be expended to any considerable extent on work not directly connected with their schools. Where this is the case it will be found that the teacher cannot devote that attention and thought to the duties of the school, which are so indispensable to successful work in the class room. Again, teachers who are always prompt to leave the school at the hour of dismissal, and who never give their work the slightest thought or study until school opens on the following morning, cannot be prepared to conduct the recitation of a class successfully, even if they have a thorough understanding of such subjects as they are required to teach.

It is gratifying to note a gradual increase in the number of pupils attending the public schools of the city. The following presents a tabular view of the number of pupils throughout the whole city, as well as the percentage of attendance for the past four years:

	No. of Pupils enrolled 1st Term.	No. of Pupils enrolled 2nd Term.	Percentage of enrolment 1st Term.	Percentage of enrolment 2nd Term.
1899..................	6832	6941	76.67	83
1900..................	6753	7160	78.23	81.9
1901..................	6947	7319	87	76.5
1902..................	6936	....	80	....

The attendance of pupils in every school throughout the city was particularly good during the months of Sept. and Oct., 1901, until the outbreak of Smallpox in St. John during the latter month, and it was even better during the same months in 1902.

From an inspection of the above table it will be seen that the number of pupils at present on the school registers is 7,329—the largest number reached since 1879. The number enrolled in the latter year was undoubtedly due to the large floating population in the city just after the fire of 1877, and did not really represent the attendance of pupils who were the children of parents residing permanently in the city. This is shown by the fact that in 1880 the enrollment dropped to 6,400, and did not again reach 7,000 until the second term of 1898. The increase of pupils at the present time is to be found mainly in the Alexandra, Winter Street, St. Peter's (Boys'), Albert and High Schools. There is also an increase in the number of boys attending grades I. and II. of the Victoria Annex. On the re-opening of the schools in August, 1902, after the summer vacation, it was found necessary to open a new department in the Alexandra School, also one in St. Peter's (Boys). Even though an additional department was opened in the Alexandra school in August 1902, the schools in that building are still somewhat overcrowded, and at the beginning of next school year it may be again found necessary to open another department there, although I am in hopes that when the fine new building on Elm St. is ready for occupation, the overcrowding in the Alexandra may be considerably relieved by a redistribution of pupils at present attending the Elm St., Newman St. and Alexandra schools.

The following table shows the enrolment of pupils at present attending grades I. to IV. Winter St., and grades I. to VI. Alexandra where the number of pupils necessarily assigned to each teacher seems excessive:

WINTER ST. SCHOOL.

TEACHER.	GRADES.	PUPILS.
Miss Gibson	III. & IV.	55
Miss Webb	III.	63
Miss Simpson	II.	64
Miss Gray	I. & II.	64
Miss Barlow	I.	63

ALEXANDRA SCHOOL.

TEACHER.	GRADES.	PUPILS.
Miss Cowan	VI.	55
Miss McAlary	V. & VI.	50
Miss Murphy	V.	50
Miss McDougall	IV.	59
Miss Forbes	III.	61
Miss Colwell	II.	57
Miss Stevenson	I.	61

When the highest educational experts give it as their opinion that no teacher can handle in an effective manner more than from 35 to 40 pupils, it will at once be seen that thorough work cannot be accomplished in some of the rooms containing the enrolment given above.

NEW BUILDINGS.

Since my last report was submitted one handsome new building has been completed. This building is situated on the west side of the harbour and bears the historic name of LaTour. This new school-house is perhaps the finest in the city, and is a thoroughly up to-date building in every respect. It contains an exhibition hall and six class rooms, four of which were occupied at the beginning of the term just closed. The rooms are all 28 ft. in breadth by 32 ft. in length, and the building was skilfully planned by the architect, Mr. H H. Mott, in such a way that the pupils in every room receive the light from the windows on their left and those at the rear. Each pupil is also provided with the adjustable seat and desk manufactured by Lordly & Co., after the pattern now approved by the Board. This building has enabled us to relieve the overcrowded condition of most of the rooms in the Albert building as well as also to afford proper quarters for the pupils, who used to occupy the small and ill-lighted rooms in the Masonic Hall. The organization of the LaTour is as follows:—Mr. Armstrong, Principal; Miss Comben, Miss Lydia Fullerton, Miss Nannery.

Another building is now in course of erection on Elm St., North End, near the site of the old Madras School. This building is named the Dufferin and will be ready for occupation in August, 1903. It will contain ten rooms and an assembly hall, and will enable us to relieve in some measure the present overcrowded condition of the Winter St. building as well as to provide suitable quarters for those teachers and pupils, who have been compelled to endure the wretched accommodation afforded by the old Madras building. The erection of this splendid new building in the place of the old school house, which has so long been a disgrace to our city, will be a lasting monument to the energy and forethought of the present Board of School Trustees.

Many a teacher has borne elequent testimony to the marked influence for good which a beautiful school room exercises on the conduct of the pupils. There is undoubtedly an intimate connection between the physical environment of pupils and their conduct ; and a pleasant school room. with its attractive surroundings, supplies one of the most effective con ditions of easy control. Many a school has been completely transformed by its removal to a new building, and every educator of experience knows that a dirty, dingy building is for the most part a constant source of temptation to disorder.

DISCIPLINE.

The discipline of the schools of the City of Saint John has been kept up to the high standard maintained during previous years and is, I believe, quite equal if not superior to that existing in the schools of any of the cities throughout the Dominion. Most of the teachers realize that the object and purpose of corrective restraints is not so much to effect immediate and temporary results as it is to establish good habits, to enable the children to act for themselves, and gradually to grow more sensitive to higher motives. It must be apparent to any visitor, who enters our school rooms, that these results are being fairly attained. I have often been delighted in my visits to the different school rooms to see the happy and busy appearance of the pupils, to note the evidences of that good understanding between children and teachers, which arises from good feeling and mutual respect, and to see that older and coarser modes of punishment are gradually disappearing. At times, doubtless, there are cases which seem to require more drastic methods of treatment, and it has occasionally been found necessary to inflict corporal punishment, but the good teacher, like a good physician, will be careful to resort to the heroic treatment only in extreme crises.

There are, however, in the schools of every city of the size of St. John some pupils upon whom ordinary incentives and punishments have not the requisite effect. It cannot be said that the acts of these pupils are vicious, but they are often really subversive of good discipline and may, if continued, develope into habits which will eventually lead to crime. These pupils are endowed by nature with strong wills, have never been effectively controlled by their parents and their example often has a very bad effect on the habits of their fellows. It would doubtless be a very easy matter to get rid of such pupils by expelling them, but inasmuch as their perversity is usually the result of improper training at home, or rather, the absence of any training at all, these are precisely the pupils who are most in need of that restraint and moral training which the school aims to give. What these pupils need is special treatment in a special school. They require to be placed under the care and guidance of some teacher who is speciallv fitted to deal with them, who will carefully study their peculiarities and ı a kind but powerful hand work a thorough reformation in their moral chı acter and habits of study. The most effectual remedy for these pup would be two or three ungraded schools in different parts of the city.

this suggestion has been made in previous reports without having received the serious attention of the Board, I would most earnestly recommend it to your careful consideration during the coming year. In my report for 1899, I suggested that the instruction in such a school must necessarily be individual and that the teacher ought not to be hampered by any cast-iron curriculum. The work would for many reasons differ considerably from that of the regular school, and the teacher might be allowed to consult to a limited extent the tastes of the individual pupils under his charge.

To render our school system still more complete we need a further school for these pupils who can no longer be controlled by their parents, and whose homes are, therefore, no longer fit places for them, but who are not yet criminals. Schools of this kind have been established in several cities of the United States. In these schools pupils are detained and completely removed from their homes. The proper location for such a school is a farm, where the scholars would have every facility for exercise out of doors, and where they would be compelled to work industriously with their hands during a portion of each day. Such a school will be an absolute necessity, if the Legislature enact a compulsory school law, as they seem likely to do at an early date, and would undoubtedly be productive of untold benefit to some young people who are now on the downward track for the want of it. It would do more than anything to effect a practical solution of the so-called 'boy problem' which has been attracting so much attention for the last few months in this city. A school of this kind could not be established without considerable expense, and no doubt there are some persons who would regard such expense as unnecessary, but that expense is surely justifiable, which saves future citizens from a life of pauperism and crime. Is it not much wiser, more economical and more humane to train the young away from crime than to punish adult criminals.

GRADING.

Pupils are still promoted from grade to grade largely on the recommendation of their respective teachers. This is entirely in line with the best educational thought of the present day. Most of the cities in the United States have abolished the examination system and now promote pupils almost entirely on the judgment of teachers, who estimate the work and attainments of their pupils by simple monthly tests. No feature of progress in the present administration of public schools is more marked than the widespread movement to curtail as far as possible the evils of what may be termed the examination system of promoting pupils. Throughout Great

Britain the change in this respect has been quite as marked as in the United States and even more so. In England the Government School Inspectors are no longer permitted to hold examinations at stated times, and the ranking of schools and pupils is no longer based on examination results. In this connection I may be allowed to quote the remarks of one of the most eminent of American educationists, Dr. Emerson E. White: "When not only the promotion of pupils but also the efficiency of teachers and the standing of schools are determined by the results of stated examinations, such examinations must, in the nature of things, largely determine the scope and character of prior teaching and study, this being especially true when the written tests are prepared by the superintendent for all classes in the same grade in the schools. Experience shows that few teachers can face such a formal test of their efficiency, and feel free to teach according to their best judgment and power. As the ordeal approaches, the burning question becomes not what is best for the pupils, but what will count in the examination. Under this pressure teaching inevitably sinks into the art of preparing pupils to pass examinations, and this often becomes a pretty fine art. Former tests are scanned for probable questions, and the arts of the coacher and crammer take the place of rational training. Teaching thus degenerates into the art of preparing wares for the examination market." What is said above, however, is not intended to prevent the teacher from making as free a use of the written test as he may find necessary for the purpose of forming an intelligent estimate of the pupils. All capable teachers must test their pupils from time to time, and the results of these tests whether written or oral must influence the teacher in forming an opinion as to the pupil's fitness for promotion. Nor can there be a surer guarantee of a pupil's fitness for promotion than the ability he shows month by month to master the work of the grade from which he desires to be promoted.

The parents, I am pleased to state, have for the most part concurred in the estimate formed by teachers as to the fitness of their children for promotion In some cases applications have been made to me for re-examination, but these have been so rare that they deserve only a passing notice. I may add that. whenever it is found that a pupil is not likely to be able to pass to the succeeding grade, the teacher is recommended to visit the parent and inform him of the fact giving at the same time the reasons for the child's failure to grade. These visits of the teacher have been in most cases productive of much good, although I am obliged to state that there have been instances where parents have been found to blame the teacher, when their child has failed of promotion.

The failure of many pupils to grade in June, 1902, was due in a great measure to their irregular attendance throughout the year. This irregularity of attendance was caused by their fear of contracting small pox which was so prevalent throughout the city during the last three months of 1901 and the early part of 1902. In many cases also the results of vaccination, which had been made compulsory by the Board on all pupils attending the public schools, were unusually severe; often keeping the pupil from school for some weeks.

SUBJECTS OF THE COURSE OF INSTRUCTION.

These have been for the most part intelligently and faithfully taught. "By their fruits ye shall know them" is an axiomatic truth that may well be applied to schools, for only in the schools themselves is it possible to determine the results of a system and the methods employed. There can be no question, in my opinion, that really excellent work is being accomplished in most of our primary grades. But at the same time an expert observer will have to admit that there is often a falling off in some of the succeeding grades, notably in the fourth and fifth. This is largely due to the lack of thorough and intelligent drill. Teachers of these grades often complain of the crowded condition of the curriculum and say that it is so full of subjects that thorough work is almost impossible. To this my invariable reply has been do not waste your time and strength on things which have little educational or practical value, teach what is essential, and then, by persistent and intelligent drill, fasten what you have taught in the mind of the pupil. There are things connected with the teaching of every subject which might well be omitted by the teacher in the first lessons, and presented only after the way has been properly paved. Hence there is the greatest need that only a person of the highest order of intelligence should fill the office of teacher.

Nothing has been more efficacious, in my opinion, in improving our schools than the meetings of the principals which have been held every month throughout the school year. By means of these meetings the work has been unified, weak places built up, and a more complete control and direction of the school work secured. In these meetings much attention has been devoted to the various subjects of the curriculum and the best mode of presenting and teaching each. These meetings have been productive of very great good in the past, and it will be my aim to make them productive of greater good in the future.

More attention has been paid to spelling in the last two years than was formerly the case. Manning's speller, a most useful little work, has been placed in the hands of pupils of the fifth and succeeding grades, and I am in hopes to see satisfactory results in the course of another year or two. Many eminent teachers have contended that accuracy in spelling depends entirely on the written test, and that oral spelling is of no use whatever. The truth of such a statement, however, has never seemed very apparent to me and recent experiments seem to show that accuracy of spelling in elementary grades is best secured by a judicious combination of both the oral and written tests. What better aid can there be than proper oral spelling in acquiring an accurate and ready pronunciation of words? And there can be no reasonable doubt that the old-fashioned system of oral spelling where a distinct pause was made after each syllable was of the greatest assistance in making pupils ready readers.

In the majority of schools there has been considerable improvement in the teaching of English composition, but there are still too many teachers who do not recognize the supreme importance of early training in this subject. When teachers require young pupils to reproduce the lesson in writing, they should be particularly careful to see that this exercise is made not simply a mere test of knowledge, but also a thorough training in the written expression of their knowledge; otherwise, careless habits are sure to be formed and the real value of such an exercise as a training in composition is largely lost. In all written work it is of the utmost importance for pupils to be trained to aim at quality rather than quantity.

The teaching of reading has been fairly up to the mark. As a rule, teachers have aimed at teaching pupils to read so as to comprehend the thought. They have likewise insisted on correct enunciation and pronunciation to a greater extent than formerly, and have made marked improvement in these respects.

PHYSICAL CULTURE.

In previous reports I have endeavored to point out the great importance of systematic physical culture in any well balanced scheme of instruction. There should be introduced into all our schools a thorough and systematic course of well graded exercises calculated to promote the bodily health of the school children and based upon scientific principles. It is scarcely possible to overrate the advantages which pupils would derive from such a course of physical training, and it is to be hoped that the Board may, duri. the coming school year, persuade our esteemed fellow citizen, Mr. Josep Allison, to renew the generous offer which he made a year or two ago, provide for a year at his own expense, a director of physical culture for th city schools. There are far too many pupils in all of our school rooms, whose awkward postures and ungraceful movements show plainly enough the necessity of such training. Nor would it take a great amount of time to correct such undesirable tendencies. Fifteen minutes of continuous training daily would be quite enough to produce a marked change in the personal appearance of an entire room, and would undoubtedly tend to promote that grace and ease of bodily carriage which everyone should try to secure.

MANUAL TRAINING AND COOKING SCHOOL.

It seems as though the time had arrived when some form of manual training work should be provided for boys of the 7th and 8th grades. The experiment has been made in connection with the schools of Fredericton under the direction of Mr. McCready and has been quite successful there. There is every reason to believe that such a school would be found to work well if established here. An effort should also be made at the same time to establish a school in which girls of the same grades could be taught how to cook. For my own part I believe the educational value of such a school would be even greater than that of a school for manual training; and nothing of greater practical worth could be imparted to the girls in those grades than a knowledge of scientific cookery. If such knowledge could be generally diffused, there would in a very short time be a marked improvement in the health, the comfort and even the morals of an entire community. Who can tell but that it might prove the best way to teach scientific temperance?

HIGH SCHOOL ENTRANCE EXAMINATION.

In June, 1901, the total number of pupils who tried this examination in St. John, was 258, a number much larger than in any previous year. Out of this number 228 passed, and 30 failed.

The following pupils succeeded in making over 800 marks out of a possible 1050. They are arranged in order of merit.

Mary Hansen	901
Louise Olive	896
Nellie Brosman	893
Stanley Bridges	874
Geraldine Coll	869
Wilbur Gerow	850
Gertrude Hannah	849

Harold Shannon	849
Effie Ingram	845
Augustus Porter	841
Winonah Brennan	839
Florence Shannon	837
Winifred Smith	834
Alice Casey	833
George Crosby	833
Lottie Mount	830
Hazel Bell	828
Mary Sweeny	827
Madeline Legere	825
Hazel Pitfield	823
Esther Lannen	822
Roy Smith	822
Nellie Gosnell	821
Helen McMurray	819
Mary Hogan	817
LeRoi Ferguson	812
Winifred Harvey	811
Sarah McGloin	809
Allen Waterbury	807
Genevieve Dever	801
Ronald Holmes	800

The regulation of the Board of Education with respect to this examination provides that the papers written by pupils in each subject shall be read and estimated by two examiners, one of whom must be a teacher of the eighth grade, and the other a teacher on the High School staff. Those who acted as examiners in each subject for this examination in June, 1901, were as follows:

English Grammar.—Miss Ward and Mr. Hayes.
English Composition.—Miss McNaughton and Mr. Barry.
History and Geography.—Miss Beckwith and Mr. Stothart.
Arithmetic and Algebra.—Mr. Myles and Mr. Montgomery.
Natural Science—Miss Wilson and Mrs. Yandall.
Drawing.—Mr. Powers and Mr. Harrington.
Latin.—Miss Bartlett and Mr. McLean.
Reading—Dr. H. S. Bridges.

In June, 1902, the number of pupils examined for entrance to the High School was 230. Of these 207 were admitted and 23 failed. The examiners in each subject for June, 1902, were the same as in June, 1901, except that in English Grammar the papers were examined by Miss Lawson and Mr. Hayes, while Miss Ward and Mr. Barry took those in English Composition. The following pupils made an aggregate of 800 marks and upwards out of a possible 1050:

Alice Kelly	905
Minerva Henderson	898
Mary O'Harra	864
Mary Mullin	863
Harry Fales	862
Margaret Sugrue	855
Gordon Kerr	849
Grace Fleming	840
George Higgins	840
Willie Brown	838
Edith Cunningham	833
Cecil Brown	832
Ellen McDonough	832
John Jennings	830
Jean Barr	829
Alfred Bardsley	828
Lillian Elliott	828
Edith Cuming	827
Regina McNeill	827
Stanley Poole	827
Florence Roberts	823
Pearl Blizzard	822
Helen Fotheringham	809
Arthur Steel	807
Etta Taylor	806
Fannie Brookins	804
Noel Lee	802
Katie Driscoll	802
Jennie Quinlan	802

HIGH SCHOOL.

There has been a marked increase in the number of pupils attending the High School during the last three years. This is due to the fact that more boys than formerly are annually seeking admission to the High School, and after entrance find it to their advantage to remain at the school long enough to secure certificates of graduation.

When the schools re-opened in August last at the close of the summer vacation, it was found necessary to transfer Grade VII. (Girls) from the High School building to the Victoria in order to secure proper accommodation for those pupils of Grade IX. who had been occupying the High School Assembly Hall for the last two years. This change proved a most welcome one both to the pupils and the teacher of this particular department of the High School, and as a consequence much better work has been done by them than was possible before. A proper room should also be provided for the pupils of Grade XII. who are now obliged to use the Principal's office as their class room. There are at the present time 17 pupils in this grade, a number entirely too large for the size of the room. Provision should also be made in the near future for opening another department for pupils taking the work of Grade XI. During the present school year there are no less than 88 pupils in the two divisions of this grade, which is really too many for two teachers to handle effectively in any year of High School work and much more so in the last year of the course, when pupils require and should receive so much individual attention.

In spite of the large numbers, I feel satisfied that the quality of the work done has been kept up to the standard which has been maintained hitherto, and which ought to be expected of a High School. No startling innovations have been attempted, but each teacher has tried in all possible ways to improve the general work of his school, and I believe there is not a single department of the High School in which real progress has not been made.

Though our needs are still many, I shall make particular mention of but three. The best work cannot be done in either history or literature without suitable works of reference, and in these the High School library is still very deficient. The Board should also at no distant day place an electric clock in the building, and provide a suitable play ground for tl girls.

The graduating exercises of the class of 1901, took place in the hall of the High School on Friday, June 28th. The graduating class numbered pupils and successfully carried out a fine programme of exercises. The followed the presentation of diplomas and honour certificates by the principal, after which the members of the class listened to an inspiring and thoughtful address by Rev. Ira Smith, pastor of Leinster St. Baptist church.

The prize winners for 1901, were as follows:

Corporation Gold Medal................Gertrude Lawson
Parker Silver Medal....................Mae Perkins
Governor General's Silver Medal..........William Morrow
Judge Trueman's Gold Medal............Mary Hansen

On June 25th, 1902, the graduating class numbered 65. The following is the programme of exercises carried out by the pupils on that occasion:

1. March—"Crack of the Whip,"................High School Orchestra
2. Essay—"Canadian Heroism,"........................Jennie Colter
3. Essay—"Nature,"..............................Hugh G. Morrison
4. Selection—"Cleanthe Waltz,"................High School Orchestra
5. Essay—"Benefits of Failure,"......................Eliza B. Smith
6. Essay—"Commercial Resources of Canada,"..........William Denham
7. March—"General Miles,"....................High School Orchestra
8. Scenes from Shakespere—"The Winter's Tale."
   Introductory and Interlude......................Miriam Hatheway

   I.—Scene at the Shepherd's Cottage.

   Florizel..John D. Matthew
   Perdita..Beatrice C. Skinner
   Shepherd..Parnell B. McCafferty
   Dorcas..Ethel Hannah
   Polixenes...William W. Malcolm
   Camillo...Ernest E. Clawson

   II.—Scene in Paulina's House.

   Leontes..S. Hart Green
   Paulina..Robina Berton
   Hermione..Mary A. Trueman
9. Selection..High School Orchestra
10. Essay—"Concentration,"..........................Jennie B. Wisdom
11. Valedictory......................................William H. Morrow

The members of the graduating class then received their diplomas and honour certificates, after which short and appropriate addresses were made by the Rev. W.O. Raymond and Senator Ellis. A very interesting feature of the closing exercises of the class of 1902, was the unveiling of a portrait of Dr. James Paterson, the distinguished head master of the St. John Grammar School, for 40 years. The portrait is an excellent likeness of Dr. Paterson and was presented to the school by Senator Ellis, who had selected Dr. W. P. Dole as the speaker on the occasion. Dr. Dole's eulogy was a fitting and graceful tribute to the merits of his former teacher and was listened to with close attention throughout.

The High School lost a very capable teacher by the withdrawal of Miss Maude Narraway, who retired from the employ of the Board in June, 1902, after a long period of faithful and devoted service. Miss Narraway's resignation was deeply regretted by all the friends of the school, as her fine scholarship, splendid teaching powers and noble ideals had left a lasting impress on the minds and characters of pupils for many years. To all old graduates the High School will not seem quite the same place with Miss Narraway no longer there. It is to be hoped that she will still retain a lively feeling of interest in the institution to the staff of which she was so long a distinguished ornament.

The prize winners for 1902, were as follows:

William Morrow................Corporation Gold Medal.
William Morrow................Parker Silver Medal.
William Woods.................Governor General's Silver Medal.
Alice Kelly...................Judge Trueman's Gold Medal.

Respectfully submitted,

H. S. BRIDGES,
Supt. of City Schools.

CITY OF MONCTON.

Board of School Trustees, 1902.

Staff of Grammar School, 1902.

GEORGE, J. OULTON, M. A., *Principal*—Teacher of Chemistry, Physics, Physical Geography, Nature Lessons, Geometry, Physiology, Arithmetic.

G. FRED MCNALLY, B. A.—Teacher of Greek, Latin, History, Civics.

H. B. STEEVES, M. A.—Teacher of Botany, Book-keeping, Algebra, Agriculture, Arithmetic, Grade IX.

W. A. COWPERTHWAITE, M. A.—Teacher of French, English Literature, Grammar and Composition.

To J. R. INCH, ESQ., LL. D.
Chief Superintendent of Education,
Fredericton, N. B.

SIR:—The Board of School Trustees for the City of Moncton have the honor to present for your consideration the annual report of the Public Schools in the City of Moncton, for the year 1902.

During the year no change has taken place in the constitution of the Board, Trustees Miss Hattie Tweedie and L. N. Bourque, M. D., whose term of office expired during the year were reappointed by the City Council. The grand total enrollment throughout the city for 1902, numbered 1795, and thirty-four teachers were engaged. Total number of pupils enrolled last year was 1778.

ABERDEEN SCHOOL.

This building accommodates sixteen schools, the grades running from I to XI, inclusive, with an enrollment of 800 pupils. The High School and the Grammar School for the County of Westmorland consists of Grades IX, X and XI; had an enrollment of 156 pupils during the year.

Some important changes in the staff of the High School have taken place during the year. During the first term of the year only three teachers were engaged on the staff, and at the beginning of the second term the services of Mr. H. B. Steeves, M. A., were engaged for Grade IX. Mr. Steeves has had long experience in other schools and came with an excellent record as a progressive teacher. At the opening of the second term, Mr. C. H. Acheson, who for several years had been one of the most successful teachers in the High School, received from the Colonial Secretary's Office in London, a flattering offer for his services. He was requested to go to South Africa and assume a position on the Normal School staff in Pretoria. Mr. Acheson accepted this offer and resigned his position in Moncton. General expressions of regret at the loss sustained by Moncton High School were made on all sides. Mr. Acheson during his term in Moncton gave universal satisfaction and was indefatigable in his efforts for the success and progress of the school. The city of Moncton, and the profession generally throughout the Province suffered a great loss in the removal of so enthusiastic a teacher. Suitable expressions of regret at Mr. Acheson's removal were formally made by the trustees, the teachers of the city, the pupils of the High School and the citizens. Mr. McNally was promoted to the position of teacher of Grade X. In filling the vacancy the trustees, were however, very fortunate in securing the services of Mr. W. A. Cowperthwaite, M. A., of Harvard University. The work in the High School has been very successfully carried on during the year. In the other departments in the Aberdeen School some changes in the staff have occurred. Mrs. Gross a teacher of long and excellent service in primary grades was given continued leave of absence and her school was successfully supplied by Miss Lottie Weldon. Owing to ill-health, at the close of the June term Mrs. M. P. Simpson an experienced teacher, who has done excellent service for many years, was compelled to ask for leave of absence. Her place was filled by Miss Mabel E. McLeod. Early in last term Miss Eva Sullivan for some years a very successful teacher in Grade IV, resigned, being about to remove from the Province. The Board expressed regret at her resignation. There being two Grades VII in the Aberdeen School, Miss Etta Cormick who holds a superior license was engaged.

ENTRANCE EXAMINATION.

In June last, entrance examination for High School was held in the Aberdeen building under the supervision of Principal Oulton, Principal Irons and the Secretary to the School Board.

79 candidates presented themselves for examination:

11 secured a place in Frst division.
42 secured a place in the Second division.
26 secured a place in the Third division.

Of the number presenting themselves, 53 were admitted to the High School. The one making the highest marks in this examination was Miss Clairence Theresa Flanagan of the Wesley Street School, who made a total of 859. She won the Silver Medal, donated by His Honor the Lieutenant Governor, for 1902. The second place in this examination was secured by Miss Ida McKay of Victoria school.

GRADUATING EXERCISES.

In June last, the closing exercises in the High School were held in the assembly hall of Aberdeen building. The following constitutes the graduating class for 1902, who received diplomas in order of merit:

1	Eva McCracken	Division	1
2	Harold Coleman	"	2
3	Florence Mackenzie	"	2
4	Eva Magee	"	2
5	Bessie Fairweather	"	2
6	Daisy Weldon	"	2
7	Ella Hannah	"	2
8	Harry Gorbell	"	2
9	Jean Welling	"	2
10	Ernest Martin		3
11	Grace Schwartz	"	3
12	Grace Steadman	"	3
13	Daisy Rand	"	3
14	Alice Burnyeat	"	3

PRIZES.

The following prizes were awarded:

Miss Eva McCracken, won the Gold Medal given by Mr. J. T. Hawke, best average Grade XI, marks 89.9.

Miss Daisy Weldon, won Math. Instruments, given by Mr. F. A. McCully, best average Grade XI, marks 93.3.

Miss Eva McCracken, won course in Business College, given by Miss Johnson, Principal, for best average in English, Grade XI, marks 95.5.

Miss Eva McCracken, won course in M. B. College, given by Miss Johnson, for best average in Mathematics, Grade XI, mark 90.

Miss Eva McCracken, won quarter lessons in French, given by Miss Smith, for best average in French, Grade XI.

Miss Stella Kerr, won prize given by His Worship, Mayor Givan, for best average Grade X.

Miss Mary Adams, won Bronze Medal, given by Governor General, for best average in Grade IX.

Miss Clairence Flanagan, won the Lieutenant Governor's Medal, given for best average entrance to High School.

VICTORIA SCHOOL.

The enrolment in this school during the year was 556, in ten departments comprising Grades I to VIII inclusive. No changes in the staff in school have occurred during the year. The work has been successfully carried on under Principal Irons.

WESLEY STREET SCHOOL.

The enrolment in this school has largely increased during the year and now comprises 445. The enrolment in this school has largely increased, as follows: In year 1898, 326; 1899, 375; 1900, 367; 1901, 413; 1902, 445.

As contemplated last year, the Board, owing to overcrowding in primary grades, engaged the services of another teacher, Miss Evangeline LeBlanc. There are now 7 departments in this building all doing goo^d work, under an experienced Principal.

Miss Clairence Flanagan, a pupil from this school, led all competito for entrahce to High School. Last year a pupil from this school also led i this examination.

INSPECTOR'S REPORT.

Early in the year written reports upon the condition of the various schools in the city of Moncton were submitted to the Board of Trustees by the Inspector of Schools for the County of Westmorland and the Secretary of this Board.

PERMANENT IMPROVEMENTS AND SPECIAL REPAIRS.

During the year the Board expended a considerable amount for permanent improvemements and special repairs which were absolutely necessary. These amounts are as follows:

1902	
Roof Aberdeen, C. O. Rowe	$44 92
Roof Aberdeen, Sumner Co	486 11
Pillars Aberdeen, (Iron)	165 00
Iron doors foul air shaft Aberdeen	38 10
Repairs to blackboards	14 16
Calcimining interior of Victoria building	119 00
Total	$ 867 29

BONDS.

During the year past, Bond No. 32, $500.00 bearing interest at 6 per cent. fell due and was paid out of Current account. During the year 1903, four bonds Nos. 34 to 37, $500.00 each fell due. In 1901, Bond No. 33, $500 00 bearing interest at 6 per cent. was paid out of the Current account. Some provisions should be made by the Council for the payment of these amounts, either by issuing other bonds or by assessment.

Attached to this report are a number of tabular and comparative statements relating to the city schools. All of which is respectfully submitted.

F. A. McCULLY, *Secretary.*

JOHN T. HAWKE, *Chairman.*

Moncton, N. B., December 31, 1902.

STATEMENT NO. 1.

Showing Increase in Enrollment.

Year.	Term.	No. of Pupils Enrolled.	No. of Schools.	Average No. Pupils to Each Teacher.
1887	First	1052	19	56
	Second	1092	19	58
1888	First	1070	19	57
	Second	1026	20	62
1889	First	1160	20	58
	Second	1271	22	58
1890	First	1237	22	56
	Second	1464	24	61
1891	First	1408	24	59
	Second	1612	28	58
1892	First	1544	28	56
	Second	1632	28	59
1893	First	1536	28	56
	Second	1621	28	57
1894	First	1572	28	56
	Second	1641	28	59
1895	First	1664	29	57
	Second	1716	31	57
1896	First	1661	31	57
	Second	1720	31	57
1897	First		31	
	Second	1749	31	58
1898	First	1678	33	
	Second	1741	33	53
1899	First	1682	33	51
	Second	1825	33	55
1900	First	1736	33	52
	Second	1717	34	50.5
1901	First	1693	34	50
	Second	1778	33	54
1902	First	1712	32	54
	Second	1795	34	53

STATEMENT No. 2.

Teachers and Grades, 1902.

Teachers.	Class	Standards.		Religions.				
		1st Term.	2nd Term.	Pres.	Cath.	Bap.	Meth.	Epis
ABERDEEN HIGH SCHOOL.								
Geo. J. Oulton, M. A.	G. S.	11	11				1	
Cyrus H. Acheson	"	10						1
G. Fred McNally, B. A	"	9	10			1		
W. A. Cowperthwaite, M. A.	"		9					1
H. B. Steeves, B. A.	"		9				1	
S. B. Anderson	Sup.	8	8	1				
Ethel Murphy	I	7	7	1				
Alice Lea	I		6				1	
Florence Murphy	II	6						
Etta Cormick	I		7					1
Agnes McSweeney	II	6	5		1			
Mame I. Smith	I	5	5	1				
Mary A. Moore	I	4 & 5	4					1
Eva Sullivan	I	4	3 & 4			I		
Miss McLeod	I	1 & 2	3 & 4	1				
Elspeth Charters	I	3 & 4	3	1				
Mrs. M. P. Simpson	III	3						
Miss Ella McKay	I	1 & 2	1 & 2			1		
Emma Condon	I	1 & 2	1 & 2	1				
Lottie Weldon	I	1 & 2	1 & 2			1		
VICTORIA SCHOOL.								
S. W. Irons	I	8	8	1				
Catherine Barton	I	7	7					1
Cora L. Simpson	I	6	6	1				
Harriet Willis	I	5	5	1				
Ella Stevens	II	4	4					1
Hazel Taylor	I	3	4	1				
G. May Forge	I	3	3					1
Eunice Brown	I	2 & 3	2 & 3	1				
Fannie McLaren	I	1 & 2	1 & 2	1				
Edith Mitchell	I	1	1				1	

STATEMENT No. 2.—Continued.

Teachers and Grades, 1902.

Teachers.	Class.	Standards.		Religions.				
		1st Term.	2nd Term.	Pres.	Cath.	Bap.	Meth	Epis
WESLEY STREET SCHOOL.								
Agnes Quirk...	I	7 & 8	7 & 8	.....	1	.....	......	....
Kate Hamilton...........	I	5 & 6	5 & 6	.....	1	.....	......	....
Natalie Allain.............	II	5	5	.....	1	.....	......	....
Elizabeth Richard.........	I	3 & 4	3 & 4	.....	1	.....	......	....
Catherine Hennessey......	I	2 & 3	3	.....	1	.....	......	....
Evangeline Bourque.......	I	1 & 2	1 & 2	.....	1	.....	......	....
Elodie Bourque............	I	. 1	1	....	1	......	......	....
Evangeline LeBlanc.......	I	.....	1	.....	1	.....	......	....
				12	9	4	4	7

STATEMENT NO. 3.

Grand Total Enrollment at Beginning of Terms in August, 1898, 1899, 1900, 1901 and 1902.

ABERDEEN SCHOOL	1898	1899	1900	1901	1902
Grade XI. High School,	44	36	33	25	45
Grade X. " "	60	43	41	51	42
Grade IX. (A) High School	39	44	47	38	32
Grade IX. (B) High School	38	47	44	38	37
	181	170	165	152	156
Grade VIII	51	49	51	48	43
Grade VII	56	49	42	46	83
Grade VI	50	52	58	93	59
Grade V	88	105	109	100	105
Grade IV	81	92	89	75	83
Grade III	79	100	99	112	89
Grades I. & II	61	66	55	63	62
Grades I. & II	60	63	53	54	60
Grades I. & II	60	62	55	59	60
	586	638	611	650	644
VICTORIA SCHOOL.					
Grade VIII	40	52	38	49	45
Grade VII	52	57	74	61	52
Grade VII. & VI	99	..	..	..	..
Grade VI	..	50	54	52	63
Grade VI .& V	..	55	..	..	..
Grade V	53	..	60	66	62
Grades V. & IV	51	56	..	..	..
Grade IV	..	..	59	57	104
Grades IV. & III	53	59	..	..	..
Grade III	50	52	55	122	71
Grade II	61	60	52	39	43
Grades II. & I	64	119	121	57	58
Grade I	...	...	..	60	58
	523	560	513	563	556

STATEMENT 3—Continued.

WESLEY ST.	1898	1899	1900	1901	1902
Grades VIII. & VII	37	44	36	38	37
Grades VI. & V	47	52	50	60	52
Grade V. IV	48	56	53	57	..
Grade V	..	..	..	..	48
Grades IV. and III	57	..	55	56	59
Grade III	..	63	..	..	58
Grades III & II	..	..	59	65	..
Grades II. & I	137	160	58	137	..
Grade II	..	..	..	...	59
Grade I	..	..	56	..	132
	326	375	367	413	435

STATEMENT NO. 4.

Term Ending June 30th 1902. Teachers and Actual Attendance Returns.

SCHOOLS.	TEACHERS.	Salaries.	Days of Session.	Pupils Enrolled.	Boys.	Girls.	Gross Days Pupils Attended	Gross Days Lost.	Average Days Pupils Attended	Percentage of Attendance
Aberdeen....	George J. Oulton......	850	114	22	3	19	2118	270	19.29	87.68
	C. H. Acheson.........	650	118	45	18	27	4338	484½	37.67	83.7
	G. Fred McNally......	500	118	70	21	49	6740	630	57.46	82
	S. B. Anderson........	480	121	46	22	24	4421	580	37.46	82.50
	Ethel Murphy..........	275	119	44	22	22	4052½	507½	35	80
	Florence Murphy......	275	119	47	30	17	4874½	384	31.9	89.2
	Agnes McSweeney....	275	119	45	21	24	4212½	989½	36	80
	Amelia J. Smith.......	265	118½	60	36	24	6063	597	52.6	87.6
	Mary A. Moore........	240	118½	54	21	33	5043	944½	43.8	81
	Eva Sullivan...........	240	118½	54	21	33	5412½	853	47	87
	Elspeth Charters......	275	118½	56	32	24	4885	805	42	75
	Mrs. M. P. Simpson....	275	118½	59	40	19	5661½	857	49	83
	Ella J. McKay.........	275	118½	61	28	33	5508½	1054	47.5	77.9
	Emma Condon.........	275	118½	60	24	36	5515½	1588½	49.35	82.25
	Lottie L. Weldon......	275	118½	63	25	38	5846½	1919	50.25	79.76
Victoria......	S. W. Irons............	850	119	41	15	26	3884½	395½	33.5	81.7
	Catherine Barton......	275	119	58	21	37	4681	1067	41	71
	Cora L. Simpson.......	240	119	51	21	30	4834	598	41.6	81.5
	Harriet E. Willis......	275	119	68	29	39	6517½	926½	56.3	82.8
	Ella L. Stevens........	275	119	53	28	25	5653	428	48.83	92.13
	Hazel Taylor...........	225	119	50	24	26	4852½	672½	41.7	83.4
	G. May Forge..........	240	119	51	34	17	5228	828	43.9	86
	Eunice J. Brown......	275	119	44	25	19	4077½	759½	34.8	79.09
	Fannie McLaren.......	275	119	60	26	34	5612½	1368½	48.5	80.9
	Edith L. Mitchell......	240	119	60	35	25	5512½	977	47.3	78.8
Wesley St...	Agnes Quirk...........	400	120	41	12	29	4167	409½	35.45	86.46
	Kate Hamilton.........	240	119	59	31	28	5620½	731½	48	81.35
	Natalie Allain.........	275	120	55	23	32	5684	723½	48.33	87
	Elizabeth Richard.....	275	120	54	32	22	5064	643	43.41	80.38
	Catherine Hennessy...	275	120	60	28	32	6024½	972½	51	85
	Evangeline Bourque...	240	120	64	25	39	5559½	1139½	47.4	74
	Elodie Bourque........	225	120	57	26	31	4880	764½	41.6	78.1

STATEMENT NO. 5.

Term ending June 30, 1902. No. of Pupils in the Several Standards of Instruction.

SUBJECTS.	I	II	III	IV	V	VI	VII	VIII	IX	X	XI	TOTALS.
Reading, Spelling and Recitation	267	226	261	207	218	166	128	102				1575
Composition			261	207	217	166	128	102				1081
Grammar and Analysis			261	207	217	166	128	102				1081
History				21	217	166	128	102	70	45	22	771
Form	267	226	261	207	217	166	128	102				1574
Industrial Drawing	267	226	261	207	217	166	128	102				1574
Print Script	267	226	261	207	218	166	128	102				1575
Writing	267	226	261	207	218	166	128	102				1575
Arithmetic	267	226	261	207	217	166	128	61	70	45	22	1670
Geometry									70	45	22	137
Mensuration												
Algebra							128	102	70	45	22	367
Geography			261	207	217	166	128	102	70	45	22	1218
Mineral, **Plant and Animal Life**	238	192	256	206	216	166	128	102				1504
Colour	267	226	261	207	217	166	128	102				1574
Singing	238	192	261	154	122	143	128	15				1253
Temperance **Teachings of Science**	238	192	261	207	217	166	128	102				1511
Physics									70			70
Physiology											22	22
Latin							122	100	52	43	18	335
French	45		34	35				20	70	38	22	264
Book-keeping									70	44		114
Chemistry										45	22	67
Agriculture and Botany									70		22	92
Greek										7		7
English									70	45	22	137

STATEMENT NO. 6.

Term Ending December 31, 1902. Teachers and Actual Attendance.

SCHOOLS.	TEACHERS.	Salaries.	Days of Session.	Pupils Enrolled.	Boys.	Girls.	Gross Days Pupils Attended	Gross Days Lost.	Average Days Pupils Attended	Percentage of Attendance.
Aberdeen ..	George J. Oulton......	850	80	45	14	31	2934	320	37.75	83.89
	G. Fred. McNally......	650	80	42	11	31	2720 1-2	302	35.04	83.45
	W. A. Cowperthwaite	500	80	37	13	24	2573	255 1-2	33.18	89.67
	H. B. Steeves.........	500	80	32	14	18	2118 1-2	254	27.1	84.7
	S. Boyd Anderson.....	480	80	43	21	22	2933 1-2	506 1-2	37 1-2	87.3
	Etta A. Cormick	275	80	40	18	22	2434 1-2	155 1-2	31.4	78.5
	Ethel Murphy.........	275	82	43	28	15	2943 1-2	392 1-2	36.	85.
	Alice Lea.............	275	80	59	21	38	4150	138 1-2	55.1	93.30
	Agnes McSweeney....	275	82	52	28	24	3542	648 1-2	44.	84.
	Amelia I. Smith.......	275	80	53	33	20	3486	538	44.96	84.83
	Mary A. Moore........	240	82	55	30	25	3613	792 1-2	45.	81.8
	Mabel E. McLeod......	275	82	58	37	21	3710 1-2	1045 1-2	45.	78.7
	Elspeth Charters......	275	80	59	28	31	3845 1-2	558	49.	83.
	Ella J. McKay	275	80	62	32	30	4102 1-2	529	52.	84.6
	Emma Condon	275	82	60	30	30	4024	787	50.08	80.33
	Lottie L. Weldon......	200	80	60	25	35	3673	1127	47.11	78.52
Victoria....	S. W. Irons...........	850	80	45	19	26	2765	366 1-2	35.1	78.
	Catherine Barton......	275	80	52	18	34	3204 1-2	496 1-2	40.94	78.73
	Cora L. Simpson	240	80	63	21	42	3960	414 1-2	50.06	80.3
	Harriet E. Willis	275	80	62	33	29	3844	576 1-2	48.7	78.5
	Ella Stevens..........	275	80	52	34	18	3352 1-2	638	42.67	82.05
	Hazel Taylor..........	225	82	52	29	23	3608 1-2	442	44.9	86.3
	G. May Forge.........	240	82	57	27	30	3708 1-2	420 1-2	46.	80.7
	Eunice Brown.........	275	82	57	31	26	4049 1-2	480 1-2	49.7	87.2
	Fanny McLaren.......	275	80	58	26	32	3567 1-2	655	45.6	78.62
	Edith Mitchell	240	82	58	29	29	4024 1-2	543 1-2	49.75	85.7
Wesley	Agnes Quirke.........	400	82	37	14	23	2620 1-2	290	32.36	87.45
	Kate Hamilton........	240	82	52	24	28	3341	637	41.47	79.7
	Natalie Allain.........	275	82	48	23	25	3210	449 1-2	39.64	82.
	Elizabeth Richard.....	275	82	53	27	26	3497 1-2	420 1-2	43.68	82.41
	Evangeline Bourque..	240	82	59	28	31	3603 1-2	524	45.1	76.4
	Catherine Hennessey .	275	82	58	30	28	3638 1-2	694 1-2	44.85	77.3
	Elodie Bourque........	240.	82	64	19	45	3727	508 1-2	46.	71.
	Evangeline LeBlanc ..	200	80	68	29	39	3876 1-2	594 1-2	49.27	72.45

STATEMENT No. 7.

Term ended Dec. 31, 1902. No. of Pupils in the several Standards of Instruction.

SUBJECTS.	I	II	III	IV	V	VI	VII	VIII	IX	X	XI	TOTALS.
Reading, Spelling and Recitation	313	219	232	329	215	151	159	101	.....	.....	.....	1719
Composition	.....	.....	202	221	215	151	159	101	.....	.....	.....	1049
Grammar and Analysis	.....	.....	202	221	215	151	159	101	.....	.....	.....	1049
History	.....	.....	.....	39	110	151	159	56	69	.....	40	624
Form	313	219	232	244	163	151	159	101	.....	.....	.....	1582
Industrial Drawing	313	219	232	244	163	151	159	101	.....	.....	.....	1582
Print Script	313	219	232	244	213	151	159	101	.....	.....	.....	1632
Writing	313	219	232	244	213	151	159	101	.....	.....	.....	1632
Arithmetic	181	219	232	244	215	151	159	101	69	42	45	1658
Geometry	.....	.....	.....	.....	.....	.....	.....	.....	69	42	45	156
Algebra	.....	.....	.....	.....	.....	.....	24	101	69	42	45	381
Geography	.....	.....	232	249	215	151	159	101	69	.....	40	1216
Mineral, Plant and Animal Life	239	171	202	198	110	151	159	101	.....	.....	.....	1331
Colour	313	219	232	244	163	151	159	101	.....	.....	.....	1582
English	.....	.....	.....	.....	.....	.....	.....	.....	69	42	40	151
Temperance Teachings of Science	278	219	193	244	215	151	1 59	101	.....	.....	.....	1560
Chemistry	.....	.....	.....	.....	.....	.....	.....	.....	.....	42	45	87
Greek	.....	.....	.....	.....	.....	.....	.....	.....	.....	.....	3	3
Latin	.....	.....	.....	.....	.....	.....	84	97	58	30	38	307
French	49	.....	.....	41	30	.....	.....	28	69	41	40	258
Book-keeping	.....	.....	.....	.....	.....	.....	.....	.....	69	42	.....	111
Agriculture and Botany	.....	.....	.....	.....	.....	.....	.....	.....	69	42	42	153
Singing	278	194	232	249	162	123	119	56	.....	.....	.....	1412

STATEMENT NO. 8.

Total School Debentures Outstanding December 31st, 1902.

DATE OF ISSUE.	Years to run	WHEN DUE	Numbers	Value Each	Total Amount	Rate %	Total Interest	INTEREST PAYABLE. Jan.	Mch.	April	July	Sept.	Oct.
August 1, 1874	20	August 1, 1894	9 to 17	$ 500	$4000	5%	$200				$200		
July 1, 1882	20	July 1, 1903	31 to 37	500	2000	6%	120	60			60		
January 1, 1885	20	January 1, 1905	38 to 40	500	1500	6%	90	45			45		
July 1, 1886	20	July 1, 1906	41	500	500	6%	30	15			15		
July 13, 1889	20	July 13, 1909	42 to 61	500	10000	6%	600	300			300		
			62 to 70	1000									
January 1, 1890	20	January 1, 1910	71 to 76	500	12000	5%	600	300			300		
			34 to 53	500									
July 2, 1890	19	July 2, 1909	54 to 57	500	10000	4%	400	200			200		
March 2, 1891	18	March 2, 1909	94 to 100	500	2000	4%	80		$40			$40	
July 2, 1891	18	July 2, 1909	1 to 20	1000	3500	4%	140	70			70		
October 1, 1897	25	October 1, 1922	21 to 27	1000	20000	4%	800			$400			$400
January 1, 1898	25	January 1, 1923	23 to 40	1000	7000	4%	280	140			140		
October 1, 1898	25	October 1, 1923			13000	4%	520			260			260
					$85500		$3360	$1130	$40	$660	$1330	$40	$660

NOTE.—Bond No. 32, $500 issued July 1,1881, fell due July 1, 1901. It was paid out of the current revenue. Bond No. 33, issued July 1, 1881 was paid in 1902 out of current revenue.

STATEMENT No. 9.

Standing Committees, 1902.

FINANCE.

MR. A. E. WALL. Mr. JAS. FLANAGAN. MR. H. S. BELL. MR. H. H AYER.

REPAIRS.

L. N. BOURQUE, M. D. MR. J. H. HARRIS. MRS. PURDY.

TEACHERS AND SCHOOL PROPERTY.

THE FULL BOARD.

NAMES OF TRUSTEES APPOINTED BY CITY COUNCIL.

Term:—Women 3 years; Men 4 years.

DATE OF APPOINTMENT.	NAMES.	IN LIEU of
1899, December 8.......	Mr. H. H. Ayer........	Mr. H. H. Ayer........
1901, March 5...........	Mr. J. H. Harris.......	Mr. G. B. Willet.......
1901, March 22.........	Mr. H. S, Bell..........	Mr. W. D. Martin......
1902, January 10........	L. N. Bourque, M. D....	L. N. Bourque, M. D....
1902, June 17............	Miss Hattie Tweedie....	Miss Hattie Tweedie....

NAMES OF TRUSTEES APPOINTED BY THE GOVERNMENT.

DATE OF APPOINTMENT.	NAMES.	IN LIEU OF
1899, March 8............	Mrs. Annie Purdy.......	Mrs. Emma R. Atkinson
1899, December 13.......	Mr. James Flanagan.....	Mr. James Flanagan....
1900, June 20...........	Mr. J T. Hawke........	Mr. D. Grant, resigned.
1900, December 26.......	Mr. A. E. Wall..........	Mr. A. E. Wall........

RECAPITULATION OF VOUCHERS, 1902.

January	$1229 66	
February	1598 64	
March	2973 35	
April	566 70	
May	1997 59	
June	3134 89	
July	543 84	
August	1011 71	
September	1096 17	
October	1372 30	
November	2722 24	
December	2383 96	
		$ 20630 99
To Bond No. 32, paid out of Current Account, May 15, 1902.		500 00
To balance due Bank, January 1, 1902 .. :		98 98
		$ 21229 97

SCHOOL TRUSTEES' RECEIPTS FOR YEAR 1902.

To Cash from City,	$2,460 39	
" " " County Fund,	1,115 67	
" " " City,	1,432 29	
" " " "	2,625 74	
" Tuition fees, Stephen Irving,	3 00	
" " " Willie Irving.	3 00	
" Cash from City,	1,116 55	
" " " "	1,349 56	
" " " "	3,480 11	
" " from County Fund.	1,244 40	
" Tuition fees, F. Bulman,	3 00	
" " " Thos. Mellish,	6 00	
" " " Birdie Tucker,	6 00	
" Cash from City,	1,119 89	
" " " "	2,898 61	
" " " "	1,016 86	
" " J. H. Harris, ashes 21 bbls. at .65,	13 65	
		$19,894 72

EXPENDITURE FOR 1902

1902.			
Dec. 31,	By Salaries Teachers and Officers		$11,708 40
"	" Janitors' Salaries, ...		1,129 00
"	" General Repairs, ...		351 51
"	" Expenses, ...		224 32
"	" Interest,..		4,387 85
"	" Insurance,.		348 00
"	" Wood		767 45
"	" School Supplies....		126 66
"	" Water,..		216 38
"	" Coal, ...		439 81
"	" Rent, Wesley St....		7 00
"	" Fuel, Wesley St....		175 00
"	" Real Estate, ...		50 40
"	" Electric Light, ...		42 00
"	" Gas, ...		5 80
	Total Expenditure for 1902...........................		$19,979 58
	Permanent Improvements........................	$651 41	
	Bond No. 32 paid out of Current Account, May 15, 1902........................	500 00	1,151 41
			$21,130 99

ESTIMATES, 1903.

	Estimates, 1902.	Estimates, 1903.
By Salaries Teachers and Officers	$ 12300 00	$ 12404 00
" Janitors	1316 00	1600 00
" Repairs	200 00	400 00
" Expenses	250 00	250 00
" Interest	4000 00	4150 00
" Insurance	308 00	50 00
" Fuel	1500 00	1500 00
" Water	75 00	225 00
" School Supplies..	120 00	125 00
" Furniture		150 00
" Rent	12 00	12 00
" Electric light and gas		15 00
" Fuel, Wesley St	200 00	300 00
" Balance due on permanent improvement		500 00
" One quarter purchase money, Victoria school play ground		500 00
	$ 20281 00	$ 22181 00
Less County Fund estimated 1903		2281 00
Total required for 1903		$ 19900 00

TOWN OF ST. STEPHEN.

To JAMES R. INCH. Esquire, LL. D.,
Chief Superintendent of Education.

SIR: I have the honor to present for your consideration the report of the Board of School Trustees of the Town of St. Stephen for the year ending June 30th, 1902.

The composition of the Board remains the same as last year.

Two changes were made in the teaching staff during the year. Miss M. Olivia Maxwell of the High School resigned at the end of the term ending June 30. Miss Ethel Hazen Jarvis was appointed in her place. Miss May B. Carter who taught Grades V and VI, after a long and faithful service on the teaching staff, sent in her resignation which was accepted with a great deal of regret by the Board and Miss Bertha M. Brown was appointed in her place.

On Monday evening, June 23rd, about twelve hundred people attended the rink to hear the closing exercises of the High School and the essays of the pupils. The class consisted of six girls and four boys and was addressed by the Rev. Mr. Goucher.

At the close of the exercises Mrs. D. F. Maxwell, on behalf of the W. C. T. U., presented to Mr. Sullivan's school a portrait of the late Frances E Willard and to the High School a portrait of the late Sir S. L. Tilley for the best essays written on alcohol and its effect on the human system. Miss Hattie Hartesy received the 1st prize for Mr. Sullivan's school and Miss Eva Clarke second prize for High School.

Respectfully submitted,

LEWIS A. MILLS, *Secretary.*

June 30th, 1902.

TABULAR STATEMENT

Showing Names of Teachers, Class, Salary, etc., for the Term Ending December 31st, 1901.

SCHOOL.	NAME OF TEACHER.	Class.	Salary.	Pupils. Boys.	Pupils. Girls.	Average Daily Attendance.	Per Cent. Attendance.	Standards Taught.
High School	P. G. McFarlane	I	$700	20	29	40.44	80.58	IX., X., XI.
	M. Olivia Maxwell	I	260	8	14	18.54	84.29	IX., X., XI.
Marks Street....	F. O. Sullivan..............	I	665	38	34	60.56	84.11	VII., VIII.
	Etta E. DeWolfe, Assistant	I	320	..	..	.....	.....	
	M. F. Boyd.................	I	260	32	20	42.58	85.06	V., VI.
	M. B. Carter...............	I	260	19	32	41.25	80.88	V., VI.
	J. D. Henry	I	260	26	23	31.32	42.	V., VI.
	Mercy Murray...............	I	260	28	22	44.54	89.03	III., IV.
Cove............	C. H. Murray	I	300	27	21	39.00	81.25	III., IV.
	Ella M. Veazey..............	I	320	26	24	42.23	84.46	I., II.
King Street.....	Emma Veazey	I	260	25	25	43.68	87.36	III., IV.
	Jessie H. Whitlock	I	320	30	23	46.85	88.00	I., II.

TABULAR STATEMENT

Showing Names of Teachers, Class, Salary, etc., for the Term Ending June 30th, 1902.

SCHOOL.	NAME OF TEACHER.	Class.	Salary.	Pupils. Boys.	Pupils. Girls.	Average Daily Attendance.	Per Cent. Attendance.	Standards Taught.
High School ...	P. G. McFarlane	I	$ 700	19	29	37.62	78.43	IX., X., XI.
	M. Olivia Maxwell	I	260	7	14	18.08	86.11	IX., X., XI.
Marks Street....	F. O. Sullivan	I	665	37	35	61.67	85.65	VII., VIII.
	Etta E. DeWolfe, Assistant	I	320	..	..	.....	.....	V., VI.
	M. F. Boyd..................	I	260	20	28	42.24	88.00	
	Jessie D. Henry	I	260	26	21	42.38	90.08	V., VI.
	Bertha M. Brown	I	260	20	29	37.	75.7	V., VI.
	Mercy Murray	I	260	28	27	44.05	80.09	III., IV.
Cove............	Charles H. Murray..........	I	320	26	20	38.47	83.65	III., IV.
	Ella M. Veazey..............	I	320	27	26	41.11	77.54	I., II.
King Street.....	Emma Veazey	I	260	25	25	41.29	82.6	III., IV.
	Jessie H. Whitlock..........	I	320	31	22	42.4	80.00	I., II.

RECEIPTS AND EXPENITURES.

Of Board of School Trustees of the Town of Saint Stephen for the Year ended June 30, 1902.

1901.			
July 3,	To amount from Town Treasurer	$3,000 00	
Aug. 21,	" " County Fund...	377 58	
Dec. 5,	" " Town Treasurer, ...	2,000 00	
" 20,	" " Town Treasurer, ...	500 00	
1902.			
Feb. 10,	" " County Fund...	465 61	
Jan. 23,	" " Town Treasurer, ...	1,000 00	
			$7,343 19

1902.	Cr,		
June 30,	By Balance,..	$2,757 50	
"	" Teachers' Salaries, ...	4,325 00	
"	" Fuel, ...	323 50	
"	" Care of Rooms,...	300 39	
"	" Repairs,..	50 00	
	" Contingencies, ...	415 00	
			$8,171 39
	Balance........................		$ 828 20

TOWN OF MILLTOWN.

To J. R. INCH, LL. D.

Report to June 30th, 1902.

For the term just ended Mrs. Bertha J. Dewar has taught the Pleasant Street Primary School formerly under instruction of Mrs. M. A. Sutherland. There has been no other change in the staff during the school year. From the Superior School was graduated a class of eight. The public exercises of graduation took place in the Presbyterian church on the evening of June 20th, on which occasion, Hon. G. W. Ganong, M. P., made an interesting and suggestive address.

Following hereto may be found the usual half yearly statements of the different schools, as well as yearly statement of expenditures.

STATEMENT, DECEMBER 31, 1901.

Schools.	Teacher.	No, Boys.	No. Girls.	Total.	Present Average.	Per Cent Average.	Standards.
Superior.	J. B. Sutherland	8	24	32	28.45	88.91	IX, X, XI.
"	I. J. Caie	10	19	29	26.1	90.	VIII.
Intermed'te.	M. C. Osborne..	7	16	23	20.8	90.43	VII.
"	B. A. Young...	11	28	39	32 3	82 8	VI.
"	M. E. Connolly..	29	14	43	38	88.3	V.
"	C. M. Caswell..	20	24	44	39.17	89.02	IV.
2nd Prim.	A. D. Young...	31	23	54	48.17	89.19	II, III..
Primary.	T. S. Kirk......	19	7	26	22.52	86.64	I, II, III.
"	M. A. Sutherland	24	24	48	43 87	91,40	I, II

STATEMENT, JUNE 30, 1902.

Schools.	Teacher.	No. Boys.	No. Girls.	Total.	Present Average.	Per Cent Average,	Standards.
Superior.	J. B. Sutherland	10	24	34	28.25	83.1	XI, X, IX.
"	I. J. Caie....	10	17	27	21,6	80	VIII.
Intermed'te;	M. C. Osborne...	7	16	23	20,28	88.1	VII.
"	B. A. Young..	23	11	34	28.28	83	VI.
"	M, E. Connolly,.	29	14	43	35.78	83.2	V.
"	C. M. Caswell..	21	23	44	38.36	87.8	IV.
2nd Prim.	A. D. Young..	31	24	55	47	85,48	II, III.
Primary.	B. J. Dewar..	22	26	48	41.18	85	I, II.
"	T. S. Kirk....	21	6	27	24.35	90.59	I, II, III.

EXPENDITURES.

For Teachers' Salaries,	$2,630 00
" Construction,	162 18
" Fuel,	104 00
" Insurance,	4 50
" Expense Account,	458 55
" Care of Rooms,	265 00
Total,	$3,624 23

Respectfully submitted,

E. H. BALKAM, *Secretary*.

W. W. GRAHAM, *Chairman*.

Milltown, N. B., June 30, 1902.

VI.—TOWN OF WOODSTOCK.

Board of School Trustees

J. R. INCH, ESQ., LL. D.,
Chief Superintendent of Education.

SIR,—The Board of School Trustees for the Town of Woodstock submit the following statement of their Receipts and Expenditure for the year ending June 30th, 1902.

RECEIVED.

Balance in Treasurer's Hands......	$ 371 05
Received from Town Treasurer.....	4,500 00
" " County Drafts	868 40
" " Rent...	48 00
" " Interest on Deposits..	6 01
	$5,793 46

PAID OUT.

Fuel......	$ 176 68	
Secretary,.	100 00	
Insurance,.	42 00	
Interest,...	308 50	
Janitors,...	383 00	
Teachers, summer term..	1,997 00	
" winter " ...	2,357 00	
Incidentals,	180 30	
Balance in Treasurer's hand,	248 98	
		$5,793 46

The attendance at the schools and the progress of the pupils during the past year was materially affected by the prevalence of disease in the Town, the schools having on two occasions been closed by order of the Board of Health.

The following is a statement of the schools under the care of the Board with the attendance, etc., during the year.

SUMMER TERM.

TEACHER.	Standards Taught.	Per Cent. Pupils daily Present.	No. of Pupils.
Minnie Carman	I. and II.	83.29	58
Ella Smith	I. and II.	75.00	52
Mary Milmore	I. and II.	73.21	51
Frances Peters	III. and IV.	81.09	66
Mary Baker	III. and IV.	74.99	39
Elizabeth J. Cupples	III. and IV.	80.63	44
Helena Mulherrin	V. and VI.	77.9	65
Kate Appleby	V. and VI.	73.04	45
Alexandra Comben	V. and VI.	70.	42
Katherine Clark	VII. and VIII.	76.29	41
N. F. Thorne	VII. and VIII.	78.66	44
Frank A. Good	VII. and VIII.	81.3	48
Julia Neales	IX.	73.03	35
G. H. Harrison	X. and XI.	82.7	25
			655

WINTER TERM.

TEACHER.	Standards Taught.	Per cent. Pupils daily Present.	No. of Pupils.
Minnie Carman	I. and II.	79.96	58
Ella Smith	I. and II.	78.19	57
Mary Millmore	I. and II.	80.16	54
Frances Peters	III. and IV.	82.2	62
Mary Baker	III. and IV.	80.45	35
Elizabeth J. Cupples	III. and IV.	88.65	44
Helena Mulherrin	V. and VI.	77.0	62
Kate Appleby	V. and VI.	85.34	43
Alexandra Comben	V. and VI.	76.83	41
Katherine Clarke	VII. and VIII.	82.	41
N. F. Thorne	VII. and VIII.	86.66	41
Frank A. Good	VII. and VIII.	80.8	47
Julia Neales	IX.	72.23	31
G. H. Harrison	X. and XI.	87.16	23
			639

Respectfully submitted,

July 3rd, 1902. A. B. CONNELL.

TOWN OF CHATHAM.

Board of School Trustees.

To James R. Inch, LL. D.,
Chief Superintendent of Education.

Sir: I herewith submit report of our schools for year ending June 30th, 1902.

In September Miss Anna G. McIntosh, the efficient principal of Wellington Street School was given leave to visit the Pacific Coast for one year. Martin J. Wallace was appointed to the vacancy and given charge of Grade VIII in Henderson Street School.

R. W. Alward was placed in charge of the Wellington Street School. On the opening of the new school in January he was again placed in charge of Grade VIII. Grade VII was also removed from Wellington Street and placed under Martin J. Wallace, in new building. Miss M. C. Edgar was appointed principal of Wellington Street School and has proved a worthy successor to Miss McIntosh.

As your report of last year made reference to the opening of our ne school building I will merely say that the necessity for same is shown b the fact that we have about 20 additional pupils enrolled in the Gramm School this year.

The new stone building also erected by the Sisters of Hotel Dieu gives us much improved accommodation for our pupils under their care.

At the examination for entrance into the Grammar School, 46 pupils presented themselves, of whom 10 passed in the first division, 29 in the second division, 5 in the third and 2 failed.

The Governor General's medal was won by Miss Jessie Fowlie for highest standing.

Attached to this report you will find statements showing names ot teachers, pupils enrolled, etc.

Respectfully submitted,

GEORGE STOTHART, *Secretary*.

Financial Statement for Year Ending June 30, 1902.

EXPENDITURES,

Balance due in 1901	$ 89 52	
For salaries	6590 86	
" Rent	560 00	
" Fuel, water and light	436 72	
" Insurance	358 75	
" Interest	1440 46	
" Bond paid	379 47	
" Incidentals	322 26	
		$ 10178 04

RECEIPTS.

County School Fund	$ 1326 45	
Town Treasurer	10960 00	
		$ 12286 45
Balance on hand		$ 2108 41

Names of Teachers, Number of Pupils and Grades Taught for Term Ended December 31st, 1901.

TEACHERS.	Salaries.	Boys.	Girls.	Total.	Grades Taught.
Philip Cox, Ph. D......	$750	13	15	28	X., XI., XII.
James McIntosh........	500	12	12	24	IX.
Martin J. Wallace......	280	24	18	42	VIII.
Miss Maggie Mowatt....	280	27	15	42	VII., VI.
" Maude K. Lawlor..	200	41	18	59	IV., III.
" Laula S. Smith....	200	39	17	56	II., I.
" Ida I. Haviland....	200	29	19	48	V.
" Bessie M. Creighton	200	22	8	30	II., I.
" K. J. B. McLean...	200	24	7	31	IV., III.
Sister Ellen Walsh......	200	..	81	81	II., I.
" E. O. Keefe......	200	..	59	59	IV., III.
" S. Jane Curry	200	..	40	40	VI., V.
" Margaret Barden...	280	..	47	47	IX., VIII., VII.
Mr. R. W. Alward......	375	25	11	36	VII.
ss M. C. Edgar	200	21	14	35	VI.
" Essie L. Keoughan	200	36	16	52	V.
" V. C. Wright......	200	31	24	55	IV.
" Mabel J. Flood....	200	25	18	43	III.
" Katie A. McDonald	200	33	18	51	III., I.
" Annie M. Curran ..	200	27	21	48	II.
" M. C. Sutherland...	200	33	30	63	I.
		462	508	970	

Number of Pupils in Grades.

I.	II.	III.	IV.	V.	VI.	VII.	VIII.	IX.	X.	XI.	XII.
191	119	136	130	121	83	68	52	42	17	8	3

Names of Teachers, Number of Pupils and Grades Taught for Term Ended June 30th, 1902.

TEACHERS.	Salaries.	Boys.	Girls.	Total.	Grades Taught.
Philip Cox, Ph. D.....	$750	14	11	25	X., XI., XII.
James McIntosh	500	10	12	22	IX.
R. W. Alward	450	24	17	41	VIII.
Martin J. Wallace.....	280	33	16	49	VII.
Miss M. Mowatt.......	280	26	10	36	VI.
" Ida Haviland....	200	27	20	47	V.
" Meude K. Lawlor	200	36	17	53	IV., III.
" Laula S. Smith ...	200	38	18	56	II., I.
" B. M. Creighton..	200	21	10	31	II., I.
" K I. B. McLean..	200	23	7	30	IV., III.
Sister Ellen Walsh....	200	..	77	77	II., I.
" E O. Keefe	200	..	57	57	IV., III.
" S. Jane Curry..	200	..	39	39	VI., V.
" Margaret Barden	280	..	51	51	IX., VIII., VII.
Miss M. C. Edgar......	280	30	11	41	VI., IV.
" Essie L. Keoughan	200	43	11	54	V.
" V. C. Wright.....	200	30	24	54	IV.
" Mabel J. Flood....	200	29	17	46	III.
" Katie A. McDonald	200	35	17	52	III., I.
" Annie M. Curran	200	30	21	51	II.
" M. C. Sutherland	200	32	28	60	I.
		481	491	972	

Number of Pupils in Grades.

I.	II.	III.	IV.	V.	VI.	VII.	VIII.	IX.	X.	XI.	XII.
188	119	140	132	123	82	69	51	43	15	8	2

TOWN OF NEWCASTLE.

Board of School Trustees,

To J. R. INCH, ESQ., LL. D.,
Chief Superintendent of Education.

SIR: The Board of School Trustees of the Town of Newcastle, submit the following statement of the receipts and expenditures for the school year ending on 30th June, 1902.

RECEIVED.

From Sale of Debentures,	$8,105 68
" J. R. Inch, Esq., Chief Supt.	7 00
" County Treasurer,	650 20
" Town Treasurer,	3,345 74
" Rebate of Interest,	4 23
" Tuition Fees,	10 00
	$12,122 85

EXPENDED.

Overdrawn 30th June, 1901,	$ 827 24	
For Salaries,	3,320 64	
" Interest,	320 00	
" Repairs,	263 28	
" Furniture,	109 65	
" Real Estate 16.00, Printing 13.00,	29 00	
" Sinking Fund 200.00, Incidentals 76.00,	276 00	
" Trustees' Note,	2,062 00	
" Rent 200.00, Fuel 486.68,	686 68	
" Maria Hennessy's Bond,	3,129 00	
" Bal. in Royal Bank of Canada,	1,099 36	
		$12,122 85

STATEMENTS FOR THE TWO TERMS.

Statement—First Term.

TEACHERS.	No. Girls.	No. Boys.	Total.	Grades Taught,
P. F. Morrissy	28	18	46	I, II, III. IV. V. VI, VII.
G. H. McNaughton	17	10	27	IX, X, XI,
M. G. Duffy	21	28	49	VII,
B. M. Bell	17	51	68	I, II,
A. O. McLeod	9	5	14	II, III, IV, V, VII,
E. McLachlan	19	25	44	VI,
L. B. Troy	21	31	52	III, IV,
I. H. Falconer	21	27	48	III' IV,
S, M, Harriman	30	41	71	I, II,
M. J. Dunnet	17	32	49	V,
B. M. Reid	16	18	34	VIII,
Totals	216	286	502	

Statement—Second Term.

TEACHERS.	No. Girls.	No. Boys.	Total.	Grades Taught.
P. F. Morrissy	13	5	18	I, II, III, V,. VII.
G. K. McNaughton	18	.10	28	IX, X, XI.
M. G. Duffy	23	28	51	VII.
E. McLachlan	23	18	41	VI.
L. B. Troy	21	31	52	III, IV.
I. H. Falconer	20	26	46	III, IV.
B. M. Reid	18	15	33	VIII.
S. M. Harriman	27	42	69	I, II.
M. J. Dunnet, H. M. McLeod	13	32	45	V.
A. J. Bell, A. O. McLeod	30	23	53	I, II, III, IV, V, VII.
B. M. Bell, A. O. McLeod, A. J. Bell	19	48	67	I, II,
Totals	235	278	503	

Respectively submitted,

. F. MORRISSY, *Secretary*. D. MURRAY, M. D., *Chairman*.

Newcastle, N. B., June 30th, 1902.

TOWN OF CAMPBELLTON.

BOARD OF SCHOOL TRUSTEES.

J. R. INCH, ESQ. LL. D.,
Chief Supt. of Education,
Fredericton, N. B.

SIR:—I beg leave to submit herewith, a statement of the receipts and expenditures of the Board of School Trustees for the Town of Campbellton, together with statistical tables and Educational work generally,in connection with our town schools, for the school year ending June 30th, 1902,

By virtue of a resolution of the Board of School Trustees, passed on the 30th day of May, all contracts heretofore existing between the Board and the several teachers in its employ, terminated on the 30th day of June following.

To fill vacancies thus created, applications from teachers in general were solicited. In all, 47 applications were received, including 6 of the former staff. These latter were re-engaged. Two of the former staff, viz: Miss Eva M. Downey, B. A. and Mr. Gustave E. Duncan, did not apply for re-engagement.

Their places were filled by the appointment of Miss Bertha J. Asker and Miss Lydia Duncan. Miss Catherine F. Mair, B. A. (Dal.) was transferred to the advanced department formerly taught by Miss Downey.

Miss Barnes of the primary department had her summer vacation extended one month, during which time her place was temporarily filled by Miss Richards of this town.

SCHOOL CONCERTS.

A series of school concerts were held during the year, and the proceeds devoted to the purchase of a piano, which the school now owns and prizes as a valuable addition to its equipment. These concerts and exhibitions have also had an excellent effect as an educational factor in the intellectual development of the pupils.

It is proposed to continue them during the incoming year, when the revenue therefrom will be utilized for equally laudable purposes.

VACCINATION.

The Act of Legislature, passed at last session, providing for the compulsatory vaccination of school children was put into operation during the summer holidays, and on the re-opening of school in August, no pupil was admitted to school privileges who had not been properly vaccinated according to law. In all cases where children had not been successfully vaccinated within the three years, required by statute, the work of vaccination was attended to during the vacation, in order that the temporary indisposition which generally accompanies this operation, would be over before opening of school term. To guard against the possibility of a plea of ignorance of the law regarding the matter being set up, the Board of Health caused the text of the act to be published in the local papers in the early part of July.

If this wise enactment of the Legislature will be properly carried into effect throughout the Province from year to year, coupled with compulsatory attendance at school, it will only be a few years at most until smallpox will have lost its grip and be a disease of the past, to be chronicled only in medical history and in the expenditure records of the municipal and provincial blue books.

INSPECTION.

Our School Inspector, Mr. Mersereau, paid his customary annual visit to our schools and spent fully one week in inspecting and examining the work in the different departments. These annual visits, by a former teacher of high educational attainments, wide experience and rare executive ability, are looked forward to with considerable interest and anxiety by teachers and pupils, as well as by all interested in the education of our children, and cannot fail to have a lasting beneficial effect in shaping the future career of the rising generation.

MANUAL TRAINING.

The most important event of the year in connection with the educational work of our school has been the establishment of a Manual Training Department. A spacious and well arranged room has been set apart for that purpose in the Grammar School building and is now thoroughly equipped with benches, tools, models and all material necessary for carrying on the work of the department. Miss Ethel I. Mersereau, a graduate of the Truro, N. S., Manual Training School, has been engaged as teacher, and evinces considerable enthusiasm in the work.

Although a radical departure from the time-honoured school curriculum of the past, Manual Training is rapidly winning its way into popular favour. Upwards of 200 of our pupils will take the course during the incoming year. This course, besides being an incentive to keeping many pupils longer at school and creating a keener interest in school work generally, can claim as a special function the cultivation of motor activities, which develop brain areas, that otherwise might remain partially inert. By this means also, pupils become more intimately acquainted with their environments, and better able to adapt themselves to the ever varying conditions of life, upon which so much of the social and industrial development of our country depends. Prof. James, the greatest psychologist in America, said—"The most colossal improvement which recent years has seen in secondary education, is the introduction of Manual Training Schools."

We trust to be able in the very near future to establish practical courses of instruction in domestic science, music, and commercial education, (including book-keeping, stenography, and allied subjects) in order that most of our boys and girls can complete their education at home and enter upon their life work, without incurring the increased cost of going abroad to learn that which they must know to enable them to earn a livelihood at home.

To make room for the introduction and successful teaching of these extra subjects, it may be necessary to dispense with some of those already in the prescribed curriculum. This can be accomplished, in part at least, by the abolition of classics from the common school course. The intellectual development of the pupils would not suffer materially thereby, while the loss, if any, would be more than compensated by the increased amount of time which could be devoted to more useful subjects. Of course it is only natural that persons, whose higher education consisted chiefly of a thorough knowledge of Latin and Greek and an almost entire ignorance of modern educational subjects, should be prejudiced in favour of the study of classics.

At the time when Latin and Greek were most prominent on the programme of studies, most of the subjects which now constitute our course of study were unknown, whereas at present the study of classics in schools is undertaken chiefly to satisfy the antiquated requirements of the colleges.

It is now admitted that even the development of "power," which at one time was supposed to be exclusively inherent in the study of classics, is equally well attained by the study of other subjects, which have as well, a practical utility, not associated with classical studies.

Colleges which fail to recognize honest work done along modern educational lines, must sooner or later be side-tracked. What suited a state of civilization that existed one hundred years ago, is now no longer tenable. The taxpayer today is master of the situation and legislation to be effective, must necessarily be the exponent of crystallized public opinion.

TEACHERS' SALARIES.

A great deal has been said and written regarding the low salaries usually paid to teachers. Now it must be admitted that teachers, like most of other public servants, can generally command par value for their services in the open market. Why do some lawyers control such high fees? Simply because of their ability to convince their clients that their services to them are worth the fees demanded. The fact that Architects, Machinists, Electricians, Engineers and Trained nurses, who, after completing the ordinary school curriculum, spend 3 or 4 years preparing themselves for their special work as skilled labourers, command a profitable income, is no argument why those teachers should receive equal remuneration who simply spend about nine months attending Normal School, and obtain a second class license, with no evident inclination to advance themselves in their chosen profession, and are only required to work about eight or nine months in the year, besides, in many cases possessing no special adaptation to the work assigned them. Let legislation elevate the qualifications of teachers along the lines of modern requirements and popular sentiment will readily respond to a demand for increased compensation. Legislators alone have the absolute control of their own salaries regardless of conditions.

STATEMENT.

Names of Teachers, Number of Pupils, Grades Taught, etc., During Term Ending June 30th, 1902.

No.	TEACHERS.	Departments.	Class.	*Yearly Allowance.	Boys.	Girls.	Total.	Grades Taught.
1	E. W. Lewis, B. A.	Gr. S.	G Class	650	17	23	40	IX., X., XI.
2	Eva M. Downey, B. A. ...	Advanced.	G Class	350	22	27	49	VII., VIII.
3	Catherine F. Mair, B. A.	Intermediate.	II	225	29	20	49	VI., VII.
4	Gustave E. Duncan......	"	II	200	32	16	48	V.
5	Mary McRae.............	"	II	200	28	29	57	III., IV.
6	Clara E. Shannon........	"	II	200	32	25	57	III., IV.
7	Mary J. Cook	Primary.	II	200	32	36	68	I., II.
8	Martha G. Barnes	"	I	275	32	26	58	I., II.
				2300	224	202	426	

*Exclusive of Government allowance.

FINANCIAL STATEMENT.

RECEIPTS.

Cash on hand June 30th 1901	17 00	
Tuition Fees, ...	12 00	
Town Treasurer	4000 00	
County Treasurer	450 56	
Board of Education Examination Funds	8 50	
		$4488 06

EXPENDITURES.

Paid.	Interest on Debentures	800 00	
"	Exchange on Drafts	2 00	
"	Interest on overdraft	7 66	
"	Contingencies	34 59	
"	Repairs	126 88	
	Fuel	242 70	
"	Supplies	1 80	
"	Water Rates	32 50	
"	Printing	2 50	
"	Sewerage	30 75	
"	Teachers' Salaries	2269 75	
"	Cartage	1 80	
"	Furniture	5 10	
"	High School Entrance Examiners	24 00	
"	Secretary's Salary	100 00	
"	Janitor's Salary	350 00	
"	Bank Nova Scotia (over draft)	444 92	
	Balance Bank Nova Scotia	11 11	
			$4488 06

Respectfully submitted,

WM. F. COMEAU, *Secretary*.

D. M. MURRAY, M. D., *Chairman*.

Campbellton, N. B., Dec. 31st 1902.

APPENDIX D.

Thirty-Second Annual Report of the Board of Managers of the School for the Blind, Halifax, Nova Scotia.

INTRODUCTION.

The Board of Managers have great pleasure in submitting to the members of the Corporation, to the Provincial Governments and Legislatures interested, and to the friends of the institution the thirty-second annual report. In doing so, they desire to express their gratitude for the support which the school has received from the Provincial Legislatures and Municipalities and from private individuals. This generous support has enabled your Board to efficiently carry on the work of the school, and under the guidance of Almighty God to make the institution a blessing to those who are deprived of sight.

SUPERINTENDENT'S REPORT.

The Superintendent's report, which is hereto appended, will be found to give some interesting details with respect to the school, its staff of teachers and the general work of educating the blind.

The members of the teaching staff have been devoted to their work, and their patience and perseverance are worthy of the highest commendation.

Mr. H. B. Campbell has been appointed Principal of the Musical Department, and his appointment will, we believe, be of advantage to the school.

A beginning has been made in the teaching of Massage and it is expected that this new occupation will give employment to a number of our graduates.

It has been the wish of your Board to make the several departments of the school as practical and effective as the means at our disposal would allow and while we have every reason to congratulate ourselves on what has already been accomplished, we fully realize that had we a larger income at our command, many advantages might be given to the pupils, which under present circumstances are impossible. We should like,, for instance, to equip reading rooms for both boys and girls, and to place within their reach all the books of reference now published in the Braille point system. To do this would involve an outlay of $2000.00 and our annual income will not at present warrant this expenditure.

DOMESTIC DEPARTMENT.

The Domestic Department of the school has been efficiently conducted during the year by the matron, Mrs. Chisholm, and her two assistants. Owing to the crowded state of the building, and the constant use of many of the rooms, the work of this department has been more difficult than usual. Notwithstanding these drawbacks and her personal bereavement, the matron has done her best to further the comfort of the teachers and pupils. The care of a household numbering one hundred and forty-six persons, the majority of whom are under fifteen years of age, involves great responsibility and requires constant and untiring supervision.

GROWTH OF THE SCHOOL.

During the past ten years the number of pupils in this school has grown from forty-six to one hundred and twenty. This is due to the increased interest taken by parents and guardians in the education of those deprived of sight, to the wider knowledge that exists with respect to the work of the school and the efforts of the graduates of the institution, who, appreciating what the school has done for them, desire to have the same privileges extended to every blind boy and girl in the country. The advance in our numbers is fortunately not due to an increase in the number of those who are blind, but simply to the fact that a largely increased number of blind persons are availing themselves of the advantages which the school, the benevolent public, and the respective Governments have placed within their reach.

LEGISLATIVE SUPPORT.

Nova Scotia sends to the school seventy four pupils, New Brunswick thirty-two, Prince Edward Island six and Newfoundland nine. In the provinces of Nova Scotia and New Brunswick statutory provision for the free education of the blind has been made by legislative enactment. Annual appropriations are made to the school by the Legislatures of Prince Edward Island and Newfoundland to provide for the education of a limited number of beneficiaries. The limit in the case of Newfoundland has hitherto been eight pupils, but as several additional applications were received and the applicants were very desirous of being admitted, your Board decided to accept them and sincerely trust that the Government and Legislature of Newfoundland will increase the appropriation so as to cover the cost of their education.

INCREASED ACCOMMODATION.

In the last annual report submitted by the Board, special attention was called to the fact that increased accommodation was urgently required. Before taking any definite steps to secure funds the question of the present needs and the probable future requirements of the school were fully considered, and it was unanimously agreed that in providing increased accommodation a new building should be erected distinct from the present buildings and connected with them by a covered way. This new building would serve as a school house for the pupils in which they would spend their hours of study and work, and in which special provision should be made for recreation rooms during inclement weather. Under this arrangement, the present buildings were to be utilized for residence purposes, and the pupils after their school work was done, would come home to their respective departments, each of which would have ample reading room, sitting room, dining room, dormitory and lavatory accommodation.

Mr. J. C. Dumaresq was then asked to prepare plans and specifications in accordance with the foregoing ideas, and these plans with a few alterations were finally adopted by your Board.

THE NEXT STEP.

In February last your Board by appointment waited upon the Government of Nova Scotia and urged upon that honorable body the advisability of making a special appropriation towards the erection of the proposed new building. The members of the Government received the deputation most kindly and assured your Board that the matter would have their favourable consideration. Subsequently the Legislature of the Province appropriated $20,000.00 towards the new building.

In the early spring we received in response to our advertisements a number of tenders from responsible contractors. These were considerably in excess of the estimates of cost previously made and the work was delayed for several months in the hope that building material would decline in price and thus enable us to secure the building for a smaller outlay. In mid summer it became apparent from the number of new applications for th admission of pupils which were being received that definite action must a once be taken. The plans and specifications were then carefully revis with a view to greater economy and new tenders were called for, resultir in the contract being awarded to S. Marshall & Son for the sum of $54,-506.00, after which building operations were commenced.

THE NEW BUILDING.

The new building which will contain four stories including the basement, will be one hundred and thirty-one feet in length by seventy-one in width. It will, we believe, be one of the most modern school buildings for the blind on the continent. Its erection will enable us to receive and educate forty pupils in addition to our present number. With this new building completed, we hope to be able to develop our literary, musical and industrial departments.

PUBLIC SUPPORT.

In undertaking this forward step to further the education of the blind, your Board have relied upon the hearty co-operation and generous support of the public spirited men and women in Nova Scotia, New Brunswick, Prince Edward Island and Newfoundland. The gratifying responses which have already been made to our appeal in the cities, towns and villages visited by the representatives of the school, prove that the public are deeply interested in the work of this institution, and are prepared to actively co-operate with us in promoting the welfare of the blind. During the coming year, other localities will be visited by the superintendent and members of the staff and we feel confident that the contributions and subscriptions received, will materially augment our building fund. All contributors and subscribers may rest assured that their donations will be thankfully received and that every dollar contributed will be carefully and judiciously expended in furthering the interests of those deprived of sight.

THE SUPERINTENDENT.

The managers have much pleasure in again expressing their sense of the invaluable services of the Superintendent, Dr. C. F. Fraser, to whose ability and devotion is largely due the confidence felt in the educational and financial management of the school, throughout the entire Maritime Provinces and Newfoundland.

ACKNOWLEDGEMENTS.

In addition to the donations elsewhere acknowledged, your Board gratefully acknowledges the following bequests; Estate of Miss Margaret Little, Halifax, $500.00; estate of M. A. Buckley, Santa Cruz, California,

$150.00; estate of E. P. Archbold, Halifax, $25.00 on account; estate of Thomas Kelly, Halifax, $10.00. These bequests which amount to $685.00 have been invested and now form a part of our endowment fund. The interest from this fund is used to supplement our current income from other sources and enables the Board to give to the pupils many special educational advantages.

The thanks of the Board are due Drs. Lindsay, Kirkpatrick and Cogswell who have during the year, and for many previous years been unremitting in their attention to the pupils, giving their services free of charge.

The Board of managers also desires to express its thanks to Mr. J. D. Medcalfe, Mr. W. E. Hebb, Mr. H. B. Clarke, the Halifax Symphony Orchestra and other individuals and organizations for kindly admitting the pupils to lectures, concerts, etc., under their respective managements.

The Exhibition commissioners have our sincere thanks for admitting the pupils to the Provincial Exhibition.

The railways and other transportation companies have our thanks for the special rates granted and for the uniform kindness and care shown to pupils while travelling to and from their homes.

All of which is respectfully submitted.

W. C. SILVER, *President.*

SUPERINTENDENT'S REPORT.

To the President and Board of Managers of the School for the Blind:

GENTLEMEN,—The table of attendance herewith submitted shows that 145 blind persons have been under instruction during the past year, of whom 87 were males and 58 females. Of these 34 have since graduated or remained at home, making the total number registered December 1st, 1902, 121, of whom 73 are males and 48 females. Of these 74 are from the Province of Nova Scotia, 32 from New Brunswick, 5 from Prince Edward Island and 9 from Newfoundland.

TABLE OF ATTENDANCE.

	Boys.	Girls.	Adults.	Total.
Registered Dec. 1st, 1901,	65	47	5	117.
Entered during the year,	15	11	2	28.
Graduated or remained at home,	11	10	3	24.
Registered Dec. 1st, 1902.	69	48	4	121.

TEACHING STAFF.

The education imparted to the pupils of a school may generally be measured by the character and attainments of the members of its teaching staff. This is specially true of a school for the Blind, where the pupils come in contact with the teachers during the hours of recreation as well as in those devoted to study. This school is fortunate in having a strong and effective staff of teachers, the members of which are devoted to the work in which they are engaged. The personnel of the staff with one notable exception, remains the same as at this date last year. In January last, the school suffered a severe loss through the death of Mr. A. M. Chisholm, who for fifteen years had been principal of the musical department. Mr. Chisholm entered this institution as a pupil in 1872, and graduated in 1879. He subsequently spent two years in Berlin perfecting his musical education. As a teacher he was skillful, zealous and energetic, and his pupils inspired by his enthusiasm, stimulated by his example and guided by his instruction, seldom failed to become thorough and practical teachers of music. Mr. Chisholm gave to his work the best that was in him and his memory will long be cherished with feelings of love and esteem by those for whose welfare he so faithfully laboured.

Mr. H. B. Campbell who entered upon his duties as principal of the musical department in September last has many qualifications which fit him for the responsible position he now fills. After taking an eight years' course in this institution, Mr. Campbell went to Leipsic where for two years he studied the piano-forte under eminent masters. On his return to this country he settled in St. John, N. B. and for the past three years has been recognized as one of the most successful piano.forte teachers in that city. Mr. Campbell thoroughly understands the difficulties with which his pupils will have to contend and the necessity that exists for their attaining a high standard of excellence both as performers and instructors. He appreciates the fact that at least forty per cent. of the graduates of the school maintain themselves as teachers of music and he realizes the great responsibility for the after success of the pupils which rests upon him and his assistants in the musical department.

The work of the literary department has been ably carried on by Miss Frame, Mr. S. R. Hussey, Miss Baker, Prof. Lanos, Miss Bowes and two assistants. Miss Josie Howe, Miss Campbell, and Miss Callanan have devoted themselves to the progress of the little boys and girls in the kindergarten and primary departments.

During the year the musical department has been reorganized under the Principalship of Mr. H. B. Campbell. Mr. Campbell is assisted by Mr. Hubley and Miss Studd as piano-forte teachers, by Miss J. Allison as vocal teacher, by Miss L. Mott and Miss B Mott as teachers of the mandolin and guitar, and by Messrs. Covey, Hanson and Warren as teachers of the cornet. clarionette and band.

The work of the tuning department under Mr. D. M. Reid, of the industrial department under Mr. D. A. Baird, of the gymnasium under Mr. James Scrimgeour and the girls' work department under Miss Campbell and Miss Mott has been satisfactorily carried on.

The pupils have fully appreciated the educational opportunities afforded to them by the several departments of the school, and with few exceptions have been diligent and persevering students.

COURSE OF INSTRUCTION.

One of the principal objects of this school is to give to the pupils a broad and practical training such as will enable them to become self-supporting. Our course of instruction has been carefully arranged with this end in view and so far as can be learned its results are well up to the average of the leading institutions for the blind in other countries. In addition to receiving instruction in all the regular branches of education as taught in the public schools, our pupils are trained as piano-forte teachers, teachers of vocal music, piano-forte tuners, basket and brush makers, chair seaters, etc. The girls receive special training in crocheting, knitting, sewing, in the use of the sewing machine, and other work. Four girls are now receiving instruction in massage and have been placed under the tuition of Miss Una Legg, a graduate of this school. Miss Legg spent eight months in London, G. B., in the studio of Dr. Fletcher Little and received a first-class certificate as a masseuse. Speaking in London at a conference of the educators of the blind, Dr. Fletcher Little referred to the many masseuses with sight employed in hospitals and other institutions. Continuing he said, "Massage is now placed upon a scientific basis, and I see no reason whatever why blind persons should not hold such appointments. I am glad to say that they are well paid and their work appreciated, and if the blind are employed in the hospitals and institutions of the country, it will be good for them and good for the institutions." Prof. McHardy of the Massage Institute of London in speaking at the conference said, "In this practice of massage by the blind there is a very real and promising opening both to help the blind and for the blind to help others."

APPLIANCES.

Dr. Dessaud of Paris has recently perfected a simple machine for writing Braille point characters. This machine promises to be of very great advantage in the education of the blind. At present when writing, a blind student proceeds from right to left and the points are embossed downwards; the paper is then reversed and the student reads from left to right. He thus practically has to learn two alphabets and moreover he cannot examine or correct his work until the paper is removed from the frame. With Dr. Dessaud's machine, the writing is done from left to right and the points are embossed from beneath the paper so that the student can correct his work as it proceeds. The great advantage of this simple device will be at once apparent to all and it is satisfactory to note that its cost will not be greatly in excess of the Braille writing frame now in general use.

HEALTH.

It is gratifying to report that the health of the pupils during the past year has been most satisfactory. Several of the pupils who came to us constitutionally weak have required the special attention of the attending physician, Dr. A. W. R. Lindsay, but these quickly responded to treatment and have since become strong and healthy. The systematic physical training of the pupils, the good wholesome diet, the regular hours, the healthy situation of the school, with abundance of sunshine and fresh air conduce to insure to the pupils a standard of health quite equal to that enjoyed by any school of its size in the country.

GRADUATES.

At the close of the last school year, certificates of competency were awarded as follows;—Vernor Jones, Pownal, P. E I., a first-class certificate as a teacher of music, also a first-class certificate as a piano-forte tuner; Edgar Hursey, Hants Harbour, Nfld., a certificate as a teacher of music; John McDonald, Mabou, C. B., a first-class certificate as a piano-forte tuner; James Rousse, Wellington, N. S., a certificate as a basket and brush maker; and James McKay, Hunter's Mountain, C. B., a certificate as a brush maker. In addition to the forgoing, Miss Rachael McLeod of Point Aconi C. B., was awarded a graduating certificate from the girls' work department. These young people have received a thorough training and are now in a position to maintain themselves.

THREE NOTABLE CONFERENCES.

During the year, three notable conferences of the instructors of the blind have been held. These were convened in London, Great Britain, Brussels, Belgium and Raleigh, North Carolina. In two of these conferences this school was represented. From the reports of these conventions that have been received it is evident that a great forward movement is now taking place in the education of the blind in Europe and America, and tl the interest in the welfare of those who are deprived of sight is stead on the increase. It is also apparent that if this school is to hold its pla among the leading institutions for the blind in the world we must be pr pared to give our pupils increased educational advantages and increa facilities for that training which will enable them to secure more lucrative employment and more responsible positions.

OUR FORWARD MOVEMENT.

The great English educator, Edward Thring, said in speaking of his school, "that proper machinery for work, proper tools of all sorts, are at least as necessary in making a boy take a given shape as in making a deal box." The machinery and tools in a school are the buildings and appliances library, grounds, etc. If the buildings be overcrowded, the appliances meagre, the library indifferent and the grounds contracted, the teachers work at a great disadvantage. The first and most important piece of machinery necessary to a well organized school, is its building or buildings in which the school is carried on. This fact has always been taken into consideration in this institution, and when the growth in the number of the pupils imperatively demanded more school room, music rooms, dormitories or other accommodation an appeal has been made to the legislature and to the public and the response has always been most encouraging. In 1890 with thirty-one pupils it was felt that additional room was required and with the help of the legislature and the friends of the school the east wing of the building was erected. In 1896 when the pupils had grown to seventy in number, the accommodation was felt to be inadequate. The legislature and public were again appealed to and the commodious west wing was erected. The pupils now number one hundred and twenty-one and many others are seeking admission. Increased accommodation is urgently required and believing that the public would support any reasonable effort that might be made to promote the welfare of those who are deprived of sight, a large up-to-date school building has been planned and the work upon the same commenced.

THE NEW BUILDING.

It has been decided to erect the new school building south of the present building, connected with it by a covered way or corridor. In the new school building will be concentrated all the regular work of the school. The building will contain in addition to school rooms, music rooms, tuning rooms and an assembly hall; a printing office, manual training department, a gymnasium for boys, a gymnasium for girls, lavatories, etc. In the southern section there are to be dormitories, and other accommodation for pupils in the kindergarten and primary divisions. The present buildings will be utilized for residence purposes, and will make it possible to provide library, reading room and sitting room accommodation which is at present urgently required.

FAITH BASED ON REASONS.

The forward movement of this school involves heavy responsibilities and persistent effort, but the work of erecting and equipping the new school building has been undertaken with strong faith that it will be carried successfully through. This faith is based on the following reasons:—First, more pupils are applying for admission; second, the school should be ready to receive all eligible blind persons who may apply; third, more accommodation is urgently required for those now in attendance; fourth, more accommodation is required for the development and equipment of the several departments of the school; fifth, the public recognize that the school is doing a practical work for the blind deserving of support; sixth, the people of the Maritime Provinces and Newfoundland are public spirited and are always willing to liberally assist any institution in which they have confidence, and in the development and progress of which they are interested.

WAYS AND MEANS.

Immediately after the Legislature of Nova Scotia had made the liberal appropriation of $20,000.00 towards the new school building, active measures were taken to secure subscriptions and contributions in all parts of the Maritime Provinces. A pamphlet dealing with the matter was prepared and widely circulated. Schools, Sunday schools and other organizations were asked to assist through brick buyers or collecting cards. Many benevolent persons obtained subscription books and were active in soliciting contributions. So far as time would permit, a personal canvass was made in Halifax and twenty-four public meetings were held in the eastern and western portions of Nova Scotia. The result of these efforts to date is a subscription of $12,057.65, upon which $5,222.28 have already been paid in; this amount is likely to be substantially increased by the subscriptions of those who have signified their inteation to contribute; by the receipts from the hundreds of brick buyers scattered throughout the country, and by the efforts of the ladies and gentlemen who still hold their subscription books and are doing their best to fill them.

ACKNOWLEDGEMENTS.

I desire to express my deep sense of obligation to the many friends the blind for all that they have done and are doing for this school, and for welfare of those deprived of sight. During the year just closed I have b more than ever impressed with the breadth and depth of the interest that is taken in this institution. My personal solicitations for aid in erecting our new building have been cordially received and liberally met. In the many large and enthusiastic public meetings which I have addressed, a deep interest in the welfare of the school has been evinced and generous contributions have been made towards our building fund. Ladies and gentlemen, boys and girls, schools, Sunday schools and other organizations in all parts of the country have co-operated by raising money through brick buyers, collecting cards or subscription books. My special thanks are due to the gentlemen who so ably carried out the arrangements for our concerts and public meetings, and to the ladies and gentlemen who so kindly opened their hospitable homes and entertained the pupils in the several localities where such meetings were held.

CONCLUSION.

In conclusion, gentlemen accept my thanks for the encouragement you have given to me in the carrying on of this work, and let me say that your deep interest in the school, your willingness to consider and solve its problems, and your strong support of my administration have made it possible to inaugurate the great forward movement now in progress.

All of which is respectfully submitted.

C. F. FRASER, *Superintendent.*

APPENDIX E.

Report of the Educational Institute of New Brunswick, of the County Institutes, and of the Summer School of Science.

I.—Report of Educational Institute.

J. R. INCH, LL. D.,
Chief Superintendent of Education.

SIR:—I beg leave to submit a report of the nineteenth meeting of th Educational Institute of New Brunswick.

The Institute convened in the Normal School, Fredericton, on June 26 1902. The Chief Superintendent of Education opened the meeting and pre sided at all the sessions.

The programme was as follows:

THURSDAY, JUNE 26th.

FIRST SESSION, 10 A. M.—Enrolment. Report of Executive Committee Election of Secretaries and Nominating Committee.

11 A. M.—Address by Chief Superintendent of Education.

11 30 A. M.—Address by Mrs. Oberholzer on "School Savings Banks."

12 15.—Visit to Exhibit of Manual Work from the Fredericton Cit Schools, the Sloyd School and the Normal School.

FRIDAY, JUNE 27TH.

SECOND SESSION, 9 A. M.—"Centralization of Rural Schools," by Inspector Carter. Discussion opened by Principal A. W. Hickson and Mr. Silas Mitchell, one of the Trustees of schools of Welshpool, Campobello.

10 A. M—"The Inductive Method of Teaching Latin," by Princip Lewis. Discussion opened by A. S. McFarlane, B. A.

THIRD SESSION, 2 P. M.—Talk on "The Teaching of Literature," by Mi Knowlton.

3 P. M.—"The Course of Instruction for High Schools," by Principal Oulton and Mr. C. H. Acheson. Discussion. Inspection of Exhibit of Manual Work.

7 P. M.—Visit to the University of New Brunswick. Address by Chancellor Harrison. Music and refreshments.

SATURDAY, JUNE 28TH.

FOURTH SESSION, 9 A. M.—"On a Graduated Scale of Salaries for Teachers" by Dr. Davidson of the University. Discussion.

10 A. M.—Election of Executive Committee and Representative to the University Senate. Unfinished and new business.

The usual afternoon session and evening meeting on Thursday were omitted so that the members of the Institute might join with the citizens of Fredericton in celebrating Coronation Day.

The financial statement of the Secretary shows the receipts and expenditures to June 26th, 1902, and was as follows:

RECEIPTS.

Balance on hand June 27th, 1901	$371 05	
Enrolment fees for 1900	94 25	
Cash from Board of Education to aid in printing a full report of the proceedings of the Institute	100 00	
		$565 30

EXPENDITURE.

Dr. A. E. Winship's fee	$ 75 00	
Mrs. A. F. Robinson's expenses	2 70	
Advertising	18 75	
Music	17 00	
Janitors	7 00	
Asistant secretary	15 00	
Stenographer	36 00	
Printing programmes, etc	9 50	
Trunk for books, stationery, ballot boxes, etc	2 25	
Transportation of same to and from Institute	90	
Printing proceedings of Institute	192 00	
Travelling expenses of Executive Committee	48 40	
ationery and postage	2 60	
ndries	82	
cretary's salary for two years	62 50	
		$490 42

Billls passed at meeting of the Executive, June 26, 1902:

Advertising	$25 00	
Printing programmes and ballots	7 00	
Expenses of Mrs. Oberholzer	25 00	
		57 00
Total expenditure		$547 42
Balance on hand		$ 17 88

John Brittain was re-elected Secretary and Miss Harriet D. Gregg. Assistant Secretary.

William Brodie, M. A., was elected as representative to the Senate of the University.

The following members were elected to serve on the Executive Committee:—

Berton C. Foster, M. A., Frank Good, Miss Ella Thorne, C. H. Acheson, P. G. McFarlane, C. J. Mersereau, A. B., E. W. Lewis, A. B., Miss K. R. Bartlett, George J. Oulton, M. A., R. D. Hanson, A. B.

The whole number of members enrolled at this meeting was 446.

The President in his opening address spoke of the high compliment which had recently been paid to New Brunswick by the Imperial Government in modelling on that of our Province the system of education about to be introduced into the recently conquered South African States; and in selecting so many of our teachers to introduce it there.

He referred to the progress along educational lines in the Province, especially mentioning the great success attending the work of the Sloyd Schools; and expressed the conviction that, with the generous measure of assistance given by the Government, Sloyd would become an integral part of our School System.

Following the address on "School Saving's Banks" by Mrs. Oberholzer a resolution was introduced in favor of giving School Boards the power to establish School Saving's Banks. The resolution, however, did not meet with the approval of the Institute, the opinion prevailing that the proposed scheme did not properly come within the scope of school work.

Following Inspector Carter's address on "The Centralization of Ru[ral] Schools," Principal Hickson and School Trustee Mitchell gave an accou[nt] of the experiment at Welshpool. Three adjacent schools were united an[d] not only has the experiment proven successful from an educational stan[d-] point, but a considerable financial saving has been effected as well. Trustees, teachers and ratepayers are well pleased with the result of centralization.

A public meeting was held on the evening of Thursday, June 26th, at which excellent addresses were made by Dr. Adams of Glasgow, and Professor Robertson, who spoke on "Manual Training in the Public Schools."

The following important resolutions were passed by the Institute:—

Moved by William McLean and seconded by Dr. H. S. Bridges,

"*Resolved*, That in the opinion of the teachers of this Province, represented by the members of the Educational Institute here assembled, all contemplated changes in the school curriculum in the Text-books for use in this Province should be submitted for consideration to a Standing Committee for such purpose; said committee to consist of the Chief Superintendent of Education, the Principal of the Normal School, one Inspector to be appointed by the Board of Education, and five members, viz., two High School teachers, two Advanced School teachers and one Primary School teacher to be elected by this Institute, and further,

"*Resolved*, That the said committee be authorized to approach the Chief Superintendent at any time with recommendations relative to either of the above subjects."

Dr. Bridges, Principal Foster, Mr. F. O'Sullivan, Mr. S. W. Irons and Miss Annie Harvey, were elected members of the above committee.

Moved by Mr. James Barry, seconded by Inspector Carter,

"*Resolved*, That the Chief Superintendent be empowered to appoint a committee not exceeding five members to report at next meeting of the Institute regarding the relative advantages of Parish and District School Boards, and that the necessary expenses of said committee be paid by this Institute.

"*Resolved*, That a committee of teachers be appointed in regard to the proper pronunciation of Latin, to confer with the teachers of Latin in the Province of New Brunswick, with the Professors of Latin in the Dominion, the United States and England, and to decide upon the best method."

Dr. Bridges and Messrs. Brodie and Tuttle were appointed upon the committee called for by the resolution.

During their visit to the university the teachers were each presented by Chancellor Harrison with specially prepared phamphlets setting out the opportunities afforded New Brunswick teachers to obtain a more liberal education at our Provincial University, especially along the lines of Electrical and Civil Engineering.

The addresses and papers presented were interesting and instructive and the discussions well sustained. Dr. Davidson's paper on "Teachers' Wages, Graded and Ungraded with a remedy therefor,' and Inspector Carter's on "Centralization of Rural Schools," will be found appended to this Report.

Respectfully submitted,

JOHN BRITTAIN, *Secretary.*

REPORT OF SUMMER SCHOOL OF SCIENCE.

To J. R. INCH, ESQ , LL. D.,
Superintendent of Education.

SIR: I have the honor to submit, for your consideration, the following report of the sixteenth session of the Summer School of Science for the Atlantic Provinces of Canada, held at St. Stephen, N. B., July 22nd to August 8th, 1902.

The enrollment was as follows:

From New Brunswick,........................	171
" Nova Scotia,........................	29
" Prince Edward Island,........................	7
" Ontario,........................	2
" Quebec,........................	1
" United States of America,........................	49
Total........................	259

The session of the school was characterized by the enthusiasm with which the students entered upon and prosecuted their studies. Much prominence was given to field and laboratory work. The presence and assistance of Dr. Fletcher, Entomologist and Botanist at the Dominion Experimental Farm, Ottawa, aided very materially in the field work.

The division of work for each day was as follows: From 9 o'clock, a. m., to 10 o'clock p. m., was devoted to work in the class-room; the afternoons to field and laboratory work, and the evenings to public lectures. This division of the work has been found to be very satisfactory.

Great prominence was given by all the instructors to illustrate methods to be employed in the teaching of the subject they were considering. In is way the teachers who attended the session received help that would be use to them in their own work in the school room.

Much interest was manifested in the work of the school by the citizens St. Stephen and also by those of the neighboring city of Calais, Maine,

Citizens of both places enrolled as members of the school, and in other ways contributed to the success of the meeting and entertainment of the visiting members,

The session of 1902, ranks among the most successful in the history of the school.

The next session will be held in Chatham, N. B., July 21st to August 7th, 1903.

Appended find a list of the officers for the ensuing year, and also the financial statement.

OFFICERS.

PRESIDENT.

PROF. L. W. BAILEY, LL. D., University of N. B, Fredericton, N. B.

VICE-PRESIDENTS.

PRIN. B. MCKITTRICK, B. A., County Academy, Lunenburg, N. S.
PRIN. PHILIP COX, Ph. D., High School, Chatham, N. B.

SECRETARY-TREASURER.

PRIN. J. D. SEAMAN, Prince Street School, Charlottetown, P. E. I.

LOCAL SECRETARY.

J. W. BAXTER, M.D., Chatham, N. B.

BOARD OF DIRECTORS.

THE PRESIDENT, THE SECRETARY.TREASUER, W. R. CAMPBELL, M. A., S. A. STARRATT, ESQ., J. B. HALL, Ph. D., J, VROOM, ESQ.

I have the honor to be, Sir,

Your obedient servant,

J. D. SEAMAN,
Secretary Summer School of Science.

Charlottetown, P. E. I., Nov. 1, 1902.

Financial Statement.

RECEIPTS.

Balance from 1901	$ 35 74	
Grant from Government of Nova Scotia	100 00	
" " " " New Brunswick	200 00	
" " Town of St. Stephen	100 00	
" " " Calais, Maine	50 00	
Registration fees	310 50	
Proceeds of entertainment	16 63	
Advertisements in Calendar	102 50	
Sundries	12 00	
		927 37

EXPENDITURE.

Printing, advertising and stationery	$ 162 35	
Calendars	62 39	
Postage, freight and expressage	43 17	
Class expenses	33 26	
Instructors and officers	398 70	
Rents and expenses of lectures	136 95	
Sundries	64 91	
Balance	25 64	
		$ 927 37

II.—REPORTS OF COUNTY INSTITUTES.

ALBERT COUNTY.

The 25th Annual Session was held at Hopewell Hill on September 25th and 26th, President T. E. Colpitts, B. A., in the chair. Fifty-one teachers enrolled as members of the Institute.

After an interesting and forcible address by the President, W. C. Anderson, of Riverside, read an excellent paper on "Discipline." This was followed by the reading of papers on "Teaching" by W. M. Burns of Hillsboro, and on "Free Text Books" by L. R. Hetherington, B. A., of Hopewell Cape.

Friday morning's session opened with a discussion on "The Best Methods of Teaching Latin," followed by a paper on "Teacher's Unions and Salaries," by E. A. Coleman of Surrey. A nature lesson on "Spiders" by Miss Mary A. Smith closed the programme.

A well.attended public meeting was held in the Methodist church on Thursday evening, at which addresses were delivered by Revs. R. H. McPherson, M. E. Fletcher and A. W. Smithers.

The officers of the Institute elected for the coming year are: T. E. Colpitts, B. A., President; Edna M. Floyd, Vice-President; W. M. Burns, Secretary.Treasurer; Grace McGorman and Bessie Horseman, additional members of executive.

CARLETON COUNTY.

[Report from the Educational Review, Jan. 1903]

The teachers of Carleton County, N. B., held their twenty-fifth annual session at Woodstock, on Thursday and Friday, the 18th and 19th December. Over eighty teachers were present; and the sessions, which were more than usually interesting, were guided by Mr. N. Foster Thorne, who made a most capable and efficient president. Inspector Meagher was present and took part in the discussions, adding greatly to the interest of the meeting. Mr. I. N. Draper read an excellent paper on "Discipline," touching the many difficult points of this question in a way that must prove helpful to [illegible] teachers present. Mr. F. A. Good read a paper on "Bird Study," illustr[illegible] ing the subject with specimens, drawings, books and papers, and, what prov[illegible] far more effective, his own admirable way of presenting this and kindr[illegible] nature study subjects in his school. One of the best discussions of the [illegible] stitute—and every paper was discussed with spirit and point—took place on Miss Lina B. McLeod's paper on "Geometry," which was followed by an illustrative lesson to a class of Grade IX. pupils from the Woodstock Grammar School. The illustrative paper—or rather talk—on "Drawing," by Mr. E. J. Branscombe, was admirable in its way. For more than an hour Mr. Branscombe held the close attention of his audience by the skillful and beautiful drawings which he executed off-hand on the blackboard. It was an illustrative lesson, *par excellence*, and the Inspector and his former pupils gave testimony to the excellent results that Mr. Branscombe had secured in his school. The editor of the REVIEW was present at all the sessions, contributing addresses on Nature Study, and taking part in the discussions.

The Institute elected the following officers for the session of 1903, which will be held in Woodstock; I. N. Draper, President; Miss Minnie Carman, Vice-President; G. H. Harrison, M. A., Secretary; Miss Ruth Reid, Mr. F. A. Jewett, additional members of the Executive.

At the public meeting on Thursday evening, a fine programme of speeches and music was carried out.

GLOUCESTER COUNTY.

Reported by President—Alfred J. Witzell.

The Gloucester County Teachers' Institute met at Tracadie on Thursday and Friday the 9th and 10th October, 1902. President A. J. Witzell in the chair. Institute called to order at 10 a. m. 29 teachers enrolled,

Mr. J. R. Doucett delivered an address of welcome.

Dr. G. U. Hay, St. John, gave a very interesting lesson on ferns, illustrating mode of reproduction.

A paper on the teaching of French Grammar was read by J. Edouard DeGrace. This paper was followed by an animated discussion.

The "Question Box" proved a success, as many questions of importance were discussed in the answers, the majority of which were given by Dr. G. U. Hay.

On Thursday evening a public meeting was held which was addressed by President Witzell, Dr. G. U. Hay, C. J. Mersereau, Inspector Doucett, P. P. Morais, Principal E. L. O'Brien.

On Friday morning the Institute opened at 9 a. m. After roll call an excellent paper on discipline was read by C. J. Mersereau, followed by discussion, Dr. G. U. Hay, Inspector Doucett, E. L. O'Brien taking part.

Mr. Chas. F. Brison also read a paper on discipline.

At the afternoon session the election of officers took place. The following being the officers elected for next Institute: President, J. Edouard DeGrace, Vice President Miss Loretta Mullins, Secretary J. A. Salter, additional members of executive Miss Bernadette Cormier, M. W. McCarthy.

KENT COUNTY.

[From the Educational Review, November, 1902.]

The Kent County Teachers' Institute met at Rexton, on Thursday and Friday, October 9th and 10th, the president, Geo. A. Coates, in the chair. Papers were read on the following subjects: "Teaching, a Profession," by E. A. Pearson; "Arithmetic," by Geo. A. Coates; "Teaching of Fractions," by Miss May Ryan; "Centralization of Schools," by A. B. Boyer; "Patriotism in our Schools," by Miss Ness Ferguson; "Geometry," by C. H. Cowperthwaite. In addition to these papers, two lessons were given—one in Geography to Grade III by Miss M. McInerney, and the other in Primary Reading, by Miss M. Farrer. The public meeting on Thursday evening was addressed by Rev. Mr. Meek, Rev. Mr. Baker and Professor MacCready, of the Manual School, Fredericton. On Friday evening the visiting teachers were given a reception at the handsome residence of Mr. G. N. Clark.

The officers for the ensuing year are: President, Geo. A. Coates; Vice-president, Miss Ness Ferguson; Secretary-treasurer, R. G. Girvan. Additional members of the executive: Miss Mary Chrystal and C. H. Cowperthwaite.

KINGS COUNTY.

(Reported by the Secretary.)

The Kings County Teachers' Institute met at Hampton on Sept. 25th and 26th. Enrollment 57. In the absence of the president, the vice president, Miss Margaret Stewart, filled the chair.

The leading features of the first session were the opening address by Inspector Steeves, and a lesson in Botany. The second session was made up of an excursion to Frost Mountain, under the leadership of Dr. G. U. Hay. This was very enjoyable as well as instructive.

On the evening of the 25th a public meeting was held in Agricultural Hall, which was largely attended. Dr. Inch gave an address on "Centralization of Schools." Prof. Raymond read a paper on "The Benefit o College Education to the Individual." The meeting was also addressed by Fred M. Sproul, Mr. Flewelling and Inspector Steeves.

Third Session.—The principal features of this session were a paper on "Nature Study" by Dr. Hay; a "Programme for Primary School work" by Miss Frances Pritchard. A few brief remarks by John March were here given on "Singing in our schools." A paper on "Manual training, by Miss Beatrice Duke, and a paper on "Discipline" by Willard Brewing.

Fourth Session.—The officers for the ensuing year were now elected as follows:—President, D. P. Kirkpatrick, Vice President Miss Seely, Sec Treas. Willard Brewing. Additional members of Executive, Miss Ada Small, Miss Ida Northrup, Mr. Orton Gray, and Mr. Rex. Cormier. Miss Margaret Evans here gave a reading on "The Ruggles Family." The last paper of the Institute was one on "History" by Miss H. S. Raymond.

NORTHUMBERLAND COUNTY.

(The Educational Review, November, 1902.)

The teachers of Northumberland County had their twenty fifth annual meeting at Harkins Academy, Newcastle, on October 2nd and 3rd, about seventy teachers being present. Ernest E. A. McKenzie, principal of the academy, occupied the chair. Chief Supt. Inch was present, and his addresses and contributions to the discussions were of great interest to the institute. Miss Mary C. Edgar gave an interesting reading lesson to a class of pupils in grade four, and Dr. Cox a practical and suggestive address on English Composition.

At the public meeting in the evening, addresses were given by Dr. Inch, Rev. Father Dixon, Dr. Cox, Rev. Mr. Palmer, and others. Dr. Inch dealt very largely with the question of centralization of schools and also with manual training. At the Friday morning session, Miss Lucas read a valuable paper on manual training.

On Friday afternoon the teachers enjoyed a trip down river in a steamer placed at their disposal by the kindness of Lieut. Governor Snowball. Dr. Cox spoke of the evidences of glacial action shown along the valley of the river. During the trip Miss Mowatt read a paper on Home Preparation of Lessons. The following officers were elected for the ensuing year: President, R. W. Alward; Vice-President, Miss Beatrice Ellis; Secretary, Ernest McKenzie. Additional Members of Executive, Dr. Cox and James McIntosh.

ST. JOHN COUNTY.

(Reported by Secretary.)

The St. John County Teachers' Institute convened in the High School, St. John, on Sept. 4th and 5th.

The Pres. Dr. H. S. Bridges called the meeting to order at 10 a. m. Thursday, welcoming the teachers, especially those from outside the city.

One hundred and ninety-four teachers enrolled.

After organization the remainder of the morning session was taken up by the reading and discussion of a paper by the President on Higher Education and Practical Life.

The afternoon was devoted to the subject of reading. Papers on primary Reading were read by Misses Barlow and Gregg, and on Advanced Reading by Miss Amy Iddles.

The third session on Friday morning was opened by a paper on Cooperation of Teachers, by W. S. Carter, A. M., Inspector of Schools. This was followed by a paper on Geography by Jos. Harrington.

All the papers were unusually interesting and fully discussed.

The fourth session was devoted to miscellaneous business, and election of officers which resulted as follows:

President M. D. Brown, Vice-Pres. J. Frank Owens, Sec.-Tres. Miss Jean Rowan, Exec. Com. H. Parlee, Miss Knowlton.

VICTORIA COUNTY.

[Educational Review, October, 1902.]

About twenty-five teachers attended the Victoria County Institute, which was held at Andover on the 25th and 26th September. Mr. John Brittain, of the Normal School, was present and gave an interesting outline of the MacDonald schools to be established in the Atlantic Provinces Mr. Brittain also conducted an outing for the study of Natural Science, which proved very profitable for the teachers. Papers were read at the different sessions—on "Practical Arithmetic," by Thos. Rogers; on the "Beauti‑ ing of School Premises," by Inspector Meagher; on "Manual Training," Miss Iva Baxter; on "Busy Work,"by Miss Maud Waldron; on "Patrioti. in our Schools," by Mr. McVain. A lesson on the "Robin" was given Standard III by Miss Bessie Scott. All the papers were followed by in esting discussions. Mr. Brittain added greatly to the value of the institute by his practical suggestions. Afterwards he met the school trustees and gained their approval to make Andover one of the group of rural schools to be established by Sir William MacDonald and Prof. Robertson.

WESTMORLAND COUNTY.

[Reported by S. W. Irons, Secretary.]

The Westmorland County Teachers' Institute met at Port Elgin on Thursday and Friday, September 25th and 26th. Miss Ella Copp, Vice-president, in the chair. About ninety teachers were in attendance, and the people of Port Elgin gave the visiting teachers a cordial welcome. Papers were read as follows: "Is the teaching of Latin Practical?" by Mr. G. Fred. McNally, A. B; on "School Organization," by Miss Janet Reade; on "Canadian History," by Miss Ella McCormick; on "Nature Lessons in Grade V, Miscellaneous Schools," by Miss Bessie Oulton; on "Reading," by Miss Louise Prescott. The public meeting on Thursday evening was addressed by speakers from the ranks of the teachers present. The officers for the ensuing year were elected as follows: President, H. B. Steeves, Moncton; Vice-president, Miss H. Ramsay, Sackville; Secretary-treasurer, S. W. Irons Moncton. Additional members of the executive, H. Burns, Petitcodiac; M. J. Wallace, Salisbury; and Miss Mary McLeod, Sackville.

The Institutes of Charlotte, Queens, Sunbury and York Counties did not meet during the last school year. On account of the meeting of the Summer School of Science at St. Stephen in July and August, and of the meetings of the Provincial Institute at Fredericton in June it was thought inexpedient to hold the County Institutes in these counties until 1903.

APPENDIX F.

Addresses delivered before the Educational Institute of New Brunswick, June, 1902.

I.—TEACHER'S WAGES, GRADUATED AND UNGRADUATED, WITH A SUGGESTION OF THE REAL NATURE OF THE DIFFICULTY AND A REMEDY THEREFOR BY PROFESSOR JOHN DAVIDSON, OF THE UNIVERSITY OF NEW BRUNSWICK.

The chief difficulty in discussing the question of graduation of teachers' salaries, which is, so far at least, in the region of aspiration rather than of practical politics, is to determine what it is we propose to gain by such a scheme. Is the aim to secure greater efficiency in the teacher? Is it merely to increase teachers' wages with or without regard to efficiency? Or is it to retain in the ranks of the teaching profession in the Province those who are leaving it or may leave it? These are some of the ends which may be proposed. They are not indeed exclusive. There is, for instance, no surer way in general of increasing efficiency than by increasing wages; and when high wages are paid the problem of retaining the best is not so difficult to solve. But still, according to the immediate aim we propose to ourselves in making such a proposal, and according to the emphasis we place upon such aims, we may come to different conclusions.

We must also recognize that there are two distinct points of view from which this question may be looked at—the point of view of the teacher and the point of view of the public. To those who are sufficiently enlightened there is no real antagonism, just as perhaps there is no real antagonism between capital and labour considered in the abstract; but, unfortunately, all are not enlightened, and wages questions are decided not in the abstract but in the very definite concrete; and we must therefore recognize a certain possible, even if temporary, divergence of teachers' interests and the public interests In this paper I propose to look at the question almost solely from the public point of view. It is true that the body of teachers are a part, and not an unimportant part, of the public; but the teacher is primarily a public servant, and the public will distinctly refuse, I think, to regard the question of teachers' wages from any point of view but its own.

I think it is better to keep to this point of view, because it is more impersonal in the first place and in the second place because the teachers' point of view is not impressive, except to the victims.

I readily admit that in many cases the wages paid to teachers are inadequate, whether considered in themselves, or relatively to the wages paid in other occupations. They are not always adequate to cover the expenses of living; and they practically restrict us to a celibate teacherhood. The higher up we go the truer it is. The third class teacher is probably paid as much as she is worth, considering the standard of living in the districts she is engaged in, considering the standard of living to which she is accustomed, and considering the standard of attainment and the period of training. It is true that she is not paid much more than, in some cases not so much as a domestic servant; but considering both occupations, I doubt whether the third class teacher has much whereof to complain. The second class teacher is also probably paid as highly as the public service demands, and relatively to what is paid first class teachers, both second and third are paid too much. This is partly due to the fact that teaching is largely a female employment—one of the observed rules of which appears to be that there is less, much less, difference between the wages of skilled and the wages of unskilled labour than there is in the case of men. So when we find that there is a comparatively narrow margin between the wages of the unskilled labour of the third class teacher and the wages of the skilled first class teacher, we have come upon a phenomenon which appears in other parts of the industrial world occupied by women. Compared with the lower classes, the first class teacher is under paid, and relatively to social and professional needs the pay is not sufficient as a permanent provision.

It must be admitted that the initial pay is high, higher than in any other profession; and it cannot be pretended that it costs as much to qualify as a teacher as it does to qualify, for instance, as a doctor. But this advantage does not continue long. The teachers' wages do not increase, and the needs of the teacher do; and what may be adequate payment for a teacher fresh from college or normal school is distinctly inadequate for the head of a family or for those who have social responsibilities.

The wages of teachers come under a well recognized type of wages,—that of the stepping-stone employments for the energetic, and even in many ways resemble the wages of those odd jobs of personal services, which modern society has provided in such numbers, which have a fairly large wage at the start and no future. The conditions of such employment are pretty definite; and there is as a rule not much industrial hope for those who enter them. The initial advantages are greater than in occupations where training is required; and a few may escape before stagnation comes, thus reaping a permanent as well as a temporary advantage; but these are few. With the teacher, the initial wage is not inadequate, but the advantages of the employment do not increase as they ought, and only those who are energetic or ambitious enough to escape before it is too late can be said to have made much from the occupation of teaching.

There is no doubt in any one's mind that, for the higher class teachers, wages are presently inadequate, and that experience does not, as in other occupations, bring its reward in increased remuneration. A careful statistical examination and comparison of the wages and length of service tables in the Educational Reports yields little result. Sometimes we have wages distinctly lower than the average, and length of service distinctly above the average; and sometimes we have just the opposite condition. Probably the statistical basis is too narrow; but, so far as I can see, there is no warrant for saying of this province that length of service means higher wages. Indeed there seems to be some reason on general grounds for concluding that length of service is not altogether desirable, so often is it the case that the efficient step out and the comparatively inefficient remain. The public in this province is not prepared to pay enough to buy the best experience, and consequently the teachers' wage remains small.

But there is not much to be made out of complaints. One may feel the inadequate pay as a bitter personal wrong, and may be conscious of being worth much more than is received; but the public cares for none of these things; and the immediate employer is content to know that the place can be filled by another victim. It is so in the University, which claims to be the head of the educational system, and it is so among the grammar and first class teachers. Experience, ability, devotion count for nothing; these may be expected, are certainly accepted, but they really count for nothing, and are seldom rewarded by anything better than fair words. It avails nothin to plead that it is impossible to live and work on the wages. The povert of the teacher, while real enough, is not picturesque enough. Over th woes of the Russian Jew sweated in the slums of London or Montreal th public grows sentimental, perhaps because it really cares about ready-made clothes and does not care about education. The protest of the individual seems to count for nothing and certainly effects little. After a short experience he finds that it is not consistent with self respect to be continually complaining of poverty and hard treatment; and he accepts his lot with more or less resignation till he can remedy it for himself. That remedy he generally finds in leaving the profession and betaking himself to an occupation where an honest wage is paid for an honest day's work. And I see no other way out for the individual but to abandon the profession.

It is true that, in the long run, the standard of living has a great deal to do with the determination of the standard of remuneration. No one who has given any attention to labour questions can neglect this side of the problem; but we must be careful to understand *how* the standard of living acts in the determination of wages. It is not because of the labourer's needs, not even because he refuses to work for less, but because the public really wants what he produces and will pay more rather than go without. If production is to be continued, the necessary labourers must be paid.

But if the public is indifferent about the product, neither the necessity of the labourer nor his refusal to work will avail. This unfortunately is too often the case with education. The public does not care much about the product; and therefore, the protest of the worker is apt to go unheeded, especially when there are many competitors who, through inexperience, are ready to accept the rate of wages of which complaint is made. An appeal to the standard of living can accomplish little for the individual even when it is accompanied by a refusal to work on poor terms: even a joint protest and threat to strike can effect little, if the public do not care enough about the product to dread even the possibility of a diminution of the supply. What is required to make the standard of living effectual as a determinant of wages is diminution of the supply of the required laborer. The teacher is in a peculiarly difficult position, when he tries to make his standard of living effectual as a determinant of his wages, because in the first place the public does not value very highly the product of his labour, and because, in the second, whatever the individual may do, the supply of teachers is kept up. I fancy that the relatively high wages of third class teachers shows that the supply there is not equal to the demand; for the best teachers the demand at a sufficient price is far below the supply.

In the long run the wages of teachers are determined by demand and supply. The teacher can only indirectly influence the demand, and his power to determine supply is also limited. There is not much hope of making the teaching profession more like a close corporation by restricting the number of those who enter it or raising the standard of qualification as the doctors do and the lawyers ought to do. There remains the possibility of reducing the supply by an exodus from the profession, which might in the end be in some degree effectual if the supply from beneath were checked; but unfortunately those who leave will be the energetic and the ambitious who are precisely those we can, from a social point of view, least afford to lose; and moreover the remanent portion is not likely to be effectual in taking advantage of their improved position because the natural leaders are the first to leave.

There is thus not much to be gained by dwelling on the teachers' side of the problem, because there is little hope of remedy for the individual unless he leaves the profession and because the standard of living, which is the teachers' side of the plea for higher wages, can be rendered effectual as a determinant of wages and a cause of higher wages only in so far as the exodus materially reduces the supply. But the reduction of the supply is at the wrong end. We lose the best and we retain in general those who are not so good. From the point of view of the public's real interest the remedy, or rather the method of the remedy, is worse than the disease; and the most depressing fact of all is that the public remains quite unconscious. But we cannot regard with equanimity a remedy which sacrifices even the unrecognized interests of the public.

When we turn to the question of demand we are faced by a very serious problem. Why is it that the public is content with that which is short of the best? The craze for cheapness which pervades the whole market is not here a sufficient explanation, for the fact is that here apparently the public is content to pay almost as much for shoddy as for genuine fabric. It pays nearly as much for third class teachers as for first class, because it does not believe that there is any essential difference between them. Whether it is that they think that the machine can do everything, and are ignorant of the fact that the more highly organized the machinery is, the greater the demands made on the skill of the labourer; is not quite obvious; and this is perhaps giving too elaborate an explanation of what, in its last analysis, is simply old fashioned greed and ignorance. But the plain matter of fact is that the average board of school trustees who are the immediate employers, and the public who are the ultimate employers and purchasers, do not apparently believe in the existence of quality in teaching and would not pay for it if they did. The educational problem for them is how to fulfil, or to evade, their duties at the least possible cost to the ratepayers.

A large part of the responsibility for this state of affairs is due to the administrative policy of the province which has been guilty at once of too much centralization and of too much decentralization. This is not the place to enter into a discussion of the reasons why our provincial administration does so much more of the work of the province than Ontario, for instance, does. Our early history partly accounts for it. It was one of the difficulties in the way of financial adjustment at the time of confederation, and governments have been criticized in our local politics for attempting to secure a better distribution of responsibilities between the province and the municipalities. In educational matters the central authority has had too much to do and has borne too large a share of the expense; and the local districts have been relieved from their responsibilities, with the result that they do not realize their responsibility. On the other hand there has been, under the stimulus of the idea that the benefits of education should be universal, too much decentralization so that there is almost a board of school trustees for every district school. (A compulsory school law would have accomplished the end more effectually but there are sinister interests opposed to a compulsory law.) It would be hopeless to expect to obtain by any system of selection within such limited areas men qualified by interest in, and knowledge of educational requirements; but by a curious anomaly in politics, these minute districts are granted a right of self-government in matters educational which is denied to the cities. The city of St. John or the city of Fredericton cannot be trusted to manage its own educational affairs, and the board of trustees has to be nominated, partly by the government, and partly by the city council, Not even the most fanatical admirer of democracy, at least if he has any interest in education, will complain of this arrangement if he has regard to the dignity and character of our city board of trustees as compared with our city councils. This principal of selection has given us generally very adequate city boards; but in the rural districts the principle of direct local election is allowed, and the result too often is beneath contempt, if all that is said be true. The area of the constituency is too small to attract men willing to serve and in many cases the board is composed of those anxious to keep down the taxes and willing to close the school, if need be, to effect their purpose. These are the immediate employers of the teacher: these are the people who pass upon the teacher's application: these are the people who adjudicate on his work, sometimes themselves illiterate, very frequently inefficient, generally indifferent to education, these men constitute the demand for teachers; and so long as the ignorant and indifferent are allowed to control, and that will be so long as the system of small districts and popular election continues, the difficulty of improving the demand will remain.

The consolidation of school districts will give us no doubt better schools but it will first give us better school trustees. The education and improvement of the school trustee is the gravest problem the modern educational reformer has to face; and the first step in that direction lies in making the present type an impossibility. In the first place the area of the school district must be enlarged so as to enlarge the area of selection. There is no reason why a proper board should not manage all the schools in a parish or even in a larger district if need be. In the second place the principle of selection must be brought into harmony with that practised in the cities. There is no reason why those who contribute what is the smaller share of the cost should have the control and management of the school. The province and the county alike are interested; and it would be in accordance with the analogous plan, successful in the cities, should the District Boards of School Trustees be appointed, half by the Local Government and half by the County Council. It is possible, as may be objected, that politics may enter into such appointments; but politics, no doubt, enter into appointments of City Boards, and yet the school board is as a rule a much more respectable body than the city council and no one need be ashamed to be a member of a Board of Trustees.

By such a consolidation we should have not only a larger area to select from but also some assurance that the best men would be selected. Most assuredly the principle would not be the present one of keeping down the cost; and since many schools might be under one Board there would be a disposition on the part of the residents to secure as much as possible from that authority rather than as at present to cut down expenses at the risk of starving the work. Another advantage would be the possibility of employing a trained and professional district superintendent who could supervise the various schools and maintain at least a routine efficiency in them.

In this way there would be secured at least the possibility of some appreciation of the value of experience. At present it is the absence of such an appreciation that makes any change for the better so apparently hopeless. These new trustees would at least not be selected on the purely negative principle of keeping down the school rate. They would have some rudimentary appreciation of the importance of education, and they might therefore be induced to understand that in education, as in other things, experience of the right sort is desirable and even worth paying for. They would also have the advantage of comparing the results o several schools and in this way it is possible they might come to an understanding that it paid the community to pay more and have the work done, rather than to pay less and have it simply attempted.

It is not probable that very much in the matter of higher wages would result from this reform. I do not think that wages would be increased to such an extent that the exodus from the profession of the energetic and ambitious would be checked. Its value would be negative rather than positive, although in the end the cumulative result might be considerable. It would at least prevent the employment of a third-class teacher where a first should be employed; and it would stop those beggarly and shameful attempts to coerce the department into issuing special licenses under threat of closing school altogether if it is not permitted to them to conduct it on the cheapest plan. In this negative way, by checking the demand for cheap teachers, and by improving the demand, it would improve the position of the teacher, and might lead to various increases of the average wage, and even to better wages, to retain an efficient teacher. How far this end would be assisted by rules and regulations prescribing some relation between the county assessment of the district and the class of teacher employed, I cannot say; though the experiment is worth trying.

The most, however, that we can expect of the rural districts is that they shall cease to be an active agent in the degradation of the teachers' position. Even with the best intentions, they cannot do much to meet the chief difficulty for which the system of grading of wages is required. They cannot prevent the exodus of the best, those whom the province has spent much money to train at Normal School and University. The rural school districts are poor, and no increase which is within their power would be effectual in retaining the ambitious. No matter how fully they recognized the value of experience and training, they cannot be expected to pay sufficient salaries to offset the attractions elsewhere. Indeed the whole system of graduated wages seems open to the same objection. It hardly considers how much has to be counteracted. We have to place the net advantages of a teacher's position in New Brunswick in comparison with the net advantages in the United States,—with the net advantages of professions which, for one reason or another, bring more social esteem,—with the church, medicine and law,—and in an increasing degree with business. We have to remember that the great and increasing majority of our teachers are women; and that no scheme of graduated wages according to experience will lessen the attractiveness of marriage, nor is it desirable from a social point of view that they should; and we must also remember that marriage usually places a term to women's industrial activity. We have to consider both the difficulty to be overcome and the means available for overcoming it. Take for instance an initial salary of say $700 paid to a grammar school teacher, which is perhaps not inadequate as an initial salary, let it be increased every three years, $100, and I am supposing an almost impossible rate of increase. At the end of twenty-one years the salary has risen to $1400, double its original figure. No graduation can ordinarily be expected to do more than double the original salary. Remuneration does certainly increase further in other occupations; but the character of the work changes and greater responsibility is added. Here experience is not worth more than double the original salary for the same class of work.

I have taken an extreme case to bring out the more clearly the improbability of a scheme of graduated salaries meeting the situation. I am informed that a first class or grammar school teacher, having our B. A. degree, may confidently expect, after one year at Harvard, long enough to get the B. A. there also, to obtain a scholastic appointment worth $1500, with the prospect of a rise in a few years to $2500. I ask what inducement does a hundred dollar increase every three years offer a young man, ambitious and energetic, to decline such an opportunity. He may take your high initial salary for a year or two to earn money to go to Harvard, but nothing will induce him to stay here permanently with such a prospect. Of late the door has been opened, and I am glad it has been opened, for the energetic teacher to better his position, and we are likely to hear more in the future of the exodus of the best of our young teachers. Again, take the case of a man who looks to the medical profession. He may have a hard struggle at first, but the success in the majority of instances is such as to make teaching unattractive in comparison. When a student does me the honour to ask my advice, I always advise him not to teach—to go into business or into some other profession; and my reason is that teaching offers no accumulated reward of experience and ability—what economists call sometimes a rent of ability—as other occupations do,

Graduation of teachers' wages will not in my opinion meet the difficulty completely (perhaps nothing can); and what of result the plan might have will be purchased at a disproportionate cost. To base the increase on mere length of service is to place in many cases a premium on inefficiency; and on what other basis it can rest, I confess I do not know. We have already graduation according to certificate and scholastic attainment; but that does not meet the situation, for it is the highest that leave, and the graduation, so far as the Educational Department is concerned, is already sufficient to mark the difference of scholastic attainment between the classes. We cannot apparently restore payment by results, and the inspectors would be the last to wish the increase to depend on their personal reports. Yet a system there must be, and time is apparently the only definite standard available; and it is a bad one. In one form it might be applied. Teachers of the second and third classes might, after seven years' service, be deprived of their certificates, for remaining so long in the ranks of the least efficient.

But we cannot rest with merely a negative result, because the situation is serious and is becoming more serious. The University, as I have said, has very wisely opened its doors on favourable terms to first class teachers; and a large proportion of its matriculated students are from the ranks of the teaching profession. That was wisely done, but we cannot stop there. We must try to keep these teachers in the province. Mere regulations will not do it. You must make it worth their while to stay; or, to use the language of the economist, you must make the net attractions of the teaching profession in the Province equal to the net attractions elsewhere or in other professions.

But how is this to be done? We may obtain some guidance by considering other occupations of a somewhat similar character, those in fact which draw from the teaching profession at present. The characteristic of professional salaries is generally a more or less prolonged period of small earnings, followed by a fair measure of success and in some cases by great success. We need not consider exceptions, though there are such, but the young doctor or lawyer must make his account with the expenses of a more or less prolonged apprenticeship or period of study, to be followed in some cases by a longer period of waiting for a practice.

The teacher after a comparatively short training of three or four years at the most if he takes a college course first, may commence with an initial salary of $700 to $1000. So far the advantage is on the teacher's side. But still the other professions draw men away, and the reason is that they offer chances of great success. It is at bottom the same instinct as the gambler's, "double or quits"; and the young men have confidence enough in themselves that the prizes will fall to them. Were it not for this confidence, the number of aspirants would be much less in some occupations. More money has been sunk in the Klondike than will be taken out of it; but there are chances of "striking it rich." In most of the professions it is, owever, not pure gambling, because ability can usually command a cometence, even if the great prizes be missed. A young doctor may never me to be entitled to a specialist's fees, but he may command a competence a general practitioner. A young lawyer may never rise to the position his profession of being able to refuse a seat on the bench because of the pecuniary sacrifice, but none the less he need not utterly fail. A teacher, however attains nearly all hissu ccess at a bound, and the wages which may seem almost princely at twenty-one may be very inadequate at forty. He has little to hope for. There are no great prizes in this profession: there are few posts which promise even a moderate competence. The doctor and the lawyer can fall back on the second best; but for the teacher there is no best and scarcely any second best to work for. Young men uuderstand these things, and it is the most natural thing in the world that they should make haste to leave the profession in this province. They may fail in the profession of their choice; but their failure, unless it is abject and due to deficiency of character, will probably be at least as good as the teacher's highest success.

The problem then is how to create inducements for the young to remain in the profession by copying the conditions of the competing occupations.

It is not necessary that the prizes of the teaching profession should be so great, or so many, as those offered in law or medicine; for teaching starts with certain attractions in its favor. I do not refer to the very real attraction which the communication of knowledge has for some minds, because every other occupation has its own similar attraction. The teacher is not in this respect any better than the clergyman or the doctor who may equally be in love with his work and derive more pleasure from his work than from any other source. I speak purely of the material returns which come to the teacher and do not come in some of the competing occupations In the first place the element of risk is comparatively small. It is a salary he receives, not an income, and salaries are, other things being equal, more easily earned than incomes. The initial salary in teaching moreover is comparatively large, and there are those so constituted that any element of risk or uncertainty, at the start more particularly, deprives the occupation of much of its attractiveness. Then there is the question of hours, where the real advantage to the teacher is by no means so large as it appears to the outsider; and there is the advantage of a fairly long and sure vacation. These are attractions which are real and must be taken into account in estimating the net advantages which an occupation offers.

But these advantages are not of a character to appeal to the ambitious and energetic. Indeed the teaching profession does not make a very strong appeal in any case to such natures; but, as things are, teaching does not make even a moderate appeal to the ambitious. Its prospects of a well spent, but perhaps somewhat monotonous life is not enlivened by the hope of achieving any striking success. I do not mean of course that the teacher cannot be successful in his work. What I do mean is that he cannot be successful in his pay. In other professions and occupations a man may be successful both in his work and in his pay. This hope of success is one of the most powerful factors in the wages question, in so far at least as regards the professions. A man will put up with many hardships and inconveniences if in the end he can really succeed. If the teaching profession is to secure its proper share of the ambitious and energetic youth of the community, it must hold out the inducement that will attract them. The prizes of the profession need not be so large as in other occupations, for reasons already suggested; but prizes there must be. At present there are no prizes in the ordinary sense of the term. There are two or three posts which offer the possibility of a moderate competence. How many young men are looking forward at the present time with any degree of equanimity, not to such posts, but to such salaries, as the very best they can do? It may be that even so little may exceed their grasp, but it is not much to aim for. Attractions do not exist at present and they must be created if we are to overcome the difficulties of the situation.

How they are to be created is perhaps beyond the subject allotted to me. The legislation increasing the salaries of the inspectors, passed during last session, was a welcome step in the right direction. But we must proceed much further to accomplish the end. The number of inspectorships should at least be doubled and the salaries attached to them further increased. Some means may be found of insisting that the head masters of our city high schools should be more adequately paid; and an entirely new class of positions of district superintendentships might be created with salaries of $1000 to $1400. Positions on the staff of the Normal School could be improved a great deal and made more attractive; and perhaps appointments in the University might be included in the list. At present no one of these positions can be regarded as sufficiently attractive to retain the ambitious and energetic. There is need, I should judge, although there is no standard for making the estimate, of some thirty or forty places in the teaching profession which could be regarded, by the class that at present practice the profession, as prizes, or at least as offering an adequate object for a life's work.

I need not say that to carry out such a proposal will cost money. But it will cost less money than the scheme, or rather suggestion of a scheme, to which the leader of the Opposition, and if I mistake not the Government also, has given a general approval, for raising teachers' salaries. No government need be afraid of spending money on education. There is no better test of the progress and enlightenment of a country, when all things are taken into account, than the actual amount of money expended on education. There is a disposition on the part of those in authority to deal with the question of teachers' wages in a broad and liberal manner. It is to be hoped that the legislation may not take the merely haphazard method of adding so much to the grant made by the department to each teacher. Such a method would be inadequate to meet the situation as it exists in this province. It would be of practically no effect in really raising wages. It would mean merely the employment of third instead of second, of second instead of first class teachers, if it demanded any sacrifice from the district boards, and if it did not, it would increase the already existing practice of fraudulently withholding, or having paid back, a portion of the district payment to the teachers. There will no doubt be many objections raised to any proposal to increase the number and the value of the upper places, and a taking appeal could easily be made on the ground that it favored the higher class teachers and did nothing for the lower But such a scheme is, to my mind, desirable because:

1. It meets the real difficulty, which is the increasing exodus of the young and energetic and ambitious;

2. Its cost would not be so great as that of a general and ineffective increase in the provincial grant;

3. It would provide for more efficient and direct supervision than is possible at present;

4. And it leaves the matter in the hands of the Department, where the most enlightened views of education, and of what education is worth, naturly prevail.

II.—CENTRALIZATION OF SCHOOLS.

BY INSPECTOR W. S. CARTER, ST. JOHN.

The most remarkable phenomenon of the century just closed has been the development of popular education, indeed, its spread may be placed in the last half century, and much of the boasted progress made by the world in that time may be traced to this cause more than to any other. It has revolutionized social and industrial polity, and countries are now ranked in importance not by their revenues, expenditures or standing armies, but by their relative expenditures per head for popular education. I need not contrast the position of such countries as Germany, United States, Great Britain; with Spain, Turkey, Central and South America. You can do that for yourselves.

It is the age of the newspaper, the magazine and the public library, the demand for which, has been created by the advancing intelligence of the masses.

In response to it, colleges, universities, high schools and university extension courses have been established throughout the land. Public and private beneficence and philanthropy flourish as they have never done before, and much of it has been poured out in the cause of education.

Witness the magnificent bequests made to educational institutions in recent years in the United States, not after the death but during the life time of the donors. It is Mr. Andrew Carnegie, who said "to die rich is to die disgraced" and he is proving his sincerity by distributing millions to colleges and libraries. After Lord Kitchener had beaten the Arabs in battle he undertook their real conquest by the establishment of a college at Khartoum. Cecil Rhodes recognized the proper mode of promoting the "nion of the British race by giving them a common education.

The United States when they wished to reconcile the Cubans to certain)nditions, sent for their teachers and instructed them. They sent to the hillipines teachers, knowing well that they would be more powerful than rmies to bring about pacification and real conquest.

In our own Empire, after the fighting, the real conquest is being made by public school teachers, and I am proud of the fact as are you all, that Canadian teachers have been placed in the van of this army as our soldiers have been in the fighting, and we are all sure that they will acquit themselves in an equally distinguished and honorable way.

Ceasar said of one of the tribes of Gaul, that while the other tribes went to battle, this tribe made war. It seems to be the function of the soldier in these modern days to conquer in battle, but that of the teacher to subdue the enemy by peaceful means.

While much has been done, much remains to be accomplished. Great good has resulted and no doubt some evil. Our systems of education are not perfect, nor will they ever be. Fifty years of popular education or only thirty, as in our own case, can bring about much good, and some mistakes are likely to be made. There can be no such thing as conservatism in education, but there may be an excess of radicalism.

It is not the object of this paper to indulge in criticism, nor is it necessary. We have our critics in abundance. In fact it is a very common-place man or woman, who does not consider himself competent to criticize the teacher in his work. The correction of this will be, I hope, a part of the education successfully imparted in the present century.

We have been favoured with the attention of professional men, authors, editors and newspapers, a few of whom have been competent and just, but many of whom could not by any possibility have any very accurate knowledge of the facts they dealt with.

It has usually been in their hours of relaxation that they have attacked a familiar subject, usually in a sensational manner, along lines which would furnish the last resistance—for popular education, while it has taught the lesson to every other body has not yet taught the teachers to co-operate for their own defense or benefit.

Popular education has developed the idea of utility possibly at too great a cost of that of citizenship. Schools for scientific, technical and commercial training are a feature of the age and must increase in numbers and importance, but surely they can exist at the same time with the study of languages.

One of the greatest civilizing and educative agencies in connection with our schools has been that of women as teachers. Is it not possible th there are too few men left in the profession?

We compel all to pay taxes but none to avail themselves of school pri ileges provided.

We shorten school hours, lengthen vacations and courses of instruction, seek to abolish home study and at the same time advocate curfew laws to keep the children off the streets at eight.

Parents send their children to school before the age of five, insist on their promotion each year, offer prizes, desire them to graduate before the age of fifteen, on no account desire them to remain two years in a grade, advocate all sorts of additions to the course of instruction, and then insist that there is overpressure on the teacher's part, and that the Board of Education is overcrowding the curriculum. There is another class of patrons of the public schools that have but little of the interest and sympathy that the parents of the olden time had for that institution. They do not visit the schools therefore they can not study them. They do not know the teacher; they are not familiar with the work done, the methods used nor the results achieved. They are content with voting money for school purposes and leaving the school officers to select lots, erect buildings, provide furnishings and supply teachers.

I ask your indulgence for digressing so far, and will conclude my remarks of a general nature which might be extended to the length of several papers, by a criticism from Supt. Stetson of Maine, which if true should make us humble and furnish work for some time to come:

"It is to be regretted beyond all possible expression that we have lost the strong features of the old time school: the maturity, the dignity, the manhood and womanhood of the teachers, the presence of the older students, who furnished examples and inspiration for the younger, the eagerness, the alertness, the anxiety of the boys and girls to be something, to accomplish something.

Those who are leaving our public schools to-day are wanting in energy, endurance and ability to stand alone and do by themselves worthy work.

They have been freed from cares, relieved of responsibilities, they have had their work done for them, their intelloctual pabulum masticated for them so long, that they have become incapable of even assimilating, elaborately prepared intellectual food. But in these days we hear so often as to be sickened by the reiteration of the sentence, 'I do not want my boys and girls to work as I had to work, to pass through the experiences I had to pass through, to be required to struggle as I had to struggle, drudge as I have drudged, and submit to the privations I have endured, I want their lives to be filled with sunshine.' One cannot have too much sympathy, too much respect for him who desires to minimize the hardships of another's life. But there is one stern lesson which parents as well as children must learn and it is that experience cannot be acquired by proxy—one must do his own work and develop his own strength."

I assume that at least three fourths of those sitting before me have been born and received the major portion of their schooling in a country district, and in consequence I deal with my subject of rural schools with some hesitation. I was brought up in the country myself and realize that while we may desire to leave it in our youth and spread our pinions, everything there is hallowed in our recollections, and no matter how long we may remain absent or how old we may live, we never lose our desire to return or our belief in the superiority of some things left behind to all else in the wide world.

The best thought of the men and women to-day interested in education is how to improve the rural school. We sometimes hear it said that we ought to stand up for the country school because of what it has done in the past, instead of criticizing it, and one would sometimes think that the effort to raise the standard of rural schools, conveyed some reproach upon rural life. No amount of assertion that he is well will cure a sick man, if he is really sick, and it cannot be denied that the rural schools, while they have undoubtedly benefitted by the general diffusion of education and improved methods of teaching, have not kept pace with the graded school, where the best attainable teaching talent is secured by the payment of better salaries, by supplying better buildings and by the holding out of inducements of attractive surroundings to teachers—an atmosphere of culture—the opportunity to be in and a part of the strenuous life of the town or city, with its many varied interests, entertainments and associations. After considerable experience both as a teacher and inspector in country schools I have no hesitation in asserting that the only advantage possessed by the rural school over the urban is that of environment, and if we can devise a plan by which the surroundings of the former can be combined with the advantages of the latter, we will have gone a long way in the directiou of the ideal school.

Man is a gregarious animal and one of the most notable tendencies of the present time is the growth of the community, and the shrinkage of the rural population. The deserted farm has become a feature in the landscape and furnishes one of the problems of the present.

Some have ascribed the cause to too much education, but I think tha it may be easily demonstrated that the absence of adequate education facilities is the more potent reason.

The country district continues, as it always has and always will, to supply an infusion of vigorous manhood and womanhood to the town. It has been said that there are "but three generations from shirtsleeves to shirtsleeves."

Let us examine more closely some of the conditions found in the rural districts at present.

Our Superintendent reports that there are in the Province something like 500 schools, with an average of less than 12 pupils. But you may say it is a comparatively poor country. It is not more true of this Province than of other places.

It happens that ungraded rural schools with very small attendance are to be found in the most thickly peopled states and often in proximity to large cities.

New York, the richest state in the union, in 1895 reported 2983 schools with an attendance of less than 10 pupils each, and 7,529 with less than 20.

Rhode Island reported 64 out of its 263 schools as having fewer than 10 pupils each, Iowa 3200 with an attendance of less than 10 and 6373 with an attendance of less than 15. Maine, I think, has been reported as having 1500 schools with an attendance of less than 10. I could add almost indefinitely to this list but so much will show that our case is not by any means exceptional.

The small school is necessarily the weak school, isolated, classification impossible, emulation unfelt, enthusiasm absent. I have often heard it said that there was a better opportunity for individual teaching in the country school than in the graded. That opinion can only be held by those who have had no experience in ungraded schools or by harking back to the experience of long ago, when the three R's were the features of the curriculum and classification was unknown. In even a very small school with eight or ten subjects to be dealt with and furnishing the same number of classes with a much more irregular attendance, individual instruction is well nigh impossible. Emerson E. White, LL. D., in a paper before the National Council of Education, U. S., 1894, says, "We sometimes hear of the old-time country school in which there were no classes, each pupil being taught by himself, if taught at all; but this school exists in imagination, I am satisfied, and not in history. If ever it had an existence, it certainly preceded the organization of the common school, if it did not precede any school composed of more than ten pupils.

My father was a pupil in one of the early common schools of New England and I was a pupil in a still more primitive school in the then backwoods of Ohio, but neither my father nor myself ever saw the wholly unclassified country school, of which the present generation of teachers is hearing.

In at least two of three common branches, i. e. branches common to all —the pupils in the old time school were classified. It is true that little attempt was made at classification in teaching the A B C's or the a-b abs, but necessity forced an early classification in reading and spelling—imperfect it is true, but necessary and helpful. I now see in my mind's eye, the row of big boys and girls, that sat on the back seats and read together in the old English reader, and I also see the rows of boys and girls who constituted the successive classes in spelling, standing on the floor and "toeing the mark." No attempt was made in the first school which I attended at classification in Arithmetic, and later the attempt was first confined to the multiplication table, which few pupils perfectly mastered, and so common drills were feasible. As a rule each pupil "ciphered" by himself, at his own gait, going to the teacher or some pupil for assistance, when needed.

The fact that most of the pupils never reached fractions, and fewer ever acquired much skill in integer processes, is evidence of the weakness of individual work, even in such a study as arithmetic."

He adds: "A few pupils who needed only opportunity for study, made good progress without instruction, sometimes remarkable progress."

It has been a common impression that the rural districts contained a smaller proportion of illiterates. It may have been true at a former period, but there is now grave reason to suppose that the fact is now often the other way. In the state of Michigan this matter has been statistically investigated, and it has been found that in cities there were 14 illiterates per 1000 and in the country 24, and the strongest reason given to account for this is the inferiority of the country schools. What is to be done? Consolidate the weak districts and centralize wherever possible.

It is no new thing. It began in Massachusetts and has spread all over the United States. The plan has been successfully carried out in Australia and there is not a Province in Canada that I am aware of but authorizes it, though there is yet but one instance of its having been carried out in the Dominion. I am proud of the fact that it has been in my inspectoral district but I will leave the details to the gentlemen to relate, who have been so largely instrumental in carrying it into effect, and who are to follow me.

I have pointed out some of the disabilities that the country schools are labouring under at present. There are many arguments in favour of the plan and many have been advanced against it. I have summarized from my own experience and from that of others the principal arguments used on both sides in order to give conciseness to the discussion which may follow.

Arguments in favour :

1. It will secure better teachers. Teachers in small ungraded schools are usually of limited education, training or experience, or are past the age of competition. The salaries paid in cities and villages allow a wide range in the selection of teachers.

2. It permits a better grading of the schools and classification of the pupils. Consolidation allows pupils to be placed where they can work to the best advantage; the various subjects of study to be wisely selected and correlated, and more time to be given to recitation.

3. It adds the stimulating influences of large classes, with the resulting enthusiasm and generous rivalry. The discipline and training are invaluable.

4. It affords the broader companionship and culture that come from association.

5. It opens the doors to more schooling and to schools of a higher grade.

6. It results in better attendance of pupils, as proved by the experience in places where it has been tried.

7. It leads to better school buildings, better equipment, a larger supply of books, charts, maps and apparatus. All these naturally follow a concentration of people, wealth and intelligence, and aid in making good schools. The wise expenditure implied in these better appointments is good economy, for the cost per pupil is really much less than the cost in small and widely separated districts.

8. It quickens public interest in the schools, pride in the quality of the work done, secures a greater sympathy and a better fellowship throughout the community.

9. It permits more thorough and more easily accomplished supervision.

10. Greater punctuality would be secured as well as a more regular ·ttendance and pupils would not need to go away from home to obtain adanced instruction.

11. It will reduce the per capita cost of education in the districts affected in nearly every case, and without exception, after the first cost of buildings has been paid.

12. It would be better for the health and comfort of the pupils to be carried in comfortable conveyances than to travel through mud and snow as they often have to do at present.

Arguments against:

1. Bad roads, especially in winter.

2. Fear that the expense will be greater than under the present system.

3. Local jealousy; an acknowledgement that some other section of the parish has greater advantages and is outstripping other sections.

4. Depreciation of property; decreased valuation of farms in districts where schools are closed.

5. Dislike to send young children to school far from home, away from the oversight of parents; and to provide a cold lunch for them rather than a warm dinner.

6. Danger to health and morals; children obliged to travel too far in cold and stormy weather; obliged to walk too far to meet the team, and then to ride to school in damp clothing and with wet feet; unsuitable conveyance and uncertain driver; association with so many children of all classes and conditions; lack of proper oversight during the noon hour.

7. Insufficient and unsuitable clothing; expense to parents of properly clothing their children.

8. Some people object to the removal of the little schoolhouse, since it furnishes the only public meeting house in many places. They say it will break up the Sunday School, the literary society and other neighborhood gatherings.

9. It is objected that the children are often wanted at home before and after school to do chores, and if they must start early for a distant school and return late, they will not be able to render this assistance and will miss learning much of the practical work of the farm, which they should acquire when young.

10. That many teachers will be thrown out of employment. It is even suggested by some of the western superintendents that some of the little district schools are kept in operation to furnish jobs for the relatives and friends of the trustees.

11. That the pupils receive less individual attention in the large school.

12. Natural proneness of some people to object to the removal of any ancient landmark, or to any innovation, however worthy the measure or however well received elsewhere.

I have already anticipated some of the objections enumerated, but a little further examination of some of these may not be out of place.

BAD ROADS.—If centralization of schools will be an agency to secure better roads, it is a consummation to be desired. A demand for such must precede the facilities and one of the instruments may well be the necessities created by centralization of schools.

COST.—There is a widespread opinion that the cost of centralization will be greater than under the present system, and every other consideration is swallowed up in this. I could quote numberless instances to show the contrary, in fact the great mass of statistics obtainable shows that the cost is less than under the present system. I am sure that it can be asserted confidently that this will be true in any sections where any adequate provision is made for the present support of schools. It may not hold in the cases of a few districts that subordinate everything to cheapness and inefficiency.

LOCAL JEALOUSY—This leads up to a large question and one that in my opinion must needs be solved before centralization can become at all general.

By our present act districts must consolidate before the government assumes half the cost of conveyance. It will be noticed that this first step had been taken on Campobello, before centralization was brought about.

I am of the opinion that this Institute should appoint a small committee of competent persons to report upon the advantages of parish or country school units instead of the present district ones.

Such a committee was appointed by the National Education Association of the United States to report on rural schools, and a more admirable and comprehensive report on all phases of the subject, I believe has never been made.

The committee was composed of twelve of the most noted educationists in the United States and included such men as Wm. T. Harris, Henry Sabin, Hon. C. R. Skinner and A. B. Poland.

The district system has been practically swept away in some of the states in the union.

The committee says, "Considering the great superiority of the Township (parish) system over the district system, it is not a little strange that its introduction in the room of its competitor should have been so steadily resisted as it should have been. This opposition is due in part to the power of conservative habit, in part to the belief that the district system is more democratic, and in part to the popular fondness for office holding, all conjoined with much misconception and ignorance in respect to the merits of the two systems. It has been urged in favour of the district system by politicians, that it is the best unit for canvassing the states for political purposes."

The great advantages of the change it seems to me would be—the equalization of the cost over a larger area, by which the weak section would be helped by the strong, broader and more intelligent school government, better school appliances of all kinds, better salaries and consequent higher qualifications for teachers, and the location of schools in the most central and convenient localities, without consulting local prejudices. The town and village are debtor to a very large extent to the surrounding country and it is a debt that has never been repaid. The proposal made a few years ago to increase the county fund was a most equitable one, and would go in a small degree to rectify this inequality.

DEPRECIATION OF PROPERTY.—The contrary has been shown to be true where centralization has been adopted. It has been the difference between the good school and the poor school.

DANGER TO HEALTH AND MORALS.—These dangers are largely imaginary and will disappear entirely with ordinary management and efficient school officers and teachers.

Children have always taken cold lunches to school with no evil results, in fact in many districts it is the practice to do so regardless of distance, because of the social inducements of the noon hour.

BECAUSE THAT MANY TEACHERS WILL BE THROWN OUT OF EMPLOYMENT.—It is notorious that the demand for third class and local licensed teachers is almost entirely created by these small, weak and often parsimonious districts. In consequence of this, salaries have been reduced more than by any other agency. Young and immature teachers of poor scholarship and little training have to be employed and the service has suffered. It would be to the manifest advantage of all teachers if this condition ceased to exist, and to a still greater degree to the districts concerned. I think it a fair proposition and one worthy, of all acceptance, that where the advantages of any plan can be shown to exceed the disadvantages, that the same should be adopted. One of the principles declared by the National Educational Association of the United States is;—"Legislation with respect to public education must not wait for public sentiment. It should lead public sentiment when necessary. Experience teaches that what people are compelled by law to do with respect to schools, they readily learn to do without compulsion, but they are usually slow to demand reforms."

I am sure that with the demands being made upon our schools, that under present conditions, the ungraded schools are not obtaining equal rights in comparison with the graded, and that more legislation is needed to bring about equality, especially in the direction of parish school boards instead of the present district ones.

Some criticisms, not without justice, have been indulged in by the writer of a previous paper at the expense of trustees, but it must be remembered that there are limitations to their powers, and they very often do better than the resources at their command permit, and incur censure thereby. Such as they are we have our responsibility in educating them.

Public sentiment needs educating in this as in other matters, and I am relying upon the teachers to do this work in as far as they may be able. It means much to them all.

Let us remember that the real value of anything is in proportion to the effort put forth to obtain it.

ANNUAL REPORT

OF THE

SCHOOLS

OF

NEW BRUNSWICK

1903.

BY THE CHIEF SUPERINTENDENT OF EDUCATION.

FREDERICTON, N. B.
1904.

ANNUAL REPORT

OF THE

SCHOOLS

OF

NEW BRUNSWICK

1902-3.

BY THE CHIEF SUPERINTENDENT OF EDUCATION.

FREDERICTON, N. B.
1904.

EDUCATION OFFICE.

FREDERICTON, N. B., March 1st.

SIR,—

I have the honour to transmit to you, to be laid before His Honour the Lieutenant-Governor, the Annual Report on the Common Schools of the Province for the School year, 1902-3.

I have the honour to be, Sir,

Your obedient servant,

J. R. INCH,
Chief Supt. of Education.

TO THE HON. L. J. TWEEDIE,
Provincial Secretary.

CONTENTS.

PART I.—General Report.

PART III.—Appendices.

Appendix A.

Appendix B.

Appendix C.

Appendix D.

Appendix E.

PART I.

GENERAL REPORT

DUFFERIN SCHOOL BUILDING,
ST. JOHN, N. B.

ANNUAL REPORT

OF THE

Schools of New Brunswick

SCHOOL YEAR 1902-3.

PART I.—GENERAL REPORT.

To His Honour, the Honourable Jabez Bunting Snowball, Lieutenant Governor of the Province of New Brunswick.

MAY IT PLEASE YOUR HONOUR:—

I beg to submit, as required by law, my report on the public schools of the Province for the school year 1902-3.

The tabular statements given in Part II are for the school year which ended June 30th, 1903. The Inspectors' Reports in Part III cover the whole of the Calendar year 1903.

It is to be regretted that the number of schools in operation during the year under review, as well as the number of pupils enrolled, shows a considerable decrease in comparison with the corresponding numbers of recent years. The causes of the falling off will be discussed on a later page.

The following summary of the statistical tables (see part II) presents a general comparison of the work of the two terms under review, with that of the corresponding terms of the previous twelve months:—

STATISTICAL ABSTRACT.

Table I. Number of Schools, Teachers, Pupils, Etc.

	First Term. 1902-3.		Second Term. 1902-3.
Number of Schools, ...	1,778	....	1,726
Decrease, ...	17	Decrease,	10
Number of Teachers, ...	1,858	....	1,815
Decrease, ...	11	Decrease,	10
Number of Pupils, ...	57,518	....	59,313
Decrease, ...	1,057	Decrease,	1,164

Table II.—Proportion of Population at School, Age and Sex of Pupils, Percentage of Attendance.

	First Term. 1902-3		Second Term. 1902-3.
Proportion of population at school	1 in 5.75	....	1 in 5.59
Number of Pupils under six years of age, ...	1482	....	1258
Decrease, ...	163	....	264
Number between 6 and 15	53746	....	54628
Decrease	882	....	722
Number over 15 years	2290	....	3427
Decrease	12		178
Number of boys	28189	....	30172
Decrease	717	....	595
Number of girls	29329	....	29141
Decrease	340	....	569
Grand total number of days made by pupils enrolled	3257733	....	4338116
Decrease	27021½	....	22681½
Average number of pupils daily present during time schools were in session	38671	....	37552
Increase, ...	100	Decrease	1184
Average number daily present for the full term....	37,019	....	34,873
Increase, ...	232	Decrease	1185

Percentage daily present during time schools were in session	67.23	....	63.31
Increase, ...	1.39	Decrease	.74
Percentage daily present during full term	64.36	....	58.79
Increase, ...	1.56	Decrease	.83

The following table shows the enrolment and percentage of average attendance for the Province for full term, from 1890 to 1903, inclusive:

Year.	Enrolment.		Percentage of Attendance for Full Term.	
	June.	December.	June.	December.
1890	58,570	55,622	50.96	57.36
1891	59,568	56,217	52.40	59.82
1892	60,786	56,547	53.45	62.38
1893	60,154	57,195	54.58	61.89
1894	61,280	57,282	56.04	63.36
1895	62,518	57,889	57.62	62.93
1896	61,918	57,200	55.64	62.68
1897	61,908	58,174	55.94	64.16
1898	63,333	59,457	57.03	61.12
1899	63,536	58,925	55.69	62.08
1900	61,444	57,629	57.52	61.87
1901	60,420	58,575	58.34	62.80
1902	60,477	57,518	59.62	64.36
1903	59,313		58.79	

The aforegoing statistics disclose the fact that while there was an increase each year from 1890 to 1899 in the number of pupils enrolled in the public schools, there has been since 1899 an annual decrease. This backward tendency is to be regretted and calls for explanation.

In my opinion the principal causes which have brought about a result so unsatisfactory are the following:

1. The scarcity of teachers, especially teachers of the higher classes. Many schools have been closed for one or more terms because of the difficulty of obtaining teachers on the terms offered. This difficulty is experienced

not only in New Brunswick but in every Province of the Dominion and to some extent in the United States. The period from 1899 to the present has been a period of marked business prosperity. Teachers of both sexes have been able to find much more remunerative employment than the teaching profession in New Brunswick has offered them There has also been an urgent demand for our highest class teachers in South Africa and in British Columbia and the North Western districts of our own Dominion, where teachers command much higher salaries than in this Province. School Trustees and ratepayers generally (especially those outside of cities and towns) have failed to recognize the changed conditions, and prefer to leave the schools closed or to employ the cheapest teachers rather than offer such salaries as would command the services of the best. There are in some parts of the Province indications that the people are awakening to the necessity of providing better salaries for teachers, but under our present system of school districts the prospect of any marked improvement is not encouraging.

The numbers who take our Normal School course and receive licenses to teach would be amply sufficient to supply all our schools were we able to retain their services; but many of them remain in the school service but a very short time.

2. Another cause of the falling off in attendance is the frequent closing of schools by Health Officers on account of the prevalence of epidemic or contagious diseases. Epidemics of such fatal and highly contagious diseases as smallpox, diphtheria and scarlatina have been, perhaps, of more frequent occurrence during the last four or five years than formerly; but whether such be the case or not it is clear that the better organization and more prompt action of Boards of Health have resulted in the closing of the schools much more frequently than in former years. Schools have occasionally been closed on account of the appearance in a community of one or more cases of the milder epidemic diseases of childhood, such as whooping cough, mumps, measles, etc. The decision as to the necessity of closing the school must, of course, in all cases rest with the local Health Officer; but it may not be out of place to suggest that before taking the extre memeasure of interrupting and seriously disorganizing the work of the schools, such exact enquiry should be made in regard to the facts as to render it clear that the public safety demands such a course.

3. A third cause for the falling off in the enrolment and attendance of pupils has been the neglect of parents to comply with the provisions of the Vaccination Acts of 1902 and 1903. Hundreds of children have thus been deprived of school privileges during the last two years. In many cases this parental neglect arises from simple indifference, in other cases from unwillingness to

incur the trouble and expense of employing a medical practitioner, in some cases from exaggerated apprehensions as to the dangers incurred by the operation, and in a few cases from alleged conscientious scruples arising from peculiar religious views. It is unfortunately true that the obligation of sending their children to school rests so easily upon the consciences of not a few parents that the slightest excuse for neglecting their duty in this regard is not unwillingly availed of. If the responsibility of leaving their children without school previleges can by any pretext be shifted upon other shoulders they feel a sense of relief, with the additional luxury of having a grievance to nurse.

4. Another cause of diminished enrolment has been the changing of the age of entrance into the schools from five years as formerly to six years by the provision of the Schools Act 1900. This change coming at a time when active business conditions in the Province tended to withdraw the older pupils from the schools at an earlier age than in periods when remunerative employment was not so easy to obtain, has still further limited the attendance at the schools, the school life having been practically shortened by at least one year.

In view of all the facts above stated, and others that could be adduced, the diminished enrolment of pupils in the public schools has really been less than might have been anticipated under the combined circumstances which have tended to obstruct progress in this direction.

The following table shows that the enrolment in the cities and towns has varied but little for the last seven years. There is no doubt that in most of these cities and towns the population has materially increased during this time. The enrolment in the schools should have increased proportionally. A census of the children of school age would establish the sad fact that in every city and town there are hundreds of children growing up in illiteracy under the shadow of our well equipped school buildings. Whatever may be the difficulties in the way of an effective enforcement of a rigid Compulsory Attendance Law in rural districts, I am convinced that such a law could be administered with excellent results in well organized towns and cities. It is principally a question of appointing competent officials to enforce the provisions of the law, and of incurring the necessary expenses of its administration.

	1895-96		1896-97		1897-98		1898-99		1899-00		1900-01		1901-02		1902-03	
	Dec.	June.	Dec.	June.	Dec.	June.	Dec.	June.	Dec.	June.	Dec.	June.	Dec.	June.	Dec.	June.
St. John	6606	6356	6566	6413	6709	6711	6986	6792	6952	6733	7160	6901	7247	6928	7331	7171
Fredericton	1225	1212	1243	1225	1209	1181	1203	1169	1231	1184	1214	1152	1196	1174	1169	1103
Moncton	1708	1660	1716	1630	1749	1678	1741	1682	1825	1736	1718	1693	1809	1712	1795	1746
St. Stephen	592	581	580	565	581	560	583	545	555	541	545	542	541	542	557	528
Milltown	369	379	381	385	389	377	370	371	371	382	368	363	338	335	315	314
Woodstock	638	643	678	688	713	712	719	674	662	644	652	652	655	630	657	660
Marysville	301	300	324	314	338	300	316	304	322	319	305	302	307	303	309	292
Campbellton	378	343	388	382	370	355	373	367	407	416	401	376	306	426	407	402
Chatham	....	941	942	973	980	1019	1024	1004	1018	989	933	934	970	972	987	955
Newcastle	....	....	....	....	....	....	....	....	....	478	497	475	502	503	526	502

TABLE III.—Subjects of Instruction.

The following summary of Table III, shows the number of pupils receiving instruction in each subject, both in the Common Schools and in the Superior and Grammar Schools:

COMMON SCHOOL GRADES, I. TO VIII. INCLUSIVE.—YEAR ENDED JUNE 30TH, 1903

	First Term.			Second Term.		
Reading, Spelling. etc.	55,405	Decrease	1,176	57,405	Decrease	964
Writing, etc.	55,100	"	1,291	57,022	"	1,198
Number and Arithmetic	55,211	"	1,159	57,035	"	1,143
Drawing, etc.	54,674	"	616	56,402	"	660
Health Lessons	51,548	"	1,331	54,239	"	269
Nature Lessons	51,047	"	585	53,175	"	810
Lessons in Morals etc	53,102	"	1,207	54,789	"	1,451
Physical Exercises	47,784	"	1,612	49,902	"	171
Singing etc	33,131	Increase	152	33,181	"	1,280
Geography	31,888	Decrease	277	34,322	"	559
English Grammar etc	31,177	"	129	33,826	"	293
History	19,810	"	222	22,109	"	387
Algebra	2,714	"	42	4,063	Increase	758
French (optional)	5,963	Increase	778	6,561	"	343
Latin (optional)	1,602	Decrease	172	1,925	"	97
Sewing (optional)	334	Increase	120	287	"	114
Knitting (optional)	154	Decrease	39	150	"	82

HIGH SCHOOL GRADES, IX. TO XII. INCLUSIVE.—YEAR ENDED JUNE 30TH, 1903.

	First Term.			Second Term.		
English Language and Literature	1,795	Decrease	39	1,753	Increase	2
Latin	1,312	"	92	1,265	Decrease	8
Greek	191	"	38	132	"	66
French	1,025	Increase	49	1,098	Increase	116
Arithmetic	1,543	Decrease	35	1,483	Decrease	53
Geometry	1,728	Increase	20	1,716	Increase	22
Algebra	1,709	Decrease	70	1,720	"	79
Trigonometry	50	"	14	72	Decrease	34
Book-keeping	885	"	109	1,167	Increase	25
History and Geography	1,765	"	84	1,710	Decrease	11
Drawing	775	"	228	843	"	23
Botany	1,511	"	53	1,652	Increase	107
Chemistry	405	"	46	804	"	138
Physiology and Hygiene	487	"	59	569	"	17
Physics	442	"	230	885	"	6

TABLE IV.—NUMBER AND CLASS OF TEACHERS EMPLOYED.

The total number of teachers employed during the year was 1858 for the first term and 1815 for the second term—classified as follows:

FIRST TERM.

	MALES	FEMALES	TOTAL
Grammar School Class	25	2	27
First Class Superior	49	5	54
First Class	76	294	370
Second Class	129	807	936
Third Class	80	330	410
Holding Local License	3	35	38
Class Room Assistants	1	22	23
	363	1,495	1,858

SECOND TERM.

	MALES	FEMALES	TOTALS
Grammar School Class	21	2	23
First Class Superior	48	3	51
First Class	77	307	384
Second Class	112	766	878
Third Class	77	317	394
Holding Local License	3	54	57
Class Room Assistants	3	25	28
	341	1,474	1,115

It will be seen that of the total number of teachers employed less than 20 per cent. are men, less than 25 per cent. hold licenses above Class II., about 50 per cent. hold licenses of Class II., and about 25 per cent. hold the lowest class of license. Since 1900 the number of untrained teachers employed has increased from 21 to 57.

Tables V, VI, VII and VIII show the period of service of the teachers employed; the time in session of the schools; the interest shown by school officials and the general public in the work of the schools as indicated by visits and the offering of prizes; the number of public examinations, and the average salaries of the teachers.

It is gratifying to note even the slight improvement in the salaries of teachers which Table VIII. indicates.

TABLE IX.—DISBURSEMENT OF PROVINCIAL GRANTS.

The total provincial grants to schools of all grades for the year 1902-3 amounted to $160,825.79, a decrease of $1,401 40 on the disbursement of the previous year. The above does not include the sum of $2,246.54 paid on account of New Brunswick pupils at the School for the Blind, Halifax, and the further sum of $935, grants to repair or build school houses in poor districts.

The following statement shows the annual expenditure from the provincial revenues since 1891, the number of schools open during the term ending June 30th, and the number of teachers of each class employed.

YEAR.	Schools. No. of	Teachers of Each Class.					Provincial Grant.
		Grammar School.	Sup. and Class I.	Class II.	Class III.	Totals.	
1891	15?6	14	274	765	579	1632	$137,679 03
1892	1585	14	304	783	568	1669	142,681 21
1893	16?4	14	345	787	547	1693	147,669 71
1894	1653	14	360	786	589	1749	150,882 20
1895	1695	13	382	827	568	1790	156,341 65
1896	1720	13	423	839	554	1829	158,135 23
1897	1737	17	440	840	534	1831	161,445 94
1998	1778	20	427	904	513	1864	163,021 86
1899	1806	25	464	894	529	1912	167,988 40
1900	1771	25	452	881	498	1856	168,224 72
1901	1741	23	429	911	478	1841	163,951 73
1902	1736	22	423	889	491	1825	162,227 19
1903	1726	23	435	878	479	1815	160,825 79

The total expenditure during the year 1902-3 for the maintenance of the Grammar, Superior and Common Schools is approximately as follows:

District Assessments (approximate).........	$374,196 00
County Fund..............................	94,969 24
Provincial Grants..........................	160,825 79
Total..................................	$629,991 03

Average amount per pupil enrolled about $9.50.

TABLES X. AND XI.—THE COUNTY FUND.

The total amount of the County Fund for the year was $97,215.78, disbursed as follows:

To Trustees of the Public Schools....	$94,969 24	
School for the Blind, Halifax	2,246 54	
		$97,215 78

The special sum apportioned to Poor Districts under the provisions of section 44 of the Schools Act was $5,001.52.

As the School for the Deaf and Dumb was not in operation during the year the amount formerly appropriated to it was distributed among the other schools.

The appropriations from the several counties to the School for the Blind were as follows:

Albert County, 3 pupils	$225 00	
Carleton County, 1 pupil	75 00	
Charlotte County, 2 pupils....	150 00	
Gloucester County, 3 pupils	218 97	
Kent County, 4 pupils	265 07	
Kings County, 3 pupils	225 00	
Northumberland County, 1 pupil, first term	37 50	
Queen's County, 2 pupils	150 00	
St. John County, 4 pupils....	300 00	
Westmorland County, 8 pupils	600 00	
		$2246 54

TABLES XII. AND XIII.—SUPERIOR AND GRAMMAR SCHOOLS.

There were 50 Superior and 13 Grammar Schools in operation during the year. Twenty-two teachers received the provincial Grammar School grant. The total number of pupils enrolled in the High School Grades (IX.-XII.) was 1827 for the first term and 1770 for the second term. Of these numbers 1084 and 1019 respectively, belonged to the Grammar Schools, and 743 and 751 to the Superior Schools.

The following statement shows the Superior Schools which had 20 pupils or upwards above Grade VIII., arranged in order of the highest numbers:

	First Term.	Second Term.
St. Stephen High School,....	68	56
Harkins' Academy, Newcastle, ...	41	43
Milltown Superior School,...	35	38
Dorchester "	37	34
Sackville "	37	29
Centreville " (Car. Co.)...	20	26
Middle Sackville "	23	22
Hillsborough "	25	19
Hopewell Hill "	25	15
St. Martins "	22	18
Moore's Mills "	20	20
Florenceville "	14	20

The following Superior Schools had from 10 to 19 pupils above Grade VIII. for one or other of the two terms: St. George, North Head, Buctouche, Hartland, Shediac, Petitcodiac, Rexton, Havelock Corner, Fredericton Junction, Salisbury, Keswick Ridge, Millerton, Grand Falls, Fairville, Bathurst Village.

The rest of the Superior Schools, (22 in number), had from 2 to 9 pupils above Grade VIII., except the four following, which had no pupils above Grade VIII.: Doaktown, Harvey, Gibson and Marysville. The two latter, Gibson and Marysville, send all pupils above Grade VIII. to the Fredericton Grammar School. As Superior Schools are supposed to provide for instruction, when necessary, up to and including Grade X., it would seem but reasonable that the Marysville and Gibson Districts should either make provision for instruction in Grades IX. and X. in their own schools, or should pay a reasonable tuition fee for the pupils in these Grades who are sent to the Grammar School in Fredericton.

By reference to Table XIII. it will be seen that the numbers of advanced pupils in attendance at each of the Grammar Schools of Albert, Kent, Queens and Victoria Counties falls below 20. It is proposed to locate the Albert County Grammar School at a more populous centre, which will, without doubt, make it accessible to a much larger number of advanced pupils.

The growth of our High School work since 1890 is shown in the following statement:

No. of Pupils in Grades IX. to XII. in Grammar and Superior Schools.

	Term Ended December.	Term Ended June.
1890-1	574	610
1891-2	701	694
1892-3	782	724
1893-4	738	806
1894-5	1155	1060
1895-6	1093	1099
1896-7	1220	1228
1897-8	1469	1523
1898-9	1495	1510
1899-1900	1565	1545
1900-1	1543	1528
1901-2	1834	1751
1902-3	1827	1770

DEPARTMENTAL EXAMINATIONS,

These examinations consist of:

(1)—The High School Entrance Examinations (See Regulation 46, School Manual) held during the month of June at the several Grammar Schools, and such of the Superior Schools as apply for the same. They cover the work of Grades I. to VIII. inclusive, or the Common School Grades. Those who successfully pass these examinations receive a certificate which is intended to serve a two-fold purpose; for pupils who do not intend to continue longer at school it serves as a diploma given under the authority of the Education Department, testifying that the holder has completed satisfactorily the course of studies of the Common Schools; for pupils who intend to continue their studies it serves as a certificate of admittance to the High School classes.

(2)—The High School Leaving Examinations (See Regulation 45, School Manual) held the first week in July at different examination stations throughout the province. They cover the work of Grades IX., X. and XI. of the Grammar Schools. Diplomas are granted to those who successfully pass these examinations.

(3)—The University Matriculation Examinations held at the same time and stations as the Leaving Examinations.

(4)—The Normal School Entrance Examinations held at the same time and places as the two former. Candidates for admittance to the Normal School and Licensed Teachers seeking for advance of Class are required to pass these examinations.

(5)—The Normal School Closing Examinations, held at the Normal School, Fredericton, and at St. John and Chatham, beginning on the second Tuesday of June, and for Third Class Candidates in December and May of each year.

The following Tables show the result of these several examinations for the year 1903.

(1)—HIGH SCHOOL ENTRANCE EXAMINATIONS.

GRAMMAR SCHOOLS.

NAME OF SCHOOL.	No. of Candidates.	Passed Division I.	Passed Division II.	Passed Division III.	Failed.
Albert County Grammar School	6	5	1	.	....
Carleton " "	54	5	21	25	3
Charlotte " "	14	6	4	3	1
Gloucester " "	11	...	5	6	....
Kent " "	7	2	5	...	....
Kings " "	10	4	3	2	1
Northumberland " "	25	....	6	19	....
Queens	11	1	5	5	....
Restigouche " "	12	2	2	8	....
St John "	254	83	110	52	9
Victoria " "	14	....	5	8	1
Westmorland " "	86	10	38	32	6
York " "	103	25	40	29	9
	607	143	245	189	30

SUPERIOR SCHOOLS.

NAME OF SCHOOL.	Number Entered for Examination	Passed Division I.	Passed Division II.	Passed Division III.	Failed.
Hopewell Hill	4	......	3	......	1
Centreville	4	......	4	......	......
Hartland	9	3	5	1	......
Grand Manan	5	4	1	......	......
St. George	15	1	10	4	......
St. Stephen	25	10	13	0	2
Milltown	12	8	4	......	......
Harcourt	6	1	3	2	......
Rexton	8	3	3	2	......
Hampton	12	9	3	......	......
Apohaqui	5	......	2	2	8
Edmundston	8	3	1	3	1
Douglastown	16	2	9	4	1
Newcastle	32	6	14	4	1
Dalhousie	6	1	5	......	......
Fairville	16	10	5	......	1
Milford	7	3	2	1	1
St. Martins	9	4	5	......	......
Fredericton Jct	4	2	......	1	1
Grand Falls	9	3	3	......	3
Dorchester	10	2	8	......	......
Sackville	22	3	6	9	4
Salisbury	8	4	2	1	1
Shediac	15	6	8	......	1
McAdam Junction	7	2	3	2	......
Superior Schools	274	90	122	36	26
Grammar Schools	607	143	245	189	30
Total 1902.1903	881	233	367	225	56
" 1901-1902	905	239	381	223	62
Increase	....	......	......	2	......
Decrease	24	6	14	......	6

(2, 3)—Matriculation and High School Leaving Examinations.

Examiners:

Professor W. T. Raymond, B. A., Greek, Latin, French, etc.
" S. W. Hunton, M. A. Mathematics.
" A. M. Scott, M. A., Ph. D. English language and Literature
" John Brittain, Natural Science etc.

The following is the report of the examiners:

Fredericton, July 31st, 1903.

To J. R. Inch, Esq., LL.D.,
Chief Superintendent of Education.

Dear Sir,—We beg to submit our Report of the Matriculation and Leaving Examinations for July 1903.

Ninty-two candidates took the Matriculation and six the Leaving Examination. Of the ninety-two Matriculation candidates, seven passed in the First Division, thirty-seven in the Second, twenty-one in the Third, sixteen in the Third conditionally and seven failed. Of the engineering candidates for Matriculation there were four; two passed in the Second Division and two in the Third conditionally. Of the six candidates who took the Leaving Examination three passed in the Second Division and three in the Third.

Respectfully submitted,

W. T. Raymond,
John Brittain,
Sidney W. Hunton,
A. Melville Scott.

The following are the names of the candidates who passed in the First and Second Divisions arranged in the order of the highest averages.

First Division.

Wm. Woods,................................St. John Gram. School.
L. Ralph Sherman,..........................Fredericton Gram. School.
Rebecca Watson,............................Fredericton Gram. School.
C. Donald McCormac,........................Woodstock Gram. School.
Annie E. V. Parks,.........................Sussex Gram. School.
Waldo C. Machum,...........................Fredericton Gram. School.
Eva M. McCracken,..........................Moncton Gram. School

Second Division

Kenneth Dunphy,......................Fredericton Gram. School.
Ethel G. Hannah,......................St. John Gram. School.
S. Jessie Weyman,......................Sussex Gram. School.
Clara Fritz,..........................St. John Gram. School.
Annie Gosnell,.......... ....St. John Gram. School.
Edna B. Bell,..........................Moncton Gram. School.
Helen C. Fraser,......................Chatham Gram. School.
A. V. Sandall,..........................St. John Gram. School.
Ronald P. Stockton,............... ....St. John Gram. School.
Tillie McClelland,......................St. John Gram. School.
Laura H. Myles,........................St. John Gram. School.
Emma E. Giggey........................St. John Gram. School.
Eldon Carruthers,......................Chatham Gram. School.
Harry E. Sutherland,..................Fredericton Gram. School.
G. Harold Edgecombe..................Fredericton Gram. School.
Alice E. Ryder,........................St. Stephen High School.
Daisy A. Belyea,........................St. John Gram. School.
Roy F. Finley,..........................St. John Gram. School.
Helen W. Gregory,.... ....St. John Gram. School.
Thos. E. DeWolfe,.... ....St. Stephen High School.
Edith M. Craig........................St. Stephen High School.
Jean P. Wilson...................... Fredericton Grammar School.
Mabel Hodge..................... .....St. John Grammar School.
Alma E. Belliveau,...................Fredericton Grammar School.
Gordon S. Macdonald.... ....St. John Grammar School.
Aulder L. Gerow.................. ....Fredericton Grammar School.
Elizabeth McBeath....................Moncton Grammar School.
Annie M. Thomas......................Fredericton Grammar School.
J. Talmage Haining ....Fredericton Grammar School.
Gordon M. Pitts.... ....Fredericton Grammar School.
Elsie O. Lawson........................St. Stephen High School.
Walter McN. Matthews................Chatham Grammar School.
Fred H. Kierstead....................Moncton Grammar School.
Hazen P. Moulton......................St. Stephen High School.
R. Gordon Warman.... ....Moncton Grammar School.
Edith K. Murphy......................St. John Grammar School.
Edna C. Tufts..........................St. John Grammar School.

Engineering.

Second Division.

Edward B. MacLean.................Moncton Grammar School.
Harry S. Day.....................St. John Grammar School.

Leaving Examinations.

Second Division.

Jean S. Welling....................Moncton Grammar School.
Arthur W. Carten...................Fredericton Grammar School.
Nellie B. Ingraham.................Fredericton Grammar School.

(4)—Normal School Entrance Examinations and Preliminary Examinations for Advance of Class, July, 1903.

Number of Candidates for Class I.		163
" " " II.		363
" " " III.		26
		552
Number gained Class I.	64	
" " II.	175	
" " III.	168	
" Failed to classify	145	
		552

Class I.

The following candidates for Class I. made 66⅔ per cent. and upward. The names are arranged in order of the highest marks.

*Jean G. Robichaud....................Shippegan.
*Elmire Girouard......................St John.
*Margaret B. McDonald.................Mt. St. Vincent, Halifax.
*Mary J. LeBlanc......................St. John.
Melbourne R. Smith....................Oak Bay.
Robert Straight.......................McDonald's Corner, Kings Co.
*Josephine Dumas......................Grand Anse.
Kate L. Colpitts......................Forest Glen, Westmorland Co.

Ruthie C Mitton.......................Hopewell Hill.
Arthur E. Floyd.......................Barnesville.
Jessie Bustin.......................Nashwaaksis.
Chauncy R. Pollard.......................Tower Hill.
M. A. Wathen.......................Harcourt.
Mary E. R. Archibald.......................Hopewell Hill.
Sara E. Hoar.......................Albert.
John Keough.......................Sackville.
Ida May Saul.......................Alma.
*Alice G. P. Clancy,.......................St. John,
E. Maude Pearce,.......................Newtown,
Otty J. Fraser, ...Lower Prince William,
Ethel J. MacMurray.......................Prince William,
Muriel L. Law,.......................Gagetown,
Nellie M. Douglas,.......................St. George,
Chas. G. Crawford,.......................Debec.

CLASS II

The following candidates for Class II made an average of 60 per cent and upwards on second class papers (arranged in order of highest marks)

*Mary Leger,.......................Bathurst,
J. Robinson Belyea,.......................Cambridge, Queens Co,
Margaret L. Johnson,.......................New Jerusalem,
*Maude E. Brophy,.......................Fairville,
Lizzie Maddox,.......................Wicklow,
Nellie R. Mallory,.......................Fairville,
Rosamond Coulthard, ...Meductic,
Lizzie J. McNair,.......................New Mills,
Howard W. Hamilton,.......................Baie Verte,
Mabel C. MacFarlane,.......................Sussex,
Clara A. Alexander,.......................F'ton Junction,
Lizzie M. Muir,.......................Belleisle, Creek.
Peter J. Caverhill,....................... Lower Southampton,
Royal Mowatt,.......................Harvey Station,
Annie G. Campbell,.......................St. Thomas,
Walter White,.......................Narrows, Queens Co.
A. Ruth Belyea,.......................Lower Gagetown,
Annie R. MacRae,.......................Black River Bridge,
*Phoebe L. O'Brien,.......................St. George,

Margaret E. Hemphill,.................... Debec,
Mary E. Coy,............................ Upper Gagetown,
Margaret E. Fraser,...................... Rexton, Kent Co,
Sarah E. Moore,......................... Moore's Mills,
Hildred Robertson,...................... Richibucto,
Mary Agnes Firth,....................... Glenco, Rest. Co,
Loretta M. McCarthy,.................... Bartholomew, North. Co.
Roy S. Parlee,.......................... Apohaqui.

*Those marked with an asterisk took French (optional.) One seventh of the marks made in French has been added as a bonus to the general average made in the other subjects.

LIEUTENANT GOVERNOR'S MEDALS FOR HIGH SCHOOL ENTRANCE EXAMINATION.

His Honour the Lieutenant-Governor has been pleased to offer thirteen silver medals to be competed for by the pupils of the eighth grade at the High School Entrance Examinations in June next, and thereafter annually during his term of office.

The examinations will be held in accordance with the provisions of Regulation 46 at the several Grammar Schools, and at such of the Superior Schools as shall make application to the Chief Superintendent not later than the first day of June.

One medal will be competed for by the pupils of each county, except that for the purposes of this competition Madawaska and Victoria will be reckoned as one county, and Sunbury and Queen's as one county.

The medal will be awarded to the pupil making the highest aggregate marks in each case, provided that no candidate falling below the second division shall be entitled to a medal. The papers of the candidates awarded the highest marks by the local examiners shall be submitted for a final examination to special Examiners appointed by the Board of Education whose decision shall determine the award.

These medals will be publicly presented to their respective winners either at the reopening of the schools in August or September, or at a later date, as determined by the local school Boards. It is intended that the medals shall be worn by the winners at all school examinations, festivals and anniversaries.

The following tabular statement gives the details of the Entrance Examinations for each examining station:

NORMAL SCHOOL ENTRANCE EXAMINATION, AND PRELIMINARY EXAMINATIONS FOR ADVANCE OF CLASS, 1903.

STATIONS.	No. Presented at Each Station for Examination.	Number of Candidates Presented for the various Classes with Results. Class I. No. Examined for this Class.	No. Obtained 1st Class.	No. Obtained 2nd Class.	No. Obtained 3rd Class.	No. that failed to Obtain any Class.	Class II. No. Examined for this Class.	No. Obtained 2nd Class.	No. Obtained 3rd Class.	No. that Failed to Obtain any Class.	Class III. No. Examined for this Class.	No. Obtained 3rd Class.	No. that Failed to Obtain any Class.	SUMMARY. Total Results for Each Class. No. Obtained 1st Class.	No. Obtained 2nd Class.	No. Obtained 3rd Class.	No. that Failed to Obtain any Class.
No. 1. Fredericton	107	24	12	6	4	2	80	26	31	23	3	2	1	12	32	37	28
" 2. St. John	75	32	6	16	5	5	41	16	14	11	2	2	......	6	32	21	16
" 3. Moncton	61	26	8	12	4	2	35	4	10	21	......	......	......	8	16	14	23
" 4. St. Stephen	60	18	5	7	1	5	41	7	13	21	1	......	1	5	14	14	27
" 5. Woodstock	72	19	8	8	2	1	50	15	21	14	3	2	1	8	23	25	16
" 6. Chatham	54	14	4	9	1	....	32	10	13	9	8	3	5	4	19	17	14
" 7. Sussex	44	13	9	4	......	......	30	8	18	4	1	1	......	9	12	19	4
" 8. Campbellton	14	2	1	1	......	......	8	5	3	......	4	1	3	1	6	4	3
" 9. Bathurst	26	6	5	1	......	......	18	8	5	5	2	......	2	5	9	5	7
" 10. Hillsboro	24	9	6	3	......	......	15	3	6	6	......	......	......	6	6	6	6
" 11. Andover	15	......	......	......	......	......	13	6	6	1	2	......	2	......	6	6	3
Total	552	163	64	67	17	15	363	108	140	115	26	11	15	64	175	168	145
1902	488	161	42	61	42	16	306	97	99	110	21	6	15	42	158	147	141
Increase	64	2	22	6	......	......	57	11	41	5	5	5	......	22	17	21	4
Decrease	......	......	......	......	25	1	......	......	......	......	......	......	......	......	......	......	......

(5)—Closing Examination for Teachers' License, held December, 1902, and May and June, 1903.

EXAMINERS.

Mathematics—CHANCELLOR HARRISON.
English Language and Literature—H. S. BRIDGES, M. A., PH. D.
Latin and Greek—H. S. BRIDGES, M. A., PH. D.
Physiology and Botany—PROF. L. W. BAILEY, M. A., PH. D., F, R. S. C.
Physics and Chemistry—PROF. A. M. SCOTT, PH. D.
School System—G. W. MERSEREAU, M. A.
Teaching and School Management, etc—G. U. HAY, M. A., D. Sc.
Industrial Drawing, Book-keeping, etc.—MR. VROOM.
French and General History—PROF. W. T. RAYMOND, B. A.

The full details of the final Examinations for License held in December, 1902, and May, 1903, for the French Department and for the Third Class Candidates of the English Department, and the closing examinations for the higher classes held at Fredericton, St. John and Chatham in June, 1903, are given in Table XV., page A 37, to which reference is directed.

The total number admitted to these examinations (including those who were examined for advance of class) was 273. The following is a summary of results ;

	No. Examined	No. Passed.
Grammar School Class............	12	8
Class I........................	82	54
Class II.......................	118	139
Class III......................	61	61
Failed to be classed.............		11
	273	273

Thirteen other candidates stood a partial examination for Grammar School Class, and six of those who gained Class I, or had previously held a First Class License, qualified for Superior School License. At the July examinations 14 other First Class Teachers received the Superior School Certificate.

The names of the successful candidates for Teachers' Licenses of all classes are given on pages A 38, A 39 and A 40, Part II.

CLASS I.

The following candidates made 70 per cent. and upwards at the Closing Examination for Provincial License.

(Arranged in order of the highest marks.)

*Margaret M. Belyea	Lily Lake, Kings Co.
*Annie McGuiggan	St. John.
*Harry A. Prebble	Butternut Ridge, Kings Co.
Helen G. McLeod	Bay Verte, West. Co.
*A. Blanche Myles	St. John.
Ruth E. Everett	Lower French Village, York Co.
Osburn N. Brown	Newcastle.
Percy R. Hayward	Ashland, Carleton Co.
*May B. Pinder	Fredericton.
*Max D. Cormier	Barachois.
Beatrice N. Richards	Campbellton.
Sarah L. Waycott	Fredericton.
Annie E. Cochrane	Petitcodiac.
Gaynell E. Long	Good's Corner, Carleton Co.
*Mary C. Creaghan	Newcastle.
Stanley Wilson	Rolling Dam, Charlotte Co.
Norman S. Fraser	Nashwaak Bridge.
Florence M. Bird	Marysville.
Paul M. Atkinson	Albert.
*Pearl Babbitt	Fredericton.
Cora H. McFarland	Lime Hill, Kings Co.
*Mary I. Finn	St. John.
Florence E. Smith	Moore's Mills, Charlotte Co.
*Madge Parkinson	Dartmouth, N. S.
Jessie McKnight	Lower Napan, Northumb'l'd Co.

CLASS II.

The following candidates made 70 per cent. and upwards at the closing examinations for Provincial License on second class papers:

(Arranged in order of the highest marks.)

*Jean G. Robichaud	Shippegan.
Ethel J. McMurray	Prince William.
Florence T. Mahood	Petersville Church, Queens Co.

Carrie E. Ayer.....................Buctouche, Kent Co.
Robt. H. Flewelling...................Chipman, Queens Co.
George Foster Camp...............Upper Sheffield, Sunbury Co.
Jennie N. Bell....................Zionville, York Co.
Nellie Harper.....................Chipman, Queens Co.
Arthur C. F. Freeze...............Doaktown.
Rheta M. Allingham...............Welchpool, Campobello.
Charles C. Crawford..............Debec Junction.
Frances J. Kinney.................Florenceville.
Bertha B. Bartlett................ Bartlett's Mills, Charlotte Co.
Damie E. Kennedy.................Hartland.
C. G. Lawrence...................Lower Dumfries, York Co.
Bessie E. Holder..................Long Reach, Kings Co.
Gertrude G. Miller................Tay Settlement, York Co.
Mary M. Lindsay..................Williamstown, Carleton Co.
Ethel A. Tait.....................North Tay, York Co.
Louise Thompson..................Chance Harbour, St. John Co.
*Madeline deBury.................St. John.
*Domitien T. Robichaud............Upper Pokemouche.
Mabel E. Perkins..................Scribner, Kings Co.
*Georgia L. Brown................St. John.
Mabel A. Estabrooks..............Chester, Car. Co.
Nellie M. Stewart.................Richibucto.
Annie L. Wilson...................Clones, Queens Co.
Sarah E. Hoar.....................Albert
J. Gladys Hudson..................Richibucto.
Lola J. Thorne....................Butternut Ridge. Kings Co.
Annie McLean.....................Charlo Sta, Restigouche Co.
Josephine Culligan................Jacquet River, Restigouche Co.
*Elizabeth Cowan.................St. John.
Lida A. Wishart...................Tabusintac, Northumberland Co.

*Candidates whose names are marked with an asterisk wrote an optional paper in French. One twelfth of the marks made on the French paper was added as a bonus to the average of the marks made on the other subjects.

The dates at which the next Departmental Examinations will begin are as follows:

High School Entrance, Monday, June 20th, 1904
High School Leaving, Tuesday, July 5th, 1904.
University Matriculation, Tuesday, July 5th, 1904.

Normal School Entrance, etc., Tuesday, July 5th, 1904.
Normal School Closing, Tuesday, June 14th, 1904.
Normal School Closing for French Department, Tuesday, May 31st 1904.
Normal School Closing for Third Class, Tuesday, Dec. 20th, 1904.

The stations at which the University Matriculation, the High School Leaving and the Normal School Entrance examinations will be held are:

Fredericton, St. John, Moncton, St. Stephen, Woodstock, Chatham, Sussex, Campbellton, Bathurst, Hillsborough and Andover.

Candidates for Superior Class Certificates may be examined either during the Closing examinations in June or the Entrance examinations in July.

TABLE XVI.—School Libraries.

The total number of new volumes purchased for School Libraries during the year was 1504, at a cost of $826.06, of which the Province paid $231.67.

This was considerably more than double the amount expended the previous year.

TABLE XVII.—Travelling Expenses of Student Teachers.

The sum of $1751.70 was paid during the year as travelling expenses to student teachers attending the Normal School, an increase of $613.20 as compared with the same account for the preceding year. The number of claimants was 253, an increase of 83.

TABLES XVIII and XIX.

These tables give a summary of all moneys disbursed by the Chief Superintendent for the School Service, for the fiscal year ended October 31st, 1902.

POOR DISTRICTS.

The whole Province is divided into 1662 districts of which about 1520 operated schools during some part of the school year. Each of the cities and towns constitutes a single district. The total number of schools in cities and towns organized under the provisions of sections 104 to 108 of the Schools Act is 288 having an enrolment of over 14000 pupils an average of about 50 to each school. Outside of these cities and towns the enrolment is about 52,000, an average to each school of about 34.

Districts having an assessable valuation of less than $12000 are classed as poor districts, and receive from 25 to 33⅓ per cent additional grants from the provincial revenues and the County Fund. The total amount of special aid granted to these poor districts during the year has been $7400.47 from the provincial revenues and $5001.52 from the County fund, or $12401.99 from both sources.

The number of districts having a claim upon the poor aid for the year 1904 as recommended by the several Inspectors is 593, as follows:

Albert County.

Parish of Alma,	Nos. 3, 6, 7, 8 (and Harvey), 9	5
" Coverdale,	" 6, 7 (and Hillsboro), *8, 9, 11, 12 15 (and Salisbury), ...	7
" Elgin,	" 4, 5, *6, 7, *9, *13, 15, 17, 18, 19, 20, ...	11
" Harvey,	" 6, 7 (and Alma), *8, *10, ...	4
" Hillsboro,	" 8, *9, *11 (and Elgin), 12, 13 (and Elgin), 15, ...	6
" Hopewell,	" *4, 5 (and Hillsboro), 9, ...	3
		36

Carleton County.

Parish of Aberdeen,	Nos. 2, (and Kent), 7, 8, 9, 10, 11, 12, 13, (and Kent), ...	8
" Brighton,	" 11, 17, 18, 19, 19½, ...	5
" Kent,	" *1½ (and Peel), *9, 19, ...	3
" Northampton,	" *8, 11 (and Southampton)	2
" Peel,	" 5, ...	1
" Wicklow,	" *8, *16, ...	2
" Wilmot,	" *14, 17, ...	2
" Woodstock,	" 11, 13, ...	2
		25

Charlotte County.

Parish of Clarendon,	Nos. 1, 2, 3, ...	3
" Dumbarton,	" 1, 4, 5, *7, *7½, ...	5
" Grand Manan,	" 7, *9, ...	2
" Lepreaux,	" 1, *2 (and Musquash), 5, ...	3
" Pennfield,	" *6, ...	1

CHARLOTTE COUNTY.—Continued.

Parish of St. David,	Nos. *2, *7, ...	2
" St. George,	" 7, 8, 8½, (and Dumbarton), 9, 10, 11, *15, ...	7
" St. James,	" *4, *4½ (and St. David), *5, 8, *10 11, *13, *19, ...	8
" St. Patrick,	" *4, *6, *9 (and St. George), *10	4
" St. Stephen,	" *2, 7½ (and St. James), ...	2
" West Isles,	" 1, *5½, 6½, 8, ...	4
		41

GLOUCESTER COUNTY.

Parish of Bathurst,	Nos. 3, 4, 6, 7, *8, 10, 11,	7
" Beresford,	" *7 (and Bathurst), 7½ (and Bath), 8, *8½, 9, *10A (and Bathurst), 11, 12, 13, 13½, 14, 15, 16, ...	13
" Caraquet,	" 1, 3, 4, 4½, ...	4
" Inkerman,	" 1, 4, 5, 7, *8, ...	5
" New Bandon,	" 1, 3, 3½, 4½, 5½, 7, 10, ...	7
" Paquetville,	" 1, 2, *4, 5, ...	4
" Saumarez,	" 2, *2½, *4, 7, ...	4
" St. Isidore,	" *8, ...	1
" Shippegan,	" 1½, *3, *3½, 5, *6½, 8, 8½, 9, 9½ 10, 10½, ...	11
		56

KENT COUNTY.

Parish of Acadieville,	Nos. 1, 2, 3, 4, *5, 7, 8, 9,...	8
" Carleton,	" 2, 4, 6, 8, 9, 10, ...	6
" Dundas,	" *5, 5½, 6A (and Moncton) *10A (and Moncton), 14, ...	5
" Harcourt,	" 1, 6, 7, 7½, 10, 11, ...	6
" Richibucto,	" 3, 5, 7, 9, 9A, 11, 13, ...	7
" St. Louis,	" 1, *5, *8, *9 (and Richibucto), 10, 11, ...	6
" St. Mary's,	" 5, 7, 7½, *14, ...	4
" St. Paul,	" 1, 2, 3, *4, 5, 6, 7 (and St. Mary's) 9, ...	8

KENT COUNTY.—Continued.

Parish of	Weldford,	Nos. 2½, 4, 5½ (and St. Mary's), 7, 11, 12, 13, 17, 18, *20, 21, 22, 23, 24,	14
"	Wellington,	" *7½, *12½, 13, 15, 16, 17, 18, ...	7
			71

KINGS COUNTY.

Parish of	Cardwell,	Nos. 4, *8, 9, 10 (and Sussex)	4
"	Hammond,	" 1 (and Waterford), 2, *3, *5, 8 (and Sussex)....	5
"	Havelock,	" *5, 6, 11, 15	4
	Kars,	" 4, 6	2
"	Kingston,	" 6, 8, 9, 14, *15	5
"	Norton,	" 9, *11 (and Sussex)	2
"	Rothesay,	" *6	1
"	Springfield,	" *4, *5, *6 (and Johnston), *11 (and Wickham), *13, 14, 18, 21	8
"	Studholm,	" 1, 2, *5, *6 *19, *26....	6
"	Sussex,	" 4 (and Waterford), *8, 11, 12, 14 15....	6
"	Upham,	" 25 (and St. Martins)....	1
"	Waterford,	" 1, 3, 4 (and Cardwell), *6, 7, 9	6
"	Westfield,	" 5 (and Greenwich), *8, 9, *10, *12 *13	6
			56

MADAWASKA COUNTY.

Parish of	Madawaska,	Nos. 3, 4, 4½, 5, 6	5
"	St. Anne,	" *2, 5, 6, 7	4
"	St. Basil.	" 2, 5, 8, 9, 10	5
"	St. Francis,	" *5, 6, 7, 8, 9, 10, 11, 13, 14	9
"	St. Hilaire,	" 5, 6, 7, 8, 9....	5
"	St. Jacques,	" 2, 3, 4, 5	4
"	St. Leonard,	" 7, 8	2
			34

NORTHUMBERLAND COUNTY.

Parish of Alnwick,	Nos. *1, *2, 8½, *12, 14	5
" Blackville,	" 1½, 3, 3½, 9, 12, 13	6
" Blissfield.	" 1, *1½ (and Blackville), *2, *2½, 3	5
" Glenelg,	" *3, 5, 6, 8, 8½, 9	6
" Hardwicke,	" 3, 6	2
" Ludlow,	" 1, *1½, 2, 4, 5	5
" Nelson,	" 6, *6½, 7	3
" Newcastle,	" *2½	1
" Northesk,	" 1, 3, 11½	3
" Rogersville,	" 1, 2, 3A (and Acadieville), 5, 10½, *11, *13, *14, *15, 16 (and Acadieville)	10
" Southesk,	" 7, *7½	2
		48

QUEENS COUNTY.

Parish of Brunswick,	Nos. *3, 4, 5, 7, 23 (and Salisbury)....	5
" Cambridge,	" *6 (and Waterboro), *7, *9	3
" Canning,	" *2, 3, 4, 5, *6	5
" Chipman,	" 2, 3, 7, *9, 12, 13 (and Waterboro), 14 (and Waterboro), 16 (and Harcourt)	8
" Gagetown,	" *1, ...	1
" Hampstead,	" 3 (and Gagetown), 10, ...	2
" Johnston,	" 2, 6, *6 (and Springfield), 8, *9, *11 (and Wickham), *12, 13, *15, (and Springfield), 17	10
" Petersville,	" 2. *13, 16	3
" Waterboro,	" *2, 3, *5, *8 (and Johnston), 9	5
" Wickham,	" *10, *13 (and Johnston)	2
		44

RESTIGOUCHE COUNTY.

Parish of Addington,	Nos. *2½, 3	2
" Balmoral,	" 1, 4, 5, 6 (and Addington), ...	4

Restigouche County.—Continued.

Parish of Colborne,	Nos. 1½, (and Balmoral), 4		2
"	Dalhousie,	" 4	1
"	Durham,	" 1½, *5, 9, 10, 11	5
"	Eldon,	" *1	1
			15

St. John County.

Parish of Musquash,		Nos. *5, *7, *8, 9, ...	4
"	St. Martins,	" 1, *3, *3½. *4, 9, *11, *12, *23 (and Simonds), 30, ...	9
"	Simonds,	" *14, *15, *16, *20, *21 (Bdr), 22 (Bdr), ...	6
			19

Sunbury County.

Parish of Blissville,		Nos. *5, *6, 7, 8, ...	4
"	Burton,	" 6, *8, 9, 10, 11, 12, ...	6
"	Gladstone,	" *2, *3, 5, 6, 8, 9 (and New Maryland), ...	6
"	Lincoln,	" 6, ...	1
"	Maugerville,	" 4 (and St. Mary's), ...	1
"	Northfield,	" 1, 2, *3, 5, ...	4
"	Sheffield,	" 1A (and Canning), 3, 6, *7, ...	4
			26

Victoria County.

Parish of Andover,		Nos. 6, 8, ...	2
"	Drummond,	" 1½, 2, 3, 5, 6, 8½, 9, 11, 12, 13, 14,	11
"	Gordon,	" *2, 3, 7, *8, 9 (and Lorne), ...	5
"	Grand Falls,	" *2, 3, *4, 5, 8, 10, *11, ...	7
"	Lorne,	" 1, 2, 5, 8, ...	4
"	Perth,	" 3, 5, 6, 7, *8 (and Drummond), 10, *11, *12, *13, ...	9
			38

WESTMORLAND COUNTY.

Parish of Botsford,	Nos. *4, 20, 22, 23, ...	4
" Dorchester,	" *4 (and Sackville), 15, 26, ...	3
" Moncton,	" *6A (and Dundas), *20, *21, 22, *24, 25, 26, *30, 32, 33, ...	10
" Sackville,	" 1, 3, 4, 15, 17, 18, ...	6
" Salisbury,	" 9, 14, 23, (and Hav. and Bruns.), 25,	4
" Shediac,	" 22, 23, 24, 26, ...	4
" Westmorland,	" 11 (and Sackville), ...	1
		32

YORK COUNTY.

Parish of Bright,	Nos. *6½, 7½, 9, *11 (and Southampton)	4
" Canterbury	" *5, 10, 10½, 12, 20, 22, 24, ...	7
" Douglas,	" 12, 14, *16, 20, ...	4
" Kingsclear,	" *7, *8, 9, 12, ...	4
" Manners Sutton	" 7, 9, 10, 11, ...	4
" McAdam,	" *7, ...	1
" New Maryland,	" *1A, 3, ...	2
" North Lake,	" *13½, 17, 18, 19½, ...	4
" Prince William,	" 6	1
" St. Mary's	" 9, 10, 11, 14, ...	4
" Southampton,	" *8, *10, 13, 14, 15, *16, 17, 18, 19,	9
Stanley,	" 1½, 2, 4, 6½, *9, 14, *16, 17, ...	8
		52
	Total for 1904	593
	Increase, ...	3

*Districts marked * to receive one quarter rate.

School House Grants to Poor Districts.

By vote of the Legislature the sum of $1000 was appropriated at the last session to assist Poor Districts in building and furnishing school houses.

The following grants from this appropriation were made during the fiscal year ending October 31st, 1903:

ALBERT COUNTY.

District No. 5, Elgin	....	$50 00	
" 6, Hillsboro,	....	20 00	
			$70 00

CARLETON COUNTY.

District No. 9, Brighton,	....	$15 00	
" 1½, Peel,	....	10 00	
			$25 00

CHARLOTTE COUNTY.

District No. 5, Pennfield,	....	$60 00	
" 5, St. George,	....	70 00	
			$130 00

GLOUCESTER COUNTY.

District No. 15, Bathurst,	....	$10 00	
" 6, Beresford,	....	10 00	
" 4, Caraquet,	....	20 00	
" 1, New Bandon,	....	20 00	
" 3, " "	....	20 00	
" 8, St. Isidore,	....	20 00	
			$100 00

KENT COUNTY.

District No. 1, Acadieville,	....	$15 00	
" 2, "	....	15 00	
" 7, "	....	15 00	
" 4, Carleton	....	15 00	
" 10, Harcourt,	....	15 00	
" 3, St. Mary's	....	15 00	
			$90 00

KINGS COUNTY.

District No. 8, Cardwell.	....	$15 00	
" 5, Waterford,	....	20 00	
			$35 00

MADAWASKA COUNTY.

District No. 8, St. Basil,	....	$15 00	
" 14, St. Francis,	....	25 00	
" 1, St. Leonard's,	....	20 00	
" 9, "	....	15 00	
			$75 00

NORTHUMBERLAND COUNTY.

District No. 6, Hardwicke,.....	....	$25 00	
" 4, Rogersville and Glenelg,....	......	25 00	
" 5, Rogersville and Huskissen,	......	25 00	
" 16A, Rogersville and Acadieville,	......	15 00	
" 7, South Esk, ...	....	25 00	
			$115 00

QUEENS.

District No. 4, Cambridge,......	....	$20 00	
" 5, Hampstead and Greenwich,	......	25 00	
" 16, Petersville,	....	25 00	
			70 00

RESTIGOUCHE.

District No. 10, Durham, ...	....		$20 00

SUNBURY.

District No. 6, Gladstone,......	....	$10 00	
" 8, Gladstone,......	....	20 00	
" 5, Northfield,......	....	20 00	
			50 00

VICTORIA COUNTY.

District No. 3, Gordon, ...	....	$25 00	
" 14, Drummond,....	....	25 00	
			50 00

WESTMORLAND.

District No. 4, Salisbury, ...	....		25 00

YORK.

District No. 9, Kingsclear,	......	......	$20 00	
" 1A, New Maryland and Lincoln,		....	20 00	
" 2, New Maryland,	......	......	20 00	
" 18, Southampton,	......	......	20 00	
				80 00
Total,	......	......		$935 00

ARBOR DAY 1903.

From the reports sent to the Inspectors it appears that 467 districts observed Arbor Day, that 1557 trees and 347 shrubs were planted, that 544 flower beds were made and other general improvements effected in connection with the school grounds and buildings of 431 districts.

If the trees planted and improvements made on arbor day from year to year had been protected by proper enclosures and looked after by successive boards of Trustees and teachers, the majority of country districts would by this time have school premises attractive to the eye, a source of pleasure to the community and a valuable means of esthetic cultivation to the pupils: but unfortunately this has not been done. In very many cases the trees and shrubs planted one year are allowed before next Arbor Day to die for want of ordinary care, the flower beds are neglected and trampled upon, and the school area presents the same uninviting scene of ugliness and desolation intensified if possible by the leafless and unsightly relics of the former well meaning but fruitless attempts at improvement. Unless there is a constant, persistent and combined effort of teachers, parents and children to protect and beautify the school home, it would almost seem better to allow Nature to adorn the surroundings in her own inimitable way with grasses and mosses and lichens and the numerous growths with which she always aims, when given a fair chance, to cover up what is unsightly and offensive.

EMPIRE DAY.

Now that Empire Day has become a public school anniversary of almost national observance, it may be of interest to record the fact that Canada has the honor of having initiated the movement. At a meeting of the Dominion Educational Association held in Halifax in August 1898 a letter was read from the Hon. G. W. Ross, then Minister of Education of the Province of Ontario, in which he suggested the establishment of a school anniversary to be known as Empire Day and to be observed throughout the Dominion. After due consideration and discussion the following resolution was unanimously adopted.

Resolved: That this association recommends that the school day immediately preceding May 24th in each year be set apart as "Empire Day," and that the Departments of Education in the provinces and territories be respectfully requested to arrange for such exercises in their respective schools as will tend to the increase of a sound patriotic feeling.

The Education Departments throughout the Dominion, within the course of a year or two thereafter, had all taken official action and issued Regulations for the due observance of the day. The New Brunswick Regulation is as follows:

Empire Day: The last teaching day preceding the Queen's birthday in each year shall be observed in the schools as Empire Day. The lessons, recitations and other exercises of the day shall be such as bear directly upon the history and resources of Canada and the British Empire, and tend to promote a spirit of true patriotism and loyalty.

It is earnestly recommended that the school trustees shall provide for the school house a suitable flag-staff and a Canadian or British flag. The flag should be raised on Empire Day, the Queen's birthday, Dominion Day, Thanksgiving Day, the Anniversaries of great National events, the days of opening and closing the school in any term and on all school festivals and examination days.

In accordance with the above quoted Regulation and recommendation Empire Day is now observed very generally in our schools by special exercises of a patriotic character. A large number of districts have been provided with flags which are displayed over the school house on special and anniversary occasions. As the children look upon the beautiful emblem of imperial power floating in the breeze, a splendid opportunity is afforded to the teacher to explain its meaning, to recount its history, to awaken stirring memories of its hallowed past, to trace around the globe the stations of British sovereignty of which the flag is the universal symbol and signal, and to impress upon their sensitive minds not only the honor and privileges they enjoy as citizens of a world wide empire, but also the responsibilities which rest upon them to defend its honor, and to maintain and extend the free institutions which have been planted wherever the flag floats. The study of history and geography is thus imbued with living interest and tends to awaken sentiments of stalwart patriotism and devotion to duty.

Since the inception of this movement in Canada it has attracted attention and discussion throughout the Empire. Chiefly through the efforts of the Earl of Meath, by his advocacy of the measure in the House of Lords, and by correspondence with the Prime Ministers and Governors of Colonies, Empire day is now or shortly will be established by statute and regulation in most of the British Colonies and dependencies in Asia, Africa, America, and Australasia, as well as in the mother country.

Notes on the Appendices.

I beg to direct attention to Part III. of this Report which contains report of the Principal of the Normal School; reports of the several School Inspectors; reports of the School Boards of Cities and Towns organized under the provisions of Section 108 of the Schools Act; reports of the Chancellor of the University of New Brunswick, of the Director of Manual Training and of the travelling Instructor and Supervisor of School Gardens and Nature Lessons; proceedings of the County Teachers' Institutes; report of the Summer School of Science; report of the Board of Directors and the Principal of the School for the Blind.

I desire to add some notes and comments on these several Reports, and to make a few suggestions on matters therein referred to.

APPENDIX A.—THE NORMAL SCHOOL.

In addition to the facts stated in the Principal's report (Appendix A.) complete statistics as to attandance, classification, staff, salaries, etc. will be found in Table XIV., Page A36.

The necessity of increased accommodation in the Normal School is becoming very urgent, especiallly since the introduction of the Manual Training courses. Durning recent years the general attendance has increased considerably beyond what was anticipated when the building was erected, and in view of the prevailing and increasing scarcity of teachers it is important that every encouragement shall be held out to qualified young men and women to prepare themselves to fill the vacant places in the schools. Further, the ever expanding subject of Natural Science in its many applied forms is demanding more attention from year to year, and this involves the necessity of enlarged space and increased equipment. In this respect the Nova Scotia Normal School at Truro is much in advance of our own. Its physical, chemical and biological labaratories are commodious and well equipped and thus the best facilities are afforded for the study of plant and animal life as well as for illustrating the best methods of teaching subjects bearing upon agricultural pursuits.

I beg, therefore, to support the recommendation of Principal Crocket that steps be taken without delay to add to our Normal School building a wing or ell sufficiently large to provide accommodation for

Manual Training and Domestic Science Departments, for Natural Science Class rooms and laboratories, and for a properly equipped gymnasium for physical exercises.

APPENDIX B.—INSPECTORS' REPORTS.

A careful persual of the Inspectors' reports impresses one with the varied conditions under which our school operations are conducted, and the complexity of the problems which the Board of education is called upon to solve.

The contrast is almost painful between the conditions of the well graded, well equipped school in city or town, with its staff of trained teachers and crowded class rooms, and the conditions often met with by the Inspector in rural districts where poorly educated and untrained teachers have charge of schools destitute of almost every essential appliance for their work. These schools, with their small and irregular attendance, are often so isolated that the union of two or more into one district seems impracticable, and yet, under existing conditions, the prospect of improvement seems far off. But notwithstanding these discouraging aspects it is pleasant to notice that on the whole the tone of the Inspectors' reports is decidedly optimistic. Progress is noted as the rule. In the pictures drawn the light dominates over the shadows. This is markedly noticed in the interest taken by teachers, trustees and ratepayers in the improvement and better equipment of school buildings.

One of the most serious facts commented upon by each of the Inspectors is the number of schools closed because teachers could not be obtained.

DEATH OF INSPECTOR SMITH.

After a long and faithful service of over twenty-three years as Inspector of Schools, Mr. George Smith was obliged to give up his work in January, 1903, on account of failing health. Though he rallied sufficiently to enable him to resume work in March, the improvement was but temporary, and he died at his home in Sackville on the 28th of October last. He was appointed Inspector of Schools in 1879 and was the senior member of the staff of Inspectors. Mr. Smith was a man of sound judgment and unflinching integrity in the discharge of his duties. The Board of Education at the first meeting after Inspector Smith's death placed upon record its high appreciation of the services he had rendered to the cause of education in his native province.

NEW INSPECTORS.

It has been evident for many years that seven inspectors were not sufficient to discharge properly the important duties imposed upon them by statute and regulation. Their visitation of the schools was necessarily hurried, and some districts failed to receive a visit even once a year. Other important duties had to be neglected, or discharged in a very unsatisfactory way. The Board decided more than a year ago to appoint an additional inspector, but it was not until last April that the appointment was actually made. The man selected for the position was Mr. Charles D. Hebert, a graduate in Arts of St. Joseph's University. In June last he was assigned work, and up to the end of the year discharged faithfully the duties which Inspector Smith was unable to attend to. The record of his inspection will be found in appendix B. Mr. Hebert has already proved himself a faithful, tactful and painstaking official, and I anticipate much benefit, especially to schools in French speaking districts, from his careful supervision.

In December last Mr. Amos O'Blenes, a teacher of long and successful experience in all grades of schools, and who had occupied for the last three or four years the position of principal of the Model School in Fredericton, was appointed as successor to Inspector Smith, and entered upon his official duties in January.

The revision of the several Inspectorates rendered necessary by the appointment of an additional Inspector is given below.

INSPECTORAL DISTRICTS.

INSPECTORAL DISTRICT NO 1.

George W. Mersereau, M. A., Doaktown, Inspector.

The County of Restigouche, except the Parish of Balmoral and Districts No. 1½ Colborne and Balmoral and No. 3 Addington.

The County of Northumberland, except the Parish of Rogersville.

In the County of York, the Parish of Stanley.

INSPECTORAL DISTRICT NO. 2.

Jean Flavien Doucet, Bathurst, Inspector.

In the County of Restigouche, the Parish of Balmoral and Districts No. 1½ Colborne and Balmoral and No. 3 Addington.

The County of Gloucester.

The County of Madawaska.

In Victoria County, the Parishes of Drummond and Grand Falls, and District No. 8 in the Parishes of Perth and Drummond.

INSPECTORAL DISTRICT NO. 3.

Charles D. Hebert, B. A., Dupuis Corner, West'd, Inspector.

In the County of Northumberland, the Parish of Rogersville.

The County of Kent.

In the County of Westmorland, the Parishes of Botsford and Shediac; also Districts Nos. 3, 4, 6, 26, 27 and 30 in the Parish of Moncton; also the Parish of Dorchester, except Districts Nos. 1, 2, 3, 4, 5, 9, 14, 20, 21, and 22.

INSPECTORAL DISTRICT NO. 4.

Amos O'Blenes, Moncton, Inspector.

In the County of Westmorland, the Parishes of Westmorland, Sackville and Salisbury. In the Parish of Dorchester, Districts Nos. 1, 2, 3, 4, 5, 9, 14, 20, 21 and 22. The Parish of Moncton except Districts Nos. 3, 4, 6, 26, 27, and 30.

In the County of King's, the Parishes of Waterford and Cardwell. In the Parish of Havelock, Districts Nos. 1, 2, 8, 10, 13, 14 and 15: also District No. 23 in the Parishes of Havelock, Brunswick and Salisbury.

The County of Albert.

INSPECTORAL DISTRICT NO. 5.

Rufus P. Steeves, M. A., Sussex, Inspector.

The County of Kings, east of the St. John River, except the Parishes of Waterford and Cardwell and Districts Nos. 1, 2, 8, 10, 13, 14 and 15, in the Parish of Havelock and District No. 23 in the Parishes of Havelock, Brunswick and Salisbury.

In Queens County, the Parishes of Brunswick, Johnston, Wickham, Cambridge, Waterborough and Chipman.

In St. John County, the Parish of St. Martins.

INSPECTORAL DISTRICT NO. 6.

W. S. Carter, M. A., St. John, Inspector.

The City and County of St. John except the Parish of St. Martins.

The County of Charlotte except the Parishes of Clarendon, Dumbarton and St. James.

INSPECTORAL DISTRICT NO. 7.

Hedley V. B. Bridges, M. A., Fredericton, Inspector.

In the County of Kings, all Districts situate west of the River St. John.

In the County of Queens, the Parishes of Petersville, Hampstead, Gagetown and Canning.

In the County of Charlotte, the Parishes of Clarendon, Dumbarton and St. James.

The County of Sunbury.

The County of York except the Parishes of Stanley, Southampton, Canterbury, North Lake and McAdam.

INSPECTORAL DISTRICT NO. 8.

F. B. Meagher, M. A., Woodstock, Inspector.

In the County of York, the Parishes of Canterbury, North Lake, McAdam and Southampton.

The County of Carleton.

The County of Victoria except the Parishes of Drummond and Grand Falls, and District No. 8 in the Parishes of Perth and Drummond.

APPENDIX C.—SCHOOLS IN CITIES AND INCORPORATED TOWNS.

It is optional with incorporated towns to have their schools operated under the general provisions of the Schools Act, or by vote of the Town Council at a meeting called for the purpose, to adopt the provisions of sections 105-117, by which the school board is increased in number and appointed in part by the Town Council and in part by the Executive Government of the province.

The latter method has been adopted by the towns of St. Stephen, Milltown, Woodstock, Campbellton, Chatham and Newcastle, and has been in force since 1872 in the cities of Fredericton, St John and Moncton.

The reports of the School Boards of these cities and towns, as given in the appendix, show a vigorous administration and successful results.

The following figures indicate the importance and magnitude of the work controlled by these Boards:

	No. Teachers.	No. Pupils.	Av. No. Pupils to Each Teacher.	Expenditure 1902-3.
St. John,	154	7,331	47	$175,884 37
Fredericton,	26	1,169	45	19,293 40
Moncton,	34	1,795	53	23,965 91
St. Stephen,	12	557	47	6,237 98
Milltown,	9	315	35	3,749 12
Woodstock,	14	660	47	5,855 85
Campbellton,	8	407	51	4,648 72
Chatham,	21	987	47	9,303 64
Newcastle,	11	526	48	4,892 08
	289	13,747	47.6	$253,831 07

It is a matter of general interest to compare the school attendance, as reported by the school Boards of these towns, with the total population as given by the census of 1901:

City or Town.	Population.	No. Pupils	Enrolled.
Saint John	40,711	7,331	1 in 5.5
Fredericton	7,117	1,169	1 in 6.1
Moncton	9,026	1,795	1 in 5.03
St. Stephen	2,840	557	1 in 5.1
Milltown	2,044	315	1 in 6.5
Woodstock	2,984	660	1 in 4.5
Campbellton	2,652	407	1 in 6.5
Chatham	4,868	987	1 in 4.9
Newcastle	2,507	526	1 in 4.8
New Brunswick	331,120	59,313	1 in 5.59

It will be seen that the attendance in proportion to population in Fredericton, Milltown and Campbellton is less than the average of the whole Province, notwithstanding the fact that many of the country schools were not in operation during the term for which the calculation is made. Woodstock, Newcastle and Chatham show the best attendance; Milltown, Campbellton and Fredericton the lowest. I am not sufficiently acquainted with the local conditions in some of these towns to warrant me in expressing a confident opinion as to the causes of the differences indicated; but it may be safely affirmed that in most of them there must be a considerable number of children between six and fifteen years of age who are not getting the benefits which the School Law provides for them, and for which the property of the country is taxed. It is not an unreasonable assumption that, under normal conditions, at least one person out of five of the population of a city, town or province is of school age. On this assumption, the numbers not enrolled in any school during the year under review were as follows: the City of Saint John, 811; the City of Fredericton, 254; the town of Milltown, 94; the town of Campbellton, 123; the Province as a whole, 6911. In my opinion, the exact facts, if known, would show a much larger number growing up without schooling than the above assumption indicates.

The interest manifested in educational matters in the cities and towns is very gratifying. Large numbers attend the terminal examinations and exhibitions, and many of the leading citizens offer prizes to be awarded to the pupils in the several departments and standards. The High School Entrance Examinations have proved a valuable stimulus both to pupils and teachers of the common school grades, and success at the Normal School Entrance and University matriculation examinations has been looked forward to by the pupils of the high school grades as a goal worthy of their best efforts.

Another handsome new school building in St. John, the fifth since 1896. has been completed and occupied during the year at a cost of about $40,000. A full description is given in the report of the St. John City School Board. A cut prepared frcm a winter photograph forms a frontispiece to this report.

APPENDIX D.—THE UNIVERSITY OF NEW BRUNSWICK.

It will be seen by Chancellor Harrison's report that the University has the largest attendance of students in its history. The total number is 134 of whom 28 are women and 47 are new students. Four ninths of the students are in the engineering department. The staff of Professors is the same as last year. Prof. Davidson to whom leave of absence was granted two years ago is still unable to resume his duties, and Prof. I. Woodbridge Riley continues to fill the chair of Philosophy and Economics.

From the reports of the several Professors to the University Senate I summarize the following:

Professor Loring W. Bailey who has for forty-two years occupied the chair of Natural History and Geology gives about fifteen hours a week to the direct work of instruction. The subjects of his lectures include Botany, Mineralogy, Geology, Zoology and comparative Anatomy. Prof. Bailey says:

"The work of the year has, within our limitations of time and equipment, been entirely satisfactory. The interest in the subjects undertaken has been well sustained, and the progress made all that I could expect. At the same time I cannot but feel that much more could be done were we provided with even a small part of what is now considered necessary for the prosecution of biological studies. We are sadly in need of a microtome, of staining agents, of sterilizers, together with many of the appliances of microscopic technique, without which many of the most interesting and instructive experiments referred to in the text books have to be wholly passed over."

Professor W. T. Raymond reports in regard to the work in Latin and Greek. He says "The Freshman Class is especially good in these subjects, perhaps because we have all the first division matriculants at the University. * * * * * * One Senior, two Juniors, three Sophomores and two Freshmen are reading the work for honors or distinctions."

Professor A. M. Scott reports in regard to the Department of Physics and Electrical Engineering. The increase in the number of Electrical Engineering students has necessitated the giving of extra lectures. The total number taking the laboratory courses in Physics is 56, of whom 13 are working for honors and distinctions. Dr. Scott refers to the generous donation of Four Thousand Dollars, mentioned elsewhere, and the further sum of fifty dollars, sent without solicitation, for the better equipment of the engineering department. Prof. Scott concludes his report as follows:—"I wish to repeat what I said last year that everything seems to indicate that it is possible for the engineering department of the University of New Brunswick to become the School of Applied Science for the maritime provinces. No effort should be spared to maintain the lead and the high standing already obtained, as evidenced by the increased attendance this year."

Prof. Ernest Brydone-Jack reports that out of 48 new students who entered the University in October last, 26 entered for the engineering courses, and that at present there are 59 in that department. He says: "The work has progressed most satisfactorily during the past year, and the students have exhibited a marked interest and ability. I am giving 22 lectures a week in addition to looking after the work in the chemical laboratory, the cement laboratory, the testing laboratory, the drafting room and the field. The engineering camp held last fall was the most successful and largely attended of any yet held."

Prof. Jack urges the Senate to provide means whereby at least two or three additional instructors may be secured, and concludes:

"While I cannot but feel that a great deal has already been accomplished in the Engineering Department, I also feel very strongly that the head of this department should have time to devote to original research, to the preparation of outside lectures, to advertising the course by personal contact with young men and practising engineers, and to the making of tests and investigations on engineering materials and engineering projects. This would go very far indeed toward making our engineering department one of the leading and best known engineering schools in the whole Dominion. In order to do this, however, the head of the department must have more time at his disposal than he has at present."

Professor W. H. Clawson reports in reference to the departments of English and French, giving a detailed statement of the work in the several classes. In addition to his regular work in French and English he has given a course of three hours a week in elementary German. The following is a summary of the enrolment of students in the several classes: Freshman, English, 34; Freshman French, 24; Freshman German, 14; Sophomore English, 36; Sophomore French, 20; Junior and Senior English, 36; Junior and Senior, French, 7. Professor Clawson says in conclusion:

"I am this year giving sixteen lectures a week. With large classes, interest and eagerness to work, and a Freshman class of very promising material, the prospects for a successful year in English, French and German are very bright."

Professor I. W. Riley of the Chair of Philosophy and Economics reports in Sophomore Logic, 42; Junior Psychology, 16; Junior Economics, 17; Senior Economics, 17; Honor Philosophy, 27: Experimental Psychology, 18. In Experimental Psychology, Prof. Riley has introduced an entirely new course in regard to which he says:

"The new psychological laboratory has opened with three hundred dollars worth of apparatus. About half of this amount was generously contributed by an anonymous donor who wishes to be known as "An American Student," twenty-five dollars was appropriated by the University Senate last year, while the balance is made up of gifts from the friends of the University. Among these gifts may be mentioned a complete set of studies from the Yale Psychological Laboratory and donations from Robert L. Gerry of New York, Dr. Murray MacLaren, W. H. Murray, Dr. J. R. McIntosh, James F. Robertson, Rev. J. de Soyres, Edward Flood, Dr. T. D. Walker, D. O. P. Lewin, Mr. and Mrs. Robert Fitz Randolph, F. B. Edgecombe, McMurray & Co and Arthur A. Shute. "So far as known no systematic experiments have hitherto been carried on among University students in the Maritime Provinces such as are embodied in the publications of the Toronto

Psychological laboratory. Much less has there been any practical application in the public schools of the most recent Pedagogical methods borrowed from experimental Psychology."

The handsome gift of four thousand dollars towards the endowment of the chairs of Civil and Electrical Engineering by a St. John lady is an event of more than usual interest. It is, I believe, the largest individual gift ever made to the University; and should stimulate others to follow so generous an example.

The first selection of a scholar from this Province under the provisions of the Rhodes bequest is to be made by the University of New Brunswick within the next few months, under conditions prescribed by the trustees of the fund. The candidate selected will enter Oxford University in October next.

APPENDIX D (II).—MANUAL TRAINING.

The progress made during the year in this new department of our public school work is explained in detail in the report of Mr. E. E. MacCready, the Director of Manual Training. A careful perusal of this report will be found interesting to all who are interested in the development of hand-work in our schools. The number of School Districts which have already availed themselves of the liberal provisions offered by the Legislature indicates the popularity of the movement. This number will be probably doubled during the next year. At present eleven districts are conducting Manual Training to a greater or less extent, and 950 pupils are taking the work. One of the most satisfactory results reported in connection with the movement is the increased interest awakened among the pupils, not only in the manual training rooms, but in the ordinary studies of the schools in which Sloyd work has been introduced. The testimony of teachers and parents in this respect is almost unanimous.

The schools at Inches' Ridge, Musquash and Fredericton were supplied with benches and tools by the MacDonald fund. The cost of equipment at the Normal School has been paid through the Public Works Department. Up to the present date (Feb., 1904) the sum total of goverment grants paid by the Chief Superintendent under the provisions of the Manual Training Act, 1902, is $1,051.80 for equipment, and $659.35 grants to teachers. The detailed statement is appended.

EQUIPMENT.

	Gov. Grant.	Total Exp'd'e
Mascarene, No. 12, St. George	$ 35 54	$ 71 08
St. Andrews	121 83	243 66
Campbellton	156 64	313 28
St. Stephen	284 04	568 08
Milltown	194 53	389 06
Florenceville	145 54	291 08
Sackville	113 68	227 36
	$1,051 80	$2,103 60

GRANTS TO TEACHERS.

Term ended December, 1902.

Bessie Kelly, Inches' Ridge	$ 18 99	
Agnes E Lucas, Musquash	14 34	
		$33 33

Term ended June, 1903.

Agnes E. Lucas, St. Andrews	$ 60 00	
Harriette Bolt, Mascarene	20 93	
Ethel I. Mersereau, Campbellton	102 43	
Sadie E. Inch, Musquash	28 60	
Bessie B. Kelly, Inches' Ridge	27 44	
		239 40

For term ended Dec. 1903.

Marjorie F. Mair, Florenceville	$ 19 17	
A. Gertrude O'Brien, Woodstock	78 64	
Ethel I. Duffy, St. Andrews	37 86	
Harriette Bolt, Mascarene	19 21	
Will Whitney, St. Stephen and Milltown	55 34	
Louise Wetmore, Campbellton	76 70	
Bessie B. Kelly, Inches' Ridge,	21 06	
Agnes E. Lucas, Fredericton	78 64	
		$ 386 62
		$ 659 35

There has also been paid for travelling expenses to teachers attending Manual Training Departments at Truro and Fredericton the sum of $75,42.

APPENDIX D (III) —REPORT OF MR. JOHN BRITTAIN INSTRUCTOR IN NATURE LESSONS AND SUPERVISION OF SCHOOL GARDENS.

As stated in my last report, Mr. Brittain was appointed by Prof. Robertson with the consent and approval of the Board of Education, as a travelling instructor to inaugurate a system of school gardens and to supervise the teaching of nature lessons with special reference to practical agriculture. Mr. Brittain was also authorized by the Board of Education to arrange, in consultation with trustees and teachers, the time tables of the schools with the view of so correlating the subjects of instruction that, while due attention should be given to the new subjects, the other subjects should not be in any degree neglected.

Mr. Brittain's report shows that he has entered upon his work with energy and success. Land for school gardens at Woodstock, Hartland, Florenceville and Andover has been secured, and the necessary preparations made for enclosing and cultivating these garden plots during the coming season. The province has incurred no expense in connection with Mr. Brittain's work, the whole cost both for salary and gardens being provided from the MacDonald fund except the amounts contributed towards the purchase of land by the districts interested. If, however, the work as is now anticipated, shall prove to be so useful as to call for measures to ensure its permanence, provision must be made in the near future for the training and remuneration of teachers to carry it on It will be but reasonable to place those teachers who may qualify themselves for imparting special horticultural and agricultural instruction, such as may be illustrated by means of school gardens, on the same footing as to provincial grants, as the law now places teachers of Manual Training and Domestic Science.

CONSOLIDATED SCHOOLS.

The suggested uniting of Districts for the purpose of forming a strong central school to which the children from a distance may be conveyed in vans is gradually gaining the attention of progressive School Boards in various parts of the province. Inquiries have been made by the school officials of Districts in Carleton, Charlotte, Kings, Queens, Northumberland Restigouche and York as to the merits and details of the system, and the conditions upon which Government aid will be given.

In Albert County I am glad to report that matters have so far progressed that the establishing of a consolidated school is assured. At a meeting of the the Trustees and other representatives of School Districts Nos. 1, 9 and 10, Hopewell and Nos. 5 and 9 Harvey, held at the call of the Chief Superintendent on the 19th of November last, it was finally decided to unite and to erect a school building between Albert and Riverside to accommodate the children of the five Districts. The school is to have Manual Training and Domestic Science Departments, to have ample play grounds and garden, and to be in other respects equal to the best city schools. It will be the Grammar school for the County, and will probably have from 300 to 400 pupils from the united Districts, besides attracting advanced pupils from all parts of the County. A staff of seven or eight teachers will be required. A central Board of Trustees in which all the uniting Districts are represented has been appointed, and steps will be taken to commence the erection of a building in the spring as soon as the frost is out of the ground. The Hon. A. R. McClellan, ex-Lieutenant-Governor, has promised a donation of $5000 towards the building fund. It is hoped to have the school opened in September. The outlook is very promising, and if nothing occurs to check the enterprise, Albert County will soon have the best school of its kind in the Province.

THE MACDONALD CONSOLIDATED SCHOOL AT KINGSTON, KINGS CO.

Under the provisions of an Act passed by the Legislature on the 9th of May, 1903, six School Districts in the Parish of Kingston and one District in the Parish of Rothesay agreed to unite for three years into one District and to maintain therein, in conjunction with Prof. Robertson as administrator of the Sir William MacDonald Rural School Fund, a graded school with special branches in nature study, manual training and household science. At the annual school meetings in June each of the confederating Districts elected a representative as member of a Central School Board to be known as "The Trustees of Kingston Consolidated School District No. 1." The Board is now organized and has charge of the property of the Consolidated District.

Plans and specifications for the new building had been prepared, when Prof. Robertson's health broke down under the pressure of over-work, and he was obliged to seek rest and recuperation on the other side of the Atlantic. Mr. R. H. Cowley of Ottawa, as the representative of Prof. Robertson, came to the Maritime Provinces in June and consulted with me in regard to the continuance of the work. At Mr. Cowley's request I assumed the responsibility of advertising for tenders, entering into a contract and supervising, with the assistance of the architect, the completion of the building.

The regrettable illness of Prof. Robertson and other unforeseen difficulties combined to delay the completion of the school building in time for occupancy during the present school year. The contract was not awarded until the month of July, and the completed building was not handed over to the Kingston School Board until February, 1904. It was then deemed prudent not to attempt to open the school until the beginning of the school year in August next. This will afford ample time in the spring and early summer to furnish and equip the building in all its departments, to grade the grounds, to make the walks and cultivate the garden plot, so that the whole institution may be ready for an auspicious opening at the beginning of the term.

The building presents a handsome appearance, as will be seen by the cut facing this page.

It occupies a commanding site, being that formerly occupied by the Kings County Court House, on the summit of the hill upon which Kingston is built.

The building is of wood of two and a half stories, and a brick basement nine and a half feet high. The roof is steep-pitched, terminating with ventilating turrets, and is shingled with creosote stained shingles. The walls are covered with clapboards and fancy cut shingles.

There are three schoolrooms of 26x33 feet, and a teachers' room on the ground floor. One of these rooms is used for "manual training" and will be fitted up with the usual appliances for that purpose.

The second floor has three rooms of 26x33 feet, a laboratory and a principal's room, to be fitted up as a library, etc. One of the rooms on this floor will be used for teaching "household science," and will be fitted up for that purpose.

In the halls of each of these two floors are cloak rooms, made of wire, six and a half feet high.

The assembly hall, 80x27 feet, is on the third floor, and there is also on the same floor a spare room over the household science room.

The basement contains playrooms for wet weather, and the hot-air furnaces and fuel.

The sanitaries are in a separate building, the dry earth system being used.

Messrs. McKean & Dunn were the architects, and the contractor was Mr. J. L. Schiefer.

The total expenditure on the building, grounds and school vans to date

THE MACDONALD CONSOLIDATED SCHOOL,
KINGSTON, KING'S CO.

is about $16,000. A large stable or shed to protect the vans will be erected in the Spring. The complete plant when furnished and equipped will probably cost in the vicinity of $20,000.

Seven vans will be required, costing about $180 each delivered at Kingston. Two of these vans have already been forwarded, the others are in Ottawa awaiting orders to be shipped. I have obtained a photo-gravure of one of the vans, loaded with school children, as it appeared standing in front of an Ottawa school. The cut faces page lxiv.

The McDonald fund is chargeable with the entire cost of the building furnished and equipped, the entire cost of the vans delivered at Kingston, half the cost of conveying the children to the school, the cost of maintaining the school and paying the salaries of the teachers for three years—less the usual provincial grants to the teachers, the County Fund grant, and a levy upon the united Districts annually, equal to the average amount voted at the school meetings for school maintenance for the years 1899 to 1901 inclusive.

The gentleman appointed as Principal of the school is Mr. D. W. Hamilton, M. A., a graduate of the University of New Brunswick, and an experienced and successful teacher. In special preparation for the duties of his new position, Mr. Hamiliton spent last year taking short courses at the University of Chicago, Cornell University, the teachers' college of the University of Columbia and at Guelph Agricultural College. Since October last, while awaiting the opening of the Kingston school, Mr. Hamilton has been rendering very efficient service at the Normal School.

School Boards in many parts of the Province are awaiting with interest the outcome of the educational experiment at Kingston. The difficulties to be met and overcome are greater at Kingston than at many other places that might have been selected. The success of the experiment there will ensure the establishing of other schools in various localities. The experience acquired during the three years' management under the MacDonald plans will furnish School Boards elsewhere with valuable lessons by means of which they may avoid mistakes inevitable in the launching of a new enterprise, and by which economy in expenditure without the imperiling of educational efficiency may be secured.

APPENDIX E.—REPORTS OF TEACHERS' INSTITUTES AND SUMMER SCHOOL OF SCIENCE.

These annual gatherings of teachers for mutual improvement and discussion of educational topics and methods have proved of special advantage to the teaching profession. The opinion has been expressed in my hearing that their chief attraction to the majority of teachers is the opportunity afforded for a pleasant outing and social intercourse with those employed in similar pursuits. If this opinion were correct the wisdom of holding teachers' conventions would still be justified; but while pleasant outings and social intercourse are quite as necessary and beneficial to teachers as to other classes, much more is aimed at and much more is gained than recreative and social pleasures. The educative influence of such associations in the interchange of experience, in the comparison and illustration of methods, and in the direct instruction imparted, is manifest in the fact that the teachers who regularly attend the meetings of the Institutes are, as a whole, the most progressive and efficient teachers we have.

The Summer School of Science, as will be seen by the Secretary's report, was held last year at Chatham with an enrolment of 90. The President, Prof. L. W. Bailey, LL. D., of the University of New Brunswick, with a staff of able instructors selected from the prominent teachers of the Atlantic Provinces, gave courses of lectures on various literary, scientific and pedagogical subjects to large classes of earnest and interested students.

The next session of the school is to be held at Charlottetown, P. E. I. opening on July 13th and closing on July 29th, 1904.

THE EDUCATIONAL INSTITUTE OF NEW BRUNSWICK

The Provincial Institute meets biennially. Its last meeting was held at Fredericton in June 1902. The next meeting will be held in the High School, Saint John, on Tuesday, June 28th, 1904, and the two following days. It is expected that 500 teachers will be in attendance, that addressess will be delivered by a prominent educationalist from the United States, as well as by leading teachers and public men of our own and other Provinces of the Dominion, and that subjects of vital interest to all interested in educational progress will be discussed.

THE DOMINION EDUCATIONAL ASSOCIATION.

The next meeting of the Dominion Educational Association will be held in the city of Winnepeg during the last week in June. Every province and territory from ocean to ocean will be represented at this important gathering of teachers convened at the growing central city of the wide Dominion. It is hoped that many New Brunswick teachers will avail themselves of the opportunity which this convention will offer to become better acquainted with the central and western portions of Canada, and especially with the vigorous educational movements which are aiming to keep pace with the rapid settlement of the country. There are many educational problems which are not merely provincial but national; and perhaps there is no more effective agency for the cultivation of a national spirit and the quickening of true patriotism than an interchange of thought and sentiment among the educators of widely separated provinces of the united country. Detailed information as to the programme of the convention, railway fares side excursions, etc., will be published at an early day.

The first meeting of the Association was held in the city of Montreal in 1891. Since that date meetings have been held in Toronto, Halifax and Ottawa. The Association will probably meet triennially hereafter.

APPENDIX F.—THE SCHOOL FOR THE BLIND, HALIFAX.

This eminently successful school continues to develop greater efficiency year after year. Though the school is situated in another province, and most of its endowments have come from citizens of that province, yet the blind children of New Brunswick are admitted to all its advantages on equal terms with the blind pupils of Nova Scotia.

For the first term of the school year which ended June 30th, 1903, the number of pupils in attendance from New Brunswick was 31, and for the second term 30. The total amount paid on account of these pupils was $4,493.08, of which one half was granted from the provincial revenues and one half from the County Fund of the several counties in which the pupils had a legal settlement.

Among the prize winners I find the names of the following New Brunswick pupils: Leon Duffy, Hillsboro'; Edward Legere, Shediac; Arthur Lindsay, St. John; Robert Rankin, Chipman; Charles Howell, Grand Manan; Frank Hanna, Moncton, Grover Livingstone, Harcourt; Alberta Kinsella, St. John.

The new building recently completed, at a cost of about $60.000, of which the Legislature of Nova Scotia contributed $20,000 and over $20,000 more has already been raised by private subscriptions, will add greatly to the comfort of the pupils and the success of the several departments of literary and industrial training.

EDUCATION OF DEAF AND DEAF MUTE PERSONS.

Following the suggestions in my last annual report, the provincial legislature in the act to revise and consolidate the general public statutes,

passed in May last, embodied a chapter authorizing the Board of Education to make an arrangement with the Directors of the Institution for the deaf and dumb at Halifax to admit New Brunswick pupils into that long established school. In pursuance of this object a deputation from the Board of Education held a conference at Halifax with the President and Directors of the Institution for the deaf and dumb, and came to an agreement by which all the benefits and privileges of that school are to be thrown open to deaf and deaf-mute persons from New Brunswick on precisely the same conditions as those on which Nova Scotia persons of the same class are admitted. Immediately after these arrangements were completed the following notice was inserted in the Royal Gazette, and a copy sent to all the parents of the children who had been in attendance at the school for the deaf and dumb in Fredericton up to the date of its closing in June 1902, so far as their addresses could be obtained:

"The parents and guardians of deaf and deaf-mute children in the Province of New Brunswick, are hereby notified that the Board of Education has made arrangements with the Board of Directors of the Institution for the deaf and dumb at Halifax, Nova Scotia, for the admission to said Institution of deaf and deaf-mute pupils from New Brunswick. Pupils of the Deaf and Dumb Institution at Fredericton, who on the 30th of June, 1902, had not completed at that Institution the full term of years' attendance to which they were entitled by statute, will be admitted to the Halifax School for the completion of their course, on the presentation of a certificate signed by the Chief Superintendent of Education of the Province of New Brunswick.

"Application on behalf of any other deaf or deaf-mute person for whom admission is desired to the Halifax School, must be made to the Warden of the Municipality, or the Mayor of the city, within which such deaf or deaf-mute person has a settlement under the provisions of Chapter 179 of the consolidated statutes, 1903, for an order for the admission of such person into the Institution for the deaf and dumb at Halifax. On receipt of such application the said Wården or Mayor, on being satisfied that such deaf or deaf-mute person is between the ages of six and twenty years, and has a legal settlement in the municipality or city, shall at once grant such order for admission under his hand and the corporate seal of the municipality or city, and forward the same to the provincial secretary for his approval to be endorsed thereon.

The parents, guardians or other friends of deaf and deaf mute persons for whom admission to the Halifax School is desired, are requested to communicate with the Chief Superintendent of Education, Fredericton, or Mr. James Fearon, principal of the Institution for the deaf and dumb, Halifax, who will give all necessary information and assistance."

In response to this advertisement many letters of inquiry were received by the Chief Superintendent, and it was confidently expected that at least twenty New Brunswick children would enter the Halifax school at its opening in September. In the meantime announcements were made that a school for the deaf and dumb was to be established at Lancaster, in the County of St. John, chiefly through the zealous efforts of Mr. Harvey Brown, supported by the generous contributions of citizens of St. John. The

Lancaster school was opened in the autumn, and most of the parents of the deaf and dumb children were induced to send to the nearer school. For the term which ended in December, 1903, there were only four New Brunswick children at the Halifax school.

EDUCATION OF THE FEEBLE MINDED.

There is another class of defective children whose guardianship and training have hitherto received but little attention in Canada. In this regard we are far behind Switzerland, France, Germany, England and the United States. Large institutions for the education and care of feeble-minded children have been in successful operation for many years in the States of Massachusetts, Connecticut, New York, Pennsylvania, New Jersey, Ohio, Indiana and probably in other States. The results of these efforts in behalf of the large numbers of mentally defective children, grading in point of intelligence from the weak-minded to the idiotic, have been on the whole satisfactory. The very worst cases are found improvable to some extent—usually to a relatively great extent. Their physical habits are trained. They are taught decency; they are made useful in many humble employments; they are raised to the level of social beings, and the tendency to further degeneration in mind and body is held in check. A considerable per centage become capable, with friendly oversight, of earning their own living and becoming useful members of society.

I can find no reliable data upon which the number of imbecile, semi-idiotic and idiotic children in New Brunswick can be determined; but there are certainly enough to appeal to the sympathy of the philanthropic and to the protective care of the legislature. This unfortunate class is not only a burden but sometimes a positive danger to society. For want of a more suitable refuge they are often sent to the Lunatic Asylum where they become a permanent charge upon the country, with but slight chances of any amelioration of their wretched condition.

An Institution for the Maritime Provinces similar to that at Waltham, Mass. might be established and maintained by the provinces of New Brunswick, Nova Scotia and Prince Edward Island, without imposing too heavy a burden upon any one province. There can be no doubt that such an Institution would call forth the benevolence of philanthropic and charitable people, who would gladly share with the state the cost of its maintenance. As the school for the Blind, and the school for the Deaf and Dumb, to both of which this province contributes, are located at Halifax, it would be but reasonable that the proposed interprovincial Institution should be located in New Brunswick.

Suggestions and Recommendations.

SALARIES OF TEACHERS.

It is universally admitted that the salaries of teachers are shamefully inadequate. The difficulty of finding a sufficient supply of teachers of any class, the unhappy alternative that constantly presents itself of allowing schools to remain closed or of placing them in charge of untrained and incompetent teachers, the fact that male teachers are being gradually but surely forced out of the profession, the constant exodus of our most progressive teachers of both sexes into other employments and pursuits or to other countries where they hope to find better remuneration in their chosen profession,—all these indicate the gravity of the crisis through which we are passing. What is the remedy? It is easy to suggest a remedy, perhaps not so easy to make it available.

There has been for many years sufficient financial encouragement held out to our young people to induce them to enter upon the work of teaching. The Normal School has been crowded, hundreds yearly pass the prescribed examinations, and most of them enter upon the work of teaching for a few terms. Then they drift out, and other novices take their place. Except in the cities, towns and a few of the larger villages, the teachers' salary is rarely if ever, increased. Experience counts for nothing; the novice commands as high a salary as the teacher who has gained pedagogical wisdom by years of honest toil in his profession. The Board of Education in its efforts to raise the standard by requiring candidates for the teaching profession to undergo professional training and rigid examinations is like a man who dips up water in a sieve only to see the sparkling drops escape nearly as fast as he has lifted them from the source of their supply.

To remedy the evil we must make it worth while for the successfu teacher to *remain* in the business of teaching as a profession. There must be advancement to look forward to, prospects of gaining positions to which salaries are attached sufficient, as to amount and permanence, to justify a prudent man in assuming the responsibility of marrying. For femal teachers the salaries should be at least equal to the amount which an intelli gent trained nurse, stenographer or shop woman can now command. Furthe the salary should be progressive—that is, it should be graded, according t experience acquired in successful teaching, up to a maximum, say, at th end of the seventh year of service. If, in addition to this, a retiring allowance could be provided for all teachers after twenty-five years of faithful service, there would be no occasion to complain of the difficulty of finding good teachers.

How are increased salaries to be provided? By an increase from each of the three sources which now contribute towards the teachers' salary—the provincial revenues, the county fund and local assessment.

In view of the large proportion of the Provincial revenues now appropriated to educational purposes—an amount which will be considerably increased by recent legislation for the promotion of Manual Training and for the encouragement of District consolidation—it is doubtful whether much larger appropriations can be made from this source. Yet, considering the importance and urgency of the case, I do not hesitate to press upon the attention and favorable consideration of the Government and Legislature the following recommendations:

(a) That the Provincial Grant to teachers of the first and second Class, after two years of sevice in the public schools, shall be increased by ten per cent for the third year, and by a further ten per cent each additional year thereafter until a maximum is reached of $200 per year for First Class Male Teachers; $160 for Second Class Male Teachers; $150 for First Class Female Teachers, and $120 for Second Class Female Teachers.

(b) That the provision now in force authorizing special grants to teachers of manual training and domestic economy be extended to include properly qualified and certificated teachers of horticulture and agriculture as illustrated by school gardens.

It will be seen that the above recommendation does not contemplate the increase of grants to Third Class Teachers, or to the teachers of Superior and Grammar Schools; nor does it provide for increasing the amount of the present grants to any class until after two years of service. Of course, all teachers who have already served two years or more would have a claim for the increase, according to their period of service, as soon as the proposed law is brought into force.

The County Fund: I recommend further that the sum of $40 per year (instead of $30 as at present) be paid directly to teachers out of the County Fund; and that in order to meet this additional claim upon the Fund, the amount levied upon each County shall be equal to Forty cents for every inhabitant of the county, instead of Thirty cents as at present.

Parish Assessment: I recommend further that each Parish (so far as may be found practicable) shall constitute a single School District, with a School Board elected or appointed as the Legislature may determine. Among the important duties of the Parish School Board would be the grouping of the present Districts and the establishing of central graded schools wherever the conditions would permit, the appointment of competent teachers, and the local supervision of all the schools of the Parish by the agency of a paid secretary. The minimum rate of assessment should not be less than one half of one per cent. of the assessable valuation of the Parish. The sum thus raised, supplemented by the County Fund Grant, and a special Provincial grant to poor Parishes equal to the amounts now paid to Poor Districts, would, in my opinion, be sufficient to provide much better school privileges for all the children than many of them now enjoy. It would assure a more intelligent and effective administration of the law. It would take the management of the schools out of the hands of illiterate and incompetent trustees, and would diminish the dissensions and factious disturbances which in not a few Districts make the annual school meeting a scene of disorder. It would enable the trustees to increase the local salaries of the teachers by at least fifty per cent. without imposing too heavy a burden upon any locality.

Unless the ratepayers and trustees of Districts can be influenced in some way to recognize the necessity of contributing much more liberally than heretofore, by local assessment, to the salaries of teachers, any possible increases from the Provincial revenues and the County Fund will fail to meet the exigencies of the case. In some localities the tendency has been apparent to diminish the local contribution in proportion to the amount of outside aid received. Indeed instances have not been unknown in which the District has contributed absolutely nothing to the support of the teacher. It might be well to require a minimum sum from Districts equal to the amount of the Provincial and County Fund grants combined.

FREE TEXT BOOKS.

The question has been raised in the discussions of some School Boards as to the expediency of providing text books and school supplies at the expense of the district and distributing them free to the school children. In twelve states and many of the cities of the American Republic text books are required to be furnished free. In others it is left optional with the school committees. Plausible arguments may be urged both for and against the practice. In my opinion permission ought to be granted to School Boards wishing to try the experiment. I beg, therefore, to recommend that at the approaching session of the legislature, section 23 of the Schools Act be so amended as to authorize any district to provide by assessment for supplying text books and other necessary materials for the use of the pupils in the school or schools of said District.

All of which is respectfully submitted.

I have the honour to be

Your Honour's most obedient servant,

JAMES R. INCH,

Chief Supt. of Education.

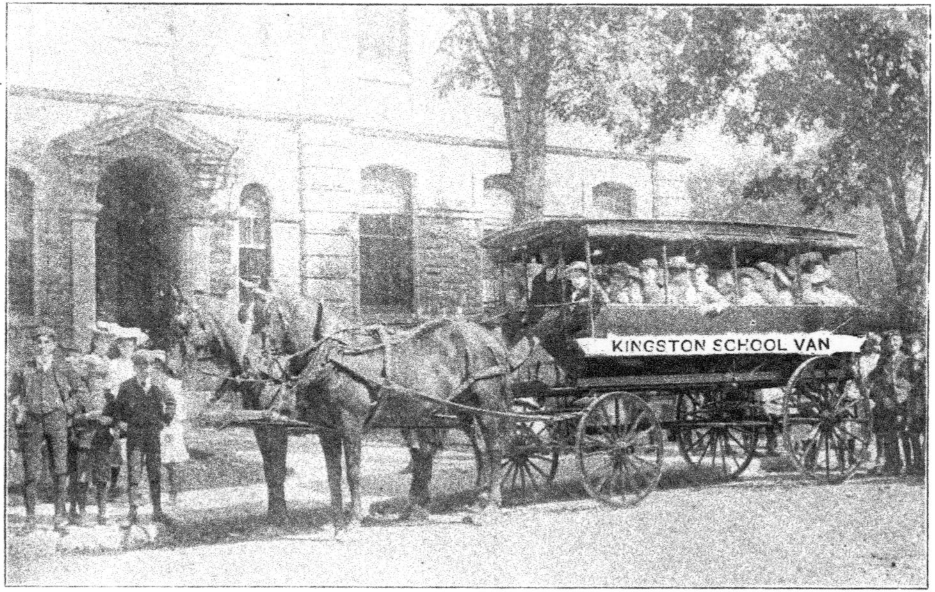

A KINGSTON SCHOOL VAN IN FRONT OF AN OTTAWA SCHOOL.

PART II.

STATISTICAL TABLES.

ERRATA.

TABLE I., 6th column, page A. 3.

In second line, instead of 4168 read 4618.
In sixteenth line, instead of 58863 read 59313.

TABLE V., Part I., 5th column, page A 18.

In fourth line and following lines,	instead of	41	read	40.
	"	101	"	38.
	"	144	"	56.
	"	50	"	37.
In ninth and folllowing lines,	"	56	"	38.
	"	41	"	17.
	"	70	"	27.
	"	40	"	18.
	"	54	"	22.
	"	168	"	72.
	"	176	"	83.
	"	1115	"	622.

In last two lines, instead of Increase 477 read Decrease 16

TABLE I. PUBLIC SCHOOLS: For the Year Ended June 30th, 1903. Preliminary.

COUNTIES.	First Term Closed 31st December, 1902.			Second Term Closed 30th June, 1903.					Year Ended 30th June, 1903.		
	Schools.	Teachers and Assistants.	Pupils in attendance at Schools.	Schools.	Teachers and Assistants.	Pupils in attendance at Schools.	New Pupils in attendance this Term, at Schools in operation both Terms.	New Pupils in attendance this Term, at Schools not in operation the previous Term.	No. of Districts having Schools in operation during the Dec. Term, that were without Schools in the June Term.	No. of Districts having Schools in operation in the June Term, that were without Schools in the Dec. Term.	Total No. of different Pupils in attendance at Schools within the year.
Albert	70	72	2,000	68	77	2,055	262	134	9	6	2,396
Carleton	141	143	3,854	151	154	4,168	697	421	15	19	4,972
Charlotte	132	139	3,944	135	146	4,336	453	125	3	6	4,537
Gloucester	108	113	4,236	105	111	4,092	382	112	8	3	4,730
Kent	119	122	3,809	116	121	4,003	484	325	13	11	4,618
Kings	153	160	3,701	148	150	3,847	506	233	18	14	4,440
Madawaska	60	60	2,091	57	58	2,179	317	69	6	3	2,438
Northumberland	149	156	4,981	141	145	4,914	513	43	11	2	5,537
Queens	86	86	1,885	83	86	2,052	285	140	12	8	2,319
Restigouche	49	51	1,823	45	47	1,734	158	....	5	....	1,981
Saint John	210	238	8,969	206	234	8,832	389	....	5	....	9,358
Sunbury	41	43	967	40	41	1,053	121	47	5	4	1,135
Victoria	57	59	1,395	53	54	1,501	231	171	9	6	1,797
Westmorland	207	216	8,146	195	201	8,094	867	55	15	3	9,068
York	196	200	5,717	183	190	6,003	769	115	17	4	6,601
New Brunswick	1,778	1,858	57,518	1,726	1,815	58,863	6,434	1,999	151	89	65,927
Cor. Terms, 1901-1902	1,795	1,869	58,575	1,736	1,825	60,477	6,688	2,162	107	139	67,681
Increase									44		
Decrease	17	11	1,057	10	10	1,614	254	163		50	1,754

TABLE II.—PUBLIC SCHOOLS: FOR THE YEAR ENDED 30TH JUNE, 1903.

PART ONE.—The First Term closed 31st December, 1902.

COUNTIES.	No. of Pupils at School this Term.	Proportion of the population at School this Term (Census of 1901).	AGE AND SEX OF PUPILS. Number under 6 years of age.	Number between the ages of 6 and 15 years of age.	Number over 15 years of age.	Boys.	Girls.	Grand total day's attendance made by the Pupils enrolled.	Number daily present on an average during the time the Schools were in session.	Number daily present on an average for the full Term.	Number daily present on an average during the time in Session per hundred enrolled.	Number daily present on an average for full Term per hundred enrolled.
Albert	2,000	1 in 5.46	58	1,852	90	972	1,028	113,616½	1,320	1,248	66.00	62.40
Carleton	3,854	1 in 5.61	136	3,501	217	1,827	2,027	213,406½	2,474	2,336	64.19	60.61
Charlotte	3,944	1 in 5.68	76	3,688	180	1,946	1,998	226,429	2,812	2,475	71.29	62.75
Gloucester	4,236	1 in 6.59	93	4,035	108	2,160	2,076	222,197	2,562	2,478	60.48	58.49
Kent	3,809	1 in 6.29	145	3,572	92	1,952	1,857	204,707½	2,385	2,312	62.61	60.69
Kings	3,701	1 in 5.85	78	3,432	191	1,812	1,889	199,430½	2,334	2,156	63.06	58.25
Madawaska	2,091	1 in 5.88	170	1,879	42	985	1,106	111,749	1,262	1,254	60.35	59.97
Northumberland	4,981	1 in 5.73	105	4,682	194	2,480	2,501	287,288½	3,370	3,2[illegible]0	67.65	65.44
Queens	1,885	1 in 5.92	44	1,742	99	899	986	95,045	1,105	1,007	58.62	53.42
Restigouche	1,823	1 in 5.80	45	1,720	58	901	922	101,883	1,220	1,180	66.92	64.72
Saint John	8,969	1 in 5.77	62	8,547	360	4,377	4,592	562,248½	7,213	7,134	80.42	79.54
Sunbury	967	1 in 5.92	33	895	39	461	506	50,577½	597	537	61.73	55.53
Victoria	1,395	1 in 6.32	53	1,305	37	689	706	68,136	689	644	49.39	46.16
Westmorland	8,146	1 in 5.16	176	7,638	332	3,966	4,180	476,888	5,475	5,338	67.21	65.52
York	5,717	1 in 5.53	208	5,258	251	2,762	2,955	324,130½	3,853	3,660	67.39	64.01
New Brunswick	57,518	1 in 5.75	1,482	53,746	2,290	28,189	29,329	3,257,733	38,671	37,019	67.23	64.36
Cor. Term, 1901	58,575	1 in 5.65	1,645	54,628	2,302	28,906	29,669	3,284,754½	38,571	36,787	65.84	62.80
Increase									100	232	1.39	1.56
Decrease	1,057		163	882	12	717	340	27,021½				

TABLE II. PUBLIC SCHOOLS: FOR THE YEAR ENDED 30TH JUNE, 1903.

PART TWO.—The Second Term closed 30th June, 1903.

COUNTIES.	No. of Pupils at School this Term.	Proportion of the population at School this Term (Census of 1901).	AGE AND SEX OF PUPILS.					Grand total day's attendance made by the Pupils enrolled.	Number daily present on an average during the time the Schools were in session.	Number daily present on an average for the full Term.	Number daily present on an average during the time in Session per hundred enrolled.	Number daily present on an average for full Term per hundred enrolled.
			Number under 6 years of age.	Number between the ages of 6 and 15 years.	Number over 15 years.	Boys.	Girls.					
Albert	2,055	1 in 5.31	41	1,884	130	1,039	1,016	144,999	1,260	1,143	61.31	55.62
Carleton	4,618	1 in 4.68	152	4,034	432	2,367	2,251	311,223	2,742	2,474	59.37	53.57
Charlotte	4,336	1 in 5.16	60	3,901	375	2,197	2,139	321,948	2,816	2,513	64.94	57.95
Gloucester	4,092	1 in 6.82	43	3,894	155	2,152	1,940	275,610½	2,338	2,243	57.13	54.81
Kent	4,003	1 in 5.98	137	3,751	115	2,074	1,929	264,519	2,335	2,124	58.33	53.06
Kings	3,847	1 in 5.62	49	3,486	312	1,991	1,856	268,254	2,297	2,109	59.70	54.82
Madawaska	2,179	1 in 5.64	147	1,980	52	1,079	1,100	140,928	1,264	1,137	58.00	52.17
Northumberland	4,914	1 in 5.80	78	4,600	236	2,543	2,371	367,828½	3,091	2,940	62.90	59.82
Queens	2,052	1 in 5.44	49	1,833	170	1,045	1,007	122,755½	1,118	996	54.48	48.53
Restigouche	1,734	1 in 6.10	28	1,615	91	896	838	119,840	1,037	957	59.80	55.19
Saint John	8,832	1 in 5.86	60	8,341	431	4,365	4,467	805,266	6,737	6,622	76.27	74.97
Sunbury	1,053	1 in 5.44	21	964	68	508	545	65,121½	615	508	58.40	48.24
Victoria	1,501	1 in 5.87	49	1,352	100	797	704	88,198	804	679	53.56	45.23
Westmorland	8,094	1 in 5.19	152	7,553	389	4,060	4,034	618,738½	5,228	5,015	64.59	61.95
York	6,008	1 in 5.26	192	5,440	371	3,050	2,944	422,886½	3,870	3,413	64.46	56.85
New Brunswick	59,313	1 in 5.59	1,258	54,628	3,427	30,172	29,141	4,338,116	37,552	34,873	63.31	58.79
Cor. Term, 1902	60,477	1 in 5.47	1,522	55,350	3,605	30,767	29,710	4,360,797½	38,736	36,058	64.05	59.62
Increase												
Decrease	1,164		264	722	178	595	569	22,681½	1,184	1,185	.74	.83

TABLE III. PUBLIC SCHOOLS: FOR THE YEAR ENDED 30TH JUNE, 1903.

PART ONE.—The First Term closed 31st December, 1902.

NUMBER OF PUPILS IN THE DIFFERENT BRANCHES OF INSTRUCTION.

COUNTIES.	Physical Exercises.	Oral Lessons on Morals, etc.	[Optional] 37		Reading—Spelling—Recitation, Etc. 38								Grammar and Analysis and Composition. 39						History. 40				
					GRADE.								GRADE.						GRADE.				
	35	36	Sewing.	Knitting.	I	II	III	IV	V	VI	VII	VIII	III *	IV *	V	VI	VII	VIII	IV *	V	VI	VII	VIII
Albert	1,547	1,924	...	...	358	295	405	318	255	119	71	74	383	310	255	119	70	77	236	234	119	70	77
Carleton	3,199	3,528	8	...	797	483	620	735	675	152	135	102	583	737	628	146	135	103	550	578	73	135	103
Charlotte	3,161	3,693	...	...	723	561	628	704	612	224	164	104	624	710	603	220	165	104	575	579	199	164	104
Gloucester	3,902	4,014	6	20	1,539	890	727	535	244	97	66	60	715	538	213	97	66	60	506	231	97	56	60
Kent	3,107	3,625	56	57	1,459	758	580	520	244	56	60	47	545	500	231	46	60	47	411	240	56	60	47
Kings	3,070	3,510	...	...	640	613	749	746	641	105	79	73	705	739	632	105	79	73	643	618	105	79	73
Madawaska	1,668	1,928	...	...	834	407	389	259	106	46	22	24	350	250	105	46	22	24	244	98	41	22	24
Northumberland	4,398	4,644	23	...	1,160	828	967	728	575	220	176	166	934	728	575	216	180	166	587	545	198	167	151
Queens	1,535	1,821	...	...	383	330	369	381	338	36	22	17	363	383	334	33	22	17	355	334	33	22	17
Restigouche	1,533	1,720	15	15	515	308	354	239	213	44	64	25	345	231	217	44	64	25	184	217	44	64	25
Saint John	7,758	8,396	176	...	1,743	1,300	1,318	1,296	1,092	740	538	402	1,308	1,296	1,092	740	538	402	1,217	1,092	740	538	402
Sunbury	777	793	...	...	242	158	171	159	130	27	11	18	142	149	120	27	11	17	143	128	27	11	17
Victoria	1,052	1,231	...	...	393	242	290	231	131	16	13	36	253	230	131	16	13	36	219	126	16	13	36
Westmorland	6,322	7,061	35	58	2,186	1,197	1,196	1,212	996	368	312	278	1,123	1,167	935	366	311	275	824	830	366	312	227
York	4,755	5,224	15	4	1,365	776	1,010	950	850	253	176	181	979	946	822	251	174	181	667	812	248	171	183
New Brunswick	47,784	53,102	334	154	14,342	9,146	9,763	9,033	7,102	2,503	1,909	1,607	9,352	8,934	6,902	2,472	1,916	1,607	7,361	6,662	2,357	1,884	1,546
Cor. Term, 1901	49,396	54,309	214	193	15,000	9,236	9,822	9,002	7,370	2,532	1,873	1,656	9,295	8,804	7,225	2,500	1,855	1,627	7,082	7,077	2,426	1,846	1,601
Increase	...	...	120	...	...	...	...	31	...	...	36	...	57	130	...	...	55	...	279	...	...	38	...
Decrease	1,612	1,207	...	39	748	90	59	...	268	29	...	49	...	...	323	28	...	20	...	415	69	...	55

* In country districts only.

TABLE III. PART ONE.—Continued.

FORM, COLOR AND INDUSTRIAL DRAWING. 41 — GRADE.

COUNTIES.	I	II	III	IV	V	VI	VII	VIII
Albert	355	297	415	303	248	119	71	67
Carleton	736	447	618	734	673	132	185	102
Charlotte	728	559	628	711	604	224	165	104
Gloucester	1526	926	737	566	244	97	66	60
Kent	1420	741	566	490	228	56	60	46
Kings	627	607	747	734	627	105	79	73
Madawaska	789	391	380	255	106	46	22	24
Northumberland	1134	819	947	724	572	228	176	161
Queens	372	828	369	371	326	36	22	17
Restigouche	512	308	357	240	298	41	64	25
Saint John	1732	1300	1318	1296	1092	740	588	402
Sunbury	240	150	168	157	129	27	11	17
Victoria	378	242	280	233	129	16	13	36
Westmorland	2137	1181	1200	1214	914	367	300	267
York	1307	765	1007	982	840	255	174	178
N w Brunswick	13993	9065	9737	8957	6840	2507	1896	1579
Cor. Term, 1901	11571	9051	9672	8008	7124	2468	1868	1633
Increase	....	14	65	49		39	33	....
Decrease	578	...	...	....	284	....	....	54

PRINT-SCRIPT AND WRITING. 42 — GRADE.

COUNTIES.	I	II	III	IV	V	VI	VII	VIII
Albert	358	297	413	309	246	119	71	77
Carleton	798	480	619	739	675	152	135	102
Charlotte	728	561	628	712	604	224	134	104
Gloucester	1515	809	709	522	232	97	66	60
Kent	1449	747	581	511	241	56	60	47
Kings	689	611	758	726	632	105	79	73
Madawaska	830	411	383	255	106	46	22	24
Northumberland	1126	832	965	718	566	220	176	160
Queens	380	330	370	381	338	36	22	17
Restigouche	515	808	353	235	209	44	64	25
Saint John	1743	1300	1318	1282	1081	720	538	402
Sunbury	248	158	171	159	130	27	11	17
Victoria	392	242	290	231	131	16	13	36
Westmorland	2164	1196	1207	1225	988	387	311	271
York	1361	778	1013	948	849	256	174	181
N w Brunswick	14246	9120	9766	8953	7028	2485	1906	1596
Cor. Term, 1901	14974	9223	9825	9001	7336	2504	1877	1651
Increase	....	...	...	....	....	..	29	....
Decrease	728	103	50	48	308	19	....	55

SINGING. ("Theory" Optional.) 43 — GRADE.

COUNTIES.	I (By Rote)	II (By Rote)	III (By Rote)	IV Rote	IV Note	V Rote	V Note	VI Rote	VI Note	VII Rote	VII Note	VIII Rote	VIII Note
Albert	143	113	171	95	....	65	....	50	....	12	....	18	....
Carleton	336	245	288	331	....	308	....	112	....	26	....	16	....
Charlotte	427	359	361	396	...	364	....	172	...	57	....	38	....
Gloucester	1079	593	482	342	87	121	35	50	18	19	20	29	....
Kent	718	339	226	216	4	129	2	27	....	30	....	15	....
Kings	329	314	346	356	....	340	....	80	....	53	...	35	....
Madawaska	554	215	240	120	15	45	....	23	...	10	5	18	...
Northumberland	700	589	672	401	14	288	83	141	17	70	....	66	1
Queens	130	103	111	120	...	102	....	23	....	10	..	9	....
Restigouche	370	283	283	163	3	168	....	14	23	8	...	1	15
Saint John	1621	1223	1245	1201	....	1016	....	723	....	525	....	381	....
Sunbury	54	47	49	32	1	37	8	6	...	2	...	5	....
Victoria	172	71	118	91	....	64	....	8	..	5	...	...	....
Westmorland	1104	783	774	712	....	526	....	252	..	175	....	89	...
York	797	489	508	516	....	418	....	88	....	55	....	52	..
N w Brunswick	8534	5616	5944	5182	74	3986	78	1787	58	1057	25	774	16
Cor. Term, 1901	8573	5749	5874	5055	35	3996	45	1744	71	1007	14	726	....
Increase	...	...	70	127	39	....	33	43	....	....	11	48	16
Decrease	39	133	....	....	....	10	....	....	13	40	....	..	..

TABLE III. PART ONE.—Continued.

COUNTIES.	NUMBER—ARITHMETIC. 44								ALGEBRA. 46		GEOGRAPHY. 47					
	GRADE.								GRADE.		GRADE.					
	I	II	III	IV	V	VI	VII	VIII	VII	VIII	III	IV	V	VI	VII	VIII
Albert	358	292	408	311	251	119	71	78	36	60	392	308	254	119	71	81
Carleton	796	483	620	731	667	152	135	103	138	109	613	746	662	146	135	103
Charlotte	717	555	632	703	601	220	165	104	193	116	652	711	609	226	168	104
Gloucester	1,534	893	727	563	244	97	66	60	48	123	727	566	244	93	66	60
Kent	1,457	758	583	518	244	56	60	48	39	48	586	528	255	56	60	47
Kings	642	612	752	743	640	105	79	73	98	76	743	747	642	105	79	73
Madawaska	836	388	377	253	111	46	22	24	15	21	398	251	108	43	22	24
Northumberland	1,060	828	967	728	574	219	182	160	91	105	937	732	567	216	188	160
Queens	380	334	374	378	284	36	22	17	78	17	368	383	337	36	22	17
Restigouche	515	308	352	239	215	44	64	25	22	35	361	235	216	44	64	25
St. John	1,696	1,285	1,318	1,296	1,092	740	538	402	60	385	1,327	1,298	1,092	740	538	402
Sunbury	245	158	171	159	130	27	11	17	33	18	150	151	130	27	11	17
Victoria	392	242	280	231	131	16	13	30	15	38	275	230	131	16	13	38
Westmorland	2,181	1,199	1,214	1,209	980	370	311	267	174	278	1,218	1,207	981	371	313	270
York	1,365	777	1,012	947	850	252	176	281	158	87	1,040	937	831	250	174	181
New Brunswick	14,174	9,112	9,787	9,009	7,014	2,505	1,915	1,695	1,198	1,516	9,787	9,030	7,059	2,488	1,924	1,600
Cor. Term, 1901	14,986	9,238	9,844	8,980	7,285	2,512	1,879	1,646	1,222	1,534	9,888	8,982	7,297	2,478	1,875	1,645
Increase	.....	.....	.....	29	.....	.....	36	49	.....	.....	.....	48	.....	10	49	.....
Decrease	812	126	57	.....	271	7	.....	.....	24	18	101	.....	238	.....	.....	45

TABLE III. PART ONE.—Continued.

COUNTIES.	Hygiene and Temperance (Health Readers). 48 — Grade. I	II	III	IV	V	VI	VII	VIII	Nature Lessons and Agriculture. Minerals—Plant Life—Animal Life. 49 — Grade. I	II	III	IV	V	VI	VII	VIII	Latin. (Optional). 50 — Grade. VII	VIII	French. (Optional) 51 — Grades I to VIII
Albert	305	252	375	304	251	115	61	71	320	265	392	300	234	108	71	90	......	10	3
Carleton	510	410	560	699	652	140	111	85	552	390	555	666	628	140	135	103	19	51	......
Charlotte	605	483	611	681	607	224	164	104	651	496	590	691	586	224	185	104	5	45	......
Gloucester	1,435	851	727	564	243	97	66	45	1,347	865	695	550	235	97	66	60	30	13	2,118
Kent	1,300	685	519	508	240	56	60	47	1,329	721	529	476	231	56	60	47	14	15	1,091
Kings	602	568	739	743	627	66	57	66	595	578	715	736	634	105	79	73	18	21	......
Madawaska	711	338	332	221	102	41	22	24	663	331	346	225	99	41	22	24	......	3	1,557
Northumberland	1,018	739	934	728	572	216	167	150	1,004	743	919	711	569	217	176	166	22	94	513
Queens	300	303	355	378	337	38	22	17	317	307	363	369	337	36	22	16	3	9	......
Restigouche	463	294	351	222	198	44	64	25	480	283	324	222	204	44	64	25	23	20	131
Saint John	1,673	1,273	1,317	1,296	1,002	740	538	402	1,662	1,267	1,311	1,286	1,092	740	538	402	369	363	......
Sunbury	197	143	159	157	125	16	2	7	194	131	155	147	124	26	11	17	2	6	8
Victoria	336	214	267	233	127	16	13	36	299	200	248	213	121	16	13	36	2	12	88
Westmorland	1,840	1,097	1,085	1,165	965	366	307	266	1,745	1,041	1,170	1,078	828	352	296	261	123	164	454
York	1,056	672	968	947	820	244	181	175	1,095	684	917	923	813	240	167	175	56	90	......
New Brunswick	12,351	8,322	9,299	8,846	6,958	2,417	1,835	1,520	12,253	8,302	9,238	8,593	6,735	2,442	1,885	1,599	686	916	5,963
Cor. Term, 1901	12,864	8,424	9,506	8,834	7,308	2,475	1,862	1,606	12,897	8,360	9,056	8,573	7,033	2,317	1,792	1,604	855	919	5,185
Increase	......	......	......	12	......	......	......	......	......	......	182	20	......	125	93	......	......	......	778
Decrease	513	102	207	......	350	58	27	86	644	58	......	......	298	......	......	5	169	3	......

TABLE III.—Superior, Grammar and other Schools having Pupils in advance of Grade VIII.

Part One.—Continued.

COUNTIES.	Language. 52 — English. IX	X	XI	XII	Latin. IX	X	XI	XII	Greek. IX	X	XI	XII	French. IX	X	XI	XII
Albert	63	37	....	....	22	11	...	..	..	...	..	..	8	4		...
Carleton	86	33	16	...	59	20	13	...	7	3	1	..	33	12	11	...
Charlotte	119	62	30	....	85	46	24	..	12	12	4	..	67	41	23	...
Gloucester	26	5	....	...	9	1	...	..	...	...	...	..	23	4	...	...
Kent	42	15	....	....	22	12	..	..	3	3	..	..	..	..	..	...
Kings	40	26	6	....	21	9	6	..	..	1	1	.	13	6	5	..
Madawaska	4	...	...	....	...	...	...	..	...	..	...	..	..	...	..	..
Northumb'l'd	87	23	6	....	67	10	15	..	...	2	2	...	31	8	13	..
Queens	10	5	3	....	9	5	3	..	..	...	..	..	..	...	..	...
Restigouche	25	16	3	....	20	16	4	..	8	8	2	...	10	5	..	..
Saint John	255	151	96	24	235	143	52	24	41	37	16	14	230	144	80	17
Sunbury	11	3	...	...	9	...	...	..	..	..	...	..	6	..	...	..
Victoria	11	12	3	...	6	4	2	...	1	2	1	..	...	..	..	...
Westmorland	163	99	51	....	120	68	46	..	..	4	3	..	72	53	45	...
York	92	5	31	...	74	..	20	..	..	...	3	..	...	17	85	...
N. Brunswick	1084	492	245	24	758	345	185	24	72	72	23	14	493	294	221	17
Cor. Term, 1901	1060	516	245	13	744	421	223	13	94	68	61	6	486	310	170	10
Increase	....	....	....	11	14	..	...	11	..	4	..	8	7	...	51	7
Decrease	26	24	....	...	..	79	38	..	22	..	28	..	..	16	...	...

COUNTIES.	Mathematics. 53 — Arithmetic. IX	X	Geometry. IX	X	XI	XII	Algebra. IX	X	XI	Book-keeping. IX	X	Trigonometry. XI	XII
Albert	63	37	44	36	....	..	57	38	..	47	32	1	...
Carleton	92	37	87	33	16	...	30	33	16	..	16	12	..
Charlotte	125	62	122	62	80	..	114	62	30	35	10	4	..
Gloucester	28	5	26	5	..	...	25	5	...	6	1	...	...
Kent	42	15	43	15	...	...	42	15	..	15	12	...	...
Kings	38	16	39	24	6	..	37	28	6	18	6	.	...
Madawaska	4	..	4	..	..	...	4	..	..	...	...	...	..
Northumb'l'd	94	23	104	23	19	..	104	23	19	23	12	..	...
Queens	9	5	9	5	3	..	10	5	3	5	5	...	..
Restigouche	25	19	25	16	3	..	25	16	3	25	.	...	..
Saint John	28	151	258	151	96	24	258	151	96	258	114	9	24
Sunbury	11	3	11	2	.	..	11	3	...	..	3	..	..
Victoria	11	12	11	12	3	..	3	5	..	..	..	..	..
Westmorland	163	99	158	94	55	..	163	99	54	150	81	...	..
York	9	5	20	5	29	..	89	..	20	10	1	..	.
N. Brunswick	1054	489	961	483	260	24	970	483	256	592	293	26	24
Cor. Term, 1901	1067	511	948	504	243	13	1080	505	244	684	310	54	10
Increase	.....	..	13	..	17	11	.....	.	12	..		..	14
Decrease	13	22	...	21	...	..	60	22	..	92	17	28	..

COUNTIES.	History and Geography. 54 — IX	X	XI	XII	Drawing. 55 — IX	Natural Science. 56 — Physics. IX	Physiology & Hygiene. X	XI	Chemistry. X	XI	Botany. IX	X	XI	Geology. 57 — XII
Albert	48	86	..	..	66	23	20	..	19	..	44	33	..	.....
Carleton	92	33	16	.	..	6	42	16	15	12	30	38	16	.....
Charlotte	119	62	30	...	[illegible]	57	40	8	50	26	91	44	21	....
Gloucester	25	5	...	..	[illegible]	5	1	..	1	..	5	1	..	....
Kent	44	15	..	...	32	24	27	..	12	..	35	12	...	....
Kings	38	28	6	...	23	17	5	..	12	6	84	28	6	.....
Madawaska	4	...	..	..	4	..	..	..	...	..	4	..	..	.....
Northumb'l'd	109	23	19	...	85	13	10	..	8	..	108	23	19	....
Queens	10	5	3	...	10	5	5	8	5	8	5	5	8	....
Restigouche	25	16	3	...	25	14	29	11	11	8	24	11	8	....
Saint John	258	151	96	24	181	213	114	9	21	96	169	151	80	7
Sunbury	11	8	..	..	14	..	8	...	..	...	..	.	...	....
Victoria	11	12	3	..	8	.	6	8	6	3	11	11	8	....
Westmorland	154	57	51	..	72	37	59	6	47	45	159	97	53	....
York	89	..	81	..	92	8	39	31	4	..	60	89	31	....
N. Brunswick	1037	446	258	24	775	442	400	87	211	194	779	488	244	7
Cor. Term, 1901	1084	508	244	13	1003	672	458	93	232	219	868	471	224	16
Increase	.....	..	14	11	.....	..	..	...	...	...	..	17	20	...
Decrease	47	62	...	..	228	230	58	6	21	25	89	..	...	9

TABLE III. PART TWO.—The Second Term closed June 30th 1903.

NUMBER OF PUPILS IN THE DIFFERENT BRANCHES OF INSTRUCTION.

COUNTIES.	Physical Exercises. 35	Oral Lessons on Morals, &c. 36	Opt'nl 37 Sewing.	Opt'nl 37 Knitting.	Reading—Spelling—Recitation, Etc. 38 Grade I	II	III	IV	V	VI	VII	VIII
Albert	1,724	1,932	...	...	382	278	384	321	327	122	74	57
Carleton	3,835	4,199	...	...	880	562	757	873	887	200	171	124
Charlotte	3,594	4,011	7	...	677	554	720	828	839	217	157	135
Gloucester	3,686	3,896	38	38	1,181	889	751	639	295	102	67	45
Kent	3,199	3,844	39	31	1,505	798	629	549	249	96	57	53
Kings	3,035	3,602	11	14	569	607	730	817	777	102	88	89
Madawaska	1,963	2,036	19	19	769	436	423	342	119	35	29	21
Northumberland	4,552	4,632	...	...	1,078	808	922	763	670	200	190	136
Queens	1,735	2,018	...	...	389	278	417	445	426	30	25	23
Restigouche	1,499	1,702	...	...	425	281	348	250	227	46	64	46
Saint John	7,931	8,189	138	...	1,608	1,372	1,308	1,324	1,101	735	497	403
Sunbury	812	892	...	...	217	174	185	218	145	143	11	15
Victoria	1,213	1,325	...	...	369	211	292	278	212	22	23	38
Westmorland	6,390	7,156	24	44	2,020	1,207	1,278	1,296	942	358	311	312
York	4,734	5,355	11	4	1,339	792	992	1,076	1,031	269	183	218
New Brunswick	49,902	54,789	287	150	13,408	9,247	10,136	10,028	8,247	2,677	1,947	1,715
Cor. Term, 1902	50,073	56,240	173	68	14,113	9,349	10,212	10,054	8,524	2,507	1,920	1,690
Increase	...	...	114	82	...	...	...	...	...	170	27	25
Decrease	171	1,451	..	..	705	102	76	26	277	...	...	...

COUNTIES.	Grammar and Analysis and Composition. 39 Grade *III	*IV	V	VI	VII	VIII	History. 40 Grade *IV	V	VI	VII	VIII
Albert	350	313	325	122	74	57	254	324	121	72	58
Carleton	716	876	849	195	171	124	704	797	196	169	130
Charlotte	655	804	837	216	157	134	638	838	217	151	134
Gloucester	730	617	295	102	67	45	527	293	102	67	45
Kent	618	517	242	96	57	52	450	233	96	57	52
Kings	718	813	765	102	88	89	694	778	102	88	89
Madawaska	365	329	111	64	29	21	349	110	40	37	21
Northumberland	913	763	662	200	190	136	504	670	200	190	136
Queens	416	432	424	33	25	23	388	431	35	28	23
Restigouche	347	256	281	46	64	46	172	225	46	64	46
Saint John	1,298	1,324	1,101	735	497	403	1,126	1,101	735	497	403
Sunbury	171	210	142	43	11	15	186	146	43	11	15
Victoria	279	274	203	22	23	38	223	190	27	24	38
Westmorland	1,150	1,301	899	358	312	299	868	898	365	304	296
York	928	1,059	1,001	260	163	193	787	970	277	178	210
New Brunswick	9,654	9,888	8,087	2,594	1,928	1,675	7,870	8,004	2,602	1,937	1,696
Cor. Term, 1902	9,741	9,883	8,396	2,498	1,926	1,675	8,082	8,334	2,486	1,920	1,674
Increase	...	5	...	96	2	...	...	...	116	17	22
Decrease	87	...	309	...	...	...	212	330	...	...	...

* In country districts only.

TABLE III. Part Two.—Continued.

Form, Color and Industrial Drawing. 41 — Grade.

Counties.	I	II	III	IV	V	VI	VII	VIII
Albert	375	278	382	314	320	122	74	54
Carleton	807	540	749	856	869	200	171	124
Charlotte	638	528	719	824	821	217	157	135
Gloucester	1153	881	745	639	295	104	67	45
Kent	1484	791	618	529	244	96	57	52
Kings	552	509	728	812	768	102	88	89
Madawaska	749	427	412	336	114	35	29	21
Northumberland	1046	796	911	763	672	200	190	134
Queens	385	265	416	447	424	33	25	23
Restigouche	425	281	348	259	225	46	64	46
Saint John	1608	1372	1308	1313	1101	735	497	403
Sunbury	217	174	181	208	143	43	11	15
Victoria	349	211	292	276	212	22	23	38
Westmorland	1937	1184	1264	1310	899	358	314	306
York	1240	782	993	1037	1008	282	188	210
New Brunswick	12965	9109	10066	9923	8115	2574	1965	1695
Cor. Term, 1902	13596	9141	10090	9858	8318	2482	1905	1672
Increase	....	....	....	65	....	92	50	23
Decrease	631	32	24	....	203	....	....	....

Print-Script and Writing. 42 — Grade.

Counties.	I	II	III	IV	V	VI	VII	VIII
Albert	373	275	384	305	315	123	74	59
Carleton	874	562	756	873	887	200	171	124
Charlotte	693	538	720	828	839	217	157	135
Gloucester	1181	889	751	639	295	102	67	45
Kent	1512	796	626	552	251	96	57	53
Kings	559	610	738	813	772	102	88	89
Madawaska	780	432	419	330	119	35	29	21
Northumberland	1068	808	922	763	672	200	190	93
Queens	386	270	419	442	422	33	29	27
Restigouche	420	278	350	257	220	46	64	46
Saint John	1596	1383	1309	1324	1101	735	497	403
Sunbury	200	158	174	197	145	43	11	15
Victoria	368	211	292	278	212	22	23	38
Westmorland	2003	1223	1271	1315	926	358	311	307
York	1277	786	992	1061	1032	267	183	211
New Brunswick	13290	9219	10123	9986	8208	2579	1951	1666
Cor. Term, 1902	14035	9301	10290	10017	8507	2493	1894	1683
Increase	....	....	....	....	....	86	57	....
Decrease	745	82	167	31	299	....	....	17

Singing ("Theory" Optional). 43 — Grade.

Counties.	By Rote. I	By Rote. II	By Rote. III	IV Rote.	IV Note.	V Rote.	V Note.	VI Rote.	VI Note.	VIII Rote.	VIII Note.	VIII Rote.	VIII Note.
Albert	184	127	194	134	...	80	...	43	..	19	..	15	..
Carleton	330	241	333	328	...	329	...	141	..	68	..	47	..
Charlotte	361	322	379	390	21	430	...	168	..	55	..	38	..
Gloucester	804	601	540	458	36	189	26	40	13	23	25	20	20
Kent	678	343	271	287	...	128	...	65	..	39	..	33	..
Kings	320	307	407	379	...	334	...	11	..	....	..	7	..
Madawaska	423	291	217	189	6	54	10	17	1	22	7	11	6
Northumberland	734	575	589	447	...	427	27	141	17	98	..	71	..
Queens	145	96	132	140	14	105	2	14	..	1	..	2	..
Restigouche	317	233	246	178	...	173	...	5	..	26	..	34	..
Saint John	1480	1300	1214	1210	9	990	...	720	..	477	..	383	..
Sunbury	56	34	63	42	...	28	...	3	..	2	..	3	..
Victoria	122	63	88	76	8	66	6	11	..	10	..	....	..
Westmorland	1100	788	759	654	...	407	...	229	..	155	..	135	..
York	738	484	565	538	10	459	48	98	24	23	40	23	20
New Brunswick	7787	5805	5907	5400	104	4257	119	1706	55	1013	72	822	46
Cor. Term, 1902	8210	5810	6277	5486	127	4628	87	1839	22	1153	29	792	3
Increase	....	....	....	....		....	32	....	33	....	43	30	43
Decrease	423	5	280	86	23	371	...	133	..	140	..	....	..

TABLE III. Part Two.—Continued.

COUNTIES.	Number—Arithmetic. 44								Algebra. 46		Geography. 47					
	GRADE.								GRADE.		GRADE.					
	I	II	III	IV	V	VI	VII	VIII	VII	VIII	III	IV	V	VI	VII	VIII
Albert	371	278	379	324	326	124	74	57	78	59	373	319	325	121	74	59
Carleton	878	562	738	883	875	199	171	124	227	148	671	783	862	199	171	130
Charlotte	675	556	720	830	837	217	157	135	301	128	732	827	838	217	157	135
Gloucester	1181	899	751	641	298	103	68	45	69	45	747	634	295	102	67	45
Kent	1482	787	631	540	244	96	57	53	40	52	652	528	241	96	57	53
Kings	572	602	743	819	761	102	91	89	182	101	743	815	769	102	88	89
Madawaska	766	438	416	339	119	35	29	21	27	21	424	840	116	35	29	21
Northumberland	1077	808	922	763	670	200	190	134	161	122	918	763	670	200	190	136
Queens	385	268	427	441	424	22	26	13	70	30	419	433	431	22	31	26
Restigouche	425	240	340	259	223	46	64	46	69	46	351	257	226	15	76	65
Saint John	1597	1383	1308	1326	1098	735	497	403	498	406	1298	1314	1101	735	497	403
Sunbury	200	158	174	199	146	42	11	15	34	13	174	209	144	43	11	15
Victoria	365	211	292	278	212	22	23	38	50	38	288	275	218	22	23	38
Westmorland	1995	1245	1272	1289	935	361	309	308	351	282	1268	1318	921	343	311	311
York	1267	786	1000	1068	1019	264	184	210	223	192	987	1062	993	277	194	219
New Brunswick	13236	9270	10133	9999	8187	2568	1951	1691	2380	1683	10045	9877	8150	2529	1976	1745
Cor. Term, 1902	13859	9361	10354	10052	8474	2504	1923	1651	1914	1391	10367	9995	8411	2508	1902	1698
Increase	.....	.....	.....	.....	.....	64	28	40	466	292	.....	.....	.....	21	74	47
Decrease	623	91	221	53	287	.....	.....	.....	.....	.....	322	118	261	.....	.....	.....

TABLE III. PART TWO.—Continued.

COUNTIES.	Hygiene and Temperance (Health Readers). 48 Grade I	II	III	IV	V	VI	VII	VIII	Nature Lessons and Agriculture. Minerals - Plant Life - Animal Life. 49 Grade I	II	III	IV	V	VI	VII	VIII	Latin. (Optional). 50 Grade VII	VIII	French. (Optional). 51 Grades I to VIII
Albert	351	254	361	319	321	117	74	59	330	251	350	300	301	123	67	73	13	1	29
Carleton	587	442	755	846	859	196	171	124	612	453	721	827	829	181	165	130	70	67	....
Charlotte	598	503	985	822	843	217	150	132	616	520	690	812	838	217	157	133	27	67	....
Gloucester	1163	874	754	642	269	92	63	45	1118	874	740	690	278	91	64	45	15	10	2404
Kent	1350	768	567	520	248	96	57	58	1334	741	570	400	244	92	57	53	13	29	1365
Kings	520	561	716	814	772	102	88	80	508	553	701	780	702	102	88	80	10	42	....
Madawaska	688	412	401	325	107	31	29	21	675	398	362	315	116	35	29	21	....	2	1579
Northumberland	1022	782	921	763	670	200	190	136	1044	796	921	763	672	200	190	134	98	71	417
Queens	317	251	407	415	405	25	31	23	328	260	423	406	411	20	25	22	....	12	....
Restigouche	399	255	337	249	229	15	70	51	416	277	325	244	221	46	64	46	45	21	143
Saint John	1582	1374	1308	1324	1101	735	497	403	1547	1347	1275	1316	1101	735	497	403	457	357	....
Sunbury	155	137	176	180	140	42	11	3	165	139	160	185	134	42	11	15	....	0	....
Victoria	302	202	284	279	205	21	23	38	317	180	234	263	205	22	23	38	....	8	148
Westmorland	1671	1070	1231	1289	914	354	308	324	1066	1033	1178	1212	858	320	310	290	165	101	470
York	1029	679	951	1076	996	260	188	210	958	687	880	1016	993	237	150	183	51	80	....
New Brunswick	11734	8564	9854	9843	8079	2508	1951	1711	11643	8468	9553	9864	7910	2400	1908	1670	970	940	6561
Cor. Term, 1902	11838	8438	10002	9847	8399	2390	1902	1692	12049	8513	9780	9511	8108	2158	1898	1708	940	888	6218
Increase	....	126	....	....	....	118	49	19	....	....	....	53	....	11	10	....	30	64	343
Decrease	104	....	148	4	320	....	....	....	406	45	223	....	183	....	....	37	....	..	

TABLE III.—SUPERIOR, GRAMMAR AND OTHER SCHOOLS HAVING PUPILS IN ADVANCE OF GRADE VIII.

PART TWO.—Continued.

COUNTIES.	Language. 52 — English. IX	English. X	English. XI	English. XII	Latin. IX	Latin. X	Latin. XI	Latin. XII	Greek. IX	Greek. X	Greek. XI	Greek. XII	French. IX	French. X	French. XI	French. XII
Albert	55	43	1		16	9	1						17	4		
Carleton	82	38	18		51	20	13		6	6	1		41	17	12	
Charlotte	121	57	31		88	41	24		7	9	3		59	34	24	
Gloucester	36	6			16								23	6		
Kent	41	9	1		24	6	1		2							
Kings	38	21	8		21	7	5			1	1		13	6	5	
Madawaska	5				5											
Northumb'land	114	13	18		92	10	14		3	2			92		12	
Queens	12	8			9	7			3	2						
Restigouche	21	15	2		11	14	2		8	8	2		11	3		
Saint John	226	135	98	25	208	130	98	25	14	13	7	7	203	130	91	18
Sunbury	12				4											
Victoria	11	16	3		6	5	2		2		1					
Westmorland	148	88	55		103	53	46		2	2	3		103	48	44	
York	88	4	30		57	3	20		11		6		40	12	30	
New Brunswick	1010	453	265	25	709	305	226	25	58	43	24	7	602	260	218	18
Cor. Term, 1902	996	505	239	11	660	389	213	11	66	68	60	6	536	272	166	8
Increase	14		26	14	49		13	14				1	66		52	10
Decrease		52				84			8	25	36			12		

COUNTIES.	Mathematics. 53 — Arithmetic. IX	Arithmetic. X	Geometry. IX	Geometry. X	Geometry. XI	Geometry. XII	Algebra. IX	Algebra. X	Algebra. XI	Book-Keeping. IX	Book-Keeping. X	Trigonometry. XI	Trigonometry. XII
Albert	64	43	51	43	1		53	42	1	60	30	1	
Carleton	82	43	82	38	18		82	38	18	63	23	13	
Charlotte	121	57	119	57	31		120	57	31	68	14	4	
Gloucester	36	6	22				38	6		36	6		
Kent	41	9	41	9	1		41	9	1	34	6	1	
Kings	43	31	38	22	8		43	22	8	42	12		
Madawaska	5		5				5						
Northumb'land	114	13	114	13	18		114	13	18	71	2	7	
Queens	9	10	43	9			18	8		20	8		
Restigouche	11	15	25	15	2		25	15	2	26	15		
Saint John	226	112	203	135	98	25	203	135	98	216	135	12	25
Sunbury	10	2	10	5			2	11	2		3		
Victoria	11	16	16	16	3		13	15	3	37			
Westmorland	148	87	143	81	54		148	85	54	127	71	9	
York	92	36	70	4	28		91	4	28	38	4		
New Brunswick	1003	480	982	447	262	25	996	460	264	838	329	47	25
Cor. Term, 1902	1028	508	975	465	243	11	963	443	235	830	312	60	46
Increase			7		19	14	33	17	29	8	17		
Decrease	25	28		18								13	21

COUNTIES.	History and Geography. 54 — IX	X	XI	XII	55 Drawing. IX	Natural Science. 56 — Physics. IX	Physiology & Hygiene. IX	Physiology & Hygiene. X	Chemistry. X	Chemistry. XI	Botany. IX	Botany. X	Botany. XI	Geology. XII
Albert	55	30	1		56	40	26	1	32	1	37	32	1	
Carleton	82	38	18		82	76	31	18	38	18	81	31	18	
Charlotte	120	57	21		96	63	25	34	51	31	96	40	22	
Gloucester	38	6			36	29			6		31	6		
Kent	41	9	1			26	17	1	16		29	9	1	
Kings	44	21	8		32	33	13		11	8	33	21	8	
Madawaska	5				5	5	5		5		5			
Northumb'land	114	13	18		114	111	18	18	13	18	112	13	18	
Queens	12	8			9	10	8		8		10	8		
Restigouche	21	15	2		21	21	15	2	15	2	21	15	2	
Saint John	226	135	98	25	226	216	135	12	203	98	226	135	94	8
Sunbury	12	3			15	12	3		12			13		
Victoria	8	6	3		11	20	15	3	6	3	8	6	3	
Westmorland	148	86	55		68	128	87	44	67	48	132	79	51	
York	65	5	30		82	85	8	30	39	55	113	37	55	
New Brunswick	980	441	255	25	843	885	406	163	522	282	884	445	273	8
Cor. Term, 1902	992	484	234	11	866	879	416	136	410	256	901	446	198	3
Increase			21	14		6		27	112	26	33		75	5
Decrease	3	43			23		10					1		

TABLE IV. PUBLIC SCHOOLS: TEACHERS EMPLOYED DURING THE YEAR ENDED 30TH JUNE, 1903.

PART ONE.—The First Term closed 31st December, 1902.

COUNTIES.	Grammar School Teachers.		MALES. Class.			FEMALES. Class.			TOTAL.			Trained.	Untrained.	No. of Assistants.		Total number of Teachers employed this Term.
	M	F	I	II	III	I	II	III	Male.	Female.	Both.			Male.	Female.	
Albert	1	.....	7	7	.....	13	38	4	15	55	70	70	.....	.....	2	72
Carleton	1	1	8	17	1	18	81	16	27	116	143	140	3	.....	.....	143
Charlotte	2	.....	18	5	1	25	69	15	26	109	135	134	1	1	3	139
Gloucester	1	.....	4	4	30	4	19	49	39	72	111	107	4	.....	2	113
Kent	1	.....	7	2	14	8	24	66	24	98	122	117	5	.....	.....	122
Kings	1	.....	15	14	2	18	95	14	32	127	159	159	.....	.....	1	160
Madawaska	.....	.....	2	1	7	.....	.....	50	10	50	60	54	6	.....	.....	60
Northumberland	1	.....	10	5	7	13	93	25	23	131	154	151	3	.....	2	156
Queens	1	.....	2	16	3	9	42	13	22	64	86	85	1	.....	.....	86
Restigouche	1	.....	1	.....	2	5	34	7	4	46	50	50	.....	.....	1	51
Saint John	4	1	21	6	1	100	91	5	32	197	229	229	.....	.....	9	238
Sunbury	.....	.....	2	5	1	5	18	12	8	35	43	40	3	.....	.....	43
Victoria	1	.....	2	3	2	6	24	21	8	51	59	55	4	.....	.....	59
Westmorland	6	.....	14	30	9	46	73	37	59	156	215	212	3	.....	1	216
York	4	.....	12	14	3	29	106	31	33	166	199	194	5	.....	1	200
New Brunswick	25	2	125	120	83	209	807	365	302	1473	1835	1797	38	1	22	1858
Cor. Term, 1901	20	3	133	123	94	810	801	366	370	1480	1850	1814	36	.....	20	1870
Increase	5	.....	.....	6	.....	.....	6	.....	.....	.....	.....	.....	2	1	2	.....
Decrease	.....	1	8	.....	11	11	.....	1	8	7	15	17	.....	.....	.....	12

TABLE IV. PART TWO.—Second Term closed 30th June, 1903.

COUNTIES.	Grammar School Teachers.		MALES. Class.			FEMALES. Class.			TOTAL.			Trained.	Untrained.	No. of Assistants.		Total number of Teachers employed this Term.
	M	F	I	II	III	I	II	III	Male.	Female.	Both.			Male.	Female.	
Albert	1	......	8	5	1	14	39	6	15	59	74	74	......	1	2	77
Carleton	1	1	14	8	1	19	85	25	24	130	154	148	6	......	......	154
Charlotte	1	......	16	9	2	26	69	17	28	112	140	136	4	2	4	146
Gloucester	1	......	4	3	31	2	18	49	39	69	108	105	3	......	3	111
Kent	1	......	7	1	14	6	27	64	23	97	120	116	4	......	1	121
Kings	1	......	12	16	1	19	88	12	30	119	149	149	......	......	1	150
Madawaska	......	......	3	......	5	......	......	50	8	50	58	48	10	......	......	58
Northumberland	1	......	9	6	3	14	91	21	19	126	145	142	3	......	......	145
Queens	1	......	3	14	2	10	38	18	20	66	86	84	2	......	......	86
Restigouche	1	......	1	......	2	7	28	7	4	42	46	45	1	......	1	47
Saint John	4	1	21	6	1	104	85	2	32	192	224	224	......	......	10	234
Sunbury	......	......	1	4	1	4	18	13	6	35	41	35	6	......	......	41
Victoria	1	......	3	2	2	5	24	17	8	46	54	50	4	......	......	54
Westmorland	4	......	12	27	9	52	62	34	52	148	200	200	......	......	1	201
York	3	......	11	11	5	28	94	36	30	158	188	174	14	......	2	190
New Brunswick	21	2	125	112	80	310	766	371	338	1449	1787	1730	57	3	25	1815
Cor. Term, 1902	19	3	127	111	89	296	778	373	346	1450	1796	1744	52	2	27	1825
Increase	2	......	......	1	......	14	......	......	......	......	......	......	5	1	......	......
Decrease	......	1	2	......	9	......	12	2	8	1	9	14	......	......	2	10

TABLE V. PUBLIC SCHOOLS: PERIOD OF SERVICE OF TEACHERS EMPLOYED DURING YEAR ENDED 30TH JUNE, 1903.

PART ONE.—The First Term closed 31st December, 1902.

COUNTIES.	No. of teachers employed in same District as during previous Term.	No. of teachers removed to a new District.	No. of new teachers this Term.	No. of teachers whose period of service is not reported.	No. of teachers not more than 3 years in the service employed this term.	PERIOD OF SERVICE OF TEACHERS OF GR., SUP. AND 1ST CLASS. Male Teachers Gr., Sup. and 1st Class. No. first Term employed.	No. second Term employed.	No. 1 to 2 years.	No. 2 to 3 years.	No. 3 to 5 years.	No. 5 to 7 years.	No. upwards of 7 years.	Female Teachers Gr., Sup. and 1st Class. No. first Term employed.	No. second Term employed.	No. 1 to 2 years.	No. 2 to 3 years.	No. 3 to 5 years.	No. 5 to 7 years.	No. upwards of 7 years.
Albert	34	21	15	....	30	....	....	....	2	....	....	6	1	....	1	2	5	2	2
Carleton	58	60	23	2	54	1	....	....	1	....	1	6	....	....	....	1	9	3	6
Charlotte	75	30	18	3	41	5	....	....	....	2	4	9	2	....	....	2	2	6	13
Gloucester	63	38	9	1	41	....	....	1	....	1	....	3	1	....	....	....	....	....	3
Kent	65	41	13	3	101	....	....	....	....	1	3	4	....	2	....	....	....	....	6
Kings	81	53	19	6	144	3	....	....	....	2	3	8	2	....	....	2	1	2	11
Madawaska	26	12	22	....	50	....	....	....	1	....	1	....	....	....	....	....	....	....	....
Northumberland	92	41	15	6	49	....	....	....	....	2	1	8	....	1	2	1	4	1	4
Queens	32	40	14	....	56	....	....	....	....	....	....	3	....	....	1	....	1	2	5
Restigouche	26	19	4	1	41	....	....	....	....	....	....	2	1	....	2	....	....	....	2
St. John	178	10	5	27	70	....	1	1	1	....	2	20	3	1	1	5	12	9	70
Sunbury	15	15	11	2	40	....	....	....	....	....	....	2	2	1	....	....	1	....	1
Victoria	30	21	6	2	54	....	....	....	....	....	....	3	....	....	....	1	1	1	3
Westmorland	119	62	25	9	168	....	1	1	4	1	5	8	3	2	4	1	10	4	22
York	86	71	32	7	176	1	1	1	....	3	1	9	1	....	1	1	5	6	15
New Brunswick	980	555	231	60	1115	10	3	4	9	12	24	91	16	7	12	16	51	36	163
Cor. Term, 1901	1055	505	158	72	638	4	....	8	11	26	20	84	6	2	21	21	53	61	140
Increase	....	....	73	....	477	6	3	....	....	....	1	7	10	5	....	....	....	....	14
Decrease	75	10	....	3	....	....	....	4	2	14	....	....	....	....	9	5	2	25	....

TABLE V. Part Two—THE SECOND TERM CLOSED 30TH JUNE, 1903.

COUNTIES.	No. of teachers employed in same District as during previous Term.	No. of teachers removed to a new District.	No. of new teachers this Term.	No. of teachers whose period of service is not reported.	No. of teachers not more than 3 years in the service employed this Term.	PERIOD OF SERVICE OF TEACHERS OF GR., SUP., AND 1st. CLASS. — MALE TEACHERS GR., SUP. AND 1ST. CLASS. No. first Term employed.	No. second Term employed.	No. 1 to 2 years.	No. 2 to 3 years.	No. 3 to 5 years.	No. 5 to 7 years.	No. upwards of 7 years.	FEMALE TEACHERS GR., SUP. AND 1ST CLASS. No. first Term employed.	No. second Term employed.	No. 1 to 2 years.	No. 2 to 3 years.	No. 3 to 5 years.	No. 5 to 7 years.	No. upwards of 7 years.
Albert	36	28	3	7	27	....	3	....	....	2	....	4	....	3	....	1	3	3	4
Carleton	89	72	10	3	58	....	2	1	2	2	2	6	1	2	....	1	5	5	6
Charlotte	84	43	7	6	49	....	5	....	....	1	3	8	....	1	....	2	2	6	15
Gloucester	82	16	7	3	33	....	....	1	....	1	....	3	....	....	1	....	....	....	1
Kent	69	40	7	4	30	....	....	1	....	1	1	5	....	....	1	....	....	1	4
Kings	91	52	5	1	53	....	1	2	....	3	3	4	1	1	....	3	1	3	10
Madawaska	34	11	12	1	36	....	....	....	1	....	1	1	....	....	....	....	....	....	....
Northumberland	118	21	2	4	41	....	....	....	....	1	2	7	....	....	2	8	3	4	2
Queens	41	36	7	2	42	....	....	....	....	1	....	3	....	1	1	1	1	....	6
Restigouche	36	8	1	1	11	....	....	....	....	....	....	2	....	....	3	....	....	1	3
St. John	186	13	2	23	21	....	....	2	1	....	4	18	2	3	1	4	14	14	67
Sunbury	22	12	5	2	15	....	....	1	....	....	....	....	....	1	....	....	1	1	1
Victoria	29	19	5	1	22	....	1	....	....	....	....	3	....	....	....	....	1	1	3
Westmorland	142	49	3	6	65	....	....	1	2	1	4	8	....	4	5	6	6	9	22
York	123	40	18	7	80	....	1	2	1	3	....	7	....	1	1	2	4	4	16
New Brunswick	1182	440	94	71	583	....	13	11	7	16	20	79	4	17	15	23	41	52	160
Cor. Term, 1902	1162	479	90	65	553	....	5	8	11	20	23	79	2	3	14	20	51	49	160
Increase	20		4	6	30	....	8	3	....	....	....	....	2	14	1	3	....	3	....
Decrease	....	39	....	....	....	....	....	....	4	4	3	....	....	....	....	....	10	....	....

TABLE V.—Continued. PERIOD OF SERVICE OF SECOND CLASS TEACHERS EMPLOYED DURING YEAR ENDED 30TH JUNE, 1903.

COUNTIES.	DURING THE TERM CLOSED 31ST DECEMBER, 1902.														DURING THE TERM CLOSED 30TH JUNE, 1903.													
	MALE TEACHERS, 2ND CLASS.							FEMALE TEACHERS, 2ND CLASS.							MALE TEACHERS, 2ND CLASS.							FEMALE TEACHERS, 2ND CLASS.						
	No. 1st Term employed.	No. 2nd Term employed.	No. from 1 to 2 years.	No. from 2 to 3 years.	No. from 3 to 5 years.	No. from 5 to 7 years.	No. upwards of 7 years.	No. 1st Term employed.	No. 2nd Term employed.	No. from 1 to 2 years.	No. from 2 to 3 years.	No. 3 to 5 years.	No. from 5 to 7 years.	No. upwards of 7 years.	No. 1st Term employed.	No. 2nd Term employed.	No. from 1 to 2 years.	No. from 2 to 3 years.	No. from 3 to 5 years.	No. from 5 to 7 years.	No. upwards of 7 years.	No. 1st Term employed.	No. 2nd Term employed.	No. from 1 to 2 years.	No. from 2 to 3 years.	No. from 3 to 5 years.	No. from 5 to 7 years.	No. upwards of 7 years.
Albert	4	1	..	..	..	2	1	8	..	3	6	7	8	6	..	1	..	..	..	2	2	...	8	3	3	15	5	5
Carleton	3	..	2	..	3	2	6	14	1	10	7	18	8	23	..	1	..	1	..	2	4	...	10	11	6	18	15	25
Charlotte	2	..	2	..	1	..	..	6	2	5	7	18	10	21	2	2	2	1	1	1	...	...	6	4	5	16	14	21
Gloucester	1	..	1	1	.	1	..	3	..	1	1	3	3	8	..	..	1	1	...	1	...	...	3	2	..	1	3	9
Kent	1	..	1	..	..	..	..	2	..	3	2	6	5	6	..	..	..	..	...	.	1	...	1	4	3	7	4	8
Kings	2	..	3	1	2	1	5	11	3	8	11	16	15	31	..	2	2	1	2	2	7	2	11	8	11	14	12	30
Madawaska	1	..	..	..	..	..	..	..	..	..	..	..	..	..	..	..	..	..	...	...	...	...	...	..	...	...	...	..
Northumberland	1	..	1	..	..	..	3	9	2	7	12	18	12	33	..	2	..	1	...	...	3	...	9	8	12	17	7	38
Queens	6	..	2	1	2	1	4	6	1	7	6	9	5	8	..	5	..	..	2	2	5	...	8	5	7	5	5	8
Restigouche	..	..	..	..	..	.	..	3	1	7	1	7	5	10	..	..	..	..	...	...	...	...	3	3	...	6	8	8
Saint John	..	..	1	1	.	..	4	2	..	3	3	13	13	57	..	..	..	..	1	...	5	...	2	3	3	6	12	50
Sunbury	1	..	.	1	1	.	2	5	..	1	2	3	4	3	..	..	..	..	1	1	2	1	3	...	1	4	6	3
Victoria	..	..	..	..	1	2	.	2	..	1	7	6	3	5	..	..	..	1	...	...	1	...	4	...	5	6	2	7
Westmorland	7	..	6	2	6	2	7	10	1	7	8	20	6	21	..	5	2	5	9	...	6	...	10	6	4	18	4	20
York	6	1	1	3	2	.	1	14	..	13	12	18	13	31	..	3	2	3	2	1	...	...	11	15	10	16	13	29
New Brunswick	35	2	20	10	18	11	33	95	11	81	85	162	110	283	2	21	9	14	18	12	36	3	89	72	70	149	110	273
Cor. Year 1901-'02	15	3	21	21	17	16	30	71	10	93	87	142	129		1	10	15	14	19	13	39	3	63	74	93	136	122	287
Increase	20	..	..	..	1	..	3	21	1	..	..	20	..	..	1	11	..	..	...	...	...	...	26	...	...	13	..	..
Decrease	..	1	1	11	..	5	..	..	..	15	2	..	19	3	..	..	6	..	1	1	3	...	...	2	23	...	12	14

TABLE VI.—PUBLIC SCHOOLS: TIME IN SESSION DURING THE YEAR ENDED 30TH JUNE, 1903.

COUNTIES.	The First Term Closed 31st Dec., 1902.							The Second Term Closed 30th June, 1903.							
	No. of Schools open this Term.	No. of Schools open less than 80 days.	No. in session 80 but less than 92 days.	Total in session less than 92 days.	No. in session the full Term of 92 days.*	Average days schools were in session during the Term.	Aggregate number of days schools open during this Term.	No. of Schools open this term.	No. of Schools open less than 80 days.	No. in session 80 but less than 100 days.	No. in session less than 100 days.	No. in session 100 days but less than 123 days.	No. in session the full Term of 123 days.**	Average days schools in session during this Term.	Aggregate number of days Schools open during this Term.
Albert	70	8	27	35	35	87.	6,113	68	9	1	10	30	28	111.6	7,593
Carleton	141	19	63	82	59	86.9	12,282½	151	15	11	26	74	51	111.	16,766
Charlotte	132	52	44	96	36	81.	10,738	135	19	7	26	67	42	109.8	14,832
Gloucester	108	4	57	61	47	89.	9,670	105	2	4	6	59	40	118.	12,406½
Kent	119	9	33	42	77	89.2	10,618½	116	11	8	19	52	45	111.9	12,987
Kings	153	24	52	76	77	85.	13,123	142	13	3	16	86	46	113.	16,749½
Madawaska	60		26	26	34	90.	5,404	57	7	4	11	34	12	110.7	6,312
Northumberland	149	12	62	74	75	89.	13,284	141	10	2	12	57	72	117.	16,521
Queens'	86	18	38	56	30	83.9	7,219½	83	14	1	15	45	23	(96	9,104½
Restigouche	49	3	20	23	26	89.	4,364½	45	2	6	8	20	17	113.5	5,110
Saint John	210	3	32	35	175	91.	19,117	206	3	1	4	51	151	120.9	24,922
Sunbury	41	9	19	28	13	82.8	3,397½	40	10	2	12	19	9	1 116	4,066½
Victoria	57	10	20	30	27	86.	4,930	53	10	4	14	25	14	104.	5,513
Westmorland	207	11	66	77	130	89.7	18,569½	195	7	4	11	75	109	118.	23,041½
York	196	23	80	103	93	87.4	17,134½	183	28	10	38	100	45	108.5	19,860½
New Brunswick	1,78	205	639	844	64	87.6	155,925½	1728	160	68	228	794	704	113.2	195,785
Cor. Terms, 1902-03	1,95	28	541	69	1,026	87.5	157,164	1736	151	67	218	849	669	113.0	196,338
Increase	.....	..	98	75	....	.1	....	.....	9	1	10	......	35	.2	....
Decrease	17	23	..	.	92	......	1,238½	10	......	....	..	55	..	......	533

*In the First Term there were 82 teaching days in Cities, Towns and other Districts having eight weeks vacation; in all other Districts there were 92 teaching days. The actual number of days the schools in the former were open is raised to the basis of 92 days for the purposes of comparison.

**In the Second Term there were 122 teaching days in St. John City, and 123 days in all other districts. The former is raised to the basis of the latter for purposes of comparison.

TABLE VII. PUBLIC SCHOOLS: VISITS—PUBLIC EXAMINATIONS—PRIZES: FOR THE YEAR ENDED 30TH JUNE, 1903.

THE FIRST TERM CLOSED 31ST DECEMBER, 1902.

COUNTIES.	Visits. No. by the Trustees and Secretary.	Visits. No. by the County Inspector.	Visits. No. by members of Parliament.	Visits. No. by Clergymen.	Visits. No. by Teachers.	Visits. No. by other visitors.	Examinations. No. of Schools holding public examinations during the Term.	Examinations. No. of Schools not holding public examinations during the Term.	Prizes. No. of prizes given to the pupils.	Prizes. Value of the prizes.
Albert	133	34	....	22	25	66	55	15	2	$ 0.70
Carleton	225	77	16	36	4	07	104	37	18	8.65
Charlotte	48	70	4	529		30	102	30	6	1.85
Gloucester	394	41	5	16	126	1410	94	14	7	5.20
Kent	359	55	....	44	99	1261	88	31	37	12.05
Kings	227	113	....	58	82	1482	124	29	38	17.49
Madawaska	177	13	6	37	55	678	54	5	45	13.60
Northumberland	396	100	9	60	108	1974	124	25	36	15.65
Queens	162	57	1	29	68	830	57	29	14	4.30
Restigouche	114	39	1	8	21	623	45	4	13	4.75
Saint John	309	128	4	89	158	1100	199	11	25	19.85
Sunbury	58	39	....	6	29	310	25	16	7	2.54
Victoria	137	39	....	16	22	303	42	15	27	5.93
Westmorland	323	125	....	66	175	2218	167	40	24	6.00
York	267	122	1	89	129	1511	62	26	21	9.50
New Brunswick	3529	1052	47	627	1400	16763	1342	327	320	$128.66
Cor. Terms, 1901-02	3958	841	37	725	1373	[illegible]	1553	242	301	132.95
Increase	....	211	10	....	27	1	....	85	19	....
Dec.	429	....	....	98	....	....	211	....	....	$4.29

THE SECOND TERM CLOSED 30TH JUNE, 1903.

COUNTIES.	Visits. No. by the Trustees and Secretary.	Visits. No. by the County Inspector.	Visits. No. by members of Parliament.	Visits. No. by Clergymen.	Visits. No. by Teachers.	Visits. No. by other visitors.	Examinations. No. of Schools holding public examinations during the Term.	Examinations. No. of schools not holding public examinations during the Term.	Prizes. No. of prizes given to the pupils.	Prizes. Value of the prizes.
Albert	150	41	1	18	54	761	62	6	4	$ 1.00
Carleton	280	141	6	56	119	1370	121	30	23	18.30
Charlotte	329	114	....	63	156	1695	105	30	5	7.75
Gloucester	408	87	3	54	125	1294	87	18	19	13.25
Kent	415	69	4	53	93	1607	97	19	25	12.46
Kings	231	147	....	36	87	1774	113	35	58	34.22
Madawaska	147	40	8	39	43	624	54	3	19	3.14
Northumberland	350	110	4	75	121	1553	110	31	127	89.85
Queens	189	74	5	32	45	989	67	17	8	3.75
Restigouche	125	32	4	22	22	602	40	5	10	2.90
Saint John	476	115	....	112	139	2009	201	5	14	9.35
Sunbury	65	33	....	9	21	398	29	11	5	1.75
Victoria	141	33	2	16	30	463	43	10	38	17.84
Westmorland	593	25	9	77	163	2355	173	22	62	34.65
York	260	160	....	77	146	1711	136	48	34	24.40
New Brunswick	4159	1221	46	739	1364	19355	1438	290	451	$274.01
Cor. Terms, 1901-02	4521	1362	51	849	1372	20236	1516	220	417	340.89
Increase	....	....	....	....	....	....	....	70	34	....
Dec.	362	141	5	110	8	881	78	....	....	$66.28

TABLE VIII.—PUBLIC SCHOOLS: AVERAGE SALARIES OF TEACHERS FOR THE YEAR ENDED JUNE 30TH, 1903.

FROM THE RATES PAID IN THE TERM ENDED JUNE 30TH, 1903.

COUNTIES.	COMMON SCHOOLS. Ave'age rate per year to Male Teachers.			COMMON SCHOOLS.* Av'ge Rate per year to Female Teachers			AVERAGE SUPERIOR SCHOOLS	AVERAGE GRAMMAR SCHOOLS
	1st Class.	2nd Class.	3rd Class.	1st Class.	2nd Class.	3rd Class.		
Albert	$402 50	$263 40	$208 00	$251 90	$215 18	$190 12	$ 541 25	See Table XIII.
Carleton	407 81	287 37	251 00	335 60	231 55	192 18	510 00	
Charlotte	439 08	318 55	249 00	332 63	245 90	196 41	570 00	
Gloucester	385 00	273 33	215 37	225 00	226 83	184 40	583 33	
Kent	315 00	308 00	206 37	261 50	216 30	179 82	525 00	
Kings	360 00	264 56	231 00	271 95	214 33	186 54	527 00	
Madawaska	267 50	....	235 20	....	....	177 13	500 00	
Northumberland	485 00	290 33	217 75	262 85	235 75	185 75	633 00	
Queens	292 50	255 85	218 62	250 73	211 06	180 54	575 00	
Restigouche	....	....	244 50	299 57	237 04	191 43	625 00	
Saint John	833 68	504 66	231 25	381 74	314 52	180 88	566 60	
Sunbury	....	299 50	188 00	261 25	207 20	172 27	500 00	
Victoria	331 50	283 50	197 00	255 00	224 51	203 51	525 00	
Westmorland	561 00	279 48	229 89	319 20	235 99	195 94	585 71	
York	566 66	282 72	206 05	327 77	227 53	186 40	575 00	
New Brunswick	$522 86	$291 22	$199 77	$328 21	$237 34	$186 30	$570 96	....
Average Salaries, 1902	510 59	286 39	220 85	315 25	232 38	180 51	569 41	....
Increase	$12 27	$4 83	....	$12 96	$4 96	$5 79	$1 55	....
Decrease	....	....	$31 08	....	....	....	....	....

TABLE IX. PUBLIC SCHOOLS: DISBURSEMENTS OF THE PROVINCIAL GRANTS FOR THE YEAR ENDED JUNE 30TH, 1903.

COUNTIES.	For First Term ended December 31st, 1902					For Second Term ended June 30th, 1903.					For the Year.	
	Common Schools. (1)	Superior Schools. (2)	Grammar Schools. (3)	Special to those teaching in poor Districts (included in amount in Column 1.)	Total.	Common Schools. (1)	Superior Schools. (2)	Grammar Schools. (3)	Special to those teaching in poor Districts (included in amount in Column 1.)	Total.	Total special aid to those teaching in poor Districts.	Total.
Albert	$2,644.44	$306.98	$140.00	$227.23	$3,091.42	$3,275.12	$143.08	$210.00	$267.39	$3,928.20	$494.62	$7,019.62
Carleton	4,841.01	405.82	280.00	118.64	5,526.83	6,653.11	589.36	420.00	111.75	7,662.47	230.39	13,189.30
Charlotte	4,437.89	490.70	138.29	175.49	5,066.88	6,446.78	743.02	198.90	223.29	7,388.70	398.78	12,455.58
Gloucester	3,626.08	308.67	140.00	414.46	4,074.75	4,666.29	421.48	210.00	504.47	5,297.77	918.93	9,372.52
Kent	3,902.07	398.78	140.00	452.39	4,440.85	4,748.05	597.56	210.00	505.06	5,555.61	957.45	9,996.46
Kings	5,417.58	42.68	138.29	[illegible]	5,998.55	6,888.79	745.74	191.22	302.16	7,825.75	608.06	13,824.30
Madawaska	1,760.34	100.00	......	[illegible]	1,860.34	1,838.30	150.00	......	94.81	2,088.30	194.63	3,948.73
Northumberland	5,[illegible]9.61	313.96	135.73	312.81	5,734.30	6,619.92	735.46	210.00	309.84	7,565.38	739.65	13,320.08
Queens	3,038.39	100.00	125.58	218.50	3,263.97	3,728.91	150.00	167.44	231.93	4,046.35	450.43	7,310.32
Restigouche	1,674.58	100.00	140.00	122.68	1,914.58	1,950.96	150.00	210.00	111.31	2,310.96	234.02	4,234.54
Saint John	7,971.08	300.00	510.91	109.37	8,812.62	11,205.32	410.24	708.76	110.07	12,534.32	225.64	21,346.04
Sunbury	1,409.29	100.00	......	129.57	1,509.29	1,582.49	143.02	......	105.96	1,725.51	235.53	3,234.80
Victoria	1,931.76	100.00	140.00	261.49	2,171.76	2,219.61	150.00	210.00	238.13	2,579.61	520.02	4,751.37
Westmorland	7,235.70	665.12	590.00	239.26	8,490.82	9,283.81	1,043.90	840.00	201.04	11,177.71	441.20	19,668.53
York	6,736.24	621.51	411.46	380.15	7,769.21	7,885.06	863.00	624.87	332.47	9,373.80	711.62	17,143.10
New Brunswick	$61,711.66	$4984.22	$3030.29	$3606.56	$69,726.17	$79,231.61	$7306.82	$4501.19	$3703.01	$91,000.62	$7400.47	$160,825.79
Cor. Terms, 1901 and 1902	62,552.48	5055.38	3051.09	3817.59	70,658.95	79,969.37	7305.28	[illegible]	4,[illegible]29.64	91,508.24	7,047.23	162,227.19
Increase							$61.54	$207.60				
Decrease	$840.82	$71.16	$20.80	$211.03	$932.78	$737.76	......	......	$335.73	$408.62	$546.70	$1,401.40

TABLE X.—PUBLIC SCHOOLS: Apportionment of County Fund to Trustees for the Year ended June 30th, 1903.

Part One.—First Term ended December 31st, 1902.

Drafts issued by the Chief Superintendent, payable by the respective County Treasurers.

COUNTIES.	Grand Total days' attendance of Pupils; rectified for County Fund Apportionment. (Term 92 days.)	In respect of the services of qualified Teachers exclusive of Assistants, for the time the Schools were in Session. [1]	Special to Poor Districts (embraced in column 1.)	In respect of the average number of Pupils in attendance, as compared with the whole average number of Pupils attending the Schools in the County and the time in operation. [2]	Special to Poor Districts (included in column 2.)	Total to the Trustees. This Term. Whole amount apportioned this Term. *[3]	Total special to Poor Districts, (included in column 3).	Rate per Pupil in attendance the full Term per colum 2. (4) In Ordinary Districts.	In Poor Districts.
Albert	123,848	$1,106 55	$110 03	$ 419 70	$ 27 74	$1,526 25	$137 77	0 31+	0 41+
Carleton	228,399	2,055 62	53 81	1,150 03	15 54	3 205 65	69 35	0 46+	0 61+
Charlotte	244,840	1,860 06	99 21	1,427 19	33 63	3 287 25	132 84	0 53+	0 71—
Gloucester	249,321	1,797 25	217 38	2,286 68	221 65	4,083 93	439 03	0 84+	1 12+
Kent	231,420	1,966 15	236 85	1,492 62	144 09	3 458 77	380 94	0 50+	0 79—
Kings	212,330½	2 297 53	157 96	838 22	32 36	3 135 75	190 32	0 36+	0 48+
Madawaska	119,129	919 51	53 41	927 14	44 90	1,846 65	98 31	0 72—	0 96—
Northumberland	312,436½	2 338 65	178 98	1,905 30	74 17	4 243 95	253 15	0 56+	0 75—
Queens	99,891	1,260 93	99 02	340 62	17 74	1,601 55	116 76	0 31+	0 41+
Restigouche	111,742	771 90	60 28	816 00	38 87	1,587 90	99 15	0 67+	0 89+
Saint John	627,368½	3,180 14	02 75	4,433 71	21 95	7,613 85	81 70	0 65+	0 87—
Sunbury	54,636	616 88	63 76	242 47	16 72	859 35	80 48	0 41+	0 55—
Victoria	78,853	945 12	130 85	393 51	42 75	†1,338 63	173 00	0 45+	0 60+
Westmorland	518,850½	3 153 99	118 24	2,855 01	60 25	6,009 00	178 49	0 50+	0 67—
York	258,347	2,607 58	201 22	1,067 87	48 03	3,675 45	249 25	0 38+	0 51—
New Brunswick	3,471,412½	26,877 86	$1,843 75	$20,596 07	$840 39	$47 473 93	$2 684 14	0 54+	0 72+

*The balance of the County Fund ($1,141.40) was paid to the School for the Blind, Halifax, N. S.
†Includes $14.88 from term ended June, 1902.

TABLE X.—PUBLIC SCHOOLS: APPORTIONMENT OF COUNTY FUND TO TRUSTEES FOR THE YEAR ENDED 30TH JUNE, 1903.

PART TWO.—Second Term ended June 30th, 1903.

Drafts issued by the Chief Superintendent, payable by the respective County Treasurers.

COUNTIES.	Grand Total days' attendance of Pupils; rectified for County Fund Apportionment (Term 123 days)	In respect of the services of qualified Teachers exclusive of Assistants, for the time the Schools were in Session. [1]	Special to Poor Districts (embraced in column 1.)	In respect of the average number of Pupils in attendance, as compared with the whole average number of Pupils attending the Schools in the County and the time in operation. [2]	Special to Poor Districts (included in column 2)	Total to the Trustees. This Term. Whole amount apportioned this Term. *[3]	Total to the Trustees. This Term. Total special to Poor Districts, (included in column 3.)	Rate per Pupil in attendance the full Term per column 2. (4) In Ordinary Districts	Rate per Pupil in attendance the full Term per column 2. (4) In Poor Districts.
Albert	153,045½	$ 989 56	$ 93 71	$ 536 69	$ 33 34	$1,526 25	$127 05	$0 43 +	$0 57 +
Carleton	314 546	2 105 31	46 93	1,100 34	15 83	3 205 65	62 76	0 39	0 57 +
Charlotte	329,097½	1 900 90	84 53	1 386 35	26 88	3 287 25	111 41	0 51 +	0 68 +
Gloucester	300,057½	1,706 88	195 76	2,371 02	195 90	4 077 90	391 66	0 97 +	1 20 +
Kent	290,095½	1,791 44	200 02	1 672 12	155 81	3 463 56	355 83	0 79 +	1 05 +
Kings	263,108	2 085 74	117 42	1,050 01	32 94	3,135 75	150 36	0 40 +	65 +
Madawaska	148,932	824 03	39 22	1,022 62	42 56	1,846 65	81 78	0 84 +	1 12 +
Northumberland	383 147½	2 168 51	153 96	2,112 94	82 79	4,281 45	236 75	0 67 +	0 80 +
Queens	128,157½	1,189 80	94 20	411 75	21 72	1,601 55	115 92	0 30 +	0 52 +
Restigouche	122,865	650 05	41 62	937 85	37 57	1 587 90	79 19	0 93 +	1 24 +
Saint John	814,618	3 090 35	51 20	4 523 50	21 32	7,613 85	72 52	0 08 +	0 91
Sunbury	68 925½	536 73	39 96	322 62	17 41	859 35	57 37	0 57 +	0 70 +
Victoria	97 623	773 71	101 40	550 04	54 12	1,323 75	155 52	0 69 +	0 92 +
Westmorland	630,247½	2,910 00	78 28	3 099 00	47 28	6 009 00	125 56	0 60 +	0 80 +
York	326,599	2,173 28	135 39	1,502 17	58 31	3,675 45	193 70	0 56 +	0 75
New Brunswick	4 371,065	$24 896 20	$1,473 60	$22,599 02	$843 78	$47,495 31	$2 317 38	$0 63 +	$0 84 +

*The balance of the County Fund ($1,105.14) was paid to the School for the Blind, Halifax, N. S.

TABLE XI.—PROVINCIAL AND COUNTY FUND GRANTS TO THE SCHOOL FOR THE BLIND, HALIFAX; AND COUNTY FUND GRANT TO THE INSTITUTION FOR THE DEAF AND DUMB.

Year Ended 30th June, 1903.

COUNTIES.	School for the Blind, Halifax. Term ended Dec. 31, 1902. No. of Pupils.	Provincial Grant, at rate of $75 per pupil per year.	Grant from County fund at rate of $75 per pupil per year.	Term ended June 30, 1903. No. of Pupils.	Provincial Grant, at rate of $75 per pupil per year.	Grant from County fund at rate of $75 per pupil per year.	Total Provincial Grant for the year.	Total from County fund for the year.	Institution for the Deaf and Dumb. Term ended Dec. 31, 1902. No. of Pupils.	Grant from County fund at the rate of $60 per pupil per year.	Term ended June 30, 1903. No. of Pupils.	Grant from County fund at the rate of $60 per pupil per year.	Total for the year.	Total County Fund Grants to both Institutions.
Albert	3	$112.50	$112.50	3	$112.50	$112.50	$225.00	$225.00						$ 225.00
Carleton	1	37.50	37.50	1	37.50	37.50	75.00	75.00						75.00
Charlotte	2	75.00	75.00	2	75.00	75.00	150.00	150.00						150.00
Gloucester	3	106.47	106.47	3	112.50	112.50	218.97	218.97						218.97
Kent	4	134.93	134.93	4	130.14	130.14	265.07	265.07						265.07
Kings	3	112.50	112.50	3	112.50	112.50	225.00	225.00						225.00
Madawaska														
Northumberland	1	37.50	37.50				37.50	37.50						37.50
Queens	2	75.00	75.00	2	75.00	75.00	150.00	150.00						150.00
Restigouche														
St. John	4	150.00	150.00	4	150.00	150.00	300.00	300.00						300.00
Sunbury														
Victoria														
Westmorland	8	300.00	300.00	8	300.00	300.00	600.00	600.00						600.00
York														
New Brunswick	31	$1141.40	$1141.40	30	$1105.14	$1105.14	$2246.54	$2246.54						$2246.54

TABLE XII.—SUPERIOR SCHOOLS: For the Year ended June 30th, 1903.

Part One.—Term ended December, 1902.

Embodied in Table IX. and Foregoing Tables.

No. and Name of District.	Parish.	County.	Teachers.	Provincial Allowance	Total to County.
Elgin Corner, No. 2.	Elgin	Albert	C M McCann	$106 98	
Hillsborough, No. 2.	Hillsborough	"	W M Burns	100 00	
Hopewell Hill, No. 2	Hopewell	"	H H Stuart	100 00	$306 98
Hartland, No. 3	Brighton	Carleton	J E Page	105 82	
Florenceville, No. 4	Simonds and Wicklow	"	F C Squiers	100 00	
Jacksonville, No. 7	Wakefield	"	C H Gray	100 00	
Centreville, No. 4	Wilmot and Wicklow	"	Ruth L Reid	100 00	405 82
North Head, No. 1	Grand Manan	"	P Girdwood	100 00	
St. George, No. 1.	St. George	Charlotte	H E Sinclair	100 00	
Moore's Mills, No. 1½	St. James and St. David	"	Bessie J Thorne	90 70	
St. Stephen, (Town)	St. Stephen	"	P G McFarlane	100 00	
Milltown, (Town)	"	"	J B Sutherland	100 00	490 70
Bathurst Village, No. 16	Bathurst	Gloucester	C J Mersereau	87 19	
			Ina F Mersereau	11 59	
Petit Rocher, No. 4	Beresford	"	Jerome Boudreau	106 98	
Tracadie, No. 3	Saumarez	"	E L O'Brien	102 91	308 67
Harcourt, No. 5	Harcourt	Kent	Miriam Kyle	98 78	
Rexton, No. 2	Richibucto	"	R G Girvan	100 00	
Bass River, No. 9	Weldford	"	A B Boyer	100 00	
Buctouche, No. 1	Wellington	"	G A Coates	100 00	398 78
Penobsquis, No. 1	Cardwell	"	G T Morton	42 68	
			Forward		$1910 95

TABLE XII.—Part One.—*Continued.*

Name and No. of District.	Parish.	County.	Teachers.	Provincial Allowance	Total to County.
			Brought forward		$1910 95
Hampton, No. 2	Hampton	Kings	R R Cormier	$100 00	
Havelock Corner, No. 8	Havelock	"	J S Lord	70 73	
" "		"	Aaron Perry	29 27	
Bloomfield Station, No. 2	Norton	"	Amasa Ryder	100 00	
Apohaqui, No. 25	Studholm and Sussex	"	G P McCrea	100 00	442 68
Edmundston, No. 1	Madawaska	Madawaska	John Barnett, Jr	100 00	100 00
Blackville, No. 6	Blackville	North'd	M R Tuttle	106 98	
Doaktown, No. 4	Blissfield	"	G A Wathen	106 98	
Millerton, No. 1	Derby	"	E A Crocker	100 00	
Douglastown, No. 6	Newcastle	"	M R Benn	100 00	
Newcastle, (Town)	"	"	A E G McKenzie	100 00	513 96
Chipman, No. 11	Chipman	Queens	A C M Lawson	100 00	100 00
Dalhousie, No. 1	Dalhousie	Restigouche	R B Masterton	100 00	100 00
Fairville, No. 2	Lancaster	St. John	Angus DeWar	100 00	
Milford, No. 13	"	"	W A Nelson	100 00	
St. Martins, No. 2	St. Martins	"	W L McDiarmid	100 00	300 00
Fredericton Junct., No. 1	Gladstone	Sunbury	F N Patterson	48 84	
" "		"	C D Richards	51 16	100 00
Grand Falls, No. 7	Grand Falls	Victoria	J C Carruthers	100 00	100 00
Dorchester, No. 2	Dorchester	Westmorland	B P Steeves	100 00	
Sackville, No. 9	Sackville	"	F A Dixon	100 00	
Middle Sackville, No. 11	Sackville	"	F S James	95 12	
Petitcodiac, No. 1	Salisbury	"	Harry Burns	100 00	
			Forward		$3667 59

TABLE XII.—Part One.—*Continued.*

Name and No. of District.	Parish.	County.	Teachers.	Provincial Allowance	Total to County.
			Brought forward		$3667 59
Salisbury, No. 24	Salisbury, Monct. & Coverdale	Westmorland	M J Wallace	$100 00	
Shediac, No. 10	Shediac	"	B H Webb	100 00	
Port Elgin, No. 1	Westmorland & Botsford	"	T J Allen	100 00	695 12
Keswick Ridge, No. 1	Bright	York	A H Schriver	105 23	
Benton, No. 23 A	Canterbury & Woodstock	"	R E McClintock	104 65	
McAdam Junct, No. 9	McAdam	"	H F Perkins	106 98	
Harvey Station, No. 2	Manners Sutton	"	J P Bulyea	104 65	
Gibson, No. 2	St. Mary's	"	Ida B Myles	76 83	
			J B DeLong	23 17	
Marysville, No. 3	"	"	W T Day	100 00	621 51
					$4984 22

TABLE XII.—PART TWO—TERM ENDED JUNE 30TH, 1903.

No. and Name of District.	Parish.	County.	Teacher.	Provincial Allowance	Total for County.
Elgin Cor., No. 2	Elgin	Albert	Clive M McCann	$143 08	
Hillsborough, No. 2	Hillsborough	"	W M Burns	150 00	
Hopewell Hill, No. 2	Hopewell	"	Henry H Stuart	150 00	$443 08
Hartland, No. 3	Brighton	Carleton	John E Page	143 02	
Florenceville, No. 4	Simonds and Wicklow	"	Fred C Squiers	150 00	
Jacksonville, No. 7	Wakefield	"	Clinton H Gray	150 00	
Centreville, No. 4	Wilmot and Wicklow	"	Ruth L Reid	119 51	
			Janie M Kinney	26 83	589 36
North Head, No. 1	Grand Manan	Charlotte	Peter Girdwood	150 00	
St. George, No. 1	St. George	"	H Ernest Sinclair	150 00	
Moore's Mills, No. 1½	St. James and St. David	"	Bessie J Thorne	143 02	
Milltown (Town)	St. Stephen	"	John B Sutherland	150 00	
St. Stephen (Town)	"	"	P G McFarlane	150 00	743 02
Bathurst Village, No. 16	Bathurst	Gloucester	C J Mersereau	149 39	
Petit Rocher, No. 4	Beresford	"	Jerome Boudreau	131 39	
Tracadie, No. 3	Saumarez	"	Edward L O'Brien	140 70	421 48
Harcourt, No 5	Harcourt	Kent	Angus Dewar	147 56	
Rexton, No. 2	Richibucto	"	Robert G Girvan	150 00	
Bass River, No. 9	Weldford	"	Fred J Carruthers	150 00	
Buctouche, No. 1	Wellington	"	Geo A Coates	150 00	597 56
Penobsquis, No. 1	Cardwell	Kings	W C Anderson	149 40	
Hampton, No. 2	Hampton	"	Rex R Cormier	150 00	
Bloomfield Station, No. 2	Norton	"	Amasa Ryder	150 00	
Apohaqui, No. 25	Studholm and Sussex	"	Geo P McCrea	150 00	
			Forward	....	$2794 50

TABLE XII.—Part Two.—*Continued.*

No. and Name of District.	Parish.	County.	Teacher	Provincial Allowance	Total for County.
			Brought forward	....	$2794 50
Havelock Corner, No. 8	Havelock	Kings	Baxter B Barnes	$146 34	745 74
Edmundston, No. 1	Madawaska	Madawaska	John Barnet, Jr	150 00	150 00
Blackville, No. 6	Blackville	North'd	M R Tuttle	142 44	
Doaktown, No 4	Blissfield	,,	Geo A Wathen	143 02	
Millerton, No. 1	Derby	,,	E A Crocker	150 00	
Douglastown, No. 6	Newcastle	,,	M R Benn	150 00	
Newcastle, (Town)	Newcastle	,,	A E G McKenzie	150 00	735 46
Chipman, No. 11	Chipman	Queens	A C M Lawson	150 00	150 00
Dalhousie, No. 1	Dalhousie	Restigouche	Robt B Masterton	150 00	150 00
Fairville, No. 2	Lancaster	St. John	Sarah Sterling	140 24	
Milford, No. 13	Lancaster	,,	W Albert Nelson	150 00	
St. Martins, No. 2	St. Martins	,,	W L McDiarmid	150 00	440 24
Fredericton Junction, No. 1	Gladstone	Sunbury	Holland R McGill	143 02	143 02
Grand Falls, No. 7	Grand Falls	Victoria	J C Carruthers	150 00	150 00
Dorchester, No. 2	Dorchester	Westmorland	Blanchard P Steeves	150 00	
Sackville, No. 9	Sackville	"	F A Dixon	150 00	
Salisbury, No. 24	Salisbury, Monct. & Cover	"	Martin J Wallace	146 34	
Port Elgin, No 1	West'd and Botsford	"	T J Allen	150 00	
Middle Sackville, No. 11	Sackville	"	F S James	147 56	
Shediac, No. 10	Shediac	"	B H Webb	150 00	
Petitcodiac, No. 1	Salisbury	"	Harry Burns	150 00	1043 90
Keswick Ridge, No. 1	Bright	York	Wm McL Barker	140 69	
Benton, 23 A	Canterbury & Woodstock	"	R E McClintock	141 86	
			Forward	....	$6502 86

TABLE XII.—PART TWO.—*Continued.*

No. and Name of District.	Parish.	County.	Teachers.	Provincial Allowance	Total for County.
			Brought forward	....	$6502 86
McAdam Junction, No. 9..	McAdam	York	Henry F Perkins......	$143 02	
Harvey Station, No. 2.....	Manners-Sutton	"	John P Bulyea	138 39	
Gibson, No. 2............	St. Marys..............	"	Ida B Myles	150 00	
Marysville, No. 3.........	St. Marys.......... ...	"	W T Day............	150 00	863 96
				....	$7366 82

TABLE XIII. GRAMMAR SCHOOLS: The Year Ended June 30th, 1903.

(Included in Previous Table.)

PART ONE.—The Term Closed December 31st, 1902.

Locality.		Names of Principals and other Teachers Receiving Grammar School Grants.	Above Grade VIII.							Legally authorized days Department was open.	Provincial Grant, &c. Salaries of the Teachers		
					Pupils.								
Counties.	Towns.		No of Dept'ments.	No. of Teachers and Assistants.	Grade IX	Grade X.	Grade XI	Grade XII.	Total No.		Provincial aid for the Term	Salary from Trustees per year.	Rate of Salary for year.
Albert	Alma	T. E. Colpitts, A. B.	1	1	9	5	....	..	14	82	$140.00	$350.00	$ 700.00
Carleton	Woodstock	G. H. Harrison, A. B.	2	2	56	15	12	....	83	82	140.00	650.00	1,000.00
		Julia Neales								82	140.00	350.00	700.00
Charlotte	St. Andrews	J. A. Allen, A. B.	2	3	23	18	9	....	50	64	109.27	450.00	800.00
		Frank Allen								17	29.02	450.00	800.00
Gloucester	Bathurst	R. D. Hanson, A B.	1	1	20	4	....	..	24	82	140.00	350.00	700.00
Kent	Richibucto	C. H. Cowperthwaite, A. B.	1	1	13	3	....	..	16	82	140.00	350.00	700.00
Kings	Sussex	A. B. Maggs, A. M.	2	2	15	12	6	..	33	81	138.29	500.00	850.00
Northumberland	Chatham	Philip Cox, Ph. D.	2	2	52	....	13	..	65	79½	135.73	750.00	1,100.00
Queens	Gagetown	D. L. Mitchell, A. B.	1	1	5	5	3	..	13	90	125.58	300.00	600.00
Restigouche	Campbellton	E. W. Lewis, A. B.	1	1	24	11	3	...	38	82	140.00	650.00	1,000.00
Saint John	St. John	H. S. Bridges, Ph. D.	11	12	206	123	87	17	433	82	....	2000.00	2,000.00
		Wm. Brodie, A. B.								81	138.97	850.00	1,200.00
		W. J. S. Myles, A. M.								82	140.69	850.00	1,200.00
		T. E. Powers, A. B.								82	140.69	600.00	950.00
		Elizabeth McNaughton								82	120.59	300.00	600.00
Victoria	Andover	Wm. M. Veazey, A. B.	1	1	8	7	3	....	18	82	140.00	350.00	700.00
Westmorland	Moncton	Geo. J. Oulton, A. M.	4	5	60	42	45	....	156	82	140.00	850.00	1,200.00
		G. Fred McNally, A. B.								82	140.00	650.00	1,000.00
		C. H. Acheson								9	15.37	650.00	1,000.00
		W. A. Cowperthwaite, A. B								73	124.63	500.00	850.00
		H. B. Steeves, A. B.								82	140.00	500.00	850.00
York	Fredericton	B. C. Foster, A. M.	4	5	75	17	49	....	141	82	140.00	850.00	1,200.00
		A. S. McFarlane, A. M								82	140.00	500.00	850.00
		H. H. Hagerman, A. M.								37	63.17	650.00	1,000.00
		Frank N. Patterson, A. B.								40	68.29	400.00	750.00
New Brunswick			33	37	575	262	230	17	1084	....	$3030.29	$15,650.00	$24,300.00
Cor. Term, 1901			32	34	546	323	187	10	1066	....	3051.09	13,850.00	21,450.00
Increase			1	3	29		43	7	18			$1,800.00	$ 2,850.00
Decrease						61					$20.80		

TABLE XIII. PART TWO.—GRAMMAR SCHOOLS: THE TERM ENDED JUNE 30TH, 1904.

(INCLUDED IN PREVIOUS TABLES.)

LOCALITY.		Names of Principals and other Teachers Receiving Grammar School Grants.	ABOVE GRADE VIII.							Legally authorized days Department was open.	Provincial Grant, &c. Salaries of the Teachers.		
					Pupils.								
Counties.	Towns.		No. of Dep'tments.	No. of Teachers and Assistants.	Grade IX	Grade X	Grade XI	Grade XII	Total No.		Provincial aid for the Term.	Salary from Trustees per year.	Rate of Salary for year.
Albert	Alma	T. E. Colpitts, A. B.	1	1	7	4	1	....	12	123	$210 00	$350 00	$ 700 00
Carleton	Woodstock	G. H. Harrison, A. B.	2	2	50	14	13	....	77	123	210 00	650 00	1000 00
		Julia Neales								123	210 00	350 00	700 00
Charlotte	St. Andrews	J. A. Allen, A. B.	2	2	25	17	9	....	51	116½	198 90	450 00	800 00
Gloucester	Bathurst	R. D. Hanson, A. B.	1	1	16	6	....	....	22	123	210 00	350 00	700 00
Kent	Richibucto	C. H. Cowperthwaite, A. B.	1	1	10	3	....	....	13	123	210 00	350 00	700 00
Kings	Sussex	A. B. Maggs, A. B.	2	2	16	9	8	....	33	112	191 22	500 00	850 00
Northumberland	Chatham	Philip Cox, Ph. D.	2	2	71	....	12	....	83	123	210 00	750 00	1100 00
Queens	Gagetown	D. L. Mitchell, A. B.	1	1	5	7	....	....	12	120	167 44	300 00	600 00
Restigouche	Campbellton	E. W. Lewis, A. B.	1	1	19	12	2	....	33	123	210 00	650 00	1000 00
Saint John	St. John	H. S. Bridges, Ph. D.	11	12	180	112	86	17	395	120	......	2400 00	2400 00
		Wm. Brodie, A. B.								118	202 45	850 00	1200 00
		W. J. S. Myles, A. M.								121	207 59	850 00	1200 00
		T. E. Powers, A. B.								122	209 31	600 00	950 00
		Elizabeth McNaughton								122	179 41	300 00	600 00
Victoria	Andover	Wm. M. Veazy, A. B.	1	1	8	7	3	....	18	123	210 00	330 00	700 00
Westmorland	Moncton	Geo. J. Oulton, A. M.	4	4	64	35	42	....	141	123	210 00	850 00	1200 00
		G. Fred. McNally, A. B.								123	210 00	650 00	1000 00
		H. B. Steeves, A. B.								123	210 00	500 00	850 00
		W. A. Cowperthwaite, A. B.								123	210 00	500 00	850 00
York	Fredericton	B. C. Foster, A. M.	4	4	67	32	30	....	129	122	208 29	950 00	1300 00
		A. S. McFarlane, A. M.								122	208 29	550 00	900 00
		F. N. Patterson, A. B.								122	208 29	400 00	750 00
New Brunswick			33	34	538	258	206	17	1010	......	$4,501 19	$14450 00	$22050 00
Cor. Term, 1902			32	35	494	298	182	8	982	......	4,293 59	13750 00	21000 00
Increase			1	......	44	......	24	9	37	......	207 60	700 00	$1050 00
Decrease			......	1	......	40	......	......	......	......	......	......	......

TABLE XIV.—PROVINCIAL NORMAL SCHOOL; FOR SESSION ENDED JUNE, 1903.

NORMAL DEPARTMENT. Students in Attendance.	No. attended.	Left through various causes.	Failed to Classify	Eligible for Examination.	English Dept. Males.	English Dept. Females.	French Dept. Males.	French Dept. Female.	Total.	Model Dept. Pupils. Boys.	Model Dept. Pupils. Girls.	Model Dept. Pupils. Totals.
Term ended Dec., 1902										78	108	186
First term ended Dec., 1902	47	1		46	5	29	1	11	46			
Session ended June, 1903	182	15		167	27	140			167			
Second term ended May '03	13		2	11			2	9	11			
Term ended June, 1903										73	104	177
New Brunswick	242	16	2	224	32	160	3	20	224			
Cor, Session last year	269			269	67	189	1	12	269			
Increase		16	2				2	8				
Decrease	27			45	35	29			45			

PROVINCIAL GRANTS TO OCTOBER 31, 1903. On Account of Salaries.	Amount.
Wm. Crocket, M. A., LL. D.	$1600 00
Herbert C. Creed, M. A., D. Lit.	1200 00
H. H. Hagerman, M. A.	1137 38
George A. Inch, B. A.	1100 00
A. Melville Scott, M. A., Ph. D.	125 00
Alphee Belliveau,	1100 00
M. Alice Clark,	800 00
Edward Cadwallader, B. A.	250 00
Amos O'Blenes,	*165 00
Mary E. Nicolson,	*150 00
M. Annie Harvey,	*183 76
Mary E. Phillips,	*45 94
Lillian Nicolson,	*183 76
Edwin E. MacCready,	466 67
Joseph V. Lynn,	133 34
Iva A. Baxter,	91 67
Total	$8732 52

*These amounts are paid by the Board of Education in addition to the Provincial Allowance and to Salaries from Trustees.

TABLE XV.—PUBLIC SCHOOLS: CLOSING EXAMINATIONS FOR LICENSE; YEAR ENDED JUNE 30TH, 1903.

TERMS AND STATIONS.	No of candidates admitted to the written examination and grounds of admission.						GRAMMAR SCHOOL CLASS.								MALE.												FEMALE.												SUMMARY.										Total Licensed
							Male.				Female.				I Class.					II Class				III Class			I Class.					II Class				III Class.			Males.					Females,					
	As classified Student-Teachers of the Provincial Normal School.	As holding License from the Board of Education.	As Graduates in Arts.	As having undergone training at a Normal School not in N. B.	As eligible for examination.	Total No. admitted.	No. examined for this Class.	No. that obtained this Class.	No. obtained 1st Class.	No. obtained 2nd Class.	No examined for this Class	No that obtained this Class	No. obtained 1st Class.	No obtained 2nd Class.	No. examined for this Class	No. that obtained 1st Class.	No. obtained 2nd Class	No. obtained 3rd Class	No that failed to obtain any Class	No. examined for this Class.	No. obtained 2nd Class.	No obtained 3rd Class.	No that failed to obtain any Class.	No. examined for this Class	No obtained 3rd Class	No that failed to obtain any Class.	No examined for this Class.	No. obtained 1st Class.	No obtained 2nd Class.	No obtained 3rd Class	No that failed to obtain any Class.	No. examined for this Class	No obtained 2nd Clas.	No. obtained 3rd Class.	No. that failed to obtain any Class	No. examined for this Class.	No. obtained 3rd Class	No that failed to obtain any Class.	No. obtained Grammar Sch. Class.	No obtained 1st Class	No. obtained 2nd Class.	No. obtained 3rd Class.	No. that failed to obtain any Class.	No. obtained Grammar Sch Class	No. obtained 1st Class.	No. obtained 2nd Class.	No. obtained 3rd Class	No. that failed to obtain any Class	Total No. Licensed.
DECEMBER, 1902																																																	
Acadian Teachers	13					13																		1	1											12	7	5				1					7	5	8
III Class temporary	34					34																		5	4	1										29	26	3				4	1				26	8	30
MAY, 1903																																																	
Acadian Teachers	13				1	14																		3	2	1										11	10	1				2	1				10	1	12
JUNE, 1903.																																																	
Fredericton	167	13	12		1	193	7	4	2	1					19	13	6			17	16	1					50	34	16			100	92	8					4	15	23	1			34	108	8		193
St John		15			1	16	1		1		4	4			1		1										9	4	5			1		1						1	1			4	4	5	1		16
Chatham		2			1	3									1		1										2		1	1											1					1	1		3
New Brunswick	227	30	12		4	273	8	4	3	1	4	4			21	13	8			17	16	1		9	7	2	61	38	22	1		101	92	9		52	43	9	4	16	25	8	2	4	38	111	53	9	262
Year end'g June, '03	268	35	11		8	312	8	5	2	1	2	2			34	20	10			38	36	2		7	6	1	55	37	14	4		125	116	9		43	38	5	5	26	17	8	1	2	37	130	51	5	306
Increase			1		1				1		2	2												2	1	1	6	1	8							9	5	4					1	2	1		2	4	
Decrease	36	5				39		1							13	7	2			21	20	1								3		24	24						1	10	22					16			44

In addition to the above, 10 candidates at Fredericton, 2 at St John and 1 at Chatham wrote a partial examination for Grammar School Class. Also 6 candidates at Fredericton and 3 at St. John received Superior in addition to Class I.

Issue of School Licenses, awarded upon Examination in December, 1902. and May and June, 1903

The number of applicants for each Class will be seen from the preceding table. The following list contains the names of successful candidates only.

DECEMBER, 1902

Third Class—Colin E Carruthers. Arthur M Foster, Reuben Getchell, Charles G Oliver, Evelyn M Akerley, Rebecca Louise Anderson, Winifred E Barbour, Myrtle E Bishop, Maggie A Boudreau, Ina E Campbell, Minnie M Davidson, Mary Dorcus, Edith I Ganong, Susie Gardiner, Jennie A Hemphill, M Hermina Hachey, Mary Loretta Meahan, Emma Miller, M Elizabeth McBean, Dorcas McConnell, Emma B Ogden, Ida Louise Pettingell, Annie Tyson Scholey, Alma R Sewell, Lily A M Sharkey, Carrie E Spragg, Laura I Stevenson, Burnetta Tobin, Nina G Williams, Jennie K Woods, Henri Cormier. Marie A Dumas, Marie Genevieve Gagnon, Mary A Hachey, Helene E Martin, Edith Michaud, Artemise Melanson, Odile Albert.

MAY, 1903.

Third Class—George J Hachey, Thimothee O Robichaud, Alma Marie Bois, Adelina J Bois, Mary Susan Cowhig, Annie Delina Cyr, Marie Emelie DeGrace, Marie Marguerite Doiron, Anna Dugnay, Eugenie Godbout, Emma Plourde, Alma C Nadeau.

JUNE, 1903

Grammar School.—Roy D Fullerton, Peter R McLean, Ward H Patterson, Charles D Richards, Mildred M Black, Maud Gibson, F Iva Thorne, H May Ward.

First Class—Fred R Anderson, Paul M Atkinson, Osburn N Brown, Lloyd A Corey, Maximilien D Cormier, Norman S Fraser, Tuttle T Goodwin, Percy R Hayward, *Charles M Hoar, H Burton Logie, Harry A Prebble, James O Steeves, Arthur F Stevenson, H. A Stanley Wilson, A Zella Alward, Pearle Babbitt, Margaret M Belyea, Florence Mabel Bird,

*First Class when passed in reading.

*L Etta Brown, Minnie I Bustin, Genevieve I Cassidy, Louella B Chapman, Annie E Cochrane, Clare Creaghan, Mary Gertrude Creaghan, Ethel E Day, Ruth E Everett, Mabel I Finn, Susie J Gilchrist, *Margaret A Gillman, Kathleen Mary Kelly, Gaynell E Long, †Marion E Moore, Annie Blanche Myles, Tillie P McClelland, Cora H McFarland, Annie McGuiggan, Jessie MacD McKnight, Helen G McLeod, Madge Parkinson, Ruth Gertrude Parlee, May B Pinder, Beatrice N Richards, *Ida May Saul, Florence Ethel Smith, Helena B Smith, †Glenna E Trenholm ‡Agnes G Waring, Mary Alethea Wethen, Sarah Louise B Waycott, Bessie May Wright, Pearl Yerxa.

Second Class—Hugh J Alward, Herbert Harris Biggar, George Foster Camp, **Peter Z Caverhill, Charles G Crawford, Joseph C Delegarde, Robert H Flewelling, Arthur G. F Freeze, Francis W Johnson, Lewis J King, Channing G Lawrence, Hugh F Linden, **James Hugh McLean, George D Macmillan, Fletcher Peacock, Domitien T Robichaud, Jean G Robichaud, Clair Willard Robinson, William R Shanklin, William J Shea, Rheta May Allingham, Emilie Alward, Carrie E Ayer, Florence Mabel Baird, Bertha B Bartlett, Margaret A Barton, **Bertha Beatrice Bateman, Jennie N Bell, Lona J Z Belyea, Helena Gertrude Bishop, Inez C Bradley, Maud Beatrice Brittain, Alice Bertha Brown, Georgia Louise Brown, **Jennie L Carson, Maude M Carter, **J May L Carter, Mary A T Casey, Elizabeth Cowan, §Mabel M Crocker, Josephine Culligan, Annette Currie, Helena A Daley, Ida M S DeBoo, Madeleine Visart DeBury, **Annie Dickie, Annie Jane Dixon, Hester L Edgecombe, Mabel A Estabrooks, Marion Taylor Estey, Mary Agnes Firth, Margaret Ellen Fraser, Isabella H Freeze, Katie A Ganong. Agnes May George, Grace M Goodspeed, Clara Grant, Nellie B Harmon, Nellie Harper, Mary B Harrington, Ada H Harkins, Sara Ethel Hoar, B. Lucretia A Hodgins, Bessie Elmina Holder, Jewel Gladys Hudson, Eva Irving, Mary Josephine Keane, Bessie Eveline Kearney, Ethel L Kierstead, Damie Eva Kennedy, Frances J Kinney, Georgia E Kirkpatrick, Nellie S Lewis, Mary Mae Lindsay, Mary Zita Lordon, Mary Elizabeth Mahoney, Florence T Mahood, Georgia C Marr, Gertrude G Miller, Lilly J Miller, Hazel Millican, Myrtle K Milne, Eva Gertrude Mitchell, Mary Emma Murphy, Margaret Hyacinthe Murphy, Maude T McElwee, Mabel C McFarlane, Annie S McGeachy, Maude Winnifred McKay, Gertrude May McKinnon, Annie McLean,

---

*First Class when passed in reading.
†First Class when Preliminary Examination is passed.
‡First Class when passed in drawing.
**Second Class when passed in reading.
§Second Class when Preliminary Examination is passed.

Grace Muriel McMaster, Ethel J McMurray, Bessie Marion McNally, May A McVey, Leola A McWha, Jennie A Nason, Ella B Oulton, Ruby B Page, Mabel E Perkins, Agnes Perry, Augusta E Perry, §Susan Isabella Reid, Margaret Reidle, Bessie M Seely, Ida Gertrude Cecilia Sharkey, Ida Evelyn Snowdon, Sara Maude Stephenson, Nellie May Stewart, Ethel Annie Tait, Louise Thompson, Lola J Thorne; Flora Margaret Tingley, Marion R Tompkins, Sade Jane Unkauf, Bertha Mae Wilbur, Maud A Williams, Annie L Wilson, Eliza Eloise Wilson, Lida Alice Wishart.

Third Class.—Le Roi A M King, Annie Lamont Clark, Kathleen Helena Dunn, Emma L Estey, Estella A Flewelling, G Norma G Goodall, Winona Hetherington, Annie Sophia Mowatt, Fannie Murray, Mary A McPherson, Georgia L Scott.

Superior Class.—Fred R Anderson, Percy S Bailey, H Burton Logie, Lloyd A Corey, Maximilien D Cormier, Miles F McCutcheon, Margaret M Belyea, Ruth E Everett, Mary McAuley McInerney.

Passed for Superior Class in the Departmental Examinations held in July, 1903.—Frank H Blake, Osburn N Brown, Tuttle T Goodwin, Walter B O'Regan, Wilford A Rideout, Clarence Shannon, Edith G Cummings, Violet E Goldsmith, Addie M Hartt, Annie Blanche Myles, Annie E McGuiggan, Helen E McLeod, Winnifred E Thompson, Beatrice N Richards.

§Second Class when Preliminary Examination is passed.

TABLE XVI.—PUBLIC SCHOOLS: LIBRARIES.

Bonuses Paid to District School Libraries During the Year Ended October 31st, 1903.

LOCALITY.			DATES OF PAYMENT.	VALUE.			Number of Volumes.
COUNTY.	PARISH.	District		Local.	Provincial	Total.	
Albert	Harvey	No. 3	August 4th, 1903	$ 19 21	$ 9 60	$ 28 81	34
"	Hillsboro'	" 10	June, 8th, 1903	18 00	9 00	27 00	124
"	Hopewell	" 1	Dec. 13th, 1902	5 43	2 77	8 20	16
"	"	" 2	March 2nd, 1903	6 19	3 10	9 29	22
Carleton	Northhampton	" 2	March 11th. 1903	2 49	1 24	3 73	18
"	Simonds	" 4	August 4th, 1903	11 39	5 70	17 09	67
"	Wilmot	" 6	May 4th, 1903	28 00	14 00	42 00	119
Charlotte	Grand Manan	" 5	June 24th, 1903	40 00	20 00	60 00	133
"	Milltown		March 19th, 1903	8 83	4 42	13 25	10
Kings	Hampton	" 2	August 4th, 1903	19 67	9 83	29 50	?
"	Kingston and Westfield	" 11	Nov. 12th, 1902	4 88	2 44	7 32	15
"	Studholm	" 4	May 21st, 1903	3 96	1 98	5 94	15
"	Upham	" 6	Oct 19th, 1903	14 02	7 01	21 03	73
Northumberland	Blackville	" 6	Dec. 8th, 1902	14 67	7 33	22 00	51
"	Newcastle	" 6	April 23rd, 1903	58 99	20 00	78 99	131
"	"	" 6	August 3rd, 1903	126 59	20 00	146 59	189
"	" Town		Sept 9th, 1903	50 44	20 00	70 44	72
St. John	St. Martins	" 1	Nov. 11th, 1902	20 23	10 12	30 35	53
"	"	" 2	June 2nd, 1903	33 67	16 83	50 50	153
"	Simonds and St. Martins	" 23	June 8th, 1903	22 01	11 01	33 02	58
"	Musquash	" 8	August 20th, 1903	10 00	5 00	15 00	18
Westmorland	Moncton	" 16	August 4th, 1903	13 00	6 48	19 48	79
"	Sackville	" 11	Sept. 22nd, 1903	56 00	20 00	76 00	25
Victoria	Andover	" 3	Nov. 3rd, 1902	7 62	3 81	11 43	29
				$595 29	$231 67	$826 96	1,504

TABLE XVII.—PUBLIC SCHOOLS.

Travelling Expenses Paid to Student Teachers Attending the Normal School During the Terms Ended June and May, 1902.

(Paid in 1903)

(Allowance of Mileage, 3 cents a mile.)

No.	Name.	County.	Amount.
1	Percy S Bailey,	Charlotte,	$ 6 12
2	Arthur W Barbour,	Albert,	9 90
3	Allen A Barter,	Carleton,	4 56
4	Frank H Blake,	Albert,	10 32
5	N Tupper Bleakney,	Charlotte,	6 30
6	John M Clindinnin,	Charlotte,	5 22
7	Harry C Cody,	Carleton,	4 86
8	Gustavus A Colpitts,	Albert,	9 12
9	Wm M Crawford,	Carleton,	4 50
10	Abram M Crookbite,	York,	2 94
11	Walter M Donahoe,	York,	2 58
12	W Orton Gray,	Kings,	5 34
13	Arnold F Jewett,	Carleton,	4 38
14	John M Keefe,	Carleton,	4 80
15	Goldwin S Lord,	Maine, U S,	7 20
16	W W Kingdon Maxwell,	Charlotte,	5 22
17	J Fraser McCain,	Carleton,	4 50
18	Wm F McKnight,	Northumberland,	7 02
19	Walter B O'Regan,	Kings,	6 96
20	Allen R Reid,	Carleton,	4 86
21	Clarence Shannon,	Carleton,	4 80
22	John S Smiley,	Charlotte,	5 88
23	Lena G Babbitt,	Sunbury,	1 38
24	Mildred M Black,	St. John,	3 90
25	Glendine Brewster,	Albert,	10 32
26	Della A Brown,	Westmorland,	9 36
27	Sarah L Brown,	Kings,	6 72
28	Muriel M Colpitts,	Westmorland,	8 22
29	Edith G Cummings,	St. John,	4 02
		Forward....	$171 30

TABLE XVII.—Continued.

No.	Name.	County.	Amount.
		Brought forward	$171 30
30	Fannie F Doyle,	Westmorland,	13 08
31	Florence Estabrooks,	St John,	4 02
32	B Marion Fraser,	Northumberland,	7 02
33	Mary E Gillman,	Charlotte,	5 76
34	Violet E Goldsmith,	Gloucester,	9 48
35	Addie M Hartt,	Sunbury,	1 32
36	Edna L James,	Albert,	10 20
37	Ethel H Jarvis,	St John,	4 02
38	Marguerite G J Legere,	St John,	4 02
38½	Annie M Loggie,	Northumberland,	7 02
39	Marjorie F Mair,	Restigouche,	13 26
40	Jessie E McLean,	St John,	4 02
40½	Margaret M Pearce,	Kings,	7 20
40¾	Mary Ryan,	Northumberland,	7 02
41	Winifred Thompson,	Westmorland,	12 00
42	E Louise Tingley,	Westmorland,	12 00
43	Glenna F White,	Carleton,	4 80
44	Margaret Wilson,	Westmorland,	9 36
45	Ada I Wright,	St John,	4 02
46	Geo H Adair,	Kings,	6 42
47	Oscar J Allen,	Westmorland,	13 86
48	Wm A R Archer,	Gloucester,	10 20
49	Fred L Bowser,	Westmorland,	12 00
50	Fred R Branscombe,	Kings,	8 10
51	J Watson Crecker,	Northumberland,	6 48
52	C Bradley Dalton,	Westmorland,	13 20
53	Wm P Day,	Queens,	3 48
54	Percy A Fitzpatrick,	Westmorland,	13 08
55	Martin G Fox,	Queens,	1 92
56	Arlington T Gunong,	Kings,	6 72
57	Louis L B Godard,	Albert,	8 88
58	Arthur E Graham,	York,	1 92
59	Chas N Gregg,	Kings,	6 72
60	Hazen W Hall,	York,	6 00
		Forward	$429 90

TABLE XVI.—Continued.

No.	Name.	County.	Amount.
		Brought forward	$429 90
61	Grant Hawkins,	Carleton,	4 86
62	H Sterling Huestis,	York,	1 44
63	Albert P Jewett,	York,	84
63½	Walter S Jones,	Queens,	3 60
64	E Stanley Knox,	Queens,	4 62
65	Medley F Miller,	York,	2 70
66	Donald L McCain,	Sunbury,	1 02
67	Ralph McKinney,	Charlotte,	5 04
68	Milton A McLeod,	York,	2 88
69	John D McMillan,	Restigouche,	11 58
70	Goldwin I Nugent,	Queens,	4 62
71	Asael W Peck,	Albert,	10 98
72	Frank C Rideout,	Carleton,	4 20
73	Frank L Shaw,	York,	4 20
74	Robt A Simpson,	Westmorland,	13 50
75	Sydney B Smith,	Sunbury,	1 80
76	Robt A Taylor,	Westmorland,	13 50
76½	Aaron E Tower,	Westmorland,	11 70
77	W J Young,	Kings,	8 76
78	V Pearl Alexander,	Carleton,	4 50
79	Cora B Allen,	Westmorland,	14 22
80	M Alberta Barton,	Queens,	3 90
81	Christina J Blake,	Restigouche,	11 58
82	Daisy A Bowser,	Westmorland,	12 36
83	Thirza Branscombe,	Kings,	5 10
83½	Clara M Brown,	Westmorland,	9 00
84	Harriet E Brown,	Sunbury,	72
85	Jessie H Brown,	St John,	6 12
86	Maude Brown,	Restigouche,	11 22
87	Alice G Cameron,	York,	1 44
88	Estella Y Coburn,	York,	66
89	Minnie E Colpitts,	Albert,	9 90
90	A M Evelyn Cook,	Charlotte,	6 12
91	Louise R Copp,	Westmorland,	12 9[illegible]
		Forward....	$651 48

TABLE XVII.—Continued.

No.	Name.	County.	Amount.
		Brought forward	$651 48
92	Rhoda J Corbett,	Carleton,	4 38
93	Bernadette Cormier,	Gloucester,	11 58
94	A Lulu Cronkite,	Carleton,	5 40
95	Agnes T Cummings,	Kings,	7 14
96	Janie S Cameron,	York,	1 44
97	Inez Daye,	Carleton,	4 92
98	Florence O DeMille,	Albert,	9 00
99	Pearl V Dennison,	York,	1 74
100	S Bessie Dycart,	Kent,	11 04
100½	Belle N Eddy,	Gloucester,	10 20
101	Daisy B M Farnham,	York,	2 70
102	Mabel I Finn,	St John,	4 02
103	Helena M Firlotte,	Restigouche,	11 58
104	Evelyn E Gallagher,	Carleton,	3 78
105	Ella M Gartley,	Carleton,	4 50
106	Della M Gauvin,	Westmorland,	9 36
107	Jessie R Gilliland,	Kings,	3 36
108	A Gertrude Gillis,	Northumberland,	7 02
109	Ethel McL Good,	Kings,	6 72
110	Annie M B Harding,	Sunbury,	48
111	Maggie A Harper,	Northumberland,	7 02
112	M Marguerite Hayes,	Kings,	7 08
113	Sadie B Hogan,	Northumberland,	6 84
114	Lizzie M Holmes,	Carleton,	4 50
115	Lydia A Jewett,	York,	1 20
116	S Alice Jones,	Westmorland,	9 00
117	Alice G Kay,	Westmorland,	12 00
118	Augusta G Kelly,	Northumberland,	7 50
119	Agnes LeBlanc,	Westmorland,	9 36
120	Hermeline LeBlanc,	Westmorland,	9 66
121	Isadore P Leighton,	Northumberland,	6 84
122	M D Clair Libbey,	York,	2 58
123	Helen M Lunnin,	Sunbury,	1 50
124	Mildred P Milton,	Albert,	11 52
		Forward....	$868 44

TABLE XVII.—Continued.

No.	Name.	County.	Amount.
		Brought forward	$868 44
125	Mary G Mitchell,	Charlotte,	7 20
126	Clara L Moore,	Albert,	11 10
127	A Laura Moore,	Westmorland,	8 04
128	Annie S Mowatt,	York,	2 58
129	Verna B Murch,	York,	1 44
130	Inez E Murphy,	Carleton,	4 74
131	Flora H McCallum,	Charlotte,	6 00
132	M Emma McCormack,	Gloucester,	10 68
133	Ethel McCrea,	Queens,	3 60
134	Jennie B McCutcheon,	Queens,	4 20
135	Beatrice A McEwan,	Gloucester,	9 60
136	Rachel McEwan,	Northumberland,	7 02
137	Emily I McFee,	Westmorland,	8 04
138	Ida M McGerigle,	Kings,	2 94
139	Mary G McGrand,	York,	90
140	Jessie McD McKnight,	Northumberland,	7 38
141	Nellie M McNaughton,	Westmorland,	8 58
142	Beatrice M M Newman,	Northumberland,	6 48
143	Sadie V Newman,	Northumberland,	6 48
144	Alice M Nickerson,	Queens,	3 42
145	Minnie E O'Brien,	Northumberland,	6 66
146	Alma L Ogden,	Westmorland,	11 88
147	Mary B Page,	Carleton,	4 86
148	R Gertrude Parlee,	Kings,	6 42
149	Verna R Perkins,	Carleton,	4 86
150	Grace A Peters,	Carleton,	4 50
151	Margaret J Phelan,	Northumberland,	7 02
152	Bertie H Plummer,	Queens,	1 44
153	Maggie B Pond,	Northumberland,	2 88
153½	Emma J Read,	Westmorland,	11 88
154	Selena M Reynolds,	St John,	4 02
155	Madge J Ricketson,	Kings,	4 20
156	Gertie Rosengren,	Restigouche,	11 58
157	Mary A B Saunders,	Northumberland,	6 48
		Forward	1077 5

TABLE XVII.—Continued.

No.	Name.	County.	Amount.
		Brought forward	$1077 54
158	Ethel A Sears,	Westmorland,	9 36
159	Ethel E Sharp,	Kings,	7 20
160	Beula M Shaw,	Carleton,	4 08
161	Georgia Sherwood,	St. John,	4 02
162	Mabelle C Sherwood,	Carleton,	3 78
163	Ruby V Sinnett.	Carleton,	4 86
164	Hester G L Sleep,	Queens,	3 12
165	Myrtle A Slipp,	Queens,	3 90
166	Mable M Steeves,	Westmorland,	8 04
167	Violet M Steeves,	Albert,	9 48
168	Helena J Tomlyn,	Kings,	7 20
169	Louisa Tomilson,	York,	1 20
170	Ella M Tompkins,	Carleton,	4 08
171	Louisa V Trail,	York,	2 70
172	Emma Walker,	Victoria,	6 72
173	Grace H Waring,	St John,	3 90
174	Mary A Weldon,	Westmorland,	10 38
175	Frances E J Wetmore,	Carleton,	3 78
176	Annie W Williston,	Northumberland,	8 28
177	Emily J Williston,	Northumberland,	8 70
178	Effie J Young,	York,	1 14
179	Minnie L Seeley,	Carleton,	4 20
180	*Willard B Kay,	Westmorland.	12 00
181	*Angelina Clowes,	Carleton,	4 08
182	*Clara McCullough,	York,	84
183	*Ethel E Swanson,	Northumberland,	7 02
184	*Susanna Lamb,	Westmorland,	13 50
185	*Margaret Anderson,	Queens,	3 00
186	*Johannah Maddox,	Carleton,	4 86
187	Jennie S Babin,	Madawaska,	8 40
188	Rosalie Barrieau,	Kent,	10 20
189	Winifred Bird,	Madawaska,	6 84
190	Philomene Chiasson.	Kent,	10 20
191	Marie M Cyr,	Madawaska,	8 10
		Forward	$1286 70

*Attended previous terms but claims just matured.

TABLE XVII.—Continued.

No.	NAME.	COUNTY.	AMOUNT.
		Brought forward	$1286 70
192	Azilda B Daigle,	Madawaska,	10 20
193	Amelia L Gagnon,	Temiscouata, P Q	13 26
194	Modeste R Lavoie,	Madawaska,	7 56
195	Alma Nadeau,	Madawaska,	6 84
196	*Mary Rice,	Madawaska,	8 40
		Gov. War. No. 605	$1332 96

*Attended previous terms but claims just matured.

TABLE XVII.—CONTINUED. TERM ENDED DECEMBER 1902.

No.	NAME.	COUNTY.	AMOUNT.
1	Colin E Carruthers	Kent,	$ 9 12
2	Arthur N Foster,	Albert,	10 20
4	Hubert H Harshman,	Westmorland,	10 62
5	Chas G Oliver,	York,	2 04
6	Evelyn M Akerly	Charlotte,	6 36
7	Winifred E Barbour,	Albert,	9 90
8	Myrtle E Bishop,	Albert,	11 22
9	Maggie A Boudreau,	Gloucester,	9 90
10	Ina E Campbell,	Carleton,	5 70
10½	Emma S Cassidy,	Victoria,	5 58
11	Minnie M Davidson,	York,	2 40
12	Edith I Ganong,	Kings,	4 20
13	Susie Gardiner,	Charlotte,	5 58
14	Jennie A Hemphill,	Carleton,	4 50
15	M Hermina Hachey,	Gloucester,	9 60
16	M Bessie Margison,	Carleton,	4 86
17	Mary L Meahan,	Gloucester,	9 48
19	M Elizabeth McBean,	York,	1 14
20	Dorcas McConnell,	Kings,	6 42
21	Emma B Ogden,	Westmorland,	11 88
22	Ida L Pettigell.	Kings,	4 56
23	Annie T Scholey,	Carleton,	4 86
24	Carrie E Spragg,	Kings,	6 30
25	Laura I Stevenson,	Queens,	4 62
26	Burnetta Tobin,	Northumberland,	6 18
27	Nina G Williams,	Queens,	3 36
28	*Arthur E Eastman,	Westmorland,	8 04
29	*Murray H Manuel,	York,	2 28
30	*Holland R McGill,	Sunbury,	1 80
31	*S Estella Carruthers,	Northumberland,	7 02
32	*Maud L Cuming,	St John,	4 02
33	*Lena M Kearney,	Carleton,	3 66
34	*Beatrice H Smith,	Charlotte,	6 12
35	*Bessie M Wilson,	St John,	4 02
		Forward	$207 54

TABLE XVII.—Continued.

No.	Name.	County.	Amount.
		Brought forward	$207 54
35½	*Dexter W Allen,	Westmorland,	13 86
36	*Arthur Mitchell,	Charlotte,	7 20
37	*Lorenzo N Wadlin,	Charlotte,	7 44
38	*Lila L Gillis,	Charlotte,	6 00
39	*Ethel M Graham,	York,	1 92
40	*Annie J Harrison,	Northumberland,	6 84
41	*Sara C McKenzie,	Charlotte,	5 88
42	*Mabel R Saunders,	Kings,	4 56
43	*Minnie P Spragg,	St John,	4 02
43½	*Elizabeth C Anderson,	Westmorland,	11 70
44	*Florence T Mahood,	Queens,	3 18
45	*Ada P Miller,	York,	1 20
46	Henri Cormier,	Kent,	11 52
47	Winifred M Bird,	Madawaska,	6 84
48	Maria A Collins,	Madawaska,	6 84
48½	Virginie M Dionne,	Madawaska,	8 40
48¾	Marie A Dumas,	Sandy Bay, Que.	13 26
49	Marie G Gagnon,	Westmorland,	10 98
50	M Agnes Guerrette,	Madawaska,	8 40
51	Mary A Hachey,	Gloucester,	9 60
52	Helene E Martin,	Madawaska,	8 10
53	Edith Michaud,	Madawaska,	9 00
54	Artemise Melanson,	Gloucester,	9 60
55	Odile Albert,	Madawaska,	10 20
56	Olive M Sirois,	Madawaska,	10 20
	Manual Training,		
57	Ethel I Mersereau,	Northumberland,	14 46
		Gov. War. No. 1157	$418 74

TABLE XVIII.—PUBLIC SCHOOLS: Year Ended 30th June 1903.

Statement of Chief Superintendent's Provincial Drafts to Teachers, and of County Fund Drafts to Trustees.

(Summarized in Tables IX., X. and XI.)

MEMORANDUM.	Provincial Drafts to Teachers.	County Fund Drafts to Trustees.
For Term Ended December 31st, 1902.		
References—Warrants Nos. 606, 607, 608...	$69,726 17	
School for the Blind, Halifax, Warrant No. 553	1,141 40	
Amount County Funds, for Term ended December 31st, 1902—Schools..........	....	$47,473 93
School for the Blind, Halifax...........	....	1,141 40
For the Term Ended June 30th, 1903.		
References—Warrants Nos. 1154, 1155, 1156,	91,099 62	
School for the Blind, Halifax, Warrant No. 1084	1,105 14	
Amount County Fund for Term ended June 30th, 1903—Schools...............	....	47.495 31
School for the Blind, Halifax..........	....	1,105 14
	$163,072 33	$97,215 78

TABLE XIX.—SUMMARY OF THE PROVINCIAL GRANTS FOR THE SCHOOL SERVICE FOR THE YEAR ENDED OCTOBER 31ST, 1903.

Schools (See Table IX for details):		
Common, ...	$140,943 27	
Superior, ...	12,351 04	
Grammar, ...	7,531 48	
		$160,825 79
School for the Blind, Halifax, (Table XI), ...		2,246 54
Normal School: Salaries (Table XIV), ...		8,732 52
Travelling Allowance to Student Teachers, (Table XVII), ..		1,751 70
Inspectors' Salaries, ...		10,383 34
" Allowance, attending Conference, ...		700 00
Education Office Salaries:—		
Chief Superintendent, ...	$2,000 00	
Chief Clerk, ...	1,200 00	
Clerk, ...	800 00	
Clerk, ...	410 00	
Clerk, ...	240 00	
Clerk (temporary)	36 55	
		$4,686 55
Travelling Allowance to Chief Superintendent, ...		400 00
Incidental expenses:—		
S W Babbitt, Stenography, ...	$ 8 00	
Jos P McPeake, do.	38 50	
Expenses to Sackville attending conference with Dr. Parkin and others re Rhodes Scholarships, ...	12 00	
Expenses to Halifax, re School for Deaf and Dumb, ...	24 00	
Telegrams, ...	1 00	
Freight on maps, ...	1 10	
Forward	$84 60	

Brought forward....$	84 60	
Lottie Kain, stenography, (Millerton),...	19 80	
G W Mersereau, expenses to Fredericton by order Chief Superintendent, ...	5 75	
J & A McMillan, index, ...	1 50	
Lillian Flewelling, work in office, ...	5 10	
Chas Toner, trucking, ...	2 40	
Chas D Hebert, assisting in investigation of charge against School Secretary in Westmorland Co, ...	10 00	
		$129 15

Examination Expenses:

License Examinations, December, 1902, and May and June, 1903,		$419 18
Departmental Examinations (Normal School Entrance, Matriculation and High School Leaving, June and July, 1903, ...	$882 28	
Less amount received in fees, ...	812 24	
		70 04
High School Entrance Examinations, ...		451 00
School Libraries, (Table XVI)....		231 67
School House Grants (see statement in Chief Superintendent's Report), ...		935 00
Conveyance of school children,....		204 07
Manual Training Teachers, ...		239 40
Equipment of Manual Training Schools,....		329 39
		$192,735 34

PART III.

APPENDICES.

APPENDIX A.

NORMAL SCHOOL, FREDERICTON.

J. R. INCH ESQ., LL. D.
Chief Supt. of Education.

SIR;—I have the honour to submit the following report on the Provincial Normal School for the year ended, June 1903.

The total enrolment for the year was 241, of whom 38 were young men. Of this total, 204 entered at the beginning of the session in September and 37 in January, the beginning of the second term. These numbers include the students attending the French Department of whom there were 13 during the first term and 13 the second.

The Counties of the Province were severally represented as follows:

Albert	11	Restigouche	12
Carleton	25	St. John	15
Charlotte	14	Sunbury	5
Gloucester	15	Victoria	4
Kent	8	Westmorland	19
Kings	26	York	42
Madawaska	12	Quebec	1
Northumberland	17	Nova Scotia	1
Queens	13	United States	1

The Religious Denominations were represented as under:

Baptists	46	Presbyterians	45
Church of England	25	R. Catholic	58
Free Baptists	26	Others	6
Methodists	35		

There were presented for examination for License:

For Class I	49
For Class II	113
For Class III	54
Not Classed	10

During the session 2 students left to teach, 13 left from sickness two of whom died.

Classification according to "Teaching ability and skill" was:—
Good, 62; Fair, 156; Not Classed, 8; Classification in vocal music was:—Rote Singing and Theory, 6; Rote Singing, 14.

GENERAL INSTRUCTION

The subjects of the course prescribed by the Board of Education—English Language and Literature, Reading, Vocal Training and Physical Culture, Mathematics, Natural Science, Drawing and Music, and recently Sloyd,—received due attention. An important feature in the instruction, more important indeed than the knowledge itself is the method pursued in its acquisition. Definitions, rules, laws, &c., are deduced from the processes which the learner is guided to adopt and thus he acquires not only knowledge but the valuable habit of connected thinking which will serve him in good stead in every sphere of life. When a student is taught in this way there is good reason to believe that he will carry similar processes into his own work when he teaches others. The chief object in view in prescribing academic instruction for a Normal School is to give its students the very best opportunity of acquiring an intimate and practical acquaintance with principles and methods of teaching. A teacher naturally follows the methods under which he himself has received instruction, however much he may be primed with professional theory. It is therefore of no small importance that whatever subject he is called upon to take up during his course in training, it should be taught according to principles fully established and methods based upon them. The recent introduction of Sloyd into the course has been of much service in many respects and eminently so in regard to sound methods. The method that must necessarily be employed in this subject compels the student to form clear ideas before he can make his hand express them. The hand tests the accuracy of the conception and goes out again, if there is error, to find the real and the true, and herein lies at least one of the educative values of manual training. Accuracy in one department of study will tend to accuracy in another and to beget those valuable habits that should characterize all the work of the student.

Many of the students come from rural schools where the conditions are not favourable to disciplinary study, and where the short cut to the minimum of knowledge is too often regarded as the best. Such students require direct instruction, and through this instruction to be taught how to learn.

how to find out their defects, and how to remove them. The instruction, so far as it goes, is intended to produce habits of observation and connected thinking, and to serve *mutatis mutandis* as models for future practice as well.

PROFESSIONAL INSTRUCTION.

The course was carried out in the usual way—by direct instruction on the principles and practice of teaching and school management. This instruction is communicated chiefly by lectures, a text book is not used, though authors are recommended to be read or consulted on special points. The principles upon which successful methods are based are discussed and methods, unless referable to well established principles, are not approved. Method is of course but the form which the instruction takes and will vary with the individuality of the teacher, but unless it is founded upon the principle of developing and cultivating the pupil's intelligence it is without educative value and as such it is useless. The outcry of a few years ago that Psychology and its applications to teaching should form a *sine qua non* in the training of the teacher has, to a large extent, subsided. The teacher will undoubtedly find that a knowledge of this science and its applications will greatly facilitate his work and prove a safe guide in his methods. But the formal study of this subject in a one year's course, especially where none of the students have any acquaintance with it, and the larger number unprepared to take it up, would be little better than charlatanry. All that this Institution, or any other similarly conditioned, can do in this regard, with any reasonable prospect of success, is to give its students some acquaintance with the well established results of mental science, so that the rationale of their methods may be fairly apprehended. To the students preparing for First Class License I have, in addition, given lectures on representative educational reformers, with a view of connecting the principles we have discussed with the principles of the educationists or teachers who originated them, or first wrought them out successfully in practice. Better facilities have of late been provided for observation and practice.

FRENCH DEPARTMENT.

The number in attendance in this Department for the year was, as stated above 26—double that of the preceding year. Candidates for admission are not required to pass the regular preliminary examination, but are examined at the Normal School for the purpose of ascertaining whether they are able to proceed intelligently with the work. Though all who are admitted are not fully prepared to take the course, I am glad to note a marked improvement in the attainments of nearly all of them, compared with former years. Instruction is given in the usual subjects of the course under the regular Instructor, Mr. Belliveau; their professional instruction and practice is under the immediate charge of the Principal. Sloyd is given in the Sloyd Department and Singing by the Instructor in music. Natural Science has heretofore been taught from a text-book which just means that "their eyes have not yet been opened." Arrangements have now been made to teach them this subject in the *natural* way, as also the ordinary subjects of instruction.

The deportment of all the students both in and out of school was so far as known to me, correct and becoming. Most of them, it was evident had come with a serious purpose and accordingly applied themselves with commendable diligence to give it effect. Their health was generally good, though I regret to say, there was more sickness than for some years past. As many as thirteen had to leave on account of continued sickness—two of whom died. Several of those who had to return home appeared from the outset delicate and sickly, and should not have entered upon the session's work. They all had, however, the required medical certificate of health. There was also more sickness in the Faculty than usual. Nearly every member of it had to intermit his work for some days at least. Dr. Creed, Instructor in English Language and Literature, was, I regret to say, laid up for some weeks, but through the kindly consideration of the Board of Education his place was supplied for the greater part of the time by Dr. Scott of the University.

The Governor General's medals for the highest professional standing in the Senior and the Junior Class were awarded respectively to Miss Margaret Belyea, of Greenwich, Kings Co., and Mr. George Camp, of Upper Sheffield.

Mr. John Brittain, who for thirteen years occupied the position of Instructor in Natural Science, tendered his resignation to accept another appointment, shortly after the commencement of the session, much to the regret of the students and every member of the Faculty. Mr. Brittain's long service to the Institution has been invaluable. His intimate acquaintance with his subject, and skilful methods in presenting it, combined with his enthusiasm and personal interest in the students, brought them in thorough touch both with himself and his subject. The Institution was singularly fortunate in securing the services of H. H. Hagerman, A. M., teacher of Natural Science in the Fredericton High School, who has already proved himself no unworthy successor to a teacher of such rare excellence

MODEL DEPARTMENT.

This department provides instruction in the first eight grades of the prescribed school course and has a staff of four regularly licensed teachers. The schools practically form a part of the city school system, the Board of School Trustees, under agreement with the Board of Education, supplying the pupils to the number of about 200, and paying a part of the teachers' salaries. The teachers are however the appointees of the Board of Education and are under its control and the schools are arranged and conducted so as to secure to the teachers in training facilities for observation and practice. The first two departments, embracing the first four grades, are of course in most frequent demand, both for illustrative and practice lessons and have been eminently serviceable in these respects. The neatness too and attractive appearance of these class-rooms cannot but have a refining influence upon those whose elementary instruction has never extended beyond the bounds of some small and remote rural district. The third department of the school is also a model of neatness and orderly arrangements.

The accommodation for all the needs of the Institution is now too limited especially since the introduction of Sloyd. I would respectfully recommend that an ell or wing be added to the building to accommodate the Sloyd Department, and having also a class room with appurtenances and laboratory for Natural Science. Some such provision is an absolute necessity for effective work in the several departments of the school and I hope that the Board of Education will be pleased to take the matter into their favourable consideration at as early a date as practicable.

My thanks are due to all the Instructors for efficient work in their respective departments and their cordial co-operation in the management of the Institution, and to yourself for your kindly interest.

I have the honour to be, Sir,

Your obedient servant,

WM. CROCKET,

Principal.

APPENDIX B.

INSPECTORS' REPORTS.

INSPECTORAL DISTRICT No. 1.

GEO. W. MERSEREAU, M. A., Inspector, Doaktown, N, B.

This District Embraces the County of Restigouche except the Parish of Balmoral and Districts No. 1½ Colborn and Balmoral and No. 3. Addington; The County of Northumberland except the Parish of Rogersville and Districts 4, 5, 12, 13, 14 and 15 in the Parish of Alnwick, in the County of Kent, the Parishes of Harcourt and Weldford and Districts 1, 2, 5, 9, 10 and 13 in the Parish of Stanley in the County of York.

JAMES R. INCH, ESQ , LL. D.
Chief Supt. of Education,
Fredericton, N. B.

SIR.—I have the honor to submit the following report on the condition of Public Schools in Inspectorial District No. 1 for the year 1903.

As anticipated in my last report, I was able to visit nearly every ungraded school in my Inspectorate each term of the school year and thus exercise a closer supervision than formerly and to give more time where the need for it existed.

I am pleased to be able to report that progress has been made in every grade of school, though not of course in every school. To my mind the ungraded schools have made the most decided advance during the year. Several of them have been closed because suitable teachers could not be secured, others were compelled to take Local Licensed teachers, but even with these drawbacks these schools have done better work than ever before in my experience. To define that improvement is not easy because it was not the same in any two Districts. The teachers seem to have broadened out, to have caught the spirit of the twentieth century, so to speak, and to have thrown aside antiquated methods and to have regarded their pupils, more than ever before, as germs to be cultivated and developed rather than cisterns to be filled. This spirit was manifested in different methods of discipline and management, and different ways of presenting lessons, and in more cordial relations between teacher and pupils. Power to think and act independently seems to be more the aim than ever before.

I have no new buildings to report this year except at Jardine's Yard in Rexton where the repairs made to the School House were so extensive as practically to make it a new building, but there has been more than the usual amount of repairs done and furniture and appliances supplied. I shall mention the most important items of this kind in my review by Parishes.

KENT COUNTY.

The Primary room of the Harcourt Superior School was ceiled throughout and walls and ceiling painted. Smith's Corner ceiled the school room inside. Railway District No. 6, Harcourt was supplied with a half dozen desks and seats by means of a Pie Social made by the teacher, Miss Fannie Murray. Adamsville school room was finished inside in wood. In Canaan, No. 20, Weldford, the outside of School House was painted and a new wire fence erected. East Branch No. 2½, Weldford, had ten new double desks, supplied. South Branch No. 1, Weldford provided seventeen new double desks. The Trustees of Richibucto Town repaired the Grammar School quite extensively, and, what is more to the credit of the people, the ratepayers increased the salaries of all the teachers of the town by an almost unanimous vote of a largely attended annual meeting. In Rexton there is one of the best primary teachers in the Province, Miss Mina B. Farrer, but her work has been hindered by the admission of pupils to the 1st grade at any and all times of year down to the middle of June, in violation of Regulation 44. I was not able to see the Trustees at the time of my last visit, but I wrote the Secretary quite fully and trust that the good sense of the Board of Trustees will prevail and that justice will be done in this matter both to teacher and pupils.

RESTIGOUCHE COUNTY.

During the year this County has hardly sustained its reputation for progressiveness in educational work. At the time of my first visit in Feb'y *eleven* of its 38 ungraded schools were closed for various reasons. Six of these were opened in April and May, three others kept closed till the month of August, and two had no school during the year, but that was because teachers could not be found. There are, however, many excellent ungraded schools in the County. One of the best of these is at Shannon Vale, No. 6 Dalhousie, where the Trustees supplied one dozen Imperial desks and an oiled hardwood floor at a cost of over one hundred dollars. Credit for this is largely due to Mr. James Wright, the Secretary to Trustees, and to Miss Susie B. MacPherson, one of the best teachers in the County. The school house at Rafting Grounds, No. 1, Eldon, was ceiled inside and painted during summer vacation. The School House at Flat Land, No. 4 Addington, was enlarged during the summer and the school was well taught during the year by Miss Melissa J. Cook. The school at New Mills, No. 8, Durham, was very satisfactorily conducted during the year by Miss Jennie A. Cook. A new Dominion flag, twelve feet long, and an International dictionary were provided at River Louison, No. 6. Durham, by the exertions of the teacher, Miss Maude Brown.

NORTHUMBERLAND COUNTY.

As I reported the work of this County generally last year, I shall review it by Parishes this year.

Alnwick.—In Bartibogue Bridge Dist. the school room was wainscoted and the walls and ceiling calsomined. Oak Point Dist. had no school during the year. McRobbie Road had no school during the year as no teacher could be found. Red Pine Island had to employ a local licensee for the short term. Tabusintac, North Side, had a good school during the year taught by Miss Olive B Jardine. Tabusintac, South Side, could not find a teacher for the short term. New Jersey had a very successful school for the year with Miss Josie Gillies as teacher. In Burnt Church there is too much advanced work attempted to allow the teacher, Miss S. Estella Carruthers, to give sufficient attention to the primary work, though she overcame the difficulty, to a large extent, by employing the more advanced pupils as monitors. Portage District has organized, levied an assessment and will, I hope, be ready to open school in August of next year.

Blackville.—At Blackville Village there is a good chance for a consolidated school. Within a radius of four miles or less, there are six small schools making, with the three departments of the village, nine schools that could be brought together. Five teachers could then do the work much better than nine can do it now, with ample provision for Manual Training, Kitchen Garden, etc. I have mentioned this to some of the Trustees and people, and am not without hope that this scheme will materialize in time. With two exceptions all the surrounding schools are small and poorly equipped and the work is of an inferior character. It would, therefore, be of great advantage to them to enter into such a scheme. The Forks school is kept open but part of each year and has very poor accommodations and equipment. Renous Bridge has a good comfortable school house and fair equipment but a small attendance. North Renous was better attended this year than for some time. Upper Renous made extensive improvements to its school property but had to take a local licensed teacher for the short term. Grainfield has a good school house well furnished but the school did not prosper as much as in former years, partly on account of changing teacher each term. The school house in Underhill District is not in the centre of the District and cannot be placed to greater advantage till a part of the District is joined to the Village District, and even then it will be difficult, the way the roads are, to place the school house so as to be equally convenient to all the children.

Blissfield—Archibald, No. 3½ is one of the most unsatisfactory of schools. The District is divided by the river and the pupils on the north side, or "Storytown," attend very irregularly. It is not altogether on account of the danger of crossing, as a ferry is provided by the District, and the distance is no hindrance. The people seem to think that the school does not belong to them and so they take little interest. If the people would consent I would divide the District by the river and join the part on the south side to the Doaktown District and let Storytown have a school of its own. Bamford, No. 3, has a very small school, but it is exceedingly well conducted by Miss Grace E. Mitchell. It would be to the advantage of the pupils, nevertheless, to have them conveyed to the Doaktown school. Cain's River, No. 1½, is doing more satisfactory work than ever before under Mr. John J. McKinnon. In the Primary Department of the Doaktown Superior School excellent work is being done by Miss Beatrice L. Ellis, a painstaking and progressive teacher, who takes a prominent place in Institute work and thus improves from year to year.

Glenelg.—The school house in Black River, No. 1, was destroyed by a cyclone on Saturday, Aug. 22nd. It was a fortunate circumstance that the loss occurred on Saturday, as the building was lifted from its foundation, hurled across the road and smashed into kindling wood. The buildings in Napan, No. 1½, Glenelg and Chatham, are kept well painted, the fences in good repair, and the grounds neat and tidy. Weldfield, No. 3, has a good school house, fairly furnished and some of the pupils are doing very well in their work. Lower Napan, No. 4, has a good new school house, but they are allowing it to become sadly out of repair for the lack of a few dollars spent in paint. Little Branch, No. 7½, has an excellent school, taught by Miss Effie A. Edmunds. Black River Bridge, No. 7, has fine buildings viewed exteriorly. Interiorly there is much to be desired. A fine set of desks was provided this year after much needless delay. Too much advanced work is required of the teacher to allow her to give proper attention to the primary classes. Point au Carr, No. 6, has a very small enrolment but the people think they cannot convey their pupils to the neighboring District, and so they do their utmost to keep their school in operation. The pupils in Sweezy's District, No. 5, were very poorly graded at my last visit. There were pupils in Grade V. unable to do the arithmetic required for Grade III. The furniture and appliances of the school are good for the location and the school should improve under good management.

Hardwick.—Escuminac, No. 1, in this Parish is a largely attended school that has been well taught during the year by Miss S. Watling. The ceiling of the building is rather low, but otherwise the classroom is fairly comfortable. The outside of the building is its worst feature. It is badly in need of being painted. Hardwoods No. 2, had a good teacher, Miss Ellen M. Donovan, but a small attendance at my last visit. The small attendance was due partly to measles and partly to it being the berry picking season. The school house is greatly in need of repair. Eel River No. 3, has a good school house kept in good repair. The children were nearly all engaged in berry picking at the time of my last visit. In Hardwick Village No. 4, Miss Robina Noble has been doing excellent work for the past four years. In Bay du Vin No. 5, a native of the District, a young lady with very little experience had been engaged, and she, though only at work a few days, seemed to be making an excellent beginning. At Bayside No. 5½. Miss Emily J. Williston took charge of the school second term and was doing excellent work at the time of my visit. The school in Bay du Vin River, District No. 6, after being closed for two years after the loss of the school house by fire, was opened again at the beginning of this year, and continued during the year.

North Esk.—Chaplin Island Road No. 1, is a small District but has a a well equipped school, well conducted, with Miss Maggie T. Daughney as teacher the last four years. Trout Brook No. 2, has a good school house and is well attended for such a sparsely peopled District. Three Islands No. 3, has very few ratepayers—not more than four, with only six pupils, but are not near enough to any other District to have their pupils conveyed. Sevogle No. 4, has a comfortable school house and the school is regularly attended. Wild Cat Brook No. 5, had no school throughout the year. Johnston's Bridge No. 6, had no school second term because no teacher was available. Allison Settlement No. 10, is a large populous District but the school is so badly managed that little benefit is derived from it. Whitneyville No. 11, has a large enrolment and the school is kept open steadily, but the best results are not attained through a too frequent change of teachers.

Protecticnville No. 11½, has a poor school house and a small number of pupils, but the school did fairly well throughout the year. In Strathadam No. 12, excellent work was done by Miss Katie Troy during first term, and Miss Annie M. Brander second term.

South Esk—Lyttleton, No. 7, and Halcomb, No. 8, employed local licensees during second term. Silliker, No. 7½, has a large school and Miss Emma M. Barron conducted it quite successfully during the year. Red Bank, No. 9, had no school during first term, but employed Miss Hester L. Edgecombe, B. A., a recent graduate of the University of N. B., second term. Miss May E. Donovan did very satisfactory work in Cassilis, No. 13, throughout the year. The trustees of South Esk, No. 14, made extensive repairs on their school house during summer vacation. Williamstown, No. 15, closes school part of each year, and the few pupils have long distances to travel, and still the pupils did well in all but the Natural History subjects.

Derby.—Wilson's Point, No. 1½, has been taught for the past three years by Miss Mabel E. Cluston, and during that time the school has been increasing in efficiency. Indiantown, No. 3, has an excellent school house, built by the exertions of Miss Lottie E. Underhill, who left the school at the end of first term. The school in Bryenton, No. 4, has a much smaller attendance than formerly. Elm Tree, No. 2, has only four children of school age and is the only school in this Inspectorate closed under section 121 of the School Law.

Nelson—The third department was opened in Nelson Village school, at the beginning of the fall term. Vye Settlement engaged a graduate in Arts for the second term. Miss Maggie L. Carmalt has done excellent work in Chelmsford District for the past five terms. This District has a good school house, well cared for outside, but the inside walls and ceiling should receive more attention. Indiantown, No. 9, has a good school house and surroundings but few pupils and the school is closed a part of every year. Barnaby River, No. 5, has an old school house with very inferior furniture. Barnaby, No. 6½, has an excellent school house, well furnished. In Semiwagan Ridge the old school building has been repaired and made comfortable. Mouth of Barnaby has a very cold schoolhouse. It is not finished outside and late in December was not banked.

Newcastle—Miss Margaret J. Phelan did a good year's work in Lower Newcastle. Little Bartibogue has a very small school but the ratepayers have no intention of closing it even for a month. The Trustees of Big Bartibogue District intend to keep their school open this winter though there are but six children of school age in the District and a few that come from Meadow Brook District, a distance of nearly four miles. Millbank No. 5 has now quite a large enrollment. Ferryville No. 8, did not have so good a school as usual this year. Miss Nora Cripps conducted the Moorfield school during the year in a very satisfactory manner.

Ludlow.—Carroll's Crossing No. 1, has had a good school during the year under Miss Estelle Crammond. McNamee No. 1½ had a Local Licensee during second term. The school at Ludlow, South Side No. 2, taught by Miss Lilian I. Price, has neither a good school house nor a generous equipment, but the pupils are clever and the teacher is devoted to her work, a combination that brings success. Boiestown No. 3, has changed teachers twice during the year, so the school has made no progress. In Ludlow, North Side, the number of pupils is so small and the ratepayers so non-progressive that the school is closed a part of every year, making the best work impossible, though the children are more than ordinarily clever. Pleasant Ridge No. 5, has changed teachers too often of late to have a satisfactory school.

Chatham—Napan River No. 5, made some improvements in its school equipment. Chatham Head No. 4, has been more successful since the Trustees employed a class room assistant. Douglasfield No. 6, had a fair measure of success during the year, though a change of teachers was made in the middle of it. The Trustees of Rock Heads No. 2, made extensive improvements both to the outside and the inside of their school house. Their teacher, Miss Sophia G. McDonald, has been with them nearly six years and her zealous services are evidently appreciated by the parents.

YORK COUNTY.

There are only five schools of this County under my supervision, They are in the Parish of Stanley. Parker's Ridge No. 11, has a very large school, with a good school house and equipment, and the school made satisfactory progress during the year. Hayesville No. 13, is a small school but the work during the year was most satisfactory. Miss Sadie A. Cameron is the teacher. Taxis River No. 10, had only four pupils enrolled at the date of my last visit. Avery's Portage No. 9, has a poor school house, and it changed teachers during the year, but still its school made a fair amount of progress.

SUPERIOR SCHOOLS.

I am pleased to be able to report that there has been increased efficiency in all these schools in my Inspectorate. The Blackville School, which was the poorest when my last Annual Report was written, has made considerable advance under Principal M. R Tuttle, B. A. The tone is better, the pupils attend better and the parents take more interest, though it is still far from what Mr. Tuttle would like to have it. By Mr. Tuttle's exertions a school library has been started with sixty-seven volumes The Douglastown school, too, has shown great improvement. Mr. Benn, the Principal, has lots of energy and enthusiasm and where these two elements are rightly directed, success must follow. He has made a specialty of his School Library and has secured the greatest number of volumes of any in my Inspectorate and is adding to it every term The Harcourt Superior School made rapid progress for one term under Mr. Angus Dewar, a young man of rare teaching ability. He left the school at the close of the year and I have not been informed of the name of his successor. The Rexton Superior School suffered a loss at the end of second term in the retirement of Mr. R. G. Girvan from the Principalship, which he had filled most acceptably for five years. He was succeeded by Mr. R. B. Masterton who, I have heard, retired on account of failing health at the close of the year.

GRAMMAR SCHOOLS.

Of the three Grammar Schools in this Inspectorate it can be said that they all maintained their efficiency throughout the year, did excellent work along the lines prescribed, and each made some improvment on the work of former years. The Kent County Grammar School, located in Richibucto, has, heretofore, been admitting pupils to the 8th standard that were very deficient in most subjects, entailing upon the Principal an amount of review work that made it impossible for him to prepare them well on the 8th grade work during the year. The consequence was that many failed to pass to the 9th standard at the end of the year and their failure was credited to the principal. By my advice the Trustees insisted on a higher percentage in grading into the 8th standard and the school has become more workable in consequence. The Northumberland County Grammar School, located in Chatham, has now the second Grammar School teacher and will, I make no doubt, do even better work than usual in grades IX, X and XI. In the Restigouche County Grammar School, located in Campbellton, I found standards X and XI well grounded and profiting to the fullest extent by the work of their grade, but standard IX seemed to take little interest and a very superficial examination disclosed the reason to be inadequate preparation to enter the standard.

ARBOR DAY.

Arbor Day was observed in this Inspectorate on Friday, May 8th 1903.

It was too early in the season for a great part of Restigouche County, where there was still much snow in the woods and the ground in the school yards was frozen. Seventy-nine Districts and Departments observed the day during which 289 trees and 37 shrubs were planted and 55 flowerbeds were made, besides much tidying up of grounds, decorating of rooms and general improvements were indulged in.

TEACHERS' INSTITUTES.

It was my good fortune to attend three County Institutes during the year and all in the short term. It took a great deal of time from my other work, but they were all profitable seasons and I did not begrudge either the time or expense incurred. I am convinced that much more good could be done at these gatherings were the inexperienced and unsuccessful under an obligation to attend and the time spent more in practical work than in reading papers that often do not reach the need of teachers who wish help in their work. I have noticed. more particularly this year, that it is only the more progressive teachers that attend these meetings. It may be that they have reached the height at which they realize their need of help or it may be that they are more independent financially, whatever the cause, there were teachers who failed to attend in each of the three Counties who had far more need of help than any in attendance.

At the Kent County Institute, which met at Richibucto, there were about 32 teachers present out of about 120 teachers in the county, a very poor showing indeed, though there is really some excuse for this.

In Chatham there were about 80 in attendance out of nearly 160 teachers in the county. This was better, but not nearly so good as it should be.

Out of 48 teachers employed in the County of Restigouche, 32 assembled at Campbellton to attend their County Institute on the last two teaching days of the year.

At all these meetings I was impressed with the earnestness of the teachers, the interest taken in the various discussions, their eagerness to ask questions and have them answered and their promptness to take part at the call of the chair. There did not seem to be any of that disposition to come late and leave early that I have observed at similar gatherings and which does more than any other one thing to dishearten aspiring teachers, make them lose interest in the proceedings and turn the whole affair into a farce and a show.

I have the honour to be, Sir,

Your obedient servant,

GEO. W. MERSEREAU.

INSPECTORAL DISTRICT No. 2.

This District comprises the County of Westmorland and the Parishes of Coverdale, Hillsborough, Hopewell and Harvey in Albert County.

Owing to the protracted illness and death of Inspector Smith, no annual report of this District has been prepared. During the first part of the month of March Inspector Smith visited and reported upon a few schools in the Parishes of Shediac, Salisbury and Sackville, but was unable to continue his work.

In June the newly appointed Inspector, Charles D. Hebert, was instructed to visit as many of the schools as possible in Inspector Smith's District. In accordance with these instructions Inspector Hebert visited the schools of the Acadian Districts of Kent County, the schools in the Parish of Rogersville, Northumberland Co., the schools in the Parishes of Coverdale, Hillsboro, Hopewell and Harvey in Albert Co., and most of the schools in the Parishes of Botsford, Shediac, Dorchester, Moncton and Salisbury in Westmorland County.

From the full monthly reports made to the Education Office by Inspector Hebert the following extracts are given:

(1) *Extracts from June Report:—*

ALBERT COUNTY.

Parish of Coverdale.—Bridgedale No. 5 has a fair school with a very good attendance. Miss Nellie McNaughton, who has lately taken charge, seems to be greatly interested in her work and will no doubt meet with success. There is room yet for improvement in reading and arithmetic. Niagara No. 6 is trying to operate a school with an enrolment of 7 and an average of 6 School was opened during the second term on April 1st. This district is a very remote one and cannot possibly be combined with any other district. The work done in No 7, Turtle Creek, is far from being satisfactory. The pupils made a very poor showing in arithmetic, reading and grammar The result of the examination in geography, however, was very good. Colpitts, No. 8, though a poor district, deserves credit for its neat school house, its clean and well enclosed grounds and its excellent furniture. Miss Ella Smith, who is in charge, is doing good work. The attendance is not very large, especially in winter, owing to the difficulty experienced by the children to reach the school. Leaman, No 9 was closed during the term for want of a teacher. No. 11, Lower Turtle Creek, has a fair school. The exterior of the building is very good, but the interior is greatly in need of repairing. The apparatus is of an inferior quality, maps are torn and shabby and the blackboards are in a very poor state. The Trustees' attention has been called to the fact, and I hope the necessary improvements will be made. Miss E. Goodhall conducts a fair school at No. 12, Nixon Settlement. The attendance is very good and discipline excellent. A good painting and other necessary repairs would greatly improve the appearance of the buildings. The house at Stoney Creek, No. 14, is badly in need of repairs. The exterior of the building presents a miserable appearance.

Parish of Hillsboro.—No. 1, Weldon, has a very good school. The apparatus is very good, furniture new and maps excellent. Miss Louisa Tingley is doing very commendable work. General repairs and a good painting would be of the greatest benefit to the school house. Mr Arthur N. Foster is doing good work at No. 4 Edgett's Landing. His classes gave evidence of good training. especially in grammar and analysis. The school house is small, poorly lighted and its exterior presents a most wretched appearance. The school in Salem, No 7, is in good order. The pupils acquitted themselves well in the various subjects. The buildings require a good painting and the grounds could be greatly improved. The school at Osborne, No. 8, is not up to the required standard. It is in charge of a zealous and faithful, but young and inexperienced teacher. New furniture was procured last summer. At the time of my visit, Mr. Judson Steeves, the Secretary, was the only Trustee in the district. The other trustees had removed from the District during the term. The school at Baltimore, No. 9, was burned last winter. Good progress is being made in the erection of a new building, which the Trustees hope to have ready for the coming term. No. 11, Berryton, operates a satisfactory school. Much, however, could be accomplished by regularity of attendance. The house is in a very good condition and the premises well kept. Rosevale, No. 13, has a very good school. The ordinary branches are very well taught. A few of the pupils worked exercises in geometry and arithmetic very well. The school house is neatly painted and surrounded by clean and well enclosed grounds. Miss Kierstead, the teacher, is to be commended for the interest she seems to take in the welfare of the school. Round Hill, No. 14, has a splendid school house and an excellent teacher, Miss Mary Smith. The tone of the school is excellent and the order almost perfect. The pupils acquitted themselves in a very creditable manner. Children from the Beech Hill District attend this school. The school at No. 15, Lower Hillsboro is in charge of Miss Edna Floyd a very successful teacher. Dicipline is excellent. The pupils acquitted themselves honorably in the various subjects. Although the attendance is not very large, I learn that the Trustees take a great interest in school matters. The well fenced grounds and the neat and bright appearance of the buildings reflect great credit on the District. Caledonia Settlement No. 12, has barely the required number of pupils to keep a school in operation. Caledonia No. 5, Hopewell Parish, is no better off so far as attendance is concerned. I understand that there is a movement on foot to combine Nos. 5 and 12. Although the schools are doing satisfactory work, the uniting of the two Districts might be a step in the right direction. The attendance is small in both and the children experience great difficulty in coming to school in winter. The matter was to be discussed at the annual meeting.

Parish of Hopewell.—Woodworth No. 3, the result of the examination showed that in all subjects the pupils were well and carefully prepared. The attendance is good, five of the scholars having a perfect attendance certificate. There has been no school during the year at Memel No. 4. Reason assigned, not enough pupils to attend. Some of the children go to the Curryville school. Curryville No. 8, has a prosperous and well equipped school, Miss Orpah West is doing very efficient work.

Parish of Harvey.—Waterside No. 1, seems to be a large and prosperous District, yet it did not have school in operation during the last year owing to neglect on the part of the Trustees and of the Secretary. Money was voted in 1902 to repair the school house and keep school in operation, Repairs were made but the school was closed. Provisions were made at this year's annual meeting to operate the school and the ratepayers seem determined to see the provisions carried out. No. 2, Lower New Horton did not have its school in operation for the want of a teacher. School will be re-opened the coming term. Miss Mildred Milton has conducted the school at Germantown No. 4, during the year with fair success. The attendance however is most irregular. Beaver Brook, No. 5 has a fair school house, good grounds but a poor School. No. 8 Brookton, could not obtain a teacher and consequently the school remained closed. The school at New Midway, No. 9, is greatly in need of general repairs and painting. There seems to be a lack of interest in school matters in this District. Miss G. McAnulty is meeting with fair success. Reading is well taught. West River, No. 10 has a fair school. Twenty-eight pupils are enrolled with an average attendance of twenty. Miss W. Barbour is in charge. The ratepayers of Waterside No. 1 send their children to the number of 7 to this school. Miss Barbour is doing as well as could be expected under this arrangement. Upper New Horton, No. 12 has a fair school, a good house and good grounds. Miss Ethel Swanson is in charge. Pupils from Lower New Horton attend school here. Miss Swanson seems to take great interest in her work.

Extracts from August Report:—

KENT COUNTY

Dundas.—No. 7, Grandigue. The school house in this District is in an excellent condition. The grounds are neat, well kept and enclosed by a good fence. The school, however, is not up to the required standard. Reading was very poor. The same applies to Arithmetic. The house in No. 12 is a new one and presents a fine appearance. When completed and furnished with all the necessary appliances, this school house will be a credit to the District. Extensive improvements are being made in No. 8, Cocagne Cape. The interior of the building is also badly in need of repairs, a new floor etc. The blackboard surface is very poor and the maps are torn and worthless. I wrote to the Board of Trustees and called their attention to the matter. No. 2. Cocagne River South, is in charge of Mr. Alfred Bourgeois, a very good teacher. The school house and outbuildings should be painted and the grounds enclosed. The blackboard surface is not what it should be and the maps are very poor. No. 5½, North West Branch, had a very small attendance at the time of my visit, 11 being enrolled. This number does not represent the regular attendance. Many of the children stay away from school during the berry season. Elementary Reading, Writing and a little Arithmetic are the only subjects receiving attention. The house is in a poor condition, furniture old fashioned and necessary appliances wanting, there being no maps in the school. Miss Viola Murray is doing excellent work in Hay's Settlement, No. 5. The result of the examination was very satisfactory. The ratepayers seem to take interest in the welfare of their school. The interior of the building has been plastered and wainscoted during the last vacation and with a few finishing touches will be highly creditable to the District. The maps and other appliances, however, are not up to the requirements. The Trustees promised to see to the matter and will provide the required apparatus. No. 10, Trafalgar, has no school in operation. The Trustees are unable to secure a teacher. They are in the meantime making needed repairs to their school. The school at No. 4, Cocagne River, South, is in charge of Mr. Aug. E. Daigle, an experienced and capable teacher. He is unfortunately handicapped in his work by a poor classification of the pupils by a former teacher. I am confident, however, that Mr. Daigle will bring the school to its required standard. The building has been recently painted and presents a neat appearance. No. 13, Cocagne Bridge, has a good school. The interior is tastefully decorated well lighted and neatly kept. Both languages are carefully taught. The pupils gave a good account of themselves in the examination. At Howard's Brook, No. 6, the work is not quite satisfactory. The result is due in my opinion, to a poor classification of the pupils. The school is poorly furnished and badly in need of maps and other appliances. The Trustees were present at the examination and I called their attention to the matter. They seemed willing to carry out my suggestions. No. 1, Cocagne, has a large attendance with an average of forty. The school is now in charge of Miss Lena Melanson, a very efficient teacher. The pupils answered readily and intelligently and showed a good knowledge of Grammar, Arithmetic and Geography. Arithmetic was especially good. Reading a little below the required mark. The Trustees and ratepayers could easily give a substantial proof of the interest they take in the school affairs by furnishing the school with maps and better black board surface. The furniture is excellent, but a few more seats are needed. Moreover the building would not suffer from the effects of a good painting. No. 11½, Ohio, Seven pupils under the required age are attending this school. Sixty-seven pupils enrolled, average forty-seven. Mr. Allain the teacher, states that the attendance is as high as 75, still the trustees do not deem it necessary to engage an assistant. The school room has been repaired, wainscoted and painted since Mr. Doucett's visit. Furniture is old fashioned and accommodation very poor, there being seven seats with three per seat at the time of my visit. Some parents have peculiar ideas and in some cases will not allow their children to learn English Grammar.

Dundas and Shediac.—No. 2½ Landry's This district has a fair building with well kept grounds. The furniture is very good but the general apparatus of very inferior quality. The furniture has been procured since Mr. Doucett's visit. The school is weak. I am told that trustees and ratepayers do not take much interest in the school. At the time of my visit, No. 17A Shediac Bridge, had an enrolment of forty nine with an average of thirty-five. But this number I am told does not represent the regular enrolment. As many as sixty-five pupils attend this school. An assistant is needed. Something mu[illegible] be done too in the way of securing more comfortable accommodation. T[illegible] school room is actually crowded, and by far too small to accommodate th[illegible] number of pupils in the district. I am told that Inspector Smith had pr[illegible]viously insisted upon better accommodation but no action has been taken [illegible] the trustees The district is a large one and the taxes are low per capita. The rate-payers could easily carry out the suggestions made them. The building is poor, apparatus deficient and the school necessarily a poor one.

Dundas and Moncton.—No. 6A, is closed for the want of a teacher. I am satisfied that the trustees did all in their power to engage a teacher, but unfortunately failed in the attempt.

No. 14A, Poirier's, is operating a very weak school; twelve enrolled, average eight. School house and appliances are poor but as good as the district can afford. The pupils are all young and the only subjects taught are Reading, Arithmetic and Writing. The trustees will provide maps and other apparatus.

Dundas and Wellington No. 11. Renaud's Mills has a fair school house but needs paint. Grounds are rough.

St. Marys No. 7. Pelering, is a new district. The school is sadly deficient in maps and blackboard surface. The furniture is old fashioned. It is a weak school. The same may be said of 7½ St. George. This school seems to have been neglected in the past, one of the pupils was unusually bright This school needs maps and blackboards. I met the trustees and talked the matter over. They ordered the necessary apparatus.

No. 13 Upper Buctouche has a splendid school house. Every one seems to take an interest in educational affairs in this district. The children take up both languages with facility, and are greatly devoted to their work. No. 14. Kings. The school in this district was not satisfactory. Reading was poor. Little attention was given to grammar and still less to Geography. Arithmetic was below the average. The children are young and do not seem to have any idea of what they are doing

Wellington.—The school house at Little River No 2, needs a good painting. The interior is in a fair condition. The furniture is excellent and the school supplied with all the necessary equipments Reading was especially good, grammar satisfactory, but arithmetic somewhat below average.

Dundas.—The school at No. 3, Scovil's Mills was closed early in the spring, owing to the prevalence of small-pox. Progress was naturally retarded. At the time of my visit Mr. E. Williams was trying to readjust things with a fair chance of success. Reading and Geography were good but grammar and arithmetic fell below the requirements. The school house should be painted.

APPARATUS, SCHOOLS, &c.

I regret to have to state that generally, schools are not provided with the necessary appliances. Trustees seem to think that a box of chalk and a bell constitute the general apparatus in a school room, maps are entirely out of the question and by some considered as luxuries. Blackboards are numerous but in some instances very unsatisfactory. In many cases the school houses, grounds and out-buildings are not well cared for. A little lime or paint would very materially improve the general appearance of some of them. Some school lots are unfenced, unimproved and entirely neglected. In all cases I endeavoured to meet the Trustees and earnestly called their attention to the important duties which the law, as well as their own interests imposes upon them.

COURSE OF INSTRUCTION.

According to notes taken during my visits the results in the several subjects of the course could be classified as follows,— Reading, in very many cases, monotonous, meaning of words neglected, and not enough attention given to the thought expressed in the lesson. Grammar, French and English, only fair, too much text book and not enough practical work Geography is fair, would be better were maps &c. provided. Spelling is very satisfactory. Writing is good generally. Arithmetic is below the average. Not enough oral and mental work.

Extract from September Report:

KENT COUNTY.—Continued.

Parish of St Paul—No. 1, Legerville has a good school and an excellent teacher Mr. Pierre Belliveau. The pupils gave a good proof of their careful training. Arithmetic, geography and reading were exceptionally good. The attendance is splendid. Extensive repairs are being made on the buildings. The grounds are to be surrounded by a wire fence. This is surely a progressive district.

No. 2, Sweeneyville is operating a fair school. Writing was not satisfactory. More time and attention should be given to this subject. The interior of the school house is neat, but the exterior needs repairing. Singing is taught here.

The interior of the school in No 3, St. Paul is in a most disgracef-l state. The attendance is most irregular. There were only young childr present on the day of my visit. Many pupils were without books, slates, e The grounds are in a miserable condition. I wrote to the trustees and call their attention to the state of their school.

No. 4, Richardville has a good house and a fair school. A few of tl pupils are without books and slates. Grammar is receiving very little attention. The school is very poorly provided with maps. etc. No. 5, Belliveau Settlement is closed. Could not secure a teacher. The school in No. 6, Devarennes, is not satisfactory. The pupils are young and do not attend regularly. Reading, Writing and Arithmetic are the only subjects receiving attention. Miss Louise Murray is doing excellent work at No. 8, McLaughlin Road. There exists a sad deficiency, in maps and general apparatus. The pupils, however, have a proficient knowledge of the several subjects of the course. The teacher with the help of the pupils manages to prepare her own maps etc. The trustees were present and seemed to be proud of their school. They had recently ordered two maps and other necessary appliances The house is small and quite well finished. No. 9, Cormier's Settlement is closed. A teacher cannot be procured.

St. Paul and St. Marys.—No. 7, McLean Settlement, has a new school house. The interior of the building is not yet finished. This is another case of a want of books and slates. As a result Geography and Grammar are receiving no attention. The pupils are not up to date in Arithmetic. Maps are wanting.

St. Marys.—The school in No. 2, Coates' Mills is closed for want of a teacher. This is to be regretted as the District is a large and important one. No. 4, Dollard Settlement is operating a very unsatisfactory school. The room is crowded with children. New furniture should be provided as that actually in use is entirely out of date. There are not enough seats to accommodate the children in attendance. Forty-five pupils are enrolled, average thirty-five, and still the enrolment is not what it generally is in the District. The Trustees have bought the necessary material to finish the interior of the house which is badly in need of repairs. I am pleased to note that new maps were procured recently. Reading in English very poor; Arithmetic below the average, No Geography and very little Grammar. Trout Brook, No. 3, has a neat little house and excellent grounds. The interior of the building is not yet completed but all the required material is on hand. The District does not feel capable of bearing the expense it would incur should the work be done at once. The ratepayers claim that this District should be classed as a poor one in consideration of its low valuation. I gave them no encouragement as I understood that the boundaries were revised some time ago or are in need of revision. Miss Sarah Bilodeau is doing good work here. Miss Esther Robichaud is doing good work at Collet Settlement, No. 5. This is her seventh term in the District The pupils are all young. The attendance is very good. The school room is neat, but the furniture is old fashioned. More seats should be provided. Maria de Kent, No. 14, has a large and commodious building. The enrolment reaches fifty with an average of forty. On the day of my last visit many pupils were absent for good reasons. The interior of the building is not as neat as it should be. I am told that the trustees intend to make some needed repairs in the spring. Reading was not up to the required standard but Grammar was good, Writing poor, attendance regular. Ste. Marie, No. 1, has a splendid school with seventy six pupils enrolled, average sixty-six. There is a class room attached with Miss Madeleine Roy as assistant teacher. The pupils have a good knowledge of the subjects of the course. Arithmetic, however, was poor in Grade V. Writing was poor in general. A report was made to the Trustees. I called their attention to the present state of the school buildings and insisted upon the necessity of better blackboard surface and a map of the world. The interior of the class room is in a very poor condition.

Wellington.—No. 11½, Mill, has a good school. A new floor has been laid and other needed improvements made to the school house. General apparatus is good. No. 15, St. Hilaire, was unable to secure the services of a teacher. The school is closed. St. Maurice No. 12, has a good school, although there exists a sad deficiency in maps and general apparatus. I wrote to the Trustees and recommended better appliances. No. 13, St. Irene, has the weakest school in the Parish. The children seem to have no idea of what they are doing. Reading, or the attempt the pupils make at reading was most unsatisfactory. Monotony, indistinctness and bad pronunciation were the special features in this subject. Apparatus, none; maps, none; furniture of the most inferior quality. I wrote to the Secretary and called his strict attention to the matter. If he does not heed the recommendation, some steps must be taken to awaken the interest of the parties concerned. The Trustees of No. 17, St. Michael wrote to me wishing to place their school in charge of a local teacher, I did not think this proper, as the District was to operate a school for the first time and stood in need of a capable and experienced teacher. I consequently refused to recommend a local license and explained to the Trustees that it was in their interests to engage a trained teacher. They followed my instructions and on the day of my visit I was pleased to find Miss Marie Boudreau in charge. No work was being done in advanc of Grade 1. The needed supply of apparatus will be provided in time The attendance is very regular; enrolled twenty-seven, average twenty-five present, twenty-three. Bay District, No. 9. has a very unsatisfactory school No. 16, St. Gabriel, is operating a fair school. The District is a weak one, onl twelve poll taxes. By revising the present boundaries and uniting Savoie Settlement, a small village, with St. Gabriels, a suitable District could be formed. Savoie is about one mile distant, none of the children attend school. The ratepayers told me it was their intention to open up a road joining the two Districts if the Government would grant them help.

Carleton.—No. 8, Sapin Point.—Arrangements had been made with this District to have the school house removed to the centre of the District and then repaired. Work was begun but had to be stopped as the delapidated state of the building did not permit of its being removed. A special meeting was held. The ratepayers decided to build in the spring of 1904, a very wise decision indeed. The new house is to be erected on a site already sanctioned by my predecessor. The efficiency of the work done here was impaired by irregularity of attendance due to a prevalence of measles in the district. No. 10, Portage River.—The building in this District is new. The exterior is well finished. The Trustees expect to have the interior completed next Christmas. The school is in a satisfactory condition and all the children are well provided with books and slates. Although the two districts just mentioned are remote and very poor it is pleasing to remark that great interest is taken by the ratepayers in the welfare of their schools. Unfortunately it happens that in consequence of the present division of the district about fourteen families are outside of the existing boundaries and at great distances from the school. No. 3, Potter's Mills.—This district has been without school for the last year. I am pleased to state that the school is in charge of Miss Henrietta Dutch, an excellent teacher. The district is divided into two sections by the Kouchibouguac. Some children can attend school but for a very limited part of the year. The attendance is, however, regular. Miss Dutch, by her enterprising and industrious way of conducting the school has however made many needed and remarkable improvements to the interior of the building Everything looks neat and bright. The furniture is excellent. The pupils are intelligent and well mannered and take a great interest in their work. Miss Dutch intends organizing a concert to buy necessary appliances. I am sorry the same cannot be said of N. 1, Kouchibouguac, so far as the interior of the school is concerned. The pupils are all huddled together. The building is greatly in need of repairs and could stand a very good painting. There is a class room attached, but not enough pupils to receive an assistant. Notwithstanding the unpleasant surroundings the pupils gave a good account of themselves. In the higher grades especially the examinations were satisfactory. No. 4, has had its troubles and very serious ones. The school has been closed for the last two years, but opened up about three weeks ago. The former building was burned under suspicious circumstances. The new building is well finished outside the interior will be completed soon. Miss Isabella Caie is doing excellent work here. The pupils are highly interested in their studies and show proof of their careful training.

Richibucto.— Richibucto Village, a special report was sent in about this school. No. 6, Cuockpish has been closed for the last two terms. I met the Trustees and enquired into the condition of the District. It was a very weak one, about six children of the required ege. The ratepayers are anxious to have the school in operation. No. 12, Aldouane, has one of the best schools in the Parish. All the subjects of the course are receiving equal attention. Pupils seem to acquire aknowledge of both languages with facility. Reading and Grammar were excellent. The attendance is very regular. Appliances were good. The house needs painting. No. 11, Cape, has a fairly well operated school. The premises are nicely kept but the buildings would require a coat of paint. The pupils are beginning to take up Geography and Grammar, but very slowly. The school is very poorly furnished and deficient in apparatus. No. 7, Lee, although a poor District, manages to keep the premises and buildings in a most satisfactory condition. The school is a good one and well provided with maps, blackboard and furniture. The attendance is fair. The school was closed during the last term. Gaspereau, No. 3, has a good school with Miss Annie Finnigan, a second class teacher in charge. The result of the examination was satisfactory. Arithmetic, however, was not up to date. The pupils of this District have not been vaccinated as required by the regulations and instructions of the Board of Health. I advised the school officials in the District to comply with the requirements of the law. The ratepayers would agree to vaccination but considered the charge too high.

St. Louis and Richibucto.—The work done in No. 7, N. W. Church, is satisfactory. The buildings are in a fair condition. The grounds are far too small. The house needs painting. No. 6, N. W. Bridge, the only subjects receiving attention are Reading, Writing and Arithmetic. Results can hardly be classified as satisfactory. Spelling was poor. Furniture is old fashioned. The buildings are greatly in need of a thorough painting. There is only one map in the school and that is of no value. The Trustee promised to see to the matter and furnish better blackboard service, as we as maps of the Maritime Provinces.

NORTHUMBERLAND COUNTY.

Rogersville.—The exterior of the building in No. 8 presents a fine ap pearance. The District, a very poor one, is to be congratulated on having such a fine house. New furniture must be provided before long. Maps and blackboards are good. The school is a fair one and the attendance good. In some respects, however, the pupils are not up to the required standard. The school in No. 3, St. Pierre, has been in operation since the 8th inst. Repairs are now being made on the building. The interior is painted and wainscoted. Furniture is good but a few more seats are needed. The appliances are good. Miss Marie Doucett is doing splendid work. Grammar and Arithmetic were excellent. Miss Melvina Godin deserves special mention for the work she is doing in No. 13, St. Marcel. The pupils are intelligent and have a good knowledge of the ordinary subjects of the course. The premises are neat and well kept, they are surrounded by a good fence. No. 14, Pleasant Ridge, has a good building and well enclosed grounds. The school is a satisfactory one. Arithmetic was below the requirements. Shediac Cape, No. 11, the school house is well finished inside but needs painting. The school is well provided with necessary appliances. The furniture is excellent. A few more seats are needed. I wrote to the trustees with reference to this matter. The work done here is satisfactory. No. 5 is closed, no teacher could be provided for this term. No. 1 Collet, a remote and lonely District. Educational progress partakes of the nature of the surroundings. The school was closed for the last year. The pupils are consequently below the average in different subjects. The teacher is painstaking and industrious and keeps the school in perfect condition. Maps and blackboards are excellent. New furniture should be provided. I wrote to the Trustees in regard to the furniture. No. 15, Vennor, is operating a poor school. The results of the examination were unsatisfactory. There seems to be no active interest taken in the school work. The inside of the house is in good condition, but the outside needs painting. Grounds are neat and well enclosed. Furniture and general appliances are up to date. No. 10½, McCool's, this school is unsatisfactory. The teacher is making efforts to bring it up to the required standard, but is meeting with very little encouragement. Grammar and geography are poor and reading a failure. The building is in a fair condition. Grounds are rough and neglected. No. 2 is closed; could not secure a teacher for the present term.

Rogersville and Acadieville.—No. 7, St. Athanase, has erected a good building. The interior has been partially finished in sheathing. The furniture is only temporary. The Trustees will purchase new desks and seats during the summer months. A map has been ordered according to my instructions. This is the first term the school is in operation. The pupils are young, but seem to take great interest in their work. Writing deserves a special notice. The school in 16A is satisfactory. Reading was good. There exists a deficiency in apparatus. I saw the trustees and called their attention to the need of maps and blackboards. They ordered the same at once. The buildings have been repaired lately and are in a satisfactory condition. The grounds should be enclosed.

Rogersville and Glen—Rosaireville No. 4, has a school in operation for the first time; the trustees and ratepayers may well take pride in the neat school house they have erected. It would be a credit to many a larger district. The interior will be finished next term and necessary apparatus supplied. The attendance is very good. A few of the pupils have already attended school in other districts. Reading and writing were very good.

Acadieville—No 5, Siding. This school is not kept in operation regularly. School closed last term. Extensive repairs have been made on the buildings during the last summer. The interior should be finished and better furniture supplied. Reading and writing were very good. McInnis Brook, No. 1, and Village St. Jean, No. 9, have unsatisfactory schools. Reading was a failure in No. 9, but a little better in No. 1. Arithmetic and writing were poor in both. Geography and grammar receive no attention. This want of efficiency is due to a poor classification of the pupils. The teachers were consequently instructed to put back pupils who had been promoted too hastily. Furniture is needed in both schools. These districts are weak and experience much difficulty in keeping their schools in operation. No. 3, the school in this district is a very weak one. Reading and arithmetic were poor. In its present condition the house is not fit to keep school in during the winter. I wrote to the trustees and recommended that the interior be finished. No. 4 is one of the neatest school-houses in the parish. The interior is wainscoted and well finished. The exterior puts up a good appearance. Better furniture should be provided. A black-board is on hand and will be in use soon. Maps have been ordered. The pupils attend school very regularly and take a lively interest in their work.

St. Louis—No. 1, Guimond, I am pleased to state that Miss Mary Guimond a local licensee is doing excellent work here. All subjects of the course are receiving due attention and the results are gratifying. The pupils are polite and intelligent. Building is in a very good condition. Furniture is good and appliances are up to date. Writing was a feature. No. 2, St. Louis, is operating a fair school. The grounds are neglected. The school in No. 10 of the Kouchibouguac Mouth, is satisfactory. Some of the pupils, however, were rather inclined to neglect the English branches.

They will henceforth confine themselves to instructions given them and take up English regularly. New furniture has been provided as well as a good blackboard. The building is small but comfortable.

Rogersville.—No. 10. A special report was sent in about the state of this school. No. 13, St Marcel, has a splendid school with Miss Mary G. Godin in charge. The pupils are bright and well trained. I listened to an excellent lesson in reading for beginners. Writing was excellent. Singing is one of the pleasing features. The school had been closed since last December. The grounds and buildings are in a good condition.

Extracts from October Report:

KENT COUNTY.

Acadieville.—At the time of my visit the school in No. 2, Acadieville, was closed on account of the teacher's illness. The buildings were in good condition. Repairs were made in connection with this school during the past year. The furniture is poor. The maps and other appliances are far from being satisfactory. The Trustees' attention was called to the matter.

St. Louis.—Upper Bridge, No. 4, is operating a fair school. The pupils are well classified and seem to be serious about their work. Reading and writing could be better. The other subjects are satisfactory. Grounds are neat and well enclosed. Building in good condition. Equipment good. Cameron's Mills, No. 5, has a weak and very unsatisfactory school. The result is fully in accordance with the management of school affairs in the district. The school is generally closed from Xmas until April. The consequence is that the pupils forget all they can possibly learn during the term. Progress is therefore greatly retarded, a fact which was clearly shown by the result of the examination. I wrote to the Trustees and gave them a full report of the state of their school.

No. 3½, McLeod's Mills, has a fair school house, very good appliances and neatly enclosed grounds. The teacher is very much interested in her work and her labour is well repaid. Reading, geography and grammar were good; arithmetic, as usual, was not up to date. Babineau, No. 11, is closed. No teacher could be secured for this term. McLeod's Mills, No. 3, maintains an excellent school. The work done here is splendid and reflects great credit upon the teacher, Miss Lucie E. Richard. She was hindered in her work by irregularity of attendance; however, the results were gratifying. Geography, especially map-drawing, was excellent. The children are good writers and take pride in their neat writing and drawing books. Better furniture is needed. The school is provided with hyloplate and good maps. General repairs will be made in the spring to the exterior of the building and good furniture provided.

St. Louis and Richibucto.—The house in No. 8, Up. N. W. Bridge, is unfit for school purposes. It is very cold during the winter months. The school has no maps, no blackboards and no apparatus. Elementary work is being done; attendance is very good. No. 9, Lake Road is in charge of Mr. Honore Maillet, an efficient teacher. One pupil is doing Grade VI. work. Results in the other grades were fair. A map of the Dominion has been ordered upon my recommendation. Hyloplate will be supplied in the near future. House needs paint. Furniture is old-fashioned and should be replaced by a more modern style of seats and desks. Ratepayers are interested in school affairs, and, with a little encouragement, will readily fall in line.

Wellington.—The school in No. 12½, Upper Chockpish, is satisfactory. The higher grades made a good showing. Writing and drawing deserve special mention. Attendance is poor owing to the children being kept home for harvest work. Building is in need of repairs, and new furniture should be provided. There exists a defiency in apparatus. No. 8, Black River, operates a fair school. Attendance is not very regular. New blackboard surface, excellent maps and other appliances have been procured since last term. This is due to the teacher's generous efforts. Buildings are in a fair condition. No. 7½, St. Anselme, and No. 18, St. Croix, are poor schools. No. 18 has a neat little house. The Trustees met me and petitioned for aid from the Board to help defray expenses on the buildings, etc. Their spirit of enterprise deserves recognition, and I would beg to recommend that a sum be granted the District. No. 4, Little River Bridge, is operating a school with an enrolment of 10. Children are all young. So far as the state of affairs in the school is concerned, the results could be classified as satisfactory, but the exterior of the building is wretched. Paint and general repairs are needed. Interior of the house corresponds with the exterior. Furniture, miserable; maps, shabby; blackboards, very poor. District is in debt and consequently cannot progress. The adjoining District, No. 5½, Dixon's Point, has its troubles. They relate to the site of the school house.

Dundas.—Cocagne Bar, No. 10½. I take pleasure in recommending this school. It is one of the best in the Parish. Buildings have been newly painted and the interior of the house renovated and provided with blackboards and excellent furniture. The work in the various standards is fully up to the requirements. Children are intelligent, well-mannered and give evidence of a careful training. Miss Leonie Cormier is doing commendable work. To fulfill the requirements of the law, this District should employ an assistant; 63 enrolled. It is too bad that more room was not provided when the house was repaired. Low average was due to irregularity of attendance during harvest time.

WESTMORLAND COUNTY.

Shediac.—Good work is being done in No. 4 and No. 1. All the subjects of the course are receiving due attention with satisfactory results. These Districts, after many years of wilful neglect and want of enterprise have suddenly decided to keep pace with progress on educational lines. The buildings have consequently been thoroughly repaired (in No. 4) and provided with splendid maps, blackboards (hyloplate in No. 1) and excellent furniture. Grounds in No. 1 are enclosed and neatly kept. I wish I could say the same for Dupuis Cor. No. 3. The school is fairly well conducted, enrolment large and attendance good. Many pupils were absent on day of visit for special reasons. The condition of the buildings and the accommodation provided are not what they should be. The District is a rich and populous one and has no reason whatever of being backward in school affairs. I have consequently suggested that more room be made, better maps procured and more blackboard surface be provided. New furniture will be supplied in time. The Trustees are in favor of improvements, and only need to be encouraged. St. Andre, No. 21, is operating a weak school. Attendance very irregular. No interest whatever is taken in school affairs, and children are allowed to stay home on the slightest pretense. The present teacher has begun work over again. Success is fair. Arithmetic, Reading and Geography are the only subjects receiving attention. House needs paint. Interior is satisfactory. The school in No. 2 is very unsatisfactory. There is a serious lack of discipline. The natural consequences are loose work, lack of thoroughness and no progress. New maps have been procured lately and hyloplate will be provided in the near future Furniture poor, house needs paint. Rivervale, No. 26, is in charge of a local licensee. Elementary work is being done with poor results. The school is poorly furnished and wanting in maps and blackboards. I was very well pleased with the result of the examination in No. 6, but not with the state of house and surroundings. The house is a disgrace to this fine populous District. The exterior is badly in need of paint, and the interior is in a miserable state. No. 25, Chapel, maintains a very good school. Equal attention is given to all subjects of the course, and the result is satisfactory. I called on the Secretary and called his attention to the necessity of better maps and more suitable blackboard surface. He promised to make the required improvements. Buildings are in good condition. No. 5 is closed. Could not obtain a teacher.

Botsford.—The schools in No. 18, Little Cape, and No. 19, Leger's Brook, are satisfactory. Both schools have bright and intelligent pupils, apparently very much interested in their work. Neatly drawn maps of the Provinces and of the Dominion ornament the walls and give proof of the work done in that line. Both schools are well provided with maps and furniture, but the blackboard surface in No. 18 is only fair. Grounds and buildings are neatly kept. No. 20, Lower Cape Bald, has a poor school, with a good attendance. Exterior of the house is good and the grounds well enclosed. The school in No. 21, Chapel, is up to date in all respects. Mr. Joseph Comeau, a splendid teacher, is in charge. No. 17, Portage, has a poor school but an excellent building. I was not satisfied with the result of the examination. The want of efficiency is due to a poor classification of the pupils. No. 23, Long Lake, does not operate a school regularly. School is closed. Bristol, No. 16, has a good school with an enthusiastic teacher in charge. Work in advance of Grade V. is being done, but does not appear to interfere with the general work of the school. The lack of discipline was a feature last term, but good order now prevails. The school is well equipped and has excellent furniture. Bayside, No. 2, has a fair school. A special report will be sent in. No. 12, Cadman, has a good school, with an excellent teacher in charge. The pupils are well advanced in all grades. Equipment is excellent. Murray Road, No. 13, and Oulton Corner, No. 14, have very efficient schools. All the subjects are receiving due attention and results are gratifying. The furniture is poor in both schools. The same applies to maps and apparatus. Both Districts have recently ordered maps, blackbourds, globes and ball frames. Miss Eva Cullins has a very satisfactory school in No. 6, Malden, 40 pupils are enroled, but the attendance is poor. The school is fairly well equipped. The school is closed in Melrose, No. 4. Could not secure a teacher. No. [illegible], Warminster has a fair school. Attendance is not very good. Repairs have been made lately. New furniture should be provided. New maps and a good hylo-plate blackboard will be supplied soon. The school in No. 3, Upper Cape, is ably conducted by Mr. Stanley T[illegible]ueman. The school has been the roughly painted and repaired, and excellent furniture procured. Cape Spear, No. 7, has a fair school and an excellent teacher in Miss Cora Allen. The pupils are young and slowly recovering from the effects of a former very poor classification. The house needs paint. There is great room for improvement so far as equipment is concerned. The Cape, No. 8, and Spence, No. 10, maintain excellent schools. Splendid work is being done. The pupils gave a very satisfactory account of themselves in the examination. No. 10 is in great need of maps. I made the necessary recommendations to the trustees. The condition of the houses in both districts is very good. Murray Corner, No. 11, has a satisfactory school. The ordinary branches are very well taught and a spirit of work seems to animate the pupils. New furniture will be bought and the house painted. The buildings in No. 1, Woodside, and No. 5, Melrose, are in need of a good painting. No. 5 should be provided with maps, blackboards, etc. The furniture in No. 1 does not meet the requirements of the law and should be replaced. Good work is done in both schools.

In bringing this report to a close, I beg leave to record a few notes jotted down during my visit to the different schools in this inspectorate :

READING IN ACADIAN SCHOOLS.

As I have already stated, this subject is receiving the lion's share of attention, but with very unsatisfactory results, especially in the Acadian sections. This is due, I think, to methods generally employed by the teachers. The majority of them atttempt to have young children learn to read English before their young minds have conquered the difficulties attending their learning to read in their own language. As a result, the child becomes confused, takes no interest in a subject he considers as a drudgery and adopts a careless, indistinct and monotonous way of reading. If extra attention were given from the start to French reading only, and English reading taken up after the child had completed Grade 1 or so, I am assured better results would follow. Where this system had been adopted in the schools under my supervision, the results were characterized by good and intelligent reading.

With references to the schools in the Parishes of Shediac and Botsford, I am pleased to be able to state that, as a general rule, the teachers are zealous and industrious and doing good work. There exists, in these schools, an energetic and ambitious way of accomplishing work which indicates good training and proper discipline. Prospects are encouraging. A great many districts still have furniture which is old-fashioned and unsuitable; but there is a decided wish on the part of the school officers to make improvements in this respect. Maps are being supplied freely; blackboard surface, especially hyloplate, is being provided, and in consequence the teacher is encouraged to make a more frequent and more extensive use of this important appliance, especially in the primary classes. I have noticed that not a few of the ungraded schools are doing work in advance of Grade V. Teachers should be cautious in this respect, as parents are sometimes inclined to say that "The many are neglected for the few."

Extracts from November Report.

WESTMORLAND COUNTY.

Salisbury—No. 3, Jones, is operating a fair school. The appliances are not quite up to date. New furniture was procured some time ago. Better blackboard surface is needed. Central Pollet River No. 4,—the ratepayers have erected a fine new building which would certainly be a credit to many a larger and more populous district. The house is large and roomy and built according to modern plans. The interior is finished in veneering and has a good hardwood floor. School will be occupied next term. The school is well supplied with excellent maps, has a globe and a splendid standard dictionary. Hyloplate will be procured. The furniture is good; more seats will be added. Miss Eleanor Fletcher is in charge and is doing good work. The ratepayers are worthy of praise for the active interest they take in their school. Kay Settlement No. 5,—a special report was sent in concerning this district The house in No. 7, Pride of the Plains, puts up a very wretched appearance. Paint should be used unsparingly. The interior of the building was sheathed, painted and ceiled during the summer holidays. Fredericton Road, No. 8. The school in this District has been closed for the last 3 terms. The Trustees have secured an efficient teacher in the person of Miss Helena Daly. The pupils are mostly young, bright, well-mannered and attend school very regularly. Good work must have been going on since the beginning of the term in order to bring the school to such a high standard. The building has been thoroughly repaired and splendid maps and blackboards provided. New furniture of a modern style has also been secured lately. Harewood, No. 9, could not secure a teacher.

Affairs in No. 10, Scott Road, must be noted down as very poor. There exists a lack of thoroughness in school work. This was clearl shown by the result of the examination. The house is in a disgrace ful condition and should be repaired without delay. I wrote t the Trustees, called their attention to the state of their schoo and recommended immediate repairs. The school in No. 11, Platform, is a weak one. Reading and Spelling were fair, but Arithmetic, Grammar and Geography were below the requirements. The appliances are good. New maps were procured lately. The school in No. 12, Wheaton Settlement, is in an unsatisfactory condition. The prevalence of whooping-cough in the District greatly hindered work in the school. The school is well supplied with all necessary appliances. The house in No. 13, Lewis Mountain, should be condemned. It is not fit for school purposes and is a disgrace to the District. Necessary steps should be taken to have the District erect a new house. The school is not in operation. The building in No. 14. Constantine, is small and greatly in need of painting. The furniture is out-of-date. A new map of the Provinces was procured lately. The school was closed last term and the usual results follow. Reading was very good in the higher grades. Elementary work was being done in all the other subjects. The Trustees spoke to me in regard to vaccination. I recommended that the regulations of the Board of Health be followed. Steeves Settlement, No. 16, is operating a fair school. The teacher had much difficulty in overcoming the evil effects of a former poor classification. The result of the examination was not up to my expectations. All the appliances are up-to-date I recommended that new maps of the Provinces and of the Dominion be procured. My suggestions were obeyed and maps ordered. The Trustees of No. 17, Fawcett Hill, intend building a new house. The present one is small and in need of general repairs. The room is poorly lighted. New furniture should be procured. Maps are new. More blackboard surface is needed. The school is a weak one. Writing was very good. The school in Glenvale, No. 20, was closed on the day of my visit. The building is in a dilapidated state. Necessary improvements will be made in the near future. Furniture is poor. The same must be said in regard to maps, I did not like the tone of the school in No. 21, Alward. There seemed to be a want of seriousness about the work. The result of the examination, however, was fair. The house was painted last fall and a new floor will be laid the coming holidays. The school has a library (81 vols.) and a case of minerals. No. 25, Blakeney Road, has a small school, old fashioned furniture, excellent maps, and very poor blackboards. The school is below the average. Readingwas poor and the same should be said of Grammar and Geography.

Salisbury and Havelock.—Hicks, No. 15. This District should not be allowed to operate a school in the building in actual use. It is in a most disgraceful state. The ratepayers take no interest whatever in school matters. I wrote to the Trustees and called their attention to the neglected

›f their house. I recommende that a new house be built, as it was ı to think of repairing the present structure. Better furniture and late maps should also be provided. Reading was good. Elementary vas being done in all other subjects. General repairs should be made house in No. 19, Kinnear Settlement. Furniture is old-fashioned, are poor, but blackboards good. The school is a fair one. Reading ammar, however, were not satisfactory. No. 22, Rockland, is oper-a fair school. Reading was below the average. The house is in a ondition. It should be painted. Money was voted to procure new ire. Maps and blackboard surface are good.

hediac —Barachois, No. 7. This District deserves credit for its of enterprise, and for the interest its ratepayers take in school matters. ouse is well kept. It has been newly sheathed and ceiled. The is well-equipped with excellent maps of the Provinces, of the Do-ı,and of the world. Furniture is very good. Miss Exelda Gallant is rge and is doing excellent work. Reading was not quite up-to-date, ithmetic, writing and drawing were exceptionally good. Some at-ı is given to singing and elocution with good results. Barachois, No. a good building. A good painting would do it no harm. The school ly provided with good maps, blackboards and up-to-date furni- A class room is attached. The interior of the building was sheathed, d and ceiled during the holidays. Progress was retarded in this by an irregular attendance. The pupils gave a fair account of them-. Reading, spelling and arithmetic were good, but writing and geog- fell below the average. No. 11, Shediac, has one of the best ›ed schools in the Parish. The school room is neat and clean and decorated. Some pupils are doing work in advance of Grade V with ctory results. Work in all subjects is very satisfactory. Mr. Percy trick is in charge. No. 16, Moncton Road, is maintaining a school following basis: enrolled, 12; average, 6. There were five pupils ıt on the day of my visit. The work done in this school can be classi-fair. The house puts up a good appearance; the interior, however, be in a better condition. Shediac Island has no school in operation; not find a teacher.

hediac and Moncton —Wissner, No. 23, has no school this term. rustees were unable to secure a teacher.

orchester.—College Bridge, No. 5½, has a fair school. The enrol-reached 66 with an average attendance of 52. Steps must be taken to have a class room laid off and a regular class room assistant employed. The room is large enough and could afford sufficient space for a separate room. I spoke to the Trustees who favorably considered the plan. They will make the necessary improvements next summer. The school has no maps, an insignificant blackboard surface and poor furniture. Time may work some needed changes.

Moncton.—Miss Maud Hopper is doing good work in No. 1, Lakeville. All the school appliances are up-to-date. Repairs were made on the exterior of the building some time ago. The interior was sheathed, painted and ceiled recently. The house puts up a fine appearance. The result of the examination was very satisfactory. No. 7, Irishtown, has an unsatisfactory school. The pupils did not show up well in the examination. Ritchie, No. 8, has no school. The District looks poor and is thinly settled. The appliances in No. 11 are very poor. More blackboard surface and better furniture should be provided. I wrote to the Trustees with reference to the deficiency in apparatus. The house needs shingling and paint. The outhouses are in very poor condition. The attendance is very regular and satisfactory work is being done. The teacher, Miss Lutz, has procured good maps by means of entertainments. No. 12, Allison, has a fine house but no school in operation. There are no children to attend school. Two pupils attend Boundary Creek school. Boundary Creek, No. 13, has a good school with a splendid attendance. The pupils are interested in their work and gave a good account of themselves in the various subjects. The school equipment is fair. General repairs should be made to the building. The furniture is miserable and not in accordance with the regulations. I wrote to the trustees in regard to this matter and hope that some improvement will be made in the near future. Some pupils are in attendance from the adjoining district. No. 14, Steeves Mountain, has a good school with Mr. A. J. Bannister in charge. An assistant should be employed. There is an enrolment of 67, with an average attendance of 44. There is a class-room attached but it is rather small. Maps are out of date and should be replaced. The blackboard surface and furniture are very good. The pupils are bright and take a lively interest in their work. Result of examinations was gratifying. No. 21, McLaughlin Road, has no school. No. 23, Caledonia, has a very weak school. The pupils are suffering from the effects of a very poor classification. Arithmetic in the lower grades was miserable. Guess work was a feature. The district experienced much difficulty in finding a teacher. The school is in operation since 3 weeks. The building is large and commodious. Furniture, maps and boards are fair.

No. 26, Lake Settlement, has no school this term. The school in No. 27, Lakeburn, is a satisfactory one. The pupils are intelligent and greatly taken up with their work. Four of them have certificates of perfect attendance. The results in the different grades were very good. The house is too small to accommodate the present number of pupils. It is neat, clean, and very well kept I wrote to the Trustees and explained matters, and hope to report progress, as a lively interest is taken in school matters. No. 30, Painsec Road, has a good school. I was greatly pleased with the result of the examination. Reading and Grammar were good, Arithmetic splendid and Drawing far above anything I have seen in any country school. The interior of the house is excellent. Maps are fair, but blackboards very poor. I wrote to the Trustees, congratulated them on the state of their school and asked them to provide good blackboard surface, hyloplate if possible. The Secretary told me he would see to the matter.

NOTES.

School Houses.

With the exception of 3 or 4, the school houses in Salisbury are in a very poor condition. In some cases new buildings should be erected, and in all cases lime and paint should be used more freely. New buildings are badly needed in the following Districts: No. 13, Lewis Mountain; No. 5, Kay; No 15, Hicks; No. 10, Scott Road and No. 17, Fawcett Hill. The Parish of Moncton and Shediac seem to keep their houses in satisfactory condition, but paint could be used with excellent results.

Apparatus.

Some school officials have no idea of the importance of maps, etc., and seem to think that teachers and inspectors are somewhat reckless in their recommendations. It is needless to say that progress in Geography is retarded wherever maps are wanting and that work in the primary grades especially suffers from the deficiency in blackboard surface.

Course of Instruction.

Reading and spelling are well taught in nearly all the schools. However, some teachers follow no method and simply let the pupils do the work No questions are asked on the lesson. Others do not attach any importance to the following: Correct posture, meaning of words and good expression.

The Acadian schools are below the average in this respect. History, especially Canadian, is taught with very satisfactory results. Progress in Geography is retarded in schools where maps are considered as luxuries and ornaments for the walls. I note with pleasure that map drawing was a feature in many schools. Too much text-book work is being done in teaching Grammar. Arithmetic as usual is below the requirements in all the schools. I have met pupils in the VI. and VII. grades who could not do problems in part 1st of Kennedy and O'Hearn. More practical work should be taken up along with the text-book. Writing and Drawing are fairly well taught and results are satisfactory.

Extract from December Report.

WESTMORLAND COUNTY.

Parish of Dorchester.—The house in No. 6, Lake District, is a shabby looking affair. A spirit of neglect seems to pervade this district. Some of the ratepayers take an occasional hand in matters educational, but it appears, only when difficulties are rife. The school is badly in need of apparatus. Furniture is poor, maps are deficient and black-board surface should be provided. The trustees were absent, and I consequently failed to meet them. The school was a weak one. The condition of affairs in No. 7, Lower Bonhomme, is very far from being satisfactory. The buildings are greatly in need of general repairs. Furniture is entirely out of date and blackboard surface very poor. The work done here partakes of the nature of the surroundings. The teaching is not up to the required standard. In the examination the pupils gave evident proofs of their want of training, and their knowledge bordered on ignorance. The well-marked irregularity of attendance testifies as to the lack of interest taken in school matters. I wrote to the Secretary of Trustees and called his attention to these matters. Other measures will have to be adopted if the suggestions are not heeded. Memramcook, No. 8,—The ratepayers of this district seem to take but very little interest in the welfare of their school. The buildings have not been repaired, and the school is still in need of maps. The Board of Trustees is now composed of three young men with progressive ideas and I confidently anticipate a change for the better. Progress in school work was satisfactory. Better results would have been obtained had discipline been enforced properly. Work in advance of Grade V is being done by three pupils, with fair results. Some of the pupils are backward in arithmetic. Reading was fair, writing poor. The only thing worthy of notice in No. 10, McGinley's, is its splendid attendance. 33 children were enrolled with an average of 32. 20

pupils have certificates of perfect attendance. The teaching is below the requirements and the school is consequently a poor one. Buildings, etc., are very satisfactory. No. 11 Mill district is operating a fair school. Results in the different subjects were satisfactory. The school is sadly in need of maps. Recommendations made last year in regard to maps were not heeded. I saw the trustees and called their attention to their neglect in this respect. Maps were ordered at once. No. 12, Mountain, has a very good building and a fair school. Furniture is excellent. New maps and better blackboard surface should be provided. I wrote to the trustees. No. 13, Chapel, has one of the best schools in the Parish. The attendance is splendid and very satisfactory work is being done. Pupils are up to date in all the subjects. Buildings are in an excellent condition and the general appliances very good. This school is surely a credit to the district. Too much guess work is being resorted to in No. 16, Belliveau Villagé, to warrant fair results. Pupils need more drill in the different subjects, especially in arithmetic and geography. The exterior of the building puts up a bright appearance, but the interior needs plaster or sheathing. Furniture is good, blackboards poor and maps are needed. I recommended a map of the provinces and blackboard surface. No. 17, Gothro, has an enrolment of 89, with an average of 67. No work is being done in advance of Grade IV. Results are only fair. This school employs an assistant.

No. 22, Taylor Villiage, is closed. No children to attend school. No. 24, Boudreau Village, is operating a fair school. The school is greatly in need of better appliances. The house needs paint. I met the secretary and insisted upon the necessity of certain improvements. He promised to interest his co workers in the matter and act according to my suggestions. No. 26, Upper Bonhomme, is a poor district. Its taxable valuation reaches $6000. Rates are $1.10 pr. hundred. Under the circumstances, I thought it better to encourage rather than recommend. House has been shingled lately and a new map of the province provided. Better blackboard surface should be furnished. Results in the different subjects may be classified as fair. The school in No. 25, Upper Memramcook is a fair one. Arithmetic, geography and writing were good, but reading was a little below the average. In this district as in many others, the school must take care of itself. Building out of repair and very cold. On certain days the school has to be closed: the room was not heated properly. There is a sad deficiency in all necessary applicances. I wrote to the secretary and called his strict attention to this wretched state of affairs. As a result a good provision of fuel was made and the interested parties promised to make the required improvements. Memramcook No. 27. Conditions in this district remain unchanged. Arrangements to proceed with the erection of a new building are about completed. I met the ratepayers. Usual difficulties on hand: many wished to have the school at their own door, I suggested that three parties measure the district and report. This was done. I am told by one of the trustees that they all agreed to the old site. Under the circumstances, the school work may be classified as fair. Attendance is excellent

Shediac.—Affairs now seem to be running smoothly in No. 10½. Point du Chene The school house was shingled and plastered during the summer, and more improvements will be made during the Christmas vacation. Miss Kate Murray, a seemingly painstaking teacher is in charge. She reports a good attendance and a much increased average. The school in No. 13, Scoudouc North is a poor one. Reading was fair, little or no attention given to grammar, geography poor and arithmetic good in higher grades. The exterior of the building put up a poor appearance, but the interior was papered lately and looks quite bright. Furniture is old-fashioned but fairly good. I met the trustees and recommended maps, blackboards etc.

INSPECTORAL DISTRICT No. 3.

R P. STEEVES M. A., Inspector, Sussex, K. C.

This District comprises the Parishes of Elgin and Alma in the County of Albert, the County of Kings east of the St. John River, and the County of Queens except the Parishes of Canning, Gagetown, Hampstead, Petersville and Chipman.

J. R INCH, ESQ., LL D.
Chief Supt. of Education,
Fredericton, N. B.

SIR,—The following is my report on the condition of the Public Schools in Inspectorate No. 3 for the year ending December 31, 1903

New school houses, replacing old and worn out structures, have been erected in Mechanic District, No. 5, and Collier District, No. 6, both in the Parish of Elgin. They will be comfortably furnished and reasonably well equipped.

In Western Narrows, District, No. 12, Cambridge, the house destroyed by fire over a year ago has not yet been replaced. The public hall is still being used for school purposes.

Summerfield District, No. 5, Studholm, voted at last annual meeting to build a new house during the fall, but owing to the high price of lumber and scarcity of workmen, the building will not be completed until next summer.

A large portion of the school buildings in this Inspectorate are kept in very satisfactory repair. There has been from year to year a marked improvement in this respect. Difficulty has been experienced this year by Trustees in getting carpenters for repairing buildings, and consequently some work has stood over that was provided for at the annual meetings. Most school houses present a neat and tidy appearance, but some Districts do not seem to recognize the importance of keeping the outside well painted. In many of these the buildings are old and the siding much weather worn.

I am able to report that much has been done in respect to additions of furniture, maps, blackboards and general apparatus. I am satisfied that the material equipment of our schools warrants the opinion that they are now more capa ble of affording a better education to the youth of the country than at any time in the past.

Scarcity of teachers still continues, and a number of schools have in consequence been closed during a part and some for the whole of the year. Districts are offering better salaries. It may be confidently expected that when salaries come up to the level of those paid in other professions demanding equal qualifications, the supply of efficient teachers will be equal to the demand.

It is my policy to resist requests frequently made by trustees to recommend the Chief Superintendent to issue third class local licenses. Consequently very few of these are found in Inspectorate No. 3, only three I think during the present year. The work done by such licensees is usually of a poor order and generally unsatisfactory.

As a rule the morals of the schools are good. In some sections and frequently where one would least expect it, negligence is apparent on the part of both teachers and trustees in the care of out buildings. Children become habituated to unseemly conditions, and as a result frequently too indifferent to the demands of modesty and decency. Trustees need to more carefully observe requirements of Reg. 9, School law manual and teachers to see that pupils use no bad language on school premises, and that they refrain from writing obscene words on walls of out-buildings, or defacing and destroying school property. Ill conditioned premises provoke immoral thoughts and lead up to vile and lawless acts. It is evident that teachers should know each day the condition of out-buildings. In connection with this duty, they will learn much of the morals of their pupils.

ARBOR DAY.

The usually large number of schools reported observance of Arbor Day this year. Although on the notices sent out the attention of teachers is directed to their duty, it would appear from reports sent in that all do not read over Reg. 20, Sec. 2, (b), School Law Manual. It is my intention in the future to exact more closely than in the past, compliance with the spirit as well as the letter of the Regulation. In view of the fact, that for eighteen years. Arbor Day has each year been observed in this province, there should be a very much larger number of school grounds well laid out, shaded and ornamented than can at present be found.

COUNTY INSTITUTE.

The Teachers' Institute for Kings County was held at Sussex on the 17th and 18th of September. A larger attendance could in future be easily secured if the Executive Committee would send out the notices a week earlier than has been done of late. Many teachers have not had sufficient notice to enable them to make arrangements to be present.

The presence of Mr D. W. Hamilton, M A., Dr G. U Hay and Mr. John March helped to increase the interest of the several sessions. The reading of carefully prepared and excellent papers, followed by full and animated discussion profitably occupied the attention of all present. The public meeting on Thursday evening in Medley Memorial Hall was addressed by Principal Hamilton, Principal Maggs, Dr Hay and others. Music was furnished by an orchestra. It was much regretted by all that the Chief Superintendent of Education was unavoidably absent.

Albert Co—No. 8, Alma, is a small district, and there seems to be little disposition on the part of the Trustees and many of the rate-payers to keep an efficient school. No. 3. Alma, has, during the year, made some improvements in equipment, Sinclair Hill, No, 6 of the same Parish, has a very small school. The pupils are within moderate distance of the Grammar School at Alma. Were it not that the district is situated on a hill, up which the road is about a mile long, the people would be willing to unite with Shore District No. 5. Kerry, No. 7, has had a school the summer term, the first in about two years. Point Wolf, No 2, has added some new furniture and made other improvements. The Grammar School of the County, which has been for upwards of twenty years located in Shore District No 5, Alma, during all of which time Mr. T. E. Colpitts, B. A., has been principal, will probably, during the coming year, be transferred to a more central place, Principal Colpitts has proved himself to be an earnest, energetic and successful teacher, and certainly is among the very few in the province who have taught for a similar period in a country village school. The high esteem in which he is held by the people of Alma attests to his many excellent qualities.

The school house in No. 7, Elgin, is very much dilapidated. This District and No. 14, which has never had any school, should be united, as should also Nos. 5 and 16. The latter, No. 16, Elgin, has never had any school, but sends several pupils each term to the school in No. 5. Nos. 4 and 15 have again opened school.

The Superior School at Elgin Corner, District No 2, is very large, and in respect to equipment is not entirely satisfactory. This District, though large, is not wealthy, and therefore the effort to keep down expenses is persistent.

Queens Co.—All the schools of Waterborough, ten in number, have been in operation this year. District No. 3 supplied new furniture, better blackboards and maps.

One of the ten districts in the Parish of Cambridge has had no school during the year. Although there are few children to attend in this District (No. 9) school will probably be opened the coming term.

The largest and wealthiest districts in the Parish of Johnston appear to be the ones to have school only a part of the time, although there are large numbers of children in each. The smaller and poorer districts have school more regularly.

All the schools in the Parish of Wickham were open this year. Some of them are fairly well equipped, others poorly.

Only four schools were open in the Parish of Brunswick this year. On account of its remote position, great difficulty is experienced in securing teachers.

Kings Co—The school at Lower Ridge, No. 7, Havelock, has been graded during the year. The secretary, Mr. John McFarlane has taken a great deal of interest in having the school well supplied with apparatus, and I confidently expect a very great improvement in educational work in that district.

The school house at Norton Station has been enlarged at a cost of about $2000, and three departments will be in operation next year instead of two, as heretofore.

The school at Lower Millstream is steadily growing in importance. Present indications point to the necessity, in the near future, of grading the school into two departments.

Several districts among which are Conner Settlement No. 25, Upham, etc. Londonderry No. 3, Hammond, and Bunnell No 22, Studholm, having had no school for some time, are making arrangements to reopen during the coming year.

Walker, No 5, Waterford, has repaired the inside of its school house so that now it is a very comfortable building.

The school house and apparatus in Sprague's Brook, No. 13, Springfield, are now quite creditable. This district is an example to be followed by many others of greater pretensions.

Sprague's Point, No. 1, Springfield, seems to have no intention of complying with the requirements of the school law. Almost continual pressure must be kept up to get sufficient equipment provided.

New furniture has been supplied in the following districts: Hampton Ferry, No. 3, Hampton (one department)· Quispamsis, No. 4, Rothesay; Titusville, No. 3, Upham; Lower Millstream, No. 13, Studholm; Lower Ridge, No. 7, Havelock; East Scotch Settlement, No. 5, Springfield.

It would unduly lengthen this report to mention all the districts in the three counties contained in this Inspectorate, that have increased their school facilities. The above statements must suffice.

It must not be supposed that what has been done has been accomplished without effort. Recommendations follow recommendations. Consultations with trustees and secretaries, letters pointing out necessities, and advising compliances for the benefit of the children, and now and then warnings of a severer nature, all are needed upon occasion.

The teachers are an important factor in securing improvements. They are always on the ground and they know the needs. Very frequently apparatus, maps and general equipment are the result of the teacher's skill and effort at a concert, entertainment or social. The number of those who do not interest themselves in this way is very small.

It has seemed to me during the year that the enrolment of pupils was in many districts smaller than in previous years, but that in these smaller schools a better average is maintained. Evidently there is a persistent effort made to make the best average possible.

There is an opinion abroad, entertained by many of the districts likely to be affected by union, that consolidation of districts is a serious evil to be resisted by every means possible. Probably the most that can be done at present is to prevent further cutting up of districts as is sometimes suggested by disaffected ratepayers.

Additions are being made to school libraries and to supplies of chemical apparatus. I believe in many cases both the above are taken better care of and used to better purpose each year.

INSTRUCTION.

In many schools the teaching of reading appears to me to be almost entirely of a routine character. Sometimes a teacher remarks apologetically, "My Fourth Reader class is just in Grade IV They had read through the Third Reader so often they became tired of it" In such cases I almost invariably find poor reading. Sometimes I find two classes in the same reader, the pupils of both classes varying but little in their ability to read. While the teaching of elementary reading—primer work—is generally quite satisfactory, the class of work done above the First Reader is not, in some cases, such as is to be desired.

Generally arithmetic is taught in a fairly satisfactory manner and the results are good. Sometimes I find that no class work is provided for in this subject on the timetable, especially in Standards IV and V in ungraded schools. Pupils are expected to work at Arithmetic when not otherwise employed. This practice is to be deprecated. Regular class work gives facility and rapidity and develops the power of accurate expression and definition, and at the same time affords to the teacher the best opportunity of testing each pupil's knowledge of the subject.

Sufficient attention is not given in some schools to oral composition. A great deal of written work is required, but the ability to orally describe, explain and narrate is not developed.

Health Reader Lessons are frequently merely read or recited.

On the whole, however, the above negative remarks apply chiefly to a small number of schools. Thoughtful, earnest work on the part of most teachers is given to the faithful discharge of their duties, and the results are in a high degree encouraging. With better school houses, with larger school grounds more tastefully laid out and cared for, with more complete equipment especially for Science teaching and Agriculture, with school gardens and Manual Training instruction, and with more thorough Normal School training for our teachers, our schools may yet do more signal service for the youth of our country, and give them greater possibilities for happy and useful lives.

Kingston Consolidated School.—A magnificent structure surpassing anything of its kind in any country section of the Dominion, is the school house not yet quite completed at Kingston Village. When the school opens in August next, as is contemplated, the pupils of seven districts will assemble to receive instruction from five carefully selected teachers. The pupils will be carried in comfortable vans from their homes in the morning and returned in the evening. In addition to the ordinary subjects of instruction, which will be taught after the most modern and approved methods, Manual Training, Domestic Economy and Household Science, School Gardening and Nature Study will be given a prominent place on the time table. The attention of those interested in education in this province will no doubt closely follow the course of the experiment that is being worked out by this school. No effort will be spared to insure its success. It is to be hoped that through its influence many such schools may at an early date be established throughout the province and that they may become centres of inspiration and usefulness, in advancing the cause of education.

I have the honor to be, sir,

Your obedient servant,

R. P. STEEVES,

Dec. 31, 1903.

INSPECTORAL DISTRICT No. 4.

W. S. CARTER, M. A., Inspector, St. John, N. B.

This District embraces the Counties of St John and Charlotte.

J. R. INCH ESQ. L L D.,
Chief Supt. of Education,
Fredericton, N. B.

SIR,—I beg to submit the following report for the year ended December, 1903.

In accordance with my practice in the past, I will give in this report a general review of what has been done in the schools of each parish in my Inspectorate in the last two years, and will try to indicate in a general way what has been done in the way of advance or improvement.

As has always been the case, the teachers have been identified with some of the more important improvements. I will mention their names and the part they have taken with apologies for any omissions.

Lepreaux.—Little Lepreaux has had scarcely any schooling in the last two years. The pupils are few and most of the ratepayers indifferent. At Lepreaux Village there are also very few pupils, but the revival of the lumbering industry there will, I hope, bring about improvement. A school was opened again last term and the teacher, Miss Sadie Carson, has been instrumental in providing some needed apparatus.

The school at Mace's Bay is a large one. Some difficulty has been experienced in securing a teacher at all times. Miss Laura Boyd has added much new apparatus. The house needs repairs and the grounds should be fenced.

The school house at New River Mills was burned by the forest fires of last June. It was not insured. There are at present less than a half dozen pupils in the District, but later I hope to see some arrangement made by which they may obtain school privileges.

Pennfield.—Pennfield Centre maintains a very regular and satisfactory school. The house has been repaired and a flag and dictionary procured.

Beaver Harbor has two departments. The primary is kept in regular operation, but the advanced, owing to the fact that the larger pupils are engaged in the factories, does not open until late in the first term, when it has not always been possible to secure a teacher. The house has been painted and much improved, and through the initiative of the teachers, Mr. King Maxwell and Miss Bessie Barry, a fine standard dictionary, maps and other apparatus have been added.

The school at Coldbrook is small but regular. Miss Kezia Maxwell has added slates, flag pole, dictionary and minerals.

The school at Pennfield Ridge is also very small, Miss Lottie G. Thompson has been instrumental in having the house refitted and adding slates, maps and other apparatus. Black's Harbor has voted for a new house, which would have been completed if workmen could have been procured Miss Mary Mitchell took much interest in her work there and added to the apparatus. Seely's Cove lost its house in the forest fires. It was well equipped in all respects. They have lost no time, and have a new one for next term.

St. George.—The schools in the village have been efficiently maintained and have been provided with some excellent apparatus. I hope in the near future to see manual training provided for. Mr. H. E. Sinclair resigned to accept a position in Milltown, after having done good work, and has been succeeded by Mr. Chas. Callaghan. The school at the Head of Letang has been regularly supported and has added some useful appliances. Breadalbane has a small school, operated for nine months. Miss Agnes Millen has added a flag, table and repairs to house. The school at the Canal has an enrolment of 40 and sittings for 26. The house is poor and the furniture worthless. I have had a conference with the Board, with a view to having a new house and I hope to be able to report improvement soon.

The house at Bonny River was burned by the forest fires. I do not regret the house so much as the excellent appliances which it contained. The trustees had no insurance, but with commendable activity they have a new house in readiness for next term. They have done this in addition to their own building concerns, as practically the whole Settlement was burned The school at Second Falls has become very small and very little interest is taken in providing school privileges. The schools at Lee Settlement, Somerville, Red Rock and Piskahegan contain few pupils and are operated very irregularly. It is often very difficult to get teachers for these Districts. The Caithness school has not been entirely satisfactory. There is a lack of harmony in the District. The house has been painted. Mascarene has had as usual a most efficient school. On the initiative of Misses Polley and Bolt, hardwood floors and new outbuildings have been added. Largely through the exertions of Miss Harriet Bolt, this District has been one of the first in the Province to introduce manual training and three benches have been supplied. At Letete the house has been painted and much excellent apparatus added through the exertions of the teacher, Miss Lizzie Knight. Back Bay has a very large school, Mr. John Clindinnin, the teacher, has added slates, some new furniture and apparatus. The school at upper Letang is not maintained regularly. There are few pupils and the house needs repairs. Mrs. Eliza Hines has returned to her old work at Letang, to the satisfaction of all. A flag pole and flag and some new apparatus have been added. A new house is needed in this District and it is proposed to build it soon.

Dumbarton.—The school at Pleasant Ridge has been maintained as usual. At Flume Ridge, Miss Fannie Murphy has been instrumental in having supplied some excellent apparatus. At Tryon, the house has been repaired. This District for its ability, makes most commendable effort to maintain a school. Mr. James Clark continues to be the efficient Secretary. There has been an excellent school as usual at Rolling Dam. The house has been painted, and one of the teachers, Miss Florence Downing, raised money for a fence in front, which up to this time the trustees have failed to build. The death of the Secretary. J. E. Peacock, is regretted. The schools at Greenock and Dumbarton have been well supported and through the exertions of the teachers, Misses Cecil Hewitt and Mary Irvine, the houses have been painted and much new apparatus supplied.

Whittier Ridge has built a very satisfactory new house. The grounds have been fenced and much interest has been taken.

St. David.—At Upper Tower Hill a good school has been operated. The house has been painted and the grounds improved. Much is due to the teacher, Miss Annie M. Holt. At Lever many improvements have been made both to buildings and apparatus. The teachers who largely contributed to these results were Miss Priscilla Read and Miss Fannie Cunningham. The school at Regan's Corner is small but very efficient. A flag has been provided. The house and grounds at Central Tower Hill are in all respects among the best in the county The excellent apparatus has been materially added to by the exertions of the teacher, Miss Mary Hawkins. At Hill's Point, a good school is maintained. The house has been painted and some new apparatus provided. Misses Bertha Dewar and Fannie Murphy have greatly assisted in promoting this. At Oak Bay there is an excellent school The house has been painted. At St. David's Hill a fairly good school is maintained. The house has been repaired and painted Miss Agnes Boyd continues to discharge the duties of Secretary most efficiently. At Oak Haven, the house has been repaired and new furniture and apparatus supplied. A good school is operated at Bay Road which is well equipped with needful apparatus. Miss Blanche Nesbitt is the efficient teacher. She has done her part in building up the school.

St. Andrews.—The town is now incorporated and though not as populous as some of the others in the province, it has ever been one of the most progressive and intelligent in the conduct of its schools. I have had occasion to point this out in many former reports, and this year is a source of satisfaction to me, as it must be of pride to St. Andrews that it was the first town in the province to introduce Manual Training, which was begun there the first of the year under the excellent tuition of Miss Agnes Lucas. St. Andrews has always been fortunate in its selection of school trustees, and none of them have been more progressive and conscientious in the discharge of their duties than Mr. W. D. Forster, whose services, I regret to say, have been lost to St. Andrews by his removal to St. John. Mr. Forster has been a trustee ever since I have held office, and in addition to giving his time and attention to a trustee's duties outside the schools, he visited them regularly and took as much interest during the last year he held office as during his first.

The school at Chamcook has been more regularly maintained than formerly. The house needs painting.

St. Patrick.—The school at Lower Bocabec has been greatly improved in appearance, furnishing and apparatus. The teacher, Miss Annie L. Adams, has greatly assisted in this work. An excellent school has been maintained at Bocabec Ridge, under the tuition of Miss Georgia McCready, who has procured minerals and a teacher's table. Miss Jennie McIntire also obtained a flag and added to the library. The secretary, Mr. C. E. Hanson, is a most painstaking officer. McMinn is a model district as to its school grounds. The house has been very tastefully painted and excellent furniture supplied. Miss Florence Cunningham has greatly aided in the improvements made. The school at Elmsville is now a small one. Miss Cecilia Craig has added to the library fund. A flag and pole have been procured for Clarence Ridge. The house at McCallum has been renovated and new furniture supplied. Through the exertions of Miss Evelyn Boone some slate blackboards have been added. Roix has painted its house and built new outbuildings. A new house will be built next year in the Burns district. It is much needed. Some excellent maps have been provided by Miss Effie Crawley.

St. Croix.—A new house is much needed at Lower Bayside. A fine book case has been added by Miss Boone and some maps and apparatus by Miss Margaret Scullin. The house at Upper Bayside has been painted. Repairs have been made to the house at Bartlett's Mills, but new furniture and blackboard surface are much needed. A globe and dictionary have been added to the apparatus of Orr by Miss Mabel Jones. The house at Waweig has been painted and a map of the world and dictionary procured by Miss Margaret Hyslop.

Dufferin.—Miss Mary Finley has been indefatigable in her efforts to improve Crocker Hill. The house has been decorated and a globe, standard dictionary, maps and other apparatus supplied. The house at the Ledge has been neatly painted, excellent outbuildings erected, and through Miss Louise Milliken some excellent apparatus procured.

St. James.—A fine new house has been built at DeWolf, and by the efforts of Miss Kathleen McPartland a flag and pole have been added. This teacher has also been the agent in purchasing enlarged school grounds for the district. Moore's Mills has maintained its excellent record as a preparatory school, sending to the Normal School larger classes than any other in the county. The house is getting out of repair and the apparatus needs renewing. Mr. Howard Moore of Somerville, Mass., has presented eighty volumes to the school library. The house at Baillie has been repaired and painted inside. The house at Lawrence has been painted and new furniture supplied through the efforts of Miss Mildred McCann. The house at Anderson has been painted and through the efforts of Miss Margaret M. Seely, slates, and some excellent apparatus, have been added to the equipment. The house at Lynnfield needs repairs and furniture. Some apparatus has been supplied by Miss Margaret Hyslop. The Robinson district needs apparatus and repairs to house. New outbuildings have been built at Oak Hill, but maps and apparatus are needed. Basswood Ridge puts forth a greater effort to support a first class school than many other districts of larger means, and the returns have been commensurate with the effort. I am informed by DrCrocket, Principal of the Normal School, that one of his most promising pupils last year was Mr. Vernard Sinclair of this school. It is a matter of deep regret to all who knew him that failing health prevented him from finishing his course there, and that he died not long after leaving the Normal School. The schools of Canous and Beaconsfield are not operated regularly and teachers cannot always be procured for them. The school at Gleason Road is a very attractive one, though the house is now rather small for the increasing number of pupils. The house has been painted, repaired and new furniture provided. The house and grounds of Little Ridgeton are among the most attractive in my district. The school is very large and the district aims to secure the best service. A new house is needed on Pomroy Ridge, or it would be better to convey the few pupils to Scotch Ridge. Miss Nellie Polley has added to the apparatus of the district. Miss Rosa B. Gray has done much for Scotch Ridge, having provided maps, dictionary and chairs. The house has been repaired and painted and new outhouses built. There is a good opportunity for centralization in this part of the Parish.

St. Stephen (Parish) The school at Mayfield has been fairly well maintained. Barterville has a very small attendance and should unite with No. 1 The number of pupils in Upper Old Ridge is small, but their regularity is unrivalled. The house at Moannes has been painted and also that at Upper Mills. In the latter district, through the exertions of Miss Mildred McCann a fine flag and pole have been provided. Miss Mildred Moore has provided Heathland with slates, dictionary and a map of the Dominion. The house at Old Ridge has been painted. The house at Valley Park has been repaired and the school again opened.

Campobello.—The schools in district No. 1, are in good order as usual. The grounds have been further improved. The conveyance of pupils continues to give satisfaction. The schools at Wilson's Beach and Head Harbor are both large. It would be in their interest to unite and grade the pupils. There are enough for three good graded departments.

West Isles.—Repairs have been made to the school on Indian Island and Miss Agnes Cummings procured a flag and pole. Repairs have also been made to the house at Chocolate Cove and a dictionary, Minerals and maps added. Messrs Bleakney and Mitchell assisted in this work. The house at Leonardsville has been painted and the fence and grounds improved. Some new apparatus has been added. Miss Gertrude Morrell procured a globe for the school at Richardson. The schools at Lord's Cove, Lambert's Cove and and Lambert Town have been well maintained. Miss Margaret S. Mc Nabb has added much to the apparatus of the school at Fair Haven—a globe, dictionary and stand, maps of hemispheres and Europe and books for library.

Grand Manan.—A fine fence has been made around the grounds at North Head and the schools have improved. At the time of my visit a very largely attended public educational meeting was held in the church hall in the place. Dr R. S. MacDougall of New York university gave valuable assistance. I hope that Manual training will soon be introduced in this and other districts on the island. Castalia has supported its school as usual. The school at Woodward's Cove has not been satisfactory through no fault of the trustees. A new department is much needed at Grand Harbor. The trustees seem slow to take action. The house at Seal Cove has been painted. Through the exertions of Mr. Jas. A. Edmonds, 150 volumes have been added to the library. The schools at Whitehead under the skilful management of Misses Maxwell and Carleton, have been of more than usual excellence. The house has been painted and a flag and pole procured. Extensive repairs have been made to the house and outbuildings on Two Islands. Deep Cove has a tidy little school. which is well equipped for the ability of the district. Mr W. B. McLaughlin still gives of his time and attention to the duties of secretary.

Milltown.—Owing to the strike in the cotton mill and the removal of many families from the town, the attendance at the schools was smaller at my last visit than formerly and it was deemed expedient to reduce the staff of teachers by one. Milltown sustains its record for attendance and the School Board continues its active and intelligent interest in the welfare of the schools. In conjunction with St. Stephen, Mr. Whitney has been engaged as instructor in manual training, giving two days in the week to Milltown and three to St. Stephen. The Cotton Mill Co. very thoughtfully gave a building for a work room to Milltown. It has been moved to the school grounds and thoroughly equipped for the purpose. During the year the schools of this town suffered severe loss by the sudden and tragic death of their Principal, Mr. J. B. Sutherland. He occupied a place in the esteem and confidence of the community that will be difficult to supply. He was succeeded by Mr. H. R. McGill, who later retiring has been succeeded by Mr. H. E. Sinclair, formerly principal at St. George. During the year two excellent teachers resigned from the staff, Misses Isabella Caie and Amy Young.

St. Stephen.—The schools of St. Stephen continue to do the best class of work and maintain their high standard of efficiency. The most notable step in advance during the year has been the establishment of a department for manual training. There have been few changes on the staff. Last year Miss Jessie Whitlock retired after having given unvaried satisfaction in her work, both in town and country districts. She was succeeded by Miss Ethel Jarvis.

Musquash.—The house at Prince of Wales has been extensively repaired and newly furnished. It had a narrow escape from forest fires, and the teacher, Miss Annie M. Hayter, lost all her effects and barely escaped with her life. The house at Musquash was burned. It was well equipped, not only with an excellent library and apparatus, but had been one of the few country districts to introduce manual training. I had hoped that a new house would have been in readiness before this, but all have been so absorbed in replacing their own buildings, that there has not been time to give attention to the school house.

Dipper Harbor has added some apparatus, and Chance Harbor, in addition to painting, has added to its library. Miss Nita Gregory has taken the lead in this work.

Lancaster.—The attendance in the advanced department in Beaconsfield has become small. This is partly owing to the proximity of the better graded schools of St. John City, and the easy terms on which outside pupils are admitted to them.

The schools in Fairville have been greatly overcrowded of late. Steps have been taken which I hope will insure a new building at the beginning of next summer term. The house has been painted and some new apparatus supplied. Mahogany has had a good school. Both the Pisarinco schools have been regularly maintained. Miss Katie Girdwood has supplied No. 12 with a globe and some excellent apparatus. The schools in Milford are most efficiently managed though the district has been crippled with some severe property losses. A fine new fence has been built around the grounds. I would like to see Fairville, Milford, Beaconsfield and Mahogany and possibly Randolph united in one district, with schools thoroughly graded and a central high school. It would be one of the finest districts in the Province. I think at least some of these districts might unite to introduce manual training as has been done in St. Stephen and Milltown. Repairs have been made to the house at Randolph and slates added. The house at Sutton has been painted.

Simonds.—The schools at Coldbrook are under much more energetic management than formerly, and the financial condition of the district has not only been improved, but many additions have been made to apparatus. A globe and dictionary have been supplied by Miss Elizabeth Maguire.

There is a good prospect of No. 2 uniting with this district and conveying its pupils to the central school. At Golden Grove Miss Isabell Patchell has been instrumental in having the grounds graded and fenced and in providing furniture, slates and apparatus. At Silver Falls the house has been painted, grounds fenced and many improvements made. The house at Lakewood has been painted. It is too small. I attended a school meeting this term at Lattimore Lake and hope that the school may soon open again. At Little River many repairs have been made and a piano supplied largely through the exertions of Miss Mildred Black. Miss May Watters has done much in the way of improving her apparatus and surroundings at Red Head, and at Mispec the house has been repaired, newly furnished and blackboards supplied. Miss J. Maud Kee is the teacher. Black River and Gardiner's Creek have not had regular schools, partly owing to the scarcity of teachers. Both districts have fenced their grounds. Garnet needs a new house badly and has agreed to build one in three years. A very excellent school is maintained at Willow Grove under the tuition of Miss Anna K. Miller, who has been in charge for some years. The building, grounds and appointments are all, owing to her exertions, of the best. The school at Otter Lake has been irregular and the house needs repairs. Grove Hill needs a better house, but it has added furniture, blackboards and maps. Fairfield is a model district in all respects. It has had a succession of good teachers who have interested themselves in its welfare and the house, outside and inside, furniture, apparatus, library, garden and grounds are unsurpassed. Miss Hannah Floyd, as a pupil and teacher, in this district, has contributed greatly to this result, and I regret that ill-health has caused her to resign.

St. Martins.—Bain's Corner is another model district in all respects. Its grounds are the best in the County. The people take much interest in their school. Miss Kathleen McPartland has been largely instrumental in building up the district. There has been a decided advance in the condition of the schools in Quaco. The houses have been painted and much new apparatus supplied. The financial condition of the district has also greatly improved. I doubt if the present standard of efficiency can be maintained under the low salaries at present paid. East Quaco has enlarged and fenced its school grounds and laid out a garden. This has been due chiefly to the interest taken by the teacher, Miss Alberta M. Brown. Mr. Geo. J. Charlton has done much for Greer in the last year. The grounds have been fenced and slate blackboards and apparatus supplied. At Wood Lake Miss Florence Debow raised money to paint the house. The trustees interpreting this liberally whitewashed it. This is the second whitewashed schoolhouse in my district and I am not desirous of having the number added to. Miss Alice M. Duhaney has added slates and a map of the Maritime Provinces to the apparatus of Hanford Brook, and Miss Florence Roberts has supplied a dictionary and maps to the equipment of Shanklin. A new house is needed in this district. There is a good chance to centralize Shanklin, Bain's Corner, Fairfield and Tynemouth Creek.

City of St. John.—I think there are few cities of the size of St. John, in which the pupils are more comfortably housed. I have reported the Aberdeen, Alexandra and La Tour schools and this year I am glad to be able to report the equal of any in the city, and which has been more needed than any other new one—the Dufferin, which takes the place of the old Madras, so often condemned in previous reports. The new building contains ten rooms and an exhibition hall. It is heated with hot water. The cloak rooms are after the same plan as those in the Alexandra and the sanitary arrangements are up to date. The rooms are not all as yet occupied but there seems to be plenty of pupils to fill them as some of the schools in the North End of the city have an enrolment as high as seventy. During my visits to some of the rooms in December, the temperature was much too low for school rooms. The reason given by the janitors was that the coal supplied was not up to specification, and that much of it was unfit for use. St. John is scarcely abreast of cities of the same size in the matters of modern business education, manual training, domestic science, musical instruction or physical training. No systematic provision is made for any of these. I do not know whether visiting the schools on the part of parents and trustees has gone out of fashion, but often—I may say usually—the visitation column in the registers devoted to these is a blank at the time of my visits.

I have called attention more than once in previous reports to the necessity of more systematic fire drill in all the large buildings. In few of them is very much attention given to this very important matter. While St. John has added many fine new buildings and provided much excellent apparatus, the salaries of the rank and file teachers have increased little, if any, since the school law. I am sure, if the School Board could see its way clear to give substantial increases to its teachers, public sentiment would heartily support its action.

Since my last report what seems to be a very vigorous Teacher's Association has been formed in St. John—indeed it is rather surprising that such a society was not organized long ago. It is too soon to form an opinion as to its work, but I feel sure it has a wide field for usefulness and that it should become an important factor in the community.

I regret to report the death of Mr. John McKinnon, principal of the Leinster St. School. Principals Dill and Armstrong of the Douglas Avenue and Latour schools retired because they considered they had not been fairly treated. These men have all been most efficient in the discharge of their duties.

During the year also, Mr. James Barry retired from the principalship of St Malachi's to accept the position of Inspector of Weights and Measures All regret Mr. Barry's retirement, but are gratified by his promotion to a more lucrative position. Messrs W. L. McDiarmid, W. A. Nelson, Miles F. McCutcheon, Angus Dewar and Maurice D. Coll, have been appointed to supply the vacancies.

Teachers.—Teachers have been scarce during at least two years and many schools have been closed in consequence. The reason is plain. Wages in every other employment have increased. I am glad to report that there is a decided upward tendency in salaries especially in rural districts, and in as far as I am able to judge, the increases are given cheerfully. It seems strange that the increases should begin in country districts rather than in the town which will have to give corresponding salaries or lower their standard. In some of them where only first-class teachers are supposed to be employed, I notice that second-class teachers are being engaged.

Some local licenses have to be issued to provide for the poorer districts I think it would be well to insist as far as possible that all candidates for this license shall have passed the preliminary examination for third class. I think also that the regulation denying third-class teachers the privilege of teaching in districts of over $15,000 valuation should be insisted upon.

The School District.—There is much sentiment in favor of centralization, but few districts care to take the plunge and unite with others without experimenting a little, and I think if the present law were altered so as to allow each district to retain its autonomy for two or three years before becoming finally united, that better results would follow. I am also convinced that local jealousies will prevent much centralization until we have Parish School Boards and I trust that your recommendations regarding them and an increased county fund may soon be carried into effect.

I hope also that permission may be given to any School Board to obtain a vote of the school meeting to provide free text books. I feel sure that the vote would be favorable in many districts.

County Institutes.—Excellent institutes were held in both counties

In Charlotte at Milltown and in St. John in St. John City. Your attendance at both places was much appreciated and added greatly to the interest. In St. John a valuable paper was read by Dr. Crocket, whom we were all glad to greet again.

Respectfully submitted,

W. S. CARTER.

INSPECTORAL DISTRICT NO. 5.

H. V. B. BRIDGES, M. A., Inspector, Fredericton.

This District embraces the County of Kings, west of St John River; the Parishes of Gagetown, Petersville, Hampstead, Canning and Chipman, in Queens County; the County of Sunbury; the County of York, except the parishes of North Lake, Canterbury McAdam and Southampton, and School Districts Nos. 9, 10, 11, 12A and 13 in the Parish of Stanley.

J. R. INCH, ESQ., LL.D.
Chief Supt. of Education,
Fredericton, N. B.

SIR—I have the honor to submit my report for the year ending 31st Dec, 1903.

I have in two former reports spoken of the difficulty which is experienced by trustees in some school districts in obtaining regularly licensed teachers. The same difficulty still exists, and has been rather augmented, and while no local licenses have been recommended until the supply of regularly licensed teachers was exhausted, the number of such licenses issued during the year has been greater. In the County of York, owing to the Provincial Normal School being within easy distance, for this county sends teachers to every county in the Province, comparatively few local licenses have been issued; but in Queens Co. the demand for such licenses is greater. I have tried to confine such recommendations to those who possess an expired 3rd class license, those who have passed the preliminary examination, and some who have signified their intention of becoming regularly licensed teachers. It is altogether too obvious, however, that we are losing particularly in our ungraded schools, from the active work of teaching in the Province, many teachers of large experience, and who possess many high qualifications for the work in which they have hitherto been employed.

In many districts the ratepayers are beginning to realize that the efficiency of their schools is to be maintained only by paying larger salaries to the teacher, but of course there are still many who are slow indeed to appreciate this fact,

One cannot help noting also the fact that there is a greater tendency among teachers themselves towards organization and professional spirit, and I think any movement along this direction should be recognized, as it will ultimately advance salaries, increase the usefulness, command greater respect, and cultivate a fraternal feeling among teachers. I have submitted a statement of valuations of school districts under my supervision with amounts of money voted at last annual meeting, for which there is hardly room in a report of this length, but which may prove of some use in any movement towards establishing parish boundaries instead of the small district system.

Following will be found a statement of a number of schools and departments in this Inspectoral District in different parishes, and also number maintaining school during whole or part of each school term of the year.

PARISHES.	No. Schools and Departments in Operation.	No. in operation during First Term.	No. in operation during Second Term.
York Co.			
Bright	13	12	12
Douglas	19	16	17
Dumfries	5	5	5
City of Fredericton	26	26	26
Kingsclear	12	11	11
Manners Sutton	12	12	12
New Maryland	5	4	4
Prince William	9	6	8
Queensbury	10	9	10
Saint Marys	24	21	22
Stanley	16	16	16
Sunbury Co.			
Blissville	8	5	7
Burton	13	11	11
Gladstone	10	9	9
Lincoln	6	5	6
Northfield	5	3	3
Maugerville	4	4	4
Sheffield	7	4	4
Queens Co.			
Canning	8	5	6
Chipman	17	13	12
Gagetown	8	7	8
Hampstead	11	9	8
Petersville	15	14	11
Kings Co.			
Greenwich	5	5	4
Westfield	6	6	6
Charlotte Co.			
Clarendon	3	2	1
	277	240	243

In No. 2, Clarendon, a new building was begun and will be completed next summer. No school has as yet been operated in this district.

In No. 6, Hampstead and Greenwich, Hamilton Mountain the ratepayers voted money for the erection of a new building, but the trustees do not state very satisfactory reasons for the delay. The contract has been let, however, and the house will be completed next summer.

A handsome new building has also been contracted for at Hoyt Station, and it will be completed next vacation.

More than the usual amount of repairs have been made upon school-houses, and the following list will give some idea of the extent of the work. I have not thought worth while to particularlize in each case, but the cost of repairs or providing new furniture, would vary from $50 to $200.

Nos. 1 and 2, Westfield; No. 5, Greenwich; No. 6, Canning; Nos. 8 and 13, Chipman; No. 7, Hampstead; Nos. 5, 11 and 12, Petersville; Nos. 3 and 8A, Gagetown; No. 7, Burton; Nos. 5 and 6, Blissville; Nos. 1 and 2A, Lincoln; Nos. 2, 4 and 7, Sheffield; No. 2, Bright; Nos. 6, 10, 11, 13 and 16, Douglas; Nos. 1 and 3, Manners-Sutton; Nos. 6 and 7, Prince William; No. 4, Kingsclear, Nos. 8 and 11, Queensbury; No 5½, Stanley.

Maps and other apparatus for school work have been provided in the following districts:

Nos. 1, 2, 6 and 12, Westfield; Nos. 3 and 5, Greenwich; Nos 4, 7 and 9, Hampstead Nos. 1, 5 and 9, Petersville, Nos. 2A and 3, Gagetown; Nos. 4 and 6, Blissville; No. 7, Burton; Nos. 1 and 8, Gladstone; Nos. 1, 6, 7, and 8, Canning; Nos. 1A, 8 and 13, Chipman; Nos. 1½, 2, 3, 9, 10, 11, 12, 13, and 14, St. Mary's; Nos. 1, 1½, 5½, 6, 7 and 8, Stanley; Nos. 1, 3, 6, 7, 8, 10, 17 and 19, Douglas; Nos. 1, 6, 6½ 7 and 8 Bright; Nos. 6, 7, 8 10 and 11, Queensbury; Nos 1 and 10, Kingsclear; Nos. 1 and 7, Prince William; Nos. 1 2, 3, 5, 7, 8, 9, 10 and 11, Manners-Sutton.

GRADED SCHOOLS—YORK CO.

City of Fredericton.—The efficiency of the schools, I am happy to report, has been steadily maintained. The excellent Teachers' Association which has been established for several years, has undoubtedly had a very beneficial effect on the character of the work of the different teachers, and there is certainly greater uniformity in the teaching in the same grades of the different schools. Mr. Good of Woodstock, succeeded Mr. Frank Patterson, B. A., as teacher of Science and French in the High School. With this exception the different departments are under the same control as formerly. The character of the teaching from primary department to High School, seemed to me fitly expressed by the word "thorough."

Marysville.—Miss Stella Clayton resigned at the close of the year her position as teacher of the department comprising V and VI Grades. I have had frequent occasion to report upon the good work done by Miss Clayton, as for years I have regarded her as one of the very best teachers of these grades in my district. Her resignation is a distinct loss to the school. Miss Fisher who has done excellent work in grades II and III has also given up the work of teaching. These positions have been filled by the appointment of Miss Minnie T. Day, who has had some years successful experiece in teaching, and Miss Bird a recent graduate of the Fredericton High School. No improvement has as yet been made in the character of the school buildings, but it is to be hoped that before long a primary department will be opened on the opposite side of the Nashwaak Stream, as the distance is too great for small pupils in cold weather. The enrollment in the Superior School under Mr. Day is increasing, although, it is interfered with by the spirit of work and wage earning which is characteristic of the thriving town.

St. Marys and Gibson.—The Superior School during the year. was under the control of Miss Ida Myles who was very successful in her work, but at the close of the year was obliged to resign on account of ill health. The trustees have made a temporary appointment in the hope that perhaps she might again be able to resume charge. The other departments of this school have also been well conducted, but Miss Bell Miles in the primary department has altogether too large an enrollment.

Harvey Station.—Mr. J. P. Bulyea resigned his position to take up the work of life insurance, and was succeeded by Miss Agnes Alward B. A. of Fredericton. I regret to report that the enrollment is not increasing.

Keswick Ridge.—Mr. William M. Barker has had charge of the Superior School, and is doing good work. There is a prospect of a good attendance during the winter months. Miss Mary Mitchell who once before taught the primary department successfully is again in charge.

Stanley Village.—As yet there is no Superior School in this Parish, Miss M. McKee B. A. was in charge of advanced department during first term. Miss Mildred Black and Miss McLeod have now charge of the two departments. Some necessary changes have been made in the seating of the departments, and a new globe provided from proceeds of an entertainment at close of term.

QUEENS COUNTY.

Gagetown.—Mr. D. L. Mitchell B. A. who for several years has worked faithfully as principal of the Grammar School resigned to study law. Mr. E. C. Weyman B. A. has since assumed charge of the school, and has entered upon the work with energy and enthusiasm.

Chipman—The departments of this school were closed during the winter for several weeks owing to the outbreak of smallpox in the vicinity. Mr. A. C. M. Lawson resigned the principalship of the Superior School to engage in the work of life insurance. Mr. Frank N. Patterson B. A. was appointed his successor who is ably assisted in the primary department by Miss Emma Porter of Fredericton.

SUNBURY COUNTY.

The Superior School at Fredericton Junction continues well attended. During the first term it was in charge of Mr. Holland McGill, and is now taught by Mr. Clindinnin. Miss Addie Hartt continues her faithful work in the primary department. This is the only graded school in the county.

UNGRADED SCHOOLS.

I have frequently reported somewhat in detail as to the work that is being done in these schools in the different parishes, and also with regard to the success that is being met with in teaching the different subjects of the course of instruction. It hardly seems necessary to go over the same ground so soon again, There is the danger, in schools that are for the most part in the hands of teachers of little experience, of the pupils being pushed too fast, faster than they can appreciate or assimilate. Of course promotion is popular, both to pupil and parent, because it suggests progress, even though the teacher who should be the judge knows that it does not always imply this. The teacher should be the educational expert, and should not yield to outside pressure in the promotion of pupils; but it requires experience and considerable moral courage to refuse to do what is known to be popular and would satisfy parents.

There is far more danger in too rapid than in too tardy promotion, for the former is a pleasurable act for the teacher, and the latter is frequently a disagreeable one. We would get on much better and there would be less friction between parent and teacher if parents would learn to regard our teachers as the proper judge of promotion, and that the best good of the child is subserved only when he is placed in the grade which calls forth all the effort of which he is capable, not beyond his power, so as to discourage him, nor below his power, so as to make him feel that no effort is necessary.

During the year I have visited all the ungraded schools in my district twice, and I have very much pleasure in stating that I do not think that I have ever visited these schools when I felt that they were doing better work than at the present time.

ARBOR DAY.

About the same number of districts celebrated this day as usual. Unfortunately the day proved very cold and windy, and programmes prepared in many instances were thereby prevented from being carried out. The mistake was made long ago in this connection that properly fenced grounds were not first insisted upon before the work of setting out trees was begun. Much of the work that has proved so unavailing would now have shown more visible results.

A Teachers' Institute was held in Fredericton on the Friday and Saturday preceding the 24th of May, and was largely attended by the teachers of York, Sunbury and Queens. An excellent programme was carried out and keen interest was manifested throughout. An excursion in the Steamer Aberdeen up the river above Currie's Mountain was by no means the least attractive part of the programme. The members of the Institute divided into parties and listened to instructive talks on rock formation by Dr. Bailey, on plants by Dr. Hay, and on birds by Mr. William Moore. The Institute for these three counties will probably convene at the same time and place next year.

I have the honor to be, Sir,
Your obedient servant,
H. V. B. BRIDGES.

INSPECTORAL DISTRICT No. 6.

F. B. MEAGHER, M. A., Woodstock, Carleton Co., Inspector.

This District embraces the Counties of Carleton and Victoria (except the Parish of Drummond) and the Parishes of Canterbury, North Lake, McAdam and Southampton in York County.

J. R. INCH, ESQ., LL. D.,
Chief Supt. Education,
Fredericton,

SIR:—I beg leave to submit the following report for the year 1903:

The scarcity of trained teachers has been severely felt during the year in this Inspectorate.

Owing to this scarcity a number of small ungraded schools have either been closed or placed in charge of local licensees. This latter course is open to so many objections that it is almost a question whether it is better to adopt it or to allow the schools to remain closed. I have at least tried to confine my recommendations to remote and isolated districts where trained teachers are ordinarily unwilling to go, and when the issue of local licenses can in no way conflict with their interests.

The parsimonious support given to their schools by the ratepayers of a large number of districts is undoubtedly the cause of this diminution in the ranks of the teaching profession, for teachers are gradually taking up more profitable occupations, and not until more liberal wages be given them, can we hope to retain them in sufficient numbers to effect a proper adjustment between the supply and the demand.

On the other hand I can say with certainty that never before during my term of office has there been such a manifest improvement in the condition of the schools at large throughout this territory as in the past year. I attribute this in part to the establishment of schools for manual training, and to the stimulus given to the study of Natural Science by Instructor Brittain in his visits to the centres which he has selected in Carleton and Victoria Counties, but the main cause lies in the teachers themselves, many of whom are exhibiting a surprising degree of energy and enthusiasm in the improvement of their school environments, in the establishment of school libraries, and in the procuring of needed apparatus by their own efforts. Nor are the evidences lacking of a corresponding improvement in the internal educational work, so that viewed from any standpoint, it seems to be evident that important and progressive influences are operating in the development of the schools, and this year I shall look for a still further increase of educational activity.

On examining the following table it will be seen that out of a grand total of 266 schools the average number closed during the year was thirty-one. In Carleton Co., the average number was fourteen; in Victoria Co., eleven, and in that section of York Co., which has been placed under my supervision, the average number was seven. The majority of these schools would have been in operation if teachers could have been procured. I might also add that the 238 districts given in the table extend from Grand Falls and remote Nictau on the North, to the Nackawick and Forest City on

the south, including also the schools in the Parish of McAdam, so that some idea may be gained of the ground gone over in my semi-annual tour of visitation. In one case I have to drive thirty-four miles to visit two schools, in another, fifty to visit five, and so on. With schools scattered in this way over a great extent of territory, it is practically impossible for me to complete my work in the first or short term of the school year.

PARISHES.	No. of organized Districts.	No of Schools.	No of Schools in operation Term ended June 30th, 1903.	No. of Schools in operation Term ended Dec. 31st, 1903.
CARLETON CO.				
Aberdeen	12	12	10	9
Brighton	19	21	20	20
Kent	18	20	19	19
Northampton	9	9	7	8
Peel	7	7	5	6
Richmond	16	16	16	16
Simonds	5	6	6	6
Wakefield	15	16	15	15
Wicklow	16	15	13	15
Wilmot	17	18	17	13
Woodstock	14	28	27	25
Totals	148	168	155	152
VICTORIA CO.				
Andover	8	9	9	9
Gordon	9	9	5 (about)	7
Grand Falls	11	14	8	14
Lorne	6	6	4	3
Perth	14	14	11	13
Totals	48	52	37	46
YORK CO.				
Canterbury & N Lake	23	24	20	20
McAdam	2	4	3	4
Southampton	18	18	16	16 (about)
Totals	43	46	39	40
Grand totals	239	266	231	238

GRADED SCHOOLS.

Benton.—Although the house at Benton has been repaired and painted it still falls far short of the requirements for a Superior School in respect to its rooms and equipment. If the Superior School is to remain at Benton, provision must soon be made for the erection of a new building.

Centreville..—Mr. J. F. Worrell has succeeded Miss Ruth Reid in the principalship of the Superior School at Centreville. Miss Reid's resignation was greatly regretted, as she was an enthusiastic teacher and devoted to the welfare of her pupils. It is probable that a new building will be erected in the near future, and if so, something will also be done in the way of manual training and school garden work.

Florenceville.—A small but serviceable building has been erected on the school grounds at Florenceville for the operation of a manual training department, which is being successfully conducted by Miss Marjorie Mair, the principal of the Superior School.

Jacksonville.—Mr. Clinton H. Gray is still the principal of the Superior School at Jacksonville, and continues to do effective work. The average attendance in the primary department is quite small.

Bath.—This district is now operating a graded school, and much more satisfactory work is being done in consequence.

Bristol.—The rooms occupied by the primary and advanced departments of the graded school at Bristol have been thoroughly repaired, and are not only more comfortable but present a much better appearance. The present principal is Mr. Abram Cronkhite.

Hartland.—Mr. John Page, B. A., after a period of successful service as principal of the Superior School at Hartland, has resigned, having been appointed Principal of the Model School at Fredericton. A vacant school-room is being fitted up as a laboratory by Inspector Brittain, in which lessons will be given in natural science, and the material for the school garden stored. Near the schoolhouse land has been set apart for a school garden and public park. A good start is thus being made in the way of nature study and improvement of the school environments.

Woodstock.—During the year a number of changes have taken place in the personnel of the teaching staff of the Woodstock Schools. Miss Clark, Miss Baker, Mr. N. F. Thorne and Mr. F. A. Good have resigned, and have been succeeded respectively by Miss Harmon, Miss Alexander, Mr. H. B. Logie, B. A., and Mr. Aaron Perry, M. A.

Some important changes have lately been made in the arrangement and distribution of the work in the two departments of the Grammar School, which, I am informed, are giving good satisfaction A department for manual training has been established under the management of Miss A. Gertrude O'Brien. This department is meeting with much success, and is continually growing in favor amongst the pupils. Next spring two school gardens will be started under the supervision of Instructor Brittain. so that the outlook from every point of view is quite bright. In very few places are such exceptional educational advantages being extended to the children of the public schools as in the town of Woodstock, but more teachers are needed and more schoolroom accommodation should be provided, as some of the departments are overcrowded.

Lakeville and Upper Woodstock.—There are good schools at these places. The principal at Lakeville, Miss Lena B. McLeod, has done excellent work. Through her efforts a school library has been established, and apparatus procured. This year Miss McLeod will have charge of the school at Bloomfield Corner.

Mr. I. N. Draper, the principal at Upper Woodstock, has also been diligent in the way of procuring school appliances, and has deservedly earned the reputation of being an efficient teacher.

Andover.—Miss Bessie E. Scott, after a number of years of faithful and efficient service in the primary department of the Grammar School at Andover, retired at the close of the last school year, and was succeeded by Miss Jennie M. Curry. Mr. W. M. Veazey, B. A., is still the principal and is doing good work. Andover is included in the group of schools visited by Instructor Brittain.

The Superior School at Grand Falls has four departments under the principalship of Mr. J. C. Carruthers. Miss O'Brien succeeded Miss Allen in the primary department. The school grounds should be enlarged and I trust that certain other recommendations which I have made to the Board of Trustees will be put into effect.

Canterbury.—The many changes that are taking place in the principalship of the graded school at Canterbury cannot but have a detrimental effect. The loss of Mr. Mauriee Coll's services is greatly felt as he was a very earnest and capable teacher.

I regret that Mr. Alfred A. Schriever has also retired. He will be succeeded by Mr. James Steeves.

McAdam—In retiring from the principalship of the Superior School at McAdam, Mr. H. F Perkins carries with him the regrets of all concerned. His successor is Mr. H. R. McGill, formerly principal of the Milltown schools. The primary and intermediate departments are being conducted respectively by Mrs. E. J. Steeves and Miss Ella Mersereau, and on the whole satisfactory work is being done.

LIST OF IMPROVEMENTS FOR THE YEAR 1903.

Bristol; Room wainscoted and other improvements.

Bedell Settlement: Room wainscoted.

Birch Ridge: Maps of British Empire and Dominion of Canada.

Bath: House enlarged so as to admit of the operation of a primary department, house painted and other improvements.

Benton: House painted.

Bloomfield: Maps British Empire, Dominion and Maritime Provinces.

Centreville: Flag and school apparatus.

Canterbury Front (No. 3): Map of Maritime Provinces.

California (Upper): Maps of the World and Dominion of Canada.

Charleston: Room painted.

Deerville: Room wainscoted, hardwood floor etc.

Elmwood: Maps and other apparatus.

Forest City: Slate blackboards.

Fosterville: Hyloplate blackboards.

Goods Corner: Hyloplate blackboards.

Gregg Settlement: Flag, blackboards.

Gillespie Settlement: Room wainscoted.

Glassville (East): Flag

Hartin Settlement: Map of Maritime Provinces.

Knoxford: Flag.

Lower Greenfield: House painted.

Lower Brighton: Chemical apparatus and Flag.

Limestone: Maps of Maritime Provinces and Dominion of Canada

Lakeville: School Library and apparatus.

Main Stream: New School House, Maps and Hyloplate Blackboard.

Maple View: House painted.

McAdam: Slate blackboarks and maps.

Oakland: General repairs on house.

Ortonville: Room wainscoted.

Pembroke: General repairs, room painted.

Plymouth: Globe.

Richmond Corner: New furniture, room painted.

Royalton: House painted, minerals and cabinet.

Rosedale: House thoroughly repaired, hardwood floor, etc.

Tracey's Mills: House and room painted.
Temple: Premises fenced.
Upper Waterville: Maps of Maritime Provinces.
Upper Woodstock: Maps of Dominion and World.
Upper Bloomfield: House painted.
Upper Greenfield: Flag.
Waterville: New furniture.
Windsor (Lower): Minerals and chemical apparatus.
West Glassville: Maps of British Empire and of Maritime Provinces.

Where "Wainscoting" is referred to in the above list it includes the ceiling as well as the walls. It is gratifying to note that many of these improvements have been effected through the instrumentality of certain teachers. Their names, amongst others, are as follows:

Ruth Reid, I. Blanch Ebbett, John M. Keefe, Ella Gartley, Bessie L. Britton, Lena B. McLeod, Clara M. Carson, Verna Perkins, I. N. Draper, Laura Burpee, Lulu Cronkite, L.D. Jones, Mrs.Geo. Estey, Myrtle Fowler, Eva S. Jacques. Alfred H. Schriever, Lucy Marston.

Arbor Day.

Arbor Day was observed by the usual number of districts in this Inspectorate. A number of trees and shrubs were planted with fairly good results in many cases. Generally speaking neither trustees nor ratepayers participate in the observance of the day, and until they do so its full measure of utility and educational value cannot be attained.

Teachers' Institutes.

Teachers' Institutes were held during the year at Grand Falls and at Woodstock. At Grand Falls the presence of the Chief Superintendent and Instructor Brittain contributed greatly to the interest of the proceedings, Under the guidance of the latter, a trip was made to the wells and rocks below the Falls, and an object lesson in nature given. The public meeting was addressed by the Chief Superintendent, Rev. Mr. Maiman, Instructor Brittain and others.

Over eighty teachers were present at Woodstock. A number of valuable papers were read and thoughtful discussions ensued, in some of which Mr. D. W. Hamilton, B. A., took an interesting and instructive part.

The public meeting was addressed by Mayor Belyea, H. Paxton Baird, chairman of the Woodstock Board of Trustees, Instructor Brittain and Wendell P. Jones, M. P. P.

In closing I wish to pay a tribute of respect to the memory of Inspector Smith. He was the oldest Inspector both in years and length of service, and I have frequently received the benefit of his advice and experience in the discharge of my duties. His death is a distinct loss to the inspectoral staff and the teaching profession.

I have the honor to be, sir,
Your obedient servant,
F. B. MEAGHER.

INSPECTORAL DISTRICT NO. 7.

J. F. DOUCET, Inspector, Bathurst, N. B.

This District embraces the Counties of Gloucester and Madawaska; the Parish of Drummond in Victoria County; the Parish of Balmoral District No. 1 1-2, Colborne and Balmoral, and District No. 3, Addington, in the County of Restigouche; and Districts Nos. 4, 5, 12, 13, 14 and 15 in the Parish of Alnwick, in the County of Northumberland.

J. R. INCH ESQ. LL D.,
Chief Supt. of Education,
Fredericton, N. B.

SIR,—I beg respectfully to submit for your information my second annual report of the educational condition of Inspectoral District No. 7, for the year ended December 31st, 1903.

During the first term of the year, when I had the larger part of Kent County under my supervision, I was unable to accomplish all the work assigned to me, and as a consequence, many schools in the Counties of Kent and Gloucester remain unvisited. During the second term, having been relieved of Kent County, I have, with but a few exceptions, been enabled to visit every school and district and to become acquainted with the state of educational affairs throughout the whole extent of my Inspectoral Division.

In the course of the year, nine new school houses have been erected in the following districts, namely:—No. 1A, Belledune River; No. 3, Waterloo, in the Parish of New Bandon; No. 4, Upper St. Simon, in the Parish of Caraquet; No. 8, Gagnon, in the Parish of St. Isidore; No. 3, Quisibis, in the Parish of St. Ann; No. 10½, Wilson's Point, in the Parish of Shippegan; No. 9, Combe's Road, in the Parish of St, Leonard; No, 3, St. Basil, and No. 2½, Lower Caraquet.

The new building at St. Basil comprises five departments and has been built at a cost of about $4,000. The rooms are spacious, well lighted and well equipped. The new school house at Belledune River is a handsome and commodious building. The one at Quisibis is not yet finished inside. The last two have taken the place of old and worn out buildings which were very uncomfortable and totally inadequate to the requirements of these districts. Schools have been opened for the first time at Upper St. Simon, Gagnon and Combe's Road, and for the first time since several years at Waterloo.

A new school house is in course of construction at Boat Landing, No. 6, Drummond.

As soon as a site is agreed upon, the people of No. 14, Salmon Beach, will begin the construction of a larger school house.

In No. 4, Saumarez, a contract has been given for the erection of a new school house to replace the one destroyed by fire last year. The new building will be ready for occupancy next August.

In No. 2, Shippegan Gully, a larger school house is needed, and I am pleased to know that there is a strong desire in the district in favor of rebuilding. New school houses are also needed in Lower Madawaska, No. 3; Beresford, No. 2; and St. Isidore, No. 7. The present buildings are small and quite dilapidated and do not compare favorably with the other buildings in these sections.

No new districts have been laid off during the year. Applications have been made by the people of St. Raphael Village, a part of District No. 4, Parish of Shippegan, and by the people living in the southern portion of District No. 13, Bathurst, locally known as Ste. Marie, but on account of the disabilities of section 6 (3), their request cannot be granted at present.

In the month of September the two Dumfries Districts, Nos 7½ and and 8½, Beresford and Bathurst, were united. The two districts together are not four miles in length. The people will find it less onerous to support a good school. It is the intention of the Trustees to engage a second or first class teacher.

Grammar, Superior and Graded Schools.

I have been very favorably impressed with the quality of the work done in the several departments of the schools in the town of Bathurst. The excellence of the mathematical subjects in the principal's room and of the primary work in Sister Stephen's department deserve special mention. The Principal, Mr. R. D. Hanson, B. A., is a very enthusiastic, thorough and popular teacher. Much to the regret of all concerned, Miss Laura Meahan, who for several years had conducted, with eminent success, the intermediate department of the grammar school, was compelled on account of failing health to tender her resignation in the month of May. Her many friends will be pleased to hear of her restoration to health. She has been succeeded ed by Miss Emma C. A. Stout, late of the Primary Department, which is now in charge of Miss Lauretta Mullins.

So frequent have been the changes in the Principalship of the Edmundston Superior School during the last few years, that the results are not as satisfactory as one would expect from an institution of this kind. The present principal is Mr. Max D. Cormier, B. A. His knowledge of both French and English renders him admirably qualified for the position he holds. Some changes have also been made in the other departments. The school has been supplied during the year with hyloplate blackboards and several up-to-date maps.

Needed repairs have been made on the Bathurst Village Superior School. The school is now in charge of Mr. J. B. Carr, who succeeded Mr. C. J. Mersereau, M. A., in the month of August. I have not yet visited this school.

The Superior Schools at Petit Rocher and Tracadie, under the direction of Mr. J. Boudreau and Mr. Ed. L. O'Brien, M. A., respectively, continue to do good work. Excepting the Superior School building at Tracadie Village, which is a creditable structure, the other school houses of these two districts, five in number, are in an advanced state of dilapidation. Mr. Joseph X. Doucet has rendered good service for the last five years in the department at Sheila. He resigned his school in August to accept a more lucrative position.

The convent at St. Basil operates six departments, all of which are giving excellent satisfaction. A seventh department will perhaps be opened during the next year to accommodate the ever increasing attendance. Too much encomium cannot be bestowed on these teachers for the wonderful development of their institution and for the services which they render to the County of Madawaska.

An expenditure of about $200 on the school house at St. Leonard has made it very pleasant and comfortable. The walls and ceiling of both departments have been sheathed and painted. The outside should now be painted and the grounds enclosed, The school is under the management of

Mr. J. C. Delagarde, B. A., who is slowly but surely bringing the school to the front.

An extension has been built to the school house at Lower Caraquet, and a primary department opened in August.

Besides these, there are graded schools of two departments each, at Nipisiquit Bridge, Nipisiquit West, St. Peter's Village No. 15, Caraquet, Middle Caraquet and Shippegan Village.

UNGRADED SCHOOLS.

As I have over 180 of these schools they take up the larger part of my time. My monthly and special reports during the year have dealt so minutely with individual cases and have exhibited so fully the points of excellence and the defects that I do not think it necessary to go into details here again.

The school house at Portage River, No. 10A, has been thoroughly renovated. The building has been enlarged by an addition of ten feet and painted inside and outside. The grounds have also been enclosed by a neat wire fence.

Extensive repairs have also been made on the houses in the following districts, viz.:—Clair, No. 2; New Denmark, No. 1; South Tetagouche, No. 5; Upper Rose Hill, No. 4; Caraquet, No. 10; St. Basil, No. 8; St. Leonard, Nos. 7 and 14; New Bandon, No. 4½; Miramichi Road, Big River, Janeville and Blue Cove.

At my visits I made it a point to see the trustees, where I found it necessary, and impress upon them the necessity of supplying their schools with the required apparatus. I am pleased to say that I found the Trustees usually willing to carry out my recommendations. A good number of the schools are well supplied with maps, hyloplate and slate blackboards, globes, etc. Some are models in this respect.

Below is given a list of the districts which have provided furniture and apparatus during the year.

Bathurst—No. 2, Maps of Canada, British Empire, Europe; No. 6, Maps of Maritime Provinces, Slate blackboard; No. 10, Map of Canada; No. 16, Map of United States, additions to the library, chemicals, etc.

Beresford—No. 2, Map of Maritime Provinces; No. 4, Map of Maritime Provinces; No. 13½, Map of Maritime Provinces; No. 6, Hyloplate blackboard.

Inkerman—No. 2, New Blackboard.

New Bandon—No. 4, 14 Paragon desks; No. 8, Map of Canada;

No. 10, 1 doz. Paragon desks; No. 11, 1 doz. Paragon desks; No. 10½, Maps of Maritime Provinces and Empire.

Shippegan—No. 1, Map of Maritime Provinces; No. 4½, 1 doz. Paragon desks; No. 8, Map of New Brunswick (Loggie's).

Balmoral—No. 3, 20 new desks; No. 1, Map of Canada.

St. Ann—No. 1, 1 doz. Desks.

St. Basil—No. 4, Map of Canada, new furniture; No. 3, new furniture; No. 2, Map of Maritime Provinces; No. 5, Map of Maritime Provinces; No. 10, new desks.

St. Francis—No. 2½, Flag, Map of Canada, fence; No. 3. 20 Paragon desks; No. 4, Slate blackboard, Map of Maritime Provinces.

St. Hilaire—No. 7, Furniture; No. 1, Bell for the tower.

Clair—No. 11, Map of Maritime Provinces.

ACADIAN SCHOOLS.

It is gratifying to note the progress which the Acadian schools of this Inspectorate are making. A plain evidence of the interest which the Acadians take in education, and of the many efforts and sacrifices which they make to keep their schools in operation is the fact that during the year just terminated all the schools in Gloucester County, with only one exception, and 64 out of 68 departments in Madawaska were kept open for some part of the year, nearly all of them for the whole year. There are yet some remote localities where schools are wanted, but the inhabitants of these places will no doubt eventually wake up to the importance of education.

In Gloucester County the number of teachers is equal to the demand but we need more second and first-class teachers. In Madawaska County, such was the paucity of teachers that during the last term I had to recommend more than the usual number of local licenses. Discouraging as this is it is pleasing to know that at the time of my last visit at St Basil Convent last September, there were thirteen young ladies in Grade VIII. preparing themselves to attend Normal School. If a like contingent from this county could be sent out every year, we would soon have a sufficient number of trained teachers for this county and the progress of the schools would not be retarded by the employment of unlicensed teachers.

With your approval, I have advised the teachers to adopt a more rational method of teaching reading to beginners. They are not to attempt the teaching of English before the pupil has mastered the chief difficulties of learning to read in his own language. This he has fairly well accomplished when he has completed his Second French Reader. It is now time to begin

English reading in the primer. Experience as a teacher and as inspector has convinced me that where this method is followed the pupil will learn to read his own language in a shorter time and that when he takes up the study of English he is enabled to learn it more intelligently. I have in my mind several schools where this method has been adopted and far better results have been obtained than where the two languages have been learned conjointly.

There is a danger, however, which the teachers following this plan must guard against, and that is in "going through" the book too rapidly. Many teachers are also wasting time in attempting to teach the elements of English Grammar to grade III as required by the course of instruction for ungraded schools. I am of opinion that more practical results would follow if the elements of French Grammar were taught to pupils in the second and third French Readers before they take up English Grammar.

INSTITUTE.

The Gloucester County Teachers' Institute was held at Grand Anse this year on the 24th and 25th September. The next meeting will be held at Bathurst. I happened to be in Madawaska then, and much to my regret, was unable to be present. By reports received, the papers and discussions were lively and practical. The public meeting was well attended and was addressed by the chairman, Mr. J. E. DeGrace, Rev'd S. J. Doucet, Mr. J. Poirier, M. P. P., and others.

MISCELLANEOUS NOTES.

The "Educational Review" is much read by the teachers of this district. Some also subscribe to the "Canadian Teacher" and to "L'Enseignement Primaire," published at Quebec.

During the year two of our teachers passed away, Ubalde Cyr of Edmunston, and Theodore Delagarde of Shippegan. The latter, though a young teacher, had been very successful in teaching and enjoyed the esteem of the community,

I have the honor to be,
Your obedient severant,
J. F. DOUCET.

Bathurst, N. B., 31st Dec., 1903.

APPENDIX C.

REPORTS OF BOARDS OF SCHOOL TRUSTEES.

CITY OF FREDERICTON.

BOARD OF SCHOOL TRUSTEES.

J. R. INCH., ESQ , LL.D.
Chief Supt. of Education,
Fredericton, N. B.

SIR.—The Board of School Trustees beg to submit for your consideration the following Report on the schools of the city of Fredericton,

We have concluded the work of another year and its character was probably as varied as that of any preceding it. Several changes occurred in our staff of teachers during the year. The work in the High School was just getting into form when Mr. Hagerman of the Science department was asked to accept the position vacated by Mr. Brittain in the Normal School. His resignation was accepted, and Mr. Frank N. Patterson, A. B. was appointed to succeed him. The vacancy in the sixth department of York street school created by the resignation of Miss Tibbits was filled by the transfer of Miss Sarah Thompson from Morrison Mill School. Miss Frances McNally was then appointed to the charge of the Mill school. Miss Holland, teacher of the second department in Regent Street School, struggled long and bravely with failing health but at last succumbed to disease. This department is now in charge of Miss Ellen McKenna, (Sr. Estelle) a former member of our staff. The first department in this school, vacated by the resignation of Miss Duffy who for more than twenty years was on the staff, is now in charge of Miss Gertrude M. Reid.

These changes in the staff are very apt to endanger the steady progress of the work, but they are unavoidable and occur year after year. Notwithstanding the fact that the interruptions during the year were unusually numerous we anticipate good results. In the early part of the year children's diseases prevailed so generally that for weeks the primary departments were largely deserted, and thus the ground work of the year was greatly retarded. Then later the other departments were affected more or less until the outbreak of smallpox in the city precipitated an order for general vaccination. This had a discouraging effect for many of the pupils absented themselves from the school room expecting to avoid the health officer. By order of the Board of Health the High and York Street School and the Model School were closed for a week while being fumigated. The attendance at the manual training department has been well maintained, the interest taken by the pupils and the progress made have been very satisfactory, and this condition of things we have no doubt is largely due to the tact, the skill, and genial management of Prof. MacCready and his associates. Through munificence of Sir William Macdonald this branch of work has been open to the children of our schools for three years, during which period some five hundred boys have had the benefits of sloyd work. This board is now making arrangements to open a manual training department in direct connection with the city schools and we hope to have it established upon the re-openings of the schools after the summer vacation.

General repairs have been made on the different school buildings, and in addition to the repairs at Charlotte Street School the building was supplied with a number of modern desks and seats. For two years and a half Mr. Jos. Mills has been the successful principal of this important school, and the Board regretted his withdrawal from the staff at the close of the present year. Nothing very practical was done this year in celebration of Arbor Day. However, lessons bearing on the objects of the day were given in the different schools, and subsequently half a dozen trees were planted. The continuous instruction through lessons on nature given to the child from admission to Grade I enables him to intelligently participate in any practical work while celebrating Arbor Day.

For several years past very little change has taken place in the number of pupils in attendance at our schools. That the city is broadening out and steadily improving in appearance is generally admitted, and the increase in population must certainly be in keeping with its environment. Our annual registered attendance varies very little, and it is just possible this may be caused by a growing carelessness on the part of parents and guardians to see that those committed to their care take advantage of the means provided by the state for the education of its youth. It is the registered pupils only for whom the teachers can be expected to accept any responsibility for attendance at school, and many of our teachers make frequent calls upon parents in their efforts to secure the presence of their children, but unsatisfactory results frequently follow. The teachers' duties are onerous and often most discouraging, but he who does not prepare for each day's work beforehand cannot expect to interest his classes or attain the progress so necessary when the test of grading is applied. With fine school buildings, attractive class-rooms, modern appliances, and a staff of teachers whose experience is extended and practical, it would seem to be the grossest carelessness that causes children to be deprived of school privileges so bountifully provided at the public expense. The minimum age for admission to school having been placed at six years caused some local opposition, but our experience has largely borne out the statement that the majority of children beginning their educational course at five years of age were not matured enough to successfully grapple with the problems presented to them five years later.

Interest in educational matters in this community is well maintained, as shown by the large attendance of the general public at the terminal examinations every year. The large assembly hall of the High School is usually crowded with visitors at each closing, and genuine interest is manifested in the proceedings. This year the graduating class numbered twenty-four, and the prize winners were as follows:

Waldo Carson Machum—Douglas Medal for Classics.

Louis Ralph Sherman—Governor General's Bronze Medal for English

Rebecca Barclay Watson—Coulthard Memorial Medal for Natural Science.

Rebecca Barclay Watson—Mathematical Prize presented by Senate, U. N. B.

Alma Belliveau—Class 1902 prize for French.

Kenneth Austin Dunphy—Class 1902 prize for highest general average among those who had won no other prize.

Louis Ralph Sherman—Class 1902 prize for History.

Celia Nichols—Highest general average in Class "B."

Fannie Vradenburg—Highest general average in Class "C."

The Graduating Class was addressed by Rev. J. A. Rogers, and his inspiring words and excellent counsel to these young persons will no doubt encourage them to reach out after high ideals. Among the other gentlemen who addressed the school or presented the prizes were Very Rev. Dean Partridge, Rev. Dr. Roberts, Rev. J. H. MacDonald, Judge Wilson, Dr. Scott. Dr. Bailey, Dr. Creed and Mr. John J. Weddall.

At this year's High School entrance examination one hundred and three applicants were present. Of these, twenty-five passed in Division I.; forty in Division II.; twenty-nine in Division III.; and nine failed to reach the pass mark.

For details respecting the schools we refer you to the appended tables.

I have the honor to be

Your obedient servant,

CHAS. A. SAMPSON,

Secretary.

STATEMENT A.

Receipts and Expenditures for 1902.

On What Account.	Amount.	Amount.	On What Account.	Amount
Permanent Account—			By Taxes from City Treasurer	$16000 00
Apparatus	$ 58 80		Debentures	4180 00
Mill School	72 50		Interest	32 62
Furniture and Furnishing	208 57	339 87	Tuition	35 00
			Damages	1 00
Annual Expenditure—			Balance, Jan., '01	5507 15
Auditors	$ 10 00			$25755 77
Rent	200 00			
Printing	54 05			
Debentures	4200 00			
Insurance	221 50			
Indigent Pupils	6 25			
Prizes	4 75			
Fuel	85 68			
Interest	2702 79			
Contingent	229 70			
Repairs	194 78			
Salaries	9933 83			
Janitors	938 00			
Unpaid cheques	172 20			
Balance	6462 37	$25415 90		
		$25755 77		$25755 77

CHAS. A. SAMPSON, *Secretary.*

STATEMENT B.

Names of Teachers, age, sex, and Number of Pupils, for Term ended 31st. December, 1902.

SCHOOL.	Teacher.	Pupils 6 to 15 years.	Over 15 years.	Boys.	Girls.	Total.
High School....	B. C. Foster........	5	26	16	15	31
	A. S. McFarlane.....	24	16	40		40
	H. H. Hagerman. } Frank N. Patterson }	14	21	10	25	35
	Ella L. Thorne.....	4	31		35	35
York Street....	Sadie Thompson....	37	4	16	25	41
	L. E. VanDine.....	49		26	23	49
	K. McCann.........	51		26	25	51
	K. E. Currie.......	53		35	18	53
	I. R. Everett.......	60		29	31	60
	L. A. Burtt........	59		28	31	59
Model.........	Amos O'Blenes.....	40		18	22	40
	M. E. S. Nicholson.	47		15	32	47
	M. A. Harvey......	49		21	28	49
	L. Nicholson.......	50		24	26	50
Charlotte Street.	Joseph Mills.......	53	3	26	30	56
	A. L. Taylor.......	52		31	21	52
	E. J. Thompson....	59		33	26	59
	N. B. Williamson...	51		24	27	51
	Ida McAdam.......	53		28	25	53
Regent Street..	Jas. A. Hughes....	26	2	14	14	28
	V. McKenna.......	33		20	13	33
	E. McKenna.......	32		11	21	32
	G. M. Reid........	44		25	19	44
Brunswick St...	C. M. McDevitt....	30		19	11	30
Mill	F. McNally........	61	5	26	40	66
Doak	R. E. G. Davies....	25		12	13	25
		1061	108	573	596	1169

CHAS. A. SAMPSON,
Secretary.

STATEMENT C.

Names of Teachers, age, sex and number of Pupils for Term ended 30th June, 1903.

SCHOOL.	TEACHER.	Pupils 6 to 15 years.	Over 15 years.	Boys.	Girls.	TOTAL.
High......	B C Foster........	....	30	15	15	30
	A S McFarlane.....	30	8	38	...	38
	F N Patterson.....	....	32	9	23	32
	Ella L Thorne......	8	21	...	29	29
York St.......	Sadie Thompson....	33	3	14	22	36
	L E Vandine,......	47	....	26	21	47
	Kate McCann......	51	....	26	25	51
	K E Currie	49	1	32	18	50
	I R Everett........	55	....	27	28	55
	L A Burtt.........	56	...	25	31	56
Model.........	Amos O'Blenes.....	36	1	13	24	37
	M E S Nicolson	45	....	15	30	45
	M A Harvey.... ...	48	....	21	27	48
	L Nicolson	47	....	24	23	47
Charlotte St....	Joseph Mills	50	5	28	27	55
	A L Taylor........	49	....	29	20	49
	E J Thompson......	56	....	33	23	56
	N B Williamson.....	49	....	23	26	49
	Ida McAdam.......	49	....	24	25	49
Regent St......	J A Hughes........	24	3	14	13	27
	V McKenna........	31	1	18	14	32
	E McKenna........	31	....	9	22	31
	G M Reid..........	43	....	24	19	43
Brunswick St...	C M McDevitt......	25	....	18	7	25
Mill	F McNally..........	60	1	29	32	61
Doak	R E G Davies......	25	....	13	12	25
		997	106	547	556	1103

CHAS. A. SAMPSON,
Secretary.

STATEMENT D.

Name and Class of Teacher, Salary, and Attendance for Term ended 31st. December, 1902.

SCHOOL.	Teacher.	Class.	Salary from Trustees.	No. Pupils.	Average Daily Attendance.	Per cent Attendance.
High School......	B C Foster.......	G. S.	$850	31	28.28	91.02
	A S McFarlane...	G. S.	500	40	38.02	95 05
	H H Hagerman. }	G. S.	650	35	31.42	89.77
	F N Patterson.. }	G. S.	400			
	Ella L Thorne.....	I.	500	35	30.34	86.06
York Street......	Sadie Thompson..	G. S.	250	41	32 35	80.87
	L E Vandine.	I.	250	49	45.05	92.08
	Kate McCann.....	I.	250	51	44.35	86.09
	Katherine E Currie	I.	250	53	42.61	86.06
	I R Everett......	I.	250	60	51.67	86.
	L A Burtt... ...	I.	250	59	53.03	90.
Model...........	Amos O'Blenes....	G. S.	650	40	36.41	91.03
	M E S Nicolson....	II.	250	47	44.	93.
	M A Harvey.....	I.	216	49	45.39	93.45
	L Nicolson.	I.	216	50	45.13	90.
Charlotte Street...	Joseph Mills	G. S.	600	56	47.08	85.35
	A L Taylor......	G. S.	250	52	44.26	85.11
	E J Thompson...	I.	250	59	50.36	85.35
	N B Williamson...	G. S.	250	51	43.68	85.64
	Ida McAdam.....	II.	250	53	45.90	86.60
Regent Street....	Jas A Hughes....	I.	600	28	24.04	87 04
	V McKenna......	I.	250	33	29.12	88.09
	E McKenna......	I.	250	32	26.64	83.25
	G M Reid........	I.	250	44	37.	84.
Brunswick Street.	C M McDevitt....	I.	250	30	23.	76 06
Mill	F McNally.......	I.	250	66	54.	81.
Doak	R E G Davies....	II.	200	25	17.	71.
				1169	39.	86.26

CHAS. A. SAMPSON,
Secretary.

STATEMENT E.

Name, salary, class of teacher, and attendance for term ended 30th June, 1903.

SCHOOL.	TEACHER.	Class.	Salary from Trustees.	No. Pupils.	Average Daily Attendance.	Per cent. Attendance.
High............	B C Foster	G. S.	$950	30	27.	90.
	A S McFarlane...	G S.	550	38	33.36	87.79
	F N Patterson....	G. S.	400	32	25.71	80.03
	Ella L Thorne....	I.	500	29	25.	86.
York St..........	Sadie Thompson..	G. S.	250	36	27.23	75.63
	L E Vandine.....	I.	250	47	39 04	83.08
	K McCann.......	I.	250	51	42.78	83.08
	K E Currie	I.	250	50	39.09	79.08
	I R Everett......	I.	250	55	43.60	79.27
	L A Burtt.......	I.	250	56	44.62	79.67
Model............	A O'Blenes	G. S.	650	37	32.39	87.55
	M E S Nicolson ..	II.	250	45	40.	88.
	M A Harvey.....	I.	216	48	43.33	90.27
	L Nicolson.......	I.	216	47	40.07	86.06
Charlotte St......	Joseph Mills.....	G. S.	600	55	46.14	83.08
	A L Taylor......	G. S.	250	49	39.75	81.
	E J Thompson ...	I.	250	56	47.33	84.51
	N B Williamson ..	G. S.	250	49	39.27	80.14
	Ida McAdam.....	II.	250	49	39.	80.
Regent St	James A Hughes..	I.	600	27	20.08	78.
	V McKenna......	I.	250	32	24.73	77.29
	E McKenna......	I.	250	31	26.44	85.10
	G M Reid........	I.	250	43	34.	79.
Brunswick St.....	C M McDevitt....	I.	250	25	19.	76.
Mill	F McNally.......	I.	250	61	46.	75.04
Deak	R E G Davies....	II.	200	25	11.	47.
				1103	34.46	80.83

CHAS. A. SAMPSON,
Secretary.

CITY OF MONCTON.

BOARD OF SCHOOL TRUSTEES, 1903.

Staff of Grammar School, 1903.

George J. Oulton, M. A., *Principal*—Teacher of Chemistry, Physics, Physical Geography, Nature Lessons, Geometry, Physiology, Arithmetic.

G. Fred McNally, B. A.—Teacher of Greek, Latin, History, Civics.

H. B. Steeves, M. A.—Teacher of Botany, Book-keeping, Algebra, Agriculture, Arithmetic, Grade IX.

W. A. Cowperthwaite, M. A.—Teacher of French, English Literature, Grammar and Composition.

J. R. Inch Esq., LL D.,
Chief Supt. of Education,
Fredericton, N. B.

Sir,—The Board of School Trustees for the city of Moncton have the honor to present for your consideration the annual report of the public schools in the city of Moncton for the year 1903.

During the year Mr. A. E. Wall, who had for some years faithfully performed the duties of trustee, removed from the city, and the government appointed Mr. James Doyle to fill the vacancy. On the 15th of July, 1903, the government reappointed Mr. J. T. Hawke chairman of the Board, and Mr. James Flanagan, Trustee.

ENROLMENT.

The grand total enrolment through the city for 1903 was 1789 pupils, and thirty-four teachers were engaged with an average of 53 pupils to each teacher.

HIGH SCHOOL.

Very successful work has been done in the various departments of the High School during the year. One important factor in the success of the High School was the fact that no changes in the staff has taken place during the year and the staff are to be congratulated on the excellent results which have accrued from their efforts.

MATRICULANTS.

The following pupils of the High School successfully passed the Matriculation examination of the University of New Brunswick in 1903 :—

Eva McCracken	Division 1
Edna Bell	" 2
Lizzie McBeath	2
Fred H. Kierstead	2
R. Gordon Warman	2
Daisy Weldon	3
Florence Mackenzie	3
Dorothy Donald	3
Bell McNairn	3
May Quinn	3
Will Hutchinson	3
Ella Hannah	3
Ed. McLean	3
Alice Burnyeat	3
Joseph P. Wood	3
G. Harry Hunter	3
Etta McLaren	3
Ida Hopper	3
Greta Northrup	3

JUNIOR LEAVING EXAMINATION.

Jean Welling passed in 2nd Division.

Of these, four, Eva McCracken, Edna Bell, Ed. McLean and Joseph Wood are in attendance at the University. Seven, viz., Ella Hannah, Jean Welling, Alice Burnyeat, Daisy Weldon, Florence Mackenzie, Bell McNairn and Gordon Warman are in attendance at the Normal School.

NORMAL SCHOOL ENTRANCE EXAMINATION.

The following students were successful in passing the entrance examination to the Normal School and are in attendance at that Institution: Mary Adams, Minnie Bishop, Jean Peacock, Jennie Woodman.

McGILL UNIVERSITY.

Two pupils of the High School J. Royden Estey and Ernest Martin succesfully passed the Matriculation examination for McGill University and have entered the Faculty of Applied Science at McGill.

One entered Acadia University, Will H. Hutchinson. And two are in attendance at Mount Allison namely:—

George S. Patterson in the faculty of Arts at the University.

Dora Duffy in the Ladies College.

GRADUATES OF HIGH SCHOOL.

The following constitute the Graduating Class for 1903, who received Diplomas in order of merit:—

1	Edna Bell	Division	1
2	Lizzie McBeath	"	1
3	Mabel Jones	"	1
4	May Quinn		1
5	Belle McNairn.		1
6	Dorothy Donald		2
7	George Patterson		2
8	Etta McLaren		2
9	Alvina Legere		2
10	Walter Bradshaw		2
11	Fred Kierstead		2
12	Greta Northrup		2
13	Iva Fairweather		2
14	Esther Nixon		2
15	William Hutchinson		2
16	Ethel Moore		2
17	Eunice Welch		2
18	Ida Hopper		3
19	Bessie Doyle		3
20	Eddie McLean		3
21	Joseph Wood		3
22	Dora Duffy	"	3
23	Karl Schaefer	"	3
24	Jennie Woodman		3
25	Eugene Bourque		3

PRIZE LIST.

The following Prizes were awarded:

For best general average, Grade XI, Gold Medal donated by J. T. Hawke, Chairman of Board, won by Edna Bell.

Second best average Scott's Poems donated by a friend won by Lizzie McBeath.

For highest standing averages in Latin and History, Kruger Sovereign, donated by C. H. Acheson of Johannesburg, won by Edna Bell.

Highest standing, a course at Moncton Business College, won by May Quinn, donated by the principal Miss Johnson.

Highest standing in English, complete works of Shakespeare, donated by Ald. J. H. Harris won by Edna Bell.

Highest in Mathematics "The Habitant" donated by Hon. C. W. Robinson, M. P. P., won by Edna Bell.

Highest in French "Johnie Courteau" donated by Hon. F. J. Sweeney, M. P. P., won by Edna Bell.

Highest in Science, Fountain Pen, donated by F. A. McCully, won by Mabel Jones.

Highest average in Grade X, Gold sovereign donated by His Worship, Mayor Givan, won by Mary Adams.

Highest average in Grade IX., Bronze Medal, donated by the Governor General of Canada, won by Clairence Flanagan.

Highest average in Grade VIII., at High School Entrance Examination, Silver Medal, donated by His Honor the Lieutenant Governor of New Brunswick, won by Mary Lumina Gauvin.

ENTRANCE EXAMINATION.

In June last Entrance Examination to High School was held in the Aberdeen building under the supervision of Principals Oulton and Irons and the Secretary of School Board.

89 Candidates presented themselves for examination.

Of the number presenting themselves, 70 were admitted to High School. The pupil making the highest average was Miss Mary Lumina Gauvin of the Wesley Street School. She won the Silver Medal presented by His Honor, Jabez Bunting Snowball, Lieutenant Governor of New Brunswick.

The Medal, by command of His Honor, was fittingly presented by Hon. F. J. Sweeney.

VICTORIA SCHOOL.

The enrolment in this School was 532. Some changes in the staff occurred during the year occasioned by the resignation of Miss Simpson and Miss Willis. Miss Mary McBeath B. A. was appointed to the vacancy in Grade VI., and Miss Florence Murphy to Grade V.

Mrs. Purdy, one of the Board of Trustees generously donated prizes for all the grades in the school. These were presented to the successful students at the closing exercises in June last, and proved a valuable spur to increase efforts during the year.

WESLEY STREET SCHOOL.

The enrolment in this school has steadily increased during recent years, being 375 in 1899, 367 in 1900, 403 in 1901, 439 in 1902, 468 in 1903.

The school has made excellent progress under the efficient Principal. A pupil from this school again led in the entrance examination to High School, making the third time in succession a pupil from this school has won this distinction.

Attached to this report are a number of tabular and comparative statements relating to the city schools. All of which is respectfully submitted.

F. A. McCULLY, *Secretary*.

JOHN T. HAWKE, *Chairman*.

Moncton, N. B. December 31st, 1903.

i 14

STATEMENT NO. 1.

SHOWING INCREASE IN ENROLMENT.

Year.	Terms	No. Pupils Enrolled.	No. of Schools.	Average No. Pupils to each Teacher
1888	First	1070	19	57
	Second	1026	20	62
1889	First	1160	20	58
	Second	1271	22	58
1890	First	1237	22	56
	Second	1464	24	61
1891	First	1408	24	59
	Second	1612	28	58
1892	First	1544	28	56
	Second	1632	28	59
1893	First	1536	28	56
	Second	1621	28	57
1894	First	1572	28	56
	Second	1641	28	59
1895	First	1664	29	57
	Second	1716	30	57
1896	First	1661	30	57
	Second	1720	30	57
1897	First	1700	30	56
	Second	1749	30	58
1898	First	1678	33	50
	Second	1741	33	53
1899	First	1682	33	51
	Second	1825	33	55
1900	First	1736	33	52
	Second	1717	34	50.5
1901	First	1698	34	50
	Second	1778	33	54
1902	First	1712	32	54
	Second	1795	34	53
1903	First	1746	34	51.3
	Second	1789	34	52.6

STATEMENT No. 2.

Teachers and Grades, 1903.

TEACHERS.	Class.	Standard.		Religions.				
		1st Term	2nd Term.	Pres.	Cath.	Meth.	Bap.	Epis
ABERDEEN SCHOOL.								
Geo J Oulton, M A	G. S	11	11			1		
G Fred McNally, B A	"	10	10				1	
W A Cowperthwaite, M A	"	9	9					1
H B Steeves, M A	"	9	9			1		
S B Anderson	Sup.	8	8	1				
Ethel Murphy	I	7	7	1				
Etta Cormick	1	7	6 & 7					1
Alice Lea	I	6	6			1		
Agnes McSweeney	II	5	5		1			
Amelia Smith	I	5	4	1				
Mary A Moore	I	4	4 & 5					1
Mabel E McLeod	I	3	3			1		
Elspeth Charters	I	3	3	1				
Ella J. McKay	I	1 & 2	1 & 2				1	
Emma Condon	I	1 & 2	1 & 2	1				
Lottie L Weldon	I	1 & 2	1				1	
VICTORIA SCHOOL.								
S W Irons	I	8	8	1				
Catherine Barton	I	7	7					1
Cora L Simpson	I	6		1				
Mary H McBeath, B A	I		6	1				
Harriet E Willis	I	5		1				
Florence Murphy	II		5	1				
Ella Stevens	II	4	4					1
Hazel Taylor	I	4	4	1				
G May Forge	I	3	3					1
Eunice Brown	I	3	3	1				
Fannie McLaren	I	1 & 2	1 & 2	1				
Edith L Mitchell	I	1	1			1		

STATEMENT NO. 2.—Continued.

Teachers and Grades, 1903.

TEACHERS.	Class.	Standard.		Religions.				
		1st Term.	2nd Term.	Pres.	Cath.	Meth.	Bap.	Epis
WESLEY STREET.								
Agnes Quirke...........	I	7 & 8	7 & 8	.....	I	.....	.....	....
Kate Hamilton..........	I	[illegible] & 6	[illegible] & [illegible]	.....	I	.....	.....	....
Nathalie Allain..........		& 5	&	.....	I	.....	.....	....
Elizabeth Richard........		& 4	&	.....	I	.....	.....	....
Catherine Hennesey......		3	&	.....	I	.....	.....	....
Evangeline Bourque.....		2		.....	I	.....	.....	....
Elodie Bourque........		1 & 2		.....	I	.....	.....	....
Evangeline LeBlanc.....		1 & 2		.....	I	.....	.....	....

STATEMENT NO. 3.

GRAND TOTAL ENROLMENT FOR TERM COMMENCING AUGUST 1899, 1900, 1901, 1902, 1903.

ABERDEEN SCHOOL.	1889	1900	1901	1902	1903
Grade XI, High School	36	33	25	45	26
Grade X. " "	43	41	51	42	44
Grade IX. (A) High School	44	47	38	32	36
Grade IX (B) " "	47	44	38	37	36
Grade VIII	49	51	48	43	50
Grade VII	49	42	46	83	45
Grade VII. & VI	..	..	..	..	42
Grade VI	52	58	93	59	55
Grade V	105	109	100	105	43
Grade V & IV	...	..	..	..	47
Grade IV	92	89	75	83	56
Grade III	100	99	112	89	89
Grade II & I	191	163	176	182	115
Grade I	..	..	..	..	58
	638	611	650	644	742
VICTORIA SCHOOL.					
Grade VIII	52	38	49	45	50
Grade VII	57	74	61	52	51
Grade VI	50	54	52	63	50
Grade VI & V	55	..	..	..	..
Grade V	..	60	66	62	52
Grade V & IV	56	..	..	..	..
Grade IV	..	59	57	104	111
Grade IV & III	59	..	..	..	..
Grade III	52	55	122	71	109
Grade II	60	52	39	43	..
Grade II & I	119	121	57	58	49
Grade I	..	..	60	58	60
	560	513	563	556	532

STATEMENT NO. 3 Continued.

WESLEY STREET.	1899	1900	1901	1902	1903
Grade VIII & VII	44	36	38	37	43
Grade VI & V	52	50	60	52	56
Grade V & IV	56	53	57	..	57
Grade V	..	..	..	48	..
Grade IV & III	..	55	56	53	56
Grade III	63	..	..	58	..
Grade III & II	..	59	65	..	59
Grade II & I	160	58	137	..	..
Grade II	..	..	...	59	59
Grade I	..	56	..	132	138
	375	367	413	439	468

STATEMENT No. 4.

Term Ending June 30, 1903. Teachers and Actual Attendance Returns.

SCHOOLS.	TEACHERS.	Salaries.	Days of Session.	Pupils Enrolled.	Boys.	Girls.	Gross Days Pupils Attended.	Gross Days Lost.	Average Days Pupils Attended.	Percentage of Attendance.
Aberdeen....	George J Oulton........	$850	116	42	14	28	4169½	390	27.	88.1
	G Fred McNally........	650	120	35	8	27	3722	319	31.69	90.54
	Herbert B Steeves.....	500	120	31	14	17	3047½	410½	26.3	84.9
	W A Cowperthwaite	500	120	33	13	20	3186½	461½	27.808	84.2
	S B Anderson..........	565	120	46	20	26	4796	521	40.	87.5
	Ethel Murphy	275	120	40	25	15	4276	470	36.	90.
	Etta Cormick..........	275	120	41	18	23	3437½	1313½	30.13	73.49
	Alice Lea.............	275	120	59	21	38	6286	562	53.28	90.33
	Agnes McSweeney.....	275	120	53	29	24	5189½	1069	44.	83.
	Mary H McBeath......	275	120	53	33	20	5082½	1327½	43.5	82.
	Mary A Moore.........	240	119	52	28	24	5010	854	43.3	88.2
	Mabel E McLeod......	275	119	55	32	23	5136	879	44.3	80.6
	Elspeth Charters......	275	120	58	27	31	5471½	832½	46.9	80.
	Ella J McKay..........	275	120	62	29	33	5678	1076½	48.6	78.
	Emma Condon.........	275	120	60	26	34	5427	1637.	46.55	77.25
	Lottie L Weldon.......	200	120	61	29	32	5621	1699	48.4	79.34
Victoria.....	S W Iron..............	850	123	45	19	26	4433	486	37.098	82.4
	Catherine Barton	275	123	48	17	31	4497½	752½	37.65	78.43
	Cora L Simpson......	240	123	56	20	36	5852½	537½	48.4	86.4
	Harriet E Willis.......	275	123	58	29	29	5922	651½	49.11	84.7
	Ella L Stevens.........	275	123	52	35	17	5508½	531½	45.46	87.42
	Hazel Taylor.........	225	123	53	28	25	5623½	644½	46.7	88.
	G May Forge..........	240	123	55	27	28	5458	788½	45.3	82.4
	Eunice J Brown......	275	123	57	33	24	5982½	629	49.	86.
	Fannie McLaren.......	275	123	60	25	35	5948½	1071½	49.81	83.01
	Edith L Mitchell.......	240	123	58	31	27	5760½	744	47.5	81.9
Wesley St...	Agnes Quirk...........	400	98	37	14	23	3115	326	31.75	85.
	Kate Hamilton........	240	98	54	27	27	3943	690	41.2	76.29
	Natalie Allain.........	275	98	43	20	23	3713½	478	39.75	92.24
	Elizabeth Richard.....	275	98	51	25	26	4169	526½	43.2	84.7
	Catherine Hennessey..	275	98	57	30	27	4458½	867½	46.	81.
	Evangeline M Bourque	240	98	58	32	26	4215	740	44.4	76.5
	Elodie E Bourque......	240	98	63	22	41	4205½	785	44.	70.
	Evangeline LeBlanc...	200	98	60	22	38	4468	792½	46.42	77.36

STATEMENT No. 5.

Term Ending 30th June, 1903. No. of Pupils in the several Standards of Instruction.

SUBJECTS.	I	II	III	IV	V	VI	VII	VIII	IX	X	XI	Totals.
Reading, Spelling and Recitation	310	213	229	244	207	145	156	101	....	....	....	1605
Composition	....	....	171	244	207	145	156	101	....	....	....	1024
Grammar and Analysis	....	....	171	244	207	145	156	101	....	....	....	1024
History	....	....	....	39	207	145	156	101	....	....	....	786
Form	310	213	229	244	206	145	156	101	....	....	....	1604
Industrial Drawing	310	213	229	244	206	145	156	101	....	....	....	1604
Print Script	310	213	229	244	207	145	156	101	....	....	....	1605
Writing	310	213	229	244	207	145	156	101	....	....	....	1605
Arithmetic	310	213	229	244	207	145	156	101	....	....	....	1605
Geometry	....	....	....	....	....	....	....	....	61	35	42	138
Agriculture and Botany	....	....	....	....	....	....	....	....	64	35	40	139
Algebra	....	....	....	....	....	....	156	101	61	35	42	395
Geography	....	....	213	244	207	145	156	101	61	35	42	1204
Mineral, Plant and Animal Life	273	131	225	220	201	145	156	101	....	....	....	1452
Colour	310	213	229	244	206	145	156	101	....	....	....	1604
Chemistry	....	....	....	....	....	....	....	....	....	35	42	77
Temp. Teachings of Science	310	213	228	244	207	145	156	101	....	....	....	1604
Physics	....	....	....	....	....	....	....	....	61	....	....	61
Physiology	....	....	....	....	....	....	....	....	....	35	32	67
Latin	....	....	....	....	....	....	100	97	49	24	36	306
French	67	....	....	40	27	....	20	10	62	32	38	296
Book-keeping	....	....	....	....	....	....	....	....	64	35	....	95
Trigonometry	....	....	....	....	....	....	....	....	....	....	3	3
English	....	....	....	....	....	....	....	....	64	35	42	141

STATEMENT No. 6.

Term Ending December 31st, 1903. Teachers and actual Attendance Returns.

SCHOOLS.	TEACHERS.	Salaries.	Days of Session.	Pupils Enroled.	Boys.	Girls.	Gross Days Pupils Attended.	Gross Days Lost.	Average Days Pupils Attended.	Percentage of Attendance.
Aberdeen....	George J. Oulton......	$850	79	28	6	22	1820½	122½	23.42	83.64
	G. Fred McNally......	650	79	45	19	26	2964	298½	38.73	86.
	H. B. Steeves..........	500	79	35	15	20	2283½	274½	29.6	84.6
	W. A. Cowperthwaite.	500	79	36	17	19	2503	206½	32.26	89.62
	S. B. Anderson........	565	79	51	23	28	3520	348	45.4	89.1
	Ethel Murphy.........	275	79	48	16	32	3140	502	40.	83.9
	Etta A. M. Cormick...	275	79	43	22	21	3013	343	38.72	90.04
	Alice Lea..............	275	79	56	30	26	3872½	330½	49.39	88.2
	Agnes McSweeney....	275	79	44	29	15	2890½	585½	37.	84.
	Mary A. Moore........	240	79	48	20	28	3263	418	41.98	87.4
	Amelia I. Smith......	275	79	55	28	27	3644½	413	47.3	86.
	Mabel E. McLeod......	275	79	49	23	26	2998½	872½	38.7	79.
	Elspeth Charters......	275	79	46	20	26	3091	448	40.	87.
	Emma Condon.........	275	79	58	28	30	3756½	836½	47.43	81.77
	Ella J. McKay........	275	79	62	32	30	3659	757½	47.5	76.6
	Lottie L. Weldon......	225	79	59	34	25	3697	964	47.81	81.03
Victoria.....	Samuel W. Irons.......	850	79	50	20	30	3450	258	44.316	88.62
	Catherine Barton......	275	79	52	17	35	3377	448	44.	84.61
	Mary H. McBeath....	240	79	51	27	24	3424	605	44.3	86.8
	Florence Murphy.....	240	79	52	30	22	3635	420	46.8	90.
	Ella L. Stevens........	275	79	53	33	20	3748½	337½	48.01	90.58
	Hazel M. Taylor......	240	79	63	29	34	4290½	572½	55.4	87.9
	G. May Forge	240	79	64	33	31	4236½	540½	54.7	85.5
	Eunice J. Brown.....	275	79	51	24	27	3556	450	45.3	89.
	Fanny McLaren.......	275	79	49	21	28	3265	489½	42.5	86.7
	Edith L. Mitchell.. ..	265	79	60	32	28	4148	370½	53.	88.4
Wesley St...	Agnes Quirke.........	400	81	43	14	29	3134	180	39.60	92.
	Kate E. Hamilton.....	265	79	59	30	29	3837	452	49.4	83.7
	Natalie Allain.........	275	81	58	25	33	4134	323	51.	87.
	Elizabeth Richard.....	275	81	56	26	30	3835	445½	48.59	86.76
	Catherine Hennessey..	275	81	61	31	30	4218	418	52.5	86.
	Evangeline LeBlanc...	200	81	71	28	43	4817½	557	60.28	84.90
	Evangeline M. Bourque	240	79	65	23	42	4193	392½	55.3	85.
	Elodie E. Bourque....	240	79	68	31	37	3885	447	53.	79.

STATEMENT No. 7.

Term ending 31st Dec, 1903. No. of Pupils in the several Standards of Instruction.

SUBJECTS.	I	II	III	IV	V	VI	VII	VIII	IX	X	XI	Totals
Reading, Spelling and Recitation	311	254	202	213	226	165	147	117	....	....	....	1635
Composition	....	....	212	158	226	165	99	117	....	....	....	977
Grammar and Analysis	....	....	212	158	226	165	99	117	....	....	....	977
History	....	....	....	42	226	165	147	117	71	45	27	840
Form	311	189	212	213	226	165	147	117	....	....	....	1580
Industrial Drawing	311	189	212	213	226	165	147	117	....	....	....	1580
Print Script	311	189	212	213	226	165	147	117	....	....	....	1580
Writing	311	189	212	213	226	165	147	117	....	....	....	1580
Arithmetic	311	254	212	213	226	114	147	66	71	45	28	1687
Geometry	....	....	....	....	....	....	....	....	36	45	28	109
Singing	211	245	212	158	105	79	147	67	....	....	....	1224
Algebra	....	....	....	....	....	....	95	117	71	45	27	355
Geography	....	....	212	162	226	114	147	117	71	45	27	1121
Mineral, Plant and Animal Life	232	254	212	158	158	79	95	117	....	....	....	1305
Colour	311	189	212	213	226	165	147	117	....	....	....	1580
English	....	....	....	....	....	....	....	....	71	45	28	144
Temp. Teachings of Science	252	254	162	213	226	114	147	117	....	....	....	1485
Physics	....	....	....	....	....	....	....	....	71	....	....	71
Physiology	....	....	....	....	....	....	....	....	....	45	....	45
Latin	....	....	....	....	....	....	131	109	71	45	28	384
French	121	....	14	44	25	....	27	14	71	44	27	387
Bookkeeping	....	....	....	....	....	....	....	....	71	....	....	71
Chemistry	....	....	....	....	....	....	....	....	....	....	28	28
Botany	....	....	....	....	....	....	....	....	71	45	27	143
Agriculture	....	....	....	....	....	....	....	....	71	45	25	141
Greek	....	....	....	....	....	....	....	....	....	....	1	1

STATEMENT No. 8.

Total School Debentures Outstanding December 31st, 1902.

DATE OF ISSUE.	Years to run.	WHEN DUE	Numbers	Value Each	Total Amount	Rate %	Total Interest	INTEREST PAYABLE. Jan.	Mch.	April	July	Sept.	Oct.
August 1, 1874	20	August 1, 1894	9 to 17	$ 500	$4000	5%	$200				$200		
January 1, 1885	20	January 1, 1905	38 to 40	500	1500	6%	90	45			45		
July 1, 1886	20	July 1, 1906	41	500	500	6%	30	15			15		
July 13, 1889	20	July 13, 1909	42 to 61	500	10000	6%	600	300			300		
			62 to 70	1000									
January 1, 1890	20	January 1, 1910	71 to 76	500	12000	5%	000	300			300		
			34 to 53	500									
July 2, 1890	19	July 2, 1909	54 to 57	500	10000	4%	400	200			200		
March 2, 1891	18	March 2, 1909	94 to 100	500	2000	4%	80		$40			$40	
July 2, 1891	18	July 2, 1909	1 to 20	1000	3500	4%	140	70			70		
October 1, 1897	25	October 1, 1922	21 to 27	1000	20000	4%	800			$400			$400
January 1, 1898	25	January 1, 1923	28 to 40	1000	7000	4%	280	140			140		
October 1, 1898	25	October 1, 1923			13000	4%	520			260			260
					$85500		$3740	$1070	$40	$660	$1270	$40	$660

NOTE.—Bond No. 32, $500 issued July 1, 1881, fell due July 1, 1901. It was paid out of the current revenue. Bond No. 33, issued July 1, 1881 was paid in 1902 out of current revenue.

Bonds Nos. 34 to 37 issued July 1, 1882, fell due July 1, 1903, and were paid out of current revenue.

SCHOOL TRUSTEES RECEIPTS FOR 1903.

STATEMENT No. 9.

Standing Committees, 1903.

FINANCE.

MR H. H. AYER. MR. JAS. FLANAGAN. MR. H. S. BELL. MR. J. H. HARRIS.

REPAIRS.

DR. BOURQUE. MR J. H. HARRIS. MRS. PURDY.

TEACHERS AND SCHOOL PROPERTY.

THE FULL BOARD.

NAMES OF TRUSTEES APPOINTED BY CITY COUNCIL.

Term:—Women 3 years; Men 4 years.

DATE OF APPOINTMENT.	NAMES.	IN LIEU OF.
1899, December 8	Mr. H. H. Ayer	Mr. H. H. Ayer
1901, March 5	Mr. J. H. Harris	Mr. G. B. Willett
1901, March 22	Mr. H. S. Bell	Mr. W. D. Martin
1902, January 10	L. N. Bourque, M D.	L. N. Bourque, M.D.
1902, June 17	Miss Hattie Tweedie	Miss Hattie Tweedie

NAMES OF TRUSTEES APPOINTED BY THE GOVERNMENT.

DATE OF APPOINTMENT.	NAMES.	IN LIEU OF.
1899, March 8	Mrs. Annie Purdy	Mrs. E. R. Atkinson
1903, February 11	Mr. Jas. Doyle	Mr. A. E. Wall (resigned)
1903, July 15	Mr. J. T. Hawke	Mr. J. T. Hawke
1903, July 15	Mr. Jas. Flanagan	Mr. Jas. Flanagan

SCHOOL TRUSTEES' RECEIPTS FOR YEAR 1903.

Tuition Fees, C. Lean, ...		$ 3 00
" " Jos Bishop, ...		3 00
Cash from City, ...		2,161 49
Cash from County fund, ...		1,236 91
Cash from City, ...		1,655 92
" "		1,381 91
" "		2,371 86
....		1,312 24
" "		3,742 20
Cash from County fund, ...		1,359 68
Cash from City, ...		2,457 35
" "		1,205 96
" "		1,269 23
B. Tucker, Tuition fees, ...		3 00
A. LeBlanc, " "		6 00
Ada McGinn, " "		6 00
B. Tucker, " "		6 00
Mary Turner, " "		5 00
B. Snow, " "		6 00
Cash from City, ...		1,703 94
" "		137 90
Cash from J. H. Harris (ashes, 25 bbls., at 65c.)		13 00
		$22,047 59
Received for Victoria play ground—		
Cash from E. A. Smith, sale of Waterloo bldg., ...	$200 00	
Cash, assessment from City, ...	500 00	
Cash, from City, sale Lutz street lot, ...	100 00	
Cash, G. Christmas, sale Lutz street lot, ...	338 00	
		1,138 00
Total receipts for 1903, ...		$23,185 59

EXPENDITURES 1903.

Dec. 31,	By	Salaries, Teachers and Officers	$12,183 20
"	"	Janitors Salaries	1,541 00
"	"	Expenses	296 05
"	"	Repairs	94 02
"	"	Interest	3,902 58
"	"	Insurance	48 00
	"	Fuel	1,420 67
"	"	Water	226 60
"	"	School Supplies	163 50
"	"	Furniture	112 20
"	"	Rent	17 00
"	"	Electric Light	45 00
"	"	Gas	8 20
"	"	Real Estate	33 00

Total Ordinary Expenditure for 1903 .... $20091 02

Dec. 31. By Bonds (4) Nos. 34 to 37, $500 each paid out of Current account during 1903 .... 2000 00

" Victoria Play Ground 1138 00

SPECIAL REPAIRS.

Furnaces, Aberdeen	$450 00	
" Victoria	61 49	
Supports, Aberdeen	87 50	
Asphalt Victoria Building	137 90	
		736 89
Total expenditure for 1903		$23,965 91

VICTORIA PLAY GROUND ACCOUNT.

		Dr.	Cr.
1902.			
Feb. 20.	By amt. borrowed at 5 p.c., Victoria P. G., ...		$2,000 00
Nov. 15.	" Interest to date, Oct. 31, 1902,		72 35
1903.			
Apr. 30.	" " "		57 36
May 16.	To Cash received from City, ...	$500 00	
July 31.	By Interest, ...		21 66
Aug. 3.	To Proceeds sale Waterloo building and lot, E. A. Smith, ...	200 00	
Oct. 31.	By Interest, ...		18 20
Dec. 31.	To Cash from City, Lutz street, 24 ft. x 8 ft., ...	100 00	
Dec. 31.	To Cash, G. Christmas, re Lutz Street,	338 00	
Dec. 31.	To Balance due Bank of Montreal,	1,025 57	
		$2,163 57	$2,163 57

RECAPITULATION OF VOUCHERS.

January	$ 642 43	
February	2508 29	
March	1277 68	
April	1326 46	
May	1312 24	
June	3392 78	
July	3 75	
August	1405 80	
September	1180 96	
October	1132 13	
November	3227 29	
December	2681 21	
		$20091 02
To Bonds Nos. 34 to 37 (4) paid out of current account, year 1903		2000 00
To Victoria Play Ground account		1138 00
To Special Repairs		736 89
To Balance due Bank January 1st, 1903		1335 25
		$25301 16

ESTIMATES MONCTON SCHOOLS, 1903 AND 1904.

	Estimates, 1903.	Estimates, 1904.
y Salaries Teachers and Officers	$ 12404 00	$ 12800 00
" " Janitors	1600 00	1644 00
" Repairs	400 00	1000 00
" Furnaces, Victoria		150 00
" Expenses	250 00	300 00
" Interest	4150 00	3900 00
" Insurance	50 00	276 00
" Fuel	1800 00	1600 00
" Water	225 00	150 00
" School Supplies	125 00	200 00
" Furniture	150 00	150 00
" Rent	12 00	12 00
" Real Estate		50 00
" Electric Light	15 00	25 00
" Gas		10 00
" Balance due Victoria Play Ground....	500 00	1000 00
	$22181 00	$23417 00
Less County Fund estimated 1904	2281 00	2281 00
	$19900 00	$21136 00

TOWN OF ST. STEPHEN

BOARD OF SCHOOL TRUSTEES.

TO JAMES R. INCH, ESQ., LL. D.
Chief Supt. of Education.

SIR: I have the honor to present for your consideration the report o the Board of School Trustees of the Town of St. Stephen for year endin June 30th, 1903.

The term of office of Miss Grace B. Stevens as trustee, having expired she was re-appointed by the Town Council, the composition of the Bo thus remaining unchanged.

Miss Jessie H. Whitlock, after a long and faithful service on the teac ing staff, resigned at the close of the term ending December 30th. Mi Ethel H. Jarvis was transferred from the High School to fill the vacancy caused by Miss Whitlock's resignation and Miss Olivia Maxwell resumed her work in the High School..

The graduation exercises of the High School were held as usual i the Rink and each year are attracting more public attention.

Respectfully submitted,

LEWIS A. MILLS, Secretary

June 30th 1903.

RECEIPTS AND EXPENDITURES

Of Board of School Trustees of the Town of Saint Stephen for the Year ended June 30, 1903.

1902.			
July 14,	To amount from Town Treasurer, ...	$4,000 00	
Aug. 21,	" " County Fund, ...	378 72	
Dec. 6,	" " Town Treasurer, ...	1,500 00	
1903			
June 26,	" " "	700 00	
Feb. 10,	" " County Fund, ...	405 91	
			$6,984 63

Cr.

1902			
June 30,	By balance, ...	$ 828 50	
1903			
June 30,	By amount paid Teachers' Salaries, ...	4,265 00	
"	" " for Repairs, ...	199 25	
	" " Care of Rooms, ...	413 72	
	" " Contingencies, ...	394 65	
	" " Fuel, ...	111 36	
	" " Interest, ...	25 80	
	Bal...........	746 65	
			$6,984 63

TABULAR STATEMENT.

Showing Names of Teachers, Class, Salary, Etc., for the Term Ending December 31st, 1902.

SCHOOL.	NAME OF TEACHER.	Class.	Salary.	Pupils. Boys.	Pupils. Girls.	Average Daily Attendance.	Per Cent Attendance.	Standards Taught.
High School	P. G. McFarlane	I	$700	32	15	39.68	82.72	IX., X., XI.
	M. Olivia Maxwell	I	260	3	17	17.78	88.75	IX., X., XI.
Marks Street	F. O. Sullivan	I	665	35	43	66.90	85.76	VII., VIII.
	Etta E. DeWolfe, Assistant	I	320					
	M. F. Boyd	I	260	28	24	43.68	68.74	V., VI.
	J. D. Henry	I	280	31	24	47.00	86.6	V., VI.
	Mercy Murray	I	300	26	17	37.73	87.74	III., IV.
	Bertha M. Brown	I	260	26	30	46.6	83.2	V., VI.
Cove	C. H. Murray	I	320	22	24	37.13	80.72	III., IV.
	Ella M. Veazey	I	320	27	30	44.34	77.78	I., II.
King Street	Emma Veazey	I	260	26	16	37.63	89.6	III., IV.
	Jessie Whitlock	I	320	31	29	48.59	80.98	I. II.

TABULAR STATEMENT.

Showing Names of Teachers, Class, Sa'ary, Etc., for the Term Ending June 30th, 1903.

SCHOOLS.	NAMES OF TEACHERS.	Class.	Salary.	Pupils. Boys.	Pupils. Girls.	Average Daily Attendance.	Per Cent Attendance.	Standards Taught.
High School	P. G. McFarlane.	I	$700	13	20	27.73	84.03	IX., X., XI.
	M. Olivia Maxwell	I	260	8	15	20.43	88.86	IX., X., XI.
Marks Street	F. O. Sullivan	I	665	30	44	59.56	80.89	VII., VIII.
	Etta E. DeWolfe, Assistant	I	320					
	M. F. Boyd	I	280	26	26	40.22	77.34	V., VI.
	J. D. Henry	I	280	30	22	42.00	82.1	V., VI.
	Mercy Murray	I	300	23	15	33.62	88.49	III. IV.
	Bertha M. Brown	I	260	26	28	46.01	88.06	V. VI.
Cove	C. H. Murray	I	320	20	24	33.83	76.88	III., IV.
	Ella M. Veazey	I	320	27	30	43.77	76.78	I., II.
King Street	Emma Veazey	I	260	26	17	38.2	88.9	III. IV.
	Ethel H. Jarvis	I	260	31	29	43.53	72.55	I., II.

TOWN OF MILLTOWN.

Board of School Trustees.

To J. R. Inch, LL. D.,
Chief Superintendent.

Report to June 30th, 1903.

No changes have occurred in the teaching staff during the year, but at the close Miss Amy D. Young and Miss Caie have terminated their engagements and Miss Bessie A. Young has applied for leave of absence for one year.

Mr. Henry E. Sinclair has been engaged. He will take in Grade VII. and together with Mr. Sutherland will teach all from VII to XI, thereby dispensing with one teacher.

The graduating exercises were observed in the Presbyterian church in the evening of June 30th. Rev. Mr. Robertson of that church very happily addressed the Graduating Class, after which followed a reception of their friends and the public, by the class, in the vestry.

The Board will start a department of manual training with the new school year. For this purpose they are fitting an excellent building given by the Canadian Colored Cotton Mills Co.

The statements of attendance, &c., half yearly, and statements of expenditures for the school year are herewith submitted as follows:

STATEMENT, DECEMBER, 31, 1902.

Days.	School.	Teacher.	No. Boys.	No. Girls.	Total.	Present Average.	Per cent. Average.	Standards.
82	Superior.	J. B. Sutherland ..	10	25	35	32.2	92.1	IX., X., XI.
82	"	I. J. Caie	4	11	15	12.81	85.44	VIII.
82	Intermediate.	M. C. Osborne....	6	23	29	24.43	84.2	VII.
82	"	B. A. Young . .	24	12	36	32.67	90.75	VI.
82	"	M. E. Connolly . ..	18	27	45	39.12	86.9	V.
82	"	C. M. Caswell.....	28	13	41	37.24	90.82	IV.
80	2nd Primary.	A. D. Young	21	24	45	36.8	81.77	II., III.
81	Primary.	M. A. Sutherland..	23	19	42	37.05	88.21	I., II.
81	"	T. S. Kirk...... ..	20	7	27	25.55	94.62	I., II., III.

STATEMENT, JUNE 30TH, 1903.

Days.	School.	Teacher.	No. Boys.	No. Girls.	Total.	Present Average.	Per cent. Average.	Standards.
122	Superior.	J. B. Sutherland.	11	27	38	34.09	89.6	IX., X., XI.
122	High.	I. J. Caie	4	11	15	11.86	79.07	VIII.
121	Intermediate.	M. C. Osborne.....	5	23	28	23.06	82.35	VII.
122	"	B. A. Young . .	25	11	36	28.95	80.	VI.
120	"	M. E. Connolly ...	18	29	47	39.15	83.2	V.
122	"	C. M. Caswell	27	13	40	33.90	84.75	IV.
121½	2nd Primary.	A. D. Young	21	23	44	33.91	77.07	II., III.
122	Primary.	T. S. Kirk.......	19	7	26	23.51	90.42	I., II., III.
122	"	M. A. Sutherland..	22	18	40	33.91	84.77	I., II.

EXPENDITURES

For School Year ending June 30, 1903

Salaries for Teachers, ...	**$2,141 50**
Construction Account, ...	**247 10**
Expense "	**365 49**
Grading Lot, ...	**121 53**
Insurance, ...	**12 75**
Fuel, ...	**93 75**
Care of Rooms, ...	**267 00**
Total, ...	**$3,749 12**

Respectfully submitted,

E. H. BALKAM, ***Secretary.***

W. W. GRAHAM, ***Chairman.***

Milltown, June 30, 1903

TOWN OF CHATHAM.

Board of School Trustees.

To James R. Inch, LL. D.,
Chief Superintendent af Education.

Sir,—I herewith submit report of our schools for year ending June 30th 1903.

Miss Annie M. Loggie, who holds a Superior Licence, was appointed to the vacancy made by the resignation of Miss Anna G. McIntosh and placed in charge of Grade VII, in the Grammar School Building.

Miss Bessie Creighton resigned from the Ellis Street School and Miss Muriel Ellis was appointed in her place.

The progress of the pupils during the year was affected by the prevalence of disease in the town. Schools were closed by order of the Board of Health all the month of May.

The Governor General's Medal was won by Miss Ellen Fraser for highest standing.

Attached you will find statements showing names of teachers, pupils enrolled, financial statement and cost of new building.

Respectfully submitted,

GEORGE STOTHART, *Secretary*.

Cost of New School Building, Chatham, N. B.

Land, fencing and grading.	$ 1,940 16	
John McDonald, contractor, building, ...	30,828 68	
McManus heating and plumbing....	6,350 00	
Inspectors and architect, ...	2,403 50	
Furniture, ...	472 59	
Electric lighting, sewers, and basement floor,	439 08	
Miscellaneous, ...	474 99	
Insurance, ...	225 00	
Interest on money borrowed and discount on bonds,	2,001 39	
Total,		$45,135 34

(Signed) ALFRED SEELY, *Auditor.*

Financial Statement for Year Ending June 30th, 1903.

EXPENDITURES.

For salaries, ...	$6,120 83	
Rent, ...	160 00	
Fuel, water and light, ...	555 88	
Insurance	58 75	
Interest, ...	1,856 85	
Bond paid, ...	250 00	
Incidentals, ...	301 33	
		$9,303 64

RECEIPTS.

County School Fund, ...	$1,544 61	
Town Treasurer, ...	7,520 00	
Tuition fees, ...	35 00	
		$9,099 61
Balance,		$204 03

Names of Teachers, Number of Pupils and Grades Taught for Term Ended December 31st, 1902.

TEACHERS.	Salaries.	Boys.	Girls.	Total.	Grades Taught.
Philip Cox, Ph. D.	$750	15	14	29	IX., XI.
James McIntosh.........	500	18	18	36	IX.
R. W. Alward...........	450	30	14	44	VII., VIII.
Miss Annie M. Loggie....	200	26	19	45	VII.
" M. Mowatt.........	280	23	18	41	VI.
" Ida Haviland.......	200	34	12	46	V.
" Maude K. Lawlor...	200	28	18	46	III. IV.
" Laula S. Smith......	200	37	19	56	I. II.
" K. I. B. McLean....	200	22	6	28	III., IV.
" Muriel Ellis........	200	29	14	43	I., II.
Sister Ellen Walsh	200	..	..	..	
Miss M. Beckwith, Asst.		..	82	82	I., II.
Sister E. O. Keefe......	200	..	56	56	III., IV.
" S. Jane Currie....	200	..	46	46	V., VI.
" M. Barden	280	..	..	..	
Miss C McDonald, Asst.		..	53	53	VII., VIII., IX. X.
Miss M. C. Edgar.......	280	22	11	33	VI.
" Essie L. Keoughan,	200	34	16	50	V.
" V. C. Wright.......	200	29	19	48	IV.
" Mabel J. Flood.....	200	32	17	49	III.
" Annie M. Curran.....	200	31	21	52	II.
" K. A. McDonald....	200	35	17	52	I.
" M. C. Sutherland...	200	30	22	52	I.
Totals		475	512	987	

Number of Pupils in Grades.

I.	II.	III.	IV.	V.	VI.	VII.	VIII.	IX.	X.	XI.
197	140	114	113	125	91	80	42	64	8	13

Names of Teachers, Number of Pupils and Grades taught for Term ended June 30th, 1903.

TEACHERS.	Salaries.	Boys.	Girls.	Total.	Grades Taught.
Philip Cox, Ph. D.	$750	15	13	28	IX., XI.
James McIntosh.........	500	17	16	33	IX.
R. W. Alward..........	450	29	13	42	VII., VIII.
Miss Annie M. Loggie...	200	26	18	44	VII.
" M. Mowatt........	280	23	16	39	VI.
" Ida I. Haviland.. .	200	33	12	45	V.
" Maude K. Lawlor...	200	27	18	45	III., IV.
" Laula S. Smith.....	200	35	18	53	I., II.
" Muriel Ellis....	200	28	13	41	I., II.
" K. I. B. McLean...	200	23	6	29	III., IV.
Sister M. Barden / Miss C. McDonald, Asst.	280	...	56	56	VII., VIII., IX.
Sister S. Jane Curry.....	200	..	44	44	V., VI.
" E. O. Keefe.......	200	..	55	55	III., IV.
" Ellen Walsh / Miss M. Beckwith, Asst.	200	..	75	75	I., II.
" Miss M. C. Edgar...	280	28	9	37	IV., VI.
" Essie L. Keoughan...	200	37	16	53	V.
" V. C. Wright......	200	28	19	47	IV.
" Mabel I. Flood....	200	29	19	48	III.
" A. M. Curran......	200	29	21	50	II.
" K. A. McDonald....	200	31	13	44	I.
" M. C. Sutherland...	200	25	22	47	I.
Totals		463	492	955	

Number of Pupils in Grades.

I.	II.	III.	IV.	V.	VI.	VII.	VIII.	IX.	XI.
172	138	110	119	125	88	82	38	71	12

TOWN OF WOODSTOCK.

Board of School Trustees.

J. R. INCH, ESQ. LL. D.,
Chief Superintendent of Education.

SIR,—The Board of School Trustees for the Town of Woodstock submit the following statement of their receipts and expenditure for the year ending June, 30th, 1903.

RECEIVED.

Balance in Treasurer's hands July, 1st, 1902, ...	$ 248 98	
Received from County Drafts	854 94	
" " Town Assessment	4,800 00	
" " McDonald Rural School Fund	200 00	
" " Rentals	8 00	
" " Interest on deposits	5 45	
		$6,113 37

PAID OUT.

Teachers, Summer Term, ...	$1,637 00	
" Winter Term, ...	2,357 00	
Janitors, ...	359 03	
Secretary, ...	100 00	
Land for McDonald School, ...	300 00	
Insurance, ...	159 50	
Repairs and Incidentals, ...	305 82	
Fuel, ...	277 00	
Interest on Debentures, ...	360 50	
Balance, ...	257 52	
		$6,113 37

SUMMER TERM.

TEACHERS.	Standards Taught.	Per cent. Pupils daily present.	No. of Pupils.
Minnie Carman	I. and II.	88.22	58
Ella Smith	I. and II.	82.69	52
Mary Milmore	I. and II.	81.71	48
Frances Peters	III. and IV.	91.42	68
Lydia E. Alexander	III. and IV.	85.217	46
Elizabeth Cupples	III. and IV.	85.68	51
Helena Mulherrin	V. and VI.	83.41	56
Kate Appleby	V. and VI.	83.071	35
Alexandra Comben	V. and VI.	82.3	36
Myrtle Harmon	VII. and VIII.	74.86	45
N. F. Thorne	VII. and VIII.	79.3	42
Frank A. Good	VII. and VIII.	79.4	42
Julia Neales	IX.	79.86	56
G. H. Harrison	X. and XI.	78.2	27
			657

WINTER TERM.

TEACHERS.	Standards Taught.	Per cent. Pupils daily present.	No. of Pupils.
Minnie Carman..............	I. and II.	79.98	61
Maud McAdam..............	I. and II.	72.72	55
Mary Milmore..............	I. and II.	69.54	46
Frances Peters..............	III. and IV.	84.81	65
Lydia E. Alexander..........	III. and IV.	86.5	47
Elizabeth Cupples............	III. and IV.	87.48	50
Helena Mulherrin..............	V and VI.	87 69	52
Kate Appleby..............	V. and VI.	81.73	38
Alexandra Comben..........	V. and VI.	76.	39
Myrtle Harmon..............	VII. and VIII.	70.02	46
N. F. Thorne..............	VII. and VIII.	78.	40
Frank A. Good..............	VII. and VIII.	75.1	44
Julia Neales..........	IX.	70.60	50
G. H. Harrison............	X. and XI.	79.82	27
			660

Sir William McDonald having, through Prof. James W. Robertson donated the sum of $200.00, the Board has procured land for school gardens in connection with the schools. The Board has also taken up the matter of Manual Training. A teacher, Miss A. G. O'Brien, has been engaged for this special work, and it is expected that on the reopening of the schools the Board will be prepared with a proper equipment to take up this important branch and carry it on successfully.

Respectfully submitted,

July 11th, 1903. A. B. CONNELL, *Secretary.*

TOWN OF NEWCASTLE.

Board of School Trustees.

To J. R. INCH., ESQ., LL. D.,
Chief Superintendent of Education.

SIR,—The Board of School Trustees of the Town of Mewcastle submit the following statement of the receipts and expenditures for the School Year ending on 30th June, 1903.

RECEIVED.

1902.			
July	1	By balance in Royal Bank of Canada,	$1,089 36
Aug.	29	Amount from County Treasurer,	401 91
Aug.	29	" Chief Superintendent,	13 50
Nov.	15	" Town Treasurer,	1,000 00
Dec.	26	"	1,000 00
1903.			
Feb'y	13	" J. J. Clarke, ...	12 84
	29	" County Treasurer....	383 33
March		" Town Treasurer, ...	1,232 61
			$5,133 55

EXPENDED.

For Salaries, ...	$3,414 02	
Fuel, ...	480 33	
Furniture, ...	113 03	
Repairs, ...	72 85	
Rent, ...	200 00	
Insurance, ...	44 00	
Interest, ...	320 00	
Sinking Fund, ...	200 00	
Printing, ...	15 50	
Incidentals, ...	32 35	
Balance in Royal Bank of Canada, ...	241 47	
		$5,133 55

STATEMENT.—First Term.

TEACHERS.	No. Boys	No. Girls	Total	Grades Taught.
A. Ernest G. McKenzie....	16	25	41	IX., X., XI.
M. J. Dunnet............	32	16	48	V.
E. McLachlan............	24	14	38	VI.
A. I. Bell	53	25	78	I., II.
S. M. Harriman..........	44	26	70	I., II.
P. F. Morrissy...........	5	10	15	I., III., V., VIII.
H. M. MacLeod..........	17	28	45	I. II. III. IV. V. VI. VIII.
J. J. Clarke, B. M. Reid, A. Craig }	24	24	48	VIII.
L. B. Troy..............	35	16	51	III., IV.
A. O. McLeod............	31	21	52	III., IV.
M. G. Duffy.............	22	18	40	VII.
Totals....	203	223	526	

STATEMENT.—Second Term.

TEACHERS.	No. Boys	No. Girls	Total	Grades Taught.
A. Ernest G. McKenzie....	17	26	43	IX., X., XI.
M. J. Dunnet, I. P. Leighton }	31	13	44	V.
L. B. Troy..............	23	12	35	VI.
A. I. Bell...............	51	25	76	I., II.
K. J. Fleming...........	46	24	70	I., II.
P. F. Morrissy...........	6	9	15	I., III., V. VIII.
H. M. MacLeod..........	16	28	44	I., II., IV., V., VI., VII
B. M. Reid..............	21	20	41	VIII.
A. O. McLeod, I. P. Leighton }	31	22	53	III., IV.
S. M. Harriman......	34	18	52	III., IV.
M. G. Duffy.........	17	12	29	VII.
Totals............	293	209	502	

Respectfully submitted,

P. F. MORRISSY, *Secretary*, R. NICHOLSON, M. D., *Chairman*

Newcastle, N. B., June 30th, 1903.

TOWN OF CAMPBELLTON.

J. R. INCH, ESQ, LL.D.,
Chief Superintendent of Education.
Fredericton N. B.

SIR,—We herewith submit for your consideration a statement showing the receipts and expenditure of the Board of School Trustees for the Town of Campbellton, together with statistical tables etc. for the school year ending June 30th 1903.

TABLE NO. 1.

Showing names of teachers, grades taught, number of pupils, etc., during term ending December 31st, 1902.

No.	Name of Teacher.	Class of License.	Department.	*Yearly Salary.	No. of Boys.	No. of Girls.	Totals.	Grades Taught.
1	E. W. Lewis, B. A.	G. S.	Grammar.	$650	15	23	38	IX., X., XI.
2	Catherine F. Mair, B. A.	Sup. I.	Advanced.	350	18	20	38	VII., VIII.
3	Bertha I. Asker	Second.	Intermediate.	225	31	17	48	VI., VII.
4	Lydia Duncan	"	"	225	26	30	56	V.
5	Mary McRae...........	"	"	225	24	24	48	III., IV.
6	Clara Shannon..........	"	"	225	36	22	58	III., IV.
7	Mary J. Cooke..........	"	Primary.	225	31	29	60	I., II.
8	Martha G. Barnes.......	First.	"	275	36	25	61	I., II.

*Exclusive of Government allowance.

TABLE NO. 2.

Showing names of teachers, grades taught, number of pupils, etc., during term ending June 30th, 1903.

No.	Name of Teacher.	Class of License.	Department.	*Yearly Salary.	No. of Boys.	No. of Girls.	Totals.	Grades Taught.
1	E. M. Lewis, B. A... ...	G. S.	Grammar.	$650	14	19	33	IX., X., XI.
2	Catherine F. Mair, B. A.	Sup. I.	Advanced.	350	19	23	42	VII., VIII.
3	Bertha I. Asker	Second.	"	225	33	17	50	VI., VII.
4	Lydia Duncan..........	"	Intermediate.	225	23	28	51	V.
5	Mary McRae............	"	"	225	22	29	51	III., IV.
6	Clara Shannon..........	"	"	225	35	20	55	III., IV.
7	Mary J. Cooke..........	"	Primary.	225	31	29	60	I., II.
8	Martha G. Barnes......	First.	"	275	35	25	60	I., II.

*Exclusive of Government allowance.

Financial Statement for year ending June 30th 1903.

RECEIPTS.

1902			
June 1	Cash on hand,	$ 11 11	
	Town Treasurer	3,750 00	
	County Treasurer	712 62	
	Tuition Fees	33 50	
1903.			
June 30	Overdraft, Bank of N. S.	141 48	
			$4,648 71

EXPENDITURES.

Paid.	Interest on debentures	$ 800 00	
	Exchange on drafts	2 00	
	Teachers' salaries	2580 00	
	Janitor's salary	320 76	
	Secretary's salary	91 63	
	Manual Training Department. (equipment.)	297 31	
	Supplies	148 10	
	Printing	16 65	
	Fuel	275 25	
	Auditors	7 50	
	Contingent expenses	9 32	
	High School Ent. Exam. fees	32 20	
	Furniture	17 00	
	Water	32 49	
	Freight	4 49	
	Interest on overdrafts	14 01	
			$4,648 72

Respectfully submitted.

S. LAUGHLAN, JR., *Secretary.*

D. MURRAY, M. D., *Chairman.*

Campbellton, N. B., June 30th, 1903.

REPORT OF CITY OF ST. JOHN.

BOARD OF SCHOOL TRUSTEES.

APPOINTED BY THE LIEUT. GOVERNOR IN COUNCIL	Retire.	APPOINTED BY COMMON COUNCIL	Retire.
Arthur I. Trueman, *Chairman*	1906	Walter W. White, M. D.	1903
James V. Russell	1903	Mrs. M. Dever	1904
W. C. Rudman Allan	1904	David H. Nase	1905
John Keefe	1905	Michael Coll	1906
Mrs. E. C. Skinner	1907	Robert Maxwell	1907
		C. Berton Lockhart	1908

Committeee.

REAL ESTATE AND BUILDINGS.	SCHOOLS AND TEACHERS.	FINANCE
M. Coll, *Chairman*	A. I. Trueman, *Chr'm.*	W. W. White, *Chr'n.*
D. H. Nase	M. Coll	W. C. R. Allan.
R. Maxwell	D. H. Nase	C. B. Lockhart.
J. V. Russell	W. C. R. Allan	J. Keefe
Mrs. E. C. Skinner	W. W. White, M. D.	R. Maxwell
Mrs. M. Dever	C. B. Lockhart	
C. B. Lockhart	J. V. Russell	
	J. Keefe	
	Mrs. M. Dever	
	Mrs. E. C. Skinner	
	R. Maxwell	

Henry S. Bridges, M. A., Ph. D., *Superintendent.*

Edward Manning, A. M., *Secretary.*

James Coll, *Clerk.*

J. R. INCH, ESQ., LL. D.,
Chief Superintendent of Education.

SIR,—We have the honor to present for your consideration our report on the public schools of the City of Saint John for the year ending June 30th, 1903, being the thirty-second report of this Board.

At the beginning of the school year Mrs. Skinner was reappointed by the Lieutenant Governor in Council, and H. J. Olive by the Common Council of the city. Shortly after Mr. Olive departed from the city for Washington State in the neighbouring Republic, after five years of faithful and unremitting service at this Board.

Mr. C. Berton Lockhart, who had previously been a member of the Board, was appointed by the Common Council to take Mr. Olive's place.

The Board met regularly on the second Monday of each month, and also held eight special meetings. Besides this the different committees and subcommittees have held several meetings on matters of local or immediate requirements. The chairmen of the Building and Finance Committees were reappointed at the beginning of the year.

THE PLAN OF VISITATION TO THE SCHOOLS WAS AS FOLLOWS:

Buildings.	Departments.	Official Visitors.
Sandy Point Road, Millidgeville, Alexandra, Newman Street, Douglas Avenue, Dufferin, St. Peter's Boys, St. Peter's Girls.	45	M. Coll, D. H. Nase.
Victoria, Victoria Annex......	19	Dr. White, J. V. Russell.
High School....	13	A. I. Trueman, Dr. White.
St. Vincent's..............	7	A. I. Trueman, J. Keefe.
Winter Street..............	12	C. B. Lockhart, R. Maxwell.
Centennial	10	J. V. Russell, R. Maxwell.
St. Joseph's...............	7	J. Keefe, W. C. R. Allan.
St. Malachi's..............	11	A. I. Trueman, J. Keefe.
Queen St., Brittain St........	2	W. C. R. Allan.
Albert, Latour, St. Patrick's, Leinster Street..........	25	W. C. R. Allan, C. B. Lockhart.
	151	

During the year one room of grade VIII pupils was removed from the High School Building to the Victoria, and one additional room opened in each of the following buildings:—Alexandra, St. Peter's Boys, St. Vincent's and Latour.

THE CHANGES IN THE TEACHING STAFF WERE AS FOLLOWS:

Resigned.	School.	Appointed.
James Barry...........	St. Malachi's, Grade VIII	J Harrington, S Peter's B
	St. Peter's Boys, Grades VIII., VI.	M. D. Coll.
	St. Peter's Boys, new school.	M. McGuire.
M. Gallagher...........	St. Malachi's, Grade IV.	Elizabeth Hayes.
A. M. Iddles...........	Victoria, Grade VII.	L. M. Kavanagh.
F. Henderson...........	" " III.	
	Alexandra, Grade V, new school.	E. McDougall.
N. H. Shaw...........	Victoria, Grade II.	E. L Colwell.
	Alexandra, Grade II.	J. McLean.
L. Wetmore...........	Leinster Street.	H. Comben.
M. Stewart...........	Victoria Annex.	L. Stewart.
L. Beckwith...........	High School Assistant.	A. Whittaker.
	Latour, Grade III, new school.	Lottie Fullerton.
	St. Vincent's, new school assistants.	Isabelle Reed. Ethel Emery. F. Estabrooks. Ida Keagin. Ella Wetmore. Ada Wright.

Besides the above changes in the staff a vacancy in the Principalship of Leinster St. School was caused by the death of Mr. John McKinnon in May last. Mr. McKinnon had been in the service of the Board for nearly twenty years and had proved himself a faithful, painstaking and successful teacher, and his death was sincerely regretted by his fellow-teachers and the members of the Board. Mr. A. L. Dykeman was transfered from the Victoria Annex to take his place. The withdrawal of Miss Amy Iddles, one of our best teachers, who went to Johannesburg to accept a position in the educational department of the Transvaal Government, as well as that of Mr. Jas. Barry who had been the efficient principal of St. Malachi's School since 1879 were regarded as distinct losses to the teaching staff of the city.

The lady Trustees have, as in previous years visited all the schools, and have exercised a special supervision over the comfort and welfare of teachers and pupils. Dr. Bridges also has efficiently performed his duties as Superintendent and Principal of the High School, and has given entire satisfaction to the Board.

The examinations at the high school at Midsummer showed the following results:—

Winner of corporation glod medal, *dux* of the school..... William Woods.
Parker silver medal, *dux* in mathematics............... Clara Fritz.
Governor General's silver medal for grade X........... E. Stanley Bridges.
Chairman's gold medal for grades VIII (whole city.)..... Lyle Kennedy
Hon. J. V. Ellis gold medal for essay.... .... Francis Bell.

No bonds matured this year, but the Board paid $2051.26 on the sinking fund account, making the amount to its credit in this fund $11,840.21.

The Board, as intimated in several previous annual reports, has long had in mind the project of replacing the old Madras School building in Elm Street by a modern building. Before the beginning of the present school year they had obtained from the Provincial Government authorization to issue bonds for this purpose.

Accordingly, on July 15th, 1902, an issue of $35,000 bonds at 3½ per cent. interest was published, which sold as follows:

$ 1,000 at ½ of 1 per cent. premium.
16,000 " ¼ of 1 " "
500 at par.

Half of the issue still remains unsold.

The erection of a fine building containing ten rooms and assembly hall on Elm Street called the Dufferin school, was the event of the year.

The lot on which the building is placed is on Elm Street, North End, near its junction with Military road and is of an irregular shape, having, a frontage on Elm Street of about 264 feet, and a width at the back of about 73 feet with a total depth of 195 feet, containing nearly three fourths of an acre.

The building is three stories and a basement, the upper storey being mainly in the mansard roof.

The arrangement of the rooms is in the manner of the "Cart Wheel" plan each room being so placed as to bring the burst of light on the left side of the pupil.

There are four school rooms on the first floor and four on the second floor of 28x32feet each and two on the third floor of 26 x 30 feet each and 12½ feet high. On the third floor is an Exhibition Hall, running from front to rear, 28 x 76 feet and 13½ feet high. A small teachers' room is attached to each room, fitted up with cupboards.

The Principal's room, 12 x 13½feet, is on the second floor and a Teachers room, 16 x 20 feet, is on the third floor.

The entrance hall, 12 feet wide, runs from front to rear with doors at each end.

At each end of this hall are the stairs from the second to the third floor.

A cross hall, sixteen feet wide, terminating at each end in a semicircular projection, contains the stairs from the first to the second floor and also to the basement. In this hall are the cloak rooms which are of steel wire grille work 6½ feet high.

The floors are deafened with "Cabot's double thick quilt."

The sloping roofs are of copper and the deck roof of gravel, the water being carried down through the building.

The walls are built of stock brick faced with selected stock. The window heads are flat arches of buff colored brick with red freestone skew-backs. The main entrance having semicircular arches of buff brick 3 feet wide and a stone label mould 1 foot wide, with dentils.

The floors are of brick and the walls are wainscoted with whitewood, about three feet high in rooms and five feet high in halls.

The stairs are built with solid strings on the slow burning plan.

The building is piped for gas.

There are slate blackboards and electric bells in each room.

The room is heated by hot water and ample provision is made for ventilation.

Large ventilating turrets terminate the two circular projections and the one on front.

The Sanitaries are in the basement and are of the latest approved style.

Large play rooms, with outside entrances are provided in the basement, with asphalted floors.

Building began early in the fall and continued throughout the school year. The contract for the mason's work was $15,470; for the carpenter's, $11,788; for the painter's, $1,000; for the metal work, $3,768 and for the heating and plumbing, $4,966. The whole amount expended on the building and lot up to date of this report is $39,632.04.

The improvements carried out during the year in the schools were:

At Albert school a new roof was provided, the walls and ceiling repaired, three new hardwood floors laid down and the outside repaired and painted.

The Douglas Avenue yard was levelled and made fit for its purpose.

At Aberdeen School new sanitaries for the girls were placed in the basement.

At Victoria the roof was mended, fire escapes provided and the building painted and kalsomined.

At the High School additional heating surface was provided.

The Leinster Street School was kalsomined and painted.

At Centennial a stone retaining wall was built in front.

The apparatus of all the schools has been much improved, new desks to the number of at least 100, maps, wall slates, teachers' cabinets, chairs for the school assembly halls have been provided, in short, whatever seemed necessary for the due improvement of the school work.

There remains now to complete the task which the Board set itself some few years ago viz. to provide the city with proper school buildings, the erection of a school building on the Weldon lot which has been owned by the Board almost since the inaurguration of the school law, but never occupied since the the great fire of 1877 destroyed the former school there. When this is done our community will possess a series of buildings of which it need not be ashamed and which will compare favorably with any city of similar size and resources. It is also desirable to enclose the different school grounds and put them in order for the childrens' use, as well as to enlarge and improve the furniture and apparatus. That their efforts may result in solid advantage to the rising generation of the city is the hearty desire and aim of the Board.

The following Table shows the average cost per School for the last seven years:

School.	No. Rooms.	Salaries.	Care.	Repairs.	Heating	Whole Cost.	Cost per Room
OWNED BY BOARD.							
Alexandra	8	$2912 00	$249 71	$145 71	$281 42	$3762 24	$470 28
*Newman St	4	1526 00	110 00	168 85	107 14	2095 42	523 85
*Douglas Ave	5	1800 85	†110 00	143 28	185 14	2344 14	468 52
Winter St	12	3765 71	373 00	483 00	395 42	5026 14	418 84
Aberdeen	7	2467 80	†200 00	121 40	295 80	3134 80	447 82
Centennial	10	3654 52	†420 00	258 42	492 42	4964 85	496 48
High	13	7707 60	†500.00	207 80	962 00	9592 40	737 87
Victoria and Annex	19	6601 71	†588 71	639 57	696 28	8739 85	459 99
*Albert	11	4084 57	†404 85	666 14	430 28	5757 28	523 39
RENTED.							
*Elm St	7	2003 57	130 00	143 57	144 42	2602 00	371 76
*S. Peter's Boys	7	2798 85	193 28	201 00	214 71	3801 42	543 06
*St. Peter's Girls	8	242/ 71	152 71	152 85	129 57	3265 00	408 12
S. Vincent's	6	1801 14	204 00	40 28	160 00	2184 00	364 00
Leinster St	5	1634 80	†200 00	106 60	230 40	2475 00	495 00
S. Malachi's	11	4006 28	326 00	194 57	205 00	5645 57	513 23
S. Joseph's	7	2000 28	†250 00	105 85	188 85	3133 14	447 57
*Mason Hall	3	1219 00	100 00	29 66	61 16	1661 33	553 66
*S. Patrick's	5	1719 57	170 57	82 85	102 71	2351 14	470 22

*Those marked thus are wooden buildings. †The janitors live in the schools marked thus.

We have the honor to be, Sir,

Your obedient servants,

ARTHUR I. TRUEMAN,

Chairman.

EDWARD MANNING, *Secretary.*

STATISTICAL TABLES.

TABLE NO. 1.—GENERAL FINANCIAL STATEMENT.

ASSETS.

Cash on hand June 30, 1903, ...		$ 2 02
Lands and Buildings, see Table	$379,020 59	
Furniture see Table	32,298 78	
		411,341 39
Sinking Funds	11,666 67	
City of St. John	23,333 33	
Water Bond, No. G.	500 00	
Ground rent due	519 00	
Assessment	45,000 00	
		81,019 00
Coal on hand	$881 04	
Supplies in office	70 00	
		951 04
		$493,811 43
Excess of Liabilities over Assets		25,396 36
		$518,707 79

LIABILITIES,

Debentures due 1908	....	$ 6,000 00	
" " 1909	....	11,500 00	
" " 1910	....	5,941 00	
" " 1917	....	20,000 00	
" " 1920	....	17,000 00	
" " 1921	....	23,000 00	
" " 1922	....	35,500 00	
" " 1925	....	34,500 00	
" " 1926	....	25,000 00	
" " 1927	....	17,500 00	
" " 1934	....	10,000 00	
" " 1935	....	20,000 00	
" " 1936	....	1,500 00	
" " 1937	....	34,000 00	
" " 1940	....	26,500 00	
" " 1940	....	43,500 00	
" " 1941	....	69,500 00	
Portland, 1906	....	7,750 00	
" 1907	....	1,000 00	
			$409,691 00
Debentures due (1913) issued by consent of Common Council and authority of the Legislature to pay off current indebtedness in lieu of unpaid assessments.	....		35,000 00
			$444,691 00
Coupons not presented	....		$10 00
Due. Bank of New Brunswick	....		74,106 79
			$518,707 79

TABLE II.—CAPITAL ACCOUNT.

RECEIPTS.

Sale of Debentures					
Issue July 15th, 1902.					
Nos. 655 and 656	....	....	$1,000 00		
at ½ p. c. prem.	....	....	5		
				$1,005 00	
Nos. 673 to 679	....	....	$3,500 00		
at ¼ p. c. prem.	....	....	8 75		
				3,508 75	
Nos. 680 and 681	....	....	$1,000 00		
at ¼ p. c. prem.	....	....	2 50		
				1002 50	
Nos. 657 to 672	....	....	$8,000 00		
at ¼ p. c. prem.	....	....	20 00		
				8,020 00	
Nos. 682 to 685	....	....	$2,000 00		
at ¼ p. c. prem.	....	....	5		
				2,005 00	
No. 687, par....	....	....	$500 00		
				500 00	
Nos. 686 to 688	....	....	$1,500 00		
at ¼ p. c. prem.	....	....	3 75		
				1,503 75	
					$17,545 00
From current account	....	....			18,705 71
					$36,250 71

EXPENDITURE.

Furniture purchased	....	.....	$983 32	
Dufferin School construction		....	35,267 39	
				$36,250 71

TABLE III.— CURRENT ACCOUNT.

Receipts.

Cash on hand June 30th, 1902, ...		$ 22 64
Due Bank of New Brunswick, ...		74,106 79
From ground rent, ...		373 00
County Funds, ...		11,910 94
For Medal Fund, ...		30 00
Assessment, 1902, ...		89,441 00
		$175,884 37

Expenditure.

Cost of schools, office and work shop as per Table	$78,767 99	
Incidental expenses, ...	203 21	
Advertising and Printing, ...	250 90	
Coupon interest, ...	17,718 10	
Coupons due, 1902, ...	312 03	
Bank interest on overdrafts, ...	1,659 88	
Sinking Fund, ...	2,051 26	
Weldon lot, fence and water rate, ...	9 60	
To Capital account, 1902, ...	1,984 77	
" " 1903, ...	18,705 71	
Paid Bank of New Brunswick due 1902	53,152 86	
Cash on hand, ...	2 02	
Coal on hand, $881 00 } Supplies in office, 70 04 }	951 04	
Special coupon interest alleged bond 277 A....	120 00	
		$175,884 37

TABLE IV.—*Maintenance for year ending June 30th, 1903, Schools, Office and Shop.*

SCHOOLS.	Salaries.	Care.	Repairs.	Fuel Water & Light.	Rent.	Insurance.	Supply.	Expense.	Totals.
Spar Cove	$	$	$	$	$ 10 00				10 00
Sandy Point Road	274 01	28 00	4 50	35 00			41		341 92
Milldgeville	368 47	42 00	89 23	15 00	20 00		91		535 61
Alexandra	3,157 06	400 00	151 77	451 46	150 00		3 72	7 50	4,322 51
Newman Street	1,600 16	120 00	194 65	99 15	80 00		2 73		2,097 69
Douglas Avenue	1,832 70	120 00	156 75	207 53	50 00		2 88		2,370 86
Elm Street	1,824 98	130 00	203 00	155 84	100 00	145 64	4 01		2,563 47
St. Peter's, Boys	3,062 51	204 00	165 52	167 77	412 50		5 64	2 00	4,020 94
St. Peter's Girls	2,495 52	192 00	180 08	135 35	412 50		6 50		3,422 95
Winter Street	3,926 44	400 00	103 51	402 14			5 36		4,838 45
Aberdeen	2,559 56	200 00	117 18	216 97			12 26		3,107 97
Centennial	3,647 69	420 00	303 47	505 83		10 00	6 67	15 00	4,909 66
St. Vincent	1,934 33	204 00	32 11	160 00	300 00		7 03	5 13	2,643 60
High Street	8,291 62	500 00	223 76	694 96		10 00	7 02	5 05	9,733 41
Leinster Street	1,807 74	200 00	35 30	225 00	350 00		4 83		2,622 87
St. Malachi's	3,930 00	372 00	157 81	189 89	833 12		9 91	6 00	5,498 73
St. Joseph's	2,117 14	250 00	69 40	146 41	425 00		13 80	6 50	3,028 25
Victoria and Annex	6,332 89	640 00	472 20	669 53		10 00	11 17	4 50	8,141 29
Albert	4,050 25	360 00	1,697 15	478 94		20 00	8 36	27 30	6,643 00
Latour	1,488 06	240 00	533 76	355 72			8 14	14 65	2,640 33
St. Patrick's	1,816 63	192 00	5 50	114 39	262 50		6 35		2,397 37
Queen Street	524 36	42 00	8 61	25 59	75 00		3 47	10 00	689 23
Brittain Street	302 67						8 11		310 78
Office	1,400 00	48 00	5 85	10 89	300 00				1,764 74
Shop			14 65	7 71					22 36
Totals	$58,744 99	$5,304 00	$5,015 76	$5,471 07	$3,780 62	$195 64	$139 28	$102 63	$78,767 99

TABLE No. V. Details of Assets in Real Estate and Furniture.

Property.		Lands and Buildings.	Furniture and Apparatus.	Totals.
Sandy Point Road School	.....	$597 40	$165 84	$763 24
Millidgeville	"	1,236 92	167 47	1,404 39
Spar Cove	" disused	355 00	....	355 00
Alexandra	"	34,553 04	2,378 90	36,931 94
Newman Street	"	2,787 66	504 33	3,291 99
Douglas Avenue	"	9,126 54	721 59	9,848 13
Elm Street	"	....	919 91	919 91
Dufferin	"	39,632 44	....	39,632 44
St. Peter's Boys'	"	....	1,311 43	1,311 43
St. Peter's Girls'	"	....	1,123 17	1,123 17
Winter Street	"	35,896 96	2,217 28	38,114 24
Aberdeen	"	20,917 41	1,066 75	21,984 16
Centennial	"	34,175 11	2,518 77	36,693 88
St. Vincent's	"	....	939 92	939 92
High School	.....	53,724 21	4,440 09	58,164 30
Leinster Street	"	....	842 38	842 38
St. Malachi's	"	....	1,769 67	1,769 67
St. Joseph's	"	....	1,475 42	1,475 42
Victoria	"	54,819 03	2,962 44	57,781 47
Victoria Annex	"	9,230 52	1,242 01	10,472 53
Albert	"	33,137 86	1,778 28	34,916 14
Latour	"	30,566 94	1,384 72	31,951 66
St. Patrick's	"	....	676 10	676 10
Queen Street	"	....	136 80	136 80
Brittain Street	"	....	95 77	95 77
Office	.....	....	1,335 84	1,335 84
Shop	.....	1,330 98	123 90	1,454 88
Weldon Lot	.....	3,000 00	....	3,000 00
Grammar School Lots	.....	13,000 00	....	13,000 00
St. Malachi's Addition	.....	668 67	....	668 67
St. Patrick's Addition	.....	283 90	....	283 90
		$379,040 59	$32,298 78	$411,339 37

Table VI.—Details of Fire Insurance in force to June 27, 1904.

SCHOOLS.	Buildings	On Furniture.	On Improvements.	Total.
Sandy Point Road	$ 400	$ 140	$......	$ 540
Millidgeville	800	140	......	940
Spar Cove	160	......	......	160
Alexandria	21,300	2,000	......	23,300
Newman Street	2,000	400	......	2,400
Douglas Avenue	5,600	600	......	6,200
St. Peter's (Boys')	......	1,000	......	1,000
St. Peters (Girls')	......	850	......	850
Winter Street	21,000	1,500	......	22,500
Aberdeen	13,000	850	......	13,800
Centennial	21,000	1,800	......	22,800
St. Vincent's	......	650	......	650
High School	30,600	3,000	......	33,600
Leinster Street	......	650	......	650
St. Malachi's	......	1,325	475	1,800
St. Joseph's	......	920	......	920
Victoria	35,000	2,400	......	37,400
Victoria Annex	5,600	850	......	6,450
Queen Street	......	110	......	110
Brittain Street	......	150	......	150
Albert	20,000	1,310	......	21,310
St. Patrick's	......	500	220	720
Latour	15,000	1,000	......	16,000
Dufferin	10,000	......	......	10,000
Shop	850	250	......	1,100
Office	......	600	......	600
	$202,310	$22,995	$695	$226,000

SPECIAL INSURANCE—ANNUAL.

Elm Street, Furniture			$ 730
Albert, 2 boilers	$2,000		
Victoria, 1 boiler	1,000		
High, 1 boiler	1,000		
Centennial, 1 boiler	1,000	—$5,000	—$5,730
Total			$231,730

i 17

TABLE VII.—School Estimates for 1903.

1. Salaries of Teachers and Superintendent			$57,500
2. Salaries of Officers			1,400
3. Fuel, Water and Light			6,000
4. Care of Buildings			5,400
5. Rent and Insurance			4,000
6. Printing and Advertising			300
7. Repairs			4,500
8. Incidental expenses and School Supplies			267
9. Apparatus			500
10. Interest on Bank Overdraft			1,600
			$81,467
Less—County Fund, say		$11,000	
Ground Rent and Interest		500	
			$11,500
			$69,967
Add for Debenture Interest:—On $ 25,250 @ 6 p. c.	$1,515		
" 6,941 @ 5 p. c.	347		
" 205,000 @ 4 p. c.	8,160		
" 226,000 @ 3½ p. c.	7,910		
" False Bond	120		
Payments on Sinking Fund	1,981		
			$20,033
			$90,000

TABLE VIII. Summary of the Year's Work.

I. BUILDINGS.	First Term.	Second Term.
Number of Buildings Occupied as Schools	24	24
" " Owned	13	13
" " Rented	10	10
" " Occupied without Rent	1	1
" Rooms owned	94	94
" " Rented	57	57
" " Occupied without rent	1	1
" High School Departments Grade XII.—IX	13	13
" Advanced Departments Grade VIII.—V	49	49
" Advanced and Primary Depart. Grades VII.—I	13	12
" Primary Department Grade IV.—I	79	80

II. PUPILS.	First Term	Second Term.
Number of Pupils Enrolled	7331	7172
" Boys "	3557	3491
" Girls "	3592	3681
" Pupils over 15 years old	318	379
" " under 15 years old	7013	6793
" " reduced by transfers	7287	7084
" daily present on an average	6043	5630
Percentage of enrolment, daily present	83	80
Grand total days' attendance	474699½	675202
Number attending High Schools	494	456
" " Advanced Schools	2398	2306
" " Primary "	4408	4410
" of pupils to each teacher (average)	47	46
" reported new to schools	1083	207
Percentage of number attending High Schools	6.94	6.37
" " " Advanced Schools	32.56	32.15
" " " Primary Schools	60.5	61.48

III. THE SCHOOL YEAR.

Number of teaching days	203
Number of pupils enrolled	7,538
Grand Total days' attendance	1,149,901½
Average number of days each pupil attended	152.6

TABLE IX.—PARTICULARS OF SCHOOL ATTENDANCE BY GRADES.

SCHOOL.	TEACHERS' NAMES.	Class of License.	GRADES.	Enrolled.	Attendance.	Per cent.	GRADES.	Enrolled.	Attendance.	Per cent.
Sdy. Pt. Road	Eya Keagin	Sup.	B & G 5, 1	17	11	82	B & G 5, 1	17	12	68
Millidgeville	J. V. Kierstead	I	" "	26	20	77	" "	23	17	73
Alexandra	H. V. Hayes	I	" 8	44	30	89	" 8	41	33	81
	Jean Scott	Sup.	" 7, 6	47	44	93	" 7, 6	48	42	88
	Ada Cowan	I	" 6	55	50	92	" 6	54	47	86
	Ella McAlary	II	" 6, 5	50	43	91	" 6, 5	51	46	90
	Grace Murphy	I	" 5	51	42	82	" 5	52	42	81
	Effie McDougal	I	" 4	59	58	91	" 4	50	50	85
	Bertha Forbes	I	" 3	61	52	85	" 3	57	48	83
	Emma Colwell	II	" 2	57	49	87	" 2	54	45	84
	E. Stevenson	I	" 1	61	53	86	" 1	61	46	76
Newman St	Malcolm Brown	I	" 7	42	37	87	" 7	42	34	82
	P. Livingstone	II	" 4, 3	52	43	82	" 4, 3	56	48	86
	Edna Powers	I	" 2	51	44	86	" 2	52	44	84
	Jean Mowry	II	" 1	61	45	75	" 1	59	44	74
Douglas Av.	Geo. W. Dill	I	" 8, 7	42	37	88	" 8, 7	40	32	81
	Alice Gale	I	" 6, 5	49	40	82	" 6, 5	48	39	83
	Louise Brown	II	" 4, 3	51	41	81	" 4, 3	51	39	77
	Helen Dale	II	" 3, 2	52	46	82	" 3, 2	52	44	85
	Ella Connell	II	" 1	47	36	77	" 1	43	33	76
Elm St	Kate A. Kerr	I	" 5	49	44	89	" 5	47	40	85
	Isabel Donaldson	I	" 4	51	40	78	" 4	51	39	77
	Blanche Alward	I	" 3	53	43	86	" 3	53	44	84
	Ethel Emery	Sup.	" 3, 2	48	40	83	" 3, 2	46	37	78
	Jessie McLean	I	" 2	55	44	80	....	..	..	..
	Sarah Gray	II	....	..	..	..	" 2	54	44	82
	Margaret Strang	II	" 1	67	50	74	" 1	56	37	63
	Jessie Munro	I	" 1	44	33	74	" 1	38	29	74
St. Peter's Boys'	Joseph Harrington	I	B 8, 6	32	27	84	B 8, 6	29	23	81
	Michael Sweeney	II	" 5	44	38	86	" 5	43	36	84
	Josephine Quinn	I	" 5, 4	46	41	90	" 5, 4	45	40	89
	Minnie McGuire	I	" 4, 3	46	35	77	" 4, 3	43	34	78
	Maggie McMillin	II	" 3	47	41	87	" 3	50	41	83
	A. B. McInnis	II	" 2	46	39	85	" 2	47	37	78
	Kate Buckley	II	" 2, 1	49	40	81	" 1	48	37	75
	Alicia McCarron	II	" 1	55	41	74	" 1	47	31	65
St. Peter's Girls'	Joanna Carney	I	G 8, 7	39	37	94	G 8, 7	37	32	86
	M. McCluskey	I	" 6	38	32	84	" 6	36	25	71
	Anne Cassidy	I	" 5	47	40	83	" 5	42	34	82
	Martina Quinn	II	" 5, 4	48	39	81	" 5, 4	47	36	78
	Marguerite Kelly	II	" 4, 3	47	38	82	" 4, 3	48	38	79
	G. Fitzgerald	II	" 3, 2	47	37	79	" 3, 2	48	36	76
	Sarah Boudreau	II	" 2, 1	50	41	81	" 2, 1	48	37	76
	Ellen Marry	II	" 1	45	36	81	" 1	44	31	71
Winter St.	Thomas Stothart	I	B & G 8, 7	44	38	86	B & G 8	42	32	77
	F. Iva Thorne	I	" 7	36	31	86	" 7	38	30	79
	Jessie Sutherland	II	" 6	52	42	83	" 6	51	41	79
	Jennie Drake	I	" 6, 5	47	39	84	" 6, 5	50	42	84
	A. A. McLeod	I	" 5	49	42	86	" 5	48	39	81
	Sarah Taylor	I	" 4	46	41	88	" 4	44	40	90

TABLE IX.—CONTINUED.

SCHOOLS.	TEACHERS' NAMES.	Class of License.	GRADES.	Enrolled.	Attendance.	Per cent.	GRADES.	Enrolled.	Attendance.	Per cent.
Winter St.	Maude Gibson.....	I	B & G 4, 3	55	49	89	B & G 4, 3	37	48	85
(*Con.*)....	Gertrude Webb...	I	" 3	63	53	83	" 3	62	54	87
	Lilian Simpson....	II	" 2	64	53	83	" 2	61	51	83
	Margaret Gray....	II	" 2, 1	62	52	84	" 2, 1	66	55	83
	Etta Barlow.....	I	" 1	63	51	80	" 1	62	50	80
	Margaret Graham.	I	" 1	49	36	74	" 1	45	34	69
Aberdeen.....	Wm. M. McLean..	G S	" 8, 7	32	26	82	" 8, 7	32	24	74
	Elizabeth Corbet..	I	" 6, 5	45	35	78	" 6, 5	44	34	77
	Anne Honeywill...	I	" 5, 4	45	37	83	" 5, 4	46	34	73
	Mary Anderson...	I	" 4	44	35	82	" 4	50	39	79
	Jessie Caird......	II	" 3, 2	53	44	84	" 3	45	38	84
	Minnie Fowler....	I	" 2, 1	50	44	84	" 2	61	46	76
	Mary Lawrence...	II	" 1	60	42	77	" 1	61	46	76
Centennial....	Henry Town.......	I	B 7, 6	47	38	87	B 7, 6	41	33	81
	Jean Rowan.......	II	" 4	46	32	84	" 4	45	36	81
	Mary Evans.....	I	" 3	52	44	79	" 3	51	43	81
	Isabel Estabrooks.	I	" 2	57	44	78	" 2	58	48	82
	Annie Allen.......	II	" 1	75	32	70	" 1	72	51	70
	Annie M. Hea.....	I	G 5	48	39	82	G 5	44	37	84
	Edith McBeath....	I	" 4	49	39	79	" 4	47	37	76
	Margaret Campbell	II	" 3	38	30	77	" 3	37	28	71
	Jessie Milligan ...	I	" 2	54	44	81	" 2	49	40	82
	Lily K. Mackay*...	I	B & G 1	53	41	76	" 1	50	43	72
St. Vincent's..	Mary McDonald...	Sup.	G 12, 10	37	31	84	" 12, 10	33	30	77
	Ellen Carey........	I	" 9	28	24	89	" 9	23	19	83
	Helen Kirke.......	I	" 5, 4	42	35	83	" 5, 4	43	35	80
	Josephine Cormier	I	" 3, 2	52	40	78	" 3, 2	57	41	72
	Rose Gallagher....	II	" 1	60	48	80	" 1	59	43	73
	Bridget Cosgrove..	II	" 5, 1	54	51	95	" 6, 2	51	48	93
High School..	Dr. H. S. Bridges..	G. S.	B & G 12	17	16	95	B & G 12	17	13	78
	William Brodie...	G. S.	" 11	43	40	94	" 11	42	35	84
	W. J. S. Myles....	G. S.	" 11	44	40	97	" 11	44	37	84
	Thomas Powers...	G. S.	B 10	45	39	87	B 10	39	35	89
	Mary Knowlton...	G. S.	G 10	41	39	94	G 10	39	28	71
	Kate Bartlett.....	G. S.	G 10	37	36	87	G 10	34	25	74
	H. May Ward.....	I	B 9	39	38	94	B 9	37	31	85
	Phœbe Van Wart..	I	B 9	41	36	87	B 9	35	29	83
	Jessie Lawson.....	G. S.	B & G 9	38	32	83	B & G 9	35	28	81
	Bessie Wilson.....	G. S.	G 9	45	39	86	G 9	39	33	84
	E. McNaughton...	G. S.	G 9	39	34	88	G 9	34	29	86
	L. H. Yandall.....	I	B & G 8	41	36	88	G 8	41	35	85
	Alice Lingley......	I	B 8	41	35	86	B 8	41	32	77
Leinster St...	John McKinnon...	I	B 7	47	43	91	" 7	47	40	86
	Edna Gilmore.....	I	" 6	43	37	85	" 6	44	35	79
	L. Ingraham......	I	" 6	44	41	88	" 6	39	33	84
	Frances Dieuade..	I	" 5	47	41	87	" 5	45	39	88
	E. Kate Turner..	I	" 4	34	29	84	" 4	34	30	90
St. Malachi's.	James Barry......	I	" 8, 7	31	29	90	" 8	31	30	90
	M. R. Carlyn.....	I	" 7, 6	40	36	86	" 7, 6	40	22	72
	Minnie Coughlan..	II	" 6, 5	37	32	78	" 6, 5	39	35	87

TABLE IX.—PARTICULARS OF SCHOOL ATTENDANCE BY GRADES.—Continued.

SCHOOL.	TEACHERS' NAMES.	Class of License.	GRADE.	Enrolled.	Attendance.	Per cent.	GRADE.	Enrolled.	Attendance.	Per cent.
St. Malachi's. (Con.)	Mary T. Sugrue	I	B 5	46	36	84	B 5	43	30	70
	Emily Bardsley	I	" 5, 4	48	40	80	" 5, 4	48	39	82
	Mary Gallivan	II	" 4	51	41	84	" 4	53	42	78
	E. F. McInerney	I	" 3	35	29	77	" 3	37	30	80
	Jas. R. Sugrue	II	" 3	37	29	85	" 3	35	28	75
	Kate A. Cotter	II	" 2	48	41	85	" 2	40	39	84
	Catherine Hogan	II	" 2	41	37	76	" 2, 1	40	30	74
	Kate E. Lawlor	II	" 1	62	46	74	" 1	65	48	74
St. Joseph's	Sarah Burchill	I	G 8	37	32	88	G 8	34	28	83
	Mary Walsh	I	" 7	47	39	83	" 7	40	32	80
	Kate O'Neil	II	" 6	46	37	80	" 6	44	33	75
	K. Haggarty	II	" 5, 4	54	47	86	" 5, 4	52	42	78
	Maggie Corkery	II	" 4, 3	50	44	89	" 4, 3	52	45	86
	Mary Legere	I	" 2	45	36	80	" 2	46	36	76
	Pauline Delaney	II	" 1	48	35	73	" 1	49	35	71
Victoria	W. H. Parlee	I	" 8	35	30	84	" 8	38	31	81
	Amy Iddles	I	" 7	43	36	84	" 7	40	33	83
	Edith Godard	I	" 7	43	36	83	" 7	38	31	80
	Maud Kavanagh	I	" 6	50	40	80	" 6	50	40	81
	Maggie Sharpe	II	" 6	50	44	89	" 6	48	39	79
	Mary Morrow	I	" 5	50	39	78	" 5	46	39	85
	Jennie Estey	I	" 5	35	29	82	" 5	32	25	78
	Louise Lingley	I	" 4	55	44	81	" 4	52	43	79
	Stella Payson	I	" 4	55	48	78	" 4	55	45	83
	Annie Robb	I	" 3	56	48	85	" 3	54	45	83
	Bessie Thompson	I	" 2	60	48	80	" 2	58	47	80
	Matilda Shaw	II	" 2, 1	54	37	68	" 2, 1	55	38	70
	Harriet Gregg	I	" 1	52	38	72	" 1	49	38	78
Vic. Annex.	A. L. Dykeman	Sup.	B 5	45	37	82	B 5	45	36	79
	Louise Wetmore	I	" 4	47	39	82	..	..	..	..
	M. A. Stewart	I	..	..	..	..	" 4	46	39	86
	Laura Salter	I	" 3	49	40	83	" 3	51	42	82
	Grace Brown	Sup.	" 3, 2	56	45	80	" 3, 2	55	45	80
	Mary Gunn	I	" 2	60	46	76	" 2	62	48	76
	Harriet Howard	II	" 1	64	46	72	" 1	62	46	75
Albert	John Montgomery	I	B & G 8	37	31	85	B & G 8	33	28	85
	Clara Fullerton	I	" 7	39	32	81	" 7	38	31	80
	Enoch Thompson	I	" 7, 6	41	35	84	" 7, 6	42	33	80
	Harriet Smith	I	" 6, 5	45	39	87	" 6, 5	46	39	85
	Margaret Emerson	II	" 5, 4	46	40	86	" 5, 4	46	38	82
	Alice Carleton	Sup.	" 4	55	44	80	" 4	54	40	75
	H. Thompson	I	" 4, 3	55	43	79	" 4, 3	53	41	77
	Annie Emerson	II	" 3, 2	55	48	88	" 3, 2	60	46	76
	Bertha Brittain	I	" 2, 1	59	51	86	" 2, 1	54	44	81
	Lily Belyea	I	" 1	65	50	78	" 1	63	46	73
Latour	George Armstrong	I	" 6, 5	48	40	84	" 6, 5	42	33	80
	Edith Comben	I	" 4, 3	55	46	84	" 4, 3	51	38	75
	Lydia Fullerton	I	" 3, 2	64	52	81	" 3, 2	63	49	77
	Mary A. Nunnary	II	" 1	[illegible]	38	76	" 1	51	34	66
St. Patrick's.	J. Frank Owens	G.S.	B 6, 4	38	34	89	B 6, 4	38	30	78
	Sarah Smith	II	" 3, 2	33	30	90	" 3, 2	31	24	78
	M. McKenna	I	G 7, 5	35	30	87	G 7, 5	33	25	77

TABLE IX.—PARTICULARS OF SCHOOL ATTENDANCE BY GRADES.

SCHOOLS.	TEACHERS' NAMES.	Class of Licence.	GRADES.	Enrolled.	Attendance.	Per cent.	GRADES.	Enrolled.	Attendance.	Per cent.
St. Patrick's	Mary Gillen.......	I	G 4, 2	41	34	84	G 4, 2	39	27	70
(Con.)...	Mary A. Doherty..	II	B & G 1	51	38	75	B & G 1	52	31	59
Queen Street..	Israel Richardson.	II	B & G 5, 1	37	26	71	" 5, 1	33	24	71
Brittain Street	Helen Adam...	I	" 4, 1	26	25	91	" 4, 1	26	25	94

TABLE No. X.—Enrolment, Daily Average Attendance, Percentage of Enrolment Daily Present, Etc., 1892 to 1903, Inclusive.

Year.	Term.	No. of Pupils Enrolled.	Average Daily Attendance.	Percentage of Enrolment Daily Present.	No. of Departments	Average No. Pupils to Each Teacher.
1892	First	6661	4891	73	143	47
	Second	6651	5432	81	142	47
1893	First	6681	4923	75	142	47
	Second	6672	5433	82	143	47
1894	First	6440	5059	79	144	45
	Second	6742	5557	83	143	47
1895	First	6580	5261	80	143	46
	Second	6636	5332	81	143	46
1896	First	6391	4853	76	146	44
	Second	6584	5466	83	146	45
1897	First	6557	4934	76	146	44
	Second	6821	5572	82	148	45
1898	First	6531	5153	79	148	44
	Second	7000	5629	80	151	45
1899	First	6832	5268	77	149	46
	Second	6941	5743	83	155	46
1900	First	6753	5783	78	150	45
	Second	7160	5849	82	153	47
1901	Half Year	6947	5590	87	153	45
1902	First	7297	5549	77	152	48
	Second	6928	5495	80	152	45
1902-3	First	7331	6043	83	154	47
	Second	7172	5630	80	154	46

TABLE XI. Subjects of Instruction.

SUBJECTS.	PRIMARY GRADES.								ADVANCED GRADES.								HIGH SCHOOL GRADES.							
	I.		II.		III.		IV.		V.		VI.		VII.		VIII.		IX.		X.		XI.		XII.	
	First Term.	Second Term.	First Term.	Second Term.	First Term.	Second Term.	First Term.	Second Term.	First Term.	Second Term.	First Term.	Second Term.	First Term.	Second Term.	First Term.	Second Term.	First Term.	Second Term.	First Term.	Second Term.	First Term.	Second Term.	First Term.	Second Term.
Physical Culture	1382	1208	1022	1108	1004	996	1030	1038	887	838	670	661	495	454	346	353								
Singing	"	"	"	"	"	"	"	"	"	"	"	"	"	"	"	"								
Reading and Spelling	"	"	"	"	"	"	"	"	"	"	"	"	"	"	"	"	230	203	144	130	96	98	24	25
Form, Color, Drawing	"	"	"	"	"	"	"	"	"	"	"	"	"	"	"	"	"	"						
Print Script, and Writing	"	"	"	"	"	"	"	"	"	"	"	"	"	"	"	"								
Number and Arithmetic	"	"	"	"	"	"	"	"	"	"	"	"	"	"	"	"	"	"	"	"				
Health, Temperance, Physiology	"	"	"	"	"	"	"	"	"	"	"	"	"	"	"	"	"	"	"	"	"	"		
Geography	"	"	"	"	"	"	"	"	"	"	"	"	"	"	"	"	"	"	"	"	"	"		
Animals, plants, minerals	"	"	"	"	"	"	"	"	"	"	"	"	"	"	"	"	"							
Morals and Manners	"	"	"	"	"	"	"	"	"	"	"	"	"	"	"	"								
Grammar and Composition					"	"	"	"	"	"	"	"	"	"	"	"	"	"	"	"	"	"	"	"
History							"	"	"	"	"	"	"	"	"	"	"	"	"	"				
Sewing		50	30	20	32	39	42	14	72	15														
Latin													343	431	338	344	219	197	142	"	52	"	24	17
Greek																	41	14	36	13	16	7	14	7
Ancient History																					"	"	"	17
Ancient Geography																							"	"
French																	230	203	144	130	89	91	17	17
Algebra													42	430	346	356	"	"	"	"	96	98	24	17
Geometry																	"	"	"	"	"	"	"	25
Book Keeping																	"	"	"	"				
Trigonometry																					19	25	"	"
Chemistry																			21	"	96	98		
Physics																							7	17
Botany and Agriculture																	144	"	144	"	89	94		
Astronomy																							7	8
Geology																								8

APPENDIX D.

I.—Report of the Chancellor of the University of New Brunswick.

(Approved by the Senate.)

To His Honour the Honourable Jabez Bunting Snowball, D. C. L., Lieutenant Governor of the Province of New Brunswick.

MAY IT PLEASE YOUR HONOUR:

In conformity with the act establishing the university of New Brunswick. I beg to submit most respectfully to your Honour, for the information of the legislature, the following report:—

One of the most important educational events of the past year was the establishment of the Rhodes scholarships. The first election of scholars under the Rhodes bequest will be made between February and May 1904. It is a matter of pardonable pride to the alumni and friends of the University of New Brunswick that the Commissioner appointed by the Trustees of the will of the late Mr. C. J. Rhodes to visit all the countries mentioned in his bequest for the purpose of formulating recommendations for the awarding of scholarships is Dr. G. R. Parkin C. M. G. a native of New Brunswick and a graduate of our own Provincial University. In the cases of Ontario, Quebec, Nova Scotia and New Brunswick it has been determined that nominations to the scholarships shall be made by the chartered universities and Colleges of these provinces in a fixed rotation based upon the number of students in attendance. The nominations for 1904 and 1905 will be made as follows:

ONTARIO.
1904, by Toronto University,
1905, by Queen's University,

QUEBEC.
1904, by McGill University,
1905, by Laval University,

NOVA SCOTIA.
1904, by Dalhousie University
1905, by Acadia University

NEW BRUNSWICK.
1904, by the University of N. B.,
1905, by Mt. Allison University.

The one thing that Mr. Rhodes thought with regard to Oxford was that the "Student should enjoy Oxford itself." What has Oxford to offer? It has been well answered. " she offers herself." There she stands in all her beauty casting a spell and a glamour; "whispering from her towers the last enchantments of the middle age.

"One of the great advantages there is this, that you have students of all kinds, of all ages, of all conditions, some rich, some poor, some older, some younger, coming from all parts of the world mixing absolutely freely, pursuing different studies but with a common aim, the advancement of knowledge. It is to the best interests of the Empire that these students should rub up against each other, and should meet and should clash in friendly collision and rivalry at the Union society and in college debates and so on.

"Where can you study so well English history and English language as in Oxford where you are surrounded with the past, where you have the traces and the relics and the remnants of the past round you, where the historical spirit and inspiration of the great men, poets and writers who have lived in these ancient halls and colleges seem still to be about us."

Such words were uttered by the Oxford representative at the Allied Colonial Universities Conference at Burlington House in London in July last.

I had the honor and privilege of representing the University of New Brunswick on that memorable occasion, and I was glad to be able to say that this University is affiliated with the ancient Universities of Oxford, Cambridge and Dublin, and that our graduates are admitted by all three of them to advanced standing without examination. The Principal of the University of London stated in the clearest way what he regarded as the corner stones on which the conference should build. The first was absolute freedom for the individual University; another he took to be absolute reciprocity among the Universities. In the third place it is very desirable that at some central point there should be a knowledge of what is going on in all the Universities of the Empire.

The following resolution was carried unanimously:

"That in the opinion of this Conference it is desirable that such relations should be established between the principal teaching Universities of the Empire as will secure that special or local advantages of study, and in particular for post graduate study and research, be made as accessible as possible to students from all parts of the King's Dominions."

During the past year the University of New Brunswick has quietly and efficiently done its work with a staff of seven Professors and with a gratifying increase in the number of students.

The complete list appended to this report shows that there are one hundred and thirty four students now in attendance. Twenty-eight of these are women. The list shows the counties and churches represented and also the line of study pursued by each student. There are now fifty-nine in the Engineering Department. Forty-seven new students came to the University at the beginning of 1903,-1904.

Of the seven candidates who stood in the First Division at the July entrance from the High Schools of the whole Province all entered the Provincial University. These facts tend to shew that a goodly number of the pick and flower of New Brunswick youth are to be found in the University of NewBrunswick. In several departments the limit of the seating capacity of our lecture rooms has been reached.

The annual reports of the Professors to the Senate testify to extraordinary activity in every branch of the undergraduate course.

An Agricultural College and a School of Forestry would prove most valuable adjuncts to the University.

In order to make a beginning, a Professor of Chemistry including Agricultural Chemistry, and a Professor of Forestry along with the existing staff might do excellent work in these popular and useful directions. It was thought at the Allied Colonial Universities Conference above referred to that Forestry as a branch of applied science would receive a completer development in the colonies than elsewhere, inasmuch as the forests are larger and forestal administration is more needed in the colonies.

The generous donation of four thousand dollars to the university by a lady of St. John who is so anxious to avoid every personal connection in the matter that she does not wish even her name to appear in any report that is to be published, deserves the most grateful acknowledgment and indicates that the work of the university meets with approval among ladies of high intelligence.

As to our needs it is admitted on all hands that the salaries of our Professors are too low, our laboratories need further equipment, our library needs more books, a new gymnasium is a pressing necessity. The needs of the engineering department have increased with increasing numbers.

The various items of income and expenditure during the past year will be found in the Bursar's statement which accompanies this report.

Respectfully submitted,

THOS. HARRISON, *Chancellor.*

II.—Report of the Director of Manual Training.

J. R. INCH LL. D.,

Chief Superintendent of Education.

Sir,—I beg to submit the following report on Manual Training in New Brunswick for the year 1903.

Since my report of a year ago there has been considerable advancement in manual training in New Brunswick.

One importent change has taken place. The three years during which Sir Wm. McDonald has borne all expenses in connection with manual training in Fredericton, for both the student-teachers at the Normal School and the boys of the city schools, expired in June 1903. During these three years Professor Robertson, who has been the leader in this advance educational movement, as he is also the leader in the movement for the consolidation of rural schools in Canada, gave much time and thought to make the work as effective as possible. His desire was to give such an object lesson of the advantages of manual training through the boys' classes that all who saw would believe in it and would work for its establishment in other schools; and, by means of the student teachers of the Normal Schools, to spread a knowledge of the work throughout the land. This, I am happy to say, is being accomplished in New Brunswick.

When the MacDonald Fund ceased to support the work in Fredericton it was only necessary to call the attention of the Board of Trustees to the matter: they voted unanimously to provide accommodations for carrying on the work at their own expense. The provincial government made arrangements for continuing the manual training at the Normal School and for special courses for teachers; also for a director of manual training for the Province; so that the work has continued without a break.

A year ago, outside of Fredericton, only two towns (Campbellton and Saint Andrews) and three rural districts(Inches Ridge, Musquash and Mascarene) had introduced manual training into their schools. During the past year St. Stephen, Milltown, Woodstock, Florenceville and Sackville have all established departments of manual training, making, in all, eleven districts in different parts of the province where manual training has been established; with about nine hundred and fifty students taking the work at the present time.

At Inches Ridge the school is taught, with much success, by Miss Bessie Kelly who is completing her second year as teacher there. Many improvements have been made in this school since the introduction of manual training though it is a "poor district."

During the past year the school house has been painted, two new hyloplate blackboards have been put up, a few new desks have been added and the woodshed has been shingled and painted. This school sent an excellent exhibit of manual training work to the Fredericton exhibition, second only to that of the Fredericton schools, and received a diploma. The interest in regular studies is greater and the percentage of attendance is higher than before manual training was introduced.

At Musquash the disastrous fire of last summer destroyed the school house, and no part of the manual training equipment was saved. The school house has not been rebuilt.

At Mascarene the school was taught last year by Miss Harriette Bolt who was instrumental in starting the manual training work there. Miss Bolt says, "having been in this school before and after manual training was introduced, I am fully convinced that the energy and zeal with which the pupils entered into all their studies are due to the new interest which the manual training created." The trustees, also, say that a great advancement has been made since manual training was introduced. Many improvements have here also been made in the school building and furnishings.

At Saint Andrews the manual training department was opened in January, 1903, with Miss Agnes Lucas as teacher. The work was effectively carried on by her for one term at the end of which time she was called to take a position in Fredericton. Miss Ethel Duffy was appointed by the school trustees of Saint Andrews to take charge of this department in September (1903) and she has been very successful with the work. The children are showing unusual interest and marked improvement. Some excellent work was sent to the Fredericton exhibition and a diploma was given to the school. Here the teacher of manual training devotes the forenoons only to the work, relieving some of the regular teachers of instruction in certain subjects during the afternoons.

In Campbellton manual training was established January 1903 with Miss Ethel I. Mersereau as teacher. After one term of very successful work Miss Mersereau resigned and Miss Louise Wetmore was appointed to take her place. Miss Wetmore has been very successful and the Board of Trustees are well pleased with this department and the work which it is doing. The members of the Board are fully alive to the educational needs of the times and we expect that the subject of domestic science for girls will soon receive their special consideration.

At St. Stephen and at Milltown manual training was started early in September of this year. A special room has been well equipped in each town and one teacher, Mr. Will Whitney, is employed by both towns. Mr.

Whitney teaches three days in St. Stephen and two days in Milltown. The interest of the boys is very great The average attendance for the term was 92 per cent. Not only are the boys delighted with the work but the citizens generally have shown their interest and approval. In Milltown alone more than one hundred persons have visited the school during the term.

Woodstock established a department of manual training and started work in September with Miss A. Gertrude O'Brien as teacher. The work progresses well. Some of the regular teachers, who, through a misunderstanding of the work, had opposed its introduction, have now become its strong supporters. The Board of Trustees say that their only regret is that they did not introduce manual training years ago.

In Florenceville manual training was started, early in September, Miss Marjorie F. Mair, the principal of the school, devoting a few hours each week to the work. The trustees had an addition made to the school building, providing a fine room large enough for ten benches and equipment. Both pupils and parents seem well pleased with the department. Miss Mair says that she is enabled to get into closer touch with the pupils through the manual training work, and that the attendance has increased sixteen per cent over that of the corresponding term of last year when they had no manual training.

At Sackville the school Trustees have provided equipment for manual training, and have made arrangements with Professor Sweetser to teach the work during the present term. Professor Sweetser has recently been appointed to take charge of this department in Mount Allison University. We expect some excellent results at Sackville.

I have already referred to the action of the Fredericton Board of School Trustees in making provision for manual training, and to the appointment of Miss Agnes E. Lucas as teacher of the department. The work continues with as great success as before. An excellent exhibit of the work of the Fredericton boys was shown at the Fredericton exhibition last fall, and a few boys were asked to work at thier benches there to give visitors a better understanding of the methods employed. The exhibition management awarded medals to eight Fredericton boys who showed the best work, and a cup to the school in appreciation of the excellent work shown.

The manual training work for the student teachers at the Normal School continues about the same as in previous years. Mr. George M. Morris, who was employed in this department under the MacDonald fund has left to take charge of manual training in Nantucket, Massachusetts. Mr. J. V. Lynn and Miss Iva A. Baxter, who were appointed by the Provincial Board of Education are both doing good work.

In the first of the three months' courses for teachers of rural districts there were ten enrolled but only six completed the course. Eight teachers now attend the second course and three others have made application to attend the third course.

There is a demand for male teachers with a knowledge of manual training to act as principals of village schools of two or three departments, and devote a few hours per week to teaching manual training. In one such district more than six months ago the trustees voted to establish the work and voted ample money to purchase equipment; but as yet they have been unable to secure a principal who could teach this subject. We hope that in future more male teachers will avail themselves of these special courses and prepare for manual training work.

The outlook, both for consolidation of rural schools and for manual training, has never been so bright as it is now. In addition to the Kingston Consolidated School and the one being arranged for in Albert County, it is expected that others will soon follow in Charlotte and Carleton Counties In these schools manual training and school gardens will be prominent features. Several other schools are planning to open departments of manual training in September, and we look forward with confidence to the steady growth of these movements in New Brunswick.

I wish here to express my appreciation of the help which, in many ways, the School Inspectors have given me in my work.

Respectfully submitted,

EDWIN E. MACCREADY,

Director of Manual Training.

III.—Report of Travelling Instructor and Supervisor of School Gardens and Nature Study.

J. R. INCH, LL. D.,
Chief Superintendent of Education,
Fredericton, N. B.

SIR, — Having been selected by Professor Robertson, with your approval and that of the Board of Education, as travelling instructor and supervisor of school gardening and nature study in a group of schools in the Counties of Carleton and Victoria, I entered upon my regular duties in that capacity in August, at the beginning of the school term.

The teachers in all the schools I visited have received me in the most kindly manner and have continued to give me their most hearty co-operation. As yet I have done most of the teaching myself—only asking the regular teachers to review the lessons with the children and to give a few lessons themselves.

As soon as the work has extended to all the grades I hope that the regular teachers, in the lower grades, at least, will be found willing to assume the responsibility of the teaching with such assistance as I may be able to give them in the short time which I will be able to spend in each department.

Five school gardens have been established—two at Woodstock, one at Hartland, one at Florenceville and one at Andover, mainly at the expense of the MacDonald Rural Schools Fund, although at Woodstock and Hartland the people have contributed a large part of the expense. At Woodstock the school board provided the ground for one of the gardens and gave $100 towards the other. At Hartland, a plot containing over two acres for garden and recreation ground was purchased at a cost of $600. The school district voted $175 towards the purchase, the MacDonald Fund gave $125, and the remaining $300 was raised by subcription, mainly through the efforts of John Barnett, Esq.

These gardens will be made the basis of nature study work in the lower grades, supplemented in the higher grades by elementary studies in the principles of agriculture and horticulture. The adjoining grounds will be adorned, with the assistance of the teachers and pupils, with trees, shrubs, and beautiful perennial herbs.

From my experience so far, and from what I have seen elsewhere, I am convinced that this work offers a valuable means of varying the monotony of school life by studies which will contribute much to render the children, more accurate and intelligent observers, more resourceful and self reliant, and more appreciative of the pleasures, advantages and possibilities of rural life.

But if school gardens and nature study are ever to become factors of any importance in our public schools, some means must be found to induce a sufficient number of teachers to qualify themselves for conducting the work, and to this end I beg to suggest that a grant equal to that now given to teachers who qualify for teaching manual training in the rural schools ($50 per year) be offered to teachers who qualify by a special course of study and practice for teaching school gardening and nature study in schools which provide a suitable garden plot and the other facilities required for the work. A much larger grant than this is given in the Province of Nova Scotia to those teachers who take a similar course. Such a grant would encourage teachers who love teaching to add to their Normal School training this special course, and would help to lengthen the term of service of a desirable class of teachers—to the advantage of the country, for no one would go to the expense and labor of qualifying unless he intended to teach for a considerable period thereafter. As the number to claim the grant would not be large, at least not before the lapse of many years, the annual expense to the province would not be great.

Besides, this seems to be a more effective means of improving the personnel of the teaching body than would be the increase of the provincial grant to all teachers, irrespective of merit or of special qualification. It would also appear to be only a fair offset to the grants now given to teachers who possess special qualifications in classics and other academic subjects.

Such a policy would tend to retain in the teaching service men of different tastes and ideals, and to save public education from becoming exclusively formal, bookish and conventional—tendencies toward which are still strong and persistent, as history shows they have always been in the past.

If the Board of Education could afford to offer, as was done last year in Ontario, a small sum to aid School Districts in providing school gardens, the difficulty of securing and preparing the necessary land would be much diminished.

Yours very respectfully,

JOHN BRITTAIN.

APPENDIX E.

Report of the County Teachers' Institutes and of the Summer School of Science.

I. Proceedings of County Institutes.

The following reports are taken from the Educational Review, St. John except when the President or Secretary of the Institute has foruarded a report of proceedings for publication with signature attached:

ALBERT COUNTY.

The 26th annual session of the Albert County Teachers' Institute convened at Surrey, on June 4th, 1903.

Forty-Six teachers enrolled themselves members of the Institute. The Institute was opened with an interesting address by the President, T. E. Colpitts, Miss Flovd then gave a model lesson on "Number" to Grade 2, which was favorably criticized,

L, R. Hetherington then read an admirable paper on "The Teachers Relation to Politics." A public meeting was held in the evening in the Methodist Church which was well attended.

The fourth session was opened by a paper "Home Lessons" by Marion Atkinson, discussed by Martha Avard and others. Dr. G. U. Hay not being present, W. M. Burns read his paper. Resolutions passed regretting illness of Inspector Smith,

Fifth Session, Miss Mary A. Smith read a paper on "English Literature as in readers III. and IV."

The following officers were elected for ensuing year; President T. E. Colpitts; Vice-Pres., Miss M. Avard; Sec'y Treas., Frank Blake.

T. E. COLPITTS,
President.

F. H. BLAKE.
Secretary.

CARLETON COUNTY.

The twenty-sixth annual session of the Carleton County Teachers' Institute met in Graham's Opera House, Woodstock, Thursday, December 11th, 1903, at 10 a. m., President Draper in the chair. The enrolment fee was placed at twenty-five cents.

Committees were appointed as follows:

Nominating—J. E. Page, C. H. Gray, A. Gertrude O'Brien.

Audit—H. B. Logie, J. M. Keefe, A. Cronkite.

The President made an address, after which Inspector Meagher, Mr. Page and Mr. Logie addressed the Institute.

Murray H. Manuel read a paper on "Multiples and Measures." An interesting discussion followed and was participated in by Inspector Meagher, John Brittain, D. W. Hamilton, J. M. Keefe, H. B. Logie and J. E. Page.

Thursday afternoon the session opened at 1.30 p. m. After roll call and reading of minutes Aaron Perry read a paper on "English Literature in Our Schools." Mr. Page opened the discussion and those taking part were the President, Mr. Hamilton and Mr. B. Perkins.

Mr. Brittain read a paper on "Gardening and Nature Study." D. W. Hamilton gave the first address on this paper and Inspector Meagher continued the discussion. Rev. L. L. Fash and Messrs. Murphy and Chas. Appleby, visitors, all addressed the Institute. This paper and discussion was one of the important features of the Institute.

The third session opened Friday morning at nine o'clock. The roll was called and the minutes of previous session were confirmed. Owing to the illness of Miss Alexander her lesson was abandoned. A question box was substituted for this and questions answered by the Inspector, Mr. Brittain and others.

Miss O'Brien read a paper on "The Place of Manual Training in Our Schools." Miss Marjorie Mair opened the discussion in a brief paper and Messrs. Harrison, Logie and Hamilton continued the discussion.

At Friday afternoon session after the preliminary work John M. Keefe discussed the "Teaching of Arithmetic." Mr. Gray and Inspector Meagher gave addresses on this subject. The Audit Committee reported the accounts correct with a balance on hand of $14.46.

The following officers were elected for the present year: President, C. H. Gray; Vice President, Julia Neales; Secretary, G. H. Harrison; additional members of the Executive, Aaron Perry, Inez Bradley. It was resolved to meet at Woodstock next year, the date of meeting being left in the hands of the Executive Committee. Votes of thanks were presented to Messrs. Brittain and Hamilton for their presence and assistance. The attendance at this annual session has never been exceeded in the history of the Carleton County Institute, there being eighty-eight enrolments. Much regret was expressed that the Chief Superintendent of Education was unable to be present.

CLINTON H. GRAY, *President.* G. H. HARRISON, *Secretary.*

CHARLOTTE COUNTY.

The Charlotte County Teachers' Institute met at Milltown on Thursday and Friday, Oct. 1st and 2nd. The attendance was a little over a hundred.

The President, Mrs Irving R. Todd of Milltown, gave a brief but earnest address to the teachers assembled. Principal Girdwood, of Grand Manan, read a paper on the lights and shades of the Teacher's Life, characterized by a broad sympathy with the life both of teacher and student. Miss Ethel H. Jarvis, of the King Street School, St. Stephen, gave a lesson in primary reading to a class of children who had been in the school only for a month. The teacher was bright and held the interest of the pupils throughout. The address of Mr. J. F. Ryan, superintendent of city schools, Calais, Me., on "What may be Gained by the Study of History," was a fine interpretation of the value of history as a disciplinary study. The discussion on the Metric System, conducted by Charles A. Richardson, was taken part in by a large number of teachers.

The public educational meeting on Thursday evening was held in the school room of the Congregational Church, and was presided over by Mr. H. E. Sinclair, Vice-president of the Institute. Addresses were given by the Secretary of School Trustees, Mr. Balkam, Chief Supt. Dr. Inch, and by G. U. Hay. Music, and refreshments served at the close by the ladies of the congregation, formed a pleasant feature of the evening.

At the Friday morning session, Mr. H. E. Sinclair read a paper on "Accuracy," which led to a profitable discussion; and an illustrative lesson on the use of the globe was given by Mr. F. O. Sullivan, followed by some valuable hints upon the care of globes and maps. A discussion on "Home Study," introduced by short papers on the subject from Mr. J.M. Clindinnin, Fredericton Junction; Miss Annie L. Richardson, St. Andrews; Miss Mary E. Caswell, Basswood Ridge; and Mr. P. S. Bailey, Moore's Mills, brought out the fact that the teachers generally approved of home lessons, while willing to admit that great care should be used in assigning them, so that they may not do more harm than good.

Mr. E. E. MacCready, who is inspecting the manual training departments of the Charlotte County schools, gave a short address, in which he spoke of making schoolrooms attractive by pictures and other decorations, and closed with an appeal to teachers to increase their salaries by taking advantage of the additional government allowance to qualified teachers who add manual training to their other work.

A paper on "Good English in the School," by Mrs. McGibbon, of St. Stephen school board, opened the afternoon session. Among those taking part in the discussion that followed was Mr. J. A. Allen, of Charlotte County Grammar School, who very strongly condemned carelessness in the every-day language of teachers, especially when in the presence of their pupils.

A paper by Inspector Carter on Co-operation Among Teachers, completed the work of the session, taking the place of a nature lesson which had been announced in the programme. Mr. Carter pointed out in a most convincing way the advantages that might come to teachers from mutual help and sympathy; and advocated the formation of social and literary clubs, and the establishment of funds for old age pensions, and for the payment of teachers during illness. He also urged that teachers acting together could have more influence upon legislation, in respect to factory laws, compulsory education and other matters that affect the welfare of children of school age, and that a teachers' library and meeting room might make the public school the educational centre of the district, to which winter lectures and other attractions would bring the grown people of the community, for pleasure and profit, and where the antagonism too often existing between teacher and parent would disappear. He approved of professional courtesy among teachers, and of associations that would promote this, increasing the interest of teachers through a mutual understanding and a common course of action; but did not approve of a union to oppose others and compel submission to its terms.

The time and place of next meeting of the Institute were left to the Executive Committee. The officers elect are Miss Annie L. Richardson, St. Andrews, President; Mr. Chas. J. Callaghan, St. George, Vice-president; Mr. J. Vroom, St. Stephen, Secretary; Mr. J. Aubrey Allen, St. Andrews, Miss Laura E. Boyd, Mace's Bay and Mr. P. Girdwood, Grand Manan, members of Executive Committee.

GLOUCESTER COUNTY.

The Gloucester, N. B., County Institute at Grand Anse, met September

24th and 25th, with a large number of teachers present from all parts of the county. President J. Edward De Grace occupied the chair. Four well prepared papers were read and discussed: The Relation that Should Exist Between Parents and Teachers, by Mr. D. T. Robichaud; Attention, by Principal R. D. Hanson, of the Grammar school; a bright paper read in French, on La Bonne Institutrice, by Miss Laura Cormier, of Caraquet; Reading for beginners, by Miss Gosnell of Bathurst· A public meeting was held on the evening of the 24th, addressed by Rev. S. J. Doucet, Mr. Joseph Poirier, M. P. P., Principal J. E. O'Brien, Principal Hanson and President De Grace. The following were elected officers for the ensuing year, President, R. D. Hanson; Vice-president, Miss Bernadette Cormier; Secretary-treasurer, D. T. Robichaud; additional members of the executive, Jean G. Robichaud and Miss Gosnell.

KENT COUNTY.

The Kent County Teachers' Institute was held at Richibucto on Thursday and Friday, October 22nd and 23rd. Inspector Mersereau was in attendance. The president, Geo. A. Coates, gave an opening address, followed by Inspector Mersereau. Miss Chrystal, teacher of the primary department of the Richibucto Grammar School, gave an instructive lesson on geography to a primary class. Dr. J. R. Inch, Chief Superintendent of Education, was then introduced. Miss Mazerall, teacher of the primary department of the Buctouche Superior School, read an excellent paper on "How to Write Correctly." Miss Caie opened the discussion, which then became quite general. Miss Carruthers, principal of Bass River Superior School, read a comprehensive paper on "Nature Study." The inspector opened the discussion on this paper.

A public meeting was held on Thursday evening, President Coates in the chair. Addresses were given by Inspector Mersereau, Dr. Inch and others.

On Friday morning a resolution expressive of sympathy for Inspector Smith, on account of his serious illness, was passed by a standing vote of the Institute.

Miss Caie gave a talk on "Plant Study," and R. B. Masterton, principal of the Rexton Superior School, read an interesting paper on "Mistakes in Teaching Arithmetic." The discussion was opened by the secretary, A. E. Pearson. Inspector Mersereau then addressed the Institute on "External Aids to Education."

The following officers were elected for the ensuing year: George A. Coates, president; Miss Kate Keswick, vice-president; A. E. Pearson, secretary-treasurer; A. Dewar and Miss Alethea Wathen. additional members of the executive. Harcourt was chosen as the next place of meeting.

After the usual votes of thanks, the Institute adjourned, immediately after which a discussion on Teachers' Union came up, and the teachers present formed themselves into a union, known as the Kent County Teachers' Union, with the following officers: A. Dewar, president; Miss Chrystal, vice-president; A. E. Pearson, secretary-treasurer. A. E. Pearson was appointed as a representative to meet with the executive of the N. B. T. U. at Moncton on December 21st.

On Friday evening a reception was held. An enjoyable evening was spent in games and amusements of various kinds.—*Condensed from Report of Secretary A. E. Pearson.*

KINGS COUNTY.

The King's County, N. B., Teachers' Institute met at Sussex on Thursday and Friday, September 17th and 18th. There was a large attendance, The first session was very profitably spent in discussing the many excellent points brought out in the address of the president, D. P. Kirkpatrick. The observance of arbor day, better methods of nature-study, a more earnest preparation for their work on the part of teachers were dwelt upon in the discussion that followed by Inspector Steeves, R. R. Cormier, D. W Hamilton, G. U. Hay and J. March.

A stimulating paper on Literature was read by G. P. McCrea, principal of the Apohaqui schools; and D. W, Hamilton, principal of the MacDonald Consolidated School, Kingston, dealt in a very suggestive and comprehensive manner with the nature-study movement. Both papers were fully discussed. Miss Ella Seely (Hampton) gave a lesson to a Grade III class on local geography, taking Sussex as a centre, and bringing out in a very interesting way the pupils' ideas on natural features, resources, industries, modes of travel, exports, imports and other topics.

Inspector Steeves presided at the evening meeting, which was enlivened by the music of the Sussex orchestra, and by the presence of many red-coated volunteers from the military camp above Sussex. Addresses were given by the Inspector, by Messrs. D. W. Hamilton, Principal A. B. Maggs, of the Sussex Grammar School, G. U. Hay, editor of the REVIEW, and by John March.

On Friday morning a nature-study excursion to the Bluffs a few miles above Sussex, had to be abandoned on account of threatening weather, The question box gave material for many helpful suggestions. Mr. W. N,

Biggar read a paper on Discipline, drawing a fine distinction between instruction and discipline. This was followed by two short papers on Correlation, and Mr. Hamilton gave an outline of nature-work and books thereon for schools.

A Teachers' Union for Kings County was formed with the following officers: W. N., Biggar, President; Mrs. M. S. Cox, Vice-president; A. B. Maggs, Secretary-treasurer; D. P. Kirkpatrick, R. R. Cormier, Frances Pritchard, Helen S. Raymond, additional members of the managing committee.

Thirty-seven members joined the Union, which will soon no doubt be largely increased. The union has not yet committed itself to any action in regard to salaries further than an understanding among its members not to underbid.

At the close of the Institute on Friday afternoon the lady teachers of Sussex entertained the visitors with a generous repast in one of the rooms of the Grammar school.

The following officers were elected for the ensuing year: President, W. C. Jonah; Vice-president, Miss Helen S. Raymond; Secretary-Treasurer W. N. Biggar; additional members of the Executive, A. B. Maggs, M. A., and Miss Eugenia Keith.

NORTHUMBERLAND COUNTY.

The teachers of Northumberland County, N. B., met at the Chatham Grammar School on the 8th and 9th of October. Inspector Meisereau addressed the Institute in stirring and effective words. The following papers were read: on the teaching of English, by principal M. R. Tuttle, of Blackville; on discipline, by Mr. C. J. Mersereau, M. A. of the grammar school; on Nature work in primary grades, by Miss Smith, Chatham; on the use of the imagination, by principal A. E G. MacKenzie, of Harkins' Academy, Newcastle; on Geometry, by Dr. P. Cox, principal of the Grammar school. Inspector Mersereau gave a talk on the Practical in Education, in which he recommended more attention to manners, facility of expression in English and accuracy in arithemetic. The following officers were elected for the year: President James MacIntosh; Vice-President, Miss Beatrice Ellis; Secretary-treasurer, A. E. G. MacKenzie; additional members of executive, Miss Stella Carruthers and C. J. Mersereau, M. A. A Northumberland County Teachers' Union was formed, with Dr. Cox, President; J. Brown, Vice-president; and M. R. Tuttle, M. A., Secretary.

QUEENS, SUNBURY AND YORK COUNTIES.

The teachers of York, Sunbury and Queens Counties held a Joint Institute in the assembly room of the Fredericton High School on the 21st and 22nd days of May last.

The Institute was opened by the President with an address of welcome to the teachers; this was followed by the enrolment, which showed that 103 teachers from York and 34 from Sunbury and Queens were present. After the completion of enrolment and miscellaneous business, the President, Jas. A. Hughes, read a paper on "The Teacher and His Mission." The Chief Superintendent of Education followed with an address of much interest to teachers, in which amongst other things of importance he spoke of the re-recent petitions for advance of salary, and the course to be pursued by the Government for the encouragement of Manual Training in this Province.

During the second session, His Honour Lieutenant Governor Snowball, accompanied by Dr. Inch, honoured the Institute with a visit, and at the end of a very excellent lesson by Miss Harvey of the Model School, on "The Effects ot Alcohol on the Heart," addressed the assembly. His Honour remained to hear the very carefully prepared paper on "Grammar," read by Mr. Geo. A. Inch of the Normal School staff.

On Friday morning Inspector Bridges delighted the Institute by reading a most excellent and exhaustive paper on "Hints on Questioning," which called forth a great deal of favourable comment and much discussion. Mr. Amos O'Blenes, Principal of the Model School, also gave a very interesting lesson on "Arithmetic," with illustrations on the blackboard.

I think the discussions which followed the different papers were of great value; and teachers preparing papers for an Institute would do well to make them short and compact so as to allow of more extended time for these discussions.

The last session was devoted to "Field Work." The Institute went on an excursion by steamer to Currie's Mountain and there divided into three sections. One led by Dr. L. W. Bailey studied Geology; a second led by Mr. William Moore studied Birds; and a third led by Dr. G. U. Hay, studied Botany. This was a most enjoyable and at the same time beneficial session.

The officers for the ensuing year are: Mr. B. C. Foster, President; Miss Sadie Thompson, Vice-President; Miss Ella L. Thorne, Secretary; Mr. Amos O'Blenes, Miss G. Reid and Miss E. McPherson additional members of the executive.

The Institute was in every respect an unqualified success.

ELLA L. THORNE, *Secretary.*

RESTIGOUCHE COUNTY.

The Restigouche County Teachers' Institute met at Campbellton on the 17th and 18th of December, 1903.

The Institute was attended by thirty-two of the forty-two English speaking teachers. Professor McCready, Director of Manual Training in schools, and Miss Louise Wetmore conducted a class of Manual Training in the presence of the teachers. Miss Melissa Cook taught a lesson on Liquid Measure, Miss C. F. Mair, B. A., one on the Metric System, Miss Beatrice Richards on Minerals, Miss Reid on Color, E. W. Lewis gave an address on Method of introducing Geometry to pupils. Miss Georgina Dickson read a paper on Grammar, and Miss Christina Richards on Primary Number. A great deal of interest was manifest in the proceedings of the meetings. H. F. McLatchy, M. P. P., was present and addressed the teachers. The success of the Institute was largely due to the energy and inspiration of the Inspector, Mr. Mersereau.

E. W. LEWIS, *President.*

SAINT JOHN COUNTY.

Over 250 teachers were present at this meeting, held December 17th and 18th, which proved to be one of the most interesting institutes ever held in the County. The impartial and prompt manner in which the president, M. D. Brown, conducted the proceedings, helped to produce this result, while the excellence of the papers read secured the undivided attention of the teachers. Papers were read by Principal Crocket, of the Normal School, on the Ideal in Education; Principal Owen, on Truancy; Miss Edna W. Gilmour, on Manual Work and Writing; Miss Florence Rogers, on Physical Culture, and Dr. H. S. Bridges on School Government. These papers were very fully discussed. The presence of Chief Supt. Dr. Inch and Inspector Carter added to the interest of the meeting. The St. John High School Orchestra and accomplished soloists furnished music. The following officers were elected: President, J. Frank Owens, B. A.; vice-president, J. S. Lord; secretary-treasurer, Miss A. M. Hea; additional members of executive committee, Miss Edna W. Gilmour and A. Lindsay Dykeman.

VICTORIA COUNTY.

The Victoria Co. Teachers' Institute met at Grand Falls on October 8 and 9. Twenty-six teachers were enrolled. The officers elected were: J.

C. Carruthers, president; Thomas Rogers, vice-president; Bessie M. Fraser, secretary-treasurer; Janet M. Curry and Edith B. Wallace, additional members of committee. Papers were read on Composition, by J. C. Carruthers: Respective duties of Parents and Teachers towards Pupils, by W. M. Veazey; Teachers' Institutes, by Miss Bessie Fraser. Additional interest and pleasure were given to the exercises by the presence of Dr. Inch, Chief Superintendent of Education, and Prof. Brittain. An enthusiastic public meeting was held in Kert..u's Hall on Thursday evening. Speeches were made by Dr. Inch, Inspector Meagher and Rev. Mr. Maimann. Music was rendered by several of the ladies of the town and by the band. On Friday morning the teachers enjoyed an outing, and derived much pleasure from viewing the beautiful scenery around Grand Falls. The executive committee was given power to decide between Andover and Grand Falls as a meeting place next year.

BESSIE M. FRASER, *Sec.-Treas.*

WESTMORLAND COUNTY.

The twenty-sixth annual meeting of the Westmorland County Teachers' Institute was opened in the Hall of the Aberdeen School, Moncton, on Thursday, October the first, at ten o'clock, the president, H. B. Steeves, B. A., in the chair. The minutes of last year's meeting held at Port Elgin was read and approved. The enrolment was then proceeded with, which showed the attendance at the first session to have been one hundred and ten. The total enrolment was 130. Roy D. Fullerton, B. A., of Port Elgin, then read a very valuable paper on the teaching and use of good English in the schools. The discussion was opened by W. A. Cowperthwaite, B. A., of the Moncton High School. He was followed by Messrs. Oulton, Dixon, Allen, McGinn and Miss McSweeney. A motion by Miss McSweeney that a committee be appointed to draft a letter expressing sympathy with Inspector Smith was carried, and the president appointed the following committee: G. J. Oulton, F. A. Dixon, R. D. Fullerton, T. J. Allen, Miss McSweeney, Miss Dickie and Miss Legere.

At the afternoon session Miss Jarvis read a paper on "Kindergarten Methods," Mr. Oulton followed in a talk in which he strongly advocated the use of globes instead of maps in the teaching of geography. In the evening the Institute listened to an interesting address on "Wireless Telegraphy" by Dr. Scott, of the University of New Brunswick.

Friday morning a lesson on algebra was given to a class from Grade VII by B. P. Steeves, B. A., followed by a paper on "Nature Study in Miscellaneous Schools," by F. R. Anderson, and on "Nature Study in Primary

Grades," by Miss Edith A. Brownell. A resolution favoring a Teachers, Union was passed and a committee appointed to perfect organization.

Officers for next year: T. J. Goodwin, president; Miss Mary Moore, vice-president; S. W. Irons, secretary-treasurer; F. J. E. McGinn and Miss Jessie McDougall additional members of the executive.

H. B. STEEVES, *President*.

S. W. IRONS, *Secretary*.

Report of Summer School of Science.

To JAMES R. INCH, ESQ., LL. D.
Chief Supt. of Education,
Fredericton, N. B.

SIR: I have the honor to submit the following report of the seventeenth session of the Summer School of Science for the Atlantic Provinces of Canada, which met at Chatham, N. B., July 21st to August 7th, 1903.

The session was opened by a public meeting held in the spacious assembly hall of the Chatham school, L. W. Bailey, LL. D., President of the School presided. Interesting and enthusiastic addresses were given by His Honor Lieut. Governor Snowball, Mayor Murdock, Inspector Mersereau Dr. P. Cox. Dr. J. McG. Baxter, the city clergy and others.

The enrolment of the school for this session was ninety—not so large as on some previous occassions, but there never was more interest manifested in the work by the student teachers present. This was a great source of pleasure to the instructors.

The sessions of the school were held in the fine new school building at Chatham, which is a source of pride to its citizens. Its cool and well-equipped rooms afforded pleasant and comfortable accommodation for the several classes.

The courtesies extended to the school by His Honor Lieut. Governor Snowball, by Mrs. Tweedie, wife of Premier Tweedie, by the members of the Miramichi Natural History Association, whose rooms and collections were open to the visitors, and the many attentions bestowed by the citizens of Chatham will always be a pleasant recollection to the members of the school.

The excursions on the broad Miramichi river, with its fertile fields gently sloping to the forest beyond the towns and villages along its banks throbbing with the hum of industry, and the opportunity to recall many scenes in the early history of this portion of the province, were eagerly taken advantage of by the visitors.

This session of the Summer School was characterized by the diligence of the students and the marked improvement made by them. As in the past great prominence was given to field work, the success of which was largely contributed to by the presence of Dr. Bailey, Dr. Hay, Dr. Cox, and Mr. McIntosh.

The financial statement is as follows:

RECEIPTS.

Balance from 1902	$ 24 64	
Refund from St. Stephen, N.B.	50 00	
Grant from Government of N. B.	200 00	
" " N. S.	100 00	
" " P. E. I.	50 00	
Advertising in Calendar	141 00	
Enrolment Fees	140 00	
Proceeds of lectures	31 45	
Sundries	25 95	
		$763 04

EXPENDITURES.

Printing, Advertising and Stationery	$ 100 84	
Calendars	141 50	
Postage, Freight, Expressage	90 53	
Class Expenses	19 10	
Instructors and Officers	224 00	
Expenses of Lectures	42 10	
Sundries	116 00	
Balance	28 97	
		$763 04

The next session of the school will be held at Charlottetown, P. E. I., July 13th to 29th, 1904.

The officers for the ensuing year are:

PRESIDENT.

James Vroom, Esq., St. Stephen, N. B.

VICE-PRESIDENTS.

F. G. Matthews, Esq., Truro, N. S.
Philip Cox, Ph. D., Chatham, N. B.
Alex. Anderson, LL. D., Charlottetown, P. E. I.

SECRETARY-TREASURER.

J. D. Seaman, Esq., Charlottetown, P. E. I.

BOARD OF DIRECTORS.

The President, The Secretary-Treasurer,
W. R. Campbell, M. A., Truro, N. S.
S. A. Starrat, Esq., Cambridge, Mass., U. S. A.
J. B. Hall, Ph. D., Truro, N. S.
L. W. Bailey, LL. D., Fredericton, N. B.

I have the honor to be, Sir,

Your obedient servant,

J. D. SEAMAN,
Secretary.

Charlottetown P. E. I., Nov. 10, 1903.

APPENDIX F.

Thirty-Third Annual Report of the Board of Managers of the School for the Blind, Halifax, Nova Scotia.

INTRODUCTION.

The Board of Managers have great pleasure in submitting to the Members of the Corporation, to the Provincial Governments and Legislatures interested, and to the many friends of the Blind, the thirty-third annual report and, in so doing, they desire to express their gratitude to a kind Providence for the many blessings vouchsafed to the school, and their appreciation of the kindness and generosity of its many friends.

SUPERINTENDENT'S REPORT.

The Superintendent's report hereto appended, deals fully with the several departments of the school. It chronicles the changes that have taken place during the past year and gives a concise account of the work accomplished. The members of the teaching staff have faithfully discharged their duties and have worked unceasingly for the advancement of the school. Their efforts to further the interests of their pupils have been most successful and the Board desires to express its hearty appreciation of the zeal and ability they have shown in their respective departments.

PERSONAL VISITS.

There are many people in the city of Halifax, as well as in other parts of the Maritime Provinces and Newfoundland, who have little or no idea of what goes on in a school for the blind. Some people imagine that it is a home in which blind people are cared for during life; others, that it is a school in which blind people are taught and trained by some mystical methods unknown to the professional educationist. Some persons imagine that the atmosphere of a school for the blind must be sad and depressing and that the consciousness of lack of sight must ever be uppermost in the minds of the pupils. Others again have no adequate conception of the capabilities of the blind individually or collectively and when a person deprived of sight comes before the public and excels in any particular respect they at once regard him as a prodigy and look upon his attainments as phenomenal. The best and surest way of obtaining a correct idea of the school and of the work it is doing is to visit the institution and thoroughly inspect its several departments. Such an inspection would at once satisfy the visitor that this is not an asylum or place of refuge for aged blind persons; that the methods of teaching are precisely the same as those employed in schools for children with sight; and that the only difference worthy of note is the substitution of appliances suited to the sense of touch for those adapted to the sense of sight. The visitor would at once be impressed with the bright and cheery atmosphere of the school, and when he fully realized that blindness has come to be second nature to the pupils, and that not for one minute in the course of the day did they fret or mourn over their lack of sight, he would begin to think, and thinking, he would come to understand, that with education four senses may be trained to do the work of five, and that the beauties of the world about us may be apprehended, appreciated and thoroughly enjoyed by one deprived of sight. If the visitor had time for periodical inspection of the departments of the school, he would learn that there is practically little or no difference in the temperament or capacity between one hundred girls and boys with sight and an equal number of blind children. He would realize that the curriculum of the school covers all the subjects taught in our public schools, and that, in addition, the pupils are receiving a practical training in special lines of work, so as to enable them to take their place in the world as useful men and women.

Your board is desirous that the school and its work should be fully understood and now that the new and commodious building for school purposes is about to be occupied they are particularly anxious that our business and professional men should visit the institution and see for themselves what is being done for the education of those deprived of sight.

LEGISLATIVE SUPPORT.

It is now twenty-one years since the Legislature of Nova Scotia adopted the Act making education free to blind children of this province. The Act has worked smoothly and satisfactorily and has proved a blessing to many boys and girls who would otherwise have been debarred from educational privileges. The Act for the free education of the blind in New Brunswick was adopted eleven years ago. Its provisions are practically the same as those of Nova Scotia and its results have been equally advantageous to the blind youth of our sister province.

The Government and Legislature of Prince Edward Island have not as yet made education free to the blind of that province, as it is to those with sight, but a small annual grant is made to this institution which, with a grant from the City of Charlottetown, amounted for the past school year to six hundred dollars. In view of the increased attendance of Prince Edward Island pupils, and the inadequacy of the past grant, your board sincerely trusts that the Prince Edward Island Government will give the matter of the education of the blind their earnest consideration, and that legislation may be enacted which will place the blind of the Island Province on the same footing as those in Nova Scotia and New Brunswick.

Your board is pleased to report an increase in the number of pupils from Newfoundland attending the school. The number of schoolable blind persons in Newfoundland will not exceed twenty-four, and it is a satisfaction to know that nearly one-half of these are under instruction. The people of Newfoundland have evinced a deep interest in the welfare of the blind, and the Government has agreed to give the matter of the education of the blind their fullest consideration and to take such steps as will place the education within reach of every blind child in the colony.

LATE MEMBERS OF THE BOARD.

During the past year your board has lost by death two of its most prominent members: the President, Mr. W. C. Silver; and the Treasurer, Mr. John Duffus. These gentlemen were appointed members of the Board of Managers at the first meeting of this corporation held in the City Council chamber, Halifax, on Monday, April 27th, 1868.

Mr. Silver had been President of the Board of Managers for the past fourteen years and had given to the work of educating the blind a large share of his time and attention. By his death the school loses a warm supporter and the blind a kind and sympathetic friend.

Mr. John Duffus took a very deep interest in the affairs of the institution and for ten years prior to his death discharged the official duties of Treasurer of the School in a most satisfactory manner.

THE NEW SCHOOL BUILDING.

Our new school building, which is so much required, will be ready for accupation early in the new year. It is a substantial brick structure, one hundred and thirty feet in length by seventy-one in breadth, and contains four stories, including the basement. The building is faced with pressed brick and trimmed with freestone. It presents a handsome appearance and is a fine addition to the property of the school. The support that has been given to us by the Legislature of Nova Scotia, and by the friends of the blind, in carrying out this work has been most timely and has enabled us to make a great step forward in the education of the blind.

THE SUPERINTENDENT.

Our Superintendent, Dr. C. F. Fraser, has continued to give to the institution that whole-hearted, methodical, businesslike supervision which has characterized his long period of incumbency and which has, under God's blessing, brought the school to a state of efficiency unsurpassed by any other institution for the blind on this continent, or perhaps in the world. He possesses in an eminent degree the respect, confidence, and affection of the managers, teachers and pupils, and of all interested in the welfare of the blind, and his efforts on their behalf have placed his name in the fore-front of the philanthropists of his native province, and his work will be a standing monument for many generations to his ability, energy and unselfishness. The tour made by him during the year in Nova Scotia, New Brunswick, and Newfoundland, accompanied by a number of the teachers and pupils, resulted in a grand success and will be fully dealt with in his report. Your Board greatly rejoice in the improved condition of the health of Mrs. Fraser, to whom the school is so deeply indebted, and they earnestly hope that she may soon be completely restored and, with her husband, spared many years to minister to the welfare of the blind.

ACKNOWLEDGEMENTS.

In addition to the donations elsewhere acknowledged your Board gratefully acknowledges the following bequests:

Estate of W. C. Silver, Halifax,	$250 00	
Estate of Mrs. T. Doyle, Halifax,	50 00	
Estate of E. P. Archbold, Halifax,	25 00	on account.

While the amount received from bequests during the past year is not large it is a material help to our endowment fund, and it is gratifying to know that this fund is steadily growing year by year. The interest of this fund is used to improve the educational facilities of the school.

Our special thanks are due to Dr. A. W. H. Lindsay, attending physician of the school; to Dr. A. C. Cogswell. dental surgeon; and t Dr. A. E. Kirkpatrick, ophthalmic surgeon, for the attention they have given to the pupils throughout the year.

The Board of Managers also desires to express its thanks to Mr. J. D. Medcalfe, Mr. W. E. Hebb, Mr. H. B. Clarke, the Halifax Symphony Orchestra, and other individuals and organizations for kindly admitting the pupils to lectures, concerts etc., under their respective managements.

The Railways and other transportation companies have our thanks for the special rates granted and for the uniform kindness and care shown to the pupils while travelling to and from their homes.

All of which is respectfully submitted.

J. C. MACKINTOSH,
President.

SUPERINTENDENT'S REPORT.

To the President and Board of Managers of the School for the Blind:

GENTLEMEN:—The table of attendance herewith submitted shows that 142 blind persons have been under instruction during the past year, of whom 87 were males and 55 females. Of these, 18 have since graduated or remained at home, making the total number registered December 1st, 1903, 124 of whom 77 are males and 47 females. Of these. 77 are from the province of Nova Scotia, 28 from New Brunswick, 8 from Prince Edward Island, and 11 from Newfoundland.

TABLE OF ATTENDANCE.

	Boys	Girls	Adults	Total
Registered December 1st, 1902,	69	48	4	121
Entered during the year,	11	7	3	21
Graduated or remained at home,	9	8	1	18
Registered December 1st, 1903.	71	47	6	124

LITERARY DEPARTMENT.

The feature of the year so far as this department is concerned has been the carrying out of a long cherished plan for the better grading of the pupils. Under the new arrangement six divisions have been formed, the work of each division covering a period of two years. The primary work, including kindergarten training, will occupy four years; the three grammar school grades, six years, and the high school course, two years. Ungraded classes have been established for the benefit of such pupils as cannot follow to advantage the regular course of study. Pupils entering between six and ten years of age will be placed in the kindergarten or primary grades. Those entering between ten and fifteen years of age will be placed in the ungraded classes and be taught to read and write in the Braille System before entering the graded classes of the school. This re-organization of our Literary Department will stimulate the pupils to increased effort, will ensure their more steady and rapid progress, and will certainly raise the general standard of the education imparted in the school.

TEACHING STAFF.

The success or non-success of the work in a school for the blind depends largely upon the members of its teaching staff. Half-heartedness, pessimism, or indifference upon the part of the instructors is speedily reflected in the work of their pupils and hence no such teachers should be retained on the staff in a school of this character. The ideal teacher requires to be thoroughly educated, to be zealous, patient and preseverving. He requires to be imbued with a spirit of hopefulness, to appreciate the special difficulties with which the pupils have to contend, and to keep ever before him the purpose for which the school has been established. Teachers of this stamp are always prepared to devote the greater part of their time and attention to the pupils placed in their care, and if they have sound judgment, high ideals, and deep sympathies, the school cannot fail to accomplish satisfactory results and to make for itself and its graduates an enviable record. The members of our teaching staff have proved by their energy and devotion, by their thoughtfulness and zeal, that they are well qualified to carry on the great work entrusted to them, and it is with pleasure that I take this opportunity of expressing my personal appreciation of the spirit of loyal co-operation with which they are imbued and of the intelligent instruction which they have given in their respective classes.

OUR PURPOSE.

The purpose of this school is to give to its pupils such a training as will enable them to become self supporting. To those familiar with the work of this institution, and with the after success of the great majority of its graduates, it will not appear in any way surprising to learn that eighty out of every hundred pupils trained in the school have been able to earn their own livelihood. This triumph of modern education has been the outcome of long years of patient experiment upon the part of the instructors of the blind both here and elsewhere. It has required much thought and long practical experience to determine what callings are adapted to the special needs of those who are deprived of sight. In our experience the teaching of vocal and instrumental music and the tuning of pianofortes can be followed with eminent success by blind persons. A fair percentage may be trained for commercial life. A still smaller percentage may be trained successfully so as to earn their living by such handicrafts as basket-making, brush-making and chair-seating. The practice of massage and shampooing has opened a new field of occupation for a limited number.

Other callings there may be, and doubtless are, which the blind could follow successfully, but they require individual aptitude and specific training such as is far beyond the scope of an institution of this character.

HEALTH.

The health of the pupils during the past year has maintained its usual fair average. Where such a large number of young people are gathered together some delicate children will always be found and occasionally the shadow of death will cross our threshold. During the past year a young boy named Frederick McDougall, of Indiantown, N. B., died at the school from meningitis after a short illness. Eleven cases of measles and two of chickenpox made their appearance during last month. Owing to the crowded state of the building, the proper isolation of the infected pupils was impossible, but this difficulty will be overcome when the increased accommodation of the new building becomes available. Dr. A. W. H. Lindsay, the attending physician, has been most untiring in looking after the health of the pupils. Dr. Lindsay's services to the school have now extended over a period of twenty years. These services have been given without remuneration and in a spirit of kindly interest which merits public approbation. Dr. Lindsay's name well deserves to be enrolled among those of the benefactors of the school, and the recent action of your Board in this direction is a graceful recognition of his years of service to the blind.

GRADUATES.

Among the graduates of the past year the following deserve special mention:

Miss Jennie Muise, of Yarmouth, N. S., graduated as a teacher of vocal music, and is now taking a special course in singing from Professor Saenger of New York.

Miss Lulu Curtis, of Onslow, N. S., graduated as a teacher of vocal and instrumental music and has been engaged as an assistant in the girls' musical department of this school.

Miss Mary McDonald, of Welsford, N. B., received a certificate as a competent masseuse and has settled in St. John, N. B.

J. Hollis Lindsay, of Woodstock, N. B., received a first-class certificate as a teacher of music and as a pianoforte tuner. In order to further his studies as a church organist he has been granted an additional year for a post graduate course.

Paul Duffy, of Hillsboro, N. B., was awarded a first-class certificate as a music teacher and as a pianoforte tuner, and has settled in his native town.

John A. McDonald, of Glassburn N., S., who graduated from our Literary department, is now in Boston taking supplementary courses in the Posse Institute and in the Emmerson School of Oratory.

Augustus Morgan, of Salmon Cove, Nfld., was awarded a certificate as a teacher of music and has received a temporary appointment in the school.

E. Chapman, of Amherst, N. S. graduated from the work shop as a brush maker, etc. He has settled in Amherst and is meeting with success.

These graduates are exceptionally bright and intelligent young people and they are destined to win many laurels for themselves and for the school.

PUBLIC MEETINGS.

During the past year thirty-one public meetings in the interests of the blind were held in Nova Scotia, New Brunswick and Newfoundland. Our reception in the cities and towns visited was most gratifying. The audiences were invariably large and appreciative and great interest was evinced in the school and musical exercises performed by the pupils. Such meetings as these keep the school well before the public. They show far better than written reports can ever do what can be accomplished by those who are deprived of sight. They widen the interest in the work of the institution and pave the way for the success of our graduates. An institution of this character, dependent as it is upon the good will of the people and their representatives in the Legislature, must not hide its light under a bushel. That light must be seen and appreciated by the people and when this is the case there is no fear of its burning less brightly or of its being extinguished.

BUILDING FUND.

Through the kindness of our many friends the subscriptions towards our new building have now reached the sum of $20,769.56, of which $12,480.80 have so far been paid in. These subscriptions and the payments on account, which have been given with such open-handed generosity, prove beyond question the breadth and depth of the interest that is taken in the welfare of the blind throughout the Maritime Provinces and Newfoundland. The public have been told of the liberality of the Legislature of Nova Scotia in appropriating twenty thousand dollars towards the building now nearing completion,, and they have been asked to supplement this grant to the best of their ability so that the work of the institution should not in any way be checked or hampered by too great a burden of debt. While still more money is required, the response of the public to date has been most encouraging. They have approved of the undertaking we have in hand and have signified their willingness to co-operate with the authorities of the school in any movement having for its purpose the improvement of the educational facilities provided for those who are blind.

The public mandate requires that this school shall be kept in the very front rank of schools for the blind on this continent, and this mandate is not to be disregarded.

INCREASED ACCOMMODATION.

The new building, which will be ready for occupation in a few weeks' time, will greatly facilitate the work of the school and will give scope for the carrying into effect of many contemplated improvements in the Literary Musical, and Industrial Departments. The plan of the building has been carefully considered and it will be found admirably adapted to the requirements of the school. The present buildings will be used for residence purposes, and the removal of all the work of the school to the new building will make it possible to provide much more comfortable home quarters for our staff and pupils during their leisure hours.

The residence buildings contain fifty sleeping rooms and dormitories for teachers, pupils and domestic staff, with adequate lavatory and hospital accommodation, in addition to which there are reading, sitting and reception rooms. The building also contains the Superintendent's apartments, the Board room and office, kitchen, dining rooms, pantries and store rooms.

The new building will contain two play rooms or gymnasiums, a swimming pool and lavatories, a manual training room, a workshop, a printing office, eight school rooms, a museum, an assembly hall, twenty-eight practice rooms and four tuning rooms. It also contains sleeping rooms and dormitories for the accommodation of forty pupils.

ACKNOWLEDGEMENTS.

I am deeply grateful to the friends of the blind for the kind interest they have evinced in the work of the school, and for the hearty and cordial way in which they have responded to the request for assistance. My special thanks are due to the gentlemen who have aided me in carrying out the preparations for the numerous public meetings to which I have alluded, and to the gentlemen who acted as chairmen at these meetings. Much of the success that has been achieved has been due to the able and impressive speeches made at the meetings by the chairmen, and in this connection I might particularly mention the admirable and sympathetic address delivered at our first meeting in St. Johns by the chairman, Sir Cavendish Boyle, overnor of Newfoundland.

CONCLUSION.

In conclusion, gentlemen, I desire to express a word of appreciation for the grand work done on behalf of the school by the late President of the Board of Managers, Mr. W. C. Silver. and the late Treasurer, Mr. John Duffus. I have been intimately associated with these gentlemen for the past thirty years and I can speak from personal knowledge of their kind interest in the welfare of the blind, and their deep affection for the school and for its work.

I sincerely trust that the happy relations which have existed between the Board of Managers and myself will continue to exist in the future as in the past, and that with your help, your support, and your encouragement, I may be of real service in my day and generation to those who are deprived of sight.

All of which is respectfully submitted.

C. F. FRASER,
Superintendent.

Lightning Source UK Ltd.
Milton Keynes UK
UKHW012021201118
332601UK00013B/2058/P

9 780260 821584